Moreton Morrell Site

# Economics
# for Business

# Third Edition

# Economics for Business

## Competition, Macro-stability and Globalisation

# Dermot McAleese

Trinity College Dublin

Prentice Hall
FINANCIAL TIMES

*An imprint of* **Pearson Education**
Harlow, England • London • New York • Boston • San Francisco • Toronto
Sydney • Tokyo • Singapore • Hong Kong • Seoul • Taipei • New Delhi
Cape Town • Madrid • Mexico City • Amsterdam • Munich • Paris • Milan

**Pearson Education Limited**

Edinburgh Gate
Harlow
Essex CM20 2JE
England

and Associated Companies throughout the world

Visit us on the World Wide Web at:
www.pearsoned.co.uk

First published under the Prentice Hall Europe imprint 1997
Second edition 2001
**Third edition published 2004**

ISBN 0 273 68398 5

**British Library Cataloguing-in-Publication Data**
A catalogue record for this book is available from the British Library

10 9 8 7 6 5 4 3 2 1
08 07 06 05 04

Typeset in 9.5/12pt Stone Serif by 25
Printed and bound in Great Britain by Ashford Colour Press Ltd, Gosport

The publisher's policy is to use paper manufactured from sustainable forests.

# Brief contents

List of boxes                                                          xiv
Preface to the third edition                                          xvii
Acknowledgements                                                       xxi

1  The economic policy consensus                                         1
2  What makes nations grow?                                             13

## Part I   The market system and competition                           43

3  The market system in action                                         47
4  Market demand and the pricing decision                              72
5  The firm in a competitive market                                    95
6  The economics of market power                                      125
7  Competition policy, privatisation and regulation                   155
8  Government intervention and the market system                      180
9  Business and the environment                                       206
10 Hiring labour and the investment decision                          227

## Part II   The macroeconomic framework                               243

11 Aggregate supply, aggregate demand and the price level            246
12 Price stability and central banks                                  276
13 Understanding interest rates and monetary policy                   305
14 Unemployment and the labour market                                 336
15 Fiscal policy, budget deficits and government debt                 370
16 Business fluctuations and forecasting                              401

## Part III   The global economy                                       421

17 Foreign trade: patterns and policy                                 424
18 Capital flows and foreign investment                               462
19 Labour migration                                                   488
20 The balance of payments: what it is and why it matters             501
21 Coping with exchange rates                                         528
22 Exchange rate regimes and the euro                                 561

Index                                                                 595

# Contents

List of boxes     xiv

Preface to the third edition     xvii

Acknowledgements     xxi

**1 The economic policy consensus**     1

Introduction     1
1.1   The economic policy consensus     2
1.2   Why policy changed     5
1.3   Implications for the future     6
1.4   Criticisms of the new consensus     7
1.5   Will the consensus last?     9
Summary     11
Questions for discussion     11
Exercises     11
Further reading     12

**2 What makes nations grow?**     13

Introduction     13
2.1   Trends in economic growth     14
2.2   Growth theories     17
2.3   Human welfare and sustainable growth     26
2.4   Policy prescriptions for growth     33
2.5   Conclusions     36
Summary     37
Questions for discussion     38
Exercises     39
Further reading     40
Appendix 2.1   The economics of the new economy     40

**Part I    The market system and competition**

Introduction to Part I     44

**3 The market system in action**     47
Introduction     47
3.1   The market system     48

Contents

3.2 The role of prices                                          53
3.3 Movements in demand and supply                              56
3.4 The role of traders and arbitrage                           61
3.5 The efficiency of the market system                         63
3.6 The free market system in social context                    65
3.7 Conclusions                                                 67
Summary                                                         68
Questions for discussion                                        69
Exercises                                                       70
Further reading                                                 71

4 Market demand and the pricing decision                        72

Introduction                                                    72
4.1 What is a 'rational' consumer?                              72
4.2 Deriving the market demand curve                            75
4.3 Elasticities of demand                                      75
4.4 Estimating the demand function                              82
4.5 Price elasticities and the pricing decision                88
4.6 Conclusions                                                 90
Summary                                                         91
Questions for discussion                                        92
Exercises                                                       93
Further reading                                                 94

5 The firm in a competitive market                              95

Introduction                                                    95
5.1 Profit maximisation                                         96
5.2 Rules for maximising profit                                101
5.3 Cost structure of the firm                                 107
5.4 The transaction costs approach                             115
5.5 From cost structure to supply curve                        119
5.6 Conclusions                                                 119
Summary                                                        120
Questions for discussion                                       121
Exercises                                                      122
Further reading                                                124

6 The economics of market power                                125

Introduction                                                   125
6.1 Firm size                                                  126
6.2 The economics of market power                              133
6.3 How to sustain monopoly power                              141
6.4 Market power with few firms – the case of oligopoly        142
6.5 Conclusions                                                146

Summary 147
Questions for discussion 148
Exercises 149
Further reading 150
Case study 6.1: The diamond cartel 151

## 7 Competition policy, privatisation and regulation 155

Introduction 155
7.1 The case for competition 156
7.2 Competition policy 159
7.3 Privatisation 169
7.4 Regulation 171
7.5 Conclusions 175
Summary 176
Questions for discussion 177
Exercises 177
Further reading 179

## 8 Government intervention and the market system 180

Introduction 180
8.1 Income distribution and the equity–efficiency trade-off 182
8.2 Market failures 187
8.3 Government intervention 193
8.4 Government failure 198
8.5 Conclusions 202
Summary 203
Questions for discussion 204
Exercises 205
Further reading 205

## 9 Business and the environment 206

Introduction 206
9.1 Economic growth and the environment 208
9.2 Environmental policies 211
9.3 Policy instruments: design and effects 214
9.4 Impact on business 219
9.5 Conclusions 222
Summary 223
Questions for discussion 224
Exercises 224
Further reading 226

## 10 Hiring labour and the investment decision 227

Introduction 227

10.1   The hiring decision                                                      227
10.2   The investment decision                                                  232
10.3   Conclusions                                                              238
Summary                                                                         239
Questions for discussion                                                        239
Exercises                                                                       240
Further reading                                                                 241

## Part II   The macroeconomic framework

Introduction to Part II                                                         244

## 11 Aggregate supply, aggregate demand and the price level

                                                                                246
Introduction                                                                    246
11.1   How is gross domestic product (GDP) calculated?                          247
11.2   Potential GDP, actual GDP, and GDP at purchasing power
       parity (PPP)                                                             252
11.3   The aggregate supply (AS) curve                                          256
11.4   Aggregate demand (AD) and money                                          261
11.5   Conclusions                                                              271
Summary                                                                         272
Questions for discussion                                                        273
Exercises                                                                       273
Further reading                                                                 275
Appendix 11.1   The money supply process                                        275

## 12 Price stability and central banks

                                                                                276
Introduction                                                                    276
12.1   What is price stability?                                                 278
12.2   Deviation from price stability 1: inflation                              280
12.3   Deviation from price stability 2: deflation                              284
12.4   Benefits of price stability                                              286
12.5   Central banks and institutional reform                                   292
12.6   Price stability and exchange rate anchors                                296
12.7   Is inflation dead?                                                        300
12.8   Conclusions                                                              302
Summary                                                                         302
Questions for discussion                                                        303
Exercises                                                                       304
Further reading                                                                 304

## 13 Understanding interest rates and monetary policy

                                                                                305
Introduction                                                                    305

13.1 Which interest rate? 306
13.2 What determines interest rates? 311
13.3 Interest rates and economic activity 315
13.4 Monetary policy and interest rates 318
13.5 The design of monetary policy 324
13.6 Conclusions 328
Summary 329
Questions for discussion 330
Exercises 331
Further reading 332
Case study 13.1 Taylor's rule for monetary policy 334

## 14 Unemployment and the labour market 336

Introduction 336
14.1 Facts about unemployment 338
14.2 Supply-side approach and the market mechanism 342
14.3 Short-run versus long-run perspectives 348
14.4 The importance of demand 352
14.5 Technology, productivity and unemployment 355
14.6 Labour market policies 357
14.7 Conclusions 360
Summary 363
Questions for discussion 364
Exercises 364
Further reading 365
Appendix 14.1 Unemployment and inflation – the Phillips curve 365

## 15 Fiscal policy, budget deficits and government debt 370

Introduction 370
15.1 Counter-cyclical fiscal policy 371
15.2 The limits of fiscal activism 376
15.3 Public debt and 'crowding out' 381
15.4 Fiscal policy in Europe 388
15.5 Conclusions 393
Summary 395
Questions for discussion 396
Exercises 397
Further reading 398
Appendix 15.1 The sustainability of debt 398

## 16 Business fluctuations and forecasting 401

Introduction 401
16.1 Business fluctuations – the facts 403
16.2 What causes fluctuations? 407
16.3 Business fluctuations and growth 411

16.4   Forecasting the business cycle                                    412
16.5   Macro-forecasts and the firm                                      416
16.6   Conclusions                                                       417
Summary                                                                  418
Questions for discussion                                                 419
Exercises                                                                419
Further reading                                                          419

## Part III   The global economy

Introduction to Part III                                                 422

## 17 Foreign trade: patterns and policy                                 424

Introduction                                                             424
17.1   Global trade and the WTO                                          425
17.2   Explaining the gains from international trade                      431
17.3   Quantifying the gains from trade                                  438
17.4   Trade policy and protection                                       442
17.5   What determines comparative advantage?                            449
17.6   Conclusions                                                       452
Summary                                                                  454
Questions for discussion                                                 455
Exercises                                                                456
Further reading                                                          457
Case study 17.1   China and the WTO: the effects of trade liberalisation   458

## 18 Capital flows and foreign investment                               462

Introduction                                                             462
18.1   Capital flows                                                     463
18.2   Basic model                                                       465
18.3   Foreign direct investment and multinationals                      471
18.4   Effects of foreign investment                                     479
18.5   Conclusions                                                       484
Summary                                                                  485
Questions for discussion                                                 486
Exercises                                                                486
Further reading                                                          487

## 19 Labour migration                                                   488

Introduction                                                             488
19.1   Recent trends                                                     489
19.2   Effects of migration – the basic model                            491
19.3   Migration, public finances and jobs                               494

19.4   Conclusions                                                           498
Summary                                                                      499
Questions for discussion                                                     499
Exercises                                                                    500
Further reading                                                              500

## 20   The balance of payments: what it is and why it matters   501

Introduction                                                                 501
20.1   What is the balance of payments?                                      502
20.2   Balance of payments problems                                          509
20.3   How to correct a balance of payments imbalance                        518
20.4   Conclusions                                                           523
Summary                                                                      524
Questions for discussion                                                     525
Exercises                                                                    526
Further reading                                                              527

## 21   Coping with exchange rates                               528

Introduction                                                                 528
21.1   How exchange rates work                                               529
21.2   Exchange rate theory                                                  536
21.3   Capital flows and exchange rate volatility                            542
21.4   Strategies for coping with exchange rate risk                         548
21.5   Conclusions                                                           554
Summary                                                                      556
Questions for discussion                                                     556
Exercises                                                                    557
Further reading                                                              558
Appendix 21.1   The global foreign exchange market                           558

## 22   Exchange rate regimes and the euro                       561

Introduction                                                                 561
22.1   The global exchange rate system                                       563
22.2   Floating exchange rates                                               566
22.3   Search for stability                                                  573
22.4   Establishing a single currency – the euro                             580
22.5   Conclusions                                                           586
Summary                                                                      587
Questions for discussion                                                     588
Exercises                                                                    589
Further reading                                                              589
Appendix 22.1   Exchange rate regimes – a brief history                      590

Index                                                                        595

# List of boxes

| | | |
|---|---|---|
| 1.1 | The economic policy consensus | 3 |
| 2.1 | Efficiency, opportunity cost and no free lunch | 18 |
| 2.2 | Production functions and economic growth | 20 |
| 2.3 | To improve GDP as a measure of welfare, ... | 27 |
| 2.4 | The human development index | 31 |
| 2.5 | The arithmetic of growth | 32 |
| 2.6 | Lessons from East Asia | 34 |
| 3.1 | The shadow economy | 52 |
| 3.2 | A market economy | 66 |
| 4.1 | The cellophane case | 81 |
| 4.2 | Estimating a demand function | 83 |
| 4.3 | Which market, which elasticity? | 86 |
| 5.1 | The principal–agent problem | 97 |
| 5.2 | Profit maximisation in action | 99 |
| 5.3 | Derivation of profit-maximisation rule | 102 |
| 5.4 | What economics means by profit | 105 |
| 5.5 | Adam Smith's division of labour | 111 |
| 6.1 | US government vs Microsoft – competition among the few? | 129 |
| 6.2 | Six factors tending to intensify competition | 131 |
| 6.3 | When competition induces pricing below cost | 139 |
| 6.4 | Price strategies and profits | 145 |
| 7.1 | The economic case for competition | 157 |
| 7.2 | Competition – definitions | 160 |
| 7.3 | EU competition law – Articles 81 and 82 | 161 |
| 7.4 | Exclusive dealing in the European motor trade | 162 |
| 7.5 | EU competition law – the Woodpulp case | 164 |
| 7.6 | Competition law with teeth | 166 |
| 7.7 | The case of the cement industry | 167 |
| 7.8 | Reasons for privatising | 170 |
| 8.1 | The equity–efficiency trade-off | 185 |
| 8.2 | Industrial subsidies in the European Union | 196 |
| 8.3 | Corruption, government and growth | 200 |
| 9.1 | Taxing unleaded petrol | 216 |
| 9.2 | Green as a selling point | 221 |
| 10.1 | Weakness of pay-back and IRR techniques | 235 |
| 11.1 | National income, gross national product (GNP) and gross domestic product (GDP) | 250 |
| 11.2 | Open market operations | 266 |
| 12.1 | The costs of deflation | 290 |
| 12.2 | The European Central Bank | 293 |
| 12.3 | Forecasting by lead indicators | 295 |

| | | |
|---|---|---|
| 12.4 | Price stability lost and gained: lessons from Argentina | 297 |
| 13.1 | Interest rates and cash-flow effects | 316 |
| 13.2 | Effects of interest rate changes on consumer wealth | 317 |
| 13.3 | How central banks define their objectives | 320 |
| 14.1 | Labour market flexibility | 344 |
| 14.2 | Technological change and employment: the lessons of history | 356 |
| 14.3 | OECD jobs policy – 10 years later | 358 |
| 15.1 | The limits of fiscal activism | 377 |
| 15.2 | Ricardian equivalence | 383 |
| 15.3 | Can fiscal contraction be expansionary? | 387 |
| 15.4 | Fiscal discipline in the EMU | 391 |
| 16.1 | Business cycles in the dynamic Asian economies | 405 |
| 16.2 | How changes in domestic activity affect economic variables | 406 |
| 16.3 | The multiplier–accelerator model | 408 |
| 16.4 | Top-down forecast of demand for personal computers | 416 |
| 17.1 | The World Trade Organisation (WTO) | 430 |
| 17.2 | Comparative advantage in action | 433 |
| 17.3 | The Uruguay Round and beyond | 440 |
| 17.4 | Adam Smith's argument for protection | 443 |
| 17.5 | Job losses and imports | 444 |
| 18.1 | Why is inward foreign direct investment to Japan so low? | 474 |
| 18.2 | Why do firms invest abroad? | 476 |
| 18.3 | Transfer pricing | 481 |
| 18.4 | Incentives and foreign direct investment | 484 |
| 19.1 | Migrants and government finances | 495 |
| 20.1 | How to interpret a current account deficit | 511 |
| 20.2 | A tale of three deficits: the US deficit, Third World debt forgiveness and deficits in Euroland | 513 |
| 20.3 | Balance of payments, country indebtedness and country risk ratings | 516 |
| 20.4 | Expenditure switching and the US deficit | 522 |
| 21.1 | The exchange rate – basic definitions | 530 |
| 21.2 | How changes in the exchange rate affect profits | 532 |
| 21.3 | The monetary approach to the balance of payments | 540 |
| 21.4 | Are foreign exchange markets efficient? | 545 |
| 21.5 | A foreign currency options contract | 551 |
| 21.6 | Example of a swap | 552 |
| 22.1 | How small countries choose an exchange rate regime | 568 |
| 22.2 | The 'tequila effect', contagion and the Mexican peso crisis, 1994–95 | 577 |
| 22.3 | The path to the euro | 581 |
| 22.4 | Economics of the euro: the story so far | 584 |

# Preface to the third edition

Economics is an integral part of the curriculum for graduate and undergraduate business programmes. Most MBA courses contain several economics modules, as do professional courses in banking, insurance, actuarial science and information technology. *Economics for Business* has been written to provide a considered, comprehensive, yet accessible introduction to economics to accompany such courses.

Although there are many good introductory economics texts, I found that none quite matched the needs of the many MBA and 'economics for business' modules that I had taught over the previous 25 years. The standard economics text is over-inclusive in some respects – for example, in the treatment of consumer choice theory, but not comprehensive enough in others – for example, in explaining interest rates or the determinants of exchange rates, which are central issues in a business-oriented economics course. Also, some texts tend to talk down to the reader in a way that is especially alienating to course participants with years of work experience.

Hence my motivation to write the original edition of *Economics for Business*. By being especially tailored for a business-oriented audience, I hoped that it would make the economics module in a business or professional programme an instructive and enjoyable experience. The fact of it reaching a third edition suggests some modest success in achieving this ambition.

## What this book offers

This third edition maintains the theme of previous editions in examining economics from a *business perspective*. We focus on concepts and information which are helpful in understanding economic performance and policy. The book is especially concerned with the interaction between business and practical economic problems. We pay attention to points of overlap and contrast between economics and other business subjects such as accountancy, strategic management and marketing.

Economic textbooks cover subjects that currently concern economists. They provide a snapshot of where economics is, without enquiring too much about whether this is a useful place to be. *Economics for Business* is *selective*. Subjects are included because they throw light on issues relevant to business. Business has to operate in an economic environment that has become vastly more competitive, more open in terms of foreign trade, investment and capital markets, and where government support to business has become more targeted and results-oriented.

Within this context, the book aims to provide a *comprehensive overview* of the three branches of economics essential to business: the economics of the market system and competition, macroeconomics, and globalisation. Managerial economics textbooks cover microeconomic aspects, and some textbooks address macroeconomic issues from a business point of view. This book covers both micro- and macro-topics. Most important of all, it focuses on the increased openness and globalisation of the economy, subjects on which every business reader needs to be well informed.

The style is non-technical and down to earth. We rely on words and diagrams to convey the message, and avoid equations. For students with a technical background who wish to probe deeper into the subject, there are references to more advanced literature at the end of each chapter.

Economic ideas do not spring from the air. They are inspired by particular economic and social events and perspectives. Further, economic ideas change. They are not set down in tablets of stone. *Economics for Business* sets these ideas in their historical and social context.

Some people find economics an infuriatingly elusive subject. Business readers often start by expecting much more precision from the subject than it can honestly provide. The questions are simple:

● How does the market system work?
● How do firms maximise profits in an open market? What should their pricing strategy be?
● What role should government play in a modern economy?
● What determines interest rates?
● What role do central banks play in the economy?
● How can we moderate business fluctuations?
● What is the balance of payments, and why is it important?
● Why do exchange rates fluctuate so much?
● What can be done to speed up economic growth?

The answers are complex – usually of the 'it all depends' type – because the issues are complex. Economics is not a body of laws, but is rather a way of thinking. Students appreciate this. In my experience, they are not afraid of complexity and do not want facile answers. They would like to know enough economic theory to make their own assessment of economic policies, without having to go through long disquisitions about the finer points of the subject. This book strikes a *balance between the theory and practice of economics*.

## What the reader should learn

Having read this book, the reader should have acquired an understanding of:

1. How the economy functions, how resources are allocated and how income distribution is determined.
2. The analytical basis of economic policy decisions and economic forecasts.
3. The role of government in the economy, both at the sectoral and firm level and at the broader macroeconomic level.
4. The linkages between economics and other subjects on a business programme.
5. The basic vocabulary of economics and its intellectual origins.

Questions for Discussion and Exercises are included at the end of each chapter to test your understanding.

## Plan of the book

Our starting point is a discussion of economic policies (Chapter 1) and the causes of economic growth (Chapter 2). The latter topic is often omitted from business economics courses, which is a pity, given the practical as well as academic importance of growth. This chapter sketches arguments, concepts and points of view, which are elaborated later in the book.

Following the introductory chapters, Part I provides an analysis of competition and the market system, with discussion of the role of markets, determinants of demand and supply, the role of the firm and how its pricing and output decisions are made, the effects of competition and privatisation on economic performance and the reasons why government intervenes in the economy. This part helps us understand why economic policy has become more focused on using the market system to achieve objectives.

Part II provides an overview of modern macroeconomics. It explains why price stability and budgetary restraint are important policy objectives, how these objectives can best be achieved and how the resulting policy decisions affect business. Interest rates, the central bank and fiscal policy enter into consideration here. We explain why rising public debt is a major source of concern to business in many countries. Unemployment and business fluctuations are also discussed.

Part III examines the role of foreign trade, the increasing globalisation of investment, the expansion of capital flows (reflected in the growth of derivatives trading) and labour migration. The balance of payments and exchange rates are discussed. Special attention is given to Economic and Monetary Union (EMU) in Europe, which is already having major implications for business.

## Appreciation

Many people have helped to bring this edition into print. My primary debt is to Ruth Gill who acted as research assistant and general advisor on all aspects of the work. Her insights, skill and commitment made an invaluable contribution. Barry Rafferty did sterling work in summer 2002, assisting with updates and new ideas. Charles Larkin provided highly percipient critiques of macroeconomic chapters and guided me to economic literature I might easily have overlooked. Colette Ding and Liam Delaney acted as sounding boards and were always helpful and ready with suggestions. To all the above production team, my warmest thanks.

This book is written by a single author, and a single author must rely heavily on criticism and conversation with fellow professionals if mistakes are to be avoided. 'It is astonishing what foolish things one can temporarily believe if one thinks too long alone,' as Keynes remarked in the Preface to the *General Theory*, 'particularly in economics where it is often impossible to bring one's ideas to a conclusive test either formal or experimental.' I owe a great deal to colleagues in the economics department and business school at Trinity College Dublin, and elsewhere, and to interactions and conversations with business people in Ireland and abroad. Also, I continue to be indebted to John Martin (OECD) for sharing his encyclopedic knowledge of economics policy issues with me.

This book has grown out of lectures to the Trinity MBA programme and to other executive postgraduate courses and undergraduate programmes in Trinity College Dublin, the Irish Management Institute, the ENPC School of

International Management, Paris, and associate courses in Tongji University, Shanghai, Ecole Hassania des Travaux Publics, Casablanca, and before that in Mendoza, Argentina and Kochi, India. The enthusiasm, commitment and probing questions of the participants in these courses have been a source of inspiration to me for many years.

The staff at Pearson Education, in particular acquisitions editor, Paula Harris, and production editor, Anita Atkinson, and her team, including the anonymous readers, were unfailingly helpful and a source of many improvements. Finally, my continuing thanks to Camilla for editorial advice and unfailing support, and to Emma and Susannah for tolerating the intrusions of this enterprise on family life.

A website to accompany this book is available at **www.booksites.net/mcaleese** see below.

*Dermot McAleese*
*Trinity College Dublin*

dermot.mcaleese@tcd.ie
www.economics.tcd.ie/staff/dermot_mcaleese.htm

## Website resources for Economics for Business

**For students:**
- An online glossary to explain key terms
- Links to relevant sites on the web

**For lecturers:**
- A secure, password protected site with teaching material
- Complete, downloadable Instructor's Manual
- PowerPoint slides that can be downloaded and used as OHTs
- Additional cases and question material

**Also:** This site has a syllabus manager, search functions, and email results functions.

# Acknowledgements

We are grateful to the following for permission to reproduce copyright material:

Tables 2.1 and 2.3 computed from Angus Maddison, *The World Economy: a millennial perspective* (Paris: OECD, 2001); Tables 2.1, 2.3 and Box 2.6 from *World Economic Outlook*, April 2002, the International Monetary Fund; Table 3.1 from F. Schneider, *'The value added underground activities: size and measurement of the shadow economies of 110 countries all over the world'*, June 2002, reproduced with permission; Figure 3.2 from Smith, S. (1986) *Britain's Shadow Economy* (Oxford, Clarendon Press), reproduced by permission of Oxford University Press; Table 4.2 from Falvey, R. E. and Gemmell, N, 'Are services income-elastic? Some new evidence', *Review of Income and Wealth*, University of Nottingham, September 1996; extracts used in Case Study 6.1 and Box 7.4 from *The Economist* (various dates); Tables 6.3 and 6.4 from *The European Observatory for SMEs*, reproduced by permission of EIM Small Business Research and Consultancy, Zoetermeer, The Netherlands. (*http://europa.eu.int/ comm/enterprise*); Box 10.1 from Gray, A. W. (1995) *EU Structural Funds and Other Public Sector Investments: A guide to evaluation methods* (Dublin, Gill & MacMillan); Figure 11.2 from *Economic Outlook*, June 2002, OECD; Tables 12.1, 12.2, 12.3 and Figure 12.3 from *World Economic Outlook*, successive issues, IMF; Figure 12.2 from *World Economic Outlook*, April 2003, the International Monetary Fund; Table 12.3 from *Transition Report 1999*, European Bank for Reconstruction & Development; Figure 12.4 from Barro, R. J., & Grilli, V. (1994) *European Macroeconomics*, Palgrave Macmillan, reproduced with permission; Table 14.1 from *European Economy*, OECD; Tables 15.1 and 15.2 from *World Economic Outlook*, May 1996 and September 2003, the International Monetary Fund; Table 15.3 from *European Economy*, Annual Reports, successive years, OECD and Vitto Tanzi & Ludger Schuknecht, *Public Spending in the 20th Century*, 2000, Cambridge University Press, reproduced with permission; Table 15.4 from *Economic Outlook*, OECD, various issues; Table 15.7 from *Economic Economy*, Autumn 2003, OECD; Figure 17.4 from *The Competitive Advantages of Nations*, Michael E. Porter ©1990, 1998, reproduced with permission of Simon & Schuster inc.; Box 17.5 from Blinder, A.S. (1989) *Macroeconomics Under Debate* (Hemel Hempstead, Harvester Wheatsheaf), originally published in *American Economic Review*, May 1988, reproduced with permission from the American Economic Association; Table 18.1 from *World Economic Outlook*, September 2002, Table 44, the International Monetary Fund; Tables 18.2 and 18.3 from UNCTAD Division on Investment, Technology & Enterprise Development, reprinted with permission; Table 19.1 from *OECD Observer* (June/July 1992), OECD and *Trends in International Migration* (Paris, 2002); Table 19.2 from *Trends in International Migration* (Paris, 2002), OECD; Box 20.4 from Krugman, P. (1994) *The Age of Diminished Expectations* (Cambridge, Mass, MIT Press); Figure 21.1 from *Economic Outlook*, (June 2002), OECD.

We are grateful to the Financial Times Limited for permission to reprint the following material:

Box 7.2 Competition – Definitions, from *The Financial Times Limited*, 7 November 2002, © John Kay; Figure 22.3 Dollar hits record low as Japan and US fail to halt slide, © *Financial Times*, 4th April, 1995.

In some instances we have been unable to trace the owners of copyright material, and we would appreciate any information that would enable us to do so.

## Chapter 1

# The economic policy consensus

## Introduction

At the start of the twenty-first century, economic policies throughout the world have converged around three basic principles:

1. There is emphasis on *using market mechanisms* to achieve objectives, with resort to state intervention on a highly selective and targeted basis.
2. Macroeconomic policy is oriented to ensuring *a stable economic framework* rather than achieving proactive counter-cyclical targets or national plan growth rates and investment targets.
3. National policies have become *more outward-looking*, as evidenced by the steadily increasing membership of the World Trade Organisation (WTO), the relaxation of controls on capital mobility and the globally more benign stance towards foreign investment.

The economic policy consensus has evolved not because the principles of economics have changed, but because over time we have learned more about the inferences that can be drawn from them. Accompanying this consensus are policy priorities, which are having a major impact on global standards of living, income distribution and lifestyles.

The global reach of the economic consensus is its most remarkable characteristic. In Europe and North America, the key turning points were the policy reforms of Prime Minister Thatcher and President Reagan in the first half of the 1980s. New Zealand and Australia developed even more radical pro-market policies. In South America, dramatic policy initiatives were taken in Chile during the 1980s, and Chile's example was followed by Bolivia, Mexico, Colombia, Argentina and Brazil. In Asia, India embraced a reform package in the early 1990s which focused on a more intensive use of market incentives in domestic labour and product markets, openness to trade and foreign investment, and fiscal stability. China too has become more conscious of the need to use market mechanisms. Throughout Eastern Europe and the former Soviet Union, policy-makers have turned away from economic planning and price controls, and are searching for ways of making their markets function more efficiently, through privatisation programmes, market flexibility measures, competition policy and more enterprise-friendly tax regimes.

Chapter outline

These policy changes are having a profound effect on the business environment. In this chapter we present:

1. A brief sketch of what the economic consensus is.

2. Why it has evolved.

3. Its likely future impact on business, employees and government.

4. Criticisms of the new consensus.

5. Its continuing relevance in the face of new challenges and stresses on the global economy.

## 1.1 The economic policy consensus

### Competition and the market system

The first pillar of the consensus concerns the role of the market system and competition in ensuring that the economy operates effectively. One manifestation of the new policy is the movement towards 'smaller' government. The share of government spending in national output in most industrial countries lies in the range 40–50 per cent. Prior to the First World War, government spending was typically below 20 per cent of GNP. Governments with high spending ratios began to query whether they were getting value for money and concluded that they were not. They responded by introducing programmes of privatisation and deregulation, two hallmarks of the new policy orientation. Also, the public sector was subjected to market-type disciplines through tendering, charging for public services, contracting out of services and extension of managerial accountability to government departments. Market mechanisms are being used in preference to regulation as a way of achieving policy objectives. For example, instead of prohibiting pollution by command and control methods, environmental policy applies market incentives, such as subsidies to cleaner production methods or higher taxes on industrial waste. In this way, the price mechanism replaces legal and administrative hassle as the means of achieving the desired reduction in pollution.

As we shall see, markets perform efficiently only if there is competition. In many countries, competition law has been strengthened and its range of application extended to hitherto protected sectors in telecommunications, transport, energy and postal services. Tendering for public contracts has become open to foreign as well as to domestic firms. Trade unions also have found their monopoly power challenged. There is an emphasis on labour market flexibility as being the way to solve the unemployment problem. Capital markets too have been affected by the new thinking. The markets have been liberalised and long-established distortions between different types of financial institutions are being removed.

Policy-makers have also become more conscious of the distortionary effects of the tax system on the behaviour of economic 'agents' in their role as buyers and sellers, savers and investors, employers and employees. High marginal tax rates tend to blunt economic incentives, as well as being complicated and difficult to enforce. Greater tax uniformity and tax 'neutrality' between different types of economic activity have become important fiscal objectives in many countries. Enterprise is being subjected to fewer regulations and lower tax rates. The buzzword is 'enterprise-friendly environment'. But business beware! Enterprise-friendly does not mean friendly to all enterprises. The new environment is decidedly *un*friendly to state enterprises that were once sheltered from private sector competition and to national enterprises exposed to competition from low-cost competitors. 'Friendly' has to be interpreted in a Darwinian sense.

---

**Box 1.1    The economic policy consensus**

**1. Competition and the market system**
- Pro-competition policies
- Labour market flexibility
- Privatisation
- Deregulation
- Enterprise-friendly environment

**2. Macro-stability**
- Price stability (independent central bank, 'hard' exchange rate)
- Budget balance
- Control of government spending

**3. Globalisation of business**
- Free trade
- Foreign investment
- Liberalisation of capital
- Labour mobility

---

## Macroeconomic stability

In macroeconomic policy there has also been a marked shift in orientation. Since the 1990s, price stability has been identified as a key objective. Central banks have the responsibility for maintaining price stability and legislation has been enacted in many countries to ensure that the monetary authorities have the degree of independence from political control needed to carry out their remit. Some smaller countries have tied their currencies to larger, low-inflation currencies as a way of maintaining price stability. Several European countries have tied their exchange rate to the euro for this reason.

Together with prioritising price stability, another key element in a macro-stability package is a commitment to low budget deficits. Fiscal policy in Europe, for example, has been dominated by the Maastricht criteria – conditions which countries must satisfy as a condition of membership of the single currency. One of these criteria stipulates that government borrowing should not exceed 3 per cent of a country's national output, a limit that continues to be imposed on those countries that participate in the euro. Many countries outside Western Europe embarked on stabilisation and structural adjustment programmes which incorporated fiscal 'balance' (i.e. low budget deficits and declining debt relative to national output) as a key objective. Even the Scandinavian countries, once regarded as enthusiastic practitioners of counter-cyclical policies, have become converts to a more cautious and conservative use of fiscal instruments. The spectre of ageing populations and unfunded entitlement programmes have combined to make governments more concerned about the future viability of public finances.

The objective of macro-stability cannot be divorced from the problem of unemployment. A central tenet of the current consensus is that better control of government finances will stimulate private investment and help to reduce unemployment. Reduction in public spending creates space for tax reductions. Tax reductions reduce disincentives to work and to hire employees. In addition, low inflation helps employees reach more rational decisions about pay. Macro-stability is an effective means of achieving sustained growth.

## Global trade in goods, services and factors of production

The liberalisation of international transactions is the third pillar of the new policy consensus. The catchword *globalisation* has been coined to describe this process. Having tried import-substitution policies, many countries concluded that they are of limited value and that openness was a superior policy. Since the 1980s, a virtual revolution in trade policy has taken place, as one country after another liberalised its trade regime. Over 140 countries have signed up to membership of the World Trade Organisation. Developing countries are now active participants in the movement towards a more liberal world trading system. Although having a per capita income only 10 per cent that of the United States, Mexico voluntarily concluded a free trade area agreement with the United States and Canada.

Likewise, the Central European countries have concluded free trade agreements with the European Union (EU). Turkey's low per capita income has not prevented it from forming a customs union with the EU. Although wedded for many decades to the idea of self-sufficiency, China has become a member of the WTO and has indicated its readiness to abide by the liberal trade rules of that organisation. In the early 1990s, India too abandoned its *dirigiste* policies and replaced them with trade liberalisation and a more open-door policy to foreign investment. Further liberalisation of international transactions has been effected through regional integration initiatives in Asia, Latin America and, more tentatively, in Africa. Most countries have abandoned the idea of development through intensive cultivation of the domestic market and have replaced it with the ambition of penetrating foreign markets and of achieving growth through exports.

The three elements of the new policy package are interdependent. The logic of the package was described by Professor Jeffrey Sachs in the context of Poland's stabilisation plan in the late 1980s:

> The basic goal was to move from a situation of extreme shortages and hyperinflation to one of supply-and-demand balance and stable prices. For this, Poland needed tight macroeconomic policies with the decontrol of prices. To have a working price system, Poland needed competition. To have competition it needed free international trade. ... To have free trade it needed not only low tariffs, but the convertibility of

currency. To have convertibility of currency at a stable exchange rate, it needed monetary discipline and a realistic exchange rate. [1]

This logic underpinned the 1990 Balcerowitz Plan, which guided Poland's successful, if by no means painless, transformation from socialism to capitalism during the 1990s. The changed perception of what makes economies prosperous has influenced economic policy in a way and to a degree which has had momentous consequences for firms, individuals and the state itself.

## 1.2 Why policy changed

Economic policy changes in response to the perceived failure of past policies. Up to the 1970s, it seemed that Russia and the other socialist economies were performing well – even outpacing many Western countries. At the same time, activist government policies were thought to have been instrumental in setting many industrial countries on a more stable and rapid growth path than ever before. That perception changed after the oil price increases and the resultant slowdown in growth. The first reason for the change in policy, therefore, was the deterioration in the industrial countries' economic performance.

Second, the socialist model lost credibility. The poor record of achievement of the socialist countries gradually became apparent. Even benign versions of socialism, such as the justly admired social market economy of Scandinavia, began to run into difficulties.

Third, the economic success of East Asia contrasted with the economic decline of Africa and Latin America. While the reasons for the former's success continue to be debated, and the currency crisis of 1997–98 removed some of the gloss on the region's 'success', the key factor in Asia's superior performance was the adoption of more liberal economic policies. For many developing countries wedded to an interventionist policy regime, the 1980s was a 'lost decade' – 'lost' because zero or even negative growth per person was achieved in that period. Reviewing the many conflicting explanations for India's 'dismal' economic performance since the 1960s, Professor Balasubramanyam concluded:

> The interventionist economic regime, with import substitution and self-sufficiency as its objectives, is largely responsible for India's poor economic performance. [2]

Fourth, developments in economic theory showed how even the best-intentioned government intervention tended to create distortions in the system, which could be even more damaging than the faults in the private sector market it was designed to correct. This is called the problem of 'government failure'. New ways of measuring the gains from foreign trade revealed the important benefits to be derived from economies of scale and competition. The potential benefits of fiscal consolidation on growth were also found to be greater than expected. Generally, countries that placed higher priority on market incentives, macro-stability and freer trade performed better.

---

[1] Jeffrey Sachs, *Poland's Jump to the Market Economy* (Cambridge, MA: MIT Press, 1993), p. 54.
[2] V.N. Balasubramanyam, 'India's trade policy review', *The World Economy* (special issue 1995), p. 80.

Fifth, advances in technology reduced the cost of communication and travel, making government restrictions on movement harder to enforce and making high taxes, and arbitrary regulation easier to evade. Also, the more countries adopting the policy consensus, the greater the practical difficulty of being an 'outlier'.

Practical experience and theoretical developments therefore conjoined to induce governments to undertake a radical review of their economic policies. Out of this review, which extended over two decades, came the economic policy programmes now being adopted in more and more countries in both the developed and the developing worlds.

## 1.3 Implications for the future

The new consensus policy regime is having major implications for the business environment and living standards. Its long-term effects are as yet a matter of speculation. For firms, it means widening opportunities, but less safety, as the domestic market becomes more exposed to competition. For employees, it means higher productivity and higher salaries for those able to adjust to the new system. Advocates of the new policy regime claim that economies adopting it will grow faster as a result.

Alongside this, there may be less job security. As domestic markets are opened to global competition, small changes in costs abroad can undermine a domestic firm's competitiveness with the result that many industries become 'footloose'. Multinationals move around seeking lower-cost locations and there is greater volatility all round. Accompanying this, we may see a widening inequality of incomes, something that is already evident in countries such as the US and the UK. The new policy regime will also mean a more flexible labour market, with less demarcation, less rigid pay scales, weaker trade unions and more varied forms of employment. This will make it easier for people to find employment, but equally it will make it less troublesome for employers to dismiss them. An optimistic view is that on balance there will be major gains for developed countries and even more so for developing countries. China and India seem to be particularly well placed to benefit from economic reform and if so we can expect to see a continuing shift in economic power towards what we now call the Third World later in the century.

The new policy consensus involves losers as well as gainers. The gainers are likely to be far more numerous than the losers but this does not rule out the possibility of temporary backlashes such as were witnessed at the Seattle trade conference in December 1999 and, before that, during the Asian currency crisis of 1997–98. Alongside this, there will be ongoing debate about the precise constellation of new consensus policies to adopt. The contest between the European labour market model (with its emphasis on job security, decent holidays and partnership) and the US model (emphasising low taxes and labour mobility) will feature prominently in this debate. Policy reform is based on ideas about both the causes of growth and the link between economic growth and economic policy. It is precisely the existence of such a link that makes economics an important subject for a business-oriented reader, and that makes the study of the principles on which economic policy is based an essential element in any business studies programme.

## 1.4 Criticisms of the new consensus

The new economic consensus has attracted strong criticism, even from those who admit to finding much that is right and helpful in its broad policy framework. Among the best-known critics are Joseph Stiglitz, a former chief economist of the World Bank and Nobel prizewinner in economics, Professors Dani Rodrik of Harvard, Robert Wade of LSE and Ha-Joon Chang.[3]

At the outset, it is worth noting that some of the most severe critics of the new consensus concede that there are important advantages to the new approach to policy advice. 'It [the new consensus] focuses on issues of first-order importance,' writes Professor Stiglitz, 'it sets up an easily reproducible framework and it is frank about limiting itself only to establishing prerequisites for development.' He goes on to comment:

> Why has globalisation – a force that has brought so much good – become so controversial? Opening up to international trade has helped many countries grow far more quickly than they would otherwise have done. International trade helps economic development ... Export-led growth was the centrepiece of the industrial policy that enriched much of Asia and left millions of people there far better off. Because of globalisation many people in the world now live longer than before and their standard of living is far better. People in the West may regard low paying jobs in Nike as exploitation, but for many people in the developing world working in a factory is a far better option that staying down on the farm and growing rice. (Stiglitz, 2000, p. 4)

What then is the problem? Two key criticisms are that policies advanced by the consensus are *incomplete* and *sometimes misguided*.[4] Let us consider each of these criticisms in turn.

First, in focusing on trade liberalisation, deregulation and privatisation, the new consensus programme has been criticised for giving insufficient attention to other important ingredients of an efficient market, most notably the ongoing need for government intervention in areas such as education, health and technology improvement. The need for government regulation of the financial sector, critics argue, has also been underplayed. Building robust financial systems is essential for an effective market system and will not be supplied automatically by market forces.

In a similar vein, critics have attacked the over-hasty, ideologically driven introduction of privatisation in countries where the regulatory and institutional

---

[3] See Joseph Stiglitz, *Globalisation and its Discontents* (London: Allen Lane, 2002) and 'More instruments and broader goals: moving toward the post-Washington consensus', WIDER Annual Lecture, United Nations University, Helsinki, 1998. Robert Wade has been a consistent and thoughtful critic of new consensus thinking for a much longer time. He has written on East Asia emphasising the positive role of state intervention in the area's development. Ha-Joon Chang, *Kicking Away the Ladder: Development strategy in historical perspective* (London: Anthem Press, 2002), criticises economists for urging developing countries to adopt policies that the present high-income countries never applied to themselves at a comparable stage of development.

[4] J. Stiglitz, *Globalisation and its Discontents* (London: Allen Lane, 2002).

structure to accompany such privatisation was absent and where income distribution issues were not addressed. The result has been a drastic overestimation of the gains from such privatisation programmes. (The Russian privatisation programme has attracted special censure in this respect.) For many transition and developing countries, in other words, the problem is one of insufficient government capabilities (independent judiciary, competitive wages for civil servants, administrative and technical capacity, incentive systems in the public sector) rather than too much government *per se*.

The macro-stability pillar of the new consensus has also been criticised for putting too much emphasis on price stability and not enough on growth. Stiglitz accuses the International Monetary Fund in particular of imposing over-severe stabilisation policies on developing countries at the expense of high unemployment and slower growth.

Finally, critics argue that the benefits of globalisation to developing countries have been oversold. In many cases, liberalisation programmes have been introduced too quickly, thereby exposing domestic industries to foreign competition before they had time to adjust. To make matters worse, industrial countries' markets remain protected, especially in the food and textiles sectors where developing country exports have a comparative advantage. To add to this, the case has been made that rich countries have benefited disproportionately from the intellectual property rules introduced by the World Trade Organisation. Likewise many developing and transition countries have been persuaded to liberalise capital movements ahead of their capacity to cope with the resultant volatility, leaving US and European financial institutions as the only beneficiaries.

What are we to make of these criticisms? First, there is a significant element of truth in many of them. They strike a resonant note in countries that have been bypassed in the growth stakes (and there are many of these, as we shall see in Chapter 2). The World Trade Organisation (WTO) conference in Doha in 2001, for instance, acknowledged the validity of developing country concerns about the costs to them of such matters as the WTO's intellectual property rules, difficulties and cost of implementing WTO procedures, and the incidence of protection in developed countries. The resultant Doha Development Agenda has placed these concerns at the forefront for future trade rounds.

Second, most criticisms relate to the manner of implementation of new consensus policies rather than to the principles of the new consensus as such. The new consensus approach itself is not extreme or doctrinaire. The proposition that government intervention is a vital element in a modern economy would be acceptable to all except the most extreme right-wing. New consensus does not imply *laissez-faire*. Nor would there be any general disagreement that a gradualist approach might have been more effective than the extreme shock therapy reform strategies applied in Russia and other countries of the former Soviet Union. (Stiglitz contrasts the programme imposed on Russia with the far more successful 'gradualist' policy adopted by China.) There is widespread acceptance that capital liberalisation should come late in the policy reform process, well after trade and services sectors have been integrated into the international economy. Most new consensus economists would accept that there is no one-size-fits-all policy blueprint for developing countries that is appropriate in all circumstances. Sequencing and timing of the policy reform is something to be hammered out on a case-by-case basis.

Third, developing countries have not been prevented from adopting policies of protectionism, extensive government intervention, nationalisation and planning. These policies have been resorted to on a major scale. One could even agree that initially these policies led to improved living standards. But the benefits were not sustained, and over time the costs in terms of rampant inefficiency and corruption outweighed the benefits. This is why policy-makers in the developing countries themselves concluded that change was needed. They switched to the new consensus policy regime because they believed it would be more effective, not because the IMF or the World Bank ordered them to do so.[5]

In short, the critics of the new consensus have performed a useful function in drawing attention to the hard fact that getting economic policies right is a complex task. It is a necessary, but certainly not a sufficient, condition for rapid growth.

## 1.5  Will the consensus last?

The new consensus consists of an integrated and coherent set of policies that promises to engender better economic perfomance than the policies of the past. Research to date suggests that this promise has been realised. Free trade and globalisation have generated more jobs and higher incomes than protection and inward-looking policies. Countries that restrained inflation and controlled goverment spending have tended to perform better than average. Emphasis on competition and the market system has paid dividends in terms of more efficient enterprises and more effective achievement of government objectives.

Economic policies, however, are means to an end and not sacrosanct in themselves. The new consensus will last only so long as it delivers on its promise of higher living standards. Clearly it has done much for the developed countries of Western Europe and North America. (The case of New Zealand, an early and radical proponent of new consensus policies, where economic growth remains sluggish and where social cohesion has been damaged by excessive income disparities, remains, however, a worrying exception.)

An important issue will be the capacity of the new consensus policies to provide convincing outcomes for developing countries. These countries comprise some 80 per cent of the world population. Most of them have adopted the new policy orientation, but many still await a level of pay-back that the general public will find convincing. India and Morocco are two cases in point, and Argentina's collapse in 2002 an even more telling example. In each instance, the 'right' economic policies in terms of the three pillars outlined in Box 1.1 appear to have been implemented but most of their inhabitants remain poor, and

[5] Ha-Joon Chang argues that developing countries have liberalised too soon. He points out that their current level of protection is far lower than that of developed countries when they were at a comparable stage of development. India's average tariff fell from 71 per cent in the early 1990s to 32 per cent today, a level below which the US tariff never fell between the Civil War and the Second World War (Ha-Joon Chang, *Kicking Away the Ladder: Development strategy in historical perspective*, London: Anthem Press, 2002, p. 68). The flaw is his argument is that developing countries have already tried many of these intervention policies, with notable lack of success.

growth is modest relative to aspirations. While there is acceptance that the old policies of indiscriminate state intervention, excessive bureaucracy, high taxation and protection were ineffective, there is continuing scepticism about whether the new policies will produce any markedly better outcome. At worst, there is a nagging suspicion that adoption of the new policy regime has been forced upon them by international organisations such as the IMF and the World Bank which are in turn excessively influenced by the US and better-off Western countries.

Several measures will be necessary to overcome this scepticism:

1. Concentration on the correct sequencing of new consensus policies, in particular delaying capital market liberalisation until the basic financial structure of the country is in good health.
2. Attention to income distribution, and focus on education and other policies designed to equip ordinary citizens to deal with the new economic environment.
3. Acceptance that economic reforms must be applied consistently and that they will take time to bear fruit.
4. Effective governance and strong domestic legal and financial institutions.

The emphasis on governance issues is plain commonsense, but it is relatively new in the literature. Clearly the best economic policy structure in the world will not produce results if business has to cope with corrupt government, has no prospect of impartial and fair treatment in legal disputes, and is subject to continuous harassment by bureaucracy. Only the developing countries themselves can resolve these issues. Developed countries also have an important part to play in providing financial assistance (despite increased capital mobility, aid flows to developing countries have been falling during the last decade) and by taking account of the special concerns of the developing world in relation to security of access to rich country markets and fair application of rules.

Threats to the new consensus have come and gone during the past decade. A succession of financial crises in Mexico, East Asia, Russia, Brazil and Argentina cast doubt on the benefits of one element in the packages – free capital mobility – as well as underlining the vulnerability of open, competitive economies to changes in 'market sentiment'. To date, most economies have managed to survive these traumas. The advent of a financial crisis occurring at the heart of the Western economy, following the stock market collapse, would be more serious. Were it to be combined with simultaneous problems in the form of oil price increases and a general economic downturn, the attractions of globalisation, competition and price stability could easily pall. This does not necessarily imply a reversion to the failed economic policies of yore but rather a move towards a more moderated and circumspect approach to the new consensus among the unconverted, and less enthusiasm for deepening global integration. In the event of the market being seen to fail either because of its inability to provide solid advances for the poor or because of the abuse of wealth and monopoly power against weaker sections of the community, a return towards more pervasive state intervention could not be ruled out. We must hope, however, that the mistakes of the past arising from excessive use of government will not be repeated.

## Summary

1. A new policy consensus has swept through the global economy. Its three principles centre on the importance of competition and market incentives, macro-economic stability and global integration. The new policies have been adopted by a geographically and culturally diverse range of nations including Australia, Chile, the Czech Republic, Hungary, India, Mexico, New Zealand and Singapore. In Western Europe, the UK has been a leader, but its example is being followed with varying degrees of enthusiasm by mainland Europe. Since Ronald Reagan's term of office, the US has espoused and promulgated the new economic doctrines.

2. The new economic policy regime has important implications for business. It has tended to bring lower taxes and a more supportive, pro-business and pro-entrepreneurial climate. On the negative side, from the point of view of the individual firm, it has also meant greater exposure to domestic and foreign competition, and less security. Individuals, too, have had to adjust to a more cut-throat economic climate, with substantial rewards for the successful and less comfort for the unsuccessful.

3. There is evidence that the change in policy has stimulated faster growth and raised living standards. Policy-makers around the world are increasingly convinced that the new policy regime, based on long-established economic principles, offers the best prospect of prosperity.

4. But the new policy regime will 'deliver' only if its introduction is correctly sequenced and it is adhered to consistently in the context of good governance and strong institutions. This will be further discussed in the next chapter.

## Questions for discussion

1. Outline the three pillars of the new economic consensus. Show how policy changes along new consensus lines can lead to better economic performance.

2. A feature of the modern economy is the growing share of the services sector in national production (e.g. financial services, recreation, information technology and communication). Discuss how the services sector has been affected by the three main elements of the new policy consensus in terms of the exposure of services to more domestic competition and market forces, greater openness to foreign competition and a context of low inflation.

3. Is the new economic policy consensus likely to last? What factors might tend to undermine it?

## Exercises

1. Outline the contemporary economic policy stance in a country of your choice and indicate how closely it approximates the prescriptions of the new policy consensus.

2. How does economic policy change impact on business? Why should a student of business take a course on economics?

3. List four questions about the economy and economic policy that you would like to have answered in an introductory course on economics.

## Further reading

A landmark study of the case for an open trading system was the *World Bank Development Report* (Washington, DC: World Bank, 1987). Robert Skidelsky's *The World after Communism* (London: Macmillan, 1995) offers an accessible, brief advocacy of the potential benefits of a free market regime. The intellectual high priest of the free market is F.A. Hayek, a prolific author and Nobel prize-winner; *The Fatal Conceit: The errors of socialism* (London: Routledge, 1989) gives the flavour of his work. David Henderson's *The Changing Fortunes of Economic Liberalism* (London: Institute of Economic Affairs, 1999) puts the new consensus into historical focus and assesses its durability. A brief, idiosyncratic and thought-provoking account of globalisation is provided by Daniel Cohen, *The Wealth of the World and the Poverty of Nations* (Cambridge, MA: MIT Press, 1998).

The literature on this topic continues to grow. For a controversial and somewhat self-indulgent critique of globalisation and new consensus policies, by a former chief economist of the World Bank, see J. Stiglitz, *Globalisation and its Discontents* (New York: W.W. Norton, 2002). The case for the consensus view is well summarised in F. Bourguignon *et al.*, *Making Sense of Globalization: A guide to the economic issues* (London: Centre for Economic Policy Research, 2002).

## Chapter 2

# What makes nations grow?

## Introduction

Before making a business decision in a foreign country, we usually ask about that country's 'rate of growth'. Fast economic growth means an expanding domestic market and higher living standards, and is associated with a changing and dynamic business environment. Slow or zero growth is perceived as stagnation and is not attractive to business. Confronted with the record of a slow-growing economy, we naturally ask what has gone wrong. From a business perspective, the cause of economic growth is an important subject.

Economic growth is desired for many different reasons. Affluent countries see faster growth as a way of maintaining their superior living standards. Governments of poor countries see faster economic growth as a means of catching up with the prosperity of the affluent countries. Faster growth makes it easier to reduce unemployment, to mitigate poverty, to improve education and health services, and to provide material well-being. There are, of course, negative aspects of growth, such as environmental degradation, the breakdown of community life and destruction of rural values. Since the Industrial Revolution in the late eighteenth century, economic growth has had its critics, some of the most trenchant of whom have been economists. The tradition of scepticism, verging on hostility, towards growth remains active to this day. Despite all this, business and governments evidently believe that the positive effects of growth outweigh its negative effects, and both groups continue to accord it a high priority.

## Chapter outline

1. The main statistical facts about economic growth.
2. The contribution of growth theories to the understanding of these facts and the political and institutional framework required for successful growth performance.
3. The relationship between economic growth and human welfare.
4. Current thinking on the economic policies most likely to encourage growth.

## 2.1 Trends in economic growth

Economic growth is measured by changes in Gross National Product (GNP). GNP is a universally used measure of the value of goods and services produced in a country. GNP divided by total population, or GNP per capita, is the economic indicator most commonly used to measure the standard of living in a country. When we say economic growth, we refer to growth in GNP measured in real terms, i.e. abstracting from the effects of price increases. Often Gross *Domestic* Product (GDP) is used instead of GNP. In practice, the growth rates of GDP and GNP tend to be very similar, but GNP is generally a better indicator of living standards (see Chapter 11 for further details). Growth data are compiled according to detailed, internationally agreed conventions.

GNP comparisons over time give a rough indication of how much better-off we have become. Table 2.1 compares GNP per capita in 2002 with its level in 1900 and 1950 for several countries. To ensure comparability, goods and services produced in those years are valued in US dollars at 2002 prices. The figures show that the value of GNP per person varies enormously between countries. For example, Japan's output per person is almost 14 times higher than India's and four times higher than Mexico's. The UK is not regarded as a high performer in the growth league, yet the table shows that output per person has increased fivefold since 1900.

Studies of economic growth reveal certain general patterns which can be summarised in a number of 'stylised' facts.

First, *economic growth was the norm rather than the exception during the twentieth century.* Despite two world wars, major increases in national output per person have been recorded in the industrial countries (Table 2.1). The period since 1950 has seen a prodigious increase in living standards. Between 1950 and 2002 national output per capita rose by an annual average of 4.7 per cent in Japan, 2.8 per cent in Germany, 3.2 per cent in France, 2.3 per cent in the UK and 2.0 per cent in the US. These growth rates may appear unspectacular, but if sustained long enough they can bring about huge improvements in output per person. For

**Table 2.1 GNP per person for selected industrial countries at constant 2002 US dollars**

|  | 1900 | 1950 | 2002 |
|---|---|---|---|
| Belgium | 5,236 | 7,670 | 26,019 |
| Denmark | 5,104 | 11,495 | 34,281 |
| Finland | 2,882 | 7,346 | 26,660 |
| France | 2,794 | 5,135 | 25,888 |
| Germany | 3,941 | 6,219 | 26,493 |
| Italy | 3,062 | 5,296 | 21,622 |
| Japan | 2,071 | 3,415 | 36,492 |
| Netherlands | 5,013 | 8,303 | 26,596 |
| Sweden | 3,941 | 10,366 | 28,993 |
| United Kingdom | 5,386 | 8,030 | 26,460 |
| United States | 5,544 | 12,753 | 36,680 |

*Source*: Computed from Angus Maddison, *The World Economy: A millennial perspective* (Paris: OECD, 2001) and the International Monetary Fund, *World Economic Outlook*, April 2002.

example, a modest 3 per cent growth rate will lead to a doubling of output every 23 years.

Second, *countries that were relatively well-off in 1900 have tended to stay well-off*. However, some significant changes in ranking have occurred:

- The UK slipped from being one of the world's richest countries in 1900 to 20th place in the league.
- Japan, a relatively poor country in 1900, has risen to be one of the most affluent.
- Argentina, once among the wealthier countries, has suffered a serious decline in its relative position since the start of the twentieth century.
- Korea has graduated from poverty to comparative affluence.

As Table 2.2 shows, the three most affluent areas of the world – the US, EU and Japan, accounting for only 13 per cent of world population of 6 billion – generate 49 per cent of world GNP.

Third, *the developing countries have achieved significant improvements in living standards since the 1950s*. Life expectancy has increased by about 50 per cent; the proportion of children attending school has risen from less than one half to more than three-quarters; and average GNP per person has doubled, albeit from an extremely low initial level. China and India, the two most populous countries of the world, have been driving forces in this improvement (Table 2.3).

Fourth, *the problem of acute poverty continues to persist*. Over 1.2 billion people, most of them living in Sub-Saharan Africa and Asia, are still struggling to survive on about $1 per day.[1] Furthermore, the economic progress of the majority of developing countries has not been smooth. Income per capita in India actually fell between 1929 and 1950. During the 1990s, no fewer than 53 out of 177 countries, most of them in Sub-Saharan Africa and former socialist countries, suffered negative growth (Tables 2.4 and 2.5). Some of these countries were quite populous, for instance Nigeria (130m), Russia (146m) and Ukraine (50m), but most were very small. The total population of the negative-growth group was 753 million. Although accounting for 30 per cent of all countries, they include only 13 per cent of the world's population. It follows that the remaining 87 per cent of

### Table 2.2 Share of world output, trade and population, 2000 (% share)

|                | Output | Trade | Population |
|----------------|--------|-------|------------|
| United States  | 21.6   | 17.8  | 4.7        |
| European Union | 19.9   | 19.9  | 6.2        |
| Japan          | 7.7    | 8.4   | 2.1        |
| **Top three**  | **49.2** | **46.1** | **13.0** |
| Rest of world  | 50.8   | 53.9  | 87.0       |
| Total          | 100.0  | 100.0 | 100.0      |

*Source*: World Bank, *World Development Indicators 2002*; World Trade Organisation, *International Trade Statistics 2001*.

---

[1] N. Stern, 'A strategy for development', in *Annual World Bank Conference on Development Economics* (Washington, DC: World Bank, 2002), p. 12.

## Table 2.3  GNP per person for selected developing countries at constant 2002 US dollars

|            | 1900  | 1950  | 2002   |
|------------|-------|-------|--------|
| China      | 561   | 461   | 4,676  |
| India      | 685   | 650   | 2,675  |
| South Korea| 939   | 964   | 19,440 |
| Argentina  | 2,977 | 5,363 | 10,091 |
| Mexico     | 1,121 | 2,089 | 8,923  |
| Egypt      | 973   | 954   | 4,087  |
| Morocco    | 1,073 | 1,934 | 3,893  |
| Ghana      | 982   | 1,491 | 3,893  |
| Nigeria    | n.a.  | 1,000 | 1,858  |

Source: Computed from Angus Maddison, *The World Economy: A millennial perspective* (Paris: OECD, 2001) and the International Monetary Fund, *World Economic Outlook*, April 2002. Purchasing power parities have been used for the developing countries (see Chapter 11 for definition).

## Table 2.4  Distribution of growth rates, 1990–2000

| Average annual per capita real growth rates | Number of countries | % of all countries | Population (millions) | % of world population |
|---------------------------------------------|---------------------|--------------------|-----------------------|------------------------|
| Less than 0%    | 53  | 29.9 | 754   | 12.7 |
| 0–3%            | 95  | 53.7 | 2,465 | 41.7 |
| Greater than 3% | 29  | 16.4 | 2,695 | 45.6 |
| Total           | 177 | 100  | 5,914 | 100  |

Source: Computed from World Bank, *World Development Indicators 2002*.

## Table 2.5  How growth rates differed, 1965–2000

|                                                  | Total real GNP 1965–2000 (% p.a.) | Real GNP per head 1965–2000 (% p.a.) | Population 2000 (millions) |
|--------------------------------------------------|-----------------------------------|--------------------------------------|----------------------------|
| Low income ($755 or less) countries (60)         | 5.9 | 3.7  | 3,722 |
| Middle income countries (78)                     | 3.7 | 1.9  | 1,433 |
| High income ($9,266 or more) countries (34)      | 3.0 | 2.3  | 903   |
| East Asia                                        | 7.5 | 5.7  | 1,855 |
| South Asia                                       | 4.9 | 2.7  | 1,355 |
| Latin America                                    | 3.4 | 1.3  | 516   |
| Sub-Saharan Africa                               | 2.6 | ‾0.3 | 659   |
| World                                            | 3.2 | 1.4  | 6,057 |

Source: World Bank, *World Development Indicators* (successive years).

the world's population experienced a rise in living standards. However, the rise in GDP per head in developing countries was in many instances relatively modest (Brazil 1.5 per cent, Mexico 1.4 per cent, Morocco 1.6 per cent, Philippines 1.1 per cent). *Absolute* living standards have risen in these countries, to be sure, but their position *relative* to the industrial countries has worsened appreciably.

Fifth, *dramatic changes have occurred in the distribution of economic activity among the developing countries since the 1960s.* Asian countries have grown at an extraordinarily fast pace, starting with Japan, followed by Korea, Taiwan, Singapore and Hong Kong, and then succeeded by a later generation which includes China, Malaysia and Thailand, among others. China, with a population of 1200 million, has recorded an astonishing annual rate of growth of almost 9 per cent per person since the early 1980s (although this figure may not be entirely reliable).

Sixth, *resource-rich countries have experienced mixed fortunes.* Being 'rich' in terms of natural resources does not guarantee prosperity. One reason is that the prices of many primary commodities, such as cocoa, coffee, sugar, groundnuts and minerals, have been on a declining trend for some decades now. Oil prices shot up to unprecedented levels in the late 1970s, but fell back in real terms to their pre-1973 levels before recovering again in the late 1990s. Many countries dependent on primary exports have suffered a decline in their terms of trade, i.e. export prices have fallen relative to import prices. Apart from this adverse price effect, *human* resources – meaning a skilled and motivated workforce – have been found to be a more significant source of economic prosperity than an endowment of *natural* resources.

The experience of the *economies in transition,* as the former socialist countries are called, shows that countries can be well endowed with both natural and human resources, and yet perform poorly because of unstable and inadequate institutional structures and a history of poor economic management. Some of these countries have recovered strongly since the introduction of market reforms, such as Russia, Poland, Estonia and the Slovak Republic, while Slovenia has recorded positive growth since 1993. But resumption of growth in the Ukraine, Romania, Bulgaria and Moldova has remained an elusive goal.

## 2.2 Growth theories

Theories of economic growth seek to identify the *long-term* determinants of growth. In this section we provide a bird's-eye, non-technical view of how economists explain growth and what policies they recommend on the basis of their analyses. Some concepts introduced here will be explained in more detail in later chapters.

Imagine an economy which produces only two goods, X and Y. Suppose we set up a list of combinations of X and Y that could be produced if the resources of the economy were fully and most effectively deployed. The *production frontier* traces the various combinations of X and Y derived in this way (Figure 2.1). An *efficient* economic system is one that operates on the production frontier (see Box 2.1). This ensures *productive* efficiency. *Allocative* efficiency is also very important. It ensures that there is no feasible redistribution of income which would permit one person to be better-off without anyone else being worse-off. We shall see later that the market system helps an economy achieve an efficient outcome. Efficiency, in turn, speeds up economic growth.

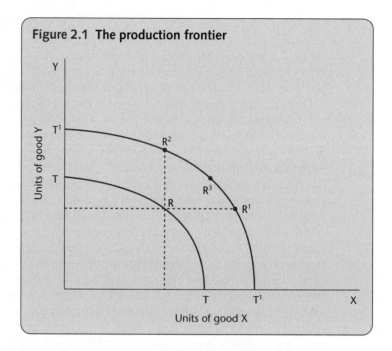

Figure 2.1 The production frontier

---

### Box 2.1  Efficiency, opportunity cost and no free lunch

Economics has been defined as the science of scarcity. Its view of the world is one where people's wants are unlimited, but the resources needed to satisfy them are limited. Provided society is at the production possibility frontier, where resources are fully employed, more of good X implies less of good Y. In order to produce more of X, scarce resources have to be transferred from industry Y to industry X. Hence the origin of the well-known maxim: *in economics there is no such thing as a free lunch.*

Again, assuming that we are on the production frontier, the cost of producing one additional unit of good X can be defined as the amount of good Y that has to be given up in order to make this possible. This is called *the opportunity cost of X*. The opportunity cost concept has many practical applications. It reminds us that 'free' education, or 'free' transport and other 'free' goods offered by politicians, convey a misleading impression. Nothing is costless. The resources used to supply these 'free' government services could have been used to produce, say, automobiles or holidays instead.

An *efficient* economy is one which (1) operates on its production frontier, at a point such as P in the figure below (*productive efficiency*); and (2) allocates the goods produced at the frontier in an efficient way (*allocative efficiency*).

*Productive efficiency*: At any point below the production frontier, society could have more of both X and Y by moving from its present position to a point closer to the production frontier. By definition, point U is not an efficient position. At that point, some productive resources are either being used inefficiently or, worse, not being used at all. Here free lunches are a possibility. If the market system is performing as it should, such situations will be rare and short-lived. Price incentives should move the economy from U to a point on the frontier such as P, where the economy has more of both X and Y than at U. Analysis of the role of prices and market structures shows how an economy reaches its production possibility frontier and stays there.

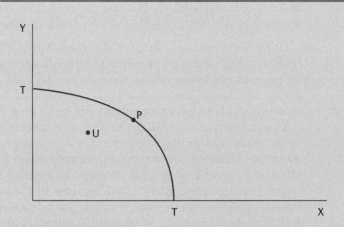

So much for productive efficiency, which has to do with getting from points like U to the production frontier. The second criterion for economic efficiency, *allocative efficiency*, requires that the goods produced at P are allocated in an optimal way between consumers. Allocative efficiency is achieved when there is no feasible redistribution of the fixed bundle of goods P which would make one person better-off without leaving anyone else worse-off. At this stage, an economy is said to have achieved *Pareto efficiency*. Not least of the attractions of a free market system is that, subject to certain assumptions, it can lead to a Pareto-efficient outcome, i.e. productive and allocative efficiency.

The productive capacity of a nation can be put to many uses. An interesting example of this is the case of the US during the Second World War. In 1939 the armed forces of the US were extremely weak. The army had more horses than tanks. The air corps and navy possessed only 1600 aircraft in total (mostly ancient biplanes), while Germany manufactured 8295 modern military aircraft in that year alone. However, the US had the world's largest industrial production capacity and was easily able to turn this to rearmament. By 1941, it was producing military aircraft at the rate of 26,277 a year. This illustrates how rapidly GNP can be switched from consumer goods to the production of the military hardware needed to win a war.

But what makes the production frontier shift outwards? This question lies at the heart of economics. It constituted the central theme of Adam Smith's masterpiece, *An Inquiry into the Nature and Causes of the Wealth of Nations* (1776). This chapter gives an overview of current thinking on the growth debate.

*Source*: US war data from R. Overy and A. Wheatcroft, *The Road to War* (London: Macmillan, 1989), pp. 258–97, 317–21.

Economic growth can be characterised as an outward shift in the production frontier, represented by the move from TT to $T^1T^1$ in Figure 2.1. This outward movement is desired because of the expanded range of options it provides society. Economic growth is regarded as a 'good thing', in so far as it enables the consumers in the economy to enjoy:

● more of X and the same amount of Y – at a point such as $R^1$,
● more of Y and the same amount of X – at a point such as $R^2$,

- more of both X and Y – at a point such as $R^3$,
- any other desired combination of X and Y on the expanded frontier.

Growth extends the range of consumption possibilities, and people choose between these different possibilities through the market system, supplemented by government intervention. Growth provides the means to enjoy more of all goods, including leisure. Economic development in industrial countries has enabled people to have more goods and services while working fewer hours.

The production frontier can be shifted outwards by two forces: first, increases in the *quantity* of productive factors; and second, improvements in the *productivity* of these factors. Since we are primarily concerned with growth per person rather than total growth, it is common to abstract from the increase in growth which is attributable solely to the increase in the population. Growth in living standards, or GNP per person, therefore, depends on (1) the *amount* of productive factors at each person's disposal (the more machinery and the more hectares of land at the disposal of an employee, the more will be produced per employee), (2) the *productivity* of these factors of production (better machinery, improved seeds and fertilisers and more advanced technology improve productivity), and (3) the skill and motivation of the workforce. We shall discuss these three elements in turn.

## Quantity of inputs

*Quantity of productive factors* (in economic jargon, 'factors of production') refers to inputs such as the physical infrastructure (roads, ports, railways, telecoms), plant and machinery (factories, machinery, tractors) and natural resources. As the quantity of inputs increases, so too does the volume of final output. The production function measures the relationship between inputs and output (Box 2.2).

---

### Box 2.2 — Production functions and economic growth

A country's output depends on its resources or productive inputs, and on the techniques it employs for transforming these inputs into outputs. The relationship between inputs and outputs is known as a *production function*. It is a technical, engineering-type relationship, which we use to conceptualise the diverse and complex influences which determine economic growth. A simple production function might be described as:

$$y = a.f(k)$$

where:   $y$ = output per person
$k$ = capital per person
$a$ = residual factor, including technology.

This relationship indicates the maximum amount of output per person ($y$) that society can produce for any given input of capital per person ($k$) and technology and other production inputs ($a$). This residual is also called *total factor productivity*.

It is possible to specify the production function in detail and to derive estimates of the effect of changes in each of these inputs on the level of output. By accumulating capital, a country can move to a higher output level per person along its production function. The greater the amount of capital available per person, the greater is output per person. The same result can be achieved by raising the productivity of this capital. Machines can be operated more efficiently, break down less often and economise on raw material inputs. The faster the pace of technological progress, the faster the increase in output – for a given capital stock, greater technological awareness allows greater amounts of output to be produced.

Estimates of production functions suggest that increases in capital per person do indeed contribute to higher output, but what really matters is the residual factor, representing the technology and other influences. Between one-third and one-half of growth in major industrial countries since 1950 falls into this unexplained 'residual' category.

*Source*: N. Crafts and G. Tonioli (eds), *Economic Growth in Europe since 1945* (Cambridge: Cambridge University Press, 1996).

Just as investment plays a key role in explaining the growth of firms, the share of investment in a country's GDP is linked closely to economic growth. A country that invested more than another would be expected, everything else being equal, to grow faster. There are some outstanding cases to support this hypothesis. Japan's average investment:GDP ratio between 1960 and 1990 exceeded the investment ratio in the EU and the US by more than 10 percentage points (31 per cent as against 22 per cent and 18 per cent respectively) and, not surprisingly, Japan's growth rate of 6 per cent up to 1990 was twice the rate of most industrial countries (Table 2.6). Within Europe, the faster growing countries, such as Spain, Italy and Germany, invested more than the slower growing countries, such as the UK. Following India's setting of a 7 per cent GDP growth target for the decade to 2007 in 1997, the IMF concluded that this would require an investment ratio of at least 30 per cent.[2] Investment ratios of this size were common in fast-growing Asian economies during the past three decades.

### Table 2.6 Investment and growth

| | Investment:GDP ratio | | | GDP growth rate (% p.a.) | | |
|---|---|---|---|---|---|---|
| | European Union | US | Japan | European Union | US | Japan |
| 1961–70 | 23.4 | 18.1 | 32.2 | 4.8 | 4.2 | 10.1 |
| 1971–80 | 23.0 | 19.1 | 32.7 | 3.0 | 3.2 | 4.4 |
| 1981–90 | 20.4 | 18.3 | 29.1 | 2.4 | 2.9 | 4.0 |
| 1991–2000 | 19.0 | 16.0 | 29.0 | 2.0 | 2.5 | 1.4 |

*Source: European Economy* (Brussels: no. 16, 1999).

---

[2] Martin Mühleisen, 'Improving India's saving performance', *Finance and Development* (June 1997), pp. 38–41.

The observed connection between investment and growth led many to believe that growth in the developing countries was mainly constrained by insufficient investment reflecting low savings and poverty. Multi-annual development plans explored ways of raising the savings ratio and allocating investment to sectors where productivity was highest. According to this way of thinking, foreign aid could make a vital contribution by supplying the additional capital input needed for sustained growth.

But how can one explain Japan's high investment rate since 1990 (29 per cent) being accompanied by GDP growth of only 1.4 per cent? Clearly, the level of investment is only one of many determinants of growth. What is called the *growth accounting approach* examines the contribution of other factors in the growth process.[3] Studies have examined historical trends in a country's productive resources, disaggregated in comprehensive detail, and have tracked the association between these inputs and the subsequent growth of output. This research has underlined the importance of *total factor productivity* and of the *quality* of the labour force as independent determinants of economic performance.

## Total factor productivity

*Total factor productivity* typically accounts for between one-third and one-half of total GNP growth in industrial countries. It is derived as a residual, after allowing for capital investment and labour force growth, and reflects the influence of factors which improve productivity but which are not amenable to exact measurement. There are many candidates for inclusion in this residual category:

● Advances in technology
● Redistribution of resources from lower to higher productivity sectors
● Terms of trade
● Institutions and political stability
● Quality of the labour force (human skills and motivation)
● Economic policy.

Low growth in total factor productivity was identified as the primary culprit for the comparative decline of the UK economy during the years 1950–73; UK TFP growth was 1.27 per cent per year compared with 3.02 per cent in France and 3.50 per cent in West Germany.

The link between *advances in technology* and economic growth involves three separate steps. First, there is invention – the scientific discovery – which often originates from pure research, not necessarily motivated by commercial factors. Second, the invention needs to be applied to the production of a good or service. Innovation refers to this application. This may involve a more efficient method of producing an existing good (e.g. quality control methods for an automobile) or production of an entirely new product (e.g. the video recorder). The third step is diffusion of the innovation to other industries and other economies. Countries in

---

[3] This approach stemmed from an investigation by Edward Dennison into the sources of growth in the US. Dennison and his followers later extended the research to international comparisons of growth experience. See E.F. Dennison, *Why Growth Rates Differ* (Washington, DC: Brookings Institution, 1967). Subsequent accounting estimates were reviewed in A. Maddison, *Dynamic Forces in Capitalist Development* (Oxford: Oxford University Press, 1991).

the early stages of economic development typically focus on this last step. Because it is cheaper to adopt new technologies that have been brought to commercial level by others than to have to discover them from scratch, poorer countries mostly borrow, imitate and adapt technology from the more advanced economies. But technological progress does not descend like manna from heaven.[4] It is costly to develop and costly to acquire. The process of technology acquisition and diffusion requires large infusions of machinery and skilled manpower. For this reason, there tends to be a close association between technological advance and investment in human and physical capital – another example of dynamic interdependence between different inputs in the growth process.

Advances in technology are not directly observable, but are measured by proxy variables such as the numbers of registered patents or the amount of spending on R&D. A country's 'system of national innovation' is seen as a critical component of economic growth. The amount of commercially oriented research undertaken in a country can contribute to the discovery and adoption of new products and new ways of producing them. But such research does not take place by accident. It needs to be nurtured by an environment that encourages innovation. The education system must provide the key personnel in terms of technological competence and motivation. Fiscal incentives also have a part to play. If these are missing, spending on research and development will fail to translate into effective innovation – as, many would say, happened in Britain through much of the postwar period.

Studies of innovation show that technological advance has a tendency to feed on itself. Innovation can be a self-perpetuating process. As more of it is carried out, a pool of skilled labour and managerial competence accumulates which reduces unit costs. It may become independently profitable and require fewer government incentives. Economic growth can be path-dependent. *Endogenous growth theories* focus on these self-reinforcing interactions between technology, human skills and economies of scale.[5]

The different influences on total factor productivity vary in importance from country to country and from one time-period to another. For example, one major source of productivity growth derives from the *transfer of the labour force from low-productivity agriculture to high-productivity industry*. In the decades immediately after the Second World War, this contributed significantly to Europe's high growth rates. The same forces are at work in boosting the growth rates of developing countries. As the proportion of the workforce in agriculture diminishes, the scope for exploiting these gains contracts, and the opportunity for really fast growth diminishes proportionately. However, opportunities for continuing productivity gains remain. Even within the manufacturing sector, productivity can grow because of movement from low-productivity to high-productivity activities. Further productivity gains are yielded by the transfer of resources from manufacturing to high-tech services. Continuing innovation, and readiness to shift to activities with the highest returns, is a characteristic of successful market economies.

---

[4] There are some exceptions such as the application of DDT or antibiotics and penicillin: very cheap to acquire and requiring little skill to apply.

[5] See P.M. Romer, 'The origins of endogenous growth', *Journal of Economic Perspectives*, VIII(I) (1994); R.E. Lucas, 'On the mechanics of economic development', *Journal of Monetary Economics* (July 1988).

Developments in a country's *terms of trade* can have a major impact on growth. The terms of trade are defined as the ratio of changes in a country's export prices to import prices. Small trade-dependent countries are more sensitive to terms of trade changes than larger countries. Developing economies dependent on just a few commodity exports are particularly vulnerable. A decline in the terms of trade of 10 percentage points over a decade reduces economic growth by 0.8 percentage points annually in that decade.[6] Since 1980, real commodity prices have declined by 45 per cent. Countries in Sub-Saharan Africa have been badly hit both by declines in export prices and by the extreme volatility of these prices. Ghana's terms of trade, dominated by cocoa, fell by over 30 per cent during this period. The post-1973 oil price increases vastly enhanced the incomes of oil-producing countries, but the increase has been reversed in real terms in the intervening period. GDP per capita in Saudi Arabia has fallen by as much as 50 per cent since 1980.

Economic growth takes place in a particular *political and institutional context*. This background can have an important bearing on productivity and growth. For example, political stability, in the sense of stable democratic government, by offering protection against arbitrary removal of property rights and confiscation of savings, is conducive to investment. Unstable political systems generate uncertainty about the future, encourage capital outflow and discourage business investment. At the same time as political stability encourages growth, so economic growth can encourage political stability. It is a chicken-and-egg problem to decide which comes first. Moreover, political stability cannot be identified with democracy in a cut-and-dried manner. Singapore developed successfully under a regime much closer to benevolent dictatorship than to democracy in a Western sense. Some dictatorships can be successful in laying the foundations of growth, such as Chile during the 1980s; others have been associated with disastrous performance, such as Romania, Zaïre (Congo) and Zimbabwe. Political stability, therefore, has to be combined with consistent and rational economic policies. In high-growth countries, the viability and credibility of growth-oriented economic policy has been reinforced by strong popular support for such policy. This support has been engendered by the widespread diffusion of the fruits of growth through society.

## Quality of the labour force

High investment and high productivity are hard to envisage without high-quality people. To produce high-quality people, however, requires investment. Every business knows this, but it has taken time for the message to be appreciated fully in economic policy. One problem is that investment in people may take decades to bear fruit and its effects are hard to measure, whereas investment in physical capital – such as a bridge or a fertiliser plant – leads to a highly visible and measurable result in a much shorter time.[7] It was not easy to get over the

---

[6] William Easterly and Lance Pritchett, 'The determinants of economic success: Luck and policy', *Finance and Development* (December 1993), p. 40.

[7] The proposition that educating a workforce improves its productivity dates back to Adam Smith. The modern concept of human capital is due primarily to the work of T.W. Schultz, 'Investing in human capital', *American Economic Review* (1961), pp. 1–17.

message that investment in education is just as 'real' and as 'profitable' from a national point of view as any other type of investment. *Human capital* refers to the development of human skills and motivation through investment in education, training and experience. Educated, skilled workers are generally more productive than uneducated, unskilled workers. High-productivity industries in the biotechnology and information sectors require a skilled and educated workforce. Simple measures of human capital such as the level of secondary school enrolment have been found to be strongly correlated with subsequent economic growth. Labour productivity growth in East Asia, three to six times the developing country average, has been credited to major investments in workers' skills. The return on investment in women's education seems to be especially high, through its effects on the health and education of the next generation, and by reducing family size.

A better-educated workforce must also be motivated. Overmanning, demarcation and poor industrial relations can retard growth just as surely as lack of physical investment. The reason why some countries have been better able to motivate their workforce than others has been much debated. One important lesson of Europe's experience has been the need to achieve a balance between the redistribution of income for social reasons and the preservation of incentives. The search by pressure groups in the developed countries to obtain a higher share of total GNP has led to the rise of what Mancur Olson has called 'distributional coalitions'.[8] Efforts by trade unions, professional groups and trade associations to increase their share of national income involve a zero-sum exercise. One group's gain is another's loss. According to Olson, the Allies performed relatively poorly after the Second World War because their distributional coalitions were left intact and even strengthened, while Germany and Japan, having lost the war, found that their distributional coalitions were discredited and destroyed. This opened the way for a better institutional framework which encouraged the workforce to abandon the old adversarial relationship with management and concentrate on building up a competitive economy instead. These ideas also help to explain why some countries seem to make little constructive use of favourable terms of trade 'windfalls'. Too much effort is devoted to working out how the windfall should be distributed. In extreme circumstances, the windfall may even damage a country's long-run growth as squabbles over income distribution lead to a deterioration in saving and excessive government spending. Tornell and Lane refer to this as the *voracity effect*.[9] Economists have become increasingly conscious of the importance of good *governance* as a determinant of economic prosperity.

The list of determinants of growth can be extended indefinitely. Business organisation and culture, the work ethic, religion and even climate have at one time or another been adduced to explain it. In the practical context of trying to improve economic performance, we have to try to identify which of the many determinants of growth are acting as a binding constraint on faster growth in a particular situation and how these constraints can be most effectively prioritised by economic policy.

---

[8]  M. Olson, *The Rise and Decline of Nations* (New Haven, CT: Yale University Press, 1982).
[9]  A. Tornell and P.R. Lane, 'The voracity effect', *American Economic Review* (March 1999).

**Population growth and living standards**

The link between population growth and economic development is a highly contentious topic. While every additional worker adds to potential output, the crucial question is how population growth will affect not just total GDP, but GDP per person. Take, for example, a country such as Nigeria with an annual population growth of 3 per cent. *Output growth of 3 per cent is needed simply to prevent living standards from falling.* To generate and support that output growth in turn necessitates a high level of investment. To obtain sufficient growth to achieve an increase in living standards means that investment must be even higher still. The mathematics of generating a growth rate high enough to outstrip the growth in population has attracted attention since the writings of Thomas Malthus in the eighteenth century.

Many argue that growth in population can depress income per person. An expanding population of young people and large family size reduce national saving and consequently limit the volume of investment. Simultaneously, a burgeoning population puts pressure on a country's infrastructure. In other words, *the rate of growth of population may interact negatively with the growth of other inputs.* As a result of this interdependence, a vicious circle of economic decline can be generated. By the same line of reasoning, lower population growth may facilitate economic growth by creating a virtuous circle of high investment leading to higher growth, which generates more saving, more investment and so on.

Affluent households tend to have smaller families than poor households and, in the same way, developed countries have lower population growth than poor countries. World Bank figures for population growth since 1980 show that higher income countries had population growth of 0.6 per cent p.a., while low income populations have been increasing by 2 per cent annually. But are affluent countries better-off because they have low population growth, or is their population growth low because they are affluent? There is no definitive answer to this question. Two general points, however, can be made. First, most governments in the developing world have concluded that population growth has damaged their efforts to raise living standards and, for this reason, official support has been given to family planning. The governments of China and India have been persuaded of the case for lower population growth and support measures to encourage smaller family size. In this they have the backing of international organisations such as the United Nations and the World Bank. Second, while Western governments are concerned about the lack of population growth and the associated problem of caring for a rising proportion of elderly people, none of them has espoused a deliberate policy of population expansion as a way out of the difficulty.

## 2.3 Human welfare and sustainable growth

The Gross National Product does not allow for the health of our children, the quality of their education or the joy of their play. It does not include the beauty of our poetry or the strength of our marriages; the intelligence of our public debate or the integrity of our public officials. It measures neither our wisdom nor our learning, neither our compassion nor our devotion to our country; it measures everything, in short, except that which makes life worthwhile. (Robert F. Kennedy, quoted in *Finance and Development*, December 1993, p. 20)

So far we have discussed economic growth as if it were the sole objective of economic policy. Growth is taken to be desirable because it enlarges the range of consumption possibilities available to society.

It is well known that GNP is an inadequate indicator of human welfare. There is no evidence that people in countries with high GNP are 'happier' or spiritually better than those in poorer countries.[10] GNP leaves out of the account many of the things that make for the good life; and some items are included in GNP that have an ambiguous effect on welfare (e.g. resources devoted to crime prevention are treated as part of GNP, but some would regard them as an input). Four specific criticisms of GNP have been made on this account. First, it puts no value on leisure and the household economy. Second, the official statistics are unable to record many useful outputs produced in the shadow or 'black' economy. Third, GNP takes no account of resource depletion and degradation of the environment and includes as outputs many activities that should properly be classified as inputs. Fourth, it ignores income distribution.

## Leisure and the household economy

Suppose that a person takes a second job. This makes large inroads into leisure time. GNP includes all the output generated by the second job but totally ignores the welfare cost of the loss of leisure. Human welfare has presumably increased as a result of this decision – otherwise the second job would not have been taken – but the net increase in welfare will be much less than the GNP indicates. The individual is likely to be more harassed and to have less time for the family. Likewise the US's higher per capita income relative to the EU takes no account of the fact that Europeans enjoy longer vacations and a more civilised and family-friendly working environment than their American counterparts. According to US

---

**Box 2.3**    **To improve GDP as a measure of welfare, ...**

*Add:*
- Leisure
- Household contribution
- Voluntary activities
- Shadow economy (positive aspects)

*Subtract:*
- Environmental damage
- Depletion of natural resources
- Inputs classified as output (defence, cost of pollution control)

*Take account of:*
- Income distribution

---

[10]  See A. Oswald, 'Happiness and economic performance', *Economic Journal* (November 1977), for a discus-

Department of Labor data, the average US employee works 1942 hours per year, 250 hours more than the British employee and 500 hours (5 weeks) more than the German worker. In addition Americans retire at an older age than Europeans. In these circumstances it is hardly surprising, and is scarcely a matter for congratulation, that US GDP per head exceeds the EU level. Suggestions that Europe should strive to 'catch up' on US levels are rather fatuous in this context.

GNP includes only transactions that involve a monetary exchange. Housework done by members of a household, being unpaid, is not recorded in GNP. As members of the household enter the workforce and household tasks, such as repair, maintenance, and care of children, are passed over to paid professionals, GNP rises. Yet all that is happening is that functions are being shifted from the traditional realm of the household and the community to the monetised economy. GNP statistics, for the same reason, ignore the output of the voluntary third sector (care for the elderly, 'meals on wheels' and other important social work).

## Shadow economy

Another source of unrecorded output is the 'shadow' or 'black economy'. The shadow economy includes a wide range of activities such as smuggled exports, personal services provided for cash and not declared to the authorities, and deliberate under-reporting of output to evade tax. To the extent that they add to welfare these should be included as part of a country's output. The shadow economy is often associated with corruption and bribery but it is not the same thing. Payment of a bribe to speed up the processing of an import licence or to avoid a traffic offence charge is an unrecorded activity but its omission is not relevant to correct measurement of GNP. We discuss the shadow economy further in Chapter 3; for the present suffice to say that estimates indicate that it constitutes a significant proportion of measured GNP.

## GNP and the environment

Conventional GNP measures do not deal satisfactorily with *environmental and ecological factors*. Higher GNP has implications for the environment on several levels which fail to be recorded in the statistics. Two aspects in particular merit attention: (1) higher levels of pollution, and (2) depletion of natural resources.

*Higher levels of pollution* can arise because higher levels of production imply more waste, including carbon dioxide emissions and other chemical waste. These pollutants should be deducted from a measure of welfare.

Second, the *depletion of non-renewable resources* such as oil and coal is not accounted for in GNP calculations. Nor is account taken of the usage of resources such as rainforests, fishery stocks, etc., which are in danger of being consumed faster than the replacement rate. Other examples include soil erosion in Sub-Saharan Africa and the decline in animal and vegetable output caused by pollution of the water supply.[11] We shall discuss these issues further in Chapter 9.

---

[11] In response to these problems, the United Nations has developed a set of 'satellite' accounts, attached to the national accounts, which incorporate adjustments for the problems mentioned above. Because of the lack of precision of these 'green' accounts, they accompany, rather than replace, the orthodox accounts.

By a perverse quirk, the cost of moderating the adverse effects of pollution is often included in GNP as an output (service provided) instead of as an input (a production cost to society). For example, the medical attention given to a radiation victim will be recorded in the national accounts as a positive entry instead of as a 'negative input' occasioned by the radiation exposure. Likewise, the introduction of catalytic converters in cars or a new waste water treatment plant adds to GNP, though arguably these activities are merely defensive protection measures. These are examples of a general problem of *'inputs' being classified as 'outputs'*.

## Income distribution

GNP per person, being an arithmetic average of total output divided by total population, reveals no information about the distribution of resources within a society. It could rise even though the majority of the population may be worse-off. For example, if the income of the most affluent one-third of a population rose by 50 billion dollars, and the income of the poorest two-thirds fell by 30 billion dollars, GNP would increase. But does it necessarily follow that society as a whole is better-off?

Some argue that the long-run sustainability of growth depends on income being shared on an equitable basis. One reason is that successful policy-making requires change, and change involves implementing measures that harm certain vested interests. A social consensus is required in order to push through such measures. This consensus can only be achieved if the majority of people believe that they have a stake in the economy and will benefit from its growth and prosperity.

For example, at the start of the century many Latin American nations enjoyed high per capita incomes under policy regimes which were favourable to free enterprise and the market system. However, income disparities were great and the power of vested interests was correspondingly strong. These interest groups resisted change and the next 80 years saw relative economic decline, as inward-looking, protectionist policies were adopted. A more liberal market regime might have benefited the majority of people but the free market regime had given them little and they saw no reason to defend it even if the alternative protectionist regime may have made matters even worse. By contrast, in East Asia, governments succeeded in moderating income disparities (without undermining incentives). The result was a social consensus behind growth-oriented policies. In addition to strong economic growth performance, East Asian countries have made what the IMF described as 'outstanding progress' in reducing absolute and relative poverty.[12] Notwithstanding the setback of the 1997–98 currency crisis, most of these countries have succeeded in cultivating a strong market system and incentives to enterprise, while simultaneously achieving widespread prosperity.

## GNP and human development indicators

In evaluating a country's growth, account should be taken of the quality of the lifestyle enjoyed by the population. We need to measure the quality as well as the

---

[12] IMF, *World Economic Outlook* (May 1993), p. 54.

quantity of economic growth. Imagine two countries. One has a lower GNP per person than the other, but has a healthier, more literate, more democratic and less crime-ridden society. In this instance, GNP is an inaccurate measure of the relative welfare of the two countries. In an effort to develop a more comprehensive socioeconomic measure, the United Nations has published a series of Human Development Indicators, which provide information on these issues. It is possible to compute a human development index consisting of a weighted average of data on GNP per person, life expectancy and educational attainment of the population (Box 2.4).

As one would expect, the new index involved some changes in ranking. The 2002 Report, for example, indicates a Human Development Index (HDI) ranking higher than the GNP ranking for Sweden, Canada, France and the UK, and the opposite for the United States and South Africa. By adding to the list of indicators, and measuring them in different ways, more radical alterations in ranking can be computed. There is ample scope for further experimentation and analysis along these lines.

Yet, the limitations of GNP as a measure of welfare must not be exaggerated. For all its defects, a higher output per person gives society the *capacity* to achieve a better quality of life. Also, there is a strong positive correlation between GNP growth and some important empirical measures of the quality of life. Countries with higher GNP tend to be healthier and better educated than those with lower GNP. They also tend to be better policed and are more secure in a financial and physical sense. Central New York is safer than central Lima, Manila or Mogadishu. Affluent Tokyo is one of the safest cities in the world. While many forms of recorded crime in the industrial world have increased since 1945, prosperity has resulted in a reduction in civil disorder. During the nineteenth century, crime rates fell as the cities industrialised.[13]

## Global convergence?

Income distribution is a source of concern at international as well as at national level. One question often asked is whether poorer countries are catching up with the richer countries. The statistics, as we have seen, show rather mixed results. In favour of the convergence hypothesis is the average 3 per cent yearly increase of GNP per person in low-income countries during the period 1980–2000, a figure considerably in excess of the 2.2 per cent achieved by high-income countries during the same period. Against this, one could argue that, excluding China and India, income per capita of the average developing country has risen by only 0.1 per cent annually and conclude with the World Bank that,

> while some poorer countries are catching up with the richer ones, just as many have failed to narrow the gap, and some are losing ground. *Overall divergence, not convergence, has been the rule.* (World Bank, *World Development Report*, 1995, p. 54; emphasis added)

Do rich countries, because they are rich, grow faster than poorer countries? Endogenous growth theories give reasons for believing that, once ahead, the more developed countries – the first-movers – will tend to stay ahead. This accords with the empirical fact that the list of industrial countries has remained

---

[13] J.J. Tobias, *Crime and Police in England, 1700–1900* (Dublin: Gill & Macmillan, 1979).

## Box 2.4    The human development index

In 1990, the United Nations developed the Human Development Index (HDI) as an alternative measure of the relative socioeconomic progress of nations. It did so in response to criticisms of GNP as a measure of welfare. The HDI is a composite index, incorporating three basic components of human development: *life expectancy at birth*, *knowledge* and *standard of living*. Life expectancy at birth is the number of years a person is expected to live at birth based on law of averages computed by demographers; knowledge is measured by a combination of adult literacy and mean years of schooling; standard of living is estimated by real income per capita adjusted for the local cost of living.

These indicators are combined in the HDI which is expressed as a value between 0 and 1. The ranking by HDI is often compared with GNP per capita.

The figures show a positive correlation between the HDI and GNP per capita rankings but it breaks down in many cases. Countries with an HDI rank ahead of its GNP rank are taking a more balanced approach to economic development. Recent experience suggests that, in the long run, such an approach will translate into faster GNP growth too.

The single HDI value for each country is a national average which can conceal inequalities at a regional and sectoral level. Work continues on constructing separate HDIs by gender, income group, geographical region, race or ethnic group. Separate HDIs would reveal a more detailed profile of living experiences in each country. Some countries have attempted to estimate disaggregated HDIs but availability of data is a pervasive problem.

*Source*: *Human Development Report 2002* (Oxford: Oxford University Press).

### 2002 HDI ranking – selected countries

| Industrial countries | HDI value | HDI rank | GNP per capita rank* | Developing countries | HDI value | HDI rank | GNP per capita rank* |
|---|---|---|---|---|---|---|---|
| Norway | 0.944 | 1 | 5 | South Korea | 0.879 | 30 | 37 |
| Iceland | 0.942 | 2 | 4 | Chile | 0.831 | 43 | 53 |
| Sweden | 0.941 | 3 | 18 | Mexico | 0.800 | 55 | 58 |
| Australia | 0.939 | 4 | 12 | Brazil | 0.777 | 65 | 64 |
| Netherlands | 0.938 | 5 | 8 | Saudi Arabia | 0.769 | 73 | 40 |
| Belgium | 0.937 | 6 | 11 | Philippines | 0.751 | 85 | 104 |
| United States | 0.937 | 7 | 2 | Turkey | 0.734 | 96 | 80 |
| Canada | 0.936 | 8 | 9 | China | 0.721 | 104 | 102 |
| Japan | 0.932 | 9 | 14 | South Africa | 0.684 | 111 | 47 |
| Switzerland | 0.931 | 10 | 7 | Indonesia | 0.682 | 112 | 114 |
| United Kingdom | 0.930 | 13 | 19 | Egypt | 0.648 | 120 | 108 |
| France | 0.925 | 17 | 20 | Botswana | 0.614 | 125 | 60 |
| Germany | 0.921 | 18 | 13 | Morocco | 0.606 | 126 | 107 |
| New Zealand | 0.917 | 20 | 28 | India | 0.590 | 127 | 115 |
| | | | | Zambia | 0.386 | 163 | 170 |
| | | | | Sierra Leone | 0.275 | 175 | 175 |

* GNP rankings derived from purchasing power parity.

*Source*: *Human Development Report 2003* (Oxford: Oxford University Press). GNP figures for 2001 in World Bank, *World Development Indicators 2003*.

fairly stable since the start of the twentieth century. Another reason for divergence is that poorer countries find it more difficult to invest as much relatively as richer countries. Yet many individual countries and regions, despite their low initial starting point, have managed to catch up on the richer countries. Indeed, one could argue that the lower a country's income, the greater is its potential to outpace the growth of the richer countries, because of the technological spillovers from rich to poor countries. Poor countries can 'piggy-back' on the findings of expensive research undertaken and exploited in the better-off countries. World Bank forecasts up to 2008 predict annual growth per capita of 6 per cent in East Asia and 4 per cent in South Asia as compared with just over 2 per cent in high-income countries.

The catching-up controversy cannot be resolved by theory. Ultimately, it is an empirical question. One much-cited empirical study estimated that the gap in income per person between a typical poor and a typical rich country diminishes at roughly 2 per cent per year.[14] This suggests that convergence will eventually

---

### Box 2.5   The arithmetic of growth

Just how slowly the catching-up process of economic growth works may be illustrated by a simple arithmetical example.

Consider country A growing at a rate of 3 per cent per annum, in contrast to poorer country B growing at the faster rate of 6 per cent per annum. The initial income of A is $26,000, while that of B is $6000. Despite Country B's faster growth rate, it will be 25 years before it reaches today's income level of country A. Moreover, since A's income is increasing each year, the absolute gap in income between the two economies increases for the first 29 years. It will take 53 years before income per head in country B finally exceeds that in country A.

| Growth rate | Country A | Country B | Absolute income gap |
| --- | --- | --- | --- |
| Year 1 | 26,000 | 6,000 | 20,000 |
| Year 10 | 33,924 | 10,137 | 23,787 |
| Year 20 | 45,591 | 18,154 | 27,438 |
| **Year 28** | **57,754** | **28,934** | **28,819** |
| Year 29 | 59,486 | 30,670 | 28,816 |
| Year 30 | 61,271 | 32,510 | 28,760 |
| Year 40 | 82,343 | 58,221 | 24,122 |
| Year 50 | 110,662 | 104,260 | 6,402 |
| **Year 53** | **120,923** | **124,181** | **−3,258** |
| Year 54 | 124,551 | 131,632 | −7,081 |

Yet, the cumulative effects of compound growth rates over the long term must not be neglected. Even small changes in the growth rate may have major cumulative effects. At a 3 per cent growth rate, GNP doubles in size every 25 years, but at a 4 per cent growth rate, doubling would occur in just under 18 years.

---

14   R. Barro and X. Sala y Martin, 'Convergence across states and regions', *Brookings Papers on Economic Activity* 1 (1991); and *Economic Growth* (New York: McGraw-Hill, 1995).

dominate, albeit at a gradual rate (Box 2.5). Perhaps the most significant advance of recent research is the finding that poor countries will converge only under certain conditions. The *conditional convergence* literature stresses the importance of openness (globalisation), education (social capability to adapt to new technologies) and governance (political stability, legal institutions, honest administration). But even here there are problems of causality: to what extent is good governance the result of economic growth as well as being its cause?

Economic convergence remains a hotly debated issue. If India and China are excluded from the data, it is possible to agree with Easterly and Levine that:

> The poor are not getting poorer, but the rich are getting richer a lot faster than the poor. Divergence – not convergence – is the big story.[15]

But the opposite case, with convergence being the 'big story' also carries considerable cogency. There is no valid reason for not giving India and China their proper weight – their combined population accounts for more than one-third of the world's total. Also, negative growth in many developing countries has been caused more by civil wars and economic policy mismanagement than by any intrinsic 'divergence' effects at work in the world economy.

## 2.4 Policy prescriptions for growth

Economic growth is the result of the confluence of many different forces, both economic and non-economic. There is no single recipe for economic success. But a review of our knowledge to date suggests certain broad guidelines (Box 2.6).

First, we are now more conscious than in the past of the need to operate the economic system in an efficient way. Economic policy must be directed towards sustained growth: in formal terms, moving the 'production frontier' outwards. But we have learned that one way of achieving such outward shifts is to ensure that the economy is operating on the frontier in the first place. In the past, it was assumed that market inefficiencies were an acceptable price to pay for faster growth. Experience has shown that this supposed trade-off is illusory. The former socialist countries allocated a large portion of their resources to raising aggregate investment but, by neglecting the efficiency of individual investment and consumption decisions, the investment yielded a poor return in living standards. By and large, countries which emphasise economic efficiency also succeed in achieving the most rapid outward shifts in their production frontier.

Second, as a consequence of the above, there is greater understanding of the need for government intervention to complement rather than replace market forces. Unless policy interventions are market-conforming, high investment and other prerequisites for growth will not be attained. (Hence the adage: getting prices right may not be the end of economic development; getting them wrong certainly is.) There is enhanced awareness of the importance of education, of a stable and transparent institutional framework, competition policy, labour

---

[15] W. Easterly and R. Levine, 'It's not factor accumulation: stylised facts and growth models', World Bank, *Economic Review*, 15(2) (2001), p. 193.

## Box 2.6    Lessons from East Asia

*The East Asian Miracle: Economic growth and public policy*, the product of a World Bank research team, published in 1993, stimulated widespread debate on the components of economic policy that underpinned the spectacular performance of the East Asian countries. From the mid-1960s to 1997 these countries registered an average yearly growth in GNP per person in excess of 5 per cent. Their export performance was particularly impressive, raising their share of world exports of manufactures from 9 per cent in 1965 to 21 per cent in 1990. Not only did these countries grow rapidly, they were also successful in sharing the fruits of growth, achieving low and declining inequality of income.

The World Bank report found that there was little that could be described as 'miraculous' about the economic performance, even though the chances of such a concentration of growth, assuming it were randomly distributed worldwide, were just one in 10,000. *Fundamentally sound development policy was the major ingredient in achieving rapid growth*, the report observed. Although each country pursued a diverse mix of policies with varying degrees of intervention, they all shared a commitment to getting the economic policy fundamentals right.

The report commented extensively on the role of government intervention in this growth process. Previous World Bank studies had tended to focus on the negative aspects of government interventions. State efforts to subsidise interest rates or to protect key industries or to encourage farming were severely criticised. By contrast, the 1993 study concluded that a combination of sound fundamentals and selective interventions was crucial to East Asia's success. Specifically, their governments focused on:

- managing monetary and fiscal policy to ensure low inflation and a competitive exchange rate;
- concentrating public investment in education on primary and secondary level schooling;
- limiting import protection so that domestic prices are close to international prices;
- supporting agriculture by assisting the adoption of 'green revolution' technologies and investing in rural infrastructure;
- encouraging exports;
- fostering effective and secure financial systems to encourage savings and investment.

There is no doubt that the post-1997 crisis has taken much of the gloss from the East Asian story. Also it is clear that earlier studies had failed to identify key weaknesses in these countries' financial systems, which left them vulnerable to the change in sentiment that swept through the global markets. Perhaps because of this faulty analysis, the IMF made several mistakes in dealing with the crisis, notably in forcing too severe

| | Population (millions) 2000 | GDP per person (US$ PPP) 2000 | Real GDP growth rate | | Exports/GDP 2000 |
|---|---|---|---|---|---|
| | | | *1991–1997* | *1998–2002* | |
| Indonesia | 210 | 3,043 | 7.4 | −0.1 | 39 |
| Malaysia | 23 | 9,068 | 8.6 | 2.8 | 126 |
| Thailand | 61 | 6,402 | 6.7 | 0.8 | 67 |
| Singapore | 4 | 23,356 | 8.4 | 3.6 | 180 |
| Hong Kong | 7 | 25,153 | 5.3 | 2.0 | 150 |
| Korea | 47 | 17,380 | 7.2 | 4.3 | 45 |
| China | 1,262 | 3,976 | 11.2 | 7.4 | 26 |

*Source*: International Monetary Fund, *World Economic Outlook*, April 2002; World Bank, *World Development Indicators Database*, 2002; *Human Development Report 2002* (Oxford: Oxford University Press).

a cutback in public spending and imposing an excessive conditionality on its assistance. Nevertheless, the Asian tiger economies have not collapsed and, with the exception of Indonesia, they have now resumed growth. Valuable lessons have been learned on the need for exchange rate flexibility, on the unreliability of short-term capital flows and the danger of contagion, and on the need for a strong domestic financial system as a complement to capital liberalisation. Meanwhile, the core facts of East Asia's sustained economic growth remain unchanged. They continue to pose a challenge to other areas of the developing world that so far have been unable to emulate the Asian achievement.

*Sources*: *The World Bank Atlas 2002* (World Bank, Washington, DC); J. Page, 'The East Asian miracle: building a basis for growth', *Finance and Development* (March 1994); Helen Hughes, 'Why have East Asian countries led economic development?', *Economic Record* (March 1995); B. Aghveli, 'The Asian crisis: causes and remedies', *Finance and Development* (June 1999). For a contrary view, blaming the crisis on premature capital liberalisation and counterproductive IMF policies, see Joseph Stiglitz, *Globalisation and its Discontents* (New York: W. W. Norton, 2002).

market policy and basic infrastructure, for which the government has a major responsibility. The information revolution has spawned a new set of 'brainpower' industries – computers, electronics, biotechnology, robotics – which rely heavily on skilled labour. Countries that have adjusted their education systems to these new realities have grown fastest and will continue to prosper.

The third lesson is that poor macroeconomic management significantly impairs growth and that outward-oriented policies have positive effects on economic performance. Countries, like firms, need to focus on becoming internationally competitive. Attack in this sense may be the best defence, as well as being the most effective way of protecting one's domestic market from foreign competition.

Fourth, the economic environment needs to encourage and mobilise individual effort in a socially productive way. Countries with a poor economic growth record do not necessarily lack entrepreneurship. Rather, they lack the right type of entrepreneurship. Entrepreneurial effort needs to be allocated towards productive activities and away from unproductive, 'rent-seeking' activities. Rent-seeking refers to entrepreneurial behaviour which improves the welfare of some individuals or groups at the expense of the welfare of some other individuals or groups. Robert Reich, US Secretary of Labor in the Clinton administration, criticised the amount of human resources devoted to 'paper entrepreneurialism', i.e. 'creative' accounting, tax avoidance, financial management and litigation.[16] These activities mostly rearrange the distribution of wealth from one section of the population to another. Much has been made of the statistic that in the United States there is one lawyer for every 400 citizens, by comparison with one lawyer for every 10,000 in Japan. This difference in the allocation of talents can be attributed to national character and culture, but often it represents the rational response of individuals to the economic incentives existing in the respective societies.

---

[16]  Robert B. Reich, *The Next American Frontier* (New York: Penguin Books, 1983).

## 2.5 Conclusions

For most of the nineteenth and twentieth centuries, formal economic analysis has focused on the problem of investment. Accumulation of capital was seen as the key to faster growth. The nineteenth-century economist worried about whether profits would remain sufficiently high to provide enough incentives to investment. Added to Malthusian concerns about growing population, this led some of the best-known nineteenth-century economists to pessimistic conclusions about the possibility of sustained growth. Hence the label of economics as 'the dismal science'.

Later models continued to lay stress on capital accumulation but added a crucial variable, technical progress, envisaged as a built-in propensity to innovate. Growth per person in this perspective was determined by (1) the level of saving and investment, and (2) technical progress which affected the productivity of that investment. What governs the *amount* of investment was still seen as the crucial element in the growth process. This way of thinking encouraged what now appears an over-optimistic and naive belief that if only investment could be raised to a sufficiently high level, growth would automatically follow. Governments formulated economic plans in which state investment projects figured prominently and, in the case of developing countries, into which foreign aid was integrated. The government was to some extent regarded as an investor of last resort, in the event of the private sector not investing as much as was warranted. Ways of thinking about growth had a very practical impact. They underpinned the era of economic planning and multi-year investment programmes, which flourished in the 1950s and 1960s.

Since then, the emphasis has shifted dramatically from concern about the *amount* of investment to *quality* of investment and to a deeper understanding of the importance of the 'knowledge economy' as well as investment activities. This change of perspective was prompted by the fact that economic planning had outlived its usefulness. Investment, if badly allocated, will yield poor results and eventually prove unsustainable. The gradual seizing-up of the socialist economies and the failure of planning regimes in developing countries encouraged the search for new and more effective approaches to development. Out of this came the revival of liberal economics.

Experience suggests that economic policy matters a great deal. While not reverting to complete *laissez-faire*, the new orthodoxy sets more critical and demanding criteria for government intervention. More than the free operation of market forces is necessary to guarantee everybody a better life. But market-oriented policies can help us on the way. And, for certain, a thorough understanding of the working of market forces is necessary for an understanding of today's business and economic environment.

In the industrial countries, postwar growth has been attributed to high investment, advancing levels of education, trade liberalisation and social consensus. The slowdown in growth since the 1970s has been blamed on excessive government spending, lax policies towards inflation and (in Europe) over-regulation of the labour market.

In developing countries, the main feature of the postwar era is the sharp contrast in performance between different sets of countries over different time periods. In the 1950s and early 1960s, the prevailing expectations were optimistic with regard to the growth prospects of Africa and Latin America, and pessimistic with regard to Asia. Asian countries, it was feared, would run up against a Malthusian 'trap', with population growth outpacing the limited availability of land and other natural resources. As it transpired, these fears have proved unwarranted. Asia's growth has been sustained, notwithstanding the 1997–98 currency crisis. The factors underlying East Asia's growth have been much analysed – success always attracts would-be emulators – and have been found to be very diverse. The priority given to education, high investment rates in both the private and public sectors, efficient deployment of the labour force and involvement in international trade seem to have combined, albeit in different ways in each country, to give Asian countries a strong competitive position. The fortunes of South Asia and Latin America are also changing for the better. Their improved prospects have been associated with the implementation of a comprehensive package of 'new consensus' economic reforms.

The central conclusion of modern growth theory is that consistent market-oriented policies, political stability and efficient institutions are essential to growth. Icelandic economist Professor Thorvaldur Gylfason expresses this view forcefully in his textbook on growth theory:

> The main point of this book is that, with appropriate economic policies and institutions, rapid economic growth is achievable almost anywhere (*Principles of Economic Growth*, Oxford: Oxford University Press, 1999, p. 15).

One is tempted to add – even in a small, remote island with as inhospitable a climate as Iceland's! *To grow or not to grow*, he asserts, *is in large measure a matter of choice*. Economic growth takes place in the first instance because of a myriad of decisions made by individual firms. Decisions on where, when and what to invest, how much to spend on R&D, the development of a new product or a new process, collectively constitute the driving forces of growth. These decisions are strongly influenced by expected profitability. Fast-growing economies are likely to be those where rewards and incentives are closely associated to activities that encourage productive entrepreneurial activity.

## Summary

1. Economic growth measures the increase in a country's material prosperity. Sustained growth is a primary target of economic policy.

2. Most countries have experienced average annual growth of between 2 per cent and 4 per cent during the past 40 years. Growth at 3 per cent sustained over 23 years results in a doubling of income. Some areas have performed much better than average, notably the high-performing economies of East Asia, but Sub-Saharan Africa and many former socialist countries have suffered an absolute decline in living standards. Economic growth is the global norm, but there are a disturbing number of exceptions to this rule.

3. The growth process is stimulated and sustained by increases in supplies of factors of production. Traditionally, emphasis was placed on physical investment and on the necessity of ensuring that capital stock grew faster than the number of people. Recent empirical studies have drawn attention to the overwhelming importance of productivity growth, in particular total factor productivity.

4. Among the ultimate causes of higher productivity growth are technological advance, quality of education, reallocation of resources from low-productivity to high-productivity sectors, political stability and business incentives. Recent growth theories stress the mutually reinforcing nature of the growth process. Thus, fast growth helps an economy achieve technological advance, which in turn speeds up growth even more.

5. Economic policy also plays a vital part. Its objective is to ensure that optimum use is made of society's resources and that there are strong incentives to improve national productivity. Under certain assumptions, it can be shown that the market system leads to a more efficient outcome than any other system.

6. The connection between income distribution and economic performance has proved difficult to quantify. Curiously, better-off societies often tend to be more egalitarian than poorer countries. Use of market incentives is not inconsistent with an even income distribution. The nature of the growth-equity trade-off is still a controversial subject and the precise direction of causality is not clear. To be sure, a country does not become rich just by redistributing income from poor to rich. But, as a result of becoming rich, it can afford to redistribute income. Neglect of equity can damage growth prospects: too much emphasis on it damages efficiency.

7. Economic growth has implications for the environment, as well as for income distribution, which impact on its usefulness as an indicator of human welfare. Standard growth measures such as average annual GNP per person are far from being perfect indicators of welfare, but they are the best available.

8. There is no magic formula for economic growth, but three lessons have been learned which have important implications for the business environment. First, the economic system must be allowed to operate in an efficient way. Second, government must intervene in the economy but, in so doing, it should seek to complement, rather than to supplant, market forces. Third, the macroeconomic management of an economy and its foreign trade policies can be an important influence for good or ill on its growth performance.

## Questions for discussion

1. Discuss the 'stylised' facts of economic growth. Analyse the applicability of these stylised facts to any three countries of your choice.

2. The present world's most pressing economic problem is that so many so-called 'developing' countries are not in fact developing. Comment on the number of developing countries that have experienced declining standards of living during the past decade and discuss the likely causes of this poor performance.

3. Is the world economy becoming more or less unequal? Which is the 'big story' – convergence or divergence of living standards between poor countries and rich countries?

4. In the 1960s Asia's income per capita was half that of Africa. Today it is double that of Africa. Infant mortality in Asia has fallen from 141 per 1000 births in 1960 to 48 in 2000 and life expectancy has risen from 41 years to 67 years. How do you explain this? Is it because of adoption of better economic policies? How 'exportable' is Asian experience to other developing countries?

5. What are the main points of similarity and difference between the determinants of the growth of a firm and the growth of an economy?

6. Effective economic policies lead to faster economic growth not only by creating a business environment conducive to investment, but also by increasing the amount of growth pay-off per unit of investment. Discuss the policy measures which would be effective in raising a country's total factor productivity.

7. It is often said that technological progress is the key to economic progress. Explain how advances in technology affect growth. What other factors are important?

8. 'To grow or not to grow is in large measure a question of choice' (Gylfason). Do you agree?

## Exercises

1. Find out the level of GDP of any country you have a special interest in. Examine its rate of increase during the past decade. Compare its growth with that of the country groups in the chapter tables. What features would you identify as critical in explaining this growth? How might you test whether your views are correct?

2. You are asked to prepare a business report on an Asian economy. In evaluating its prospects for future growth, what variables would you consider most important, and why?

3. Between 1960 and 1990, Korea and Zambia had the same ratio of investment to GDP. Yet Korea's GDP grew by 9 per cent per year, while Zambia's grew by just 1 per cent. What factors would you consider in trying to explain this difference in performance?

4. Two economies, Lilliput and Oz, exist beside each other. Last year Lilliput experienced an annual growth rate of 8 per cent in GDP, while Oz experienced annual growth of 5 per cent. 'The citizens of Lilliput are clearly better-off than the citizens of Oz', claimed a local journal. Explain what further information you would require before accepting this assessment as valid.

5. An elderly parent leaves the family home, where the family looked after them, to a nursing home. Explain what happens to GDP.

→

6. India's per capita GNP was $2675 in 2002 (PPP basis). Assuming a growth rate of 3 per cent per person was sustained, how many years will it take India to reach average GDP level in the industrial countries of $28,744? Supposing industrial countries continue to grow at 2 per cent, how long would it be before India catches up with the industrial countries? Comment on the plausibility of these projections.

7. Suppose people increase their consumption of cigarettes, what happens to GDP? Because poor people spend proportionately more on cigarettes than rich people, this increase in cigarette consumption could easily appear as a decline in the country's poverty index. Thus while World Bank reports repeatedly deplore the consequences of smoking in developing countries, its poverty measure treats the increase in smoking as contributing to the decline in poverty. How can this paradox be resolved?

## Further reading

The World Bank's *World Development Indicators*, published annually and available on CD-ROM, is a goldmine of economic statistics for developed and developing countries. Information on the growth performance of developed economies and up-to-date estimates and forecasts are provided by the OECD (Paris), by the European Commission (Brussels) and by research institutes such as the UK's *National Institute of Economic Review*. The World Bank's publications provide regular reviews and assessments of growth performance and constraints. The causes of economic growth have occupied the attention of economists since the foundation of economics and are the subject of continuing analysis and controversy. T. Gylfason offers a concise and non-technical overview of recent growth theory in *Principles of Economic Growth* (Oxford: Oxford University Press, 1999). Jeffrey Sachs has written extensively on the empirical determinants of growth: see J. Sachs and A. Warner, 'Economic reform and the process of global integration', *Brookings Papers on Economic Activity* 1 (1995). One of the more controversial topics has been the negative aspects of economic growth, on which both E.J. Mishan, *The Costs of Economic Growth* (Harmondsworth: Penguin, 1967) and Fred Hirsch, *The Social Limits to Growth* (London: Routledge, 1977) are standard references. A more recent addition to this literature is R. Frank, *Luxury Fever: Why money fails to satisfy in an era of success* (New York: Free Press, 1999). For a discussion of green GDP estimates, see Joel Darmstadter, *Greening the GDP – Is it Desirable? Is it Feasible* (Washington, DC: Resources for the Future, 2000).

## Appendix 2.1 The economics of the new economy

The 'new economy' refers to a range of new industries and activities, mostly in information technology (IT) and biotechnology, that have grown at breakneck speed during the past two decades, have generated (and post-2000 dissipated) vast fortunes on the stock market and have revolutionised the way work is done in many sectors of the economy. The new economy has been fed by a once- or twice-in-a-century surge in technology that has boosted productivity-enhancing and cost-reducing investment and raised long-term economic growth. The Internet is an example of the rapidity of change. It had fewer than 3 million users worldwide in 1991 and its application to e-commerce was non-existent. Ten years later, an estimated 366 million users accessed the Internet and about one-quarter of them made purchases online from electronic sites, worth approximately $160 billion. At present this amounts to well under 5 per cent of total business-to-business (B2B) and business-to-consumer (B2C) transactions, but the potential for e-commerce growth beyond this figure is enormous. Computer-related spillovers, increasing returns in the production and use of computers, and network effects are fundamentally changing the US economy (Jorgenson and Stiroh, 1999).

Initially some believed that IT-related advances in technology were part of a continuum of change: capable of generating productivity improvements, but not at a rate that was any different from the past. The 'new economy' was seen more as a phenomenon affecting trends in the stock market than trend growth in the real economy. By the turn of the millennium, however, the consensus had shifted to the view that the IT revolution has made an important contribution to trend change in both labour productivity and total factor productivity and that these have translated into an increase of 0.5 percentage point in trend GNP growth.

To date the US has been the laboratory test case. It is the world's largest producer and consumer of high-tech products. According to World Bank figures, the US has 625 personal computers per 1000 people compared with only 366 in the UK and 382 in Germany (Table A2.1). Comparisons between e-commerce transactions and other indicators of IT use, such as availability of Internet hosts, show the US to be vastly more developed than most other countries. However, this superiority has been slow to translate into higher US productivity growth. The expected surge became evident only since the mid-1990s, when labour productivity began to grow at 3 per cent annually, double the rate of previous decades. Some sightings of a similar acceleration have been observed in the UK; and euro-optimists expected this to pass through to other member states in the EU that had invested heavily in IT. IT raises productivity in several ways: capital-deepening via investment in high-tech activities; total factor productivity increases in these activities; and spillover effects on 'old economy' activities as new technology is applied to them.

The new economy has important indirect effects on the economy. First, high-tech industries have a strong appetite for skilled computer-literate labour, while

### Table A2.1  Access to new technology

|  | Mobile phones per 1000 people | Personal computers per 1000 people | Internet hosts per 10,000 people |
|---|---|---|---|
| United States | 398 | 625 | 2420 |
| United Kingdom | 727 | 366 | 348 |
| Germany | 586 | 382 | 233 |
| France | 493 | 337 | 167 |
| Italy | 737 | 195 | 273 |
| Argentina | 163 | 91 | 47 |
| Morocco | 83 | 14 | 0.3 |
| Brazil | 136 | 63 | 39 |
| China | 66 | 19 | 0.7 |
| India | 4 | 6 | 0.3 |

Source: World Bank, *World Development Indicators 2002 and 2003*.

at the same time diminishing the relative demand for unskilled employees. This tends to raise the remuneration of the skilled and better-paid employees relative to the unskilled. US Department of Labor statistics show that the real weekly earnings of graduates have risen by 15 per cent compared with a 12 per cent fall in pay for those who left education after high school. In Europe the trend is much less pronounced, partly because it is less advanced in IT investment and partly also because the supply of skilled labour has been increased through investment in education (supply and demand analysis is outlined in Chapter 3). The new economy requires, and stimulates, massive investment in education.

The advance in technology also has implications for competition. This effect applies especially to activities where 'new' economies of scale and scope (network economies) apply. Robert Metcalfe, founder of 3Com, the network vendor, has argued that in a network the value of intercommunication among participants increases with the square of the number of participants, while the costs increase only linearly. Metcalfe's law applies especially to electronic marketplaces and helps to explain why many new economy industries such as software (Microsoft) and media (Time-Warner) tend to be dominated by a few firms. (Economies of scale and monopoly are discussed in Chapters 5 and 6 below.) At the same time, IT tends to enhance competition in activities where small firms can benefit from access to data and information sources that formerly were limited to the better off. It falls to the competition authorities to weigh the balance between these opposing forces in specific cases.

New economy activities have raised measurement problems for GNP statisticians. IT products have fallen dramatically in price. The price of PCs fell by an annual average of 24 per cent during the 1990s. The acquisition price of IT equipment for investment fell 16 per cent during the same period. Statistical problems arise when it comes to assessing the price equivalent of dramatic improvements in quality, as in the case of PCs and Intel chips. The US authorities estimate these effects in a different way from the EU statisticians. For this reason, a Bundesbank report published in 2000 revealed that EU growth would be half a percentage point higher if US statistical methodology was applied to EU GNP calculation.

How will new technological developments affect poorer countries? Optimists argue that latecomers enjoy the luxury of being able to 'catch up' without incurring all the development costs that richer countries have had to pay in bringing the product to market. A business in India, for example, can avail itself of the Internet to access the same information that is available to citizens of the richest countries. New, 'weightless' goods and services have caused the 'death of distance' that gives remote and marginalised peoples a better opportunity of boarding the high-tech bandwagon. On the other hand, economies of scale often tend to benefit first-movers, through exploitation of network economies of scope, and thus to reinforce the income gains of the richer countries. Research indicates that on balance the positive effects on developing countries outweigh the negative effects, subject to one proviso: that developing countries ensure basic levels of education and skills that enable their people to utilise and understand the new technologies being imported from the industrial countries.

*Sources*: 'E-commerce: impacts and policy challenges', OECD *Economic Outlook*, June 2000; C. Leadbeater, *Living on Thin Air* (New York: Viking, 1999); 'The new economy', *The Economist*, 23 September 2000; D. Jorgenson and K. Stiroh, 'Information technology and growth', *American Economic Review*, May 1999.

# Part I

# The market system and competition

**3** The market system in action

**4** Market demand and the pricing decision

**5** The firm in a competitive market

**6** The economics of market power

**7** Competition policy, privatisation and regulation

**8** Government intervention and the market system

**9** Business and the environment

**10** Hiring labour and the investment decision

How does the market system function? We begin (in Chapter 3) with an overview of forces of demand and supply, and show how these interact to determine prices. Prices in a free market act as a signalling device. A rise in the price of a product indicates that this product has become scarcer. The price increase signals to consumers the need to purchase less, by seeking cheaper substitutes, for instance, and it signals to business the need for more supply. Consideration is given to the institutional background required if the free market system is to operate efficiently. In long-established market economies this background tends to be taken for granted, but the experience of the newly liberalised economies of Europe has shown the importance of an adequate institutional framework of law, custom and behaviour.

Next (Chapter 4) we study the determinants of demand. Students of marketing will find many points of similarity and contrast between the marketing and the economics approach to this issue. The meaning and usefulness of the concept of elasticity of demand and its relevance to the firm's pricing decision is explained.

This is followed by chapters detailing the determinants of supply and the response of the individual firm to changes in the economic environment. We study the firm's cost structure, paying particular attention to economies of scale and scope (Chapter 5), and also to the extent of competition in the market (Chapter 6). As competition intensifies, goods tend to become cheaper and businesses tend to be managed more efficiently. The economic case for competition and the market mechanism is analysed.

Under conditions of competition companies make profits, but in equilibrium these will be just sufficient to service the capital invested in its assets and to keep the firm in business. Competition from new entrants makes it impossible to earn any more than this. Thus a company can make 'real' money only when there is imperfect competition. A firm will strive to move away from the 'ideal', perfectly competitive market. It can build up a degree of monopoly power by a number of strategies: product differentiation, innovation, creation of a patent or brand name.

There is a tension between the imperative of exploiting economies of scale and keeping a sufficient number of firms in the industry to preserve competition. In some industries, the cost of developing new products has become so large that small independent producers have been driven out of the market. Scale economies have led to the absorption of many formerly independent firms into much larger entities. The rising cost of market entry has driven many firms to seek out new forms of organisation. Multinationals have found it possible to compete fiercely with each other in some markets, while agreeing cooperative sales and distribution arrangements in other markets.

The marketplace needs to be policed. Fair trading rules have to be enforced in order to protect the consumer. They are also needed to protect small firms that are vulnerable to unfair and unscrupulous competition from financially powerful rivals. For this reason, most countries have established institutions to enforce competition. Where monopoly cannot be avoided, public intervention is also needed to regulate the monopolist's behaviour. These issues are discussed in Chapter 7. Also, we analyse the privatisation programmes, which have been such a distinctive feature of the economic scene in the recent past.

Although there is a strong movement towards smaller government, public intervention can and does contribute significantly to the market system. Business complains of taxes, as does everyone else, but knows that some level of taxation is essential if the fabric of society, and the market system itself, is to be preserved. The question is less one of whether government intervention is *needed*, than what type and how much government intervention is *optimal* (Chapter 8).

Economic policies relating to the environment have a serious impact on many firms. Chapter 9 examines the relevance of the economic concepts developed in this section to this topical and important issue.

Finally, we outline (Chapter 10) how simple demand and supply analysis can be used to explain the determination of pay at plant level and industry level, and also to illuminate the nature of a firm's investment decisions.

Microeconomics, as the type of economics used in this section is called, provides useful and practical insights for business. The material in this section is not designed to teach the reader an easy way of becoming either an economist or an entrepreneur. But it will help budding entrepreneurs – and those who in the future will advise and assist them – to understand the market system and to participate in the ongoing task of improving it.

## Chapter 3

# The market system in action

## Introduction

The free market comprises a series of interconnected markets. These markets are assumed to be highly competitive and to operate free of government interference. This is an initial simplifying assumption, which will be relaxed in later chapters. In reality, many markets are subject to monopolistic influences, and government intervention in the market system is a feature of even the most enthusiastically capitalist society. Indeed, in some circumstances, such intervention can be shown to be a necessary condition for achieving economic efficiency. Additionally, we assume a stable institutional framework of law and order within which market transactions can be conducted in an orderly and predictable way.

What is a market? There are many types of market, but the one we start with is a *competitive market*. It has the following characteristics:

- Large numbers of sellers and buyers, each acting independently and exerting no individual monopolistic power.
- Full information – everyone knows what the going price is and can evaluate the quality of the good or service being produced.
- Free entry and exit of firms in the market.
- Consumers aim to maximise utility (i.e. personal satisfaction) and firms aim to maximise profits.
- Prices are flexible in all markets.

Given these conditions, the market system allocates resources between different uses and among different people. It acts as an equilibrating mechanism between supply and demand. Prices act as *signals*; and the price system is the coordinating mechanism which ensures that markets 'clear', i.e. that supply equals demand in each market.

The operation of the price system is by no means obvious. The fact that a free market system works at all may be considered, if one stops to think about it, as somewhat miraculous. Millions of individual decisions are taken daily in a market economy by producers and consumers. These decisions are independent and uncoordinated. Yet, by and large, goods and services are available in the shops to meet consumer demands as they arise. The market system is the mechanism which brings this about in an automatic and efficient manner.

**Chapter outline**

1. Description of the overall market system.
2. The functioning of prices in the context of a single market.
3. What causes demand and supply to change, how the price system responds to such changes, and the effect of taxes, subsidies and price limits on market quantities and prices.
4. The role of traders and middlemen in the system.
5. The efficiency of competition and the free market.
6. The social and institutional conditions necessary for the market system to operate smoothly.

## 3.1 The market system

The market system can be sketched by reference to three major markets – the product market, the labour market and the capital market – and two primary sets of participants: firms and households (see Figure 3.1). The *product market* comprises the markets for individual goods and services; the *labour market* involves the buying and selling of labour; and the *capital market* deals with the lending and borrowing of capital. Each market involves the participation of *firms* and *households*. Thus, households sell their labour to firms; and, with the salaries so earned,

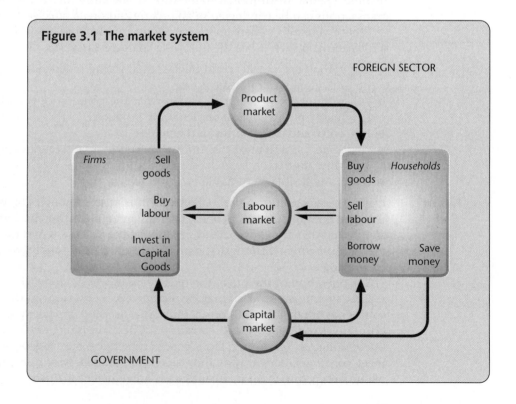

**Figure 3.1 The market system**

FOREIGN SECTOR

Product market

Firms     Sell goods

Buy labour     Labour market

Invest in Capital Goods

Buy goods     Households

Sell labour

Borrow money     Save money

Capital market

GOVERNMENT

they buy goods and services from firms. Firms produce goods and services by hiring labour and capital from households (and other firms). Households and firms also interact on the capital market. If individuals choose not to spend all their income, their savings are channelled to firms by intermediaries such as banks and pension funds. If they choose to spend more than their income, loans will be supplied by the same intermediaries. The lines in Figure 3.1 run both ways. However, the savings arrow from households to firms is thicker than the reverse arrow from firms to households in recognition of the fact that the corporate sector is the key investor and borrower in an economy. Households are generally net suppliers of funds to firms.

This is a much simplified conceptualisation of the market system as we know it in the real world, but it is sufficient to illustrate the strong interconnections between markets. Households need to sell their labour to firms in order to be able to buy goods. Unless households spend their incomes on purchases of goods and services, there will not be any demand for their labour. Or, to take another example, if firms do not invest, there will be no demand for household savings: savings are useful only in so far as there is an investor somewhere ready and willing to use them for investment. Clearly, a mechanism must exist to bring these disparate and independent decisions into equilibrium. A sustained dis-equilibrium in one part of this closely interconnected market system can have serious repercussions on other parts of the system. The market system is, in other words, a general equilibrium system. If anything goes wrong with the market mechanism, an economy could run into serious trouble.

Two other market participants must be considered – the *foreign sector* and the *government sector*. Firms do not have to sell their entire output to domestic consumers. They also have the option of exporting. Likewise, households can import goods and services instead of buying the output of domestic firms. Imports, exports and the foreign trade market are an integral part of an analysis of the market system. Factors of production such as capital and labour can also be traded internationally. The rise in global capital mobility, especially between developed countries, has meant that the domestic economy is no longer restricted to domestic savings for its supply of investment funds. The foreign sector has been growing rapidly in relative importance during the postwar period.

The government is also an important participant in the market. Government spending amounts to about 40 per cent of total national expenditure in industrial countries generally and exceeds 50 per cent in a number of European countries. Sweden's ratio is 50 per cent (and it reached 70 per cent in 1993). Even in an economy as free market-oriented as the US, the government's share of total spending ratio is 30 per cent (2002). The spending ratio, however, gives only a rough impression of the extent of government influence in the market system. Public intervention takes many forms in addition to government spending. Official regulations impinge on all areas of economic life – planning requirements for new buildings, health and safety regulations and environmental restrictions, for example. State-owned commercial companies are another vehicle of government influence not reflected in the spending:GDP ratio.

Economics is primarily about the market economy. The market economy includes all those goods and services that are sold on the market at a price determined by supply and demand. In the market economy, price plays the key role in determining production and allocation of output. The market economy, however, is not coterminous with total economic activity.

This point is illustrated in Figure 3.2. Total economic activity is divided into two components: the *formal economy*, the activities of which are measured and recorded in national economic statistics; and the *shadow economy*, the activities of which largely escape classification and measurement. The market economy extends over a large section of both these economies, but it does not include all their activities. Thus, in the shadow economy, unpaid housework, do-it-yourself repairs, and the activities of voluntary organisations are useful and important activities, but they are not part of the market economy. Housework includes childcare, cooking, cleaning, household repairs and decorations. Voluntary activities include activities such as mountain rescue, the lifeboat services, and unpaid administration of clubs, churches and agencies for the elderly and the handicapped. The distinctive features of these activities are that their output is not marketed (hence they are not part of the market economy) and that they are not recorded in GDP (hence they belong to the shadow economy). By contrast, several components of the shadow economy are included in the definition of the market sector. Black market activities such as double-jobbing, casual service work and the production and distribution of illegal goods fall into the marketed category. A conspicuous example is drug trafficking.

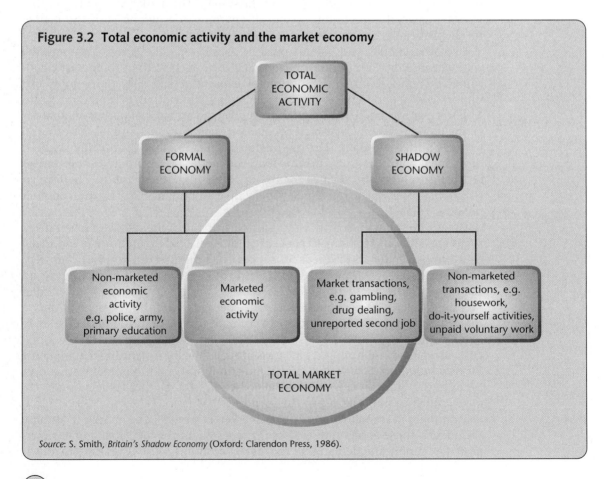

**Figure 3.2  Total economic activity and the market economy**

TOTAL ECONOMIC ACTIVITY

FORMAL ECONOMY

SHADOW ECONOMY

Non-marketed economic activity e.g. police, army, primary education

Marketed economic activity

Market transactions, e.g. gambling, drug dealing, unreported second job

Non-marketed transactions, e.g. housework, do-it-yourself activities, unpaid voluntary work

TOTAL MARKET ECONOMY

*Source*: S. Smith, *Britain's Shadow Economy* (Oxford: Clarendon Press, 1986).

Estimates of the importance of the shadow economy vary between countries and, for obvious reasons, they are subject to large margins of error. Underground economy estimates for 2002 range from 28 per cent of GDP for Greece and 27 per cent for Italy to a low of 9 per cent for Switzerland and the USA[1] (Table 3.1). These figures show how important the shadow economy can be even for well-run and modestly-taxed countries. Where central government is weak and corrupt, or is simply becoming more intrusive and regulation-minded, the value of 'hidden' transactions can be expected to rise. Schneider reports figures of 62 per cent for Georgia, 39 per cent for Romania and 54 per cent for the Ukraine. Equally hair-raising estimates have been derived for many developing countries (Box 3.1).

Most activity in the formal economy is part of the market economy. The major non-marketed section is the provision of government services. There is no market for defence, for example. Government does not offer to sell the services of its soldiers to the highest bidder! Likewise the judiciary and the police are not part of the market economy. In the EU, about one-fifth of the workforce in the formal economy is employed in producing non-marketed services.

The non-marketed sector makes an important contribution to society's welfare. That some activities are not marketed means it is difficult to value them, not that they are without value. Yet a crucial strength of the marketed sector, as a way of providing goods and services, is that its activities are kept under competitive scrutiny and subjected repeatedly to the test of the marketplace. Producers of a

### Table 3.1 Size of the shadow economy (% of GDP)

| Country | 1990 | 2002 |
| --- | --- | --- |
| Austria | 5 | 11 |
| Belgium | 20 | 22 |
| Canada | 14 | 16 |
| Denmark | 11 | 18 |
| Germany | 12 | 16 |
| Greece | 27 | 28 |
| France | 9 | 15 |
| Ireland | 12 | 16 |
| Italy | 23 | 27 |
| Netherlands | 14 | 13 |
| Norway | 15 | 19 |
| Spain | 21 | 23 |
| Sweden | 16 | 19 |
| Switzerland | 7 | 9 |
| UK | 10 | 13 |
| USA | 7 | 9 |

Source: F. Schneider, 'The value added of underground activities: size and measurement of the shadow economies of 110 countries all over the world', June 2002, see:
www.economics.uni-linz.ac.at/members/schneider/publik.html

---

[1] R. Mirus, R.S. Smith and V. Karoleff, 'Canada's underground economy revisited: Update and critique', *Canadian Public Policy* (September 1994) reported that about 15 per cent of the underground economy represents illegal income, the remaining 85 per cent comprising income from legal activities.

## Box 3.1 The shadow economy

The 'shadow', 'underground' or 'black' economy is a feature of most economies. It is part of the market economy because it involves marketed transactions freely entered into by third parties. Shadow market activities are motivated sometimes by the desire to evade legal restrictions (for example, illegal gambling, drug dealing), sometimes by the desire to evade tax or avoid loss of state payments (for example, part-time work by the unemployed, casual earnings, unreported rental income, tips, baby-sitters' earnings, sales of home-grown produce, 'skimming' cash receipts by shopkeepers). Sometimes the two motivations coexist. For example, smuggling can be a way of simultaneously evading the law and the tax authorities.

The key characteristic of the shadow economy is that its activities are not officially reported. The question is often asked: to what extent are official estimates of output (Gross Domestic Product) distorted by this omission?

### How to measure?

By its nature, measurement of the shadow economy is difficult and uncertain. Estimation of the shadow economy has been described as a 'scientific passion for knowing the unknown' (Schneider and Enste, 2000). Most methods rely on indirect procedures. One method is the *monetary aggregates method*. Market activities in the shadow economy involve mostly cash transactions, since payment in cash is the safest and surest way of keeping them unrecorded. Hence, the larger the shadow economy, the greater the use of currency relative to bank deposits. Data on the currency/deposit ratio can be used to estimate the value of the shadow economy. Another approach is to use econometric models. These can be supplemented by *special investigations* based on household surveys, labour market surveys and tax audits. They are undertaken from time to time by the statistical authorities.

### How large relative to official GDP?

Estimates of the shadow economy show wide variations among countries (10–30 per cent of GDP in developed countries and much higher in developing countries) and, more worryingly, also between different methods of estimation. To some extent this is an ineradicable problem because of the nature of the activity being measured.

### Causes

The main factors contributing to the black economy are:
1. High taxes and a perceived lack of 'fairness' of the tax system.
2. Onerous regulations (health and safety, employment legislation).
3. High unemployment combined with high unemployment compensation.
4. Cultural and personal behaviour characteristics.

### Cures

First, the most effective cure is to reduce tax rates and to make them simpler to comply with. Many countries are seeking to achieve this without detriment to overall tax revenue by measures to 'broaden' the tax base. This reduces the rewards of tax evasion.

Second, regulation and legal restrictions can be made less onerous and more focused. Small businesses are particularly affected by many employee protection and other regulations which involve high compliance costs. A better system would diminish the often high degree of public acceptance of black economy activities.

Third, compliance can be enforced by better internal monitoring and by international cooperation among tax authorities.

*Sources*: F. Schneider, 'The shadow economies of western Europe', *Economic Affairs* (September 1997); F. Schneider and D. Enste, 'Shadow economies around the world – size, causes and consequences', *Journal of Economic Literature* (March 2000); F. Schneider and D. Enste, 'Hiding in the shadows: the growth of the underground economy', IMF *Economic Issues*, 30, Washington DC (2002).

good or service usually think highly of the product they provide and believe that it is good for, and will please, the consumer. The market subjects this perception to an acid test. It provides an instant poll of whether the consumer agrees or disagrees with the provider's assessment. The verdict of the market is impersonal, decisive and measurable. It is conveyed to the producer through the price mechanism.

## 3.2 The role of prices

*Price is determined by demand and supply. If demand exceeds supply, price tends to rise. If supply exceeds demand, price tends to fall.* This description of the role of price is familiar to most people. It can be illustrated by a simple example. Consider the demand for laptops and the supply of laptops, and how changes in the price of laptops bring supply and demand into equilibrium.

The first step is to draw a demand curve. This shows how many laptops will be demanded at each price level. We make the reasonable assumption that the relationship is negative. As laptops become cheaper, they become more affordable and are purchased at a higher rate. As price falls, demand rises. The corollary also holds: as laptops become dearer, quantity demanded falls. This is termed the law of demand. The demand curve in Figure 3.3 illustrates this point. As we *move along the demand curve, we refer to a rise or a fall in demand.*

The next step is to construct a supply curve. This indicates the amount supplied by firms at each price level. We assume that the curve is upward-sloping: that is, the supply of laptops increases as price rises, and falls as price declines. A higher price enhances the profitability of laptop production and makes it economical for producers to offer overtime to their workers or to hire extra employees, even if they are less productive than the existing workforce. Another option made possible by higher price is to shift production from other products to laptops. Lower prices are assumed to have the opposite effect. Hence the supply curve in Figure 3.4 slopes upwards.[2]

---

[2] The sequence of events may not be so simple in practice. Thus, many firms find that more demand leads to a fall in unit costs which allows them to sell at a lower, not a higher, price. Their supply curves might be downward-sloping rather than upward-sloping. For a plant of given size, however, unit costs will rise after a certain point (machines will be operated too intensively, there will be administrative bottlenecks, etc.).

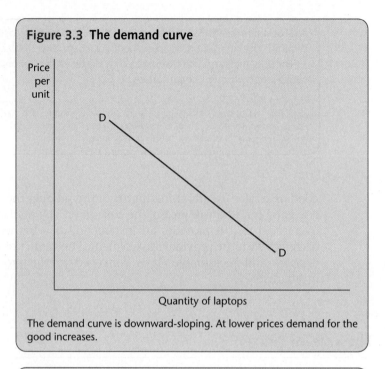

**Figure 3.3  The demand curve**

Price per unit

D

D

Quantity of laptops

The demand curve is downward-sloping. At lower prices demand for the good increases.

**Figure 3.4  The supply curve**

Price per unit

S

S

Quantity of laptops

Now place the demand curve and supply curve together (Figure 3.5). Suppose price happened to be at $P_1$. At this price the amount supplied, OH, exceeds the amount demanded, OQ. Retailers will find inventories of the product rising. Producers will find orders slowing down and their own inventories will increase. Inevitably, someone will give the order to 'move' the product by reducing the price.

As price falls, two things happen. First, demand tends to rise: more laptops are purchased because existing owners take advantage of the reduction in price to buy

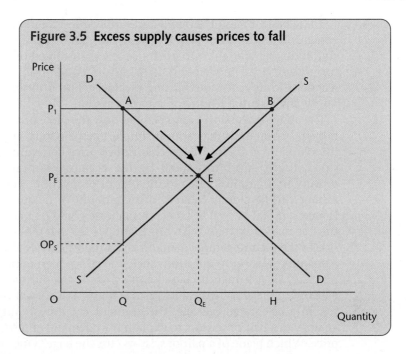

**Figure 3.5 Excess supply causes prices to fall**

a new model and new customers appear on the scene. This effect is captured by the movement downwards along the demand curve from A to E. Second, supply tends to fall. The decline in the price spills back into lower profits. Some producers will go out of business; others will operate at a reduced output level. This effect is captured by the movement downwards along the supply curve from B to E. Eventually, demand and supply are brought into equilibrium. *Market equilibrium* is reached at price $OP_E$ and quantity of laptops $OQ_E$. At this point, there is no tendency for price to either rise or fall. Provided the assumptions of the competitive market hold, there will be continuous pressure to move towards the equilibrium point.

The above analysis contains an implicit assumption about the adjustment process. We have assumed that if supply exceeds demand, price declines, and if demand exceeds supply, price increases. In other words, adjustment occurs via changes in price because of disparity between quantity supplied and quantity demanded at a particular price. An alternative adjustment process is via *changes in quantities*. We consider price disparities at a given output level instead of quantity disparities at a given price level. If, for any given quantity supplied, the supply price exceeds the price at which that quantity is demanded, then the quantity supplied will decrease. If the demand price exceeds the supply price, quantity supplied increases. For example, consider a given supply $OQ$ in Figure 3.5. The price at which that quantity is demanded, $OP_1$, is higher than its supply price, $OP_S$. This means that quantity supplied will increase. Note that, as the curves are drawn, it makes no difference to the equilibrium outcome which of the two adjustment mechanisms is chosen.[3]

---

[3] This is called the Marshallian adjustment process; that based on price movements is the Walrasian adjustment process. With differently shaped curves, specifically if the supply curve happens to be downward-sloping, it makes a difference which adjustment process is assumed from the point of view of the stability of equilibrium.

These basic forces of demand and supply affect all markets – not just consumer goods and services, but also raw materials, land, capital and labour. In all cases, equilibrium is brought into existence and is sustained by movements in price. In turn, these price movements help restore equilibrium by eliciting predictable reactions from profit-maximising producers and utility-maximising individuals. This is the essential feature of a market system.

The above discussion has explained how the price of a good or service is determined. The analysis may appear simple, even obvious, and so in a sense it is. Yet it took many years for the mechanism of price determination to be fully understood. Much effort was spent by the classical economists of the nineteenth century trying to link price to the cost of production. The cost of a product was assumed to be closely related to the amount of labour required to produce it. Hence, a moral as well as an economic case could be made for the superiority of the free market system. With hindsight, we see that cost of production is just one side of the picture. Simple demand and supply analysis also enables us to provide a definitive answer to questions such as: Is price high because a good is expensive to make? Or is it high because people prize it greatly? Or does one go to a lot of expense to make it because its price is high? The answer to all three questions is *yes*. In a celebrated passage, the eminent economist Alfred Marshall used the analogy of a pair of scissors to explain how demand and supply jointly determine price. Which blade of a pair of scissors cuts the page? One cannot say: both blades together do the cutting.

While prices are determined by supply and demand, they also act as *incentives* and as *sources of information*. They play an active as well as a passive role in the market system. Changes in price *bring about* equilibrium between demand and supply. When a gap threatens to appear between demand and supply, prices act as a signalling mechanism to bring them closer together. These signalling and incentive functions of price play a vital role in making the market system work.

## 3.3 Movements in demand and supply

Demand and supply curves do not stay permanently in the one position. Over time, demand will shift because of changes in:

- the level of income available to consumers,
- the price of substitute or complementary goods,
- the distribution of income among different classes of consumers,
- the demographic structure and age-trends,
- expectations of *future* price and income changes,
- advertising.

Each demand curve is defined relative to its own price for given levels of these other variables. If they change, the demand curve will shift. The term an 'increase' or 'decrease' in demand, by conventional usage, is used to denote an outward or inward shift in the demand curve.

Suppose real income in a country rises by 10 per cent. Demand for laptops will increase. In Figure 3.6 we depict this as a shift in the demand curve from DD to $D^1D^1$. At the initial equilibrium price $OP_E$, demand now exceeds supply by EB.

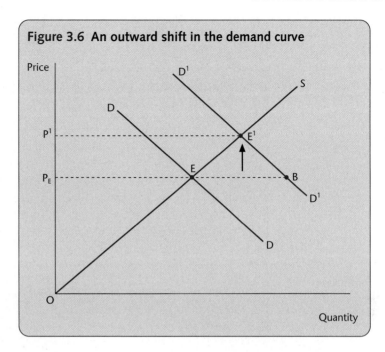

**Figure 3.6 An outward shift in the demand curve**

This excess demand, D > S, will cause price to be bid up. It keeps rising until a new equilibrium $E^1$ is reached. This rise in price has caused a fall in demand, but only in the special sense that one moves upwards along $D^1D^1$ by the amount $BE^1$. At $E^1$, price is higher, having risen to $OP^1$. Output too is higher, having responded to the higher price by moving *along* the supply curve. The amount demanded has also risen, despite the higher price, reflecting the power of the income effect.

Supply curves also shift position. Among the reasons for a shift in supply are:

● technological innovation,
● change in prices of labour, capital and material inputs,
● natural calamities and man-made disasters (war, weather, fire),
● strikes and government regulations,
● organisation and management restructuring.

Suppose scientists discover a cheaper way of producing a good. This means that, at each price level, more output can now be produced. We represent technological innovation of this type as an outward shift in the supply curve from SS to $S^1S^1$ (Figure 3.7). At the original equilibrium price $OP_E$, there is an excess supply of EB. Applying the adjustment-process rule (S > D ⟹ price declines), price starts to fall. This stimulates demand which moves downwards *along* the (unchanged) curve DD to $E^1$. A new equilibrium is established at $E^1$. More is supplied (and demanded) at a lower price as a result of the cost-reducing innovation, just as one would expect.

These examples illustrate the flexibility of the market system and its adaptability to change. Demand and supply curves can shift outwards and inwards. Provided prices are sufficiently flexible, markets will 'clear'. Everyone who wants the product, whether it be laptops or wine or rented apartments, and is prepared to pay the prevailing price, will be able to buy it.

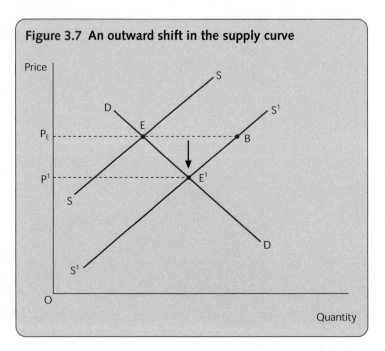

**Figure 3.7 An outward shift in the supply curve**

The practical significance of price flexibility within the market system needs to be emphasised.[4] For example, in former socialist countries, where the market system was absent, willingness to pay and the availability of goods in the shops were quite distinct concepts. One's pockets could be bulging with money, yet many products were unobtainable. Everything had to be booked well in advance; shop shelves were often bare; many products were unavailable because of administrative decisions. The system did not respond to market incentives but to bureaucratic dictates. The existence of excess demand was not easy to detect and was certainly not crucial to the supply decisions made by producers.

Attempts to replace the price system with administrative decisions, whereby suppliers were instructed how much to produce, led to major distortions and systematic inefficiency. Figure 3.8 illustrates what happens when there is interference with the price system. Thus, suppose a maximum price (or 'ceiling') of OP was set, administrators having (incorrectly) assumed that at price OP demand would have equalled supply at output OR. The mistake leads to excess demand AB. What happens? Utility-maximising individuals will rush to purchase more

---

[4] Commenting on the transition in Moscow to 'free-for-all capitalism', *The Financial Times* journalist Leyla Boulton listed among the advantages of the new lifestyle:

the queues and the shortages at the local food shop have disappeared since the abolition of price controls in January 1992. Thanks to the liberalisation of imports decreed at the same time, Muscovites today are far better-dressed than in the Soviet Union and, despite (justified) grumbling at still very high prices, can find whatever they need in the shops and in the kiosks which have mushroomed in the capital. There is little that is not for sale in Moscow today. 'Afghan war veterans available for all manner of security services' says the advertisement on the trolley buses. ('Capitalism grew in my courtyard', *Financial Times*, 25 August 1994)

As the author makes clear, there is also a negative side. Because of the weak institutional framework, identified later in this chapter as essential to the market system, Russia suffered many economic and social ills arising from an unbridled free market.

Figure 3.8 Effects of a price ceiling set at OP

laptops. Laptops will be siphoned off the official market into the more profitable black market. The resultant price will rise towards OM, evidently offering ample scope for profitable dealing. The price cannot exceed OM, but it will lie well above the officially determined price OP. The authorities are likely to blame speculators for the resultant rise in price, but the blame is misdirected. Even in the absence of a black market, long queues and waiting lists will occur. The problem is that the official price is not permitted to perform its coordinating function. By being artificially depressed, it is signalling a much greater abundance of the product than is in fact the case. With market liberalisation the equilibrium price would be $OP_E$ with sales of $OQ_E$.

Suppose, to take another example, the authorities choose an administrative price with the intention of maintaining producers' income. They set a minimum price above $OP_E$ and undertake to buy all the supply at that price. Now excess supply appears. Stocks accumulate in shops (a familiar sight in countries with extensive price control; huge stocks of unwanted produce appear alongside lines of bare shelves). The surplus stocks will have to be: (1) sold off at lower prices, thus causing the administrative error to be explicitly exposed; (2) stored in warehouses in the hope of a shift in demand occurring at some future date; or (3) effectively destroyed in some manner (e.g. fish dumped in the ocean, fruit and vegetables fed to animals, wine converted into pure alcohol). These solutions are not theoretical curiosities. They have been resorted to on a regular basis in many countries. The EU's Common Agricultural Policy has led to an accumulation of surpluses, large unwanted stocks (butter mountains, wine lakes, etc.) and subsidised or 'dumped' exports, just as economic theory would lead us to expect.

Demand and supply curves can be useful in answering a question which business often has to address. Suppose a tax is imposed on an industry's output, who bears the burden? Is it the consumer, or the producer, or both? This is known as the problem of determining the *incidence of the tax*.

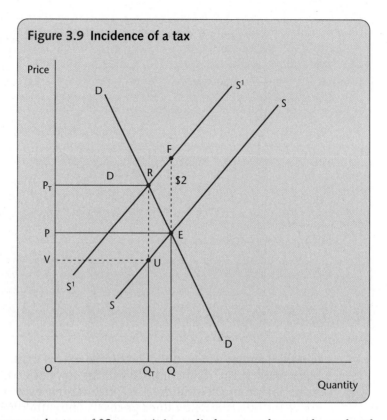

**Figure 3.9 Incidence of a tax**

Suppose a sales tax of $2 per unit is applied to a product such as a bottle of wine (Figure 3.9). This can be depicted by a shift in the supply curve to the left. At the initial output OQ, the selling price rises to QF = (OP + $2), where FE represents the tax. At that higher price, supply exceeds demand and price falls. Eventually, equilibrium is restored at $OP_T$ and $OQ_T$. From this it can be seen that: (1) quantity supplied and demand after the imposition of the tax falls to $OQ_T$; (2) government tax revenue is the area $P_T RUV$, i.e. tax of $2 per unit ($P_T V$) multiplied by the amount sold ($OQ_T = UV$); (3) the price to the consumer has risen by $PP_T$, *not by the full amount of the tax*; and (4) the price has fallen by PV (to OV). Hence the burden, or the incidence, of the tax has been shared between the consumer and the producer.

The amount of tax raised depends on the slopes of the demand and supply curves. If the demand curve is steeply sloped, the government gets more tax and most of the incidence falls on the consumer. If, on the other hand, the demand curve is flat, the government gets less revenue and the incidence falls mostly on the producer. The slope of the demand curve depends on the availability of substitutes and/or of alternative sources of supply such as the shadow or black markets. Tax incidence problems loom large in industries such as alcohol, tobacco and petrol, and also in the labour market, where the incidence of income and social security taxes can have serious implications for labour costs and for demand for labour. In determining tax incidence effects, we need to know the precise shape of the relevant demand and supply curves.

A sales tax, or any other type of tax, affects not only the allocation of output but also income distribution. Economists take a close interest in the *incentive effect* of taxation. They spend a great deal of effort measuring the responsiveness of supply and demand to changes in price. Companies (and politicians) are, of course, interested in this aspect, but they will also be concerned with the *endowment* (or income distribution) *effect* of a tax. Thus, in Figure 3.9, the imposition of the tax leads to a decline in wine producers' revenue (net of the sales tax) from PEQO to $VUQ_TO$. This loss of revenue could have serious repercussions on the overall profitability of firms in the industry.

The above analysis of taxes can be extended to subsidies. Subsidies to certain types of goods and services are common: food, petrol, fertilisers, domestic heating. Often the intention is to reduce the price of goods that are important for the less well-off. Sometimes the objective is to reduce congestion and pollution (subsidies to urban transport). The incidence, incentive and endowment effects of a subsidy can be traced in exactly the same manner as taxes. Note that a subsidy involves an *outward* shift in the supply curve whereas a tax involves an *inward* shift.

Demand and supply conditions are in the process of constant change. Provided prices are flexible, the market system generates a new equilibrium price after the initial equilibrium has been disturbed. However, markets vary with regard to the timespan required for adjustment to take place. Financial markets, such as those in foreign exchange, adjust very rapidly – often within minutes. Others, such as the labour market, may take years to adjust. While the equilibrating characteristics are plausible and readily understood in the context of a single market, it is more difficult to show that the market *system* as a whole will possess these equilibrating characteristics. How can we be sure that markets for all goods and services together will succeed in generating a mutually consistent, unique and stable general equilibrium? To Adam Smith this was the work of the 'invisible hand', guiding market actors towards a socially efficient outcome. A formal proof of the stability of the market system was not worked out until the 1950s, but the assumptions required for this proof were highly restrictive. Experience shows, however, that the market system seems to react to changes in a broadly stable way and it has so far coped with disequilibrating shocks reasonably well. This gives grounds for confidence that our simple theoretical model captures important features of real world markets.

## 3.4 The role of traders and arbitrage

The analysis of demand and supply has so far assumed that producers deal directly with consumers. As we know, this is far from being the usual case. The ex-factory price often amounts to only a fraction of the final retail price paid by the consumer. The difference between price ex-factory and price over-the-counter to the consumer represents payments to the 'middleman': wholesalers, agents, accountants, transporters, retailers. Is this margin between the two prices a reflection of inefficiency, or exploitation, or does it simply represent a fair reward for the effort and risks of distributing goods?

Some people regard trading and arbitrage as somehow inferior to 'real' work, such as actually producing a good. The tendency to deprecate the role of the distributive sector has a long pedigree. The Physiocrats of the eighteenth century, for example, viewed agriculture as the only true source of a country's wealth, with distribution playing a derivative role. Adam Smith himself, normally a rock of common sense, made a distinction between productive and unproductive (i.e. services) labour which sounds very contrived to modern ears:

> The sovereign, for example, with all the officers both of justice and war who serve under him, the whole army and navy, are unproductive labourers. ... In the same class must be ranked, some both of the gravest and most important, and some of the most frivolous professions; churchmen, lawyers, physicians, men of letters of all kind; players, buffoons, musicians, opera-singers, &c. ... Like the declamation of the actor, the harangue of the orator, or the tune of the musician, the work of all of them perishes in the very instant of its production.[5]

He justified this view on the grounds that service workers did not produce a physical surplus which could be reinvested. Not only did service sector workers not add to the surplus, their wages were paid out of it, reducing the amount available for accumulation.

From a market perspective, classifying the service sector as unproductive or second class makes no sense. The reason was explained by Professor Alfred Marshall as follows:

> It is sometimes said that traders do not produce: that while the cabinet-maker produces furniture, the furniture-dealer merely sells what is already produced. But there is no scientific foundation for this distinction. They both produce utilities, and neither can do more: the furniture-dealer moves and rearranges matter so as to make it more serviceable than it was before, and the carpenter does nothing more.[6]

If the end of all economic activity is consumption, then the production of wholesale and retailing services is as 'useful' in economic terms as the production of goods.

The information industry is a case in point. It includes activities such as the compilation of massive financial databases, stockbrokers' information sheets for clients, reports on firms, industries and economic surveys. There are consumer guides of various types, ranging from the *Which?* magazine reports of the Consumers' Association to travel guides, designed to help the consumer make informed decisions. All this activity helps to make the market operate more efficiently. Advances in communications technology have played an important role in easing the problem of *asymmetric information*. This problem arises when one party to a transaction possesses more information of its true value than another.

Consider, for example, a small firm seeking a bank loan. The firm has intimate knowledge of its own financial state of affairs, but the bank knows much less. In an effort to correct this asymmetry, the bank must engage in protracted information-gathering on the past financial performance of its prospective borrowers. It will ask for audited accounts and a business plan before making a decision on the loan. These services inputs are a valuable and necessary element in an efficient market system, not a superfluous frill.

Popular opinion in some countries persists in viewing manufacturing as the key to prosperity, with other related activities regarded variously as derivative – or, worse, exploitative – and as such either irrelevant or harmful to growth.

---

[5] Adam Smith, *Wealth of Nations* (1776), Book 2, Chapter 3, p. 352.
[6] Alfred Marshall, *Principles of Economics* (London: Macmillan, 1920), p. 53.

**Table 3.2 Employment in services as a percentage of civilian employment**

|  | 1960 | 1980 | 1990 | 2000 |
|---|---|---|---|---|
| US | 56.2 | 65.9 | 70.9 | 74.5 |
| Japan | 41.3 | 54.2 | 58.7 | 63.7 |
| Germany | 39.1 | 51.0 | 56.8 | 62.7 |
| France | 39.9 | 55.4 | 64.0 | 71.5 |
| UK | 47.6 | 59.7 | 68.9 | 73.0 |
| Italy | 33.5 | 47.8 | 58.6 | 62.2 |
| Canada | 54.1 | 66.0 | 71.2 | 74.1 |
| EU | 39.1 | 52.7 | 61.1 | 66.7 |

Source: OECD, *National Statistics*; OECD, *Employment Outlook* (June 2000); and author's own estimates.

Former socialist countries went so far as to exclude services from GNP altogether, using the gross material product concept instead. The practical significance of this exclusion is far from trivial.

The proportion of the EU workforce employed in services exceeds 60 per cent, up from 53 per cent in 1980. In the US and the UK, over 70 per cent of the workforce is employed in the services sector. Furthermore, the percentage of employment in services is increasing rapidly (Table 3.2) and has risen by about 50 per cent since 1960. Many of those so employed are facilitators, intermediaries and arbitrageurs. It makes no sense to suggest that these people do not contribute to GDP. Such an attitude, if carried over into policy, can cause governments to underestimate the importance of an efficient and productive services sector in a modern economy.

## 3.5 The efficiency of the market system

In Chapter 2 we defined the concepts of productive efficiency and allocative efficiency, and mentioned that, under certain conditions, the free market could be shown to bring the economy to an efficient point so defined. The analysis of the market system in this chapter enables us to provide an intuitive explanation of why this might be the case.

Consider, first, the demand curve. It shows how much people are willing to purchase at each price. The person who bought the OQth unit of the good in Figure 3.10 did so because the utility received from it made it just worth the price OP. The consumer tries to ensure that the extra utility obtained from an additional purchase is proportional to its price. This extra utility is termed *marginal utility*. When deciding how to allocate our income among competing desirable items, we implicitly compare marginal utility and price. If pears cost twice as much as oranges, we assume that, in a free market, utility-maximising consumers will arrange their purchases so that the marginal utility provided by the last kilogram of pears purchased is double the marginal utility of the last kilogram of oranges. Suppose this condition were breached and the utility of pears were four

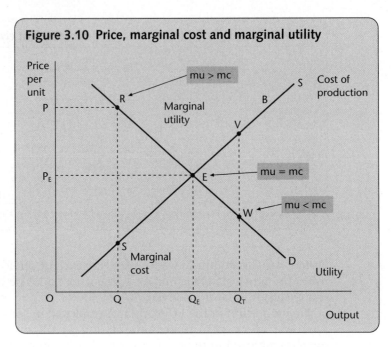

**Figure 3.10 Price, marginal cost and marginal utility**

times the marginal utility of oranges. Then the consumer could add to utility, within a fixed budget, by buying more pears and fewer oranges. The utility-maximising assumption will dictate a continuance of this reallocation until the 2:1 ratio is reached. Free market prices reflect marginal utilities.

Next, consider the supply curve, SS. This represents the cost of producing the product. The extra cost of producing the OQth unit of output, otherwise known as its *marginal cost*, is QS. The supply curve slopes upwards because, in the short run, unit costs are assumed to rise as output increases. Hence, at a higher price it becomes profitable to produce more output and firms continue producing more until marginal cost equals that higher price. The connection between costs and price at firm level will be explained fully in Chapter 5. For the present, all we need to understand is that the supply curve indicates the marginal cost of producing any given level of output.

Consumption at R (of output OQ at price OP) is not efficient. This is because the marginal utility derived from consuming the OQth unit exceeds the marginal cost of producing the OQth unit. Ideally, we would want to expand production until the point is reached where price and marginal cost are equal. That is, the marginal cost of producing the last unit of output is exactly proportional to the utility derived from it. In Figure 3.10, such a point is reached at E, where output is $OQ_E$ and price is $OP_E$. That equilibrium is clearly superior to the OQ–OP combination, because for each unit between OQ and $OQ_E$, the marginal utility exceeded marginal cost. It would not be desirable to produce beyond $OQ_E$ because then the marginal cost would exceed the marginal utility. At output $OQ_T$, for instance, marginal cost $Q_T V$ exceeds marginal utility $Q_T W$.

If points such as E are reached for every product, then we know that marginal utility (which is proportional to price) will also be proportional to marginal cost.

As we have seen, *the free market system with competition will provide precisely that outcome*. Market forces drive each market to equilibrium at points such as E. This is achieved not because market participants are consciously striving to achieve an efficient outcome in the economist's sense. Rather, they are being driven by the desire on the part of consumers to maximise utility and on the part of producers to maximise profits. We are back to Adam Smith's 'invisible hand', leading market agents to a socially beneficial outcome which was no part of their original intention. Competition leads profit-seeking producers to provide what consumers want to purchase at the lowest possible price. While free market competition tends to lead the economy towards *static* efficiency, it also has important *dynamic* efficiency effects. Over time, pressures of competition will ensure that costs are kept to a minimum. A free market with competition gives firms a powerful incentive to seek more effective ways of producing and distributing their output, through rationalisation and innovation. For most industries, we think of this process as involving continuing shifts of the supply curve to the right.

The case for competition and the free market as a generator of economic efficiency is subject to many qualifications. The 'invisible hand' is itself in need of guidance. Discussion on these matters is a live issue as many industrial countries attempt to become more market-oriented and as countries in transition decide on the type of market institutions most suited for their needs.

## 3.6 The free market system in social context

This chapter provides an explanation and analysis of the market system. Later chapters will expand on the demand and supply framework. Before proceeding further, however, it is useful to consider the institutional conditions needed if the market system is to operate efficiently. These conditions are easy to take for granted, but the transition from socialism to a market system in many countries has shown just how important the social context of the market can be.

First, the price system presupposes a *stable and reliable medium of exchange*. This implies the existence of a secure and widely acceptable currency. A monetary economy differs from a barter economy in that it allows exchange to occur even in the absence of a coincidence of wants between the buyer and the seller. For example, a car worker can sell labour to the employer in return for money, which can then be spent on goods and services at the individual's discretion. By contrast, exchange will take place in a barter economy only if someone is willing to take exactly what another has to offer – one needs what is called in the jargon a *double coincidence of wants*. Also, if the general money price level is rising rapidly and unpredictably, people get confused about the *real* price level and are unable to distinguish between an absolute rise and a relative rise in the price of a good they are interested in trading. Rapid price changes involve great uncertainty.[7]

---

[7] A business graduate from the National University of Cujo, Argentina, explained the frustrations of trading during the period of hyperinflation of 1989–90 as follows. To purchase an automobile tyre, one had to seek quotations from a number of suppliers. Wide price variations – of as much as a 3:1 ratio – were not uncommon, even within the same city. After spending considerable time obtaining the various quotations, it often happened that the lowest price supplier had changed the price in the interim and the search had to be started all over again.

> **Box 3.2** **A market economy**
>
> In a market economy,
>
> *Exchange is mediated through markets in which prices play a decisive role.*
>
> To work smoothly and effectively, a market needs:
>
> - A medium of exchange –stable and reliable.
> - Competition – free entry and exit of firms into the industry.
> - Full information – transparent prices and well-informed consumers.
> - Strong institutions – a body of law which protects property rights and ensures that contracts are enforceable.
> - A supportive framework of social custom – markets will not function efficiently without standards of truth, trust, acceptance and obligation.
> - Income redistribution – sufficient to create consensus and to confer legitimacy on social order without destroying incentives to perform.

Second, there must be full information. The market cannot work well if consumers are ignorant of the qualities of the good or service being purchased – lack of such knowledge explains why so much of the health service has been taken over by the state and why there is such intensive regulation of the banking and insurance industries. Third, competition is needed in order to ensure that firms respond quickly and efficiently to price signals and that best production techniques are utilised and waste avoided (see Chapters 6 and 7).

Fourth, we need strong institutions, in particular the *institution of private property* and a *legal framework*. At one time, proponents of market socialism believed that market mechanisms could apply while retaining state ownership. But experience showed that this was not a practical proposition. Bureaucrats 'bargaining' with other people's goods and services will rarely act in the same manner as consumers and producers would in a free market. Individuals will save only if there is a real prospect of their being able to use their savings at a later date as they wish. Entrepreneurs will invest only if the profits they earn can be retained, either to reinvest or to pass on to future generations – or even to 'waste' on luxuries. Private property is needed if the investment and saving decisions of the market system are to be efficient. In addition to private property, one needs a broad legal framework covering bankruptcy, competition law and contract enforcement. Limited liability, patents and the public company are examples of legal constructs which have exercised enormous influence on the process of industrial development. Without them, the market system as we know it today could not have developed.

Fifth, markets will not function properly without *certain minimum standards of truth, trust, acceptance and obligation*. Where these are missing, either transactions do not take place or else they take place at great cost in terms of legal, financial and security precautions. Such costs inhibit the ability of the price system to signal scarcities and surpluses. The growth of business ethics courses reflects an appreciation of the practical importance of ethical standards in the market system. Where such standards are high, customers trust a label, believe that freshly baked bread means just that, accept a buyer's word. Likewise, in an ethical world, investors accept the word of executives and the endorsement of accountants, without the need for endless rechecking. In a practical way, this saves resources and enhances efficiency.

Finally, one needs an equitable distribution of *wealth and income* to confer legitimacy on the social order. To some extent, this involves a curtailment of the right to private property. Private property can, and may even have to be, compulsorily acquired by the state in order to ensure social harmony. The extent of state involvement needed to achieve this objective is a matter of debate. What is clear is that governments can affect income distribution in a myriad of ways: by imposing progressive income taxes (rich people pay a higher proportion of tax on their income than poor people), by targeted spending on education, health and housing, and by the provision of social welfare income 'floors' and 'safety nets' for the poor. These measures are not always as effective as appears, and they can have unwanted and often unexpected side-effects such as the adverse effect of highly progressive taxation on entrepreneurial incentives. Some critics argue that the search for social justice is a mirage. An individual's income, they claim, is acquired by hard work, luck and inheritance; attempts to alter the balance between rich and poor will turn out to be counterproductive and ineffective in the long run.[8] Clearly, there is room for much disagreement on these issues.

## 3.7 Conclusions

One of the best-known passages in the *Wealth of Nations* (1776) describes how the pursuit of self-interest leads to social benefit:

> It is not from the benevolence of the butcher, the brewer or the baker that we expect our dinner, but from their regard to their own self-interest. We address ourselves, not to their humanity, but to their self-love. (Adam Smith, *Wealth of Nations*, Book 1, Chapter 2, p. 18)

In retrospect, we see that the imposition of centralised decision-making on an economy can achieve short-term successes. Among them might be included the transformation of the Soviet economy under Stalin and the restoration of the Chinese economy under Mao. But history suggests that the successes of such centralisation soon reach a limit. The postwar experience of Central Europe confirms this conclusion. Decades of socialism left this region weakened by an inefficient allocation of resources, by the erosion of innovation and by technological obsolescence.

One striking consequence of the neglect of the price system by the socialist countries was the dramatic contrast between energy consumption patterns in Eastern and Western Europe. Between 1965 and 1985, the energy intensity of GDP fell from 0.52 to 0.38 per cent in the West, while actually rising in the East over the same period from 0.73 to 0.78 per cent.[9] Because internal energy prices in the

---

[8] F.A. von Hayek, *The Fatal Conceit: The errors of socialism* (London: Routledge, 1989).

[9] B. Heitger, 'Comparative economic growth: East and West', in B. Heitger and L. Waverman, *German Unification and the International Economy* (London: Routledge, 1993).

Eastern economies were not set at the prevailing international levels, the increase in world energy prices in the early and late 1970s, 'signalling' the need for energy conservation, was not transmitted to their firms and consumers. As a result, industrial energy intensity in the 1990s was five times higher in Poland than in the US, and five times higher in Hungary than in Germany. The high level of energy intensity not only implied a waste of energy due to underpricing, but also encouraged the growth of heavy pollution industries and gave insufficient incentives to the development of less energy-intensive methods of production.

Writing of the contrast between East and West Germany, John Kay has remarked that:

> Whatever the superficial attractions of central direction and control, in practice it literally failed to deliver the goods. The immediate contrast between East and West Germany provided as close to a controlled experiment as social science is ever likely to see. The results of that experiment, and its dramatic end, imply that for the foreseeable future the private value-maximising corporation will be the principal engine of commercial activity in Europe.[10]

The 'private value-maximising corporation' is the same as the profit-maximising firm which determines supply. Given the increasing range and scope of the market system, it has become more important than ever to understand this system and the role of the firm in its working.

Where the institutional prerequisites are absent, however, market capitalism can get a bad name. Essentially, the point is that the free market will not perform efficiently without moral restraints. A legal system based on the principles of profit maximisation would deliver little justice. Judges would make judgments on the basis of the highest bribes. Paradoxically, the market system and the pursuit of self-interest will operate effectively only when a significant proportion of the workforce puts duty and propriety ahead of personal advancement and prosperity. It has often been remarked that the *definition of property rights based on the market system depends precisely on the lack of universality of motivations of the market system*. An efficient economy needs an incorruptible judiciary and civil service. An interesting question is whether the market itself tends to undermine some of the values of trust, incorruptibility and restraint which we have identified as essential to its proper functioning. Evidence from the history of economic development suggests that, while it may be relatively easy to pull down the monolith of central economic control and to reinstitute private property and free exchange, it takes longer to develop the cultural and social structures necessary to sustain a truly successful society.

## Summary

**1.** The market system comprises three major markets – the product market, the labour market and the capital market; two primary sets of participants – firms and households; and two subsidiary participants – government and the foreign sector. The market system is characterised by a set of interconnecting relations.

---

[10] John Kay, *Foundations of Corporate Success: How business strategies add value* (Oxford: Oxford University Press, 1993), p. 321.

The interdependence of the market system is reflected in the circular flow of income between the different market participants and from one market to another. Households sell their labour to firms and use their earnings to purchase the output of these firms. Households save for the future and their savings are deployed by firms, thereby adding to society's capital stock. Failure of any one market to 'clear' affects the other markets.

2. Many useful economic activities are not included in the market economy, such as household duties or voluntary community work. Other shadow activities are included in the definition of the market economy, but they often fail to be recorded in official estimates. The shadow economy has been estimated to account for up to 30 per cent of officially recorded national production in developed countries.

3. Price is determined by supply and demand. Provided prices are flexible, markets will 'clear' automatically, meaning that the amount supplied just equals the amount demanded. The market system also ordains that price changes act as a signal or incentive. Thus, a rise in price calls forth additional supply and gives consumers an incentive to reduce consumption and to divert expenditure to substitute products. Shifts in the demand or supply curves cause a change in price. In the real world there is no single stable equilibrium price because demand and supply curves are in a constant state of flux.

4. Demand and supply curves can be used to analyse the effects of the imposition of a sales tax or subsidy, or to estimate the consequences of different scenarios of shifts in incomes, technology and similar factors.

5. Agents and middlemen make a positive and important contribution to the functioning of a market system. Generally, the provision of services is the largest sector by far in industrial countries, much of it consisting of facilitator-type activities. In the US and Britain, over 70 per cent of the total workforce is now employed in this sector. There has been sustained growth in service activities such as transportation, recreation and personal services – ranging from hairdressing, health and education to banking and insurance.

6. Competition and the market system lead profit-seeking entrepreneurs to produce what consumers want to consume and secure an economically efficient level and distribution of output. But to do so, there must be an appropriate institutional background and value system. Capitalism, although useful, is unlovely and badly needs the protective social framework it constantly tends to undermine.

## Questions for discussion

1. Discuss the preconditions necessary for the smooth functioning of the market system.

2. Does the existence of a shadow or 'black' economy imply that the price system is not working? Is its existence consistent with the laws of demand and supply?

3. Discuss what you would consider to be the main determinants of demand and supply of rented apartments. Suppose the government decides that rents are too high and sets a maximum rent. What would you expect the consequences of this action to be for (a) apartment owners, (b) existing renters, and (c) future renters?

➜

4. The government gains revenue by imposing a sales tax. Who stands to lose the most, the consumer or the producer, or both?

5. Discuss the role of the 'middleman' in the distribution of goods and services.

6. It is often claimed that market forces, with their emphasis on selfish motivation and profit maximisation, undermine ethics, yet arguably an ethical approach towards contracts and employees by business is essential for the market system to function. Is the first assertion simply wrong?

## Exercises

1. At the beginning of January 1992, price controls were lifted in Russia. Within a day food prices had increased by 250 per cent, but the food queues vanished overnight. Using demand and supply curves, explain what happened. How would you expect the supply of food to have been affected – in the short term and in the long run? Which groups in society gained, and which lost, as a result of the abolition of food price controls?

2. We know that the number of personal computers being sold has increased, yet the price is falling. Use supply and demand curves to explain how this can happen.

3. Consider the supply curve of oil for central heating. In each of the cases below, indicate whether there is a movement along the supply curve (and in which direction) or a shift of the supply curve (and whether left or right): (a) new oilfields start up in production; (b) the demand for central heating rises; (c) the price of coal falls; (d) oil companies anticipate an upsurge in the demand for central heating oil; (e) the demand for petrol rises; (f) new technology decreases the costs of oil refining.

4. The table contains data on price, quantity supplied and quantity demanded.

   (a) Draw a diagram showing the demand and supply curves.
   (b) With this diagram, estimate the new equilibrium price and quantity after the imposition of a tax of £2 per unit.
   (c) Comment on the incidence of the tax.
   (d) Show how producers' sales are affected and how much tax revenue accrues to government.

   | Price £ | Quantity supplied (units per week) | Quantity demanded (units per week) |
   | --- | --- | --- |
   | 10 | 500 | 800 |
   | 11 | 550 | 750 |
   | 12 | 600 | 700 |
   | 13 | 650 | 650 |
   | 14 | 700 | 600 |
   | 15 | 750 | 550 |
   | 16 | 800 | 500 |

5. Suppose buyers' tastes change in favour of fresh vegetables and simultaneously there is an advance in vegetable-growing technology. Show how the supply and

demand curves would be affected. What would be the effect on the equilibrium price and quantity? Do we know?

Suppose instead of an improvement in technology, vegetable producers were hit by adverse weather. How would your diagram change? Would you be able to say whether the new equilibrium price would be higher or lower than the original equilibrium? What would be the effect on equilibrium quantity?

6. (a) Consider the economic consequences of a prohibition on the consumption of alcohol. What happens to the supply curve? What happens to the demand curve? How will the prohibition affect equilibrium consumption and price? What further indirect effects are likely to follow? (According to some writers, 'prohibition is likely to raise the level of violence by increasing the marginal benefits, and lowering the marginal costs, of breaking the law'.)

   (b) Suppose the head of an anti-drugs enforcement agency reports, as evidence of the agency's success in deterring drug users, that the street price of drugs has fallen. Is this evidence conclusive? What other factors might have caused the fall in price?

7. The minimum price set by the European Commission for many foodstuffs and dairy products is set above the market clearing equilibrium price. The objective of this price floor is to support farm incomes. Use a supply and demand diagram to illustrate the effects of setting the minimum price on (a) food prices; (b) farm incomes; (c) government spending.

8. Suppose the average cost of a legitimate software package is €150. The owner of the software complains of pirated software in developing countries. The estimated number of pirated packages sold is 20 million copies. The firm argues that it is losing 20 million × €150 = €3 billion in sales revenue. What is wrong with this estimate of loss?

What would be the correct way of estimating loss?

## Further reading

There is an extensive literature on what has been variously called the 'shadow', 'black' or 'hidden' economy. A useful, if rather inconclusive starting point is the special feature 'Controversy; On the hidden economy', *Economic Journal* (June 1999). Professor Friedrich Schneider is a leading authority on the subject (see Table 3.1 for reference). Demand and supply curves and the determination of price are standard fare in introductory economic textbooks. The relationship between economics and business morality is discussed in W. Baumol, 'Smith vs Marx on business morality and the social interest', in W. Baumol (ed.), *Microtheory: Applications and origins* (New York and London: Harvester Wheatsheaf, 1986). John Kay, *The Truth about Markets* (London: Penguin Books, 2003) offers a readable if somewhat disjointed account of the strengths and weaknesses of the market system.

## Chapter 4

# Market demand and the pricing decision

## Introduction

The market demand curve is important for business in two practical ways. First, the decision to invest in expanded production capacity or in a marketing campaign requires a close analysis of the expected growth of demand over time. Second, the firm's pricing decision depends on the nature of the demand curve for the firm's products. The pricing decision, of course, is not determined solely by demand-side considerations – the company's cost function and profit objectives, and the reaction of competitors, have also to be taken into account – but demand analysis plays a crucial part in the decision.

This chapter provides an economic analysis of market demand. This is an important starting point, both for understanding the economy and for the study of marketing.

## Chapter outline

1. Assumptions about the behaviour of 'rational' consumers.
2. How to construct a market demand curve from a set of individual demand curves.
3. The concept of elasticity of demand: price, income and cross-price elasticity.
4. How demand curves are estimated in practice.
5. The relevance of market demand characteristics to the firm's pricing decision.

## 4.1 What is a 'rational' consumer?

The theory of demand explains how an individual responds to changes in key economic variables such as prices and income. Five major assumptions about consumer behaviour are made which elaborate on the hypothesis that consumers are utility-maximisers. These assumptions can be summarised under the headings of *comparability*, *non-satiation*, *consistency*, *convexity* and *independence*.

- *Comparability*. Consumers can, and do, compare and rank different combinations of goods and services in terms of utility. If offered two baskets, A and B, of goods, the individual is sufficiently well informed to be able to declare a preference for A over B or for B over A, or express indifference between the two.
- *Non-satiation*. Consumers' wants are unlimited. More is always preferred to less. If basket A contains more of every good and service than basket B, then A must be preferred to B.
- *Consistency*. Consumers are consistent. If A is preferred to B, and B is preferred to C (where C is a third basket of products), then A must be preferred to C.
- *Convexity*. As an individual consumes more of a particular good relative to other goods, its utility falls relative to those products. Consider the example of a cyclist returning home after a long journey. The first glass of water tastes wonderful; the second glass, great; the third glass, good. Note how the extra utility per glass progressively declines. By the tenth glass, it may be near zero or even negative![1]
- *Independent utilities*. Independence of individual utilities means that the utility a person derives from a good is independent of how much others may possess of the same good. In other words, the value attached to a good by a consumer is not affected either by its value to others or by the quantity consumed by others.

These assumptions are reasonable, but nobody would claim that they provide a completely realistic description of consumer behaviour. For example, when information is costly or difficult to acquire, we may not have sufficient knowledge to rank preferences in a comprehensive and consistent manner. When consulting professionals (for example, doctors and lawyers), we are often unable to assess the quality of the services they are offering. The cost of acquiring information may lead the consumer to use a rule of thumb, or to follow the crowd. In such instances, recourse may be had to a less ambitious definition of rationality, such as 'bounded' rationality, whereby the consumer is assumed to be able to rank *relevant*, *feasible* and *known* options rather than all possible options.

Another problem arises when the utility derivable from the consumption of a particular good or service is unknown or uncertain. Liberal and authoritarian ideologies clash as to whether people are the best judges of their own interests in such circumstances. For example, one reason often cited for supporting unpopular innovative cultural products is that they will generate better returns in the long run when people learn how to appreciate them. Such a 'failure' of appreciation on the part of the individual is ruled out by the assumption of comparability.[2] Of course, the current preferences of the arts lobby may not be necessarily more long-sighted than anybody else's. The point is that people do not

---

[1] The convexity assumption is consistent with the highly diversified character of most people's consumption patterns. If the assumption were invalid, a utility-maximising individual would spend all income on a single product. Such behaviour is not generally observed. An exception may be addictive goods which have increasing marginal utility; spending tends to concentrate heavily on the object of addiction.

[2] The debate about subsidies to the arts generates much controversy. See D. Sawers, *Should the Taxpayer Support the Arts?* (London: Institute of Economic Affairs, 1993). John O'Hagan, *The State and the Arts: Key economic policy issues* (London: Edward Elgar, 1998) provides an authoritative overview of these issues.

always have a well-defined preference field. Tastes and preferences change over time and the consequences of many decisions in economic life cannot be predicted. We try to weigh uncertain future benefits against certain present benefits.

The assumption of independent utilities has also been challenged. The opposite proposition has been propounded: that much of the satisfaction we obtain from the consumption of a particular good or service derives precisely from the fact that others are unable to afford it. A large house in a good neighbourhood, or a Rolls-Royce, yields much less utility if everyone has one. Similarly, we give certain gifts because their cost is widely known and will be appreciated by the receiver rather than because of any intrinsic usefulness of the gift. This type of interdependence has important implications for pricing policy. 'Position', 'gift' or 'snob' goods may be positively, rather than negatively, related to price. Yet an upward-sloping demand curve is an exceptional case and valid only within fairly limited price ranges. At a price of £1 million each, even the demand for Rolls-Royces will start to decline!

Keeping in mind these qualifications, the type of behaviour implied by the above 'rationality' assumption is a reasonable approximation of reality. Consumers weigh up alternatives, seek out and choose larger and better 'baskets' whenever possible. More consumption is better than less consumption. There is sufficient independence of utilities to make economic growth and increased consumption a source of higher welfare. Formally, we can imagine each consumer as maximising utility, subject to a budget constraint (income). One interesting result of this exercise shows that this idealised consumer will maximise utility when the *ratio of marginal utility to price is the same for all products consumed*. This confirms the point outlined in Chapter 3 in our discussion of the efficiency of the free market.[3]

---

[3] Suppose the consumer's utility function is $U = U(X, Y)$, where $X$ and $Y$ refer to volumes of each product. (We assume a two-product economy for simplicity.) The consumer is then assumed to maximise utility subject to the budget constraint, where $M$ is the consumer's income and $P_x$, $P_y$ are the prices of $X$ and $Y$, respectively:

$$P_x X + P_y Y = M$$

To maximise $U$ subject to this constraint, we form the Lagrangian function

$$L = U(X, Y) - \lambda(P_x X + P_y Y - M)$$

where $\lambda$ is the Lagrangian multiplier. The first-order conditions for a maximum are

$$\frac{\partial L}{\partial X} = \frac{\partial U}{\partial X} - \lambda P_x = 0$$

$$\frac{\partial L}{\partial Y} = \frac{\partial U}{\partial Y} - \lambda P_y = 0$$

from which it follows that

$$\frac{\partial U}{\partial X} \div P_x = \frac{\partial U}{\partial Y} \div P_y$$

or

$$\frac{\text{marginal utility of } X}{P_x} = \frac{\text{marginal utility of } Y}{P_y}$$

## 4.2 Deriving the market demand curve

The assumptions of economic rationality enable us to conclude that, if the price of a good falls, other things being equal, the consumer will respond by demanding more. At worst, the consumer will not respond by demanding less. Hence, the individual demand curve will be downward-sloping or vertical, as shown in Chapter 3.

The *market demand curve* is derived by the addition of individual demand curves in a process of *lateral summation*, described in Figure 4.1. Suppose there are two individual consumers in the market. We begin by taking a price (OP) and asking how much each individual will demand at that price. At a given price per unit (OP), individual J demands OJ of a given product and individual H demands OH. Market demand at price (P) is therefore equal to (OJ + OH) denoted by point R (see Figure 4.1). This gives a point K on the market demand curve. Other points can be generated by setting new prices and adding J and H's consumption at each price. Thus, if price rises to $OP^1$, market demand falls to OS ($=OJ^1 + OH^1$).

Given that individual demand curves have a negative slope, the market demand curve should also be downward-sloping. This property, however, could be jeopardised by a large shift in income distribution between individuals with different tastes and priorities. Suppose that a society was divided into two groups – book-lovers and food-lovers. Any redistribution of income from book-lovers to food-lovers will have an impact on demand. Hence the demand for books depends not just on price and total income, but on the distribution of income. This potential difficulty must be kept in mind when analysing market demand in the context of changing macroeconomic aggregates.

## 4.3 Elasticities of demand

Elasticity of demand is a shorthand way of characterising the sensitivity of demand to changes in price, the level of income and other determining variables. Three types of elasticity are especially relevant to demand analysis: (1) price elasticity of demand, (2) income elasticity of demand, and (3) cross-price elasticity of demand. We shall discuss each type in turn.

**Figure 4.1 Derivation of the market demand curve**

(a) Individual J

(b) Individual H

(c) Market demand

## ◯ Price elasticity of demand

A fall in price has two opposing consequences for sales revenue. First, sales revenue *increases* because more units are sold to existing customers, and new customers will be tempted to make purchases as a result of the lower price. Secondly, revenue *decreases* in that the price obtained on the original volume of sales has fallen. The balance between these two forces determines whether the reduction in price leads to an overall increase or decrease in total sales revenue. For example, suppose the figures are as follows:

| Unit price | Quantity sold | Total revenue |
|------------|---------------|---------------|
| $5 | 4 | $20 |
| $4 | 6 | $24 |

The reduction in price from $5 to $4 involves an *increase* in revenue of $8 arising from the sale of two extra units at a price of $4 each, and a *loss* of $4 revenue because of the price decline of $1 on the original four units sold. The net revenue effect is ($4 × 2) – ($1 × 4) = $4.

In this example, the reduction in price yields a net revenue gain. In other circumstances, customers will not respond equally strongly to the fall in price and net sales revenue may fall. Depending on the degree of sensitivity of quantity demanded to price, we know that (1) cutting prices can sometimes be a mistake, (2) on occasion it may be possible to raise price and increase sales revenue at the same time, and (3) there may be a time-lag before the reduction in prices has its full effect on the quantity sold, because customers are slow to realise that price has fallen and to adjust their purchasing habits.

Price elasticity of demand measures the sensitivity of quantity demanded to changes in price and is defined as:

$$E(p) = \frac{\%\text{ change in quantity demanded}}{\%\text{ change in price}}$$

Since price and quantity changes are negatively related, $E(p)$ is negative. However, in discussing critical values of the formula, it is customary to use absolute values. Thus, we say that a good with a price elasticity of 5 has a higher elasticity than a good with elasticity of 2, notwithstanding that $-2 > -5$.

Reverting to the above arithmetical example, as price falls from $5 to $4 $E(p) = [(6 - 4)/4]/[(4 - 5)/5] = 0.5/-0.2 = -2.5$.

Elasticities are defined exactly only for small changes in price around the prevailing level, i.e. to changes *in the neighbourhood* of existing prices. The sensitivity of the elasticity estimate to the base can be illustrated by considering the effect of raising price from $4 to $5, instead of reducing it from $5 to $4, as in the above example. Elasticity then becomes:

$$E(p) = [(4 - 6)/6]/[(5 - 4)/4] = -0.33/0.25 = -1.32$$

Also, price elasticities can change as one moves up or down the demand schedule. In the case of the linear demand curve of Figure 4.2 and Table 4.1, the slope is constant. Every one unit rise in price leads to a loss of one unit of quantity sold. But a rise in price from 1 to 2 involves a decrease in volume sold of only 10 per cent (from 10 units to 9 units), while a one unit rise in price, from 6 to 7, results

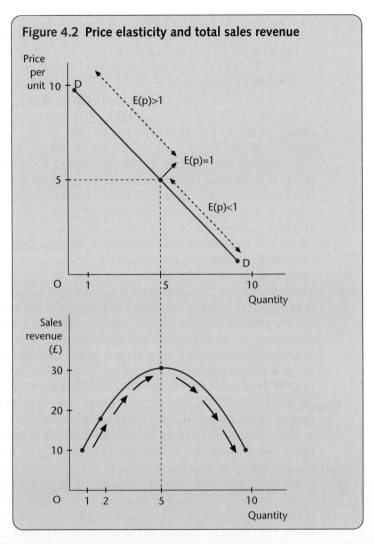

Figure 4.2  Price elasticity and total sales revenue

## Table 4.1  Price elasticity and total revenue

| Price | Quantity sold | Sales revenue | Marginal revenue | Price elasticity of demand* |
|-------|---------------|---------------|------------------|-----------------------------|
| 10 | 1 | 10 | 10 | |
| 9 | 2 | 18 | 8 | |
| 8 | 3 | 24 | 6 | >1 |
| 7 | 4 | 28 | 4 | |
| 6 | 5 | 30 | 2 | |
| 5 | 6 | 30 | 0 | =1 |
| 4 | 7 | 28 | −2 | |
| 3 | 8 | 24 | −4 | <1 |
| 2 | 9 | 18 | −6 | |
| 1 | 10 | 10 | −8 | |

* Elasticities are defined in absolute values; negative sign is ignored.

in a 20 per cent cutback in sales volume. Hence, as price increases, we see that the value of the price elasticity rises. Although it is common practice to list different products according to '*the*' value of their price elasticities (as if they were unique), this is a convenient approximation and caution should be exercised when using such elasticity estimates.[4]

A crucial cut-off point in price elasticity analysis is a value of unity. If the value of the price elasticity of demand for a good exceeds unity (>1) in absolute terms, the demand for that good is said to be price-elastic. This means that a given percentage decline in price will elicit a larger percentage increase in sales, and total sales revenue will increase. If the price elasticity is less than unity (<1), a given percentage decline (rise) in price will stimulate a less than proportionate rise (decline) in quantity demanded, the demand for the good is said to be price-inelastic, and sales revenue will diminish (rise) as price declines (increases). If the absolute value of price elasticity is equal to unity (=1), prices and quantities demanded move in inverse proportion; sales revenue for small changes around the prevailing price remains constant.

Price elasticity of demand can be further explained with a simple arithmetical example (Table 4.1). Suppose we take a range of prices from £10 per unit to £1 per unit and, at each price, estimate how many units would be demanded. *Total sales revenue* at each price is price times quantity. *Marginal revenue* is defined as the additional, or incremental, revenue obtained from the sale of the last unit. Referring to Table 4.1, we see that at price £10 only one unit is sold. Total sales revenue is £10. If price is reduced to £9, two units are sold. The marginal revenue obtained by reducing price from £10 to £9 is (£18 – £10), or £8. If we cut price to £8, three units are sold and sales revenue increases from £18 to £24. Marginal revenue from selling the third unit is (£24 – £18), or £6, and so on.

This information can be translated into price elasticities by noting that for prices above £6 per unit, the percentage change in quantity demanded exceeds the percentage in price. For example, a 10 per cent reduction in price, from £10 to £9, leads to a 100 per cent increase in quantity demanded (from one to two units). Marginal revenue is positive. The elasticity is 10. By contrast, at the bottom of the table, a 50 per cent fall in price from £2 to £1 results in only an 11 per cent increase in quantity demanded. Marginal revenue is negative and the elasticity is 0.2. Elasticity is equal to unity at a price of £5. At this price, quantity demanded is six units. The marginal revenue from the sale of the sixth unit is zero. Sales revenue is maximised at this price.

There are four main determinants of a product's price elasticity. The first is the range of available substitutes for a good – the more close substitutes there are for the product, the greater is the price elasticity of demand. If the price of a product increases, buyers will switch to these substitutes. If its price decreases, buyers will switch to it from the substitutes. For example, if the price of a software program rises, buyers can easily turn to alternative software packages. At the other extreme, the demand for life-saving drugs such as insulin and beta interferon is likely to be highly price-inelastic, since there are few alternative treatments.

Second, the narrower the definition of the product, the higher is the price elasticity. Thus, the demand for Irish whiskey is more price-elastic than the total

---

[4] By translating value into logs, demand curves of constant elasticity can be constructed. Elasticity estimates are often derived from such data transformations.

market demand for whisky. In turn, the demand for whisky is more price-elastic than the demand for spirits as a whole.

Third, the share of spending on the good in the consumer's budget affects elasticity. The larger the share of one's budget spent on a good, the greater the elasticity of demand for it. A 10 per cent increase in the price of pepper or salt will have little effect on consumers' behaviour, given the small fraction of income spent on these products. By contrast, a 10 per cent increase in the price of clothing or automobiles will impact more severely on the average consumer's budget. Consequently, demand for such products may be expected to be more price-elastic.

Fourth, elasticities are generally higher in the long run than in the short run. People need time to adjust to a new price, to find acceptable substitutes and to alter spending patterns.

Price elasticities have several important practical uses:

● *Governments* have a keen interest in price elasticities. They help to determine both the products on which to levy taxes and the rate of tax to impose. Clearly, products with low price elasticity of demand, such as tobacco, alcoholic drinks and energy, are the ones to tax. Imposition of a tax on such products has a small effect on quantity and hence proves a lucrative source of tax revenue. Luxury goods are attractive to tax authorities for the same reason. Knowledge of demand theory and empirical estimates of the shape of the demand curve also help to determine the rate of tax to levy. As prices rise as a result of indirect taxes, price elasticity tends to increase. After a point, a rise in tax could lead to a fall in total tax revenue. This is particularly likely where taxes can be evaded by smuggling.
● *Business organisations and industry associations* use elasticities to estimate the effects of changes in price and taxes on their members' sales revenues. Also, in advocating lower corporate tax rates, recourse might be had to estimates of the elasticity of investment in response to such tax changes.
● *Central banks* use elasticities to estimate the effects of changes in exchange rates on imports and exports, and more broadly in assessing the effects of movements in an economy's cost competitiveness on GDP and employment.
● *Energy pricing policy* would be difficult to formulate in a coherent way without good information on the relevant price elasticities of different products.
● *Trade economists* use elasticities to estimate the effect of trade liberalisation on imports, exports and domestic production. Price elasticities are also intensively used in evaluating agricultural policy options.

Thus, there is practical value in understanding the interactions between tax rates, the consumer price, the producer price, sales revenues, and profits. As we saw in Chapter 3, an indirect tax can be represented as an inward shift in the supply curve. The *incidence of the tax* is shared between producers and consumers, and depends on the slope and position of both the demand and the supply curves. In general, the more inelastic the demand for the product, the larger the proportion of the tax shifted forward to consumers, and the smaller the decline in equilib-rium quantity. For those reasons, it pays industries affected by indirect taxes to keep close watch on such matters.

## Income elasticity of demand

The income elasticity of demand is defined as:

$$E(y) = \frac{\% \text{ change in quantity demanded}}{\% \text{ change in disposable income}}$$

This measure indicates the responsiveness of demand for a particular product to changes in income. Interpretation of the coefficient is straightforward: if $E(y) > 1$, the percentage demand for the product grows faster than the percentage change in disposable income and the product is defined as a *luxury good*. If $E(y)$ lies between 0 and 1, demand for the product grows, but at a less than proportionate rate than income. A product with such an income elasticity is called a *necessity*. Demand for some goods actually declines as income rises ($E(y) < 0$). These are called *inferior goods*. Examples include potatoes, dairy products, black-and-white television sets and table wine. Beef consumption in the US peaked at 96 lbs per person in 1976. Today, despite much higher incomes, it has fallen to 86 lbs. Knowledge of how demand responds to changes in income is a vital ingredient in long-term planning. But, as in the case of price elasticity, the larger the company's share in the overall market, the more useful the information will be. If a company has only 1/1000th share of the total market for a particular product, it is likely to concentrate more on expanding its market share than in expanding the total market. Estimating the expansion or contraction in the total market response to price would be an academic exercise for such a firm. By contrast, a trade association, representing the entire industry, would be extremely interested in the overall income elasticity.[5]

## Cross-price elasticity of demand

The cross-price elasticity of demand measures the relationship between the quantity of a product demanded and the price of related products. The related products can be *substitutes* or *complements*.

$$E(x,y) = \frac{\% \text{ change in quantity demanded of } x}{\% \text{ change in price of } y}$$

A good $x$ is a substitute for $y$ if an increase (decrease) in the price of $y$ causes an increase (decrease) in the demand for $x$. A good $x$ is a complement for $y$ if an increase (decrease) in the price of $y$ causes a decrease (increase) in the demand for $x$. The relationship should be reciprocal for the effects of changes in the price of $x$ on the quantity demanded of $y$.

An example of substitutes is two competing personal computers such as Gateway and Dell. A rise in the price of one leads consumers to buy more of the

---

[5] Sometimes income and price effects interact in a curious manner. A famous example is that of the Giffen good, where a fall in price could, in theory, lead to a decline in demand. If the product absorbed a large proportion of an individual's income, a major fall in price could have a significant impact on income. Now suppose that the good is 'inferior', so that the rise in income caused by the price decline would lead to a fall in demand. For sufficiently large income effects and price changes, it is conceivable that a fall in price could lead to a fall in quantity demanded. In other words, the demand curve could be upward-sloping. Although of great theoretical interest, the Giffen good case is virtually irrelevant from a practical point of view.

## Box 4.1    The cellophane case

The use of cross-price elasticities of demand for the purpose of market delineation received the endorsement of the United States Supreme Court in a landmark judgment, *U.S.* v *E.I. Du Pont de Nemours and Company* (1956).

At that time, Du Pont produced 75 per cent of total sales of cellophane in the US and received royalties from the remaining 25 per cent, which were produced under licence. Prices of cellophane were between two and seven times higher than those of substitute products. Du Pont was accused of using monopoly power to maintain this price differential. It defended itself against the anti-trust suit on the grounds that the market in which it was competing was not that for cellophane itself but for all feasible wrapping (e.g. aluminium foil, wax wrappings, and so on). In that broader market, Du Pont held only an 18 per cent market share. Clearly, whether Du Pont had monopoly power would depend on how the relevant market was defined.

Goods belonging to the same market have high substitutability. A key measure of the degree of substitutability is the cross-price elasticity of demand. In this case it was decided that the cross-elasticity between the price for cellophane and other wrappings was sufficiently high to justify the broader definition of the market, and this allowed Du Pont to win the case. The judgment proved to be controversial: there was reference to the 'Cellophane fallacy'. The decision as to when a particular cross-elasticity becomes 'large' must, of necessity, be arbitrary. The US Supreme Court has adopted a 'reasonable interchangeability' criterion for defining the extent of a market, measured by reference to cross-elasticities.

The issue of defining the relevant market is crucial to competition law, mergers control legislation and business strategy. It regularly features in competition cases. An example is the protracted legal dispute between the Anglo-Dutch conglomerate, Unilever, and the US private corporation, Mars. Legal proceedings began in 1990. Mars complained that Unilever had created barriers to entry to the impulse-purchase ice-cream market. The legal battles were fought in two jurisdictions of the European Union: Germany and Ireland. Unilever had a dominant share of the impulse-purchase ice-cream market in both these countries, which Mars was anxious to break into. In the Irish case, Unilever (through its subsidiary HB) pleaded that the relevant market was not the total sales of impulse ice-cream, but rather sales of all convenience products sold through small stores. This meant that soft drinks, candy and other confectionery belonged to the same market as ice-cream. Unilever's evidence was based on qualitative and opinion-based estimates. Mars argued that the narrower definition of the market was the correct one to use and adduced econometric estimates of cross-elasticities in support of its case. In this case, the trial judge took the view that, in contrast with the Du Pont case, the narrower definition should prevail: the relevant market was defined as the impulse sales of wrapped ice-cream products. It is not clear to what extent this decision was based on the economic evidence. According to McDowell, European case law has not been based to any significant extent on the evaluation of statistical and econometric estimates in defining the relevant market.

*Source*: William F. Shank and Noel Roy, 'Market direction in the analysis of United States groundfish demand', *The Antitrust Bulletin* (Spring 1991); Moore McDowell, 'An ice-cream war: bundling, tying and foreclosure', *European Journal of Law and Economics*, 3 (1996).

other. An example of complements is printers and personal computers. A rise in the price of computers leads to a fall in demand for printers. Why? Because fewer computers are demanded and each PC user needs access to a printer. Cross-price elasticities of demand provide a useful point of departure for defining the market of a particular good and indicating which products should be included in a given market. This can be important in cases involving competition law, where a firm's share of 'the' market can be relevant evidence (see Box 4.1 for the famous cellophane case).

## 4.4 Estimating the demand function

A firm might want to quantify the relationship between sales volume, product price, price of substitutes and complements, national income, advertising expenditure, etc., for several reasons. For example:

- A tobacco company might want estimates of the effect of an increase in government taxes on sales.
- An electricity company may be planning to build a new power station and would like to know how demand for electricity is expected to develop over the next 10 years.
- A brewery might want an estimate of the effect of income growth and a changing age-structure of the population on the demand for beer.
- An automobile industry association might want an estimate of the future increase in demand for imported automobiles as restrictions on imports are relaxed.
- A computer firm might want to know the consequences of lower price and high national income growth on the demand for microcomputers.

To derive this information, it will be necessary to estimate a demand function for the product concerned.

### ⬤ How to estimate demand functions

There are six steps involved in estimating a demand function and using it for forecasting purposes (Box 4.2). First, the variables likely to influence demand for the product must be identified. Own price, income and price of substitutes are obvious candidates, but there may be other specific factors influencing demand. The next three steps are technical in nature. They concern the form of the demand function, the statistical estimation techniques used (usually regression analysis of some type) and the derivation of statistically reliable estimates of the parameters. Thus, in the equation in Box 4.2, an actual number will be estimated for the value of $a_1$, $a_2$, etc. These parameters will enable quantitative statements to be made (within a defined range of possible error) about how demand for the product will be affected by changes in the independent variables. This information is often presented in the form of elasticity estimates. Step 5 involves careful evaluation of the results, including comparison between the economic consultant's estimates and those of other studies. If the objective of the study is to

---

Box 4.2    **Estimating a demand function**

Think of a demand function of general form:

$$Q_i = a_0 + a_1 Y - a_2 P_i + a_3 P_s - a_4 P_c + a_5 Z + e$$

where:    $Q_i$ = quantity demanded of good i
$Y$  = real income
$P_i$ = price of good i
$P_s$ = price of substitute(s)
$P_c$ = price of complement(s)
$Z$  = other relevant determinants of demand
$e$  = error term representing random factors
$a_1, a_2 \ldots a_5$ can be interpreted as elasticities (assuming logs instead of absolute values are used).

Then follow these steps:

1. Identify independent variables: income, own price, price of substitutes and complements, other influences.
2. Decide on form of function: linear, log linear, translog; lag structure; prior constraints.
3. Determine statistical estimation techniques: ordinary least squares is one of a large number of possible estimation techniques.
4. Derive parameters: often reported as short-term and long-term elasticities.
5. Evaluate results and cross-check with other procedures: surveys, marketing tests, managers' opinions.
6. Set up different scenarios of future Y, P and Z. Use simulations to derive forecasts for Q.

---

examine the sensitivity of demand to a particular variable(s), the exercise might end here. However, if the objective is to derive a demand forecast, the final step – step 6 – is to construct a range of scenarios involving prices, income and other (Z) variables such as advertising and demographic changes, and to estimate the level of demand corresponding to each scenario.

Clearly, liaison is required between management and the consultant in deciding what variables are relevant for the estimates of each good, how such variables should be measured, what statistics are relevant and for which period. Attention should be drawn to any unusual features of the data due to exceptional events such as strikes, adverse weather or changes in compilation methods. The statistical procedure will then generate estimates of the net effect of each variable on quantity demanded. In the case of elasticities, while their derivation is largely technical, evaluation will require dialogue and cross-checking with other procedures such as consumer surveys, marketing tests and the opinions of management. At all times it is important to bear in mind that econometric results are highly tentative and sensitive to the specification of the equation. Normally a range of estimates should be compiled on the basis of different assumptions about the future evolution of income and so on. If the company is the sole seller in the market, the market demand for the product will be the same as the company's demand curve. If, however, as is usually the case, the company is one of a number of suppliers, additional analysis is required. The effects of a change in the company's price will be influenced not by the nature of the market demand curve alone, but also by the reaction of competing firms to any change in the firm's price.

Forecasting demand for a firm's product is a necessary exercise, but is fraught with uncertainty. The statistical analysis provided by economists helps to identify the structure and driving forces of market demand. Knowing these basic determinants of demand, the manager is in a better position to react to a changing future environment. But statistical analysis relies on historical market data. It should be supplemented by qualitative analysis based on customer interviews, market surveys, managers' views, regular monitoring of current sales volumes and trends, and price experiments. As an example of the last, Dolan and Simon (1996) cite the case of a German mobile phone manufacturer who kept price constant in one region but allowed it to vary upwards and downwards in other regions. By studying the regional response rates, this experiment enabled the firm to implement a successful nationwide price strategy.[6]

## Empirical findings

Empirical studies show that price and income elasticities tend to vary considerably between different goods and services. In general, price elasticities for food, fuel, health and housing services are found to be low (<1); while price elasticities of demand for clothing, communications and purchased transport tend to be high (>1). Even at this broad level of generality, there are sharp differences in elasticity values for the same products across countries. Elasticities are also sensitive to the precise specification of the product. The price elasticity of demand for haddock has been estimated at 2.2, much higher than the price elasticity of fish and higher still than the elasticity of food (estimated at zero for the UK and 0.87 for the US).[7] Services have been found to have a low price elasticity in general (0.32), but individual items have much higher elasticities, such as recreation (0.97). Within recreation, the price elasticity of demand for movies has been estimated at 3.7 (Table 4.2).[8]

Income elasticities tend to be higher than unity for books, health services, communications, consumer durables and recreation, while significantly below unity (but positive) for food (0.17 in the UK, 0.95 in the US). A selection of estimates for service industries is provided in Table 4.2.

A detailed study of car ownership and use in Britain provides further insights into the usefulness of elasticity estimates.[9] A summary of the short-run and long-run demand elasticity values for the income, motoring cost and bus fare variables with respect to ownership and use of automobiles is given in Table 4.3. The dependent variables are per capita car ownership and per capita car use. Annual

---

[6] R.J. Dolan and H. Simon, *Power Pricing: How managing price transforms the bottom line* (New York: Free Press, 1996).

[7] A. Deaton and J. Muelbauer, *Economics and Consumer Behaviour* (Cambridge: Cambridge University Press, 1980).

[8] Edwin Mansfield, *Applied Microeconomics* (New York and London: W.W. Norton, 1994), p. 4.

[9] Peter Romilly *et al.*, 'Car ownership and use in Britain: a comparison of the empirical results of alternative cointegration estimation methods and forecasts', *Applied Economics*, 33(14) (2001).

### Table 4.2 Price and income elasticities for the service sector

|  | Price | Income |
|---|---|---|
| Housing | −0.73 | 1.186 |
| Health | −0.82 | 1.582 |
| Purchased transport | −1.11 | 0.955 |
| Communications | −1.63 | 1.315 |
| Recreation | −0.97 | 1.410 |
| Education | −0.55 | 0.959 |
| Government | −1.36 | 1.071 |
| Total | −0.32 | 0.979 |

Source: R.E. Falvey and N. Gemmell, 'Are services income-elastic? Some new evidence', *Review of Income and Wealth*, September 1996.

### Table 4.3 Short-run and long-run elasticities for car ownership and use in Britain

|  | Short run | Long run |  | Short run | Long run |
|---|---|---|---|---|---|
| **Car ownership:** |  |  | **Car use:** |  |  |
| Income | 0.39 | 1.84 | Income | 0.67 | 2.38 |
| Motoring costs | −0.25 | −1.76 | Motoring costs | −0.52 | −1.94 |
| Bus fares | 0.14 | 1.70 | Bus fares | 0.23 | 2.33 |

Source: Peter Romilly et al, 'Car ownership and use in Britain: a comparison of the empirical results of alternative cointegration estimation methods and forecasts', *Applied Economics*, 33 (14) (2001).

observations were taken for the period 1953–96. To explain movements in car ownership and car use, a number of determinants (independent variables) were tested including:

- Per capita real disposable income
- Real motoring costs
- Real bus fares
- Real interest rate
- Unemployment rate.

Five alternative estimation methods were used to estimate these relationships.

Income elasticities are positive – the higher the income, the more cars are owned and used. As economic theory would suggest, the long-run income elasticities are greater in absolute value than their short-run counterparts. Cars emerge as a luxury good in the long run, a finding that is consistent with simple observation of the increasing congestion on British roads as people become more prosperous. Car use income elasticities are greater in absolute values than the corresponding car ownership elasticities – adjusting car use is easier than adjusting car ownership. Motoring costs can be interpreted as a proxy for the 'own' price of car ownership and use, and hence increases in costs have an expected negative effect on demand.

Bus journeys are substitutes and an increase in bus fares has a positive effect on demand for car ownership and use. The size of this effect is surprisingly large, but surprises are not uncommon in empirical studies of this nature.

Econometric estimation rarely 'lets the statistics speak for themselves'. Quirky and idiosyncratic results are not unusual and the researcher who is frank about them deserves credit rather than censure. There is a danger of trying too hard to find estimates which the researchers will consider 'plausible' and accord with 'intuition' based on economic theory.

Finally, some further warnings about the reliability of elasticities should be noted. Most elasticities are estimated on the basis of historical experience. They may prove to be unstable, since the past is not always the best guide to the future. Also, elasticities are defined in relation to a particular market but, as we have seen, the relevant market segment has to be found by careful analysis. The manager of a football stadium, for example, may find that different groups have quite different price elasticities, depending on how stadium seats are organised and segregated. Similarly, a theatre or a hotel will explore opportunities for segmenting the market (see Box 4.3). From a revenue-maximisation point of view, the more

---

**Box 4.3**  **Which market, which elasticity?**

When markets are segmentable, the definition of the market to which the elasticity applies becomes rather complicated. The relevant elasticity in the use of the football stadium is not tickets as such, but each particular *type* of ticket.

The complexity can be illustrated by an example, drawn from the hotel industry.

Most capital cities offer the traveller various types of accommodation. The traveller can either stay in a hostel or make use of the wide range of one- to five-star hotels.

The four- and five-star categories are typically represented by a small number of hotels all belonging to well-known domestic or international chains, usually situated in or near the city centre. The demand for accommodation in four- and five-star hotels comes from various types of buyers, from the 'classic' tourist who books a room directly at the hotel to the business executive whose secretary organises the trip and the wholesaler who asks for big discounts. The choice of each buyer for one particular hotel of this category is not only a question of personal preference, but also of the buyer's budget. Buyers will try to maximise their utility, and hoteliers their profits. The following table roughly outlines the main segments of the market for four- and five-star city hotels and their prices in London:

| Segment | Average price of room per night |
|---|---|
| Individuals | £285 |
| Corporate clients | £250 |
| Packages | £210 |
| Wholesaler/travel trade | £170 |
| Government | £150 |
| Airlines | £100 |

Although a hypothetical case, the range of price variation is similar to the range found in many capital cities.

To attract each market segment efficiently, the hotel must differentiate its rates according to the type of consumer. It is not unusual for a hotel to quote around 60 different prices for the same room, depending on the client, the number of room nights and the time of the year. The individual visitor, for example, may be willing to pay the highest rate for luxury accommodation, but the demand of this segment is not large enough to fill a hotel. Only about 5–8 per cent of the yearly occupation can be secured from this source. In contrast, an airline which contracts to purchase 15 room nights daily and stay with the chain on a worldwide or national basis throughout the year will demand, and obtain, a much lower price. This leads to differences in rates of up to 200 per cent for the same room. The most important customers for the four- and five-star hotels are corporate clients. They promise the largest volumes at a relatively high average rate. Companies sometimes book high-class hotels in order to give their employees an incentive and for prestige reasons. Normally hotels offer one-year contracts with fixed rates to this segment, in order to bind the company to the hotel. The graph shows a market demand curve that might characterise this market in simple terms.

The demand curve is non-linear. Since only a few customers are willing to pay the highest rates, a rise in price results in a relatively small loss of room nights sold to this segment of the market. At the lowest end of the market, demand is more price-sensitive. Customers who normally stayed in three-star hotels are more willing to switch hotel grade. As can be implied from the graph, the demand for rooms can be very price-elastic and differs from segment to segment.

The hotel has to consider how many rooms it will offer to each segment without losing customers and impairing its image as a first-class hotel. A business executive, for example, would be disturbed by a busload of tourists causing congestion at the reception desk. The individual tourist would be upset on discerning that most of the other guests are paying less. With low-budget tours organised by a tour operator, the hotel is fully booked, but other bookings are jeopardised. These situations can lead to long-term problems in the high-price segment of the market. The development of a strategic business mix requires knowledge of the market, experience, and risk awareness. Elasticities are only one of a number of ingredients which go into determining the price structure of the hotel. However, they are an important element in the equation. The point of the exercise is to increase margins (maximise profits) by selling as many bookings as possible to the high-price segments such as corporate clients and individual tourists. Bookings from airlines and the lower-price segments are taken only in order to maintain good business relationships or to promote one's 'image'.

degrees of segregation the better. Another important point is that markets are dynamic entities. Demand for products can be cyclical, leading to systematic changes in elasticity values over time. Sometimes, though rarely, the advent of a new product can lead to an increase in demand for a product which is consumed jointly with it, such as happened to the cassette market following the success of the Sony Walkman. Elasticities change in value over time. Markets are evolutionary, not static. Finally, businesses that are interested in elasticities of a much narrower segment of the market than is amenable to standard econometric analysis will have to resort to more informal estimation methods.

## 4.5 Price elasticities and the pricing decision

Elasticities are of most interest to larger firms and to trade and industry organisations. Such firms are, by definition, important players in the market and their sales constitute a significant portion of total demand.

If the firm is one of many and each firm accounts for a minute part of the market, each firm's demand curve will be very flat and its price elasticity of demand will be very high. In such circumstances, there is a 'going price' in the market. If a firm charges above this price, customers will vanish. If it reduces the price below the going rate, it is inundated with customers. Such a firm is unlikely to be interested in having its demand curve estimated. The product's income elasticity of demand is also of little concern to the firm since its share of the total market is so small.

Firms are always trying to escape the bind of perfect competition, to make their demand curves inelastic to some degree, to enhance their market range so that they can raise their prices above the going rate. This is what finding a *market niche* means. Once the niche has been found, price elasticities become highly relevant. Firms with well-established market niches must constantly review possibilities of market segmentation in order to exploit any opportunities for revenue increases. Although firms may not express it that way, they are, in effect, seeking to separate high and low price elasticity segments of the market. This is the basis of the distinction between business and economy-class air travel, between 'reserved stand' seats and terraces in a football match, between the dress circle and the stalls in theatres.

Take, for example, the case of the owner of a football stadium who is organising a special charity match. The objective is to maximise gate receipts for the good cause. The question is what price, or profile of prices, to charge in order to achieve this objective. The additional costs of opening the stadium and operating it for the match are small in relation to the expected revenue. For simplicity, let us assume that they are zero. The problem then becomes one of maximising sales revenue.

Suppose that the market demand curve is estimated as DD in Figure 4.3. What price will maximise revenue? To answer this question, we need to construct the *marginal revenue curve*. Marginal revenue is the net change in total sales revenue resulting from the sale of an extra unit of a good. It equals the price obtained from sale of the marginal unit *less* revenue lost as a result of having to reduce the price

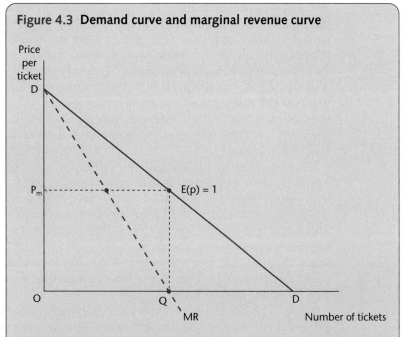

**Figure 4.3 Demand curve and marginal revenue curve**

The marginal revenue curve (MR) measures the change in total revenue corresponding to a marginal change in quantity of sales. More quantity can be sold only by lowering price. To the right of Q, MR > 0 implies that such a strategy increases sales revenue. After sales volume, it leads to lower sales revenue.

on existing sales. Hence the marginal revenue curve is below the demand curve in Figure 4.3; that is, the marginal revenue received by the producer for each extra ticket sold is less than the price charged for that ticket.

Sales revenue will be maximised when marginal revenue equals zero. In the case of a linear demand curve, such as Figure 4.3, this happens when OQ tickets are sold. At that point, marginal revenue has fallen to zero and elasticity of market demand is equal to unity.[10] If price were lowered any further, more tickets would indeed be sold, but total sales revenue would fall.

That might seem to be the end of the story. However, suppose the market could be segmented further. Instead of charging a uniform price, different prices could be charged to different groups of spectators. Essentially, we offer slightly superior seats in the stadium at a much higher price to one segment of the market which is less price-sensitive than the other segments. When the markets are segmented,

---

[10] This can be explained also by simple calculus. Sales revenue ($R$) is, by definition, price ($p$) times quantity ($q$): $R = p.q$. To find the revenue-maximising price, differentiate with respect to $p$:

$$dR/dp = q + (dq/dp)p = 0$$
$$1 + (dq/dp)p/q = 0$$
$$(dq/dp)p/q = -1$$
$$(dq/q)/(dp/p) = -1$$

But this last expression is the definition of the price elasticity. So the price which maximises revenue is reached when the price elasticity equals (minus) unity.

the definition of the market to which the elasticity applies becomes rather complicated. The relevant elasticity in the case of the football stadium is not tickets as such, but rather each particular type of ticket. Segmentation is enforced easily by checking tickets against seats and ensuring that the lower-price ticket holders cannot occupy the high-price seating. The lower the price elasticity of demand of a group, the higher the price it will be profitable to charge. Hence the effort to segment the market, and to reinforce the loyalty of each segment by relatively inexpensive ploys, such as frequent-flyer miles allowance to business class airline travellers, greeting passengers by name, provision of free in-flight programmes and roomier seats.

In attempting to understand the effects of price changes on volume sold, however, customer reactions are not the only factor for a firm to consider. Competitor reactions also need to be taken into account. If competitors feel threatened as a result of the price cut, they may follow with cuts of their own. This could lead to a price war. Competitor reactions are also relevant in estimating the consequences to the firm of raising its price. If they keep their price constant, the firm may lose customers. If they do follow, the net effect on demand may be very small – at least in the short run. In the longer run, the price increase may stimulate new entrants.

These considerations underline the inevitable uncertainty surrounding the price–volume relationship at firm level. The demand curve facing the firm is unknown, apart from one point: the present sales volume and price. It is unlikely to have the nice smooth features of the textbook market demand curve. Also, it will be likely to change over time and to be sensitive to the stage of the business cycle. To add to the complexity, it can change over the course of the product cycle of the good itself.

## 4.6 Conclusions

Demand analysis can make an important contribution to a firm's understanding of its market. It helps to identify the key variables that can influence demand for a product and provides an empirical quantification of their influence. But it is only one of a number of techniques that managers use in formulating sales and pricing strategy. It needs to be combined with other methods of assessing the market. Statistical analysis is designed to complement, not act as a substitute for, liaison with those close to the market.

Elasticities of demand are an essential element in the toolkit of an economic analyst. They are a shorthand way of summarising the degree of sensitivity of sales volume or quantity demanded to changes in designated variables such as price, income, or prices of related goods.

Price elasticities quantify the association between prices, sales volume and sales revenue. They are important to business whenever a firm has some degree of market power and can exercise discretion over price. Companies producing or distributing goods and services subject to indirect taxes also have good reason to take an interest in elasticity analysis. The incidence of the tax as between producer profits, sales volumes and the consumer is to a substantial extent determined by the product's price elasticity of demand. By contrast, in a competitive market there is a 'going' market price from which no single producer can stray. The price elasticity of demand is, by definition, infinite when viewed from the perspective of an individual firm.

Income elasticities are important in developing scenarios for growth of sales volume as consumer income increases. They summarise the effects of income growth on sales. Again, they are relevant mostly to larger firms or to industry-level analysis. They are used extensively by business and governments for forecasting. Cross-price elasticity of demand has been employed in anti-trust (fair competition) cases and in investigations of the sensitivity of the demand for one good to the price of others. The elasticity concept can be used to measure the effects of other variables on demand as well as price and income.

We have emphasised the need for caution in using elasticity estimates. Great care must be taken to define the market one wants to have investigated and to allow for changing market structures and elasticity values over time. Elasticity analysis is only a subset of a fully-fledged analysis of demand.

The economic analysis of demand is sometimes criticised for focusing too much on price and not enough on quality. It seems to suggest that price, and price only, keeps demand and supply in line with one another and that price competition between firms is the only kind of competition that matters. There is some validity in this criticism. In economics, 'price' is used for purposes of simplicity as a proxy for non-price variables as well as price. These non-price factors include product quality, after-sales service, prompt delivery and suchlike. In practice, we know that getting the quality decision right may be as important, and often is more important, for sales and profits as getting the pricing decision right.

A business student will also be struck by the way economic analysis of demand tends to take the demand curve as given. By contrast, strategic management and marketing theory is all about finding out how to change the demand curve. The inventor of Coca-Cola, John Pemberton, confided to his nephew in 1887 that, if only he had the proper capital, he could make a fortune out of Coca-Cola: 'If I could get $25,000', he wrote, 'I would spend $24,000 on advertising and the remainder on making Coca-Cola'.[11] Advertising and sales promotion are powerful tools in influencing a firm's demand curve. Product innovation is also important. When launching a new product, a firm will have to forecast demand without having historical data to guide its pricing decision.[12] We discuss ways of promoting and protecting market power in Chapter 6. But while advertising and sales promotion are powerful tools in influencing a firm's demand curve, price still matters and the market can be highly price-sensitive.

## Summary

1. Economics assumes that the typical consumer is 'rational'. That is, the consumer is capable of making comparisons between different groups of purchases, has

---

[11] Mark Prendergast, *For God, Country and Coca-Cola: The unauthorised history of the world's most popular soft drink* (London: Weidenfeld & Nicolson, 1993), p. 73. Coca-Cola has learnt the lesson. It spends hundreds of millions of dollars on advertising and public relations annually.

[12] One way of resolving this problem is to break down the new product or service into its component parts or *characteristics* (which pertain to currently produced goods and services) with known price elasticities.

consistent preferences and always prefers more to less, has a diversified pattern of spending, and derives utility from consumption independently of what others consume.

2. The market demand curve is conceptualised as the sum of individual demand curves for the good or service. It shows the relationship between changes in price and change in quantity demanded.

3. Price elasticities of demand are a shorthand method of describing the sensitivity of consumer demand to a change in price. Income elasticities of demand refer to the association between changes in income and quantity demanded. Cross-price elasticities of demand refer to the effect of a change in the price of one good on the amount purchased of another good. Each of these elasticities provides useful information to business.

4. Firms, industry associations and governments go to considerable trouble to estimate demand functions. The estimates so obtained yield insights into the market profile of the good which can be useful in production, marketing and pricing decisions. They are frequently used as a basis for forecasting exercises. Statistical estimation techniques have become immensely sophisticated, but unfortunately are highly prone to error. They need to be supplemented by on-the-ground information and managers' judgement.

5. Market segmentation is an important element of pricing and marketing strategy. If different groups of consumers have different price sensitivities, it pays to identify and separate them and to charge them different prices. Hotels, theatres, football stadiums and airlines utilise such policies in their pricing. For instance, it is not unusual for a hotel to quote as many as 60 different prices for the same room, depending on the type of client, the time of the year and the number of room nights.

## Questions for discussion

1. Define the concepts: (a) price elasticity of demand; (b) cross-elasticity of demand; and (c) income elasticity of demand. How are these elasticities estimated? Explain why it might be important for a firm to know their values.

2. In what respects would you expect determinants of the demand for computers to differ from the determinants of the demand for milk?

3. A study of electricity consumption shows that the income elasticity of demand is 0.3 in the short run and 0.6 in the long run, and that the price elasticity is −0.1 in the short run and −0.3 in the long run. Why, in your view, are long-run elasticities usually higher than short-run elasticities?

4. Regarding the cellophane case outlined in Box 4.1, Du Pont claimed that cellophane had close substitutes such as aluminium foil, waxed paper and polyethylene, and cited in evidence the high cross-elasticity of demand for cellophane. Against Du Pont, it was argued that a high cross-price elasticity between Du Pont's cellophane and other products would be expected since Du Pont would have an incentive to keep increasing price until some good became a substitute. Which argument do you find more convincing?
   The Supreme Court found in favour of Du Pont.

5. In May 2003, a five-star London hotel quoted a midweek nightly rate of £285. The same hotel was offering an Easter weekend rate of £165 per night. What does this tell you about the hotel's assessment of the price elasticity of demand of week-enders relative to midweek occupants? (See Box 4.3.)

   Is there any rate (price per night) below which hotels would not be prepared to sell rooms?

## Exercises

1. Draw a graph showing the demand curve and the supply curve of personal computers. How would your graph be affected by:

   (a) a rise in the price of software,
   (b) a rise in the price of electric typewriters,
   (c) a fall in the price of desktop printers,
   (d) an expected increase in next year's PC prices,
   (e) a 10 per cent sales tax on computers,
   (f) a fall in income tax?

2. A retailer has purchased 500 software packages, which are non-returnable to the distributor. The retailer's supply curve of these products is therefore vertical. It finds that the equilibrium price is £150. Draw a supply and demand curve diagram showing this equilibrium.

   Suppose there was a fire at the store and 100 packages were destroyed. Show the new equilibrium position on the diagram. If you are told that the price elasticity of demand is 2, by how much will price rise as a result of this fall in supply?

3. Which of the following are likely to have a positive cross-elasticity of demand?

   (a) Fishing rods and fishing permits
   (b) Imported rice and domestically produced rice
   (c) Taxi and bus fares
   (d) Automobiles and tyres
   (e) Beer and wine
   (f) Cameras and films.

4. Suppose a government wanted to reduce petrol consumption by 10 per cent. You are told that the price elasticity is 0.3. You are asked to evaluate two possible ways of achieving the target:

   (a) by means of a tax on petrol, or
   (b) by rationing.

   Which policy would you recommend and why?

5. Suppose for health reasons a tax is placed on tobacco consumption, with the objective of reducing the demand for cigarettes. The cigarette industry objects to this tax and argues that, since the price elasticity of demand is very low, the only effect of the tax will be an increase in government revenue. Use diagrams to analyse this situation. What other measures could the government use to achieve its objectives?

→

6. Imagine that you are responsible for running a bus company and you have access to the following information about the elasticities of demand for bus travel:

   (a) Income elasticity = −0.4
   (b) Own-price elasticity = −1.2
   (c) Cross-price elasticity with respect to rail fares = +2.1.

   How might this information be of use to you in circumstances when your company is running a service which is currently making a loss?

7. You have been hired as an economic consultant by OPEC and given the following statistics showing the world demand for oil:

   | Price (dollars per barrel) | Quantity demanded (millions of barrels per day) |
   |---|---|
   | 10 | 60,000 |
   | 20 | 50,000 |
   | 30 | 40,000 |
   | 40 | 30,000 |
   | 50 | 20,000 |

   Your advice is needed on the following questions:

   (a) If the supply of oil is decreased so that the price rises from $20 to $30 a barrel, will the total revenue from oil sales increase or decrease?
   (b) What will happen to total sales revenue if the supply of oil is decreased further and the price rises to $40 a barrel?
   (c) What is the price that will achieve the highest total sales revenue?
   (d) What quantity of oil will be sold at the price that answers (c) above?
   (e) What are the values of the price elasticity of demand for price changes of $10 a barrel at average prices of $15, $25, $35 and $45 a barrel?
   (f) What is the elasticity of demand at the price that maximises total sales revenue?
   (g) Over what price range is the demand for oil inelastic?

## Further reading

The analysis of consumer behaviour can be extended in many directions, including indifference curve analysis, allocation of consumption over time, choice in the face of risk and uncertainty, and the effects of advertising. These issues are treated in S. Estrin and D. Laidler, *Introduction to Microeconomics* (London: Harvester Wheatsheaf, 1995) and H. Varian, *Microeconomic Analysis*, 3rd edn (London: W.W. Norton, 1992). The price–quantity relationship which economics focuses on is only one of many aspects of the firm's pricing decision. N. Hanna and H.R. Dodge, *Pricing: Policies and Procedures* (London: Macmillan, 1995), offer a marketing specialist's review of these issues and place the price–volume relationship in a broader marketing perspective. R.J. Dolan and H. Simon, *Power Pricing: How managing price transforms the bottom line* (New York: Free Press, 1997) provides a lively practitioners' perspective on this subject.

## Chapter 5

# The firm in a competitive market

## Introduction

In Chapter 4 we examined the determinants of market demand. Now we ask what lies behind the market supply curve. This involves a study of the motivation of firms and their cost structure. We maintain the assumption of market competition, but this will be relaxed in later chapters.

It is easy to see why a demand curve is downward-sloping. The reasons for a supply curve being upward-sloping are less straightforward. In one scenario the upward slope can be explained easily. A rise in price will induce firms to supply more. A rise in price may even be a necessary condition of more output in the short run, since employees may have to be paid overtime and material inputs may have to be purchased on less favourable terms. As output increases, so too does unit cost, and hence the firm's supply curve slopes upwards. By adding together the supply curves of the individual firms we derive the market supply curve, and it too slopes upwards.

Complexities arise if increases in output lead to a fall in unit cost. This happens quite often because of *economies of scale*, and it is especially likely in the long run. As markets expand, the scope for exploiting economies of scale expands. To be able to exploit scale economies and to have vigorous competition at the same time requires even larger markets. Scale economies have implications for the competitiveness of national industries and for the viability of national markets, as well as for the slope of the supply curve.

The textbook model of competition assumes that all firms are profit maximisers, that they all produce the same product and that each firm accounts for a small fraction of the total market. Thus, the individual firm has no market power. This assumption is rather extreme, but approximates the position facing many firms which operate in highly open and competitive markets. Exposure to global competition means that they have to supply at world market price or else lose sales. By assuming zero market power initially, we are able to explore important features of the market system. One such feature, familiar to business strategists, is the tension between the individual firm's efforts to acquire market power (through product differentiation, takeovers and alliances) and the prevalence of market forces tending to undermine that power.

Chapter outline

1. Profit maximisation as the objective of the firm.
2. The implications of profit maximisation for the behaviour of the firm.
3. The cost structure of the firm, economies of scale and scope.
4. The role of transactions cost in explaining firm size and organisational mode.
5. Empirical evidence on cost functions.
6. The derivation of the market supply curve from individual firm supply curves.

## 5.1 Profit maximisation

Firms seek to maximise profits. Like the assumption of utility maximisation, this assumption has to be interpreted as a general tendency, a reasonable hypothesis, rather than a statement that all firms are guided only by this consideration. In the short term, the acquisition or defence of market share may often necessitate taking price and quality decisions which conflict with profitability and may even involve short-term losses. Also, opportunistic behaviour is rarely the best foundation for long-term profits. The firm that avails itself of every opportunity to take maximum advantage of its customers, employees and suppliers will sooner or later ruin its reputation and lose business.

When originally conceived, the idea of profit maximisation applied to a world of owner-managers of small firms. Provided the owner-manager did not have too strong a preference for leisure and the good life, the assumption that he or she would try to maximise profits seemed reasonable. Difficulties arose with the growth of the public limited liability company and the replacement of owners by professional management. Owners (the shareholders) might still safely be presumed to want maximum profits. But managers might want to maximise something different – their salaries, for instance, or their executive power. Since, in a typical limited liability firm, ownership is often fragmented, shareholders are unable to monitor and judge performance as closely as the executives. With the possibility of conflicting objectives between owners and managers, the firm might not always behave in the way one would expect on the basis of the profit-maximisation assumption. In the words of Herbert Simon, a pioneer in the theory of organisational behaviour:

> Most producers are employees, not owners of firms. Viewed from the vantage point of classical [economic] theory, they have no reason to maximise the profits of the firms, except to the extent that they can be controlled by owners. (H. Simon, 'Organisations and markets', *Journal of Economic Perspectives*, Spring 1991)

The divorce in objectives between owners and managers gives rise to a *principal–agent problem* (see Box 5.1). A firm's profits are assumed to be related to managerial effort, but owners are unable to monitor and measure this effort. Hence they must think of ways of motivating executives to maximise profits rather than their own utility.

One start to resolving this problem is to appoint a Board of Directors, elected by and answerable to the shareholders. But this redefines rather than resolves the principal–agent problem since non-executive directors, like any other agent, may

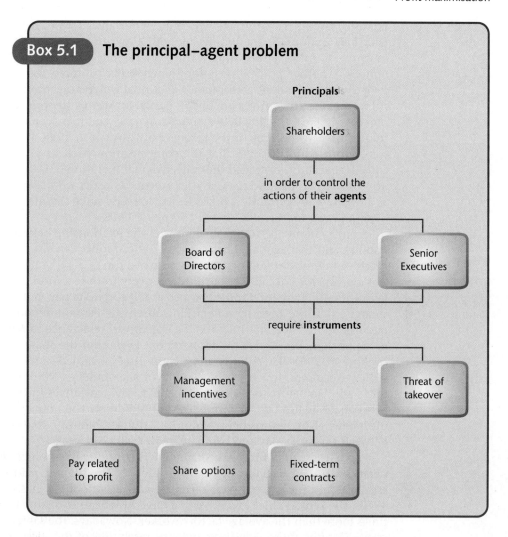

**Box 5.1** **The principal–agent problem**

Principals

Shareholders

in order to control the
actions of their **agents**

Board of
Directors

Senior
Executives

require **instruments**

Management
incentives

Threat of
takeover

Pay related
to profit

Share options

Fixed-term
contracts

have their own agenda (including the desire to 'keep in' with the management). They have limited time to devote to board business and their financial stake in the company may be relatively modest.

There are two further ways of tackling the problem. First, owners (the principal), through the Board of Directors, can devise 'price' incentives which will motivate executives (their agent) to pursue the principal's objectives of profit maximisation. Second, if they are unable to do this, owners can sell their shares to other owners who will find ways of utilising the firm's assets more profitably. The threat of a takeover, and the consequent prospect of a new management team, can be a powerful spur to performance by executives. We consider each of these possible solutions in turn.

## Management incentives

Owners pay executives a base salary, but they also tie remuneration to profits by payment of various forms of profit-related incentives. Examples include profit bonuses, fixed-term contracts which are renewable if a profit target is reached, and share options. Share options are both a reward for past performance and an incentive to future effort, since a rising share price will increase the value of the options. Another possibility is for shareholders to apply the 'stick' of critical review of management performance at annual general meetings.

Profit-related incentives are only a partial answer to the problem of divergent objectives.[1] First, the link between executive pay and managerial effort is difficult to quantify. At the time of the takeover of Chrysler in 1998, Daimler executives were surprised to discover that the compensation package given to one senior Chrysler executive exceeded the collective remuneration of Daimler's entire executive Board ($13m). Did the Chrysler executives really work all that much harder as a result? They certainly worked less effectively, since Daimler was taking them over (*International Herald Tribune*, 14 August 1998).

Second, a more difficult problem is that the relationship between a firm's profitability and managerial effort can be erratic. Profits can rise or fall because of macroeconomic developments or because of a run of good or bad luck. The 1990s was a prosperous decade for business: recovery from recession, low inflation and falling unemployment. Profits boomed as did corporate pay, but it would be hard to argue that the high remuneration caused the economic boom. Proof of the pudding in this instance may well be executives' reluctance to rely too much on profit or share-price-related remuneration. Even after the share price and profits collapse of 2001–03, remuneration committees awarded hefty pay increases to senior executives, much to the chagrin of shareholders. Minimum service contracts and 'golden parachutes' (payments to the executives in the event of their being made redundant or dismissed) also moderate the impact of profit-related incentives. Not surprisingly, empirical studies indicate that the correlation between executive pay and company performance is weak.[2]

Despite these qualifications, shareholders continue to pay high levels of remuneration to their executives. Compensation of the highest paid executives has escalated and the gap between executive and shopfloor pay has widened. In the 1970s, the typical chief executive of a large American company earned about 40 times more than the average factory worker. Nowadays, the same executive earns over 475 times more. Executive pay was rarely out of the news in the UK, with attention focusing on the pay of senior executives of several privatised industries. Executive share option schemes were particularly popular in the US. In 1998 alone, 92 of America's 200 leading chief executives were given options with an average minimum value if exercised of $31m.[3] Of course, high executive remuneration may prove a good bargain for the owner-shareholders if they achieve

---

[1] Kevin Murphy, 'Executive compensation', in O. Ashenfelter and D. Card (eds), *A Handbook of Labour Economics* (Amsterdam: North Holland, 1998).

[2] A survey of 169 companies by the National Institute of Economic and Social Research (NIESR) in the UK concluded that the pay of top executives responded positively to growth in sales, but was only weakly correlated to returns for shareholders. Another finding was that executive directors' pay grew faster in firms which grew by acquisition rather than by organic growth, and in firms which funded their expansion by borrowing rather than by use of shareholder funds. Inclusion of the value of executive share options in the calculations would, by definition, have brought executive remuneration and company performance (defined often in terms of share value) less out of line. But the link between even total executive compensation and company performance remains extremely weak.

[3] 'Share options', *The Economist* (7 August 1999).

---

### Box 5.2   Profit maximisation in action

A history of the Coca-Cola Corporation reports that Roberto Goizueta, newly appointed CEO in 1981, was frustrated by Coke executives' varied reactions to competition in setting their goals: 'some going after increased sales, some market share, and *only a few concerned over return on capital*' (my emphasis). Goizueta believed something had to be done. At the heart of his new strategy lay the profit target: 'a rate substantially in excess of inflation, in order to give our shareholders an above average total return on their investment'. This emphasis on profitability was instrumental in raising earnings per share by 10 per cent per year. The price of Coca-Cola stock shot up from $35 in 1980 to $120 in 1986, an increase well above the stock market average for the period. The value of management share options followed suit, bringing significant benefits to the chief executive and to his team in the process. The moral of this story is that failure to maximise profits will eventually be detected and corrected by market forces.

*Source*: Mark Prendergast, *For God, Country and Coca-Cola* (London: Weidenfeld & Nicolson, 1993), p. 374.

---

even a mild motivation effect. Shareholders may also acquiesce in high pay for their executives because, being dispersed and numerous, they have little economic incentive to monitor management directly. An individual shareholder will bear heavy costs for organising such monitoring, but the benefits will accrue to all other shareholders. Hence each individual shareholder has an incentive to sit tight and hope that another shareholder will take the initiative. This is an instance of a pervasive problem in economic life called *the free-rider problem*.

The need to bind executive pay more closely to profit performance has been a prevailing theme of debate during the past few years. The rash of corporate scandals in the US, in companies such as Enron, WorldCom, Tyco International, Global Crossing and Adelphi Communications to name but a few, exposed the vulnerability of shareholders and employees to malpractice by top executives and accountants. Misstatements of profits through what were euphemistically called 'aggressive' accounting practices and the abuse of executive incentive schemes were exposed. Share option schemes were often set up with blithe disregard of the interests of shareholders, and their cost to the firm was not charged in a transparent way against the profit and loss account. The Sarbanes–Oxley Act of 2002 was enacted in order to redesign the regulation of US publicly listed firms, the composition of their boards and their reporting practices. A new Accounting Oversight Board has been set up to review company audits. Europe has to a large extent avoided American-style excesses. In Britain, the Cadbury Committee (1992) recommended that executive remuneration committees should be composed primarily of non-executive directors, and the Greenbury Report (1995) on corporate governance made further recommendations, one being full disclosure of directors' remuneration as a way of enhancing accountability.

### Threat of takeover

Even if all the above measures fail, the threat of takeover acts as one further discipline on management. If management persistently underutilises the company's resources, the threat of a takeover by another management team will be accentuated, with potentially adverse consequences for incumbent executives. While even the best-run companies can become a takeover target, the probability of this unpleasant outcome can be minimised by earning high profits. This raises the share price and makes the firm too expensive for predators.

The takeover threat is particularly relevant to countries with a highly developed stock market culture, such as the US and the UK. Of course, management has devised many ingenious ways of reducing the potency of this threat. Among the more familiar schemes are *greenmail* (where incumbent management buys off the raider with company money), *white knights* (where the assistance of a friendly outsider is enlisted to ward off hostile bidders) and *poison pills*. Poison pills refer to provisions whereby, in the event of a merger/takeover, shareholders can acquire shares in the surviving firm at a substantial discount from market price. This acts as a disincentive to such takeovers by making them more expensive. Executives are aware that these measures offer no foolproof defence. Replying to a question about a possible takeover of the company, the chief executive of a major materials multinational, CRH (Cement Roadstone Holdings), commented:

> A company is always vulnerable if it performs badly. A good performance is the best protection against acquisition. It means that someone else has to prove to shareholders that they can run your business even better.[4]

Market forces, in the form of both the 'carrot' of incentives and the 'stick' of the takeover threat, impose a discipline on management and penalise the systematic neglect of profit maximisation. However, the threat of takeover, like executive compensation, is not foolproof against abuse. Good performance does not provide immunity against takeover. Often takeovers are motivated by personal egos of chief executives rather than objective pursuit of profit, as the dismal performance of most large mergers demonstrates. At the limit, however, there is the threat of bankruptcy, a real danger for an underperforming firm. Even in the public sector, state-owned commercial enterprises can be given an incentive to act like a profit-maximising firm through the imposition of 'hard budget constraints' linked to a targeted return on capital.

In recent years, the power of institutional investors has risen relative to that of individual investors, giving greater weight to shareholder interests over those of corporate executives. Large pension fund and mutual fund investors are more able to wield power and are better organised than traditional small private shareholders. Investment managers are themselves under pressure to perform well. Investment and pension fund trustees compare the performance of different fund managers and are more prepared to shift their funds from one manager to another than are small private investors. Thus, while the volume of capital available to investment managers has reached unprecedented heights, so too has the competition for managing it. This makes fund managers more demanding in terms of shareholder returns.

---

[4] Cited in J.A. Murray and A. O'Driscoll, *Managing Marketing* (Dublin: Gill & Macmillan, 1999), p. 378. Note, however, that good performance does not guarantee immunity from hostile bids. See T. Franks and B. Mayer, 'Hostile takeovers and the correction of managerial failure', *Journal of Financial Economics*, 40 (1996).

Alternatives to the assumption of profit maximisation have been explored, for example, that executives try to maximise sales, subject only to a minimum level of profit to keep shareholders happy. This assumption is plausible in certain circumstances, but as a generalisation it is hard to argue its superiority over profit maximisation. Unless long-run profits are maximised, the forces of competition threaten not only the jobs of management, but the survival of the firm.

Besides, profit maximisation does not necessarily conflict with the objective of keeping or expanding market share. The firm making the largest sustained profits will be best equipped to survive in the long term. Of course firms will continue to emphasise factors such as product quality, but this preference for product quality might reflect a contrasting management style and time horizon, rather than deviation from the long-run objective of profit maximisation. The contemporary profit-maximising firm may have a sophisticated agenda. A former chief executive of the Bank of Montreal explained that:

> In rating my bank's performance, I assign only 40 per cent weight to the bottom line. Customer satisfaction, employee competence and public image count for 60 per cent for they are the indicators of future profit and future shareholder value.[5]

Thus, most firms remain profit maximisers. Some just place more weight on future profits than others.

## 5.2 Rules for maximising profit

The profit-maximisation assumption is important, because it has strong implications for how firms behave. These implications apply both to the pricing decision and to the output decision. Where competition is intense, the firm has little or no discretion over price. It takes price as given. The key decision becomes how much to produce. The company must also decide what techniques to use in its production: how much labour, what type of machinery, buildings and raw materials. In making these decisions, a profit-maximising firm will be guided by certain rules.

A first rule is that a *technically inefficient (in an engineering sense) production technique should not be used*. If 100 units of output could be produced by using (a) 80 units of labour and 100 units of capital, or (b) 60 units of labour and 90 units of capital, technique (b) will always be chosen by the profit maximiser. This profit maximisation objective dictates that the firm will seek out best practice technologies and avoid waste.

Second, the firm *minimises the cost of producing any given level of output*. It minimises costs by applying the rule: *purchase each input up to the point where the net value of the output produced by that input equals the cost to the firm of purchasing it*. The input might be the services of an employee, a new machine, additional quantities of raw materials or more warehousing space. The marginal cost of the input to the firm is the price paid (assuming price is insensitive to the amount of the input demanded by the individual firm). The value of the extra output produced by each

---

[5] M. Barrett, 'Practical idealism in banking', *Irish Banking Review* (Autumn 1994), p. 77.

input to the firm equals the extra output multiplied by price (in technical jargon, the value of its marginal product).

Suppose this were not the case. Say the value of the marginal product of an employee is £100 per day (net of material costs), while the cost of hiring him or her is £60 per day. At the same time, the marginal product of the new machine is £60, but the cost of running it is £100 per day. Then, assuming no other costs, the firm is making £40 per day profit from the marginal employee and losing £40 per day from the marginal machine. The profit-maximising firm should hire more labour and fewer machines!

The third rule is that the firm must produce up to the point where *marginal revenue (MR) equals marginal cost (MC)*. Recall from Chapter 4 that marginal revenue equals the increase in total revenue derived from the sale of one additional unit. Marginal cost is defined analogously as the increase in total cost incurred by the production of one additional unit. Suppose the marginal revenue from an additional unit of sales is £10 and marginal cost (the extra cost of producing that unit) is only £5. Clearly, it is profitable for the firm to produce that

---

### Box 5.3  Derivation of profit-maximisation rule

The profit-maximisation rule can be derived formally as follows:

By definition
$$\pi = TR - TC$$

where:  $\pi$ = profits
TR = total revenue
TC = total costs.

The first-order condition for profit maximisation is:

$$\frac{\partial \pi}{\partial q} = \frac{\partial TR}{\partial q} - \frac{\partial TC}{\partial q} = 0, \text{ where } q = \text{unit of output} \tag{1}$$

i.e.
$$\frac{\partial TR}{\partial q} = \frac{\partial TC}{\partial q}$$

$$MR = MC$$

This is the rule that *marginal revenue must equal marginal cost*.
The second-order condition for a maximum is:

$$\frac{\partial^2 \pi}{\partial q^2} < 0$$

i.e.
$$\frac{\partial MR}{\partial q} - \frac{\partial MC}{\partial q} < 0$$

$$\frac{\partial MR}{\partial q} < \frac{\partial MC}{\partial q} \tag{2}$$

This means that the MC curve must cut the MR curve from below. From a practical point of view, it is not important. Businesses are highly unlikely to choose minimum profit points!

unit. Suppose that the next unit also earns a marginal revenue of £10 but that its marginal cost rises to £8. It is profitable to produce that unit also. The firm will increase production up to the level where the marginal cost and the marginal revenue are equal. At any lower output, marginal revenue exceeds marginal cost and unexploited opportunities for profit would be ignored. At any higher output, marginal cost exceeds marginal revenue. The firm incurs losses at the margin, and that too is inconsistent with profit maximisation. This rule is derived formally in Box 5.3.

The logic of the MR = MC rule is illustrated in Figure 5.1. An individual firm in a competitive market, by assumption, faces a given market price. Each additional unit it produces can be sold at a constant price OP. Hence the extra revenue earned by an additional unit of production (marginal revenue) equals price. The firm's demand curve can be depicted as a horizontal straight line. In this instance, the demand curve and the marginal revenue curve are the same. Profits are max-imised when MC intersects the firm's MR line, PD, at S. At that point, OQ is pro-duced and sold at price OP. Profit per unit is ST, which is the difference between price QS and average cost per unit (TQ).[6] Total profits are PSTV.

A perfectly competitive industry is one where entry and exit are free. If firms in an industry make profit, this attracts new entrants to the industry. Although no

**Figure 5.1 Cost curves of the firm**

Total sales revenue   OPSQ
Total costs           OVTQ
Total profits         PSTV

---

[6] The relationship between average costs and marginal costs can be explained as follows. Average total costs include fixed costs plus the sum of marginal costs. If the marginal cost is above average cost, average cost must rise; if below, average cost must fall. This point can be illustrated by a simple example. Suppose a person of 7 feet is added to a class with an average height of 5 feet. The average height of the class is raised. Likewise, if a person 4 feet tall joins the class, the average class height falls. For the same reason, if marginal cost is lower than average cost, average cost is falling.

individual firm can affect the market price, collectively their entry does have an impact. Eventually, expansion of supply by the new entrants will cause price to fall and, possibly, also raise costs in the industry as the price of inputs is driven up by the industry's growth. In the long run, equilibrium will occur when profits are reduced to the bare minimum needed to retain firms in the industry. This minimum level is called *normal profits*. *Supernormal profits* are bid away by new entrants to the industry and by output expansion within the industry. The price line, PD, shifts downwards and the AC curve shifts upwards, until eventually AC is at a tangent to PD. At this point, MC = MR and average cost (including a normal rate of return on capital) equals price. Firms make no 'excess' profits. There is no incentive for firms either to enter or to exit the industry. We have reached equilibrium price and quantity for the industry.

This analysis can be related back to the supply and demand analysis of Chapter 3. Starting from initial price/output equilibrium at E, suppose there is an outward shift in the demand curve to $D^1D^1$ (Figure 5.2). Assume that at first supply remains fixed at OQ. Price rises to OP. Large 'supernormal' profits of PAEC are earned by the industry at that price, just as they are by our individual firm in Figure 5.1. These profits attract new entrants to the industry as well as encouraging existing firms to expand. Supply increases along the SS curve. As it does so, downward pressure is brought to bear on price. Eventually equilibrium is reached at $E^1$, where there are no longer supernormal profits.

Hence an important paradox of the market system: *the imperative of profit maximisation drives firms to innovate and to minimise costs in order to obtain supernormal profits. But such profits tend to be eroded sooner or later by the process of competition*

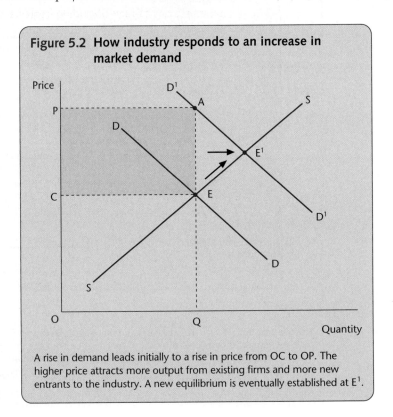

**Figure 5.2 How industry responds to an increase in market demand**

A rise in demand leads initially to a rise in price from OC to OP. The higher price attracts more output from existing firms and more new entrants to the industry. A new equilibrium is eventually established at $E^1$.

*and free market entry*. From the point of view of the firm, this outcome is both unintended and undesirable. From society's perspective, it is the great advantage of competitive markets.

The rules for profit-maximising behaviour are plausible, but they need to be interpreted with care. First, 'profits' in an economic sense are not the same as profits in a company's profit and loss statement (see Box 5.4). Second, empirical measurement of marginal costs and of the marginal product of an input may be subject to a wide margin of error. Third, firms may have insufficient information on demand conditions to determine marginal revenue. This last problem can be particularly acute in circumstances where the reaction of competitors has to be

---

### Box 5.4    What economics means by profit

Profits are defined as the difference between total revenue and total costs. The key to understanding the distinction between economic profits and profits as defined by an accountant lies in the interpretation of costs.

The *accounting definition of profits* is, of course, far from straightforward. A simple pro-forma profit and loss account might look similar to that below, with six possible versions of profit.

**Pro-forma Profit and Loss Account**

|  |  |  |
|---|---|---:|
| | Turnover | 1000 |
| | *less* direct cost of sales (including depreciation) | 900 |
| (1) | **Gross profit** | **100** |
| | *less* overheads (distribution and administration) | 60 |
| (2) | **Operating profit** | **40** |
| | *less* exceptional items[1] | 2 |
| (3) | **Operating profit before interest and taxation** | **38** |
| | *less* interest | 4 |
| (4) | **Operating profit before tax** | **34** |
| | *less* corporation profits taxation | 10 |
| (5) | **Operating profit after tax** | **24** |
| | *less* (net) minority interests[2] | 4 |
| (6) | **Profits attributable to ordinary shareholders** | **20** |
| | *less* extraordinary charges[3] | 3 |
| (7) | **Profits for the financial year** | **17** |
| | Dividends | 10 |
| | Balance to reserves | 7 |

*Gross profits* are defined as the difference between sales revenue and variable costs. *Operating profits* are obtained by deducting overheads (or fixed costs in our terminology).

The existence of operating profit does not *per se* indicate that other firms would be eager to enter the business. The reason is that capital has been invested in the firm, in respect of which investors expect a certain level of return. This expected or 'normal' rate of return would *at minimum* equal the yield on a fixed-interest government bond. Instead of investing in the company, investors could have obtained this (riskless) return by buying government bonds. Given that business is risky, some premium over the

➡

Box 5.4 continued

bond rate would be required to keep investors satisfied. This risk premium will differ from industry to industry. Compared with, say, a government bond yield of 5 per cent, return on capital of between 8 per cent and 15 per cent would be the expected norm in industries. Return on capital employed (ROCE) equals operating profits before interest and tax divided by the value of total assets.

From operating profit before tax, therefore, we should deduct an amount representing a 'normal' return on capital to shareholders before profit, in the economist's sense, is earned. It is the presence or absence of economic or supernormal profits which determines whether firms will enter or exit the industry. *Supernormal profits*, not operating profits in the accounting sense, perform the signalling function of the market system.

The *economic definition of profits* incorporates the idea of *opportunity costs*. It takes into explicit account that capital employed in a firm has alternative uses. There is a cost to society of deploying it in the firm. That cost is determined by considering the 'best' alternative use – defined in terms of the best cash yield ratio – to which it could have been put.

Two aspects of economic profit merit comment. First, the standard economic analysis of the firm focuses exclusively on profits. *Cash flow* does not appear in the calculations. Yet many firms argue that a cash-flow statement showing movements of cash within a company reveals more about the firm's viability than declared profits. In theory, a profitable firm ought to be able to raise cash, given a perfect capital market. In practice, this is not always the case, especially in instances where the firm is part of a group which is cash-negative or where there is a long gap between the timing of initial investment and inflow of cash return. Being wholly dependent on shareholders or financial institutions for cash is not a sustainable long-term position and may be difficult even in the short term. The importance of cash flow tends to be neglected in the economic analysis of the firm.

Another qualification concerns the *role of taxation*. Economic profits are defined before deduction of tax. We assume that all firms face the same tax regime and that different initial positions regarding tax credits and write-offs can be ignored. We also assume that corporation profits tax does not affect the profit-maximising level of output. These initial assumptions can, however, be relaxed to take account of both regional tax incentive schemes – 'signals' devised by national or regional authorities to attract inward investment – and of the complex interplay between corporate profits tax, depreciation and inflation on the cost of capital to the firm.

To conclude, there is no single universally applicable measure of profits in either accountancy or economics. The substantive conceptual difference between the two disciplines' approach is the deduction in the economics definition of normal return to shareholders on operating profits. The resultant (positive or negative) 'supernormal' profits perform the signalling role for enterprises that prices perform for individuals.

*Notes*:
1. Defined as material items of a non-recurrent nature arising out of the ordinary activities of the business.
2. Profits arising from activities in which the firm has a minority shareholding.
3. Defined as highly abnormal, non-recurring items arising from transactions which fall outside the ordinary activities of the company.

estimated as well as the reaction of customers. Intuition and guesswork then have to supplement more systematic information.

Given these practical difficulties in making the MR = MC rule operational, it is not surprising that firms use rules of thumb to determine sales and pricing. *Mark-up pricing* or cost-plus pricing is one such commonly used alternative. However, the size of the mark-up varies considerably by product which indicates that, in deciding on the mark-up, managers may implicitly be using the marginal rules. Another pricing strategy, the Japanese practice of *target pricing*, consists of taking a competitive market price as given and working backwards to determine the target cost for the product. This proactive approach to costs is also compatible with adherence to the marginal rules for profit-maximising behaviour. Finally, some forms of widely observed price behaviour such as *below-cost selling* superficially appear to contradict the profit-maximisation rule. But such is not necessarily the case. The practice of loss leading by large multiples is based on the concept of an extended MR. The loss leader attracts customers to the store and, once there, further purchases are likely. The MR of the loss leader must take account of this indirect effect of the discounted price.

## 5.3 Cost structure of the firm

A firm's costs are divided into *fixed costs* and *variable costs*. Fixed costs consist of pre-committed outgoings, which are payable regardless of the level of output. Variable costs represent outgoings, such as materials, energy and distribution costs, which rise and fall in accordance with the volume of output. Fixed costs can be subdivided into *sunk costs* and *other fixed costs*. Sunk costs refer to past expenditure on fixed assets which have no alternative use and the cost of which can be amortised or recouped only by trading. Examples of sunk costs include the costs of a nuclear power station, large steel plants or the Channel Tunnel. By contrast, the cost of the lease of an office building is a fixed cost, but is not a sunk cost, since the building could be sub-let to another firm. Sunk costs play an important role in determining the firm's output and price strategy. Over time, all costs except sunk costs become variable. In economics jargon, the long run is defined precisely as that period of time over which fixed costs can be converted into variable costs.

The cost structure of a firm is illustrated in Figure 5.3. Costs are measured on the vertical axis and level of the firm's output on the horizontal axis. Fixed costs have to be paid regardless of the level of sales and are depicted by a straight horizontal line. Total variable costs are shown as an upward-sloping line, reflecting the fact that variable costs are a positive function of output. Thus, a rise in output from 500 units to 600 units raises total costs from £10 million to £12 million. The variable costs incurred in adding 100 units of output amount to £2 million.

In calculating the contribution of a new product to profits, variable costs are sometimes assumed to be linearly related to output (i.e. they are assumed to rise by a constant amount per unit of output). The *breakeven chart*, for example, includes information on costs and revenues, and depicts a situation where a

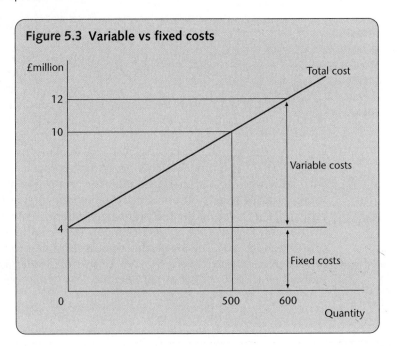

**Figure 5.3 Variable vs fixed costs**

certain minimum level of sales is required for the firm to break even (Figure 5.4). After this point, the firm enters a profit zone, with profits being calculated as a constant contribution per unit. Breakeven charts are used to estimate the effects on profits of variations in sales volumes around the breakeven point.

Studies of cost structures, however, suggest a more complex picture than the linear relationship suggests. The key point is that variable costs per unit of output are not constant as output increases. In the short run, they tend to fall. Then, beyond a certain output level, they begin to rise. A simple starting point is to depict the relationship between unit costs and sales volumes by a U-shaped curve (Figure 5.5). The initial cost decline is attributed to *economies of scale*: the flattening, and eventual rise, of the unit cost curve is explained by the growing weight of *diseconomies of scale*. These concepts, which occupy a central role in our understanding of the size and cost structure of firms, now need to be explained.

## Economies of scale and scope

First, there are *indivisibilities*. Indivisibilities are costs incurred in large non-incremental amounts, such as the cost of constructing a tunnel or a nuclear energy plant. A half-built tunnel is costly to make, but useless. A half-built nuclear reactor is likewise costly, but dangerous. Each project becomes useful when the entire project is completed. Completion may be a large-scale and expensive exercise. The Channel Tunnel between England and France cost more than £10 billion sterling to construct. These *sunk costs* had been incurred, and the accompanying debt remained to be serviced, without a single train or passenger having passed through. As the 'output' of the tunnel increases, the fixed costs are spread over a larger volume of traffic. *Average fixed cost per unit of output* (AFC) falls. Hence *average cost*, i.e. total cost per unit, declines. The more passengers using the tunnel, the lower the cost per unit.

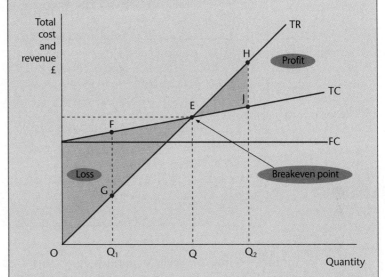

### Figure 5.4  The basic breakeven chart

The breakeven chart is a graphic representation of the relationships between costs, volume and price and shows the effects of short-run variations in output upon a firm's profitability. A typical breakeven chart might look as follows:

Total fixed costs (FC) are constant over a range of output, while total variable costs start at zero when output is zero and increase with output thereafter. Total costs (TC) are the sum of fixed and variable costs. Since selling price is constant, the total revenue (TR) line starts at zero and increases proportionately with output and sales volume.

The firm breaks even (makes neither a profit nor a loss) at output $OQ$. At output less than this, say $OQ_1$, total cost $FQ_1$ exceeds revenues $GQ_1$, resulting in a loss of FG. At outputs greater than the breakeven output, say $OQ_2$, total revenues $HQ_2$ exceed costs $JQ_2$, resulting in a profit of HJ. Profits or losses at other output levels can be similarly determined.

Indivisibilities are encountered in many areas of business. For example, the costs of R&D and product design have to be incurred long before production begins. As the product reaches the market and is sold, these initial fixed costs are spread over a larger volume of output. The cost of developing a new car and bringing it to the market can involve an outlay of more than $1 billion over a period of two or more years before a single car is sold.[7] The average pre-tax cost of developing a successful drug is $150m, which rises to $500m if costs of failures are included. As test procedures become more demanding and as science tackles more complex diseases, these indivisible costs are rising all the time. From the author's point of view, it costs the same to get one copy of a book ready for publication as 1000 copies. To get a new food product onto a UK supermarket shelf can cost as much as £3 million in marketing, advertising and promotion expenditure. The essential feature of these expenditures is their 'indivisibility'.

---

[7]  K.B. Clark and T. Fujimoto, *Product Development Performance: Strategy organisation and management in the world auto industry* (New Haven, CT: Harvard Business School Press, 1991).

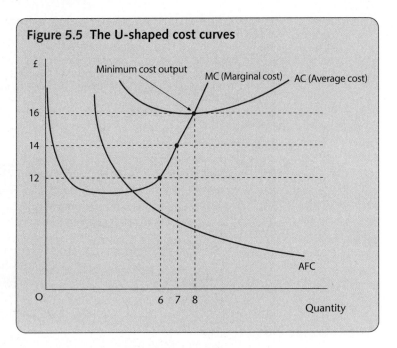

**Figure 5.5 The U-shaped cost curves**

Another source of scale economy is *increased specialisation*. Adam Smith observed that, as a firm's output increased, its cost per unit declined because employees would become more dextrous and skilled and, by focusing intensively on a narrow range of activities, would be able to suggest improved ways of performing their work and even devise better machinery to assist them (see Box 5.5). Skinner's concept of a *focused factory* puts these ideas into modern garb:

> A factory that focuses on a narrow product mix for a particular market niche will out-perform the conventional plant, which attempts a broader mission. Because its equipment, supporting systems and procedures can concentrate on a limited task for one set of customers, its cost and especially its overheads are likely to be lower than those of a conventional plant. But, more important, such a plant can become a competitive weapon because its entire apparatus is focused to accomplish the particular manufacturing task demanded by the company's overall strategy and marketing objective.[8]

Two modern versions of Smith's scale economies through specialisation focus on *core competencies* and *learning-by-doing*. Core competencies state that a firm can use specialised skills across many products to exploit acquired competence. Learning-by-doing economies arise because of growth in the firm's *cumulative output*. The longer the firm remains in business, the more technical and marketing experience accumulates, which translates into lower unit costs. A 'learning'

[8] Wickham Skinner, 'The focused factory', *Harvard Business Review* (May–June 1974), p. 41. Skinner went on to observe that focused manufacturing plants are 'extremely rare' in the US. The conventional US plant, in his view, undertook a multiplicity of tasks motivated by the desire to achieve economies of scale and utilise its overheads to the maximum. Adding more products to the firm's product range yielded scale economies in one sense – more intensive use of capital equipment – but it undermined them in a more important sense by distracting human and organisational resources from the core task.

> ### Box 5.5   Adam Smith's division of labour
>
> Adam Smith's classic text, *An Inquiry into the Nature and Causes of the Wealth of Nations*, was published in 1776. A major theme of the book, sketched in the opening chapters, is that wealth consists of a nation's productive power, not its stock of gold. In Smith's view, the source of 'the greatest improvement in the productive powers of labour' is the *division of labour*. Nowadays, we use 'specialisation' and 'economies of scale' instead of 'division of labour'.
>
> Smith identified three ways in which increased specialisation leads to higher productivity: first, it enhances the dexterity of the workforce; second, it saves time lost in passing from one type of work to another; and third, it leads to the invention of 'a great number of machines which facilitate and abridge labour and enable one man to do the work of many'. Interestingly, Smith believed that inventions were likely to be suggested by the workers 'who, being employed in some simple operation, naturally turn their thoughts towards finding out easier and speedier methods of performing it' (p. 13).
>
> To illustrate the benefits of specialisation, Smith took the celebrated example of the pin factory. By specialising the tasks of each worker, the factory produces 4800 pins per worker per day, but if each worker tried to produce pins on an individual basis they could produce only a fraction of that amount. More than 200 years after the publication of *The Wealth of Nations*, the output of pins per worker in Britain had risen to 800,000 per day. This converts to an annualised average 2.6 per cent growth rate in labour productivity (close to the national average for all industries!).
>
> Not all of this productivity growth can be ascribed to specialisation within the pin industry. For instance, employees are now better educated than in the past – though this superior education reflects specialisation in a separate sphere itself. Technical progress also derives from division of labour.
>
> The figures illustrate the immense significance of an apparently modest productivity growth – if it is sustained over a sufficiently long span of time. The structure of the pin industry has also changed markedly since Smith's time. Whereas in 1776 there were 100 or more small firms in Britain producing pins, in 1976 all pins in the United Kingdom were produced by just two firms.
>
> *Source*: C.F. Pratten, 'The manufacture of pins', *Journal of Economic Literature* (March 1980).

elasticity of 0.2 has been estimated for the aircraft production industry; production costs decrease by 2 per cent, with a 10 per cent rise in output. Know-how and technological expertise embodied in the workforce rise with the number of aircraft that have been produced.[9]

The statistical *law of large numbers* is another factor helping to reduce unit costs. The optimum level of inventories grows with the square root of sales (the stock inventory rule), not proportionally with sales. *Economies of increased dimension*, or *'engineering' rules*, also account for the reduction in unit costs with extra sales volume. This source of scale economies is important for storage and transport

---

[9] G. Klepper, 'Entry into the market for large commercial aircraft', *European Economic Review*, 34(4) (1990), p. 777.

activities. Capacity increases with *volume*, while cost is more closely related to *area* – hence the economies of huge warehouses, supertankers, pipelines and beer-vats. Imagine a box $2 \times 2 \times 2$ with a volume of 8 m$^3$. The area of the box consists of six sides, each of which is 4 m$^2$. Total area = 24 m$^2$. Now consider the effects of doubling the dimensions of the box to $4 \times 4 \times 4$. Each side of the box now measures 16 m$^2$. Total area = 96 m$^2$, but cubic capacity increases to 64 m$^3$. Thus, while storage capacity increases eight-fold, costs (assumed to be related to area) increase only four-fold. Another example of this phenomenon is the tendency for the cost of operating a machine to vary by the capacity of the machine raised to the power 0.6 – the Haldi–Whitcomb '0.6 rule'.[10]

Finally, *economies of scope* arise when the cost of providing two or more distinct goods from the same firm is less than the cost of producing them separately. Economies of scope are common in distribution and retailing. In the case of photocopiers, for instance, it is more economical for one firm to supply toner and paper together rather than to have them supplied separately by different firms. Likewise, it is sometimes more cost-effective to distribute different but related products, say refrigerators and washing machines, together than to distribute each separately. Economies of scope are crucial to understanding the cost–benefit of developing global brands. Hamel and Prahalad explain this by citing the example of Yamaha.

> Yamaha makes and markets a broad range of musical instruments under a single brand (including guitars, pianos, trumpets, organs and violas). It is inherently better positioned to build a significant market share than single-instrument competitors ... which cannot amortise their brand investments across multiple product categories. (*Competing for the Future*, Boston, MA: Harvard Business School Press, 1994, p. 282)

Economies of scope are also common where networks exist. Information technology and telecommunications are outstanding examples of networks which allow the owner of the network to push down unit costs as the network's facilities can be employed in more uses (e.g. a fixed-line fibre optic network can accommodate telephone, television, cable and Internet connections). Joint distribution of bank and insurance services makes it possible to spread costs by using distribution networks more intensively. The removal of rules restricting the provision of these products led to the development of the bancassurance industry in Europe in the 1990s. Another example is the benefits to an airline of an extended flight network. Although some services may not be individually profitable, they may still add to overall company profits if customers using them are attracted thereby to profitable parts of the airline's network. Airlines often offer highly competitive fares for short-distance flights to hub airports in order to induce customers to avail themselves of the firm's more profitable long-haul flights.

---

[10] The Haldi–Whitcomb study researched the cost structure of 687 plants. They found that 94 per cent had economies of scale. They proposed the equation $C = ax^b$, where $C$ = cost of operations and $x$ = output capacity of plant. The value of the exponent $b$ was estimated as 0.6 – hence the 0.6 rule. Another example concerns the cubic capacity (output) of a pipeline which increases with the radius of the pipe ($\pi r^2$), whereas the cost of production is related to the diameter ($2\pi r$) and increases less than proportionately to the output volume.

These varied sources of scale economies explain why average cost per unit of output can fall when total output rises.[11] After a certain level of output, however, the forces reducing costs cease to dominate. The average cost curve flattens out and then starts to slope upwards. In technical jargon, diseconomies of scale begin to outweigh economies of scale.

Economies of scale and scope are important in most economic activities. According to OECD estimates, economies of scale are the primary factor affecting competitiveness in about 30 per cent of manufacturing output in the major industrial countries. Scale economies are also important in the services sector, particularly banking, insurance, telecoms and the media.[12] Where the minimum average cost of a firm is large relative to the national market, there will be few firms in the industry and this makes the measurement and analysis of scale economies highly relevant to competition authorities. Analysis of scale economies can also act as a warning to business of the need for restructuring if the size of domestic firms in an industry is significantly smaller than that prevailing in competitor countries.

## Diseconomies of scale

Unit costs tend to rise in the short run because, among other reasons, employees will have to be paid overtime. A point may even be reached where they start to get in each other's way. As output increases, there is a build-up of stress and friction on managers, machines and materials as they are pushed to the limit. Also, standard scale economies become less effective. Learning-by-doing in any particular activity occurs at a declining rate and eventually reaches zero. Employees too can become over-specialised, leading to loss of adaptability and initiative.

In the long run, these problems can be addressed by expanding the size of the plant, buying more machines and adding to staff. Management systems can be developed, and bottlenecks and constraints can be systematically addressed. The long-run overall average cost of the firm may continue to slope downwards for a considerable range of output. Successful firms tend to see a continuous downward trend in unit costs. Yet the constraints on minimum efficient size eventually become binding, at different scale levels in different industries. (In other instances, unit costs continue to decline until a monopoly position is reached, at which juncture competition legislation rather than scale constrains the size of the firm.)

---

[11] It is tempting to add the economies of bulk order purchasing as another source of scale economies. These are called pecuniary economies of scale. To be sure, bulk ordering provides the keenest input prices to the larger firms, and businesses identify this as a major advantage of larger size. But lower price through bulk orders reflects, rather than constitutes, an economy of scale. Alternatively, it could represent exploitation of market power (monopsony) which has nothing to do with scale economies, although both reduce costs for the firm.

[12] This assessment may be qualified somewhat by John Kay's observation: 'I have yet to encounter a firm or an industry where managers did not initially overestimate the importance of scale economies' (p. 172). One explanation for this may be that firms often find they are profitable when overtrading and incorrectly ascribe this to economies of scale. Also, when recommending a merger or takeover to shareholders, executives often have a strong incentive to exaggerate the potential cost savings to be reaped from making the firm bigger in size. See John A. Kay, *Foundations of Corporate Success: How business strategies add value* (London: Oxford University Press, 1993).

After a certain output level, *diseconomies of scale* swing into action. These involve *increases* in unit costs as output rises. Diseconomies of scale take a number of forms.

1. *Informational requirements* grow as the firm becomes larger. Instead of the informal communication system of a small firm, larger firms have to employ special systems to disseminate information.
2. *Management control* becomes more difficult as firms get bigger, leading to higher unit costs.
3. *Industrial relations problems* can become more acute, and disproportionate effort has to be devoted to motivating staff and cultivating corporate *esprit de corps*.
4. As firms become larger they suffer a *loss of flexibility*. Customised demand becomes harder to cater for.
5. *Transport costs set limits to size in some industries*. For this reason, corrugated cardboard manufacturing and construction materials, such as cement and gravel, usually have to be installed nearer the consumer than in many other industries. This sets a limit on plant size.

The scope for exploiting scale economies and for avoiding diseconomies of scale is in a constant state of flux. 'New wave' manufacturing strategies, variously labelled as world-class manufacturing, lean production, flexible specialisation, post-Fordism and Total Quality Management, can restore economies based on new forms of work organisation. To raise productivity, teams or groups can be formed around the production of common parts or the search for customers.[13] Lean production, for example, is based on teams of multi-skilled workers and flexible automated machines. It is 'lean' in that it uses fewer inventories, less space and more teamwork, with an objective of zero defects and minimum inventory. It strives to combine the advantages of mass production and craft production.

In some industries the optimum scale of operation (from a cost per unit perspective) is increasing, but in others the advent of new technology has given a renewed lease of life to smaller firms. Computerised reservation systems provide special advantages to larger airline carriers, but information technology has improved the ease and cost of access of smaller firms to data which previously only a large firm could have afforded to acquire. Major drug companies find that they can control the rising cost of innovation by contracting out research to smaller specialised medical research companies. Chiroscience and Celsis, two of Britain's most successful medical research companies in the 1990s, founded by biotechnology entrepreneur Chris Evans, were started in this way. Quality control, likewise, in the sense of quality assurance and strategic quality management, has become less expensive at smaller scales of output as a result of computer-aided design and the microcomputer. Flexible batch production has reduced the plant size at which the minimum cost point, or the minimum efficient scale of operations (MES), is attained. Changes in telecommunications technology, such as the development of mobile phones and satellite communications, exposed many former state-owned monopolies in Europe to competition

---

[13] J. Storey (ed.), *New Wave Manufacturing Strategies: Organisational and human resource management dimensions* (London: Paul Chapman, 1994).

from smaller competitors. The telecoms industry no longer requires enormous sunk costs in the form of cables linking every receiving household.

## The shape of the cost curves – short run and long run

Thus, both managerial and technical factors explain why the average cost curve may, after a certain level of output, level, flatten out and then slope upwards. Firms, of course, try to circumvent these constraints. Much organisational innovation and experimentation, ranging from franchising to cooperatives and multi-divisional planning, is targeted at overcoming potential diseconomies of scale. The net effect of these measures on the evolution of optimum firm size defies simple generalisation. As we shall see in the next chapter, there is no universal trend towards larger firm size. There indeed seems to be a large range of output where the average cost curve is flat and the optimum firm size remains indeterminate. Many different sizes of firms can be equally efficient. This is consistent with the observation that both small and large firms are able to coexist profitably in many industries.

A second implication is that the long-run average cost curve is likely to be much flatter than the short-run cost curve. In the long run, firms can adjust their plant size and try to deal with congestion problems. Hence the rise in costs will be less pronounced. Fewer costs will be fixed in the long run.

## 5.4 The transaction costs approach

A curious feature of a market economy is that the price system is used to allocate resources everywhere – *except within the firm itself*. Within the firm, the allocation of resources, the assignment of functions and the distribution of rewards are determined by management. Professor Ronald Coase elaborated on this point in a well-known passage:

> Outside the firm, price movements direct production, which is co-ordinated through series of exchange transactions on the market. Within a firm, these transactions are eliminated and in place of the complicated market structure with exchange transactions is substituted the entrepreneur co-ordinator, who directs production. It is clear that these are alternative methods of co-ordinating production. ('The nature of the firm', *Economica*, November 1937)

Why is coordination the work of the price system in one case and of management in another? Coase's response was that firms exist because they economise on *transaction costs*. For example, an employee in a firm agrees to work for a certain remuneration and, in return, undertakes to carry out whatever reasonable tasks are assigned by management. This saves two types of cost, which would have been incurred had each of these tasks been negotiated through an item-by-item market contract: (a) special contracts do not have to be made with each factor with which labour works (owner of machinery, landowner, supplier of inputs); and (b) the cost of specifying future duties is avoided (the services to be provided by the employee are expressed in general terms). Thus, by hiring an employee on an annual or permanent basis, the firm economises on transaction costs.

Two types of transaction costs are of particular relevance to the firm:

1. *Motivation costs*, which arise because of asymmetric information. For example, by hiring on a long-term basis, with a promotional 'ladder', the employer hopes to give the employee a stake in the business which will cut down on monitoring costs and minimise costly arrangements for protecting the firm against *opportunistic* behaviour, or *shirking*, on the part of employees.

2. *Imperfect commitment*. Two parties may wish to bind themselves to honour promises they would like to make but which, having made, they may later have an incentive to renounce (e.g. a housebuilder's guarantee). The market system may not be able to provide them with such an arrangement. A firm can get around this difficulty, however, by building up a reputation for reliability through repeated execution of contracts and fair dealing with customers and staff.[14]

The diverse nature of transaction costs enables us to explain the reasons why firms exist, why the optimal size of the firm is bigger in some industries than in others, and why firms choose different modes of organisation. Certain types of activity will be conducive to the formation of cooperatives; others to cottage industry; some to public ownership; others to private ownership. The transactions approach can be used to explain why some people are hired on one-off contracts, while others are offered long-term contracts. Tasks can be subcontracted through the market system and agents motivated by *franchises* and *licences* rather than by outright hiring as employees. Another implication of the theory is that, as technology and markets change, the organisational mode can also be expected to change.

Transaction costs explain why different *size* of firms will be a feature of a market system, complementing the analysis of economies and diseconomies of scale. Consider, for example, the analysis of the takeover of a supplier's business in preference to procurement of these supplies through the market system. The advantages, from a transaction cost perspective, of such forms of vertical integration arise for three reasons:

● Better coordination and better protection of specific investments can be achieved, especially where specialised know-how is involved.
● The supplier may not be able to assess the value of its market power and hence it can be taken over at a cost less than its value to the buyer.
● Scale and transaction economies can be obtained. These will enable the firm to consolidate its market power. (This topic is treated in Chapter 7.)

After a certain stage, the larger firm begins to encounter diseconomies of size. Not just because of the type of managerial diseconomies described earlier in this chapter, but also because of problems such as the loss of the benefits of competition among suppliers, distraction from the 'core competencies' of the firm and the problem of 'double marginalisation'. All these, taken together with the growing demand for customised goods and services from a more affluent society, diminish the appeal of vertical integration and add to the attraction of contract-

---

[14] P. Milgrom and R. Roberts, *Economics, Organisation and Management* (Hemel Hempstead: Prentice Hall, 1992).

ing out. The *core competence* argument, useful as a source of scale economies up to a point, can be converted into an argument for downsizing after that point is passed. Many corporations have explained their reduction in scale on this basis.[15]

## 5.5 From cost structure to supply curve

### Marginal cost and supply

Suppose one accepts the general proposition that costs per unit initially decline and after a certain point start to rise. Two implications follow. First, an optimal firm size becomes possible to determine analytically. It is located at the level of output where MC = MR and AC = price. Second, a link can be directly established between the firm's supply and the industry supply.

The link between the individual firm's supply curve and the industry supply curve can be illustrated by imagining the reaction of the firm to changes in price. Returning to Figure 5.5, at a price of £12, six units are produced. A higher price of £14 leads to seven units; at £16, eight units are produced, and so on. Thus, the MC curve can be interpreted as the supply curve of the firm.

To derive the market supply curve, the supply curves of the individual firms are laterally summated (see Figure 5.6). This is depicted in just the same way as individual demand curves were laterally summated in order to derive the market demand curve. The resultant upward-sloping market supply curve reflects two main influences. First, a rise in price elicits more supply from each firm in the industry in accordance with the profit-maximisation rule. Second, a rise in price, by raising the profitability of the industry, *attracts new entrants*. These two effects – more output from firms in the industry and still more from new entrants – are incorporated in the industry supply curve. They illustrate how a shift in market demand can, through the price mechanism, attract more supply from the industry.

As the industry gets larger, various influences begin to impinge on the firm's MC curve. First, the price of inputs into the industry might be bid up. If this

**Figure 5.6 Deriving the market supply curve from individual firm supply curves**

(a) Firm 1    (b) Firm 2    (c) Industry (= Firm 1 + Firm 2)

[15] G. Hamel and C.K. Prahalad, 'Core competences of the corporation', *Harvard Business Review* (1990); *Competing for the Future* (New Haven, CT: Harvard Business School Press, 1994).

happens, the supply curve will shift upwards. Second, scale economies will also have to be taken into account. They could involve downward shifts in the supply curve over time.

## External economies of scale

As an industry grows, an additional class of scale economies often emerges, namely *external economies and diseconomies of scale*. Although internal to the industry, they are external to the individual firm. External or *agglomeration economies* are relevant to understanding the pattern of location of industries, the tendency of some industries to form clusters, and the reinforcing of competitive advantage through clusters of activities related to a specific industry.

Expansion of a particular sector in a location means that skilled personnel are attracted to that location and a specialised R&D capacity may develop. Subcontractors find it worthwhile to locate nearby. The development of a centre of excellence reduces costs for all firms in the industry, but the cost reductions happen only because of the expansion of the industry as a whole in the region. Growth feeds on growth, in a virtuous circle of cumulative and circular causation. Instances of the practical significance of external economies of scale are easy to list:

- The cases of the flower industry in the Netherlands, ceramic tiles in Italy, the Swiss watch industry and the German printing press industry are much cited examples of industries that have drawn competitive strength from external scale economies. Their experience has been documented in Michael Porter's classic study, *The Competitive Advantage of Nations*.[16]
- The regions of north-central Italy (the Third Italy) are another much studied instance of external economies in action.[17] For example, the growth of the Emilia-Romagna region, based on small, heavily localised firms with a high proportion of owner-managers, owes much to regional support mechanisms which generate substantial external economies of scale. Trade associations provide marketing, technical information and training facilities. Financial cooperatives are a vehicle for guaranteeing loans to individual artisans. External economies of scale enable small firms to compete and to attain very high levels of productivity.
- The concentrated location of the entertainment industry in Hollywood, high tech in Silicon Valley and international banking centres in London, Luxembourg and Dublin is heavily influenced by external economies of scale.
- Similar effects have been observed in the Languedoc-Roussillon region of France and in the Jutland region of Denmark, where inter-firm cooperation has

[16] M.E. Porter, *The Competitive Advantage of Nations* (London: Macmillan, 1990).

[17] M.H. Best, *The New Competition: Institutions of industrial restructuring* (Oxford: Polity Press, 1990). The benefits of extended market size can be illustrated also from the example of Koni, a major producer of shock absorbers. Koni can concentrate on R&D on shock absorbers today, better than Ford could in the early days of automobile production when the market was so small that Ford had to produce every component for itself (the engine, gearbox, steering wheel, shock absorbers and so on). Only with an increased size of market does it become profitable for a separate firm like Koni to specialise in shock absorbers, producing them more efficiently than Ford ever could – this advantage further enhanced by concentrating on R&D for this component alone. Division of labour at work once again! (I am indebted to Professor Jacob Kol of Erasmus University, Rotterdam, for this example.)

been found to play a vital role in overcoming the disadvantages of small firm size.

External scale economies can be incorporated into the supply curve by imagining outward shifts in the curve occurring as output expands. The key feature of external scale economies is that they impact favourably on *all* firms in the industry and, therefore, do no violence to the assumption of a competitive market. They can be treated more or less the same as technology improvements. Such improvements lead to a downward shift in the cost curves of all firms in the industry.

## 5.6 Conclusions

The chain of causation, from market demand to the supply decision of an individual firm, is simple in outline. But to establish the link, assumptions have to be made concerning the motivation of the firm as expressed by the actions of its executives, the nature of the firm's cost structure and the degree of market power. Each assumption is open to modification. Nevertheless, the actual behaviour of many firms in a modern economy conforms quite closely to the theoretical model outlined in this chapter. Shifts in demand elicit changes in supply more or less automatically, sooner or later, motivated primarily by the dictates of profit maximisation.

In a competitive market, management's objectives and the firm's cost structure determine the size of the firm. Economies and diseconomies of scale, both at firm level and at industry level, are key determinants of this cost structure. Indirectly, they help to explain why some industries are more concentrated (i.e. have fewer firms, accounting for a larger share of industry production) than others. But new ways of exploiting these economies, and of overcoming diseconomies, are constantly being discovered. Also, the scope for exploiting them differs markedly between industries, with aircraft production at one end of the spectrum and *haute couture* fashion clothing at the other. As the possibility of applying scale economies increases, even comparatively large countries, such as the UK or Germany, do not offer sufficient size to permit complete exploitation of scale for some industries. National markets are too small to support enough firms to ensure a healthy degree of competition. In order to help their domestic industries to achieve optimal scale and minimum costs, governments are being driven to negotiate better access to export markets. In return, they are obliged to reduce their own trade barriers against foreign goods and services. The pursuit of unit cost reductions through greater scale is a major explanatory factor underlying the growth of the multinational firm and the globalisation of business.

Yet the trend towards bigness is not uniform across countries. Technology and customised demand are moderating influences. They enable small firms to engage in activities where bigger is not better. Small and large firms can coexist within the same industry, each category operating profitably. External economies of scale can also help small firms to overcome the disadvantage of small size.

The cost structure of firms and industries, and consequently the shape of the industry supply curve, has a strong time dimension. Throughout this chapter, the distinction is repeatedly drawn between *short-run* and *long-run* cost profiles. The short run is characterised by the dominance of fixed costs. The firm's location, its plant and machinery, its managerial staff and structure are relatively fixed and cannot be altered in response to surges or restrictions in demand. In the short run, once capacity levels are reached, the supply curve is upward sloping, as more expensive labour time, less efficient workers and/or less efficient firms have to be brought in to increase output. Over time, however, a firm can exercise discretion over these fixed price costs. The plant can be closed and production transferred to another location. New machinery can be ordered to replace the old and the structure of the workforce can be altered. Formerly fixed costs can become variable. As we have seen, the long run is defined as a period when all costs, except 'sunk' costs, have become variable. The long-run cost function shows the minimum cost at each output level, when the desired plant size, technology and human resources structure can be freely chosen. Generally, this function will be flatter than the short-run cost function. It could even be downward sloping. Costs will rise less steeply as output increases beyond the minimum-cost point because, over time, it will be possible to build a larger plant and also external economies may develop, both of which will tend to reduce unit costs.

This chapter has focused on the competitive market model. Most managers, however, operate in markets in which they possess some degree of market power. Faced with aggressive competition, firms try to evade it by repositioning themselves in the market. The essence of this repositioning is a search for monopoly power. We shall discuss what happens in these less competitive markets in the next chapter.

## Summary

1. Just as consumers are assumed to maximise utility, so firms are assumed in economic analysis to maximise profits. The profit-maximisation assumption is justified on the basis that firms which neglect profitability either become vulnerable to takeover or run the danger of becoming bankrupt. Executives can be induced to maximise profits on behalf of owners by specially designed managerial incentive schemes. But corporate scandals of the early 2000s have demonstrated that these schemes do not always function as shareholders expect and are subject to abuse. Also, takeovers and mergers can be motivated by executive egos rather than by the dictates of profit maximisation.

2. If a firm is a profit maximiser, it must act according to certain key rules. First, the firm must reject all technically inefficient production techniques. Second, the firm minimises the cost of producing any given level of output. It will combine intermediate and factor inputs in such a way that the extra profit brought into the firm by the last unit of each input equals its cost to the firm. Third, it will sell output up to the point where the marginal revenue obtained on the last unit sold exactly equals the marginal cost of producing it.

3. A firm's cost structure is conventionally depicted as being U-shaped, or L-shaped, with declining unit costs being succeeded by a tendency for unit costs to rise or, at least, to flatten out. The main reasons for declining unit costs are economies of scale and scope. Standard economies of scale are those arising from indivisibilities,

greater exploitation and cultivation of specialised skills, learning-by-doing and economics of increased dimension. Economies of scope apply to networks which allow different products to be supplied more cheaply through a common network than through a separate network for each service.

4. Diseconomies of scale set limits to the expansion of large firms. They are evident in the loss of operational flexibility and the mounting informational requirements as firms grow in size.

5. The long-run average cost curve is likely to be flatter than the short-run curve because, in the long run, non-sunk fixed costs can be transformed into variable costs. Fixed assets, plant and labour can be sold off and redeployed in line with a firm's changing needs.

6. The optimal size and organisation structure of the firm can be analysed by the transactions costs approach. This approach enables us to weigh up the merits of buying in a good from outside the firm versus making it itself, and proceeds to study the strength and weakness of different modes of organisation: long-term contracts, joint ventures and franchising, for example. This approach asserts that the firm is not merely a profit-maximising entity responding to a fixed set of opportunities and constraints. It is also a set of governance structures in which diverse motives operate. Transactions analysis complements the standard economic analysis in a significant way.

7. Scale and scope economies are an important feature of economic life, and they play a crucial part in determining industrial structure and the size distribution of firms in different economic sectors. Empirical measures of economies of scale have been used to estimate the effects of the opening of internal markets to competition (such as the EU's single market programme or the effects of WTO membership).

8. External economies of scale can explain why small firms may coexist with, and even thrive against the competition of, very large firms. Examples include the Marche regions of northern Italy, Jutland in Denmark, Languedoc-Roussillon in France and Silicon Valley, California.

## Questions for discussion

1. Economics assumes that firms try to maximise profits. Review the arguments used to justify this assumption. Do you find them convincing?

2. It is often argued that the MR = MC rule is of no practical use because firms do not know the values of the marginal cost and marginal revenue of their output. Is this a criticism of the economic theory of the firm, or of the firm's accounting system?

3. In industries such as the automobile industry, economies of scale have increased enormously as a result of vertical integration and automation. New entry to the industry has virtually stopped. Yet Jaguar (which was taken over by Ford in 1989) announced a major investment programme in 1995 for two new luxury models with annual volume of a modest 70,000 cars per year. If a model can be viable with such a small production run, why do large firms dominate the market?

4. In banking and insurance, economies of scale, obtained by the takeover and control of distribution networks, deter new entrants. Banks and insurance companies have been amalgamated into giant bancassurance companies. What types of economies of scale are likely to be most relevant to this sector? What types of diseconomies of scale would you expect?

5. 'Rarely is a firm efficient because it is big. Rather, it becomes big because it is efficient.' Do you agree?

6. Does the existence of economies of scale and scope mean that small- and medium-sized firms will no longer be able to survive?

## Exercises

1. 'The mere threat of a takeover acts as a powerful force motivating top corporate managers to pursue value-maximising business strategies.' Explain why this should be so. What takeover defences can management devise to reduce the threat of takeover?

2. 'In the economists' perfectly competitive industry, jockeying for position is unbridled and entry to the industry very easy. But this kind of industry structure offers the worst prospect for long-run profitability' (Michael Porter). Identify some industries which are close to being perfectly competitive. Why do new firms enter them if the long-run profits outlook is so poor?

3. Show with the aid of diagrams how firms in a competitive industry will respond to a decrease in market demand.

4. Suppose that a firm, with a total cost structure as shown in the table, can sell as much output as it wants at a price of £10.

   (a) Derive its MC curve.
   (b) At what level of output will the firm reach the point of maximum profits?
   (c) Compute the average costs per unit at each output level. Is the firm making a profit or a loss at the 'profit-maximising' level of output?
   (d) Suppose price were to rise to £14, what difference would this make to output and profit?
   (e) If a firm is making a loss, should it close down?

   | Output | 0 | 1 | 2 | 3 | 4 | 5 | 6 | 7 | 8 | 9 | 10 |
   |---|---|---|---|---|---|---|---|---|---|---|---|
   | Total cost (£) | 10 | 25 | 36 | 44 | 51 | 59 | 69 | 81 | 95 | 111 | 129 |

5. The following table shows a firm's total costs over a range of output and the price corresponding to each quantity sold. Find out its profit-maximising level of sales and the corresponding price. (Compute the firm's total revenue, marginal revenue and marginal cost schedules.)

| (1)<br>Output<br>(goods produced<br>per week) | (2)<br>Total costs<br>(£ per week) | (3)<br>Price<br>(received per unit) |
|---|---|---|
| 0 | 10 | – |
| 1 | 25 | 21 |
| 2 | 36 | 20 |
| 3 | 44 | 19 |
| 4 | 51 | 18 |
| 5 | 59 | 17 |
| 6 | 69 | 16 |
| 7 | 81 | 15 |
| 8 | 95 | 14 |
| 9 | 111 | 13 |
| 10 | 129 | 12 |

6. (a) Calculate the marginal and average costs for each level of output from the following data.

(b) Explain how marginal and average costs are related.

(c) Costs of £12 are incurred in the initial position, even though no output is being produced. How can this be explained?

| Output | 0 | 1 | 2 | 3 | 4 | 5 | 6 | 7 | 8 | 9 |
|---|---|---|---|---|---|---|---|---|---|---|
| Total cost (£) | 12 | 40 | 53 | 64 | 73 | 83 | 93 | 104 | 120 | 145 |

7. Suppose a firm discovers that the marginal product of a unit of machinery is twice the marginal product of a unit of labour. You are told that the cost of labour is £6 per unit and the cost of machinery is £3 per unit. Is the firm minimising costs in accordance with the rules for profit maximisation? If not, how can it reduce them?

8. Suppose two firms produce the same product and have exactly the same marginal cost curve but their average fixed cost is different. Will they produce the same level of output?

9. Assume that a manufacturer of food-mixers has the following costs and price:

| Food-mixer price | £70 |
|---|---|
| Variable cost per unit | £40 |
| Unit contribution | £30 |
| Total fixed costs | £60,000 |

Assuming both price and unit variable costs are constant, how many food-mixers would the manufacturer have to sell in order to break even? (See Figure 5.4.) Suppose it was judged impossible to attain a sufficient sales volume to break even, what should the firm do?

10. (a) Sketch the average fixed cost curve, the average total cost curve and the average variable cost associated with Figure 5.3.

(b) Is this cost structure consistent with the widely observed association of higher profits with higher levels of economic activity?

(c) What are the limitations of the breakeven chart approach in comparison with the U-shaped analysis?

(d) Is the U-shaped analysis also consistent with the cyclical behaviour of company profits?

11. Examine Figure 5.1 carefully to show that maximising total profits is not the same as maximising average profit per unit. Explain why this is the case.

## Further reading

A good place to start is Adam Smith's *Wealth of Nations* (1776), notably the still interesting and percipient introductory chapters on the division of labour and the size of the market. Topics such as economies of scale and market power are addressed comprehensively in texts on the economics of industrial organisation. R. Clarke, *Industrial Organisation* (Oxford: Basil Blackwell, 1985), is a good general treatment. On transaction costs, a classical source is O.E. Williamson, *Markets and Hierarchies: Analysis and anti-trust implications* (New York: Free Press, 1975). For a more up-to-date assessment, see the conflicting exchanges between S. Ghoshal, Peter Moran and Oliver Williamson in the *Academy of Management Review*, 21(1), 1996. An excellent review of business and organisation is provided in P. Milgrom and J. Roberts, *Economics, Organisation and Management* (Upper Saddle River, NJ: Prentice Hall International, 1992), especially Chapter 16. Further developments – especially in relation to the economics of the vertical integration of firms – are comprehensively outlined in D. Besenko *et al.*, *Economics of Strategy* (New York: John Wiley & Sons Inc., 2004).

## Chapter 6

# The economics of market power

## Introduction

Competition is an enduring and pervasive fact of business life. Although the intensity of competitive pressure varies according to type of industry and stage of the business cycle, most managers recognise a broad similarity between their own experience and many aspects of the competitive model of the previous chapter. High profits attract new entrants; losses lead to exits. Prices cannot be realistically altered without regard to the 'market' rate, and so on.

Yet one important aspect of business reality is *market power*. Up to now, we have assumed that firms have negligible market power. Each firm is so small in relation to the total size of the market that it takes the going market price as 'given' and can safely ignore other firms' reactions to its sales or price decisions. There are too many (uncoordinated) producers to make any such interdependence worth considering. This assumption is now relaxed. Firms are allowed to have monopoly, or market, power.

The way firms use, and maintain, market power is the subject of this chapter.

## Chapter outline

1. Evidence on the proportion of economic activity that can be classified as monopolistic.

2. How firms behave in situations where they possess market power; the case of a *single-firm monopoly*, the most extreme instance of market power.

3. How monopoly profits act as a magnet to new entrants. In trying to gain a share of these profits, the new entrants tend to erode them. In a dynamic market system, monopolies are always under threat. How firms protect a monopoly position – or 'market niche'.

4. The analysis of *oligopoly* markets, where a few firms have a significant share of the market.

5. Competition versus monopoly – an economic assessment.

## 6.1 Firm size

### The facts

'Corporate giantism' is a feature of many parts of the economy. In the auto-mobile, aircraft and oil industries, large scale is the norm rather than the excep-tion. The top four meat-packing firms in North America slaughter 84 per cent of US cattle. Wal-Mart employs over one million people – a workforce more than half the size of the total working population of a small country such as Ireland, and held over 60 per cent of the retail discount trade of the US in 2001. Among Europe's major employers, DaimlerChrysler, Siemens and Unilever have become household names (Tables 6.1 and 6.2), as have the state-owned communications and transport companies.

At the opposite end of the spectrum are the small and medium-sized enterprises (SMEs), defined as enterprises employing fewer than 250 persons. In 2000, there

**Table 6.1 The world's 10 largest corporations, 2001**

|  | Employees (000s) | Revenue US$bn |
|---|---|---|
| 1 Wal-Mart | 1383 | 219.8 |
| 2 China National Petroleum | 1167 | 41.5 |
| 3 State Power | 1163 | 48.4 |
| 4 Sinopec | 937 | 40.4 |
| 5 US Postal Services | 891 | 65.8 |
| 6 China Telecommunications | 566 | 22.3 |
| 7 Agricultural Bank of China | 500 | 10.6 |
| 8 Siemens | 484 | 77.4 |
| 9 Industrial and Commercial Bank of China | 430 | 19.8 |
| 10 McDonald's | 395 | 14.8 |

Source: Global Fortune 500, Fortune (July 2002).

**Table 6.2 Top employers in Europe, 2001**

|  | No. of employees |
|---|---|
| 1 Siemens | 484,000 |
| 2 Carrefour | 382,821 |
| 3 Vivendi | 381,000 |
| 4 DaimlerChrysler | 372,470 |
| 5 Compass Group | 344,830 |
| 6 Volkswagen | 322,070 |
| 7 Sodexho Alliance | 314,000 |
| 8 La Poste | 313,854 |
| 9 Deutsche Post | 283,330 |
| 10 Unilever | 279,000 |

Source: Global Fortune 500, Fortune (July 2002).

## Table 6.3 Size-class structure by industry, Europe-19, 2000

| | Average enterprise size | Size-class dominance | Relative labour productivity of SMEs* |
|---|---|---|---|
| **Extraction** (including energy) | 36 | LSE | 135 |
| **Manufacturing** | 14 | LSE | 90 |
| – Food products, beverages, tobacco | 13 | LSE | 91 |
| – Textiles, wearing apparel, leather | 10 | SME | 98 |
| – Chemicals, chemical products, coke, refined petroleum, nuclear fuel | 51 | LSE | 97 |
| – Electrical and optical equipment | 19 | LSE | 96 |
| – Transport equipment | 54 | LSE | 89 |
| **Wholesale trade** | 5 | SME | 101 |
| **Retail distribution** | 4 | Micro | 104 |
| **Transport and communication** | 8 | LSE | 82 |
| **Personal services** | 5 | Micro | 85 |
| – Hotels and restaurants | 5 | Micro | 100 |

* Labour productivity (value added per occupied person) of SMEs as a percentage of industry average.

Source: 'SMEs in Europe, including a first glance at EU candidate countries', *Observatory of European SMEs*, no. 2, 2002 (http://europa.eu.int/comm/enterprise).

were 19 million such enterprises in Europe-19 (the EU countries, Iceland, Liechtenstein, Norway and Switzerland). Although comprising only a fraction of the total number of enterprises, the 40,000 enterprises with 250 or more employees accounted for 34 per cent of the EU's workforce in services and industry of 122 million.[1] Enterprises employing fewer than 10 persons ('micro'-firms) employ 42 million or just over one-third of the total. Micro-firms are heavily represented in retail distribution, construction and personal services (Table 6.3).

Almost half of all US firms are SMEs. Firms with fewer than 250 workers account for 46 per cent of private sector employment.[2] The vast majority of US firms had sales below $10 million per year.

## Firm size, concentration ratios and market power

Some rough indication of the proportionate strength of competitive forces in the economy can be gleaned from examining the proportion of small relative to large

[1] 'SMEs in Europe, including a first glance at EU candidate countries', *Observatory of European SMEs*, no. 2, 2002 (http://europa.eu.int/comm/enterprise).

[2] 'SMEs in Europe, including a first glance at EU candidate countries', *Observatory of European SMEs*, no. 2, 2002 (http://europa.eu.int/comm/enterprise). William Shepherd, *The Economics of Industrial Organisation* (Hemel Hempstead: Prentice Hall International, 1990), p. 128.

firms in an economy. Suppose one starts with the assumption that sectors with large numbers of small enterprises are more likely to have the characteristics of a competitive market than sectors dominated by the larger enterprises. On this basis, since 66 per cent of the EU workforce is employed in SMEs, we could infer that 66 per cent of total marketed activity approximates the conditions of the competitive market and the remaining 34 per cent could be classified as monopolistic. This is a crude indicator, however, since, as we have seen, on the one hand large firms are not incompatible with competition and on the other the prevalence of small firms does not guarantee competition.

Another approach is to focus on *concentration ratios*. Concentration ratios are a commonly used measure of the degree of market power at industry level. These ratios measure the percentage share of industry sales, or employment, accounted for by the largest companies. A C4 of 70 per cent, for example, indicates that the largest four firms account for 70 per cent of industry sales. A C10 of 85 per cent indicates that the 10 leading companies account for 85 per cent of industry output. The concentration ratio is a widely used measure of the degree of market (or monopoly) power in an industry.[3] Typical illustrations of information expressed in this way: six firms (including Polygram, Sony, EMI, Warner, BMG and RCA) accounted for 80 per cent of worldwide music sales in the mid-1990s, while one firm (Unilever) accounts for 40 per cent of the global tea distribution market.

Inferences based on concentration ratios are subject to many caveats. For one thing, they *overestimate* the degree of market power in so far as they ignore the exposure of even the largest enterprises, and the most concentrated sectors, to foreign competition. In a world of free trade and mobile foreign investment, the strongest European enterprises can no longer treat their domestic market as safe. Domestic sales meet with stiff competition from Japan and the United States at one end of the market and the newly industrialising countries at the other. Global competition has also affected the giants of the American market such as General Motors, General Electric and IBM. A significant proportion of these firms' product range is sold in highly competitive markets. IBM's strong market power in mainframes, for example, does not extend to other products in its range such as PCs and software. For this reason, high domestic market shares may be a misleading indicator of market power. This caveat is particularly necessary in the case of small open economies. Their small size means that concentration ratios are likely to be high; their openness means that they are bound to be far more exposed to competition than the concentration ratios will suggest. Thus a high concentration ratio in a sector is a necessary, but not a sufficient, condition for monopoly power (Box 6.1).

Some degree of *underestimation* of market power arises to the extent that small enterprises are under the direct or indirect control of a larger company. An enterprise is defined as the smallest unit which has a separate legal entity. Parent companies often deliberately subdivide their operations into semi-autonomous enterprises as a means of avoiding organisational diseconomies of scale. The

---

[3] Many other ways of doing this have been proposed. The Hirschman–Herfindahl index, for example, measures the degree of monopoly power as the sum of squared values of market share of all firms. Use has been made of other 'comprehensive' indices, but none has proved demonstrably superior to the standard concentration ratios. The HHI tends to be used in the US, while the concentration ratio is more used in the EU.

**Box 6.1**  **US government vs Microsoft – competition among the few?**

Small numbers of firms in the industry is a necessary but not a sufficient condition for market power. And possession of market power is not the same thing as abuse of market power. Both these issues came to the forefront during the competition case, *US government v. Microsoft*, initiated in 1998 by the US government which sued Microsoft, the world's largest software company, on grounds of abusing its market power. The main focus of the case was on Microsoft's response to the emergence of Netscape's Navigator browser. In response to the threat, Microsoft developed its own browser (Internet Explorer) and gave it away for free. In addition, the US Justice Department argued that Microsoft had forced PC makers to install Internet Explorer as a condition for obtaining a Windows operating licence (i.e. a case of 'bundling' Internet Explorer and Windows).

Microsoft's Windows operating system dominates the personal computer (PC) market. It is installed on 8 out of 10 PCs in use. Apple and Linux are also competitors. Rivalry exists between makers of PCs themselves as well as among software firms producing products such as spreadsheets and operating systems.

The case revealed interesting evidence on the forces leading to large size in high-tech industries. Some years ago, Professor Brian Arthur identified three in particular:

- *Up-front costs* – the first disk of Windows to be sold cost Microsoft $50m. The second and subsequent disks cost $3.
- *Network effects* – the more users, the more likely the language or a standard emerges as *the* standard. Hence the more people who use the standard the more useful it becomes. Consumers of a product gain from it being used by *other* consumers.
- *Customer groove-in* – high-tech products are difficult to use. Training costs are high initially but thereafter only updating is needed (e.g. learning to use Word or teaching pilots to fly Airbus planes).

These scale economies act as a barrier to entry for any newcomer and explain why first movers in the sector are hard to displace.

The barrier to entry that was judged to favour Microsoft was termed the *applications barrier*. It arises because operating systems provide value to the consumer through running applications. Since the development of software in applications involves high sunk costs in preparation but low marginal costs in production and distribution, applications developers have a strong incentive to write for the operating system with the most users; that way, the fixed costs will be recoverable from a larger number of users. This network externality effect enhanced the power of the largest firm, Microsoft, and was bad news for producers of competing operating systems. US anti-trust officials argued that the integration of Microsoft's Internet browser with its operating system was stifling competition in Internet software. Thus monopoly power in one segment of the market (operating systems) could be used to expand dominance in other areas such as Internet software. In short, Microsoft was able to use network externalities and lock in to exert market dominance and exclude competitors.

The case poses a certain dilemma. On the one hand, market power can be abused to keep out competitors with predictable consequences for price and quality in the long run. On the other hand, as Microsoft CEO Bill Gates argued, government

➜

regulation could curb innovation. There are three main possible responses to these arguments: (a) do nothing, on the grounds that one operating system may be the most efficient outcome, (b) regulate Microsoft's prices and practices, as is done in the case of utilities, or (c) split Microsoft into two separate companies in order to create competition. Industry economists have different views on the merits of each response.

*Sources*: Brian Arthur, 'Increasing returns and the new world of business', *Harvard Business Review*, July–August 1996; Findings of fact (5/11/99) *USA v. Microsoft* (www.usdoj.gov); R. Schmalensee, Direct testimony in *USA v. Microsoft* (www.microsoft.com); contributions by N. Economides and F. O'Toole to special issue of *Journal of Industry, Competition and Trade*, March 2001.

bargaining power of a large company can be underestimated by mistakenly regarding its small subsidiaries as fully autonomous entities. Concentration is always greater if calculated by reference to firm size rather than enterprise size. Account must also be taken of the many formal and informal links between major suppliers and retail outlets in some sectors, which may give a misleading impression of the degree of competition. McDonald's franchisees, petrol stations and 'tied' UK pubs are subject to much less competition than might appear.

Assessing the 'amount' of competition in an economy, therefore, cannot be decided on the basis of a simple formula. A broad overview based on firm size analysis and concentration ratios suggests that as much as 75 per cent of the European and US markets could qualify as 'effectively' competitive. 'Effectively competitive' means more than four competitors, all with small (<50 per cent) market share. On this definition, relatively high effective competition is found in the wholesale and retail trades, finance, insurance and real estate services. This leaves the remaining 25 per cent of market activities being transacted in monopoly or oligopoly market structures.

## 'One capitalist always kills many'

The share of major conglomerates in economic activity appears to have been declining rather than increasing over time. Total employment in the 500 largest US companies fell from more than 14 million in 1984 to 12 million in 1994, during which time employment in business services doubled to over 6 million.[4] Figures for the UK reveal a similar picture. While between 1935 and the 1970s the share of the 100 largest UK firms in total manufacturing output rose from 24 to 41 per cent, the concentration ratio declined significantly in the 1980s, especially if allowance is made for the increased exposure of the UK market to foreign trade.[5] This is reflected in the increase in the proportion of UK manufacturing employees at work in plants with fewer than 200 employees from 27 per cent to 39 per cent between 1976 and 1987. US Bureau of the Census figures show that the share of small firms in total manufacturing employment rose from 24 per cent in 1972 to 38 per cent in 1991.[6]

---

[4] 'Outsourced and out of luck', *Business Week* (17 July 1995).

[5] Roger Clarke, 'Trends in concentration in UK manufacturing 1980–89', in M. Casson and J. Creedy (eds), *Industrial Concentration and Economic Inequality* (Aldershot: Edward Elgar, 1993); S.J. Prais, *The Evolution of the Giant Firm in Great Britain* (Cambridge: Cambridge University Press, 1976).

[6] William J. Dennis Jr, Bruce D. Phillips and Edward Starr, 'Small business job creation: the findings and their critics', *Business Economics* (July 1994), p. 25.

That concentration ratios, measured in terms of numbers employed, sales or capital assets, appear to be on a downward trend is an important finding. It contradicts the Marxian prediction that big business, driven by the interaction of economies of scale and the single-minded pursuit of profit, would eventually dominate the industrial economies. In this view, larger firms, with low unit costs, would have been expected to put smaller firms out of business. 'One capitalist always kills many' (Karl Marx, *Capital*, vol. 1, p. 36) – the prediction being that economic power would become steadily more concentrated. This has not happened, notwithstanding popular concern about the sheer size and power of the new global corporations.

Monopoly power and the relative growth of big business has been restrained by six factors (see Box 6.2). First, in the previous chapter we referred to the role of technology in facilitating small businesses. Second, this effect is strengthened by the growing demand for customised goods. Third, the shift in demand in industrial countries towards services may also be a significant factor. Concentration is considerably lower in services than in manufacturing. For instance, establishments with fewer than 100 employees account for 64 per cent of non-manufacturing employment, but only 28 per cent of manufacturing employment. Fourth, deregulation has exposed many formerly closed sectors to competition. Fifth, the globalisation of trade and investment has impacted very strongly on the market power of domestic firms. Sixth, and finally, anti-trust and merger legislation has made monopoly power more difficult and costly to maintain (see Chapter 7).

These trends are consistent with the empirical finding that bigger size does not always imply better profitability. The performance of industrial conglomerates in profit terms has been very mixed. Mergers have had modest long-run effects, suggesting that efficiency gains from mergers are small. Periods of merger frenzy tend to be succeeded by downsizing and a reversion to smaller-scale and more focused activity. Successful conglomerates do exist but they are the exception rather than the rule. Perhaps the only consistent beneficiary of all the takeover activity has been the deal-maker. Size alone, even within a single industry, is neither a necessary nor a sufficient condition for sustained competitive advantage.

Contrasting with the performance of large firms, SMEs have been a major source of job creation and entrepreneurial innovation. The Birch Report found that two-thirds of the increase in US employment between 1969 and 1976 was in

---

**Box 6.2**    **Six factors tending to intensify competition**

1. Technology factors favourable to small firms

2. More demand for customised goods

3. Shift to service industries

4. Deregulation

5. Globalisation of trade and foreign investment

6. Anti-trust and competition policy and merger restrictions

enterprises with fewer than 20 workers.[7] This finding has attracted intense scrutiny. Subsequent studies whittled down the contribution of small enterprises to one-third rather than two-thirds of the increase in employment in later periods. Nevertheless, these statistics continue to confirm the important role played by small business in new job generation.[8]

In the EU, micro and small enterprises have generally proved more dynamic in creating job opportunities than larger firms. The superior performance of SMEs has been attributed to active labour market measures and tax concessions, in addition to the long-term forces referred to above.[9] Growth rates of employment for SMEs exceeded those of larger firms through the period 1988 to 2001 (Table 6.4). This dynamism derives from the flexibility of production methods and labour deployment in these enterprises. To assist their continued growth, the European Commission (1) supports cooperation between firms, (2) provides financial facilities for SMEs, and (3) subsidises measures to improve management quality.

This positive assessment of the dynamism of small business is subject to one major qualification: small firms generate new jobs at a faster rate than big firms, *but they also have a high mortality rate*. A study of small firms in the German economy, for example, showed that only about 40 per cent of establishments in each cohort were still operating eight or nine years after start-up.[10] Again, this conclusion is quite general: there is an exceptional amount of 'churning' in the employment record of small firms.

The era of the mega-plant employing thousands of workers seems to have ended some time in the 1970s. Nowadays, the typical large firm is no longer associated with giant manufacturing plants, but rather with a multitude of decentralised, moderate-sized and specialised manufacturing and distribution units

---

**Table 6.4 Growth of employment, output and productivity in European enterprises, 1988–2001**

| | *Average % growth p.a.* | |
| --- | --- | --- |
| | *SMEs* | *LSEs* |
| Employment | 0.3 | −0.1 |
| Real value added | 2.1 | 2.6 |
| Labour productivity | 1.7 | 2.8 |

*Source*: 'SMEs in Europe, including a first glance at EU candidate countries', *Observatory of European SMEs* (http://europa.eu.int/comm/enterprise).

---

[7] D.L. Birch, *The Job Generation Process* (Cambridge, MA: MIT Program on Neighborhood and Regional Change, 1979). See also D. Storey, *Understanding the Small Business Sector* (London: Routledge, 1994).

[8] For a critical view of Birch's and subsequent authors' estimates, see Steven J. Davis, John Haltiwanger and Scott Schuh, 'Small business and job creation: dissecting the myth and reassessing the facts', *Business Economics* (July 1994).

[9] European Network for SME Research, *The European Observatory for SME Research Second Annual Report* (Brussels, 1994), p. 13.

[10] T. Boeri and U. Cramer, 'Employment growth, incumbents and entrants', *International Journal of Industrial Organisation*, 10 (1992), pp. 545–65.

managed from a small and equally specialised head office. And side by side with that large firm, a surprisingly large number of independent small firms compete and coexist.

## 6.2 The economics of market power

### The theory of monopoly

All firms seek to obtain, consolidate and expand market power. Many firms have some degree of market power but, in the majority of cases, it is not sufficient to cause significant deviations from a competitive market outcome. Other firms occupy strong monopoly positions. Firms in this category account for a significant, if not strictly determinable, proportion of total marketed activity. To understand the market system in its entirety, therefore, we need to know how the system functions when individual firms possess significant market power. Specifically, we need to know (1) the consequences of this power for the firm's price and output decisions, (2) how market power is attained and sustained, (3) the systemic implications of market power, and (4) how policy-makers should respond to it. We discuss the first two issues in this chapter and the others in Chapter 7.

The consequences of market power can be explained with the analysis of the firm described in Chapter 5. For simplicity, we take the extreme case of a single-product monopoly. We assume its costs are U-shaped (Figure 6.1). Demand conditions are represented by the demand curve DD, from which the marginal revenue curve MR can be derived. Applying the profit-maximisation rule MR = MC gives the equilibrium output of $OQ_m$. The market-clearing price for that output is $OP_m$.

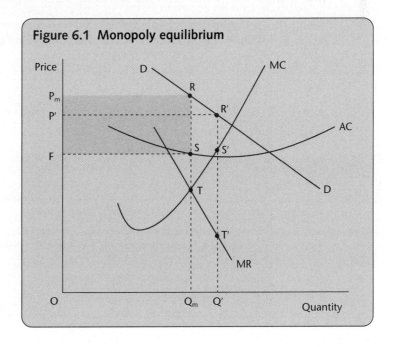

**Figure 6.1 Monopoly equilibrium**

The average cost at that output level is $SQ_m$. Monopoly profits are then the average profit margin RS multiplied by output $OQ_m$. They are represented by the area of the rectangle $P_mRSF$.

Market power means that an individual firm's output affects price. Thus, suppose production were raised above $OQ_m$ to $OQ'$. Price would have to fall to $OP'$. Corresponding to that price and output, we have $MC = Q'S'$ and $MR = Q'T'$. Note that $MR < MC$. This implies that the net increase in revenue obtained by raising output by $Q_mQ'$ is less than the cost of producing that extra output. Hence total profits must be lower at output $OQ'$ than at $OQ_m$. The profit-maximising monopolist, therefore, will cut back sales to $OQ_m$. The profit-maximising rule prevents the firm from selling either more or less than $OQ_m$. This is why $Q_m$ and $P_m$ are monopoly equilibrium price and quantity.

The economic consequences of the monopoly are estimated by reference to the benchmark case of competition (Figure 6.2). We start off from the monopoly equilibrium. Only this time, for convenience of exposition, constant costs over the relevant output span are assumed (i.e. $AC = MC$). (We can imagine the monopolist as a multi-plant firm, able to increase output by adding to the number of plants without affecting unit costs.) The monopoly sells $OQ_m$ at price $OP_m$. Now assume that competition is introduced into the industry. Each plant is taken over by an independent owner. The plants are numerous, so each single owner can have no influence on price. Hence, $MR = P$ for each individual firm. The profit-maximising rule leads each firm to produce up to the point where $P = MR = MC$. In Figure 6.2, this corresponds to point S, with output $OQ_c$ (higher than monopoly output) and price $OP_c$ (lower than monopoly price). The welfare loss of monopoly is the triangular area RTS. Intuitively, this represents the total utility derived from the addition of $Q_mQ_c$ to extra output, measured by $Q_mRSQ_c$ *less* the actual resource cost of producing it represented by the area under the MC curve, $Q_mTSQ_c$. The creation of this so-called 'dead-weight' loss of monopoly (the triangle RST) constitutes the standard 'static' argument against monopoly.

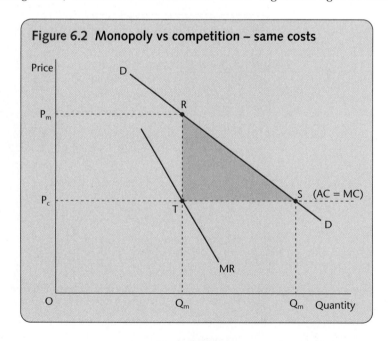

Figure 6.2 **Monopoly vs competition – same costs**

*It captures what most people believe is wrong about monopoly: price is higher and output lower than would be the case if competition were introduced.*

One core issue has been left offstage. Figure 6.2 assumes that costs are the *same* under both market structures. But if, as seems likely, cost levels *differ* between the two situations, the net welfare effects will have to be revised accordingly. Suppose, for example, that monopoly leads to 'managerial slack', defined as a lackadaisical attitude to costs and innovation. The cost curve in conditions of monopoly would then lie *above* the cost function for competition (Figure 6.3). The change from monopoly to competition would in these circumstances yield not only the welfare triangle RTS, but also a significant cost-saving *rectangle*, ASVB, plus an extra small triangle SVZ. These combined elements can amount to a significant efficiency gain. Competition among firms is one of the most powerful forces stimulating innovation and investment in technology in modern industries.[11]

The economic losses of monopoly have to be analysed on an empirical case-by-case basis, as is done every day by law courts and by competition authorities. The weight of evidence is that monopoly frequently involves *higher* costs than the welfare triangle because costs under monopoly are higher than under competition. This is particularly likely in state-owned monopolies or in companies that are insulated from the threat of takeover, since elsewhere the desire to avoid attracting predators will force the monopolist to be as cost-efficient and profitable as possible.[12]

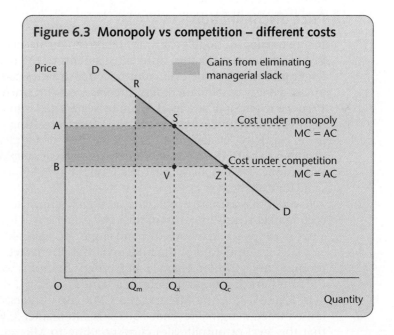

**Figure 6.3 Monopoly vs competition – different costs**

---

[11] Michael Porter, *The Competitive Advantage of Nations* (London: Macmillan, 1990), p. 636. If, however, scope for exploiting economies of scale and innovation capacity is greater under monopoly than under competition, these dynamic gains would also have to be included in the cost–benefit analysis of monopoly. We shall discuss these further in Chapter 7.

[12] A potential disciplining mechanism on a monopoly firm in the private sector is the fear of takeover. Any sign of management taking life too easy will attract the corporate raider. A monopolist does not always enjoy a quiet life.

So far, the economics of monopoly have been analysed in terms of its *efficiency* effects. The effects on *income distribution* must also be taken into account. Clearly, the *owners* of the firm benefit; indeed, the analysis of Figure 6.2 suggests that they obtain all of the monopoly's profits. In reality, monopoly profits, or 'rents', tend to be distributed more widely than that. For example, *employees* gain a share of the benefits in the form of better working conditions and above-average remuneration.[13] Managers and staff, being under less pressure to perform and to keep up with best practice, can enjoy a utility-generating, easy-going lifestyle. The 'managerial slack' or 'X-inefficiency' thereby created absorbs considerable amounts of monopoly rents. Sometimes monopoly profits may not be that high because of wasteful use of raw materials and poor maintenance of machinery. A portion of the excess profits might also go to ensuring that the monopoly position of the firm is sustained. Strategic entry deterrence techniques involve some dissipation of the maximum attainable profits. Prices may be cut. Lobbying costs may be undertaken to keep regulators on side. Activities that serve no social function other than to acquire and protect rents or quasi-rents have been called *rent-seeking* or *directly unproductive profit-seeking (DUP) activities*. The costs of resources used and decisions distorted in this way are called *influence costs*. A private sector monopoly, however, must ensure an adequate return on influence costs. If the financial return does not justify the spending, profits will decline and the monopoly again leaves itself vulnerable to takeover.

## Price discrimination

A single-seller monopoly can profitably exploit its market power by practising *price discrimination*. That is, different segments of the market can be charged different prices; hence their different price-sensitivities can be exploited. Wherever price elasticity of demand differs, there is scope for price discrimination.

To see why, suppose a market can be segmented into two parts: one representing high-elasticity customers and the other consisting of customers with a low price elasticity of demand. The respective demand curves are $D_1$ and $D_2$ (Figure 6.4), with the corresponding marginal revenue (MR) curves $MR_1$ and $MR_2$. We assume, for simplicity, that the monopolist's MC curve is constant and the same for each market.

In order to maximise profits, the monopolist must set price such that its MR in each market equals its constant MC. The exercise will involve computing the MR curve corresponding to each demand curve. A combined MR curve can be derived as a lateral summation of the MR curve in each market. The combined marginal revenue curve, CMR in Figure 6.4(c), is derived in this way. When CMR cuts MC, the firm's maximum profit point is attained.

In Figure 6.4(c), the MC and the CMR curve intersect at E. Profits are maximised when marginal revenue equals OC. In market 2, we see from Figure 6.4(b) that the level of output/sales corresponding to $MR_2 = OC$ is $OQ_2$. At that sales level, a price of $OP_2$ can be charged. In market 1, marginal revenue of OC is

---

[13] This does not imply that competitive firms must necessarily be worse employers than monopoly firms. There are sound microeconomic efficiency arguments for being a 'good' employer. Competition gives firms an incentive to think more carefully about the optimum remuneration pattern for employees.

**Figure 6.4 Monopoly price discrimination**

(a)

(b)

(c)

earned on the $OQ_1$th unit of sales. The price obtainable in this price-sensitive market is only $OP_1$. The firm's profits are therefore maximised by selling:

- $OQ_1$ at price $OP_1$ in market 1,
- $OQ_2$ at price $OP_2$ in market 2.

Price discrimination is common practice wherever monopoly power exists. In Chapter 4 we introduced the theory of market segmentation and the pricing decision in the case of hotel rooms, football stadiums, theatres and suchlike. Utility companies, such as gas, electricity and telecoms, also resort to elaborate forms of price discrimination, and successful exporters are regularly accused of 'dumping' – i.e. selling cheaper in the (price-elastic) world market than in their (price-inelastic and protected) domestic market. But a price-discriminating firm must be careful that the markets are truly segmented, i.e. it must not be possible to arbitrage between them. Otherwise, an intermediary could make money by buying the good in market 1 at $OP_1$ and selling it into market 2 at $OP_2$. Assuming zero impediments between markets, this arbitrage would continue until the prices in each market were equalised. The presence of impediments, or transaction costs, gives scope for divergence in price between one market and another. A firm obviously has an incentive to spend resources on *creating* market segmentation, through advertising campaigns and improved quality. Cosmetic changes to the product may be made in order to avert accusations of exploitation or unfairness. This would mean that the MC differs in each market and allowance would have to be made for this in deciding the optimal sales level in each market. But the principles guiding the decision would remain unchanged – it boils down to ascertaining the level of MR through careful demand analysis, supplementing it with reliable cost information and applying the appropriately adjusted marginal cost = marginal revenue rules.

Price discrimination can also be incorporated into a monopolist's pricing strategy through charging two-part tariffs. Typical examples include telecom charges involving a fixed rental per quarter plus a price per call, or professional associations charging a membership fee allied to a concessionary members' fee for conferences, journal issues and other services. The net effect is that different users are charged different amounts for the same service. The practices of 'bundling' or 'full-line forcing', whereby a firm requires the customer to stock a range of its products or sells them on a 'bundled' as well as on a single-item basis, are other forms of price discrimination. These practices all presuppose the presence of some monopoly power.

Price discrimination is widely practised. This is because it can be important for the bottom line. Dolan and Simon observe that, for given cost structures, a 1 per cent boost in average price yields a net profit increase of 12 per cent to the average US corporation.[14] Readers can check this by taking 1 per cent of net sales of any company and adding it to net profit. At the same time, price discrimination can be hard to document. Fear of adverse consumer reaction and of attracting the attention of the competition authorities makes firms cautious about publishing details. They are more likely to try to explain price discrimination by claiming that the dearer product is of superior quality or that the costs of supply and distribution vary between markets, or by offering complicated pricing structures and elaborate bundling. Of course, if the products are not identical, prices could diverge without this constituting price discrimination in the economist's sense.

## Multi-product and multi-plant monopolists

Occasionally, some parts of a monopolist's product range are sold under highly competitive conditions, while other items are sold under monopoly conditions. In that event, the MR = MC rule continues to apply, with allowance being made for the different demand conditions in each market.

Take, for example, the pricing policy of a large supermarket. Part of its sales consist of products whose price is well known, such as milk, bread and hamburgers. These are called known-value items (KVIs). Also on the supermarket's shelves are many goods whose price is not familiar to the average customer (non-KVIs). Once inside the store, the customer is likely to purchase both types of good. In a one-stop shop, KVIs and non-KVIs are complements. The supermarket can be viewed as being able to exercise a certain degree of monopoly power (spatial monopoly) over its customers, *once they are inside the store*. In such circumstances, it can be shown that the supermarket's profit-maximising strategy might lead it to charge below-cost prices for the KVIs in order to attract customers and recoup these losses through sales of non-KVIs at monopoly prices (see Box 6.3).

A loss-leader price strategy can, therefore, be compatible with profit maximisation. In this instance, the important point is to ensure that the MR of KVIs is properly defined so as to include the revenue obtained from additional sales of non-KVIs to customers attracted to the supermarket as a result of the loss leaders.

A multi-plant monopolist, by contrast, faces a single MR, but a different MC schedule in each plant. The profit-maximising rule ordains that the cost of producing the last unit in each plant should be the same for all plants and equal to the common MR:

$$MR = MC_1 = MC_2 = MC_3 = \ldots = MC_n$$

where $n$ is the number of plants. Suppose this rule were breached. MR was £10; $MC_1$ was £8 and $MC_2$ was £12 in plants 1 and 2. By transferring production from plant 2 to plant 1, profits could be increased. Such allocation will continue until

---

[14] R.J. Dolan and H. Simon, *Power Pricing: How managing price transforms the bottom line* (New York: Free Press, 1996), p. 4.

## Box 6.3   When competition induces pricing below cost

Loss-leading is a pricing strategy which is widely used in multi-product retailing. It involves the sale of a subset of 'traffic building' items at below-cost prices. This appears to contradict the rule of profit maximisation. Another interpretation is that it is an outcome of anti-competitive behaviour, i.e. large firms price below cost in order to drive the weak out of business. However, closer analysis shows that it is perfectly consistent both with profit maximisation and with competition in the market. The critical issue in selecting the optimal price of a retail product is the correct definition of marginal revenue. In multi-product retailing the marginal revenue of any one product must incorporate the spillover effects arising from the pricing of other products in the store. These effects include the mark-up earned on goods purchased by customers attracted to the store by loss leaders.

Loss-leading is an inherent feature of supermarket retailing. The distinguishing feature of the retail market is the vast range of product categories and different brands offered to the consumer. The average American supermarket of 40,000 square feet typically carries between 20,000 and 30,000 different products ('Survey of retailing', *The Economist*, 4 March 1995). Consumers will only have prior knowledge of prices in a subset of known-value items (KVIs) that are characterised by frequently purchased standardised staple products such as bread and milk. The prices of all other products, non-KVIs, will be unknown to the customer prior to entering the store.

Consumers are rational and enter stores that are deemed to offer lower retail prices. Given the costs and disutility associated with acquiring price information, customers' entry decision will be based upon their *perceived* value for money from shopping in a particular store, as indicated by KVI prices. Retailers will therefore compete for market share on the basis of KVI prices. The information costs that are associated with finding out the relative price of non-KVIs in different stores generate switching costs for consumers. Once consumers have entered the store, therefore, switching costs result in spatial market power that allows the retailer to extract price–cost mark-ups on non-KVIs.

Thus retailers sell certain 'traffic building' KVI items below cost in an endeavour to attract consumers into the store, and to charge higher prices on other (non-KVI) goods.

**Box 6.3 continued**

The optimal KVI pricing strategy for the multi-product retailer under conditions of imperfect information is illustrated in the figure.

In the absence of interdependent demands, aggressive price competition between stores for market share results in continual price undercutting on KVIs that ensures pricing at marginal cost and zero economic profit at $q_0$. However, optimal pricing of KVIs must take into account the demand interdependency between KVIs and non-KVIs. For complementary products this has a positive impact on revenue. The greater the market share attracted by KVI pricing, the greater the sales of non-KVIs with high price–cost mark-ups due to retailer market power once the customer has entered the store.

The marginal revenue curve must be amended to incorporate this additional net revenue impact from non-KVI products, and hence the corrected marginal revenue curve CMR will lie above the original MR. The effective marginal revenue resulting from selling $q_0$ KVIs thus exceeds marginal cost by $(p' - p_0)$, and the retailer earns profits $(p'abp_0)$. Given these profits, the retailer has an incentive to undercut its rivals' prices by reducing the price of KVIs slightly below $p_0$ in an endeavour to increase market share. All retailers face the same incentive. Once again intensive price competition between stores for market share results in continual price undercutting on KVIs by all retailers until this is no longer profitable. The additional profits generated by the complementary sale of non-KVIs are fully dissipated by price cuts on KVIs. These are priced below cost ($p^*$ is below MC) to protect market share. In equilibrium, the resultant loss on KVIs ($p_0 bcp^*$) will just equal the profit ($p'abp_0$) earned on non-KVIs. Competition over the consumer base ensures that overall profits remain at zero and output at $q_0$. We make the realistic assumption, in other words, that the market price elasticity of demand for KVIs is close to zero, while being very high for any individual retailer.

The extent of below-cost selling depends upon the spillover effect that the pricing of KVIs has on non-KVI products. This will be contingent upon the cross-price elasticity of demand and share of expenditure on non-KVIs relative to KVIs. Higher cross-price elasticity values will result in a greater impact on sales volume for non-KVI complements and hence on effective incoming revenue. This positive effect is enhanced for high prices of non-KVIs, where a larger unit increase in revenue is obtained for a given rise in sales volume. The scope for below-cost selling is therefore apparent. The benefits of one-stop shopping and the costs associated with shopping around result in a high cross-price elasticity between KVIs and non-KVIs. In addition the extensive range of products carried by retailers and the limited capacity of consumers to remember all of these prices imply that the proportion of non-KVIs to KVIs is large, while the ability of retailers to exercise some degree of market power over non-KVIs once customers have entered suggests that the mark-up on non-KVIs exceeds that on KVIs.

Overall, competition for consumers will reduce margins on KVIs to the lowest possible value so that the sum of margins over all products will just cover costs and retailer profits will be zero. Below-cost selling on certain known-value items is an outcome of competition under conditions of imperfect consumer information, interdependent demands, and intensive price competition over the consumer base.

*Source*: Dr Ciara Whelan; P.P. Walsh and C. Whelan, 'Loss-leading and price intervention in multi-product retailing: welfare outcomes in a second best world', *International Review of Law and Economics*, 19(3), 1999; B. Ortega, *In Sam We Trust: The untold story of Sam Walton and how Wal-Mart is devouring the world* (London: Kogan Page, 1999).

the MCs are equalised. This rule can have important practical application when allocating quotas between different participants in a cartel (see Case Study 6.1).

## 6.3 How to sustain monopoly power

Monopoly power can be achieved in a number of ways:

- *Economies of scale*, if sustained over a sufficiently large range of output, give big firms a cost advantage over smaller competitors. Eventually, this could result in just one firm serving the market (single-firm monopoly). More usual is the situation where a few firms dominate the industry.
- *Government policies* such as provision of a patent, nationalisation or regulation, create monopoly situations. For example, until recent times, private buses were prevented from competing with the state-owned bus monopoly in many European cities.
- *Ownership of know-how* can confer market power even in the absence of specific legislation and economies of scale. This know-how could embody organisational, marketing or financial procedures, as well as technological leadership.
- *Ownership of natural resources* – such as oil, diamonds, uranium, etc., where the number of producers is limited by physical constraints.

Monopoly profits act as a beacon to potential entrants to the industry. If they succeed in gaining entry to the industry, monopoly profits will be competed away. Strategic management textbooks advise firms on how to protect and insulate themselves from potential entrants. Hence a paradox of the market system: *profit maximisation drives firms to seek to acquire monopoly power; at the same time this self-same drive for profits attracts new entrants and makes monopoly power hard to sustain.*

The way in which market power can be sustained, once it has been acquired, needs careful attention. Many firms fail to sustain market power. In Britain, GKN, Courtaulds and British Leyland, and in Germany, AEG and Mannesman, are examples of once great companies which survive in much diminished shape or have fallen by the wayside. Sustaining market power involves three primary elements:

- *Architecture*. The network of relational contracts written by or around the firm. Companies such as IBM and Marks & Spencer exemplify strong architecture in that they have established a *structure*, a *style*, a *set of routines*, which motivate employees and suppliers. These routines resulted in exceptional corporate results over many years and through many changes in the economic environment.
- *Reputation*. Relevant in markets where quality is important, but verifiable only through long-term experience. Examples include car hire, accountancy services and international hotel chains. In these markets, reputations are costly and difficult to create but, once established, can generate substantial market power. Reputation is bolstered by advertising and development of brand names.
- *Innovation*. Development of product differentiation and patents, as already noted, are a source of market power, but many types of innovation are not protected by patent. The key issue is how to protect a specific innovation in a world where innovations – from software to personal stereos to cream liqueurs

– are difficult and expensive to protect through legal measures. The most powerful means of protection usually is to combine innovation with architecture and reputation, much as, say, Microsoft combines its constant innovation with sedulously created marketing and distribution.

Architecture, reputation and innovation together give a firm what Professor John Kay has termed *distinctive capability*, which in the long term sustains its monopoly power.

Market power can also be preserved by *strategic entry-deterrent measures* such as (1) setting price deliberately below the profit-maximising level in order to reduce the attractiveness of the industry to outsiders (limit-pricing), (2) concealing profit figures for monopolised parts of its business – a common practice in the case of subsidiary operations of large companies, (3) below-cost selling, predatory pricing and dumping, and (4) deliberate over-investment in capacity and extension of product range.

To sum up, what matters in terms of exercising market power is the firm's ability to earn above-average profits while keeping potential new entrants out of the industry. If entry is not too costly and cannot be deterred, even a 100 per cent market share may leave the incumbent firm with little market power. A high firm concentration ratio will signal market power only if it is accompanied by a low degree of *contestability*.

## 6.4 Market power with few firms – the case of oligopoly

The case of monopoly, in which just one seller dominates the entire market, is useful for illustrative purposes. However, in reality single-seller monopolies are the exception. More common is the case of markets dominated by a few large firms. Economists call this oligopoly. Oligopoly and monopoly are close cousins from an economic viewpoint. For example, a firm needs to supply only one quarter of the total market in order to be characterised by the UK's Office of Fair Trading as possessing a 'monopoly position'.

Oligopolies come in many guises. There are different ways in which market power can be exercised when interdependence between the small number of firms prevails in the market. Firms might try to form a *cartel*, whereby price, market share and investment decisions are made collectively, with the objective of maximising profits. At the international level, the best-known cartels include OPEC (once a dominant force in the oil industry, but now greatly weakened) and the De Beers diamond 'monopoly'. Within the EU, cartels have been found in a diverse range of industries: cases involving dyestuffs, quinine, vitamins and cement have come to attention in recent years.

Suppose there are two producers, firm 1 and firm 2. They form a cartel in order to avoid competing away their profits. Total profits are maximised when MR = MC for the industry as a whole. This is the level of profits the profit-maximising cartel will seek to earn. To determine the marginal cost curve for the industry, each firm's MC curve is laterally summated by finding out how much output can be produced in each firm at each MC level. The MR curve is derived from the industry demand curve, estimated by the techniques described in

Figure 6.5 How a cartel determines profit-maximising output

Chapter 4. The profit-maximising output for the two-firm cartel in Figure 6.5 is OQ and price OP. Total industry profits are represented by the area PRSF.

The cartel then has the task of determining production quotas for each firm (market-sharing). This is not an easy task. One possibility would be to order each firm to sell at OP and to allocate a quota of $OQ_1$ to firm 1 and $OQ_2$ to firm 2. Because of firm 1's lower cost structure, however, it earns more profits than firm 2. Some haggling might take place as to the share-out. Each participant has a selfish interest in the other participant being reasonably satisfied with the outcome, but the unbalanced nature of the distribution in Figure 6.5 may lead to tension. If this imbalance is not corrected, firm 2 will be tempted to 'cheat', i.e. to sell a few extra units at OP, in order to obtain a larger share of the cartel's profits. This will be a profitable exercise for firm 2 if undetected, since MC is well below OP at its assigned production level $OQ_2$. Of course, if everyone cheats, the cartel's effectiveness is undermined. Hence a mechanism for detecting and limiting cheating is an essential requirement for a cartel. Many cartels have self-destructed because of their inability to implement such a mechanism. (We explain in Case Study 6.1 how the troubled but still surviving De Beers diamond cartel has coped with this problem.)

In some instances, rather than form a cartel, oligopolists may decide to allow a dominant firm to assume a leadership role. If the leader raises price, the others follow, and vice versa in the event of a fall in price. The *price leader* then decides on the price that maximises its profits, on the assumption that all other producers will sell as much as they find profitable at the price chosen by the leader. The net result is a higher price and more profits for all in the industry. It is not as advantageous for the producers as a cartel, but it is less transparent and, therefore, less likely to encounter legal problems. Too blatant price leadership behaviour can, of course, attract attention. In the US, the Department of Justice has taken exception to 'conscious parallelism' of price decisions, even in the absence of overt collusion – and hence can object to the leader advertising price changes.[15] A well-publicised example of price leadership is the case of ICI and British Salt. The two firms accounted for a 45 per cent and 50 per cent share, respectively, of the UK market. In its 1986 *Report on the UK Salt Market*, the Monopolies and Mergers Commission criticised British Salt for having chosen to 'follow' the price

[15] H. Michael Hayes *et al.*, *Business Marketing: A global perspective* (Chicago: Irwin, 1997), p. 297.

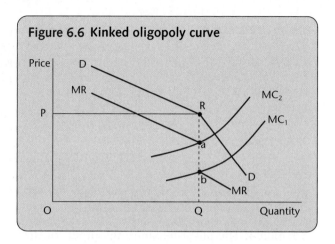

Figure 6.6 Kinked oligopoly curve

increase of ICI. The Commission recommended that the price of salt should be controlled through the use of an index, based on the costs of the more efficient producer, British Salt.[16]

A variant of the price leadership model is the kinked oligopoly model. According to this model, if, at a given ruling price OP, an oligopolist reduces price, the fall in the price will be followed by its competitors, but if it increases price, competitors will not follow. They will prefer to see their market share increase at the expense of the firm which raised price. Hence the demand curve is relatively flat above price OP (Figure 6.6) and relatively steep below OP. The *kinked oligopoly curve* model explores the consequences of this rigidity. One consequence is that, at the ruling price, there will be a break in the MR curve. At this point, an upward shift in the MC curve from $MC_1$ to $MC_2$ may not be passed on to price. An aggressive trade union, therefore, could demand a rise in remuneration without any repercussions on output or price. The theory tells us nothing about how the going price itself is determined, only that once set it will tend to be stable. Firms in the industry will be slow to pass on increases in costs of production to the consumer. Price changes in such circumstances are likely to occur in discrete jumps and to be accompanied by uncertainty and even 'price wars' before a new 'going' price becomes accepted.

Price competition is often shunned by oligopolists. Because of a fear of the unpredictable consequences of price changes and the danger of sparking off a series of disequilibrating 'follower' price-cuts, the ambitious firm may prefer to engage in less quantifiable, less transparent and consequently less easily followed forms of *non-price competition*: advertising, provision of better quality service and marketing strategies designed to create customer loyalty and tie in more customers.

The analysis of interdependence can be extended well beyond the standard cases of cartel, price leadership and kinked oligopoly demand curves. The implications of strategic interdependence in markets with few producers have been extensively explored in game theory. Game theory analysis develops the idea

---

[16] J. Sutton, *Sunk Costs and Market Structure* (Cambridge, MA: MIT Press, 1991), p. 195. The salt market is dominated by two firms in the UK (a *duopoly* case) and, in the US, the four-firm concentration ratio approximates 100 per cent.

that, if interdependence exists, firms' decisions on production and pricing will be affected by what they believe their competitors will do in response.

A standard example starts with a two-firm industry. Each firm can choose a 'high' or a 'low' price (Box 6.4). If they both choose high prices, they make profits of $3 million each. With low prices, they make only $2 million each. But if one sets a high price and the other a low one, the low-price firm makes $4 million while the high-price firm gets only $1 million. Although the firms would do best if they both set high prices, they will not do so. If firm A sets a high price, firm B's best strategy is to undercut it. Firm B will then make $4 million, rather than $3 million. If firm A sets a low price, firm B's optimal strategy is to do the same. It will earn $2 million instead of $1 million. Thus, each firm will be driven to opt for a low price regardless of what the other firm chooses. They each choose the low price and make only $2 million each. This is called a *Nash equilibrium*. No firm wants to change strategy, given full knowledge of the other firm's strategies.[17]

---

**Box 6.4    Price strategies and profits**

In each box, firm A's profit is on the left and firm B's profit is on the right. Firm A's dominant strategy is low price and high output. (This is better for A whether B's price is high or low.) Likewise, firm B's dominant strategy is low price. Hence, low–low is Nash equilibrium. It is the strategy which is best for each firm when the other firm's strategy is taken as given. We assume a non-cooperative game. If the two firms cooperated, they could reach (3,3), a superior outcome for the firms, though not for the consumer.

A cooperative solution is possible provided there is:

1. pre-commitment, i.e. an agreement is made;
2. credible threat, i.e. the commitment will be *binding* and enforceable.

---

[17] This case is otherwise known as the prisoners' dilemma. Two prisoners having committed a crime are kept in separate cells. If they both keep silent, they will be acquitted – hence the importance of keeping them apart and ensuring that there is no collusion. If one confesses and the other keeps silent, all the blame falls on the latter, who gets a heavy sentence, while the prisoner who confesses receives a light sentence. Each prisoner is likely to conclude that to confess is the optimal strategy. This is the Nash equilibrium. Thus they both confess, they incriminate each other and get a moderate sentence each. The optimal position from their joint perspective is not chosen – much to the relief of the honest citizen, one may add! The more prisoners involved in the crime, the more likely they are to confess. From society's perspective, large numbers make for a superior outcome, though each prisoner acts solely out of self-interest. This echoes Adam Smith's analysis of the market system.

A key aspect of this situation is that firms cannot make *binding commitments* to collude. Even if they did make a commitment to charge the higher price, they would each have an incentive to cheat. And the commitment, since it involves collusion, could not be enforced in the courts. (On the contrary, if discovered, the parties to the agreement could end up in trouble since any such agreement might be deemed illegal.) Game theory has gone on to explore ways in which a more advantageous outcome from the firms' point of view could be achieved. If the game is repeated often, as happens usually in real life, each firm can find ways of testing each other's good faith. Firms might be able to keep profits up by setting high prices and building up a reputation for keeping them there, regardless of how other firms react (the price leadership model). Game theory has also been applied to monopoly theory to explain how the monopolist is likely to respond to new entrants and how it might plan to neutralise rivals. Although game theory addresses problems with which business can readily identify, it has been less successful at giving governments and firms practical advice. Game theory was given a signal boost by the award of a Nobel prize in 1995 to the three economists most closely associated with its development over the past 50 years: two Americans, John Nash and John Harsanyi, and a German, Reinhard Selten. Business too has become more aware of the usefulness of a game-theoretic approach in deciding whether to enter a market, or how to defend a market position. Game theory can also be useful in devising bid systems. The design of the multi-billion auctions of the radio spectrum for mobile phones in the UK in 2000 and in the US in 1994–95 was influenced by game theory, as was the mobile phone companies' participation in the auction. The application of auction theory to such practical transactions continues to the present day.

## 6.5 Conclusions

Market structures vary a great deal. They range from perfect competition at one extreme to a single-firm monopoly at the other. In between there is a continuum. At one end of the range there is monopolistic competition, where there are many firms, each with some small degree of product differentiation but with little ability to fix price, and relatively easy entry and exit. Small retail businesses, restaurants and small clothing firms have these characteristics, and are included in the 'effectively competitive' sectors. At the other end of the spectrum are cases of oligopoly, where a few firms exercise a dominant position in an industry and where the actions of each individual firm have a perceptible impact on market price.

It is easy to describe a market morphology in general terms. More problematic is the task of identifying the extent of market power exercised by individual firms in specific industries. We conclude that large sections of modern industrial economies can be described as 'effectively competitive' in the sense of being highly exposed to competitive pressure and with individual firms having limited market power. Moreover, the proportion of the economy falling into the effectively competitive category seems to be increasing. With increased prosperity there is a shift to the services sector, where the optimum scale is smaller than in industry. Technology also seems to be helping the survival and growth of many small firms. Also, as the world economy becomes more open, more firms are exposed to competition. For example, in the late 1950s the automobile industry counted four or five major world players. Today, about 20 automobile firms are capable of competing on a global scale, although at a national level there is continuing rationalisation of the industry. In the European market, the removal of trade barriers following the 1992 Single Market programme has led to a significant erosion of individual companies' market power. Another factor contributing to a higher incidence of competition is the break-up of large, state-owned companies as part of many countries' privatisation programmes and the deregulation of the telecoms, post, energy and transport industries. The growing customisation of the market also opens opportunities for an increased number of market participants. The top-selling auto model in the US market in the 1990s sold 400,000 units, compared with 1.5 million units in the late 1950s. Automobile manufacturers produce more models than previously and enjoy a smaller volume of sales of each model.[18]

Yet monopoly influence and market power are important realities in the business world. The flourishing amount of anti-trust and competition law cases testifies to that fact. Analysis of monopoly theory shows why there is a general presumption that monopoly will be inefficient relative to competition. Reference was made to both the static inefficiency losses and to the potentially more important, but difficult to measure, dynamic efficiency losses. Objections to monopoly are also frequently made on equity grounds. Establishing a sense of 'fairness' is essential to the proper operation of the market system. Consequently, the general presumption is that monopoly has detrimental effects on economic performance. But each case has to be judged on its merits. In some circumstances, scale economies and an innovation programme can best be developed within a monopoly market structure. In such cases, without monopoly there may be no market and hence it makes good economic sense to treat the monopoly as the lesser of two evils.

## Summary

1. Monopoly in various forms is a common feature of a modern economy. At least a quarter of economic activity in the EU and US is transacted in what can be described as predominantly non-competitive markets. The proportion of manufacturing that can be characterised in this way is higher than the economy average. However, in an economy, there is a continuum between perfect competition and the single monopolist at opposite ends of the spectrum. Neither model is completely 'realistic'. Which activities are grouped at each end of the spectrum has to be decided case by case.

2. Forces of competition have been kept strong by advances in technology and the growth of the services sector, which have been conducive to the development of small independent firms. Other factors underlying this trend are trade liberalisation, the deregulation and privatisation of the former state-owned monopolies and

---

[18] This does not *necessarily* prove that the market has become more competitive, since brand proliferation could reflect an entry-deterrent strategy on a non-competitive market. The above data are taken from Kim B. Clark and Takahiro Fujimoto, *Product Development Performance: Strategy, organisation and management in the world auto industry* (Boston, MA: Harvard Business School Press, 1991).

the demand for customised products. Competition policy has played a role (to be further discussed in Chapter 7).

3.  Monopoly involves the redistribution of income from the consumer to the monopolist. It can also lead to static and dynamic efficiency losses for the economy. It is a *negative-sum game*; the monopolist's gain is less than the economic losses of the rest of society.

4.  Monopoly profits attract would-be entrants. In order to survive, the monopolist must continually upgrade and maintain technological leadership. It must build up and sustain its competitive architecture.

5.  Oligopoly exists where an industry is dominated by a few firms which have to take account of interdependence between their decisions. Industrial organisation theorists have outlined many possible modes of strategic behaviour and interaction. The measurement of market power in such cases can be difficult, and instances of the abuse of such power hard to detect. Each case must be examined on its own merits.

6.  Economic analysis helps us to understand how monopolists and oligopolists will behave under different market conditions. Non-competitive behaviour is generally expected to lead to an inferior outcome relative to competition, although there are some exceptions. Sometimes economies of scale and scope require very large size relative to the extent of the market. Also, as the development of patent, copyright and trademark law testifies, innovation is often stimulated by non-competitive market structures.

## Questions for discussion

1.  Suppose a firm acquires a monopoly position in an industry by buying out all previous suppliers in the market.
    (a) Give three reasons why a Competition Authority might object.
    (b) What arguments may the firm use to justify the takeover?

2.  'The key to growth – even survival – is to stake out a market position that is less vulnerable to attack from opponents, whether established or new, and less vulnerable to erosion from substitutes and other competitors.' What methods can a firm use to establish such a position?

3.  'Collusion is difficult to achieve and even more difficult to maintain.' Explain these difficulties.

4.  Large firms usually account for a much greater share of a country's exports than of its domestic market. Can you suggest reasons why this should be so?

5.  (a) A monopolist sets a lower price in one market than in another for the same good. Is this consistent with profit maximisation?
    (b) You are now told that the lower price has been set below both average and marginal costs and that the firm is engaged in *predatory pricing*. Should the firm be prohibited from setting price this way? Could this price behaviour be consistent with profit maximisation?

6.  Discuss the main factors tending to intensify competition in the global economy. Are there any countervailing forces tending to undermine competition?

# Exercises

1. Consider an industry with which you are familiar. How would you assess the degree of competition in that market? Is the market becoming more or less open to competition? What are the consequences of this for economic efficiency?

2. The table shows a demand curve facing a monopolist who produces at a constant marginal cost of £5 per unit.

| Price (£) | 9 | 8 | 7 | 6 | 5 | 4 | 3 | 2 | 1 | 0 |
|-----------|---|---|---|---|---|---|---|---|---|---|
| Quantity  | 0 | 1 | 2 | 3 | 4 | 5 | 6 | 7 | 8 | 9 |

Calculate the monopolist's marginal revenue curve and its profit-maximising price and output. What would be the equilibrium output and price for a competitive industry with an identical cost structure (MC = £5 at all levels of output)? Explain why a monopolist produces a lower output and charges a higher price.

Suppose that, in addition to the constant marginal cost of £5, the monopolist has a fixed cost of £20. What difference would this make to the monopolist's output, price and profits?

3. Suppose there are 10 identical producers of spring water. The constant marginal cost of extraction of the water is £1 per litre. The maximum extraction rate for each firm is 10 litres per day. Suppose the market demand curve for this water is as follows:

| Price (£ per litre) | Litres per day demanded | Price (£ per litre) | Litres per day demanded |
|---------------------|-------------------------|---------------------|-------------------------|
| 11 | 0 | 5 | 6 |
| 10 | 1 | 4 | 7 |
| 9  | 2 | 3 | 8 |
| 8  | 3 | 2 | 9 |
| 7  | 4 | 1 | 10 |
| 6  | 5 |   |   |

(a) If the firms form a cartel, what will be the profit-maximising price and output for the industry, and for each firm?
(b) Suppose that one of the firms secretly breaks the rules of the cartel and reduces its price. What effect will this have on its profits?
(c) How might the remaining nine producers respond?
(d) If the cartel breaks up and firms compete against each other independently, what will be the equilibrium amount of water supplied and demanded, and what will be the price? How much will each firm produce?

4. An author receives a royalty equal to 10 per cent of the revenue obtained by the publisher from sales of a book. Use a straight-line demand curve to illustrate the point at which the author's royalties will be maximised. Show that the author's preferred price will always be lower than the price level which maximises the publisher's profits.

→

**5.** An industry has a demand curve as follows:

| Price (£) | 10 | 9 | 8 | 7 | 6 | 5 | 4 | 3 |
|-----------|----|----|----|----|----|----|----|----|
| Quantity | 1 | 2 | 3 | 4 | 5 | 6 | 7 | 8 |

(a) Suppose the industry is composed of a monopolist with a constant MC equal to £3. What price and output are chosen?

(b) Now suppose there are two firms, each with MC = AC = £3. What price and output will maximise profits if they collude?

(c) Why do the two firms have to agree on the output each will produce?

(d) Suppose a third firm entered the industry which could supply the industry at a constant MC of £4. How would that affect the monopolist/cartel's calculations?

## Further reading

There are numerous texts on the economics of industrial organisation. An overview of the basic models of monopoly and oligopoly, and the pricing behaviour of firms in different market structures, is provided in William Shepherd, *The Economics of Industrial Organisation: Analysis, markets, policies* (Hemel Hempstead: Prentice Hall International, 1997), and D. Hay and D. Morris, *Economics of Industrial Organisation* (London: Oxford University Press, 1993). An excellent discussion of how firms can best sustain their monopoly power is John Kay's *Foundations of Corporate Success: How business strategies add value* (Oxford: Oxford University Press, 1993). For a detailed discussion of the role of small firms, see contributions to the July 1994 issue of *Business Economics*. John Vickers provides a summary of advances in oligopoly and competition theory in 'Strategic competition among the few – some recent developments in the economics of industry', *Oxford Review of Economic Policy* (1985), reprinted in S. Estrin and A. Marin, *Essential Readings in Economics* (London: Macmillan, 1995). William Baumol urges anti-trust authorities to judge innovative oligopolists less harshly in his engaging book *The Free-Market Innovative Machine: Analysing the growth miracle of capitalism* (Princeton, NJ: Princeton University Press, 2002).

# The diamond cartel

'A diamond is forever' boasts the glamorous advertisement of De Beers. But diamonds are valued mainly because they are considered a sound investment, relatively immune from the vagaries of economic ups and downs. Diamonds are cheap to produce and would be lower in price but for the global cartel operated by De Beers. The cartel has protected its market monopoly by flattening out short-term fluctuations in supply, and to some extent demand, with the aid of a huge buffer-stock.

The diamond cartel was set up by Sir Ernest Oppenheimer, a South African mining magnate, in 1934. The cartel is the vehicle through which over 80 per cent of world rough sales are marketed and administered.

Unlike other commodity cartels, the diamond cartel both controls supply and influences demand, combining the roles of major distributor, marketing agency and buffer-stock manager. It has developed an expertise in matching supply to demand and the financial strength to hold diamonds temporarily off the market.

## Structure of the diamond market

Diamond mines are relatively few in number, are easily identified and cannot be increased at will. The major producers are South Africa, Botswana, Namibia, the former Soviet Union and Australia. Owing to the wide variation in diamond quality, a country's volume of output is not an accurate indicator of the value of its production. For example, Australia is the world's largest producer of diamonds in volume terms but, because of the low average price of its output, it ranks much lower in terms of value.

The industry's major producer is the De Beers corporation, which has direct and indirect interests in mines throughout the world, as well as in South Africa.

**The major diamond producers ranked by volume and value**

| | Per cent share of world production (volume) | Volume in 2000 | | Value in 2000 | |
|---|---|---|---|---|---|
| | | Carats (m) | Rank | US$m | Rank |
| Australia | 24 | 26 | 1 | 360 | 6 |
| Botswana | 23 | 25 | 2 | 2126 | 1 |
| Russia | 18 | 20 | 3 | 1595 | 2 |
| Congo | 15 | 17 | 4 | 585 | 5 |
| South Africa | 9 | 10 | 5 | 1110 | 3 |
| Angola | 4 | 4 | 6 | 740 | 4 |
| Others | 7 | 8 | – | 923 | – |
| Total | 100 | 110 | – | 7439 | – |

*Source*: www.worlddiamondcouncil.com and author's own estimates.

The structure of supply is quite complex. Each diamond has to be classified and valued individually, and different diamonds of the same price are not necessarily

151

tradeable substitutes. At the micro-level, the diamond market is not a single market, but embraces many sub-markets with different prices and distinctive supply and demand characteristics. Price differentials exist for different product grades in most commodity markets. The lack of homogeneity in diamonds is such that there is no single price which acts as a reliable benchmark for the market as a whole. The market is highly segmented and prices range from $1 to tens of thousands of dollars. This has important implications for their marketing by the cartel.

Good stones are relatively scarce – around 10 per cent of the market by volume accounts for 50 per cent of the market by value.

Industrial diamonds refer to stones that are too small or flawed and too opaque and imperfect to be saleable as polished stones. Historically, industrial diamonds have formed about 80 per cent by volume and 20 per cent by value of all diamonds found. This segment of the market is also served by synthetic diamonds. Natural industrial diamonds nowadays probably account for less than half of all diamonds sold by volume and for less than 5 per cent by value. De Beers and General Electric dominate the world market for industrial diamonds.

De Beers sorts diamonds into boxes and sells them to sightholders who represent the main cutters. These cutters and polishers of diamonds are spread around three main centres: Antwerp, Tel Aviv and Bombay. They sell the polished stones to polished diamond buyers who in turn supply the retail trade. China is a recent newcomer in this part of the business and could also be an important new source of demand.

**Producers**
Australia, Botswana, South Africa, Congo, Russia and others. Most rough diamonds are sold to De Beers under contract. De Beers also buys on the open market and sells output from its own mines
↓
**De Beers**
Sorts diamonds into boxes
Sells them at 'sights' to:
↓
**Sightholders**
Who represent the main cutters
↓
**Cutters and polishers**

Antwerp          Tel Aviv          Bombay
↓
**Polished diamond buyers**
↓
**Retail trade**

Certain key characteristics of the market make it susceptible to cartelisation. First, there are a small number of significant suppliers and rigorous physical barriers to entry. De Beers directly produces nearly half of the world's high-quality diamonds by value. Second, the product is durable, has a high value to volume ratio and is easy to store. Third, the demand for jewellery-quality gems, which make up 90 per cent of the $5 billion rough diamond market, is relatively price-inelastic. The rewards to a cartel from controlling supply are therefore likely to be considerable.

## How the system operates – control production, dominate the trade, influence demand

The Central Selling Organisation (CSO), based in Switzerland and London, is the collective name of companies controlled by De Beers and its associates. It buys rough diamonds from the mines, valuing them and selling them to sightholders. CSO sales peaked at $6.7 billion in 1997. By keeping rough prices at the highest sustainable level, the cartel aims to achieve long-run profit maximisation over the demand cycle rather than short-run market clearing at spot prices. The key characteristics of the cartel are:

1. The system of *producer quotas*. Most significant producers have a long-term and exclusive contract to supply a certain proportion of De Beers' annual diamond sales.
2. The cartel has created a strong antidote to any individual producer's *incentive to cheat*. De Beers backs up the carrot of higher prices with a powerful stick – its ability to release from its stocks a supply of any type of diamond. Every diamond mine has its own characteristic output. If De Beers chooses to release more stones of this characteristic from its stockpile, the stockpile-supported price can drop dramatically.
3. De Beers acts as a *swing producer*. In a buoyant market, De Beers benefits from both higher prices and stock appreciation as goods are sold from the buffer-stock. But in a depressed market, it absorbs excess supply and reduces its own production. It can play this role credibly since its mines are among the cheapest sources of fine diamonds in the world and because of the company's financial strength. De Beers holds stocks worth US$4 billion (which it would like to cut to $2.5 billion or less).
4. The cartel pays careful attention to *demand management*. It spends over $150 million a year on advertising. Rather than ride out cyclical fluctuations the company wants to drive incremental demand through targeted marketing campaigns.

## Threats to the system

Any interference with the market system runs the danger of encouraging unintended countervailing and competing reactions. An official price ceiling gives an incentive to sell diamonds outside the system (to 'cheat'); while minimum prices encourage over-supply. The diamond cartel is not exempt from these tendencies and its operations are under periodic threat.

1. Advertising can influence demand, but its effects can easily be overwhelmed by business cycles and by the ebb and flow of fashion. If De Beers expects a glut of a certain type of diamond, it will stop putting it in boxes, but months can pass before the effect of the move is felt in the market for polished stones.
2. De Beers' sway over customers for rough diamonds is not matched by its influence on customers for polished diamonds – jewellers and their suppliers. This makes it difficult for De Beers to control prices to the end-buyer.
3. New entrants add uncertainty to the diamond market. The new Ekati diamond mine in Canada accounts for 6 per cent of world supply. Political instability in

Africa and Russia can also create problems by magnifying the incentive to cheat and favouring short-term over long-term perspectives of national interest. This explains why De Beers has embarked on a marketing campaign to create a De Beers brand rather than to promote diamonds in general.

4. De Beers' main concern is the confidence of its members. If they sense that the cartel lacks the strength needed to fulfil its role as swing producer, cartel members will be tempted to sell their diamonds before others do the same. The main cement to this cartel, as to others, is the conviction that centralised selling and buffer-stock management are in its collective interest.

*Sources*: 'The cartel lives to face another threat', © *The Economist* (London, 10 January 1987); 'The diamond business: glass with attitude' and 'The diamond business: washed out in Africa', © *The Economist* (London, 20 December 1997 and 3 June 2000). I am grateful to Roderigo Carillo de Albornoz for assistance with this case study.

## Questions for discussion

1. Suppose you were asked to estimate a demand curve for diamonds, what variables would you include? In what respects would you expect the demand for a long-lasting good such as diamonds to be different from the demand for non-durables such as wine and food?

2. How would you draw up a supply curve for the diamond industry? What relevance would such information have for the cartel?

3. How might the cartel determine the profit-maximising price?

4. Who gains and who loses from the cartel? Is there an economic case for trying to break it up? If so, is there any way of doing it?

## Chapter 7

# Competition policy, privatisation and regulation

## Introduction

When competition prevails, firms have limited discretion over price. Profit maximisation leads them to equate marginal cost to marginal revenue and, because price is more or less 'given' in a competitive market, price equals marginal revenue. Also, competition forces firms to minimise costs and to search relentlessly for new and better ways of doing things. Competition encourages innovation. For these reasons, maintaining a market structure that is open to competition is of the utmost importance to an efficient economy.

Our first task in this chapter is to assess the case for competition and to define the characteristics of a market that encourages competition.

Our second task is to analyse competition policy. Competition policy refers to the rules governing the conduct of firms in a market. Without well-developed and effective competition rules, the market system will not function properly. Yet a competition regime has to balance the need for active competition on the domestic market with the equally pressing need to allow firms to attain a minimum efficient scale and be able to match international competition. On occasion, it may make sense to tolerate, even encourage, high concentration ratios in the domestic market. The extension of competition policy to deal with state aids to industry, and particularly support for state-owned enterprises, is also examined. We illustrate these issues with examples from the competition policy of the EU.

Third, the move to privatisation is analysed. Starting in the 1980s in the UK and New Zealand, privatisation programmes have been implemented throughout the world economy. 'New consensus' thinking goes far to explaining the rapid spread of these privatisation programmes. They have been motivated by the desire to introduce competition where it was absent as well as assisting governments to improve their financial situation.

The degree of popular enthusiasm for competition has waxed and waned. Proponents of competitive market structures are now in the ascendant. In order to understand why, we must understand the origin of this pro-competitive viewpoint. It is not necessarily pro-business, though it has coincided with a strongly pro-business trend in other areas of economic policy. Most businesses feel under threat from competition. They are more likely to believe that their problems derive from excess competition rather than an insufficiency of competition. They argue for space and time to adjust to the pace of technological advance and to build up competitive advantage. Getting the balance right between sectoral strength and optimal competitive pressure is vitally important for economic performance.

## Chapter outline

1. The case for competition.
2. The main features of competition policy.
3. Privatisation programmes, their rationale and effectiveness.
4. Regulation.
5. Conclusions.

## 7.1 The case for competition

Competition policy is based on a belief in the *economic* benefits of competition. The starting assumption is that market forces are the most effective means of ensuring efficiency in the allocation of resources, of adapting to change and, ultimately, of maximising consumer welfare. A much-quoted passage from the European Commission's first report on competition policy (1972) reflects this basic philosophy:

> Competition is the best stimulant of economic activity since it guarantees the widest possible freedom of action to all. An active competition policy ... makes it easier for the demand and supply structures continually to adjust to technological development. Through the interplay of decentralised decision-making machinery, competition enables enterprises continually to improve their efficiency, which is the *sine qua non* for a steady improvement in living standards and employment prospects within the countries of the Community. From this point of view, competition policy is an essential means for satisfying to a great extent the individual and collective needs of our society.[1]

Competition has several major advantages over monopoly (see Box 7.1). First, it provides static benefits through elimination of deadweight losses illustrated in Figure 6.2. This figure shows how competition can lead to more output at a lower price – and it accords with the practical experience of falling prices and higher sales volumes that followed the introduction of competition to formerly monopolised industries ranging from air transport to telecoms. Estimates of the importance of this static effect vary widely, but some have reached as high as 1 per cent of GDP.[2] Second, competition brings *dynamic* benefits:

---

[1] European Commission, First Report on Competition Policy (Brussels, 1972).

[2] R.A. Posner, 'The social costs of monopoly and regulation', *Journal of Political Economy*, (83)4 (1975), found large costs, most of them attributable to government-created restrictions in competition as it happens, and even larger losses have been estimated by subsequent studies.

---

> ### Box 7.1   The economic case for competition
>
> - **Static benefits:**
>   - More output at lower price (eliminates deadweight loss).
> - **Dynamic benefits:**
>   - Makes firms more *cost efficient*.
>   - Allows more-efficient firms to expand and inefficient firms to exit (*selection process*).
>   - Stimulates innovation.
> - **Equity:**
>   - Small competitors, suppliers of inputs and consumers protected from abuse of monopoly power.

- It makes organisations internally more efficient by sharpening incentives to avoid slackness.
- It allows the more efficient organisations to prosper at the expense of the inefficient (the selection process).
- It improves dynamic efficiency by stimulating innovation.

The above arguments emphasise *efficiency*. *Equity* is another important consideration in competition policy. Governments enforce competition policy in order to protect weaker companies against the abuse by monopolies of their dominant market position. Support for the free market presupposes 'fair' trading rules and a level playing field. Defining 'fairness' is not, of course, always easy. Moreover, the dictates of fairness, efficiency and competition sometimes pull in different directions. Efficiency may require a more concentrated industrial structure than a government concerned with equity might want to tolerate. Somehow, consistent rules must be formulated which encourage competition and allow business a reasonable degree of certainty, but have enough flexibility to deal with cases where market power may be necessary on technical grounds.

Market structure is defined in terms of a set of market attributes:

- numbers and size distribution of sellers and buyers,
- characteristics of the product and degree of market segmentation,
- barriers to entry into the industry,
- barriers to exit from the industry.

The textbook definition of a competitive market is one where there are large numbers of firms selling a homogeneous output in an industry with no entry or exit barriers. At the other end of the spectrum is monopoly. In between, there is a large array of complex market structures. These are defined by reference to the industry's concentration ratios and the characteristics of the product, the latter being measured in terms of degree of differentiation, price elasticity of demand, and sensitivity to business cycles. Account must also be taken of the degree of vertical and horizontal integration within the industry (i.e. the extent to which firms own or control 'downstream' intermediate goods industries or related, horizontal products and services), and ease and expense of entry and exit.

Two points must be made about this market structure approach. First, a business reader will appreciate the contrast between the economic approach to markets and the approach taken by strategic management theory. The latter urges management not to take market structure as 'given', as part of an unchangeable 'external' environment. Rather, corporate strategy analyses how corporate conduct can be framed so as to bring about *changes* in that environment. It shows how management can restructure the market in a partisan fashion and establish a monopoly niche. There is clearly a two-way process at work. More generally, business decisions about pricing and other matters are often determined less by the present market structure than by the structure the firm is seeking to establish in the future.

Second, the link between market structure and a firm's conduct and performance can be more complex than the simple model suggests. Firms may be few in number and yet competition and rivalry can be intense. As we have seen (Box 6.1), the software market is dominated by Microsoft, but small firms continue to chip away at the leader's sales. This rivalry could be all that is required for efficiency. Hence, Schumpeter's famous assertion that 'the textbook case of perfect competition has no title to be set up as the ideal model of efficiency'.[3]

Also, whereas the standard approach emphasises the efficient allocation of a *given* set of resources, Schumpeter stressed the importance of innovation as a vital generator of the *growth* of resources. Successful firms are typically characterised by a capacity to engage in research, to innovate, to hire entrepreneurial managers and to enjoy sufficient profit margins to finance such overheads. These firms are often large corporations enjoying large market shares. Unlike the stereotypical monopoly, however, this market share does not necessarily insulate them from competition. Pressure on the Schumpeterian firm comes from:

> competition from the new commodity, the new technology, the new source of supply, the new type of organisation ... competition which strikes not at the margin of the profits and output of existing firms but at their foundations and very lives. (Schumpeter, 1942, p. 84)

The free enterprise system is one of a continuously uncertain and shifting equilibrium:

> The essential point to grasp is that in dealing with capitalism we are dealing with an evolutionary process. ... Capitalism never can be stationary. ... The fundamental impulse that sets and keeps the capitalist engine in motion comes from the new consumers' goods, the new methods of production or transportation, the new markets, the new forms of industrial organisation that capitalist enterprises create. (Schumpeter, 1942, p. 85)

Any weakening in the firm's impulse to innovate will lead to its displacement by new, aggressive competitors, searching for enhanced market share. Leadership and dominant market position do not necessarily provide a safe refuge from competition – unless state regulation protects existing firms by creating artificial barriers to entry.

---

[3] J. Schumpeter, *Capitalism, Socialism and Democracy* (London: Allen and Unwin, 1942), p. 106.

Thus one needs to use a broad perspective in assessing market structure and its consequences for efficiency. What matters is that the threat of competition and new entrants is kept alive, while existing firms are not denied the means of defending themselves against the threat. Regulation should not be based solely on rules about numbers of competitors and concentration ratios but should take account of the overall degree of contestability from domestic and international competitors.[4]

There is continuing debate, however, over the long-run dynamic effects of competition on productivity growth and innovation.[5]

> Some argue that more competition produces greater incentives to innovate, some that monopoly power is a necessary condition for innovativeness and some that the truth is in the middle. Important assumptions explaining the differences in results pertain to the likelihood of technology spill-over and to capital availability. Empirical evidence on the issue is conflicting.[6]

This conflicting evidence may arise because some industries use high profitability to finance innovation, while others deploy their profits largely to the protection of their monopoly. In the pharmaceutical industry, for example, some persistently profitable firms with high market shares derive their profits from the discovery of new drugs. Most patent applications emanate from large firms. Companies with more than 1000 employees account for two-thirds of Europe's new patents. But against this, a large number of market leaders do not conform to the image of a Schumpeterian innovator but behave like the textbook monopolist – building their market position on advertising, brand loyalty and distribution chains, and generating very few social benefits in the process. Clearly the ideal market structure will vary from industry to industry. The key requirements are that the markets should be *contestable* – new entrants should not be excluded by monopoly pricing or other strategies – and that they should *encourage innovation*. These guiding principles are worth keeping in mind when evaluating competition policy and when devising a privatisation programme.

## 7.2 Competition policy

### General principles

Competition law is one of the most important points of interaction between business, law and economics. Firms need to understand the rationale and practice of

---

[4] The notion of hypercompetitive rivalries has Schumpeterian overtones. D'Aveni describes the process in these terms in his much acclaimed book: 'As long as one wild-card player may try to enter the market, the market is contestable; so it is no longer a safe haven. Thus, even where we observe that entrants have not attacked yet, we can't be sure that they won't enter in the future. The mere threat of their entry is enough to force firms to act like they have entered.' Richard D'Aveni, *Hypercompetitive Rivalries: Competing in highly dynamic environments* (New York: Free Press, 1995), p. 96.

[5] Recent research on this question is summarised in *A World Class Competition Regime*, White Paper from the UK Department of Trade and Industry, July 2001.

[6] P. Stoneman and P. Diederen, 'Technology diffusion and public policy', *Economic Journal* (July 1994), p. 923.

> ### Box 7.2    Competition – definitions
>
> 'Competition is a dynamic and inherently uncertain process, one in which some innovative business strategies succeed and others fail; and in which the process of continuing rivalry between firms gives consumers new products and better-run businesses. ...
>
> Competition is a mechanism of disciplined pluralism, which rewards success and penalises failure. The purpose of competition policy is to protect that mechanism.'
>
> *Source*: John Kay, *Financial Times*, 7 November 2002.

competition legislation and rules. Competition law is also important because it impinges so closely on the welfare of the consumer and the dynamism of the business sector. Badly framed competition policy will bring relatively few benefits to the consumer at a high cost to business. These costs include not only the costs of taking or defending a competition case, but the costs arising when a firm is uncertain about the applicability of the law to its behaviour.

While individual countries have their own distinctive competition regimes, four general principles underlie competition policy:

1. Highly concentrated market structures are more likely to be monopolistic than less concentrated structures. Competition policy tends to focus on the former.
2. Competition law is applied to a wide range of markets, i.e. to public sector commercial services and non-profit organisations, as well as to the private sector.
3. The benefits of competition include direct benefits to the consumer. But its indirect effects on upstream and downstream markets have also to be taken into account. An inefficient telecoms industry, for example, affects both the individual telephone user and also the pattern of comparative advantage, through raising communication costs.
4. Case-by-case studies are necessary to quantify the net economic benefits and costs of a monopoly.
5. Care needs to be taken in devising remedies which can include sanctions, declarations, structural and behavioural actions.

## Competition policy – the example of the European Union

The EU's competition regime provides a practical illustration of the general principles of competition policy.[7]

The principles of the EU's competition policy are contained in Articles 85 to 94 of the Treaty of Rome. Since the Treaty of Amsterdam came into effect in 1999,

---

[7] Within the EU, national competition rules coexist with the common EU regime but, in the event of conflict between them, EU law takes precedence. For a good summary, see W. Santer, 'Competition policy' in A. El Agraa (ed.), *The European Union: Economics and policies*, 6th edn (Financial Times Prentice Hall, 2001).

these have been renumbered Articles 81 to 90. To avoid confusion, we use the post-1999 numbering in this chapter. These articles cover both uncompetitive behaviour between firms and state aids that affect trade between Member States. The objective of keeping the EU market open and free from distortion is addressed by two key articles, Articles 81 and 82 (Box 7.3).

---

**Box 7.3**  **EU competition law – Articles 81 and 82**

### Article 81 (Agreements)

1. The following shall be prohibited as incompatible with the common market: all agreements between undertakings, decisions by associations of undertakings, and concerted practices which may affect trade between Member States and which have as their object or effect the prevention, restriction or distortion of competition within the common market, and in particular those which:

   (a) directly or indirectly fix purchase or selling prices or any other trading conditions;
   (b) limit or control production, markets, technical development or investment;
   (c) share markets or sources of supply;
   (d) apply dissimilar conditions to equivalent transactions with other trading parties, thereby placing them at a competitive disadvantage;
   (e) make the conclusion of contracts subject to the acceptance of other parties of supplementary obligations which, by their nature or according to commercial usage, have no connection with the subject of such contract.

2. Any agreements or decisions prohibited pursuant to this article shall be automatically void.

3. The provision of paragraph 1 may, however, be 'declared inapplicable' in the case of any agreement, decision or concerted practice which contributed to improving the production or distribution of goods, or to promoting technical or economic progress, while allowing consumers a fair share of the resulting benefits, and which does not:

   (a) impose on the undertakings concerned restrictions which are not indispensable to the attainment of these objectives;
   (b) afford such undertakings the possibility of eliminating competition in respect of a substantial part of the products in question.

### Article 82 (Dominance)

Any abuse by one or more undertakings of a dominant position within the common market or in a substantial part of it shall be prohibited as incompatible with the common market in so far as it may affect trade between Member States.

Such abuse may, in particular, consist in:

   (a) directly or indirectly imposing unfair purchase or selling prices, or other unfair trading conditions;
   (b) limiting production, markets or technical developments to the prejudice of consumers;
   (c) making the conclusion of contracts subject to the acceptance of supplementary obligations which, by their nature or commercial usage, have no connection with the subject of such contracts.

## Box 7.4   Exclusive dealing in the European motor trade

EU law bans any agreement between firms intended to prevent or distort competition. But 'selective and exclusive dealerships' (SEDs), the arrangements which govern all new car sales, are exempt under what is known as Rule 123/85. A typical European new car dealer offers models of only one make, or a few select makes. The customer cannot cross the street and buy the same car more cheaply because, by agreement, the next dealer will probably be located several miles away. The rule also applies to spare parts. Manufacturers can refuse to sell to wholesalers or can 'advise' their equipment producers against reaching agreements with them unless certain terms are agreed.

SEDs are examples of what economists call *vertical restraints*. Vertical restraints involve agreements between producers of complementary goods. They are distinguished from *horizontal restraints* which relate to agreements between producers of the same good or close substitutes. Thus if a car manufacturer places a limit on what retailers sell and how they sell the product, that is a vertical restraint. Agreements between car manufacturers themselves as regards price or market share is a horizontal restraint. *Generally, vertical restraints are considered innocuous for competition (but see below for qualification). By contrast, there is a presumption that horizontal restraints are harmful to competition.*

An SED typically specifies what retailers sell and how they sell it. Under 'selective dealership', a producer uses only those retailers who agree to support its brand in specified ways – perhaps by giving information to potential customers or providing after-sales service to those who buy. 'Exclusive dealerships', as the name suggests, commit retailers to selling one brand. They often go hand-in-hand with 'full-line forcing', under which retailers stock a manufacturer's whole range, not just one or two products.

Other vertical restraints include 'exclusive territories', which limit a retailer's sales to a particular area (hotel firms or fast-food chains rarely put two outlets in the same part of town) and 'franchise fees', which are sometimes paid to manufacturers for the right to sell their wares or to put their logos above the shop door (some high street shops are run this way). Producers may also try to fix retail prices, either by controlling discounts or by demanding that retailers sell minimum quantities of their products.

At first sight, these devices look like a conspiracy against consumers. But sometimes they can benefit the consumer, because contracts with vertical restraints are often the most efficient way for producers to get their products to the customer and to ensure good after-sales service.

A manufacturing firm can sell through an independent retailer or by setting up its own retail network. Independent retailers have stronger incentives than employees to maximise retail profits and they may know more about local markets.

However, retailers may set prices higher than producers (and consumers) would like. Suppose producers sold their goods to retailers at a uniform wholesale price. If retailers have some monopoly power in their local markets, they can set retail prices above wholesale prices (plus retail costs). But manufacturers would like prices to be lower: that would expand retail sales, reduce unit costs, and boost the manufacturer's sales and profits. One of several ways around this is to set up a SED, i.e. insist that retailers pay a franchise fee for the right to sell the product and, in return, cut wholesale prices. Payment of a franchise fee does not affect the dealer's profit-maximising level of sales. But a lower wholesale price does, and gives an incentive to the dealer to cut the retail price and raise sales volume.

Complaints against vertical restraints might still be valid in that consumers' range of choice is being restricted. However, if there are many competing producers, retailers, even with exclusive territories, do not have much market power. While they face no competition from others selling the same brand, other local retailers are selling competing brands, curbing their ability (and that of producers) to exploit consumers.

Hence the rationale for exempting SEDs under the competition regime. This exemption has been extended to 2004. Current economic thinking stresses the importance of market structure. The more competition between brands, the more likely that pro-competitive and efficiency effects of vertical restraints will outweigh any anti-competitive effects.

*Sources*: 'Restraints of trade?', © *The Economist*, London, 24 September 1994; D. Salvadori, 'The automobile industry', in D. Mayes, *The European Challenge: Industry's response to the 1992 programme* (Hemel Hempstead: Harvester Wheatsheaf, 1991). For an updated account, see European Commission, 'Competition in Europe: the competition rules for supply and distribution agreements' (Luxembourg, 2002).

Article 81 prohibits *restrictive agreements* relating to price, market shares or production controls, *unless specifically exempted or licensed*. Exemptions can be given by the Commission if the restrictive agreements can be shown to (a) improve efficiency, (b) allow consumers a 'fair' share of the resulting benefits, and (c) preserve some degree of competition. The exemption clause has been frequently and successfully invoked.[8] For example, selective and exclusive dealerships for new car sales are permitted by virtue of this clause (Box 7.4).

Article 82 addresses the problem of *abuse of dominant position*. It outlaws unfair trading practices, unjustified tie-in clauses and similar arrangements. Concepts such as 'dominant position' and 'market abuse' have been subjected to different interpretations. Some indication of the complexity of the issues is given in the summary of the judgment in the *Woodpulp* case (Box 7.5).

These articles apply in principle to vertical as well as horizontal agreements between firms. *Vertical restraints* (VRs) are contracts between firms at different stages of the production chain that specify more detailed commitments on the parties than simply to exchange a given quantity of goods or services at a given price per unit. Examples include selective and exclusive dealerships (SEDs) discussed in Box 7.4, retail price maintenance, service requirements, e.g. undertakings to spend on advertising and after-sales service, and two-part (non-linear) pricing involving a fixed charge and a fixed price per unit. VRs essentially involve agreements between producers of complementary goods. They are distinguished from *horizontal restraints* (HRs). HRs relate to agreements between producers at the same stage of the production chain.

Competition law tends to take a permissive view of VRs. The reason for this is that abuse of market power by one producer (say the car manufacturer) damages the producer of the complement (the dealer). Thus any limit to sales by the manufacturer to exploit monopoly power reduces sales and profits of the dealer, and vice versa in case of use of monopoly power by the dealers. Hence both parties are driven by self-interest to an efficient outcome, very much in the spirit of Adam

---

[8] Case of *Vacuum Interrupters* [(0) 1977 L48/32]. The Commission declared the joint venture a restrictive agreement, but granted an exemption on the grounds that technological and economic progress would be enhanced by the joint venture.

## Box 7.5   EU competition law – the *Woodpulp* case

According to the Commission, whenever a producer has charged the same price as another producer for a given product in a given region and during a given quarter, it must, in principle, be regarded as having 'concerted', i.e. colluded with the other producer. But parallel conduct cannot be regarded as furnishing proof of collusion unless collusion constitutes the only plausible explanation for such conduct. Also, although Article 85 of the Treaty prohibits any form of collusion which distorts competition, it does not deprive economic operators of the right to adapt themselves intelligently to the existing and anticipated conduct of their competitors. (European Court of Justice ruling on *Woodpulp*, 1993)

This case gives the flavour of the problems that can arise in trying to resolve difficult economic issues in a legal framework. In March 1993, the European Court of Justice finally closed one of the longest-running cases in competition law, the *Woodpulp* case, nine years after the original decision by the Commission! This was a case where the Commission had found that a group of Scandinavian, Canadian and US woodpulp producers had operated a price cartel over a sustained period. The parties challenged the Commission's decision.

First, they challenged it on grounds of jurisdiction. However, because the arrangements challenged in the decision had *effects* within the Community, the Court found that the Commission had been perfectly entitled to make a ruling on it, regardless of the place of origin of the parties or of where the agreements were actually drawn up and signed.

Second, the parties claimed that 'parallel price behaviour' did not amount to collusion. They claimed that it could be explained by the operation of legitimate market behaviour. This turned into the key issue.

Eventually, the Court commissioned two reports by economic consultants to help them come to a ruling on the case. The first report dealt with parallelism of prices and, in particular, whether the evidence justified the findings of parallelism of announced prices and transactions prices. The second report analysed the woodpulp market during the period in question.

According to these reports, the system of price announcements agreed between the parties to the arrangement was introduced in response to the producers' customers. The quarterly cycle was the result of a compromise between the consumer's desire for a degree of predictability as regards the price of pulp and the producer's desire not to miss any opportunities to make a profit in the event of a strengthening of the market. The simultaneity or near-simultaneity of the price announcements could be explained as reflecting a high degree of market transparency.

On the parallelism of announced prices, the experts concluded that this could be plausibly explained by market conditions rather than collusion. The market in question was oligopolistic on the producers' side and also on the customers' side. This led to a situation where prices were slow to react in the short term.

On the basis of the expert reports, the Court upheld the appeal by the companies and quashed the fines imposed by the Commission.

This case illustrates the complexity of competition cases. The judicial process on competition cases can be protracted and uncertain. Note also that the remit of the economic consultants advising the Court was to discover whether a restrictive arrangement existed. Had they been asked to quantify the effects of such a possible arrangement, the exercise would have been even more prolonged.

Smith, and no intervention by the Competition Authority is needed. In judging VRs, the EU takes a permissive view provided efficiency is in fact achieved. It adds two other criteria: (a) equity – protection of small enterprises; and (b) promotion of market integration – hence any measure preventing 'parallel' imports (imports of the same product from different national markets) is unfavourably regarded. The more inter-brand competition in the market, the less the danger of a VR being in breach of competition law.

## Mergers and state aids

Another instrument for maintaining competition is *control of mergers* regulation. A merger comes within the scope of this regulation if it exceeds a certain size – the aggregate world turnover of the merged units must exceed €5000 million and the Community-wide turnover of at least two of the undertakings must exceed €250 million. Proposed mergers have to be notified to the Commission. Sometimes they are rejected, sometimes approved, and on other occasions approved with qualifications. Merger policy in the EU, as in many other countries, is predicated on the assumption that, provided no significant increase in market power ensues, mergers are efficiency-enhancing. Entrepreneurs are considered better equipped to judge the future economies to be gained from a merger than outsiders – though they are far from being infallible in this regard, as we have seen. (According to one authority, the 'only effect' of many mergers is 'to increase company size and to produce economic inefficiency'![9])

*State aids* have been an intrinsic component of the industrial and regional policies of many states. Government aid which distorts competition and which affects cross-border trade is regarded as incompatible with the common market. The main thrust of policy has been to ensure that state aids are transparent, monitored and subjected to upper limits. Any new state aid likely to affect trade between Member States has to be approved by the Commission. The thrust of policy has been to curtail the amount of subsidies and other indirect supports provided by Member States. Of course, political and economic considerations can conflict on these issues, and the Commission has been criticised for being overly influenced by political pressures, particularly where powerful state companies are involved (such as the state airlines).

The European Commission sometimes acts on its own initiative and at other times responds to complaints from the public or competitors concerning the abuse of monopoly power. Sometimes action is triggered by tip-offs from insiders. Its investigative powers are considerable. These include 'dawn' raids whereby its officials arrive without prior notice at the premises of companies in order to search for evidence. Executives can have their offices searched, an alarming experience, and can be subjected to oral questioning even before any charges are brought against the company. Telephone print-outs, possession of competitors' business cards and even invitations to business lunches can be used as indirect evidence of 'concertation'. The scale of the dawn raids can be considerable. A dawn raid was carried out in April 1995 on the offices of 40 newsprint producers

---

[9] D.C. Mueller, 'Mergers', in *The New Palgrave Dictionary of Money and Finance* (London: Macmillan, 1992), p. 705.

> ### Box 7.6 Competition law with teeth
>
> Breaches of competition law can carry severe penalties. In 1999, two top European companies, Roche and BASF, were fined $725 million in the US for their part in a worldwide conspiracy to control the market in vitamins. According to US investigators, the executives met once a year to fix the annual 'budget' of a fictitious company Vitamins Inc. In practice this involved setting prices, sharing geographic markets and setting sales volume. The annual summit was followed by meetings, quarterly reviews and frequent correspondence. The cartel controlled the most popular vitamins including vitamins A and C and vitamin premixes. A former executive of Roche agreed to serve a four-month prison sentence; he was the first European national to submit to such a sentence for anti-trust offences. Following its investigation into the case, the European Commission concluded in November 2001 that 'the participants of the cartel fixed prices for the different vitamin products, allocated sales quotas, agreed on price increases and also set up machinery to monitor and enforce their agreements'. The Commission imposed record fines of €855m on eight members of the cartel.
>
> These fines, and the attendant adverse publicity, are an effective deterrent, but are they sufficient? In the US, price-fixing, for example, is a felony, with a potential penalty of three years' imprisonment, as some eminent members of the US business community have found to their cost (e.g. *United States v. Taubman*, filed 20 April 2002). Some European countries have followed the US lead. In Ireland, for instance, a maximum prison term of five years can be imposed. Other European countries, however, are loath to go this far.
>
> Source: *Financial Times*, 24 May 1999, 21 November 2001.

in seven European countries suspected of price collusion. After all this, the Commission can order firms to refrain from certain practices which it deems anti-competitive. It can also impose fines of up to 10 per cent of a company's world-wide turnover, as some major EU firms have discovered to their cost. Fines of €248 million (equivalent to about 6 per cent of turnover), for example, were imposed on 33 European cement producers in November 1994, on the grounds that they used secret agreements to reduce price differences between them in order to protect their national markets. Prestigious companies such as Blue Circle (UK), Italcementi (Italy) and Lafarge (France) were among the accused (Box 7.7).[10]

The monopoly power of public utilities has been the subject of special attention. Often what is required is the application of competition law combined with specific legislation. The Rail Directive of December 1991 is one of many examples of action to enhance competition in Europe's state-owned infrastructure companies. The Directive sought to introduce greater financial discipline and more operational competition within Member States and across borders. National railways were pressed to separate track infrastructure from train operations and to produce transparent accounts revealing the respective costs and revenues attributable to *infrastructure* and to *services*. This approach was based on the belief

---

[10] This case has been appealed by the producers.

---

**Box 7.7**  **The case of the cement industry**

Competition is the underlying principle behind the Single Market and is paramount to building an integrated market between the European economies. The European Commission has the task of safeguarding the competitive climate. On occasion, it has taken a tough stance with firms or undertakings which it believes have violated EU competition law. Large penalties have been imposed on firms which breach these rules. At the same time, competition policy is heavily politicised, much more so in the EU than in the US.

The authorities usually learn of violations of competition law through voluntary notification or through complaints from aggrieved third parties.

Following extensive investigation, penalties were imposed on a cement producers' association, called CEMBUREAU, during 1994. It was ordered to pay a fine amounting to €248 million, equivalent to 6 per cent of its members' turnover.

CEMBUREAU is the European Cement Association. Its members included eight national cement associations and 33 European cement producers, among them prestigious companies such as Blue Circle (UK), Italcementi (Italy) and Lafarge (France). The firms accounted for almost half of the Community supply. Supply in the cement industry is particularly concentrated at a national level, with only one producer in operation in some countries. Economies of scale and high entry/exit costs make the industry prone to high levels of concentration. This might explain why the alleged collusion can occur, despite comparatively high (33) numbers of firms. Usually, a cement works is located close to its raw materials, due to the heavy transport costs. However, investigation showed that varying cost structures in different firms made exports profitable for some firms. Hence there was an incentive to arrange market-sharing deals and take joint action to prevent 'disruption' of the market. In the case of CEMBUREAU, the Commission alleged that the members of the cartel had agreed to confine sales within their own national borders, allowing each producer to maintain their dominant position in their national market. The nature of the alleged infringements originated from market-sharing agreements, transnational restrictive practices and restrictive practices relating to exports. EU law forbids any agreement or collaboration between businesses or individuals which could affect the trade between Member States.

The investigation took five years to complete, which shows how difficult it can be to gather evidence of anti-competitive practices. The case was appealed in the European Court, and the fine was reduced to €110 million.

*Source*: 'Press releases issued on the most important developments', *EC Competition Policy Newsletter*, Vol. 1, No. 3 (Autumn/Winter 1994).

---

that the provision of rail services on that infrastructure, for freight and passengers, can, and should, be opened to competitive tender.[11] Similar initiatives were taken in the case of energy, telecoms and postal services.

In addition to the 1992 programme, the EU is committed to further trade liberalisation (see Chapter 17). Liberalisation of foreign trade can be a potent antidote

---

[11] Some separation of track and service operations has been implemented in Germany, the UK, Scandinavia and New Zealand, among others. France is opposed on the grounds that separation involves loss of economies of vertical integration. In retrospect, the French view appears to have been the correct one.

to monopoly power. The expectation is that exposure to global competition – increasing the degree of contestability of the domestic market – will make industries more efficient. More concentration and rationalisation at a domestic level may be a fall-out of this policy and need not necessarily be a cause of concern. A more open market is, by definition, a more competitive market and the competition authorities' job is done for them by the market. This saves on the high compliance costs attached to enforcement of competition by legal means.

Competition law is being applied with increasing rigour across a growing number of countries. The 1998 Competition Act, regarded as the biggest shake-up in British competition law in 25 years, brought UK competition law into line with that of the European Union for the first time. It gave sweeping new powers of investigation to the Office of Fair Trading (OFT) and opened the way for massive fines if companies break the rules. Directors and employees can be sent to prison for obstructing investigations. The OFT has been given powers to demand information and carry out dawn raids if it suspects anti-competitive behaviour. Interestingly, earlier that year (1998) the loss to the UK economy from monopolistic behaviour was estimated at 1 per cent of GDP or about £7.6 billion at 1996 prices.

In 1999 the mighty Microsoft ran foul of the US anti-trust authorities. Judge Thomas Jackson began his 207-page ruling with a four-word sentence: 'Microsoft enjoys monopoly power' (in November 2002 it was exposed that Microsoft had an 86 per cent profit margin on its Windows operating system, which is on 90 per cent of all desktops). He went on to rule that the company used its power to eliminate competition from a range of rivals across the industry, particularly from Netscape. Emerging relatively unscathed from the American anti-trust proceedings, Microsoft faced a new assault from competitors on the European front. An umbrella organisation representing Sun Microsystems, Oracle and Nokia, among others, filed a complaint against the latest version of the Windows operating system. The European Commission expressed concern that Microsoft was leveraging its Windows monopoly into the servers and audiovisual software markets.

## Competition and globalisation

Domestic markets are becoming more and more exposed to foreign competition. This increased globalisation of national economies is having several different effects. First, it means that high concentration and rationalisation at a domestic level need not necessarily be a cause of concern. A more open market is by definition a more competitive market. Openness may encourage concentration of production in the domestic market but it simultaneously prevents concentration translating into market power. Second, national industries are becoming more sensitive of the need for a 'level playing field'. If country A has strict competition rules and country B has lax rules, this could mean that B's producers are able to set up arrangements to reserve B's markets for themselves, while enjoying free access to A's market. This will not seem fair to A's producers. For this reason pressure is growing for similar competition rules to be introduced in countries participating in world trade. Third, as the global reach of firms in many industries extends, the danger of abuse of monopoly power by giant multinationals becomes more potent. Mega-mergers between companies in different parts of the world create corporations of global dimensions. Even without an actual production presence in countries, firms can form strategic alliances that enable them to penetrate foreign markets with international partners. This is particularly true of the information technology, entertainment, air transport and pharmaceutical industries, but high levels of global concentration are also found in less glamorous products such as tea and bananas. In these circumstances, coordinated action by competition authorities on an international scale is necessary if the enhanced opportunities which free trade provides are not to be undermined. The formulation of global competition laws is high on the agenda for many countries, including those of the EU.

## 7.3 Privatisation

Privatisation has become an integral part of most countries' pro-competition programme and is a familiar feature of new-consensus economic policy. It is defined as the transfer of state-owned assets to private control. This can be achieved through direct sale of the assets to the private sector. Another possibility is to transfer the administration of these assets to the private sector (by competitive tender, for example) but for the state to retain ownership. This section focuses on privatisation in the former sense.

The move to privatisation began in the UK and New Zealand in the 1980s; it spread to continental Europe in the 1990s and is now taking a front seat in developing and transition economies. The US was a significant absentee from this trend, largely because it had so few nationalised industries to privatise. European government receipts from privatisation amounted to $675 billion between 1990 and 2002 (*The Economist*, 29 June 2002). Cumulative privatisation revenues had exceeded $1000 billion by 2000. However, following the stock market crash there has been a marked slowdown in the rate of privatisation worldwide.

There is something paradoxical about privatisation of state-owned companies in Western countries. After all, these companies were originally set up to resolve an economic problem, not to cause one! Many were established in response to situations of private monopolies or of 'excessive' competition among private firms. Nationalisation was designed to encourage exploitation of scale economies and to ensure that monopoly profits, to the extent that they existed, would accrue to the state, which would distribute them in a socially optimal way. In retrospect these expected advantages failed to materialise. Too often nationalised firms abused their monopoly power. They gave bad service at high prices. They suffered extensive X-inefficiencies. Although they tended to 'featherbed' their employees, they were prone to surprisingly bad industrial relations. They also suffered from political interference, mixed managerial signals and sometimes outright corruption.

### Effects of privatisation

Privatisation programmes come in diverse forms and it is not always easy to determine their success or failure. Studies of the UK experience suggest mixed results. Some privatised companies achieved a highly successful turnaround, notably British Telecom and British Airways, but the verdict on the privatisation of British

---

**Box 7.8** **Reasons for privatising**

The motivations for privatisation have been diverse.

- A major objective of privatisation was to make companies more efficient and change their ethos. This resulted from a certain disillusionment with the capacity of nationalised industries to deliver efficient services to the public and to achieve the social goals they were set up to attain.*
- Closely related to the above, governments wished to introduce competition into sectors hitherto dominated by state utilities. From the state's viewpoint, the revenue maximising strategy was to sell the company first, with monopoly profits to inflate its value, and liberalise the sector afterwards.
- Many nationalised industries were notorious losers of money. The liberalisation of trade threatened even further losses. Selling them was seen as a way of stopping the haemorrhage from the current state budget. Fiscal benefits could also accrue on the state's capital account from the sale of assets.
- Many developing countries saw privatisation as a golden one-off opportunity to reduce public sector debt and to set in motion a lower tax environment without damaging increases in budget deficits.
- Politicians, supported by public opinion, became converted to the view that the balance of the mixed economy has shifted excessively towards the public sector. This belief was fortified by the abuse of power by many public sector trade unions with frequent use of the strike weapon and outmoded attachment to demarcation and other restrictive practices in the workplace.

* Assets of UK public companies constituted 12 per cent of GDP in 1979, but only 2 per cent in 1997 when the Blair government came to power. Assets of state-owned enterprises in industrial countries amount to 5 per cent now, about half the figure at the start of the privatisation programme.

---

Rail, the water industry and the health service is far less flattering.[12] *The Economist* described the privatisation of British Rail as a disaster. Experience also differs between countries. In a highly generalised way, one might say that privatisation has been successful in the UK while unsuccessful in Russia.

The effects of privatisation can be evaluated under several headings: effects on *efficiency*, effects on *government revenue* and effects on *income distribution*.

A key consideration is the effect of privatisation on efficiency, i.e. on measured labour productivity or, better still, total factor productivity. The resultant fall in unit costs can be passed on to the consumer in terms of lower prices and better quality. In the UK, telephone charges fell by 35 per cent in real terms between 1984 and 1994, whilst electricity prices for business fell by 30 per cent during the period 1990–99. According to the US Department of Justice Antitrust Division Annual Report 1994, increased competition in the US telecoms industry hastened the introduction of fibre optic technology and spurred an increase in technological innovation. Electricity charges also declined in real terms. As a general rule, experience shows that the more competition in the privatised companies the greater the likelihood of a positive outcome. This is just as economic theory would predict. A policy environment that encourages long-run investment in the privatised companies is also important.

---

[12] Experience differs between countries. In France, 75 per cent of the population is now supplied with water by the private sector (Vivendi and Lyonnaise des Eaux), so far without complaint.

The effect on government revenue is more complex than might appear. In the case of an outright sale, the gain to the state cannot be equated with the sale price. The state has just replaced one asset (the state company) with another (cash). To calculate the net financial gain to the state, we must compare the present value of the stream of net revenue expected from the firm had it remained in state ownership with the proceeds from the sale. (The concept of present discounted value is explained in Chapter 10.) The price paid for the company is thus a crucial variable. If under-priced, the privatisation programme could end up worsening instead of improving government finances in the long term. Also there must be some assessment of how this extra cash accruing to the government is being used. It is being spent on building up military power or on consumer handouts or on long-term investments for the future?

Last, one must consider the income distribution effects. There are at least four parties to consider: the state, employees of the privatised firms, the consumer, and the new owners. The mode of privatisation has an important bearing on the outcome. Share flotation is one mode, often associated with a certain predetermined allocation to existing employees (British Telecom 1984, British Gas 1986). Direct sale to private sector business has also been used (National Coal Board 1994, Rover cars to British Aerospace). Management buy-outs are another possibility (National Freight Corporation 1982 and several bus companies). In each case, careful analysis is needed in order to assess the resultant income distribution effect. It is obviously easy for the state that is strapped for cash to be induced into selling too cheaply (as happened in Russia and in many other transition countries). Also shares can be sold too cheaply to the public in order to curry popular favour or to ensure that the flotation will be a 'success', as happened in several Western European countries.

There is little doubt that in most instances privatisation has brought benefits to the consumer, not just in terms of lower price but also in terms of improved quality of service and efficiency. There are many areas of the economy to which the ethos of a state company is particularly unsuited and where privatisation has yielded unambiguous benefits. Examples are state-owned hotels and restaurants or manufacturing industries, where quickness of response and an entrepreneurial approach is especially important. State farms, created on the grounds of economies of scale, have never become successful enterprises. To some extent, governments have voted with their feet. The number and scope of privatisation programmes around the world shows that finance ministries are convinced that the potential benefits exceed any potential losses. Experience to date would support this verdict. But it will take time before the dynamic efficiency effects of privatisation can be fully evaluated.

## 7.4 Regulation

### Regulatory reform and natural monopolies

Regulatory reform is designed to promote competition, regardless of whether the industry is in state or private ownership. In principle it is a separate issue from privatisation. Yet, in practice, reform of government regulation of industries, particularly state-owned utilities such as electricity, gas and telecoms, has been associated with the issue of privatisation. For that reason we introduce the subject at this stage of the discussion.

Suppose a state-owned company exists in a context where competition is not apparently possible. Economies of scale are so preponderant that it is not profitable for more than one firm to operate in the industry. This is the case of a *natural monopoly*. The state may still wish to privatise in the hope of securing a change in the 'managerial culture' of the organisation, or to add to government revenues, even though the privatised firm will continue to retain monopoly power. How do costs and benefits stack up in this instance? Clearly there are benefits from privatisation, but these will be achieved only if there is also some state regulation of the privatised entity. How should the privatised monopoly be regulated? The economics of regulation now enter the picture.

Natural monopolies were until recently regarded as dominant in the energy, transport and telecoms industries. In addition, private sector competitors were often excluded by law from trying to compete with the state monopoly in these sectors. But banning competitors would be redundant if economies of scale were really that powerful, so the existence of legal restrictions suggests that the monopoly was not so 'natural' after all. When such is the case, one solution is to remove the restrictions on entry, subject to the new entrants satisfying some basic minimum operating criteria such as prudential reserve ratios, safety provisions, and so on. Privatisation can then proceed, though whether *deregulation* comes before or succeeds privatisation can have an important bearing on how much revenue is obtained from the sale.

Deregulation has been applied to many industries in addition to those controlled by state monopolies. Major changes have been made in the rules governing banks, stockbroking, insurance, and radio and television broadcasting. These initiatives were inspired by belief in the merits of the free market. No less important was technological change. In some industries, it has made restrictions on new entrants unenforceable; in others it has made small production units more efficient. For example, technical advance has now made even very small electricity generating plants more efficient than previously. The combined effects of deregulation and technology have opened up many hitherto restricted markets. The resultant increase in contestability has brought about huge improvements in efficiency.

However, there remain some important sectors where the monopoly proves to be genuinely 'natural' and where consequently the degree of competition is limited. There are two major steps in dealing with the situation. The first step is to break down or 'unbundle' the services provided by the monopoly into component parts so as to isolate the core natural monopoly element in the industry. In electricity, for example, the real monopoly element is not power generation or power distribution but the transport of electricity through a network. By unbundling the industry into its different potentially competitive and natural monopoly components, efficiencies can be secured through the market system. The potentially competitive parts can be sold to the private sector, or put into competitive play by out-contracting or competitive tendering.

The second step is how to deal with the natural monopoly element. This involves three interrelated strands: pricing, access and quality of service. We briefly review each of these, recognising that the relevance of each aspect will differ according to sector and the period of time since the liberalisation process was begun.

## Pricing

*Incentive regulation* refers to the design of incentives to ensure that producers keep prices and costs as low as possible. The underlying assumption is that costs are not given but are influenced by the incentives set by the regulatory authorities. If there was no regulation the privatised monopoly might well slip into the same bad habits as the state company it replaced. Whether the new regulation achieves a superior outcome to direct provision of the good or service by the state company depends on the effectiveness of the regulatory system.

In the UK, following the privatisation of telecoms, gas, water, electricity and railways, regulatory bodies were set up for each industry (with acronyms such as Ofgen, Ofgas, Ofwat and so on). Their task was to prevent the abuse of monopoly power and to find ways of promoting competition. This sounds easy, but regulators frequently get into hot water in trying to achieve this objective.

There are several ways of regulating a privatised industry with strong monopoly elements:

1. *Price = marginal cost.* One simple way would be to oblige the monopoly firm to charge a price equal to marginal cost, and provide a subsidy for any ensuing loss. The drawback is the cost of the subsidy and the difficulty of determining marginal cost.

2. *Breakeven or average return on capital.* Alternatively the regulator could insist on a price that allows the firm to just break even. This eliminates 'monopoly' profits but leaves wide open the opportunity to reap the rewards of monopoly in other guises (such as the quiet life and X-inefficiency). Some regulators use a formula related to *rate of return on capital* which the monopoly would not be permitted to exceed. This avoids the problem of direct price control, but has the disadvantage of reducing the incentive to firms to minimise costs, once the permitted profit rate has been attained. Rate of return controls have been applied extensively in the US. Not surprisingly there have been frequent disputes over the definition and measurement of rates of return in these cases.

3. *RPI minus X.* Another possibility is to set maximum prices. The UK authorities have taken this approach. Various types of price-capping formulas have been used, known as '*RPI minus X*', whereby the regulator permits the firm's price to rise by no more than $x$ percentage points below the retail (consumer) price index (RPI). In a multi-product monopoly, such as telecoms, the regulator may opt for a tariff-basket method, whereby the authorities decide which products are placed in the basket and how the various prices are to be weighted. This usually means permitting lower prices for price-elastic services (say international phone calls by business customers) and relatively higher prices on the price-inelastic part of their provision (say to domestic customers). While providing flexibility, regulation can be highly controversial. The public will often perceive such pricing structures as unfair, even if based on sound economic principles. Where the output is more homogeneous, such as gas and electricity, the regulator may use an average revenue target, whereby the predicted rise in average revenue in the firm is not permitted to exceed RPI minus X.

A key problem of incentive regulation is to determine the efficiency factor X. If X is set too low, the firm will make excessively large profits ('rents') and the regulator will lose face. If it is set too high, the firm will become unviable. In deciding on the right value of X, the regulator may have to be guided by the expert, but hardly disinterested, knowledge of the regulated firm. Relations between the regulated and the regulator may become too close and cordial (this phenomenon is called *regulatory capture*). Another problem is that the formula could act as a disincentive to efficiency if more efficient performance were to lead to subsequent upward revision of X. In practice, rate of return considerations are implicit in setting X. Even the most expert and experienced regulator can make mistakes. The UK electricity regulator, for example, had to undertake a full-scale review less than a year after establishing new price-caps because the regulated firms' financial performance was much better than estimated. Opportunistic behaviour by the regulator can be highly destabilising.

## Access and quality of service

Each of the above techniques refers to ways by which the regulator can prevent abuse of monopoly power in the form of excessive charges to the consumer and excessive profits. But monopoly power can also be curbed by determining the conditions of access to the service or sector. For example, in the case of network operators in electricity, gas, telecoms or air transport, the monopolist has an obvious incentive to provide access to its network on unfavourable terms. To counteract this, the regulator must devise and open a fair and transparent licensing scheme for new entrants. Considerable research has gone into establishing how *access charges* for connection to networks should be determined. The *efficient component pricing rule* (ECPR) has been developed to deal with such situations. It provides that new entrants must pay an amount to cover the marginal cost of access to the network plus some contribution towards fixed costs of setting it up which were borne by the original state firm. This rule has many flaws, and there is no simple rule of thumb for determining the relevant fixed and marginal costs. Another factor here is that some providers may have universal service obligations, i.e. an obligation to provide a minimum set of services of specified quality to all users at an affordable price. The regulator must also have regard to the quality of service offered by existing and new operators to the consumer and by the network owner to competing operators. The existing operator must not be allowed to favour its own downstream (retail) arm over competitors. Finally, there is usually provision for complaints procedures and for the development of customer charters.

The above considerations demonstrate that regulation may be necessary, and better than no regulation, but it is by no means costless. Regulators do not come cheaply. They need large staffs of economists and lawyers. Regulators can be of variable quality and regulatory capture is an ever-present danger. Their decisions can always be subject to long and expensive appeal, just as in the case of competition law. Regulation cannot be considered a satisfactory substitute for competition. The high cost of imposing regulation underlines the importance of competition as an alternative, more efficient, policing device for curbing excessive profits. In short, the best regulator will often be one that succeeds in making itself redundant. Over time, emphasis must be placed on deregulation and exposure to international competition as the most efficient way forward.

## 7.5 Conclusions

When thinking of competition most businesses see their problem as one of excess competition, not a lack of it. This is understandable from the perspective of an individual firm already established in an industry. Competitive pressure has increased in most economies. But the notion of competition being 'excessive' sits uneasily with economic thinking on the role of free markets. Competition affords opportunities for new firms to enter the industry. From these firms' perspective, the problem may appear one of too little, not too much competition. Competitive pressure, however, gives firms an incentive to search more vigorously for ways of protecting their domestic market, by developing market niches and, if necessary, by circumventing competition legislation. As a result, new entrants to an industry can be deterred by unfair trade practices, and financially weaker (often small) firms can be discriminated against in the process, unless protected by law. The consumer, too, can suffer discrimination as larger firms build up their war chests and tighten their hold on their market share. In short, competition policy is still needed.

Competition policy should aim to be transparent, easy to implement and predictable. The need for case-by-case assessment, taking account of each market's special features, can result in complex legal cases and much uncertainty. Competition policy is not a flawless set of precepts which can impose competition in a costless way. It can be expensive and inefficient to enforce and can be subverted and distorted. Yet, for all that, the secretary general of Unice, the federation of European industry, reflected the weight of business opinion in his assertion that *the essential corollary of competitiveness [is] strong competition policy.*[13]

State-owned enterprises in formerly nontraded sectors of the economy – telecoms, transport, energy and public utilities – have become a focus for competition policy in recent years. These enterprises were once regarded as 'natural' monopolies, but thinking has changed. Governments have become convinced of the efficiency gains that can be obtained through a more market-oriented framework. The European Commission has been particularly active in promoting competition in these sectors through the use of competition law.

Competition policy has been further bolstered by setting limits on the amount of state aid provided by EU Member States to various industrial and regional initiatives. This type of action is welcomed by the weaker Member States because they are unable to afford the cost of matching the subsidies offered by richer Member States. The EU's strategic policy to favour competition is also evident in its support for SMEs.

A degree of tension between competition and industrial policy is to be expected. Prior to the Second World War, cartelisation was seen as a way of building up more efficient and technically progressive industries in Germany and Switzerland. Japan also had a tradition of looking with suspicion on 'excessive' competition because of its possible detrimental effects on an industry's capacity to exploit fully the economies of scale. According to one authority, the Japanese authorities feared 'excessive' competition as much as monopoly as a potential

---

[13] Reported in *Financial Times* (5 December 1994).

source of inefficiency.[14] Their predilection for limiting competition and encouraging mergers, vertical and horizontal firm groupings, and inter-firm operating agreements, has been fundamentally at odds with anti-trust policy. In the case of the automobile industry, for example, the Ministry for International Trade and Industry (MITI) sought to limit production to one firm and, failing that, a target of 'at most' three firms was set. It proved impossible to restrict competition in this way, however. The vigorous competition between domestic firms that prevailed in postwar Japan proved to be an important source of vitality for the Japanese economy. Yet, to this day, some countries maintain a more tolerant approach to cartels than would be countenanced by most European countries. Keeping the domestic market contestable often entails an element of compromise between the objective of avoiding market dominance and allowing a technically efficient size of firm.

The suggestion has been made that internal competition rules should be extended to incorporate an international body of rules on competition law, under the framework of the World Trade Organisation (see Chapter 17). In a globalising economy, stronger enforcement against the abuse of monopoly power by powerful multinationals will need to be established.

Competition policy, by correcting market distortions, is designed to maintain the efficiency of the market system. Firms need to be careful that they do not infringe competition law. Economics and law interact very closely in relation to market power, and managerial decisions on restructuring, mergers and acquisitions should take this into account.

## Summary

1. Competition law derives motivation and sustenance from economic principles. But putting these principles into a legally coherent framework is not easy. Application of competition law can be complicated, uncertain and highly expensive.

2. EU competition law applies to restrictive agreements, abuse of dominant position, control of mergers and state aids. The European Commission sometimes acts on its own initiative and at other times acts in response to complaints. It has played a very proactive role in introducing competition into Europe's state-owned service industry monopolies such as telecoms, post, air and rail transport, and energy.

3. One important motive for privatisation is the promotion of competition but fiscal and political considerations have also prompted countries at all levels of development to adopt privatisation programmes. Like competition policy, they are being introduced in conjunction with new consensus policies. On balance, they are seen as a way of improving the structure of the economy. Evidence to date suggests that privatisation has on balance been successful in raising efficiency. But the privatisation experience has not been universally beneficial.

---

[14] R. Komiya, *The Japanese Economy: Trade, industry and government* (University of Tokyo Press, 1990), p. 297. For an early treatment of 'excessive' competition, see also K. Rothschild, 'The waste of competition', in E.H. Chamberlin (ed.), *Monopoly and Competition and their Regulation* (London: Macmillan; New York: St Martin's Press, 1954).

4. Regulatory reform is another key element in a pro-competition policy. The regulator has the task of setting objectives and targets for profits and prices. There is no easy formula to guide action in this area and the performance of the regulator has proven a contentious issue. In Britain, there has been sustained criticism of the regulators for allowing privatised firms to earn too much profit, pay over-generous executive salaries and provide poor quality service. This has stimulated interest in finding ways of replacing regulation by market forces – by de-bundling the services of such natural monopolies and exposing them to competition.

## Questions for discussion

1. Suppose a group of firms organises a market-sharing agreement. They arrange not to compete with each other in their local markets. What would be the effect of such an agreement on the industry's profits? Why should a competition authority object? What arguments might the chief executive of the new group use to defend the agreement?

2. Why is it necessary to have competition legislation? What would prevent market forces from eroding the market power of a monopoly or oligopoly?

3. Innovation is a core ingredient of faster economic growth. What contribution can competition policy make to encouraging innovation?

4. Comment on the motivations for privatisation in your country and compare them with those outlined in this chapter.

5. What gains can be expected from a policy of privatisation? Which, if any, of these gains arise because of the transfer from public ownership to private ownership? Do you agree with the argument that what really matters is that competition is introduced or extended as a result of the privatisation?

6. Suppose a state-owned monopoly has been privatised. After privatisation, the problem of regulating the now private sector monopoly rests with a regulator appointed by the government. What guiding rules would you suggest for the regulator? Should the objective of the regulator be to call the shots in pricing or to try to introduce competition into the industry? Would the latter policy have the same effect in the long term as price controls would have in the short run?

7. According to the British Nobel prize-winner, Sir John Hicks, 'the best of all monopoly profits is a quiet life'. Compare this view with Schumpeter's hypothesis that firms with monopoly power are the driving force in innovation.

## Exercises

1. Write a memo to a newcomer on a competition authority explaining why and under what circumstances monopoly is inferior, from an economic point of view, to competition. In your memo, comment on the EU Competition Commissioner's assertion that 'competition policy plays a key role in creating an environment that is favourable to business, this being crucial to lasting growth and job creation' (*XXVth Report on Competition Policy*, Brussels, 1995).

→

2. Early in 2000, Brazil's Economic Defence Council, the anti-trust agency, was asked to approve a merger between Brazil's two top brewers to form a powerful new company AmBev (*Business Week*, 27 March 2000). The new company would have a 70 per cent share of the Brazilian beer market. The argument in favour of the merger was that scale economies would enable AmBev to become sufficiently strong to withstand competition on the home market from imported beers and to prevent them being taken over separately by foreign multinationals. AmBev would also have the financial power to invest abroad and achieve multinational status itself. Brazil's number 3 brewer, Cervejarias Kaiser, objected that the merger would reduce competition and raise prices. The issue was a sensitive one, since an upsurge in foreign investment inflows had resulted in a sell-off of large numbers of Brazilian-owned companies. Mergers were proposed in airlines and steel for reasons similar to those prompting the formation of AmBev. The Council approved the merger in March 2000. From an economic point of view, did it do the right thing?

3. In March 1996, two Swiss giants of the drugs industry, Ciba and Sandoz, announced a merger. This was a merger of record size, the combined market values of the two companies being $64 billion (£42 billion). By contrast, the value of Glaxo's bid for Wellcome in 1995 amounted to only £9 billion.

After the merger, the new company, Novartis, would rank as the world's second largest drug company, next to Merck and ahead of Roche and Johnson & Johnson, with a 4.4 per cent share of the prescription drugs industry.

The case for the merger was that (a) synergies created by merging with another Swiss company would be greater than with an American, British or German giant, (b) the merger would create a single company with vast financial resources, (c) cost savings worth an estimated £1 billion could be made – mainly through shedding 10,000 jobs worldwide, (d) pressures on healthcare costs have brought profit margins under pressure and have forced drug companies to seek savings through consolidation, and (e) the rising cost and complexity of medical science means that huge sums (amounting to £1 billion per year in the case of Novartis) have to be spent on R&D.

After the announcement of the merger, the stock of Ciba and Sandoz rose by 28 per cent and 20 per cent respectively.

The deal had a wide-reaching impact on other firms in the industry. Shares in Zeneca and Warner Lambert rose because of their prospect of becoming takeover targets. Shares in companies such as Glaxo fell because the market suspected it might make a bid for other firms in response to the Swiss merger.

The chief executive of Zeneca, a firm with a market value of some £30 billion and 1.4 per cent of the prescription drugs market, commented that large size is irrelevant because success in this industry depends on scientific innovation and there is no evidence that R&D productivity increases with size. Small companies such as Astra of Sweden and Amgen of America had grown rapidly in the decade to 1996. But other industry experts argue that only giant firms will be able to survive in such a fast-changing, R&D intensive industry.

(*Source: The Sunday Times*, 10 March 1996)

(a) Comment on the possible benefits of the merger.
(b) Evaluate the possible downsides of the merger.
(c) Was the rise in the share prices of Ciba and Sandoz linked to the announced downsizing of the workforce? If so, could this be viewed as evidence of conflict of interest between capital and labour?

(d) How do you explain the initial rise in Zeneca's share price?

(e) What light does this example throw on the existence of economies and dis-economies of scale?

4. In Box 7.4, the statement is made that 'payment of a franchise fee [i.e. a fixed amount of money regardless how much of the product is sold] does not affect the dealer's profit-maximising level of sales. But a lower wholesale price does'. Explain this assertion with the aid of a diagram, using U-shaped cost curves.

## Further reading

J.S. Bain's *Barriers to New Competition* (Cambridge, MA: Harvard University Press, 1956) is a classic, and still highly readable, source on this subject. For a good contemporary review, see D. Jacobson and B. Andréosso-Callaghan, *Industrial Economics and Organisation: A European perspective* (Maidenhead: McGraw-Hill, 1996). The reports of national competition authorities such as, in Britain, the Monopolies and Mergers Commission are the best source of information on recent cases and illustrate how cases are adjudicated in practice. *Competition Policy Newsletter*, published by the European Competition Policy Directorate, contains summaries of recent competition cases and also special articles on EU competition policy. For analysis of vertical restraints, see EU Commission, *Green Paper on Vertical Restraints in EC Competition Policy* (Brussels: EU Commission, 1997).

*Competition Policy in Europe: The competition rules for supply and distribution agreements* (Luxembourg: Office for Official Publications of the European Communities, 2002) gives a good overview of the competition rules for supply and distribution agreements within the EU. Important advances have been made in public policy towards firms with market power, in particular regulatory theory. These aspects are presented in a non-technical manner in F.M. Scherer and David Ross, *Industrial Market Structure and Economic Performance*, 3rd edn (Boston, MA: Houghton Mifflin, 1990). For an *ex-post* review of the experience of privatisation, see W. Megginson and J. Netter, 'From state to market: a survey of empirical studies on privatisation', *Journal of Economic Literature*, June 2001. A readable and insightful account of the application of new thinking on competition policy and regulatory reform to transition economies is provided in J. Fingleton *et al.*, *Competition Policy and the Transformation of Central Europe* (London: Centre for Economic Policy Research, 1996). For a good summary of the Microsoft case up to 2001, see R.J. Gilbert and M.L. Katz, 'An economist's guide to U.S. v. Microsoft', *Journal of Economic Perspectives*, 15(2), Spring 2001.

## Chapter 8

# Government intervention and the market system

## Introduction

Government plays a major role in the economy. Among industrial countries, the share of government spending in GDP ranges from 32 per cent in the US to 53 per cent in Sweden.[1] In addition to this, the authorities affect the business environment through a myriad of taxes, rules and regulations. The purpose of this chapter is to analyse the contribution of government to economic welfare and the business environment.

The objectives of government and business are to some extent in opposition. The social objectives of government policy can impose restraints on a firm's behaviour in relation to employees and investment. Competition policy limits the scope of business to acquire and exploit monopoly power, environmental legislation can impose heavy financial burdens on industry, and progressive income taxes impact severely on executive salaries. However, governments and business also share much common ground. Both have an interest in fostering growth, securing high levels of employment and promoting social harmony. Hence, business should not allow itself to be cast in the role of opposing all public intervention. Much of this intervention is desirable, necessary and directly beneficial to business. This much has always been recognised in economics. Adam Smith himself devoted a long chapter to discussing the various functions of government. In addition to the provision of defence and justice, he asserted that 'the sovereign or commonwealth' had a duty to erect and maintain

> those public institutions and those public works which, though they may be in the highest degree advantageous to a great society, are however of such a nature that the profit could never repay the expense to any individual or small number of individuals. (Adam Smith, *Wealth of Nations*, 1776, Vol. 2, p. 244)

The debate has come a long way since then, as we shall see.

For four decades after the Second World War, the influence of government in the economy grew at an unprecedented rate. Some of this growth was fuelled by

---

[1] *OECD Economic Outlook* (December 2002).

Keynesian ideas of macroeconomic management. We defer discussion of this aspect of government intervention until Part II. This chapter focuses on the microeconomic considerations that prompted governments to play a more active role in the economy.

The economics of government intervention have undergone extensive review in recent decades and the tide of government expansion has turned. Whereas 50 years ago governments regarded nationalisation as a solution to market imperfections, nowadays the debate is about privatisation. Many no longer see the welfare state as the solution to the problem of poverty, but rather as a possible source of its exacerbation. Instead of providing people with pensions, governments are encouraging people to make provision for the future for themselves. Changing ideas have spilled over into changing budgets. Government spending as a percentage of GDP has stopped increasing and in some countries has declined (see Chapter 15).

## Chapter outline

1.  The case for *income redistribution*. A large proportion of public spending is motivated by the desire to help the poor. This is because the free market system may result in considerable income inequalities. Intervention then may be desirable as a means of securing social solidarity, and thereby helping to secure faster and more sustainable growth.

2.  The problem of *market failure*. Four types of 'failure' are discussed: (a) monopoly power, (b) externalities, (c) public goods, and (d) lack of information. Business will certainly be familiar with these reasons for government intervention. The case of monopoly, discussed in Chapters 6 and 7, touches many firms directly or indirectly. Also, business benefits from government subsidies – this subvention being justified by the externalities argument or by the desire to redistribute jobs and incomes to poor regions. Correction of market failure for reasons of public good and information may have less agreeable consequences for business. Thus, firms may find themselves subject to regulations and controls regarding pollution, consumer protection, fire and health provision. A manager needs to understand the economic causes and consequences of the market failure that gives rise to such intervention.

3.  The instruments of *government intervention*. Should intervention take the form of tax and subsidy incentives, regulation, or direct state provision?

4.  The problem of government *failure*. Although a case for intervention may exist on first principles, in practice government intervention may create its own equally damaging set of distortions. This possibility could arise if, say, income taxes had to be raised in order to provide industrial or regional assistance. The gains to the economy through provision of this assistance could be offset by the disincentive effects and compliance cost of the higher taxes. Government intervention often opens the way to corruption and to subsequent damage to economic growth. The cure might end up being worse than the disease.

## 8.1 Income distribution and the equity–efficiency trade-off

Economics seeks to improve society's material welfare. This seems a reasonable definition of the aim of economic activity, although at various times in the past other objectives have taken precedence. To some, economic activity was useful primarily as a means of securing and maintaining political power. Colbert, the influential finance minister of Louis XIV, saw as the main purpose of his subjects' labour not the increase in their own happiness, but the enhancement of the glory and power of their sovereign, who personified the nation. Despots, through the centuries, have viewed economic activity primarily as a means of securing and extending their power rather than of improving the welfare of the masses. Even those who agree with the objective of maximising individual utilities may disagree over the interpretation of what truly gives utility to us as human beings and who is best equipped to judge.

The value judgements underlying modern economics are derived from a philosophy of individualism and liberalism. *Individualism* means that what ultimately counts is the utility every individual attains and that the utility of each individual should be given an equal weight. *Liberalism* signifies that individuals should be free to decide what provides the greatest utility. Individual preferences are taken as given. The task of the economist, in this view, is to advocate structures which ensure that they are satisfied to the maximum extent, not to pass judgement on them.

It is important to distinguish between utility and income. The standard assumption underlying economic reasoning is that the marginal utility of income is positive, but decreases as income rises.[2] 'Economic man' always prefers a higher income to a lower one, but the intensity of this preference diminishes as income rises. Ascetics, who are happiest with a minimal income, and Scrooges, for whom income becomes more important the more they have of it, are both excluded by this definition. A systematic relationship thus links utility to income. On the face of it, the individualist principle of treating the utility of every person equally, coupled with the assumption of declining marginal utility for all individuals, would seem to imply that the total utility in society is maximised when income is distributed perfectly evenly. However, few would advocate total income equalisation.

There are two reasons for this. First, different people derive different amounts of satisfaction from the same income levels. Material wealth does not matter equally to all. Second, policies to achieve greater equality have an adverse effect on incentives to work and enterprise and may, after a point, lead to a fall in total income. The size of the cake to be distributed may be affected by how the cake is sliced. In this metaphor, the slicing pattern represents the egalitarian or equity factor and the size of the cake stands for the second major criterion of economic judgement: efficiency.[3] If the unweighted utility sum in a society can only be

---

[2] This is the axiom of dominance, as described in Chapter 3.
[3] Utilitarian political philosophy considers a third major criterion for judging economic systems: individual liberty. We assume in this chapter that governments are democratically elected and civil rights are respected. Hence, the 'state vs market' distinction does not mark a choice between an authoritarian and a liberal system.

maximised by allowing a degree of inequality, then the inequality outcome might be preferred to perfect income equalisation.

There are, none the less, strong egalitarian tendencies in popular debate on economic issues, dating back to the eighteenth-century English philosopher Jeremy Bentham, the founder of utilitarianism. The assumption of decreasing marginal utility implies that when we take an equal amount from the rich to give to the poor, the rich will have suffered less of a utility loss than the utility gain enjoyed by the poor. Egalitarian predispositions also emerge from other philosophies and schools of thought. Some argue that society should give the utility of the poor greater weight than the utility of the rich on grounds of need, regardless of fine points about diminishing utility.[4] Others, such as the philosopher John Rawls, have pushed this line of judgement to the extreme, arguing that any economic change which increases inequality would be acceptable only if it serves to make the poorest better off also.[5] This implies that the utility of the worst-off individual takes precedence over all others. In opposition to the egalitarian presumption, Robert Nozick and others argue that what matters is not how much utility individuals currently attain, but how they have got to this point. If the individual's income has been obtained legally, no one is entitled to deprive him or her of any of it, hence *ex-post* redistribution of income is unjustified.[6] Note that these are all individualistic philosophies. None of them, however, has rivalled the impact on economic thinking exerted by utilitarianism.

The equity–efficiency trade-off remains a controversial topic. There are undoubtedly situations where the criteria of equity and efficiency conflict. Too much equality reduces the incentives to work and can thus lead to inefficient outcomes. Yet too much inequality can lead to a waste of human resources and lack of productive investment. The even spread of the fruits of growth has been identified by the World Bank as a factor favouring rapid development (see Chapter 2). There is increasing concern about the growth in inequality in countries such as the US, the UK and New Zealand, which have been at the forefront of free market policies. As Box 8.1 shows, two of the most unequal societies in terms of income distribution are the US and Switzerland. In Switzerland's case, the inequality can mainly be attributed to the presence of a small number of extremely wealthy people, against a background of a very broad well-off middle class and little absolute poverty. In the US, the high inequality index arises because of major population groups at both extremes of the income spectrum. There is a sizeable group of very rich, a more numerous cohort of very poor people, and a large middle class in between. This shows how difficult it is to measure and assess the degree of inequality in a country. Perhaps the more fruitful line of enquiry is to examine how assistance might be most efficiently channelled to those most in need, rather than what abstract degree of inequality society should be prepared to tolerate.

Such reasoning has motivated policy-makers to focus on the efficiency criterion. Efficiency is less ambiguous an objective than equity. An improvement in efficiency produces a net increase in income and, hence, it is in principle possible

---

[4] Abram Bergson, 'A reformulation of certain aspects of welfare economics', *Quarterly Journal of Economics*, 53 (1938).
[5] John Rawls, *A Theory of Justice* (Oxford: Oxford University Press, 1971).
[6] Robert Nozick, *Anarchy, State and Utopia* (Oxford: Basil Blackwell, 1974).

## Box 8.1   The equity–efficiency trade-off

Economics is the study of trade-offs between different uses of scarce resources. Firms continuously trade off current benefits from the distribution of dividends against future benefits from retaining these profits and reinvesting them in the business. Managers and workers trade off the career fruits of long and hard working hours against the joys of leisure time. Consumers trade off the utility that could have been attained by buying good X or Y for the utility derived from purchasing good Z instead.

Arguably, the most important, and certainly the most hotly debated, economic trade-off is the political choice between equity and efficiency. Conventional wisdom suggests that more equity leads to less efficiency, because equalisation of income and wealth among individuals can reduce work incentives, as well as the aggregate level of savings and investment (since rich people tend to save more). Conversely, unrestrained market forces result in inequitable outcomes or, in the famous words of Arthur Okun, 'dollars transgress on rights'.[1]

Economists have attempted to check the link between equity and efficiency empirically. This entails finding satisfactory measures of the two concepts. Efficiency is usually measured by reference to average GNP per capita.

Measuring equity is trickier. Economists associate equity with an even distribution of income and wealth among individuals. The main measure of income distribution is derived from the Lorenz curve, presented in Diagram 1.

The Lorenz curve plots the cumulative share of income and wealth in ascending order against the cumulative percentage of population. In Diagram 1, for instance, 80 per cent of the population receives only 50 per cent of the total income, while the richest 20 per cent enjoy the remaining 50 per cent of the pie. The poorest fifth of the population receives a mere 3 per cent of national income and wealth. This Lorenz curve thus

**Diagram 1 The Lorenz curve**

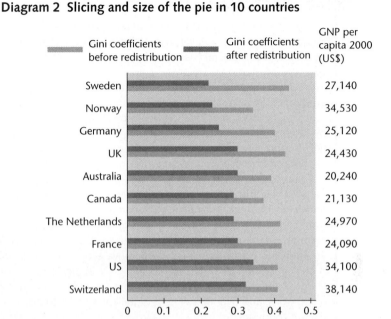

**Diagram 2  Slicing and size of the pie in 10 countries**

Sources: A. Atkinson, *Income Inequality in OECD Countries: Evidence from CIS data* (Paris: OECD, 1995); *2002 World Development Indicators* (Washington, DC: World Bank, 2002).

depicts a society with considerable inequality. A country with perfect equality of income and wealth, where each individual controls the same amount of material goods, exhibits a straight Lorenz curve, called the 'line of equality'.

The more strongly the Lorenz curve diverges from the line of equality, the greater the degree of inequality. This can be captured by a simple measure. The Gini coefficient is the proportion of the area delimited by the line of equality and the Lorenz curve, relative to the total area between the line of equality and the horizontal axis. The index can take values between 0 and 1, where 0 means perfect equality and 1 represents complete inequality (one individual gets the whole pie).

Diagram 2 shows Gini indices for a selection of high-income countries. The upper bars represent the distribution of disposable income among individuals. The lower shaded bars show what level of income inequality would have prevailed in the absence of government redistribution through progressive taxes and welfare benefits.

Two important conclusions can be drawn from Diagram 2.

1. Market forces alone produce highly unequal income distributions. The 'before redistribution' Gini indices for the 10 sample countries are contained in the range 0.33–0.44.
2. Post-tax distributions are much less unequal than pre-tax distributions. The 'after redistribution' coefficients lie in the range 0.20–0.34. Tax and welfare payments reduce inequality to a significant extent.

Box 8.1 continued

Wealthy countries tend to be more equal in overall income distribution than poor countries.[2] The UK, however, has experienced deteriorating inequality in recent years. Up to the 1980s its Gini coefficient was 10 points below the US level; by the 1990s the gap had fallen to only 5 points.[3] Equity and efficiency do not necessarily conflict. The 10 countries in Diagram 2 are all among the world's very richest and some are quite egalitarian. In developing countries, higher inequality in income or land ownership tends to be associated with lower growth. It is argued that big income and land ownership differentials reflect underinvestment in education, divert government efforts from investment and growth promotion towards the abatement of social conflict, and reduce the majority's incentive to save and invest.[4]

The relationship between equity and efficiency depends to some extent on individual attitudes and culture. In some societies, income inequalities are condemned less, and financial work incentives valued more, than in others. A political philosopher stated that 'the combinations of equity and, say, economic growth attainable in a competitive market economy full of individualistic materialists might be rather different from those attainable in a co-operative economy run by and for ascetic altruists'.[5] A poll conducted in 1990 showed that only 29 per cent of Americans thought it was the government's job to reduce income differentials, while 60–70 per cent of Germans and Britons, and over 80 per cent of Italians and Austrians, were of that opinion.[6] The debate continues.

*Notes*:
1. Arthur M. Okun, *Equality and Efficiency: The big trade-off* (Washington, DC: The Brookings Institution, 1975).
2. M. Bleaney and A. Nishiyama, 'Economic growth and income inequality', University of Nottingham CREDIT Research Paper, December 2002. Data on world income inequality are available from the World Institute for Development Economics Research (WIDER) database.
3. K. Forbes, 'A reassessment of the relationship between inequality and growth', *American Economic Review*, September 2000.
4. Torsten Persson and Guido Tabellini, 'Is inequality harmful for growth?', *American Economic Review*, 84 (1994).
5. Julian Le Grand, 'Equity versus efficiency: the elusive trade-off', *Ethics* (1990).
6. Reported in *The Economist*, 5 November 1994.

by income distribution to make all people in the community better-off – or at least to ensure that nobody is made worse-off. An outcome is defined as efficient when it is impossible to make one person better-off without making at least one other individual less well-off. Devised by the nineteenth-century Italian economist Vilfredo Pareto, any outcome which passes this efficiency test is said to satisfy the *Pareto criterion*. A corollary to the Pareto criterion is the *compensation principle*, which says that if an outcome is more efficient, it should be feasible for the gainers to compensate the losers. The implicit assumption is that compensation can be, and is, arranged for the losers from economic change. The arranger in this instance is the government. In that case, if the entire cake grows bigger, everybody's slice will also grow.

The above approach focuses on the degree of equality of *outcomes* of the market process. But the *process* may be fair, even if it generates unequal outcomes. Much modern debate focuses on this – i.e. inequality may be less objectionable if the process is fair (equality of opportunity, level playing field) than if it is unfair. For example, people with different levels of stamina, ambition, attitudes and willingness to work engage in market activities. Provided there is equality of opportunity, a meritocratic approach would not object to inequality of outcome in such circumstances.

## 8.2 Market failures

Economic theory has shown that a perfectly competitive economy, guided by Adam Smith's 'invisible hand', attains a Pareto-efficient allocation of resources. But most real-world markets violate at least some of the assumptions which underlie the economists' idealised free-market model. Such deviations of real markets from the efficient model economy are called 'market failures'. Market failure can arise for four main reasons: (1) monopoly power, (2) externalities, (3) public goods, and (4) information asymmetries.

### Monopoly power

The distortionary effects of monopoly have already been analysed (Chapter 6). Monopoly involves a breach of the rule that marginal cost = price by introducing a wedge between marginal cost of production of a good and the utility it provides the marginal consumer as measured by prices. Monopoly pricing also creates an income distribution effect. Monopoly profits are earned at the expense of the consumers, who pay a higher price relative to what they would pay in a competitive market. This is the reason why consumer organisations oppose monopolies and cartels, and lobby their governments for stricter competition legislation.[7]

However, the gain of monopoly producers at the expense of consumers can involve serious losses at both domestic and international level. The World Bank has estimated that cumulative overcharges to developing countries over the life of the cartels in vitamins, citric acid, lysine (a food additive), steel tubes and graphic electrodes ranged from $3bn to $7bn.[8] Uncompetitive behaviour also reduces economic efficiency. As we move from a competitive situation, with a large quantity supplied at a low price, to a monopoly, where a smaller quantity is supplied at a higher price, what occurs is not a zero-sum redistribution of income from consumers to producers, but a net loss of utility to society at large. This is the 'deadweight loss' of monopoly.

The deadweight loss, as described above, is a static phenomenon relating to the market situation at one point in time. Empirical estimates of the deadweight losses caused by existing monopolies or oligopolies typically amount to only a few percentage points of the values of total sales in the particular industry.

---

[7] Another redistributive effect of monopoly power is that rival firms might be pushed out of a market by a more powerful competitor, not because of the latter's superior product, but because of the monopolist's ability to enhance a dominant position even further, be it through advertising, below-cost pricing or government lobbying.

[8] World Bank, *Global Economic Prospects and the Developing Countries 2003* (Washington, DC: World Bank, 2003), p. 137.

A forerunner in trying to measure the deadweight loss, Arnold Harberger was surprised to find that such welfare losses amounted to a mere 0.1 per cent of US national income in the 1920s.[9] Later, detailed studies have come up with much higher estimates, though these have been subject to a wide range of variation.

As readers will recall from Chapter 7, the efficiency losses from monopoly occur over time. Monopolists or oligopolists have less of an incentive than competitive firms to maintain efficiency, to innovate and to improve their services. Indeed, as Hicks once noted in a famous dictum, 'the greatest of monopoly profits is a quiet life'.[10] This is a central theme of the Austrian School. The pressure of competition forces firms to aim at lowering their (marginal) costs continuously, while sheltered firms do not have to be so concerned about their costs and the improvement of output quality. The losses due to such so-called X-inefficiencies are even more difficult to estimate empirically than deadweight losses. Nevertheless, in many circumstances they outweigh the deadweight losses stressed by economic theory. The Cecchini Report, for example, estimated that the X-efficiency losses of nontariff barriers on intra-European trade amounted to 2 per cent of GNP in the late 1980s.

## Externalities

A second important source of market failure is *externalities* or 'spillover effects'. These arise when an economic activity affects a third party directly rather than through the market. The competition model assumes that both producers and consumers bear the entire cost and enjoy the entire benefit created by their economic actions. This assumption is frequently breached in practice. The resulting spillover effects reflect an inefficiency of the free-market system.

Externalities can be either positive or negative. Positive externalities, also called external benefits, bestow a benefit on a third party (e.g. a firm trains an employee in computing technology, which skill can then be passed on at zero cost to another firm if the employee changes job). Correspondingly, a negative externality, also referred to as an external cost, imposes a cost on a third party, involving a loss of utility (a classical example being the chemical plant which causes water pollution – see below). A further distinction can be made between producers and consumers. Externalities can result either from the consumption activities of some individuals or from the production process of firms.

The different types of externalities are summarised in Figure 8.1. Examples are given for each of the four categories. All four types of externalities lead to inefficiencies when the market system is left to operate freely. The free market provides too little of the activities providing positive externalities and too much of those with negative externalities. In that sense, 'positive' externalities are just as 'inefficient' as 'negative' externalities.

To illustrate the efficiency loss from spillover effects, we begin with the example of a *negative production externality*. Imagine a chemical plant which channels its polluted effluents into the nearest river. Imagine also that, downstream,

---

[9] Arnold Harberger, 'Monopoly and resource allocation', *American Economic Review*, 44 (1954); K. Cowling and D. Mueller, 'The social costs of monopoly power', *Economic Journal*, 88 (1978) estimate a deadweight loss for the UK in the range 0.2 to 7.2 per cent of private sector output.

[10] J.R. Hicks, 'Annual survey of economic theory: the theory of monopoly', *Econometrica* (1935).

## Figure 8.1 The four categories of external effects

Origin

| | Production | Consumption |
|---|---|---|
| Positive | Training employees in transferable skills | Vaccine against contagious disease |
| | Aesthetic company headquarters building | Neighbour's well-kept garden |
| Negative | Air, water and noise pollution | Congestion Noise from mobile phones |
| | Waste disposal | Cigarette smoke |

(Effect — labelled on left axis between Positive and Negative)

there is a factory which needs clean water, and, therefore, must incur costs in cleaning the water. Finally, assume that the resulting loss in profits for the downstream factory can be measured in money terms and is a constant fraction of the factory's output. This situation is represented in Figure 8.2.

Assume for simplicity that the chemical factory can sell at a given price OP, i.e. it faces a horizontal demand curve and thus price = marginal revenue. Its marginal costs increase with output. The production costs borne by the firm are denoted by PMC, which stands for private marginal cost. Profit maximisation drives the firm to produce up to OP = PMC, hence the amount $OQ_1$ of chemicals is produced. However, the factory's operating costs do not encompass the totality of costs created by the manufacture of its output. Costs borne by the downstream factory in cleaning the water need to be accounted for. Suppose these amount to EF per unit of chemical output. In order to represent total production costs per

Figure 8.2 A negative production externality: chemical plant polluting river

unit, we add EF to PMC to obtain SMC, the social marginal cost. In the case of a negative production externality, the social cost is greater than the private cost of production. From society's point of view, the costs to the downstream factory should be added to the outlays of the chemical company. Hence, the optimality condition is that OP = SMC. It would be socially optimal to produce $OQ_2$ rather than $OQ_1$.[11]

This example shows that, in the presence of negative externalities, the free market leads to an over-provision of the goods concerned. In the opposite scenario – where the production or consumption of a certain good creates external benefits – a free market results in too low a level of production or consumption.

Note that economics tends to resist any absolutist approach to the pollution problem. The existence of external costs such as pollution does not generally provide an economic justification for the total suppression of the underlying activity. In our example, the closure of the chemicals plant is not required for efficiency, merely a reduction in output (and its associated pollution) to the level $OQ_2$. There is a trade-off between the utility lost by the sufferers of pollution and the utility gained by the producers and consumers of the good whose production gave rise to the externality. In this sense some pollution is, for this reason, usually better than no pollution. Only if the negative spillover EF were so large as to push up SMC beyond the demand curve over the whole range of output would it be most efficient to shut down the factory completely. This is not just a theoretical possibility – several polluting plants of Central Europe were closed down during the 1990s for this reason.

## Public goods

The third main category of market failure arises because of the existence of *public goods*. A public good is defined as being *non-excludable* and *non-rivalrous* in consumption. A private good, by contrast, is both excludable and rivalrous in consumption.

For the explanation of these concepts, consider the example of an army, representing a pure public good, and an apple, a private good. A good is excludable if individuals can be prevented from enjoying its benefits. It is easy to withhold an apple from someone, hence it is excludable. However, if an army successfully defends a country against an invading force, then all inhabitants of the protected country necessarily benefit (assuming none of them sympathises with the invader) and no one can be excluded. National defence is thus non-excludable.

Non-rivalry means that the consumption of a good by an additional person does not preclude someone else also consuming it. Put more technically, a non-rivalrous good is subject to a zero marginal cost of consumption. If one individual eats the apple, this precludes anyone else from eating it. Apples are thus rivalrous goods. If the army protects the nation, however, all citizens are free to enjoy the feeling of security that protection engenders. The fact that I feel secure does not in any way preclude your feeling secure, nor does it add to the security bill. Consequently, national defence is also a non-rivalrous good.

---

[11] The net welfare gained by a move from $OQ_1$ to $OQ_2$ is equal to the shaded triangle. This could also be described in the deadweight loss caused by the existence of the external effect.

Public and private goods do not constitute sharply delineated categories. There is a continuous range of products between the two opposite poles, pure public goods and pure private goods. Figure 8.3 tentatively places some examples of different goods within this continuous range, differentiating between the intensity of rivalry and the degree of excludability of these goods. The fact that most goods are roughly situated around the diagonal starting at the origin illustrates that there is a strong link between (non-)rivalry and (non-)excludability.

In the bottom left corner of the diagram are listed some pure public goods. If a country's air is clean, if its territory is safe from foreign armies and if its currency is stable, then the benefits of these achievements can be withheld from no citizen of this country, nor does it cost more to provide them if the resident population grows. They are, therefore, unambiguously non-excludable and non-rivalrous. At the other extreme are pure private goods, situated in the top right corner of Figure 8.3. Apples, cars and books are clearly excludable and rivalrous. The most interesting cases, however, are located between these two poles. Museums and art galleries are to some extent non-rivalrous. My enjoyment from viewing a Caravaggio today in no sense diminishes the possibility of your enjoying it tomorrow – hence it is non-rivalrous. But if everybody crowds into the gallery at the same time, each person's enjoyment will diminish and, in that sense, the art gallery becomes a rivalrous good. It is also excludable – one can change the admission fee to the gallery.

Another example of a good which is only partly 'public' by nature is a motorway. Again, up to a certain point of congestion, additional users cause only minor, if any, diminution of existing users' utility. It is also possible to exclude certain drivers from the use of these roads by setting up checkpoints or toll booths. Obviously, it is more costly to control the access to a motorway than to monitor the entrance of a museum or art gallery. A motorway is thus less 'excludable' than a museum. This is important, because very few things are technically non-excludable. As technology changes, some things become less excludable (e.g. defence) and some more excludable (e.g. urban roads, pay TV). The real issue is the *cost* of exclusion, which is an example of *transaction costs*. Also, improved technology and income growth have made some hitherto non-rivalrous goods become rivalrous (e.g. air space for planes, ocean fishing).

**Figure 8.3 Private goods and public goods**

Markets fail in the presence of pure public goods because of the so-called 'free-rider' problem. It may be very costly to provide a public good (think of an army!), but everyone can benefit from it no matter whether he or she has contributed to its financing. Self-interested individuals have an incentive to avoid paying for the good in the hope that others will provide it. In other words, utility-maximising individuals try to free-ride on the others. If all individuals reason in that fashion, none of the public good is produced, even if the aggregate cost of providing the good is much lower than the sum of potential utility gains. The market, a system based on non-cooperative interaction of selfish individuals, leads to zero provision of pure public goods. If the aggregate benefit potentially derived from the public good exceeds its total cost of provision, this could be a very inefficient outcome. The non-rivalrous character of a public good means that the market should produce more than it does, while its non-excludable character means that the market will never have the incentive to do so.

Markets fail not only in the presence of pure public goods, but whenever a good shares some of the characteristics of a public good. For example, suppose a good is excludable but non-rivalrous (MC = 0). Provision by the free market at a positive price is non-optimal. Since MC = 0, P should also equal 0, i.e. the good should be provided free of charge. Market provision implies prices above the socially optimal level. Take the example of a bridge. If the bridge is provided by a private firm, then a fee has to be charged to the crossing vehicles so that the firm can cover the costs of building the bridge and earn a profit. As we have shown, however, once the bridge has been built, the most efficient outcome occurs at the point where the social marginal cost and marginal benefit curves intersect. Since the marginal cost curve of a bridge is virtually zero for all additional crossings up to the point of traffic congestion, the price charged should be zero. Obviously, no private firm will be prepared to build the bridge without charging a toll for all crossings. The levy of a toll has two effects. First, it implies a transfer of resources from the users of the bridge to the supplying firm (a redistributive effect). Second, charging a fee also implies a deadweight loss of efficiency, conceptually similar to the deadweight loss arising from monopoly. Therefore, compared to the potential optimum, provision of such a public good through the market system leads to a net loss of economic efficiency. [12]

Public goods are not the same as publicly provided goods. Even though public goods are usually provided by the government, many goods and services currently provided by the state do not conform to the economic definition of a pure public good. Services such as health, education and housing all come under the heading of *merit goods*. Merit goods are goods that society wishes everyone to consume, regardless of what an individual's preferences for that particular good are. For instance, most countries have a law which dictates that children must attend school until they reach a certain age; this is society's way of ensuring that everyone consumes a certain amount of education, because it is seen as good. There also exist *merit 'bads'* (e.g. heroin) which society believes that each individual should not consume (because they are bad), regardless of the individual's preferences. With merit goods, society can have a different view of the consumption

---

[12] This is a frequently used example, but it is tricky because the concept of MC is ambiguous when the unit of production is different from the unit of consumption. The same applies to seats on a train.

of these goods than the individual. The case for merit goods implies some qualification of the basic assumption that social welfare is an aggregate of individual welfare and that the individual is the best judge of the latter.

## Information failures

The fourth type of market failure arises because real-world consumers and producers are not perfectly informed about all goods and prices. Where lack of such knowledge is significant, *information failure* leads to an inefficient outcome in a market system. A good example is the health effect of tobacco consumption. In a free market, no firm has an incentive to circulate information about the hazards of smoking. The demand curve for cigarettes has shifted outwards above what the level would be if information was symmetric. It is obvious that tobacco companies have no incentive to rectify the asymmetry. Nor will any individual have an incentive to provide such enlightenment. Hence the need for government to step in. Information failures also provide a rationale for public sector involvement in activities as diverse as drugs testing, health inspection of restaurants, banking regulation, insurance and the provision of job search centres for the unemployed.

These four sources of market failure point to the need for government intervention. The form of such intervention is the subject of the next section.

## 8.3 Government intervention

The public sector constitutes the major alternative to free private markets. Hence, a call for government intervention is generally regarded as the logical consequence of the diagnosed market failures. As we have seen, public sector activity accounts for sizeable proportions of all countries' national output. Even in a country as market-oriented as the US, government expenditure accounts for a third of GDP.

Governments can influence economic activity in three major ways: *taxation and subsidisation*, *regulation* and *public provision*. Together, they constitute the main elements in the government's microeconomic policy.

In evaluating the different modes of intervention, attention is focused on their efficiency effects rather than the income distribution effects. Of course, in many instances the modality of intervention may be determined by equity or, indeed, purely political considerations. For example, it may be 'easier' in political terms to boost farm incomes by raising food prices than by providing highly transparent subsidies of an equivalent amount. For that reason, arguments about the inefficiency of one mode of transfer over another may often fall on deaf ears. Yet research on more effective ways of intervening, and on the costs and benefits of different forms of intervention, clearly helps rational decision making.

## Taxes and subsidies

Taxes and subsidies are used extensively to distribute income (food subsidies, education grants to the lower-income groups, progressive income taxes, etc.).

Subsidies require taxes to finance them, and this raises questions concerning the optimal structure of taxes. We have already referred to the rules which should govern indirect taxes: impose high tax rates on activities with low price elasticity of demand and low broadly-based rates on all other activities (Chapter 3), assuming that the motivation for imposing taxes is simply to obtain revenue for the government.

While most taxes are imposed for this reason, there is another motivation which merits discussion. Taxes can sometimes be imposed not primarily in order to collect revenue, but to direct resources in a particular direction – e.g. a pollution tax. In other instances, the two motives overlap (a tax on tobacco yields large revenue and also discourages consumption of cigarettes).[13] By the same token, while the bulk of subsidies are transfer payments to lower-income groups, many are provided in order to encourage particular activities and regions (industrial grants and regional assistance).

Returning to the example of the polluting chemicals factory (Figure 8.2), it is easily shown that, if the government taxes the plant by the amount EF for every unit produced, the firm's private marginal cost is increased and equals the social marginal cost, leading the firm to produce the socially optimum output level of $OQ_2$. By taxing the polluter by the value of the damage caused, the government is said to have 'internalised' the externality. In general, an optimal government policy taxes firms or individuals for the value of the external cost they cause and subsidises them to the value of the external benefit they create. This is the rationale underlying, for instance, taxes on fuel, and subsidies for education and industrial training.

The desirability of government intervention in the presence of externalities has been questioned by Ronald Coase and his successors. His work in this field, resulting in the formulation of the 'Coase Theorem', earned him a Nobel prize in 1991. Coase's theorem states that the market system can be efficient even in the presence of spillover effects, provided that property rights on these effects are clearly defined and that negotiation between the concerned parties is costless. Returning to the example of the polluting factory, the Coase Theorem states that the optimum output level $OQ_2$ of Figure 8.2 would be achieved if the property rights for the clean river were assigned either to the chemical plant or to the downstream firms (and any other parties affected), and if negotiation among them was costless. If the plant is given the right to pollute the river, the downstream users can get together and 'bribe' the firm to reduce its output and the ensuing water pollution. Starting at output level $OQ_1$, the downstream users' gain in utility from reduced effluents (EF per unit of output) exceeds the firm's forgone profit from reduced output up to the point $OQ_2$. At production levels below $OQ_2$, the firm's forgone profits through further output reductions (OP – PMC) are greater than the downstream additional utility gains (EF). Hence the plant will be 'bribed' to limit its output to point $OQ_2$. If the property rights for the river are allocated not to the firm but to the downstream users, then the starting point is at zero output, because the latter's preferred situation is one of no pollution. However, up to point $OQ_2$ the chemical plant gains more in profits by increasing its production than the others lose in utility. Hence, the firm will find it profitable to 'bribe' the

---

[13] Note that these objectives conflict.

downstream users to allow output up to a level $OQ_2$. In consequence, the efficient output level $OQ_2$ will be attained independently of who owns the rights over the river.

The Coase Theorem provides a fascinating insight into the complexity and ingenuity of the market mechanism. But it is subject to two major qualifications. First, while for Coase's model the distribution of property rights does not affect efficiency, it certainly does matter in terms of equity. There is a distributional difference between the scenario where the downstream users have to compensate the firm for reducing pollution, and the situation where the firm is forced to compensate the downstream users for directing its effluents into the river. Society at large might have a preference in this respect, and thus expect the government to intervene. An example of such a state-imposed allocation of property rights is the 'polluter pays' principle enshrined in Article 130r of the Maastricht Treaty:

> Community policy on the environment shall aim at a high level of protection taking into account the diversity of situations in the various regions of the Community. It shall be based on the precautionary principle and on the principle that preventive action should be taken, *that environmental damage should be rectified at source and that the polluter should pay*. (emphasis added)

Society at large is implicitly given the property rights for clean air and water, and it is up to the polluter to pay compensation rather than society having to 'bribe' the polluters to reduce emissions.

Second, Coase's result hinges on the assumption of zero costs of negotiation. Such transaction costs, however, are a considerable obstacle to many negotiated settlements in the real world. It might be a costly and time-consuming endeavour for the downstream factory, anglers and others to organise themselves and to negotiate with the firm. If we think of external costs such as air pollution, it is obvious that to organise all consumers of air is a sheer impossibility. Furthermore, anybody trying to coordinate the public interest would have to confront the free-rider problem, since reduced air pollution is non-excludable.

This leads to the conclusion that government intervention is still needed to deal with externalities, particularly where these spillovers affect large numbers of otherwise unrelated individuals. Box 8.2 analyses the rationale for government assistance to industry. Most countries offer support to industry in one form or another and EU Member States are no exception to this rule.

## Regulation

Regulation involves, first, direct control or prohibition of certain actions; and second, the creation of incentive programmes using taxes, subsidies and other measures in order to guide behaviour to socially superior outcomes. Competition policy is a form of regulation, and we have already seen in Chapter 7 how it can be applied to moderate uncompetitive behaviour of private firms. Environmental and planning legislation is an everyday feature of life for a modern business (to be discussed in the following chapter). Regulation of natural monopolies and the supervision of the bank and insurance industries are familiar examples of government interference in the market system. Even though regulation involves an infringement on the workings of the market system, it may be justified on efficiency grounds.

### Box 8.2  Industrial subsidies in the European Union

The European Commission produces periodic estimates of the value of subsidies to industry. These estimates include not only the grants paid, but also implicit subsidies in the form of soft loans, which are very important in France and Denmark, and tax concessions, which are used relatively more by Germany and Ireland. According to this comprehensive definition, the average rate of industrial subsidy in the EU amounted to 3.7 per cent of value added in the early 1990s.

**State aid to manufacturing in the European Union (yearly averages 1998–2000)**

|  | Million euro | Value added (%) | Euro per person employed |
|---|---|---|---|
| Belgium | 675 | 1.7 | 1034 |
| Denmark | 786 | 3.0 | 1784 |
| Germany | 9,718 | 2.3 | 1199 |
| Greece | 442 | 3.4 | 720 |
| Spain | 1,376 | 1.5 | 487 |
| France | 4,560 | 1.9 | 1215 |
| Ireland | 548 | 2.1 | 1866 |
| Italy | 4,147 | 2.0 | 801 |
| Netherlands | 657 | 1.1 | 608 |
| Austria | 444 | 1.2 | 656 |
| Portugal | 210 | 1.0 | 215 |
| Finland | 416 | 1.5 | 931 |
| UK | 1,318 | 0.6 | 305 |
| Total EU (15) | 25,781 | 1.7 | 854 |

Source: State Aid Scoreboard, Spring 2002. Available at:
http://europa.eu.int/comm/competition/state_aid/scoreboard/

There are wide variations in subsidy rates (see table) among EU countries, but state aids for selected businesses are a favourite dish on the microeconomic policy menu of most European governments. Why do they subsidise industry to this extent?

The major justification is provided by the externalities argument. For example, R&D brings benefits which the firm undertaking it cannot fully appropriate, hence the subsidisation of 'techno-parks'.

A special case of externality is employment creation in depressed areas. In Europe, the biggest subsidies have been flowing to declining industries such as coal, steel or shipbuilding, which often happen to be located in economically disadvantaged areas. While unbridled market forces would have driven many firms in these industries out of business long ago, governments have supported them in order to slow down the process of job shedding and to provide time for alternative employment sources to replace the declining industries. The externalities corrected by the support of declining industries in depressed areas relate to (a) excess of private over social cost of labour if the alternative to a job in supported industries is unemployment, and (b) congestion costs avoided in the centre by keeping employees at work on the periphery. There may also be non-economic considerations such as social harmony and regional balance in the country. *Efficiency* arguments can be complemented by a case on *equity* grounds, particularly if employees in declining industries possess skills that are specific to their jobs and cannot be transferred to alternative employment.

Another reason invoked to justify industrial subsidies is asymmetric information. Take, for example, the case of SMEs seeking investment finance. It is often asserted that SMEs have to pay too high a rate of interest because lenders have a less clear appreciation of the riskiness of their projects than borrowers. As the firm grows, and establishes a track record and *reputation*, the problem eases considerably. But in the early stages some intervention may be warranted, such as the provision of interest relief on loans to SMEs. The action can be rationalised as a response to (a) the information problem – the government might have a better idea of private and public returns on SME investment than private lenders, (b) externalities – small firms, if they manage to survive and grow, may confer social as well as private benefits because of their flexibility and regional dispersion and (c) the need to encourage competition.

Many other arguments, some quite ingenious, have been invented to justify state subsidisation. Yet often subsidies are disbursed not for rational and high-minded reasons but because of politically motivated alliances between politicians and the lobbying firms. The European Commission is trying to make subsidies more transparent, so as to bring them within the ambit of public debate, and to limit their amount, in order to minimise their distortionary effects on the private sector and to prevent the spectacle of rich regions outbidding poorer regions for much-needed investment projects. The Commission has achieved some success in this endeavour. Subsidies, as a percentage of value added, have fallen from 3.7 per cent in the early 1990s to 1.7 per cent at the start of the new millennium.

Regulation is never costless and frequently involves a perpetual game of leapfrogging between the regulator and the regulated. The former sets down rules of behaviour which the dictates of profit maximisation often lead the regulated to circumvent. For this reason, the belief is gaining ground that 'command-and-control' regulation should be replaced as much as possible by regulation based on taxes/subsidies and other incentives. The less pollution the firm causes, the less tax it pays, hence the *incentive* to adopt cleaner production technologies. This amounts to harnessing the coordinating powers of the price mechanism on the government's behalf. Taxes and subsidies will often not be a feasible option for practical and administrative reasons. In that event, direct intervention may be necessary.

## State provision

The main policy instrument to achieve an efficient procurement of pure public goods is *state provision*. We have shown above that the free-rider problem inhibits private markets from providing pure public goods, even where these are clearly in demand. For this reason, for instance, national security is never left to private provision. Much government spending on justice, defence or fundamental research could be attributed to public goods. Next to social welfare, these tend to absorb a high share of government spending in most industrial countries.

Many goods fall into the intermediate class between the purely public and the purely private in nature (see Figure 8.3). For these, various forms of public and private provision can be appropriate, depending on the extent and nature of the good's 'publicness'. Thus, there are strong efficiency grounds for assigning responsibility to the public sector for keeping our cities clean – but does this mean that all street cleaning and rubbish collection must be undertaken directly by the public sector? For a long time the answer was thought to be yes. It is now realised that many of these activities can be contracted out to the private sector, with major savings in cost without losses in service quality.

How government intervention can help a country to get on board the knowledge economy is another important topic. One way is for the state to provide more education, especially at second and third level. Another possibility is to establish research institutes that would be required to liaise with industry as, for example, agricultural research institutes with the food industry. An alternative to direct provision of new technological activities is to provide tax incentives to 'new economy' activities in the hope of obtaining knowledge spillovers from domestic and foreign-owned 'new economy' businesses.

There is room for debate about the desirable levels and types of government intervention in these different situations. In most cases, the probability of the government's achieving an efficient and equitable outcome must be balanced against the efficiency of private markets in terms of cost minimisation and speed of innovation. The latter aspect indicates that government intervention, like the market system, is susceptible to various failures.

## 8.4 Government failure

So far we have implicitly assumed that governments are omniscient, altruistic bodies striving to lead the economy to equitable and efficient outcomes where private markets fail to do so. This is obviously an unrealistic assumption. Led by William Niskanen at the University of California in the 1970s, economists began to scrutinise the behaviour of public sector employees more closely. Rather than assume bureaucrats know everything and aim only at the social good, recent studies have applied the same behaviour assumptions to public sector workers as to those in the private sector. Public servants – like private sector workers – are assumed to look for high pay, high job security and good promotion opportunities. Once this is done, one finds that, unlike in a competitive market, there is no 'invisible hand' in a bureaucracy to lead self-interested individuals towards an efficient output mix. In the private sector, managerial advancement is correlated with the profitability of the employing firm, albeit somewhat imperfectly, through the takeover threat and profit-related performance incentives. In the public sector, however, no such constraints apply. The main source of advancement lies in the growth of the agency or the commercial state company in which the individuals are employed. Self-interested public sector employees thus strive towards the expansion of their department or company. Niskanen has formalised a 'Parkinson's Law' of ever-increasing numbers of government officials into a theory of public sector that has an insatiable tendency to grow, and hence to interfere with the economy beyond the point of optimal intervention.

Niskanen's model captures an important part of the truth, but hardly the whole truth. Many politicians and civil servants act impartially and unselfishly. Yet, even if bureaucrats were altruistic, government failure might occur. The problem lies in the absence of full information being available to the authorities to enable intervention to be imposed at just the right level. How, for instance, can a government find out the value of the external cost caused by the chemicals factory discussed above? Even a perfectly well-intentioned government, aiming to levy a unit output tax corresponding to the distance EF in Figure 8.2, will find it difficult to estimate EF in practice. If the officials ask the downstream firms for their valuation of the river pollution, they are likely to obtain an exaggerated estimate. These firms have an incentive to overstate their utility losses in the hope of greater compensation or greater output reduction. The chemicals firm, on the other hand, will do its best to understate the value of the external costs it causes in order to minimise the tax it will be charged. Imperfect information in the real economy prevents governments from intervening in an optimal fashion.

Government failure can also arise because of lack of correspondence between politicians' objectives and those of the electorate. The *theory of public choice* explores the implications of the idea that politicians, like voters, are rational utility-maximising individuals. Political representatives, however, are motivated by the desire to be re-elected into office. They maximise utility by maximising votes, and this may lead to different actions and different outcomes than those required by the long-run interests of society. The fundamental hypothesis has been described by one of the early writers on this topic, Professor Anthony Downs, as being that *political parties formulate policies in order to win elections, rather than win elections in order to formulate policies*.[14] Politicians may wish to be elected so as to benefit from the power, prestige and perks associated with a particular political office. Political parties may be inclined to put policies in place which will enhance the party's popularity and win votes for the next election, rather than those based on macroeconomic prudence.

To complicate the analysis even further, government intervention may not only be incapable of relieving market failures, it might even give rise to new ones. The classic example is taxation. Subsidies, losses by state enterprises and the costs of public sector employees in regulatory activity have all to be financed sooner or later by taxes. Taxation of income, however, creates obvious distortions. It encourages leisure relative to work, the shadow economy instead of the official economy, and tax avoidance rather than productive market-driven activity. Indirect taxation can also, after a certain point, lead to high compliance costs, avoidance and evasion. Another problem with both taxation and regulation is to enforce and oversee compliance by all firms. Large corporations frequently complain that smaller firms find it easier to avoid certain taxes, safety standards or social regulations.

Because government intervention is subject to inefficiencies, there are situations where the cost of attempting to 'correct' the free-market distortion is greater than the cost of the original distortion itself. There was indeed a widespread belief

---

[14] A. Downs, *An Economic Theory of Democracy* (New York: Harper, 1957), p. 57.

## Box 8.3  Corruption, government and growth

Requiring business to pay bribes is a direct tax on production; it deters investment and inflates government spending. Not surprisingly, it has a negative effect on economic growth. Corruption exists in virtually all economies, as we have seen in Chapter 3's commentary on the shadow economy. For those who dislike calling a spade a spade, the polite term for corruption is 'problems of governance'. Governance is seen as a particularly pervasive problem in today's developing countries.

Quantifying the extent of corruption is as difficult as quantifying the scale of its close cousin the shadow economy and for much the same reasons. Most measures rely on business opinion surveys. The *International Country Risk Guide* measures the degree of corruption using opinion surveys where executives are asked about their perception of corruption in different countries. The World Bank and the World Economic Forum also conduct periodic reviews of executive perceptions of the problem of irregular payments. The *Transparency International Index*, produced annually since 1995 by an international agency dedicated to fighting corruption worldwide, bases its index on a weighted average of such surveys.

### Transparency International Index, 2002

| Rank | Country | CPI 2002 score |
|---|---|---|
| **Top ten + US** | | |
| 1 | Finland | 9.7 |
| 2 | Denmark | 9.5 |
| | New Zealand | 9.5 |
| 4 | Iceland | 9.4 |
| 5 | Singapore | 9.3 |
| | Sweden | 9.3 |
| 7 | Canada | 9.0 |
| | Luxembourg | 9.0 |
| | Netherlands | 9.0 |
| 10 | United Kingdom | 8.7 |
| 16 | United States | 7.7 |
| | | |
| **Lowest ten** | | |
| 93 | Moldova | 2.1 |
| | Uganda | 2.1 |
| 95 | Azerbaijan | 2.0 |
| 96 | Indonesia | 1.9 |
| | Kenya | 1.9 |
| 98 | Angola | 1.7 |
| | Madagascar | 1.7 |
| | Paraguay | 1.7 |
| 101 | Nigeria | 1.6 |
| 102 | Bangladesh | 1.2 |

*Source*: Adapted from *Transparency International Corruption Perceptions Index 2002*. Available at: www.transparency.org

The rankings invariably show industrial countries in the top ranking (low corruption) and a predictable set of low-performing developing and transition countries nearer the bottom (Bangladesh, Honduras, Indonesia, Kenya, Nigeria, Russia, Uganda, etc.). United Nations' indicators tell a similar story. Using standardised indicators with mean zero and standard deviation of unity, the indicators of what is termed (with unusual bluntness) *graft* are −0.95, −0.32 and +0.24 for low, medium and high human development countries respectively.

Corruption comes in two forms: centralised and decentralised. With centralised corruption a government leader organises systematic corruption and determines the 'take' of his various underlings. Under decentralised corruption, there are many bribe takers and the imposition of bribes is not coordinated. This type of corruption can be especially damaging because of its unpredictable and chaotic nature. A kleptomaniac dictator, by contrast, will be aware that too much corruption will destroy the economy and kill the goose that lays the golden egg, and hence will levy the corruption tax in a more rational manner. Such is the theory. In practice, many dictators stand all too ready to drive their economy into the ground.

Corruption is the ultimate form of government 'failure'. It constitutes another reason for circumspection in urging proactive government policies in developing countries. Such intervention provides more opportunities for graft, and is sometimes enthusiastically proposed by corrupt politicians and bureaucrats for exactly this reason. Measures of regulatory burden and government ineffectiveness are closely correlated with the graft index: high in low HDI countries, low in high HDI countries. One important disadvantage of import protection, for example, is that it generates incentives for corrupt distribution of import licences and quotas and other forms of 'rent-seeking' activity.

Research on how to restrain corruption is continuing. Four factors are vital to the business environment: rule of law, quality of bureaucracy, government adherence to contracts and freedom from expropriation. A high quality and adequately paid bureaucracy, employed on meritocratic terms, helps to provide an honest and efficient framework for effective government. Governments in developing countries should be careful to keep state commitments in line with bureaucratic capacity. Economists in developed countries should be careful not to adopt a high moral tone in analysing these problems. Italy continues to prosper despite extensive corruption of the body politic; the US lobby system invites huge abuse of economic power; and there have been well publicised incidents of corruption in the administration of the EU's Common Agricultural Policy.

*Sources*: W. Easterly, *The Elusive Quest for Growth* (Washington, DC: MIT Press, 2001); P. Mauro, 'Why worry about corruption?', *Economic Issues*, No. 6 (Washington, DC: IMF, 1997); United Nations Development Programme, *Arab Human Development Report* (New York, United Nations: 2002), Table 35; *Transparency International Corruption Perceptions Index 2002* (available at www.transparency.org). For a readable account of corruption in a contemporary developed country, see T. Jones, *The Dark Heart of Italy* (London, Faber and Faber: 2003).

that the European economies in particular had become overtaxed in the 1980s for these reasons.

In developing countries, the problem of government failure is particularly acute. This is because state intervention gives increasing opportunities for corruption. Research has recently focused on this problem. It tends to favour the common-sense view that corruption is a powerful disincentive to investment and has a strong negative effect on growth (Box 8.3). Hence the general movement towards (a) targeting government intervention only in areas where it is indispensable and (b) implementing much stronger control over public expenditure.

Subsidies also lead to problems by cultivating a dependence mentality in their recipients. Subsidised intervention designed to correct a particular externality can take on a life of its own and continue in existence, even if the original cause of the externality has ceased to exist. Rather than adapting to change, firms and individuals may find it easier and more lucrative to devote their efforts to obtaining special government concessions. Such behaviour of 'grantepreneurs' is yet another instance of 'rent-seeking' and can be extremely inefficient. It can also lead to bribery and corruption, and thereby undermine the quality of governance. This has proven to be a major problem in many transition and developing economies.

## 8.5 Conclusions

Asked how big government should be, a British politician, Enoch Powell, once answered:

> This is one of those questions which have the appearance of being capable of an experimental or objective answer, but which, on examination, refer us back to matters of opinion and intent. It is a proposition in a debate which mankind will never conclude and in which the tides and currents will continue to flow back and forth.[15]

This chapter has shown that there are good reasons for not expecting easy answers to such general questions. Government intervention exists in all countries and successful countries tend to have widely divergent degrees of intervention. The optimal degree of intervention varies among countries and within countries over time. There is some evidence based on World Bank studies, referred to in Chapter 2, that lower government:GDP ratios are associated with higher growth. There is also evidence that, while the huge postwar growth in the public sector in Western Europe was at first highly successful in stimulating economic growth, by the 1980s it had started to produce diminishing and even negative returns. Public sector trade unions became more powerful, bad industrial relations and inefficient practices became institutionalised, and tax burdens became too heavy.

There is nothing in economic theory to support the view that business should be 'opposed' to government or relentlessly hostile to its expansion. The case for some government intervention in the economy is strong. Provision of education and physical infrastructure are obvious examples, no less than public support for R&D. The achievement of regional balance in an economy and the minimising of congestion are important objectives which government alone can address. But too much interference can do serious damage to an economy. Professor John Sutton of the London School of Economics has noted that one of the most striking handicaps that firms in developing countries encounter is the additional costs incurred as a result of excessive and inappropriate regulatory controls, and in the petty corruption that develops around their compliance – or non-compliance – with such restrictions.[16]

---

[15] P.H. Douglas and J.E. Powell (eds), *How Big Should Government Be?* (Washington, DC: American Enterprise Institute, 1968), p. 41.

[16] John Sutton, 'Rich trades, scarce capabilities: industrial development revisited', *Economic and Social Review*, Spring 2002, p. 2.

Business can play an important role in stimulating and leading debate on how government could be made more efficient and how intervention can be effected with least cost.

Even though it acknowledges a role for state intervention, economics takes a more favourable view of the potential of competitive markets than of public sector involvement. This predisposition lay at the heart of the general policy shift towards stronger emphasis on market forces. Wherever feasible, state-provided services are being privatised and competitive elements are being introduced into the most unlikely quarters, even into the workings of the civil service itself.

Efficiency is only one of the two criteria framing economic judgement. Equity considerations often favour more rather than less state intervention. Real-world free markets generally may maximise the size of the economic cake, but they also tend to produce some very small slices. The decision on what level of equity to aspire to cannot be made by either the economist or business, but must be decided by the electorate.

## Summary

1. The free-market system may bring about considerable income inequalities which, if widely perceived as 'unfair' outcomes, may require intervention to correct. Government intervention to protect the poor through disaster relief and basic anti-poverty programmes is quite consistent with 'new consensus' policies. In redistributing income, however, account must be taken of adverse effects on incentives and efficiency. Also, there is much ambiguity associated with conventional measures of income distribution. Inequality may be less objectionable, for instance, if the *process* is fair, even if it generates unequal outcomes. There may be a trade-off between equality of opportunity and equality of outcomes.

2. A Pareto-efficient outcome is defined as one such that nobody can be made better-off without making at least one other individual less well-off. Free markets can fail to deliver efficient outcomes for four main reasons. First, when firms attain monopoly power, economic efficiency is reduced as monopolies tend to produce lower quantity at a higher cost than a competitive situation. Second, positive or negative externalities can be an important source of market failure if the market system is left to operate freely. A third source of market failure arises because of the existence of public goods and the associated free-rider problem. Fourth, information asymmetries lead to market failure when consumers and producers are not perfectly informed about all goods and prices. These sources of market failure point to the need for government intervention to bring about equality between social costs and social benefits.

3. Governments can influence economic activity in three major ways: (a) taxes and subsidies, (b) regulation, and (c) public provision. Taxes and subsidies are used extensively to distribute income. Both can also be used in order to direct resources in a particular direction or activity. Regulation involves direct control or prohibition of certain actions. Even though regulation involves an infringement on the workings of the market system, it is justifiable in certain circumstances. Public provision is the main policy instrument to achieve efficient procurement of pure public

goods. However, the provision of many goods which fall between purely public and purely private goods can be contracted out to the private sector, with major savings in cost and without losses in service quality. In any particular instance, the precise form of intervention may be determined by equity or political considerations, as well as by the efficiency effects.

4. The public sector is prone to 'government failures' just as the incentives driving the private sector can lead to market failures. Governments often do not know the 'right' level of intervention. There may be a lack of correspondence between politicians' objectives and those of the electorate. Government intervention may not only be incapable of relieving market failures, but might give rise to new ones. One notable example is the opportunity for corruption. The cost of attempting to 'correct' free-market distortions can be greater than the cost of the original distortion itself. Even though economics acknowledges a role for state intervention, it commends the potential of competitive markets and warns of the dangers of excessive public sector involvement.

## Questions for discussion

1. What is the economic case for government intervention in a market economy?

2. What is meant by government 'failure'? Why does such failure happen?

3. The Delors White Paper (1993) identified as one of the 'fundamental imbalances' in the EU economy the fact that

> current levels of public expenditure, particularly in the social field, have become unsustainable and have used up resources which could have been channelled into productive investment. They have pushed up the taxation of labour and increased the cost of money … . As a result, the level of long-term investment has fallen and the lack of confidence among those involved in the economic process has caused demand to contract. (p. 40)

Is this assessment still valid?

4. Give reasons in support of the view of EU business organisations that government spending's share of GDP in Europe should be reduced to the United States' level in order to speed up EU growth. Do you agree with this view?

5. Using the arguments for state intervention outlined in this chapter, make a case for government support for:
   (a) small and medium-sized enterprises (SMEs),
   (b) urban transport,
   (c) railways,
   (d) education.

6. Sometimes government intervention to correct an externality (say, a subsidy to university education) has an adverse impact on its income-distribution objective (children of the better-off have a disproportionate probability of entering universities). What combination of measures might a government use to deal with this problem?

## Exercises

1. Give examples of government interventions affecting your business that have been (a) helpful, and (b) unhelpful to the firm. Justify or criticise these interventions by reference to the analytical framework of this chapter.

2. Compare cleaning an office building with improving the air quality of a major city. Which is a public good and which a private good? Why?

3. The Commission for Social Justice Report, November 1994 (London: HMSO), drew attention to the following:

   (a) The richest 20 per cent of the UK population had 7 times the post-tax income of the poorest 20 per cent in 1991, compared with a multiple of 4 in 1977.
   (b) The 1991 multiple of the richest 20 per cent over the poorest 20 per cent was 25 in terms of pre-tax income.
   (c) Between 1973 and 1991, the income of the bottom 10 per cent of Britain's population rose by 10 per cent; the income of those in the top 10 per cent of the income distribution rose by 55 per cent.
   (d) The most pronounced increase in income inequality was observed in the UK, New Zealand and the US.

   Comment on the implications of each of these findings. With the benefit of hindsight, how would you respond to the Commission's argument that further tax reductions will increase inequality and social divisiveness instead of promoting enterprise?

4. 'While competition and entrepreneurship are essentially private sector activities, they require markets that function well, and it is up to governments to ensure an environment in which markets remain contestable and entrepreneurship is rewarded' (World Bank, *Global Economic Prospects and the Developing Countries 2003*, p. 107). Examine the extent to which the government fulfils this function in a country of your choice.

## Further reading

There are many good texts on the economics of government. C.V. Brown and P.M. Jackson, *Public Sector Economics*, 4th edn (Oxford: Basil Blackwell, 1990), provides a comprehensive analysis and list of references. The first systematic attempt to apply economic theory to bureaucratic organisation was W. Niskanen's *Bureaucracy and Representative Government* (Chicago: Aldine Press, 1971), which has been reprinted and updated in W. Niskanen, *Bureaucracy and Public Economics* (Aldershot: Edward Elgar, 1994). A witty and forceful statement of the need for state intervention and of the consequences of its absence ('private affluence, public squalor') is provided by J.K. Galbraith, *The Affluent Society* (Harmondsworth: Penguin Books, 1950). For a withering attack on the abuses to which state intervention can lead, see Deepak Lal, *Against Dirigisme* (San Francisco: ICS Press, 1994) and *The Depressed Economy* (Aldershot: Edward Elgar, 1993). The World Bank view is presented lucidly in *World Development Report 1997*, 'The state in a changing world' (Washington, DC, 1997), and an updated assessment is provided in *Global Economic Prospects and the Developing Countries 2003; Investing to unlock global opportunities* (Washington, DC, 2003).

## Chapter 9

# Business and the environment

## Introduction

As industrial output and world population continue to grow, people are becoming more conscious of the strains being placed on the environment. Business too is affected by these concerns. Environmental laws and policies have been adopted in virtually all industrial countries and they impinge profoundly on many sectors of industry. Spending by industry on pollution control has averaged 3 per cent of total sales revenues, and this figure has risen to 20 per cent or more for some of the more polluting industries such as chemicals, paper and mining.[1] But while some firms have seen their costs escalate as a consequence of having to conform with more rigorous environment regulations, other firms have been favourably affected. Suppliers of pollution abatement equipment and pollution monitoring systems have found themselves in a rapidly growing market. Many companies have discovered that going 'green' can be a profitable way of doing business.[2]

Environment problems relate primarily to issues such as water reserves and water quality, air quality, soil contamination, disposal of waste and depletion of natural resources. At one time, depletion of non-renewable resources, in particular fossil fuels, was regarded as the major physical constraint on economic growth. Today, the focus of concern has shifted towards the deterioration in air and water quality, the disposal of waste and the protection of natural areas.

The environment has a strong economic, as well as scientific, dimension. From an economics perspective, the problem is that ownership of fresh air and good water supplies is not clearly vested. Access to ocean fisheries and large tracts of natural rainforest is unrestricted because there is no clear owner of these resources. Environmental goods and services are not supplied in the shops like

---

[1] Jean-Claude Paye, 'Investing in a clean environment', *OECD Observer* (February/March 1996), p. 4.

[2] There is strong competition among large, consumer-oriented firms for leadership on environmental issues. What began for many firms as a government-regulated burden has become a way of reducing waste, conserving resources, improving public image and making profits.

apples or computers. Consumers might care desperately about the quality of the environment, but there is no market through which they can express their preferences. Environmental quality confronts us with extreme examples of public goods, externalities and market failure as outlined in Chapter 8. Because there is no well-defined market for environmental goods, nobody has an incentive to ensure that these resources are carefully husbanded. *The absence of a market price means that the scarcity value of these resources is not signalled to the consumer. This means that they will tend to be abused and overexploited.*

Because the optimal allocation of vital environmental resources cannot be assured by the free market, government intervention is necessary. But for government intervention to be effective and efficient, ways have to be found of inferring the value consumers place on non-market goods, and then of imposing the requisite taxes and subsidies to correct these externalities, where feasible, and using direct regulation where it is not. Finding the optimum mix of these measures is important for economic efficiency.

There is a global, as well as a national, dimension to the environmental problem. Traditionally, economists took an unending supply of clean water and air for granted. These were labelled 'free' goods, to which no price was applied because there was no scarcity. This was an acceptable assumption when world population was little more than a billion and when industrialisation and energy consumption were a fraction of their level today. We know now that these resources are not infinite. The water table in many parts of India and China has fallen steeply in the past two decades, as it has in southern Spain, the Aral Sea and in parts of the US. Under the North China plain, including Beijing and Tienjin, the water table is disappearing by 1–2 metres per year. The area covered by the Aral Sea has dwindled by 60 per cent since 1960, mainly because of the draw-down of irrigation waters from the rivers flowing into the sea. As world population continues to grow – it has now reached 6.3 billion people and is predicted to reach 10 billion by 2050 – the air quality in the world's mega-cities and the quality of water supply have become major issues. Acid rain, global warming, through the release of greenhouse gases, and the depletion of the ozone layer have also entered the debate. These problems have a predominantly international dimension and need to be tackled on a multilateral basis. They also raise deeper issues concerning the extent to which the global ecosystem, which has finite absorptive and accommodating capacities, will impose an ultimate limit to economic growth.

## Chapter outline

1. The relationship between economic growth and the environment.

2. Setting and attaining environmental objectives.

3. Instruments of environmental policy, distinguishing between market incentives and the traditional regulatory approach of setting quantity-based pollution emission standards.

4. Implications for business.

## 9.1 Economic growth and the environment

It is sometimes argued that economic growth and improved environmental quality are irreconcilable objectives; that economic growth must inevitably lead to further environmental degradation. However, this view takes account of only one of the links between the environment and economic growth. In reality, the environmental impact of economic growth is more complex than this.

1. Economic growth entails increased pressures on the environment if there are no changes in the way the economy operates. Hence it leads to a decline in environmental quality via a *scale effect*.
2. The *composition* of economic activity changes with the various stages of economic development. When economic growth takes off, economies move out of agriculture and into manufacturing, thereby increasing the resource and pollution intensity per unit of production. As income levels grow even higher, service activities increase their share in the economy. Because services are generally characterised by low pollution levels per unit of production, this slows down pollution.
3. As economies expand, *technology* reduces pollution per unit of product. In market economies, the drive to minimise production costs gives an incentive to energy efficiency and reduced material intensity.
4. *Environment policy* comes into play. The willingness to pay for environmental quality grows with income. Environmental policies affect behaviour. They mandate price incentives in favour of clean activities and penalise pollution-intensive activities. Technology and innovation are stimulated in a certain direction by the resulting change in explicit and implicit price structures. Higher energy prices, for example, stimulate research into more fuel-efficient cars and machinery. Consumers may also directly affect this trend by increasing their demand for environmentally friendly products.

Empirical data show a complex set of correlations between economic growth and different types of environmental pollution. Air and water quality indicators reveal considerable diversity in effluent patterns as countries become richer. In Figure 9.1, the quantity of effluents is graphed on the vertical axis and GDP on the horizontal axis. In the early stage of development, the strain on the environment grows rapidly. Industrialisation initially inflicts severe damage on air quality and the physical urban environment. Yet the graph indicates that, while some aspects of the living environment change for the worse, some basic indicators of local pollution (such as access to safe drinking water) improve at a very early stage in the growth process.

Once a certain income level is reached, growth not only tends to raise citizens' preferences for a clean environment, but also provides the financial resources for taking effective policy action. The output of certain effluents has an inverted U-shaped pattern over time. Pollution levels rise, stabilise and then decline. The turning point for the majority of pollutants occurs at an income per capita level of around $10,000. Suspended particle matters, sulphur dioxide, airborne lead, carbon monoxide, nitrogen dioxide, faecal coliform and oxygen-depleting substances in rivers follow such an inverted U-shape. Smoke and lead emissions emanating from some of Europe's main cities (London, for example) are about half what they were 30 years ago, and the quality of European rivers and lakes has

## Figure 9.1  A stylised view of the relations between economic growth and the environment

**(a) Typical local pollution** (e.g. population without safe water)

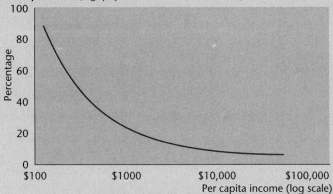

**(b) Typical regional pollution** (e.g. sulphur dioxide)

**(c) Typical global pollution** (e.g. carbon dioxide per capita[a])

[a]Emissions are from fossil fuels.

*Source*: Based on World Bank, *World Development Report* (1992).

also improved in certain respects during this period. The layout of housing estates and urban landscapes has improved as a result of tighter and more enlightened planning requirements. The concentration reversal shown by the inverted U is due, in order of importance, to: (a) the compositional effect, i.e. the shift from manufacturing to services, (b) tighter regulations, and (c) new technologies. In industrial countries, the inverted U-shape has largely hinged on the changing composition of aggregate production.[3]

In contrast with this reassuring picture, some types of effluent concentrations increase monotonically with development, e.g. greenhouse gases (carbon and nitrous oxides) and municipal wastes. Problems of diminished biodiversity, depletion of the ozone layer, acid rain and, in certain areas, a falling water table also continue to worsen. Transport pollution, in general, has proven resistant to control. Road-vehicle traffic continues to grow and the energy intensity of transport has not improved.

Industrial countries typically spend around 1.5–2.0 per cent of their national income on pollution abatement.[4] Provided pollution abatement policies are based on proper cost–benefit analysis, however, the benefits from improved environmental quality should outweigh the costs and there should be a net welfare gain. Contrary to common belief, environmental protection is not job-destroying. If account is taken of new jobs generated by the environment protection industry itself, environmental policies have had, overall, *a beneficial (although small) impact on employment.*[5]

### Table 9.1 Carbon dioxide emissions*

| | Total (million metric tonnes) | | Per capita (metric tonnes) | |
|---|---|---|---|---|
| | 1980 | 1998 | 1980 | 1998 |
| China | 1,476.8 | 3,108.0 | 1.5 | 2.5 |
| India | 347.3 | 1,061.0 | 0.5 | 1.1 |
| Japan | 920.4 | 1,133.5 | 7.9 | 9.0 |
| Russian Federation | — | 1,434.6 | — | 9.8 |
| United Kingdom | 580.3 | 542.3 | 10.3 | 9.2 |
| EU-15 | 1,565.2 | 2,431.9 | 7.5 | 8.0 |
| United States | 4,626.8 | 5,447.6 | 20.4 | 19.8 |
| Low income | 772.4 | 2,416.1 | 0.5 | 1.0 |
| Middle income | 4,266.1 | 9,211.7 | 2.3 | 3.5 |
| High income | 8,814.2 | 11,197.2 | 12.4 | 12.6 |
| World | 13,852.7 | 22,825.0 | 3.4 | 3.9 |

* Carbon dioxide ($CO_2$) accounts for 49 per cent of total greenhouse gas emissions.

*Source*: World Bank, *World Development Indicators 2002*.

[3] G. Grossman and A. Krueger, 'Economic growth and environmental quality', *Quarterly Journal of Economics*, 110 (1995).

[4] R. Turner, D. Pearce and I. Bateman, *Environmental Economics: An elementary introduction* (Hemel Hempstead: Harvester Wheatsheaf, 1994), p. 240; B. Field and M. Field, *Environmental Economics*, 3rd edn (London: McGraw-Hill, 2002), p. 9.

[5] Jean-Claude Paye, 'Investing in a clean environment', *OECD Observer* (February/March 1996), p. 5.

As countries become richer, they first clean up the most pressing environmental problems that pose direct health hazards and fall exclusively within the national domain. At a later stage they turn to the more complex threats to the regional and global environment. Economic growth assists this process by generating the means to finance pollution abatement and to consider environment-improving strategies.

It is clear from the above that the environment is not just a matter of concern for developed economies. It also affects developing countries. Developed countries are responsible for more than two-thirds of greenhouse emissions at present, but developing countries are growing fast and are consuming more energy. China's carbon dioxide emissions, for example, already exceed those of the entire EU (Table 9.1) and show no signs of abating. By 2025, today's *developing countries will account for two-thirds of global greenhouse emissions*. This will have major implications for their own citizens as well as for the global ecosystem.

## 9.2 Environmental policies

### Setting objectives

It is not easy to set quantifiable objectives for environmental policy. First, scientists disagree about the extent and consequences of environmental degradation. Anyone attending a public hearing on the environmental impact of a motorway, a chemical plant or a new mine will be struck by the contradictory evaluations of the different parties' environmental impact statements. Second, the impact on the *global* environment is even more complex to evaluate than the *national* or the *local* impact. Third, it can be difficult to disentangle disagreements about the consequences of pollution from objections to the income distribution effects of measures to deal with them.

To illustrate the problem, consider the topical issue of how to deal with greenhouse gases. The *greenhouse effect* refers to the concentration of greenhouse gases (such as carbon dioxide, methane and nitrous oxide) in the atmosphere leading to global warming. Fossil fuel industries and agriculture are the two industries most likely to generate such emissions. According to some mainstream scientists, the greenhouse effect is already having a visible impact on the economy through flooding and extreme weather conditions across Europe and elsewhere. Initially, global warming may have a favourable impact on parts of the world (higher agricultural output, less need for energy) but, as temperatures increase, the costs will become apparent as populations in low-lying areas are displaced and drought begins to affect many regions. There are likely to be serious income distribution effects. Low-lying Bangladesh, Egypt and the Netherlands will be adversely affected, while higher-lying areas in cold climates will benefit. Other countries may experience extremes of heat and cold, with unpredictable consequences.

In such circumstances, the objective of policy is determined by weighing the benefits to society of reducing greenhouse emissions against the cost of controlling them. In order to do this, first we need to estimate the benefits to be

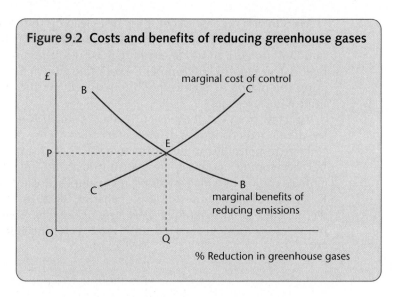

**Figure 9.2 Costs and benefits of reducing greenhouse gases**

obtained from reducing/avoiding damage due to greenhouse gases; and, second, estimates must be made of the cost of controlling these emissions.

The benefits to society of control of greenhouse gases are represented by BB in Figure 9.2. BB is downward-sloping because, once emissions have been reduced beyond a certain level, the marginal benefits of further reductions in greenhouse gases decline. The marginal social cost of reducing emissions is drawn as the upward-sloping curve CC, reflecting the hypothesis that increasing amounts of economic activity would have to be curtailed in order to squeeze out the last vestiges of greenhouse gases. The two curves intersect at E, indicating an optimal level of reduction in pollution of OQ. To insist on a higher rate of reduction would involve greater marginal costs than benefits. To choose a lower rate than OQ would mean allowing more pollution than is socially desirable.

By this reckoning, OQ is the objective, the optimal level of greenhouse gas emissions. By conceptualising the problem in this way, we find, repeating the lesson of Chapter 8, that from an economic point of view a complete ban on emissions would be sub-optimal. The optimal level of emission is not zero.

But how do we assign actual numbers to costs and benefits? Often, we do not have sufficient empirical information to identify the exact location of point E. In the greenhouse gases case, there have been many estimates of the CC curve. Most economic studies of global warming have focused on ways of minimising the cost of achieving a given reduction in greenhouse gas emissions, through a combination of fiscal and regulatory instruments. But estimating BB has proven difficult.

One way forward is to adopt a *'no regret'*, or *precautionary, principle*. Thus, even a very low risk of catastrophic damage should induce society to take countervailing action. In the case of greenhouse gases, the Kyoto conference (December 1997) attempted to restrain greenhouse gas emissions to 5 per cent below the 1990 level by 2012, while the Montreal Protocol (1987) and its successive amendments envisaged the complete phasing out of chlorofluorocarbon (CFC) emissions.[6] Progress could also be made by governments correcting local externalities which have an incidental effect of reducing emissions. That way, even if concern about greenhouse gases were to turn out to be mistaken, minimal economic loss would be incurred because the measures taken would be justifiable in their own right. For example, the removal of subsidies to coal could be justified on the grounds that coal-burning causes local air pollution.

Various methods have been proposed to measure the benefits of an environmental resource. Take, for example, the recreational use of a lake created by a dam. One way of finding out its value to the public would be to ask individuals, by means of a questionnaire, how much they would be prepared to pay for such use. This is the *contingency valuation method*. Another method of inferring values is by *hedonic pricing techniques*, used to estimate the disutility of airport noise, bad air quality in cities or the value of a woodland amenity. Here we compare house prices near airports (say) with those, equal in other respects, in a quiet area. The difference can be indicative of the capitalised value of a quieter environment. A *production function approach* can also be used whereby we assign a value to the environment equal to the amount consumers pay in order to produce substitutes themselves. For example, the amount spent by consumers on domestic water purification apparatus for tap water could be taken as a rough indicator of the value to them of higher water quality. The amount spent on noise insulation may be an indicator of the value people in cities place on being insulated from traffic noise. Depending on the problem, one might use one or a combination of these three methods of assessing the social value of the environment.

The depth and extent of reaction to a diminution in environmental quality *from those who are themselves unlikely to be directly affected by it* can be surprisingly strong. People who have never gone on a safari worry about wildlife, and stay-at-homes can get just as upset as seasoned travellers by the erosion of the Nepalese valleys. The resultant value is called *the non-use value of a resource*. The utility of non-users accounts for more than half the total economic value of wilderness areas and better water quality in lakes and rivers.

Setting measurable environmental objectives places a heavy demand on statistics. The development of environmental indicators, satellite accounts to existing national accounts and, in the long run, integrated economic/environmental national accounts are essential to this exercise and are being developed. Environment impact studies are now compulsory for state-aided projects in the EU and are helping to provide a statistical foundation for a national accounting exercise. From a business perspective, it is important to ensure that there is a strong economic input in specifying the optimal level of pollution and quantifying the economic costs of attaining environmental objectives.

---

[6] The Kyoto agreement has enjoyed limited success. Although signed by 110 countries, they mostly comprised countries unlikely to be affected by the Kyoto restraints or likely to ignore them. The US pulled out in 2001, arguing that it would cost the American economy $445 billion to implement (4–5 per cent of GDP). China and India did not contract into Kyoto, also on grounds of expense. Their share of greenhouse emissions is estimated by the OECD (1998) to rise from 13 per cent in 1990 to 38 per cent in 2050. The agreement was ratified by the EU in 2002. By contrast with Kyoto, the Montreal protocol has been highly successful.

## 9.3 Policy instruments: design and effects

Government environmental policy has been described as *an effort to put a green thumb on Adam Smith's 'invisible hand'*. In the past, the emphasis was on regulation rather than prevention and on administrative controls in preference to market-based incentives. Over time, these regulations have become increasingly onerous because of:

- high administrative costs,
- insufficient flexibility in implementation,
- stultifying effects on industrial innovation.

The economic reasons for preferring market incentives to regulation can be illustrated with a simple example (Figure 9.3). Imagine a paper mill, the output of which is linearly correlated with the amount of pollution. On the horizontal axis we measure quantity of the firm's output, for which there is a corresponding amount of pollution generated. Draw the marginal profit curve of the firm, MP. It is downward-sloping because, as output increases, profits per unit are assumed to fall. The firm continues production up to output OQ. At that point, any further increase in sales will yield negative profits (loss). In terms of Chapter 5, it represents the point where private MC = MR.

Next, the marginal social cost of the pollution created by the factory is represented by the upward-sloping curve MSC. These social costs are external to the firm – private costs are already taken account of in the firm's profit-maximising calculus.

The socially optimal equilibrium point is reached at output OQ*. However, the private profit-maximising firm will want to produce at OQ. To reduce the firm's output, the government could use regulation or market incentives.

**Figure 9.3 Regulation vs tax to reduce pollution**

Output of paper mill (units)

*Source*: Adapted from R. Turner, D. Pearce and I. Bateman, *Environmental Economics: An elementary introduction* (Hemel Hempstead: Harvester Wheatsheaf, 1994).

The government could tackle this problem by setting a fixed emission standard for each firm in the industry. Assume it had perfect information and chose the right level OQ\*. Each firm is instructed not to produce more than OQ\*. What is wrong with this solution? First, the firm has an incentive to evade the regulation. Profit maximisation requires output OQ, not OQ\*. Profits forgone as a result of this restriction amount to the area QEQ\*. Second, as a consequence of this incentive structure, firms will have to be monitored. Forms will have to be filled in, factory visits made, etc. This will involve compliance costs for the firm and administrative costs for the authorities. Third, penalties will have to be introduced in order to ensure compliance. If the financial cost per unit of these penalties to the firm is less than OR per unit, it will pay the firm to produce more than OQ\*. At penalty level OR' per unit, it would be profitable for the firm to produce $OQ_p$, thus breaching the optimal level.

Suppose that a tax OR were imposed instead of the 'command and control' fixed emission standard. The firm would respond to the tax by cutting back output to OQ\*, the optimal output level. One advantage of the tax is that the firm will be *motivated* to reduce output by the dictates of profit maximisation. At output OQ\*, marginal profits are zero; hence the introduction of tax of OR makes production beyond OQ\* uneconomic. The same applies to all output in the range Q\*Q. Second, because of this, close monitoring of each firm's output will not be necessary. Government can focus on the problem of getting the overall tax and pollution level right and let individual firms produce as they like.

A disadvantage of a tax relative to command and control regulation is that it may give the authorities insufficient control over the *absolute* level of pollution. Suppose, for example, the MP curve shifted outwards because of an increase in demand or a reduction in input costs for paper. For a given tax level, the firm's output will increase and also the level of pollution. In cases where it is important that absolute levels are not breached, say for reasons of community health, this would be a consideration in favour of regulation (see below). Another disadvantage of the tax in the above paper mill example is that it is levied on output of paper rather than on the direct output of pollution. Ideally, the tax should be imposed as close to the source of pollution as possible – in order to give maximum incentive to the producer to find ways of reducing the pollution generated by each unit of paper output.

Over and above these theoretical issues, the rising cost of environmental regulation has forced governments to reconsider the merits of market incentives. Market-based instruments refer to price incentives such as pollution taxes, subsidies, deposit-refund systems and tradeable permits. (*Tradeable permits* consist of permits for a specified level of pollution, allowing firms to trade the permits to the highest bidder.) The US, Canada and the Scandinavian countries have been to the fore in employing these measures and their use is being extended to developing countries, including Chile and Mexico. The European Commission has also proposed to use tradeable permits with the aim of helping to cut emissions of greenhouse gases by 8 per cent between 1990 and 2012. The incidence of such measures has grown in recent years. The most pronounced increase was in energy taxes aimed at reducing carbon emissions in the Scandinavian countries and the Netherlands. *Deposit-refund systems* in packaging have also become more common. They are designed to encourage people to return empty bottles and cans. Some countries offer subsidies on trade-ins of old cars in order to prevent owners dumping them in the countryside.[7]

Market-based incentives have many advantages over the 'command-and-control' approach of direct regulation. Use of the price mechanism enables costs and benefits to be weighed by each individual firm and consumer, thereby increasing the probability of achieving a given pollution abatement at least cost. Environmental measures which use the price mechanism have the added advantage of integrating environmental concerns into the design of products and into process innovation (see Box 9.1). A European Commission report expresses it in terms of the polluter pays principle as follows:

> By ensuring that prices reflect underlying scarcities, governments can give consumers, as well as industries, incentives to limit the environmental consequences of their behaviour. The principal advantage of this approach is that the right signals are given to decision-takers. Instead of mandating specific technologies, this policy integrates the environment into everyday decision-making and leaves it to individual agents to find the most promising solutions to environmental problems without compromising their international competitiveness. By drawing upon the full knowledge base of society

---

### Box 9.1  Taxing unleaded petrol

Pollution arising from exhaust emissions is one of several examples of externalities associated with motoring. Motorists take no account of the effect on society of this pollution unless they are charged for it. One way of charging them is to tax petrol. Furthermore, if the emissions from leaded petrol are more dangerous than emissions from unleaded petrol, leaded petrol should be taxed more heavily than unleaded petrol. The rationale behind this action was that lead pollution had adverse effects and, in particular, that it might inhibit children's intellectual development.

Applying the *precautionary principle* and the *polluter pays principle*, governments tried to persuade people to buy less leaded petrol. This was done through a combination of tax and subsidy incentives, and also by regulation.

In the UK there is a tax differential in favour of unleaded petrol. Germany also has a tax differential and, in addition, provides a subsidy to catalytic converters. (Once fitted with a catalytic converter, a car has to use unleaded petrol as lead poisons the catalyst.) An EC directive ruled that, from 1990 onwards, all new cars sold in the EC have to be able to run on unleaded petrol. Many other countries have introduced a tax differential between leaded and unleaded petrol.

These measures resulted in a rise in the share of unleaded petrol in total petrol sales between 1990 and 1998 from 34 per cent to 78 per cent in the UK and from 68 per cent to 100 per cent in Germany. When goods are close substitutes, as are leaded and unleaded petrol, market incentives can be very effective. Differentiation of fuel taxes enabled most EU countries to phase out completely the use of leaded petrol by 1999. Developing countries are introducing similar measures. By 2005, India plans to have completely phased out the use of leaded petrol and China is following close on its heels.

*Source*: Laura Blow, 'Fuel for thought', *Economic Review* (September 1995); Jean-Philippe Barde and Jeffrey Owens, 'The evolution of eco-taxes', *OECD Observer* (February/March 1996).

---

[7]  OECD, *Managing the Environment: The role of economic instruments* (Paris: OECD, 1994).

rather than upon the technical know-how of a limited number of regulators, such a strategy is often likely to generate least cost solutions. Furthermore, as environmental improvements are rewarded, a powerful incentive is given to develop clean technologies and production processes. This, in turn, might trigger further improvements in technology via a trickle-down effect and bolster the position on international markets.[8]

The European Commission has introduced a macroeconomic rationale for more intensive use of green tax/subsidy measures by pointing out that they could have the added advantage of alleviating unemployment, if revenue from eco-taxes could be applied towards reducing taxes on labour. In its 1993 White Paper, *Economic Growth, Competition and Employment*, the Commission referred to the 'under-use' of labour combined with 'over-use' of environmental resources. Yet taxes on labour, a factor we want business to hire in greater numbers, yield ten times more tax revenue than taxes on the environment, which we want business to utilise less intensively (Table 9.2).

In a speech on 2 August 1995, the British Chancellor, commenting on his new landfill tax proposal, said that by raising revenue from waste disposal, Britain would be able to make further cuts in employers' insurance contributions and so create more jobs: '*We will tax waste more and jobs less.*' The benefits from such reorientation of policy could be significant. By relieving the unemployment problem, economic growth in Europe could be increased at the same time as improving the environment. Furthermore, the quality of economic growth could be enhanced and the connection between growth and human welfare brought closer together.

By far the most widely discussed economic instrument for the environment in Europe has been a carbon tax. The idea was to levy a tax on the carbon content of fuels in order to cut back the amount of carbon dioxide released into the atmosphere. This proposal has been criticised on several grounds. The first is inadequate

**Table 9.2 Tax structure in the European Community**

|  | Total revenues (per cent) | GDP (per cent) |
|---|---|---|
| Taxes on consumption | 26.3 | 10.9 |
| Taxes on labour | 56.7 | 23.4 |
| Taxes on capital | 17.0 | 7.0 |
| **Total** | **100.0** | **41.3** |
| *Of which*: |  |  |
| Revenues from taxes linked to environmental problems | 6.33 | 2.66 |
| – Transport (vehicle ownership and purchase, vehicle fuels) |  | 2.37 |
| – Energy |  | 0.21 |
| – Pollution and others (e.g. soil, air, water, noise) |  | 0.07 |

*Source*: European Commission, *Economic Growth and the Environment: Some implications for economic policy-making* (Brussels, 1994).

8 European Commission, *Economic Growth and the Environment: Some implications for economic policy-making* (Brussels, 1994, COM 94/465), p. 10.

'ring-fencing' – critics argue that additional revenues from carbon taxes would be used to bolster government spending instead of reducing labour taxes. Second, if Europe introduced stiff carbon taxes without parallel action in competitor countries, energy-intensive sectors could suffer competitive losses, with potentially damaging consequences to jobs. Third, to achieve carbon reduction targets, high tax rates would have to be imposed. According to one estimate, an increase in oil prices of 128 per cent in real terms would be required in order to bring about a 20 per cent reduction in the carbon content of fossil fuels in the UK.[9] Although the Scandinavian countries have introduced a form of carbon tax, agreement on the desirability, not to mention the level and application, of such a tax has still to be achieved at EU level. A new Directive on Taxation of Energy has, however, come into force in 2004 that sets minimum tax levels in Member States for coal, electricity and oil products.

## Effects of intervention

Despite the many advantages of market-based measures, regulatory intervention, enforced by penalties, is necessary in some cases. Regulation may be superior where:

- major health risks are involved (e.g. toxic waste),
- risks of catastrophic failure are present, such as nuclear power plants,
- the amount of pollution generated by the polluter (i.e. at the level of an individual plant) cannot be measured precisely.

However, government intervention, whether market-based or regulatory, can 'fail'. Lack of information, the danger of regulatory capture, intrusiveness of bureaucracy and rent-seeking by lobby groups all serve to diminish the effectiveness of such intervention. 'Failure' can apply both in the process of specifying the target levels of pollution (which may be set too high in response to green lobbies or too low in response to industry lobbies) and in deciding the level of incentives or penalties needed to attain these targets. Often, intervention in one sector of

### Table 9.3 Energy efficiency

|  | GDP per unit of energy use (PPP $ per kg oil equivalent) | |
| --- | --- | --- |
|  | 1980 | 1999 |
| United States | 1.6 | 3.9 |
| EU-15 | 2.8 | 5.9 |
| Japan | 3.4 | 6.3 |
| China | 0.8 | 4.2 |
| India | 1.9 | 4.7 |

*Source*: World Bank, *World Development Indicators 2003*.

---

[9] A. Ingham and A. Ulph, 'Carbon taxes and the UK manufacturing sector', in F. Dietz, F. van der Ploeg and J. Van der Straaten (eds), *Environmental Policy and the Economy* (Amsterdam: Elsevier, 1991).

the economy frustrates the effectiveness of environmental efforts in another. Agricultural supports have led to overuse of chemicals, overgrazing and water pollution. Subsidies to irrigation have accentuated the problems of salination and water shortage in many developing countries. Energy subsidies have led to overuse of fossil fuels, thus exacerbating the pollution problem.

But, for all the qualifications, intervention has been superior to inaction. One of the success stories is the reduction in lead and smoke emissions in urban areas in many industrial countries. Also, because European post-tax energy prices have been 25 to 50 per cent higher than in the US, the EU can produce 60 per cent more GDP per unit of energy than the US (Table 9.3).

## 9.4 Impact on business

The new approach to environmental issues has had a profound impact on business. Although originally the concerns of environmentalists and industrialists were regarded as antithetical, attitudes have changed considerably. Many firms now pride themselves on their green image. Business organisations have pledged their support for environmental improvement. Groups such as the Business Council for Sustainable Development (BCSD) and the 'Responsible Care' programme set up by US chemical manufacturers have compiled 'good practice' guidelines for environmentally friendly behaviour by companies. Some involve firms committing themselves to tracking the environmental impact of their products right through their lifecycle, from manufacture to final disposal.

Frances Cairncross has identified five positive motivations for this about-turn in business attitudes:[10]

1. *Employee morale*: employees want their firm to have an environmental record of which they can be proud. They dislike being associated with a 'dirty' industry.
2. *Consumer tastes*: shoppers are more interested in 'green' products (though often unwilling to pay for their green preferences) and respond positively to favourable publicity.
3. *Good publicity* strengthens the corporate image. It can be important for multinationals selling directly to the consumer (such as McDonald's), to companies subject to government taxes and hence vulnerable to political pressure (petrol companies, brewing), and to firms in the mining, oil and chemical business, which frequently interact with planning authorities where their 'reputation' may be an important aspect of the final decision. The fear of bad publicity, even if undeserved, led Shell to abandon its plans to sink the Brent Spar oil rig at sea in 1995.
4. *Cost savings*: companies have found that reducing waste and conserving energy and raw materials can be profitable, especially in view of the rising costs of waste disposal. 3M's 'Pollution Prevention Pays' scheme claims to have saved some $500 million since 1975. Tough environmental policies can save firms money.

---

[10] Frances Cairncross, *Green Inc.: A guide to business and the environment* (London: Earthscan, 1995), p. 64.

5. *Market niche*: a 'green' image can be important for sales of food and disposable products, and can be an effective way of establishing a strong market niche.

These positive factors are important for firms which are subject to public scrutiny and where information on their 'greenness' can be compiled. But, given the unwillingness of many customers to pay a premium for green products, the movement would have been much slower and less decisive in direction had it not been buttressed by government legislation and enforcement. In this regard, the *threat of litigation* has added a powerful incentive to firms to conform to environmental regulations. Litigation has become a major worry for firms, and for their insurers, because it can be immensely costly as well as generating negative publicity (regardless almost of the verdict). It also creates uncertainty; firms can be liable for damages and clean-up costs of not only present but also past pollution, for which the current management of the firm may have had no responsibility. Litigation can be initiated by environmental authorities and even by individuals who take action against the authorities for not enforcing their rules with sufficient zeal.

Environmental policy affects business in many different ways. First, it reduces costs for some business inputs. A fishing hotel on a lake will benefit from tighter rules on sewage disposal in nearby towns. German paper companies have benefited from the recycling laws which have increased the supply of cheap recycled pulp. A country's food and drinks industry may gain from the improvement of its green image.

Second, environmental consciousness may encourage innovation, with the possibility of discovering new and more efficient processes and products, and/or creating new markets for a company's products. Johnson Matthey benefited from the growth of catalytic converters since it mines platinum and palladium, key ingredients in a catalyst. By adjusting its product design, Procter & Gamble benefited from the shift in preferences to greener products (Box 9.2). Professor Michael Porter, a strong advocate of the benefits of environmental regulation for industry, cites other cases of what he calls *innovation offsets*:

> Process changes to reduce emissions frequently result in increases in product yields. At Ciba-Geigy's dyestuff plant in New Jersey, the need to meet new environmental standards caused the firm to re-examine its waste water streams. Two changes in its production process – replacing iron with a different chemical conversion agent and process changes that eliminated the release of toxic products into the waste water stream – not only boosted yield by 40 per cent but also eliminated wastes, resulting in annual cost savings of nearly $1 million.[11]

Generally, firms involved in innovative techniques for waste disposal, energy efficiency improvements, leisure industries with minimal adverse environmental effects, firms specialising in environmental audits, environmental impact studies, eco-labelling and suchlike can be expected to have improved opportunities. Automobile firms which are successful in developing environmentally friendly cars can anticipate substantial returns. Case studies confirm that it is possible that innovation offsets, even under a strict regulatory regime not intended to

---

[11] Michael E. Porter and Claas van der Linde, 'Towards a new conception of the environment–competitiveness relationship', *Journal of Economic Perspectives* (Fall 1995), p. 102.

> ### Box 9.2  Green as a selling point
>
> During the 1980s, detergent manufacturers began to find ways to use the environ-mental properties of their products as selling points. One was Procter & Gamble (P&G). In the early 1980s, a technician at its French division came up with the idea of the flexible plastic 'dosing' ball. It had two advantages: it stopped powdered detergent from blocking the dispenser and it allowed a highly concentrated washing solution to engulf the clothes for the first 10 minutes of a wash. The ball stimulated P&G to develop concentrated liquid detergent that could be sold in a recyclable plastic con-tainer. Also, the firm developed a refill carton, thereby reducing household packaging waste. As a result, liquid detergents increased their market share. Refill cartons proved popular with environmentalists and also with the supermarkets, partly because they take up much less shelf space per wash than concentrated powders.
>
> *Source*: Frances Cairncross, *Green Inc.: A guide to business and the environment* (London: Earthscan, 1995).

encourage innovation, can provide benefits in excess of compliance costs to the affected firms. Early development of new products with attractive environmental features can give companies an 'early mover' advantage, such as that enjoyed by Scandinavian pulp and paper manufacturers, and by some German firms in package-intensive products. A key requirement for this to happen is that national environmental standards should anticipate international trends in environmental protection.

Third, tighter environmental regulation can in some circumstances give one company or industry a lead over its rivals. Thus, the major chlorofluorocarbon (CFC) producers, such as DuPont and ICI, were influential in backing the Montreal Protocol, the treaty to reduce the use of CFCs through aerosol propel-lants, refrigerants and solvents. As well as producing CFCs, these firms also hap-pened to be the main producers of the nearest chemical substitute to CFCs. But since the substitute was also more expensive than the CFCs, they had an obvious interest in securing a properly enforced global agreement on CFCs. A national ban by one government alone would have exposed domestic producers of the expensive substitute to unfair competition from CFCs made in other countries. Hence a company that has developed substitutes will do well from tighter regula-tions or changes in tastes, provided the regulations or taxes are universally applied and consistently enforced. Environmentally clean firms may also benefit by attracting ethical mutual funds. This could be advantageous to these firms' reputation, albeit not necessarily providing them with cheap capital. Ethical funds to date have not earned notably lower rates of return than other funds.

Since the establishment of the Toxic Release Inventory in 1986, more than 20,000 American manufacturing plants have a legal obligation to publish details of their releases of some 320 hazardous chemicals. In the belief that attack is the best method of defence, a growing number of American companies have responded by including an environmental audit in their financial statements. In Europe, this practice has gained some adherents. Norsk Hydro, for example, a chemical and fertiliser manufacturer, publishes reports with detailed figures on emissions and discharges, measured against authorised limits. British Gas publishes an environmental review of its approach to subjects such as contaminated land and energy efficiency, and the Chartered Association of Certified Accountants holds an annual competition for the best environmental reports.

Fourth, environment policy can have an important impact on a firm's international competitiveness. High product standards can sometimes restrain foreign competition. For example, the European Commission's ban on the use of certain growth hormones prevents US hormone-treated meat from competing with EU producers. In other circumstances, rules relating to production processes and methods applied in the home country can give a competitive advantage to firms producing in countries with less stringent standards. As noted above, environment policy has strong sectoral effects. Firms in polluting industries find their cost structure has risen. The consequences can be seen in the opposition to the proposed carbon tax in Europe from energy-intensive building materials and transport industries which perceive (rightly) that the measure will lead to higher energy costs, and hence to higher prices and diminished demand for their products. The nuclear industry, on the other hand, is supportive of the proposal since it sees the carbon tax as promoting its cost advantage relative to power generators using coal or oil. These sectoral conflicts are an inevitable consequence of any economic change.

Environment policy has implications for income distribution within countries. A tax on energy may make sense in environmental terms, but it will be unpopular with those directly affected. Unfortunately, many eco-taxes hurt the poor proportionately more severely than the better-off. They are examples of *regressive* taxes.[12] The attempt by the UK government to raise value added tax on energy consumption in the mid-1990s generated such an electoral backlash that the proposal had to be effectively abandoned. Attempts to compensate the losers proved ineffective, and the gainers – the environmental lobby – failed to support the measure.

## 9.5 Conclusions

The concept of an environmentally sustainable growth rate has captured the attention of economic policy-makers. The Earth Summit at Rio de Janeiro in 1992 exposed an entire generation of politicians and citizens to environmental ideas. However, the relationship between economic growth, the environment and human welfare is more complex than headlines or political slogans suggest. Higher GDP and a better environment can in many respects be complementary objectives. Prosperity allows people the luxury of becoming more environmentally conscious and makes them better able to afford higher environmental standards. It is extreme poverty (i.e. the lack of GDP) that creates the mind-set of short time-horizons and a lower propensity to plan far into the future.

---

[12] In calculating these income distribution effects, one has to have regard of the ultimate incidence of the tax. As we saw in Chapter 3, just because a tax happens to be levied on the supplier (say, an electricity generating station), that does not mean that the supplier suffers the whole incidence of the tax. The incidence will depend on the price elasticities of demand and supply.

Improving environmental performance is not inconsistent with a firm maintaining competitive advantage. At the extreme, environmental catastrophes such as at Bhopal (1984), the *Exxon Valdez* (1989) and *Diamond Grace* (1997) can have dramatically adverse effects on a firm's financial viability, and environmental strategies are needed to find cost-efficient ways of minimising these risks. Moreover, environmental regulation often encourages firms to use their resources more efficiently. Many forms of environmental pollution by firms, whether in the form of discharges, toxic materials or discarded packaging, are simply waste in a different guise. Opportunities exist to eliminate such waste through redesigning products and processes, and through innovative ways of reorganising operations. Through innovation, some environmental problems at least can be reduced or eliminated without incurring substantial costs. There are instances where a reduction in environmental pollution has even reduced business costs and improved product quality.

Throughout Part I of the book we have emphasised the role of the market and the importance of competition in an efficient economic system. Environmental economics addresses the problems that arise when the market 'fails' – either because property rights are not defined, as in the ocean fisheries, or because of the intrinsic nature of environmental goods. Government intervention becomes essential to an optimal outcome. But government intervention does not mean ignoring altogether the market mechanism. Good environment policy consists in setting objectives and using market mechanisms to achieve them. This is easier said than done. A strong state sector does not guarantee a good environment, as the degradation of the environment in many countries testifies.

## Summary

1. The integration of environmental and economic policies is important for achieving sustainable growth. Measures in place are already having a major impact on business. Business cannot afford to neglect environmental concerns.

2. The relationship between quality of the environment and economic growth is complex. After a certain level of prosperity has been reached, some forms of pollution seem to abate. This happens partly because of shifts in the composition of demand away from manufacturing towards less polluting services and partly because richer countries are able to afford to give higher priority to pollution control. In many respects – water quality and clean air in urban areas, for instance – the quality of the environment in the advanced industrial countries is better than it was at the start of this century. In developing countries, by contrast, the early stages of industrialisation and the development of agriculture have been associated with environmental degradation. One billion people still lack adequate supplies of drinking water.

3. The relationship between economic growth and problems such as global warming is still not known with precision. Yet there is support for countervailing action on the basis of the precautionary principle.

4. Environmental priorities should be set so as to equate the cost of cleaning up, or preventing, an additional unit of pollution with the benefit of higher output to

society. Various techniques for measuring these benefits and costs have been developed. There is a need for an extensive statistical base on environmental quality to make environmental impact assessments more accurate and useful.

5. The instruments of environmental policy include market incentives and regulation. Both have a role to play in achieving policy objectives. Regulation has been costly to implement, and there has been a swing towards market-based incentives through policies of the 'polluter pays' type.

6. The impact of environmental policy on business is a thorny question. Some argue that environment policy can be a spur to innovation and can force industries into efficiency. Others worry about the costs and the delays caused by this policy. All agree that there are strong sectoral effects and, as with economic policies generally, well-defined losers as well as gainers. Firms with a positive approach to environmental issues can benefit through improvements in reputation, in employee morale and in product quality.

## Questions for discussion

1. The costs of environmental protection are perceived as being too burdensome for many businesses confronting international competition in an increasingly open economy. It has also been argued that many governments struggling with large budget deficits cannot afford high environmental standards. Yet there is a bedrock of public support for environmental goals. Discuss the economic costs and the benefits of environmental improvement from:

   (a) a business perspective,
   (b) an overall economy perspective.

2. Give examples of ways in which environmental protection can be profitable for business. Under what circumstances can environment policy damage business?

3. Outline the main advantages and limitations of the 'polluter pays' principle.

4. Discuss possible sources of 'government failure' in the application and administration of environmental policy.

5. 'Market prices should as far as possible be made to reflect the external costs to society of economic activity.' What methods can governments use to 'internalise' the social costs of environmental damage?

6. Many studies have shown that the application of nitrogen fertilisers to agricultural land causes pollution. What measures could be taken to reduce this pollution?

7. If people travel on a bus that causes pollution, should government try to reduce the emission from the bus by taxing the transport company or the bus passengers?

# Exercises

1. Many corporations, especially those in environmentally sensitive industries, allocate a section of their Annual Report to explaining their environmental policy. Describe and evaluate such a policy statement in a firm of your choice.

2. According to some estimates, a $200 carbon tax would cut carbon dioxide emissions by four to five times as much as an equivalent $200 devoted to subsidising energy conservation. Why might this be so?

3. Waste management has become a major priority for governments in the 2000s. A new EU Directive (The Waste Electrical and Electronic Equipment Directive) makes business responsible for the electrical and electronic products they produce and obliges firms to recover and recycle their products when they reach the end of their useful life. Consumers are entitled, as from 2004, to return waste equipment either to the place of purchase or to an authorised collection point *free of charge*. From this point, firms will be responsible for collection, recovery and recycling.

    (a) Apply the 'polluter pays' principle to an analysis of this regulation.
    (b) The affected industries have argued that they should be permitted to impose a collective tax on the products to cover the costs of complying with the Directive. Examine the economic case for and against such action.

4. Consider a tax on petrol, imposed because of concern about air quality. The objective of the tax is to reduce vehicle emissions. Given that the price elasticity of demand for petrol is well below unity, examine the effects of the tax under each of the following headings.

    (a) Does it discourage an activity that causes environmental harm?
    (b) Does it place a burden on those responsible for the environmental problem?
    (c) Does it minimise administrative costs to government and to payers of the tax relative to the benefits expected?
    (d) Does it provide a dynamic incentive for petrol refineries and car manufacturers to innovate and upgrade product quality?

5. It is often claimed that multinational subsidiaries apply higher environmental standards in the host country than domestically owned competitors. Give reasons why this might be the case. Would you expect multinationals to apply different standards in plants in the host country to those in the home country?

6. Two approaches could be used to protect endangered species such as elephants.

    (a) Developing countries impose restictions on *exports* of ivory.
    (b) Developing countries impose restrictions on ivory *imports*.

    Use demand and supply analysis to find out which of these two policies a developing country would prefer. (Assume for simplicity that demand for ivory comes from developed countries only.)

7. The city of Taiyuan in North China is looking to the market to help solve its air pollution problem. With nine times the air pollution level considered safe for humans, Taiyuan is considered one of the most polluted cities in the world. It proposed to introduce emissions trading in order to achieve a 50 per cent decline in sulphur dioxide output in five years. The source of pollution is concentrated in 24 large

companies that account for half of all emissions. Significantly, these firms have divergent clean-up costs ranging from $60 to $1200 per tonne of gas emitted

(a) Analyse the case for trading permits.

(b) Discuss how such a system might operate.

(c) Explain why it might be considered a more efficient method of reducing pollution than across-the-board direct controls.

8. Water is becoming an increasingly scarce resource. About 70 per cent of water supplies in countries such as China and Morocco is consumed by farmers for irrigation at below-cost prices. Instead of such subsidisation, should farmers be charged the full economic costs of the water they use?

## Further reading

A readable introduction to environmental economics is provided in R. Kerry Turner, David Pearce and Ian Bateman, *Environmental Economics: An elementary introduction* (Hemel Hempstead: Harvester Wheatsheaf, 1994). For an overview of the issues from a business perspective, an excellent source is Frances Cairncross, *Green Inc.: A guide to business and the environment* (London: Earthscan, 1995). The OECD has an ongoing stream of publications on this topic, as does the European Commission. See, for example, 'Economic growth and environmental sustainability – a European perspective', *European Economy*, Brussels, 71/2000. Those interested in environmental project appraisal should consult *The Economic Appraisal of Environmental Projects and Policies: A practical guide* (Paris: OECD, 1995). S. Barrett, *Environment and Statecraft: The strategy of environmental treaty-making* (Oxford: Oxford University Press, 2003) is a brilliant exercise in political economy that casts light on why the Montreal agreement succeeded where Kyoto failed. For a well-informed and slightly iconoclastic view of the environment literature, see B. Lømborg, *The Skeptical Environmentalist: Measuring the real state of the world* (Cambridge: Cambridge University Press, 2001).

## Chapter 10

# Hiring labour and the investment decision

## Introduction

Previous chapters have been concerned with how much output a firm produces, what price it charges and, when discretion over price is lacking, what other measures can be used to boost profits. This chapter considers how the firm should determine the amount of inputs to purchase. By this we mean the number and quality of employees, the amount of plant and machinery, the quantity of energy and commodity and intermediate materials, and so on. Since the same basic principles apply to all inputs, we confine discussion to the economics of hiring labour and the investment decision. Both these subjects are treated in depth in human relations, industrial organisation and corporate finance courses, and no claim is made in this chapter to provide a comprehensive analysis. Yet much light can be thrown on these subjects by the application of the simple economic principles developed in the previous chapters.

## Chapter outline

1. The hiring decision.
2. The firm's investment decision.

## 10.1 The hiring decision

### The classical theory

It follows from the principle of profit maximisation that the firm's demand curve for labour is driven by the rule: hire employees up to the point where

total remuneration costs = the marginal revenue product of labour

That is, the firm should first compute all the costs of hiring an extra unit of labour; second, calculate the net value to the firm of that unit of labour's output;

and third, continue hiring up to the point where costs and benefits are equal. If the cost of hiring an extra employee is £1000 per month and the output of that employee contributes £1500 to profits, the firm should add to its staff. If the marginal revenue product is only £500, the firm should reduce its staff. Equilibrium is reached at the point where costs equal extra revenue.

The marginal revenue product (MRP) depends on several variables. First, it depends on the degree of competition in the product market. If the firm operates in a perfectly competitive market, all its output can be sold at the going market price, and hence the value of the marginal employee is found by multiplying the employee's marginal product by the market price, i.e. $MRP = MP \times P$. If the marginal employee produces 10 units of output at a price of £150, its marginal revenue product is equal to the value of its marginal product, i.e. $10 \times £150 = £1500$. (For simplicity, we assume zero materials cost.)

If, on the other hand, the price were to fall as a result of the extra 10 units being offered on the market, the loss in revenue on existing sales would have to be incorporated in the calculations, by computing marginal revenue (as discussed in Chapter 4). The marginal revenue product from these 10 units is then:

$$MRP = MP \times MR$$

Second, account must be taken of the decline in marginal productivity as more units of labour are applied. If the law of diminishing marginal productivity applies, after a certain point successive increments of labour yield a diminishing return, assuming all other factors such as size of plant, number of machines, etc., remain unchanged. Hence the marginal product curve is assumed to slope downwards. Since the firm's demand curve for labour (DD) depends on the marginal product of labour, it too is downward-sloping (Figure 10.1).

Third, the supply of labour to the firm must be considered. If the firm is a small player in the market, it takes the going 'rate for the job' as given. It can obtain all the employees it wants at that rate, and so will not offer more. Were it to offer less than the going rate, nobody would be willing to work for it. In such circumstances, the supply curve of labour to the firm is a horizontal line ($W_1W_1$ in Figure 10.1). Equilibrium occurs when the firm's supply and demand curves for labour intersect, at point $E_1$.

**Figure 10.1 Demand and supply of labour to the firm**

This simple analysis yields important but familiar conclusions about the relationship between pay and numbers employed by the firm:

1. A rise in pay leads to a fall in the demand for labour. If the ruling pay level were to be $OW_2$ instead of $OW_1$, the equilibrium would change to $E_2$, with $OL_2$ instead of $OL_1$ units of labour demanded.
2. A fall in pay, for the same reasons, leads to a rise in the amount of labour demanded.

## From firm to industry

It is possible to progress from the individual firm's demand and supply of labour to an industry supply and demand curve. The industry demand curve is obtained by the lateral summation of individual firm demand curves. The procedure is the same as that used in deriving market demand curves. The aggregation exercise, however, relies on several strict assumptions about the independence of a firm's demand from the overall level of demand for labour. The industry demand curve, like the individual firm's, is downward-sloping.

The industry supply curve is different from the firm's supply curve. It is no longer horizontal because, while labour might be available to an individual firm at the going rate, the going rate itself is determined by supply and demand at the industry level. Instead, it slopes upwards, reflecting the assumption that higher pay will attract more labour supply. As pay levels increase, more people are attracted to the industry, existing employees are more reluctant to leave the industry and also some may work longer hours. All this is consistent with our model of the rational individual, maximising utility in the workplace.

In this way, we obtain the industry's supply and demand curve. Equilibrium pay is OW, and OL units of labour are demanded and supplied at that pay level (Figure 10.2).

## Disequilibrium in the labour market

The above analysis depicts a market-clearing situation. Pay flexibility ensures that

**Figure 10.2 Industry demand and supply curves for labour**

In a free labour market, demand equals supply. The labour market clears at equilibrium wage OW and employment OL.

everyone who wants work can find it, provided they are prepared to accept an appropriate level of pay. In practice, there are many impediments to adjustment.

Labour markets, for example, can be affected by *trade unions* which exert monopoly power in order to raise pay levels. The labour supply curve then no longer reflects the sum of independent individual utility-maximising decisions, but rather the collective preferences of unions. It becomes a pay-setting schedule, determined by union–management bargaining strategies.

Labour supply can also be distorted by *minimum wages*, by the *tax system* and by other *cost-increasing rigidities*. These prevent, or slow down, the process of adjustment between labour demand and labour supply, and can exacerbate the unemployment problem (we discuss this further in Chapter 14).

Suppose, for example, the labour market was in equilibrium at point $E_1$ where the pay level is $OW_1$, and $OL_1$ are employed (Figure 10.3). The government now decides that this is the minimum pay which employees should ever be asked to accept and enacts legislation accordingly. Pay $OW_1$ becomes the minimum rate.

Now assume that the demand for labour curve shifts downwards from $D_1D_1$ to $D_2D_2$. This could happen because of the announcement of slower growth, which leads to pessimistic expectation for future sales. With a free market, the fall in demand leads to:

- a new equilibrium at $E_2$
- a fall in pay to $OW_2$
- a fall in employment to $OL_2$
- a decline in labour supply of $L_1L_2$ in response to lower pay level.

As a result of the minimum wage legislation, however, the new equilibrium is at $E^*$ instead of $E_2$. Pay does not fall (which is good news for the 'insiders', $OL^*$, who are fortunate to hold on to their jobs). Numbers employed fall to $OL^*$. The burden of adjustment to the decline in demand, in other words, falls entirely on the numbers employed rather than on pay.

In discussion of this type, the term *pay rigidity* is used as an umbrella term to denote all conventions, institutions and legal measures which set an externally imposed 'floor' to pay levels. Some European governments are concerned that the EU's Social Charter, by imposing minimum standards for working and living conditions (hours worked, treatment of part-time workers, provision of benefits), will

Figure 10.3 Economics of the minimum wage

tend to aggravate the unemployment problem. Considerations such as this prompted the British government to insist on an 'opt-out' clause enabling it to reject initiatives based on the Charter. These fears have proved unfounded. European governments are conscious of the need to reduce the indirect costs of hiring labour. France and Germany have both made efforts to roll back some of the more significant cost-increasing features of their social welfare systems.

## Extending the model

The textbook model is a useful starting point, but it needs extensive modification before becoming a useful guide to the operation of the real-world labour markets.

One obvious objection is that labour should not be treated as analogous to a commodity. Employees depend on pay for their livelihood and on their jobs for a feeling of well-being and inclusion. There is a social as well as an economic dimension to the labour market.

Even more serious is the objection that the demand–supply model conceptualises labour as something that can be bought and traded at will, more or less as farm workers once were at hiring fairs, or dock labourers. Hiring a new staff member in today's world is a different matter, for the following reasons.

1. The firm is purchasing a stream of labour services over time, often over many years. It has to assess the pattern of productivity during this period. The productivity pattern can itself be affected by the type of pay structure the firm offers. If a firm does not want to hire an employee, it can call on the services of a consultant or it can decide to contract out. This gives it the flexibility envisaged in the model.
2. The productivity of the employee cannot be known with certainty in advance of actually being at work in the firm and, even after that, productivity is difficult and expensive to monitor. An employee is not a machine which performs according to instructions. A firm has to consider how to motivate its staff. Compensation schemes have to be devised that will encourage maximum participation by the employees and transform them from 'compelled performers' to 'willing contributors'.
3. Employees, like machines, have to be upgraded (trained) but, unlike machines, they can choose to leave their employer after the upgrading.

The standard analysis of the labour market treats marginal productivity of labour as given, once the amount of capital, land and training made available to an employee is given. Business, by contrast, sees marginal product as something that is the manager's job to raise. The level of remuneration is seen as a crucial instrument for raising productivity. Also, it is clear that the whole remuneration 'package' has an important bearing on employee morale and motivation. An attractive pay structure, defined in terms of its progression over time, pension contributions, procedures for promotion and separation, etc., can help a firm to attract and retain the right people in the business. These considerations are especially important when work itself requires intellectual effort and commitment, which cannot be accurately measured and is more difficult to monitor. This is the typical case in high-tech industries. For them, human relations (devising ways of motivating highly skilled and mobile staff) is as much a part of the firm's technology as its patents and machinery.

In deciding how many people to employ, the firm must consider more than the current pay. It needs to calculate the stream of net revenues likely to be generated by the employee over time. From this it must deduct the stream of costs associated with that employee (pay, employer social security, social provision such as holidays, maternity leave). Further deductions must be made in respect of up-front outlay for searching, screening and interviewing. All the above must be discounted at an appropriate rate (see below), and then the impact on profits after tax must be assessed.

From the employee's perspective, accepting a position with a firm also involves long-term consequences which an investment approach is best suited to analyse. Hence a recent graduate may be happy to accept a job in a well-known accounting or law firm for lower pay than in a less prestigious firm, because higher future earnings are expected to result from the prestige of having passed the former's stricter screening process. Also, skilled employees, on leaving their jobs, do not necessarily take the first alternative offered. To take a job which fails to utilise their skills could lead to an erosion of these skills, and also to a loss of status and reputation. Instead, they search around until a better option is found, balancing the lost revenue from being unemployed (net of any unemployment benefits) against the prospect of a better job and a superior flow of future earnings. This leads to the phenomenon known as *search unemployment*, a voluntary withdrawal from the workforce which is entirely consistent with utility-maximising principles.

## 10.2 The investment decision

### Rental cost of capital

Investment consists of an addition to capital stock. Net investment refers to the accretion of capital in a firm, after deducting depreciation. We have seen that, in the case of labour, a profit-maximising firm will apply the wage = marginal revenue product rule, subject to the various qualifications just outlined. The same rule applies to its purchase of raw materials or intermediate materials. In any well-run company, details of marginal revenue product and marginal cost will be properly recorded.

An investment decision by the firm involves the purchase of a machine or a new plant (*physical* investment), or allocating funds to training and upskilling the workforce (*human* investment). In principle, the familiar profit-maximising rule applies. We work out the marginal revenue product of the capital used for the investment and compare it with the cost of capital. Because investment involves a long time-dimension, future returns are hard to define and to measure. Marginal revenue product refers to the stream of net earnings generated by the project over its lifetime. We must find a way of expressing this profile as a single average annual return.

In addition, we must find a formula for deriving the cost of capital. In simple terms, what is called the *rental cost of capital* is determined by three main factors. The first is the rate of interest. Suppose the investment cost the firm £C. Had the firm invested the cash in bonds (or given it to shareholders to invest as they wished), this capital would have earned $i.£C$ annually. If the investment fails to earn more than this, management should not proceed with it. Second, account must be taken of the depreciation of the asset, which we might compute as an annual charge of $\delta.£C$. Third, an adjustment might have to be made for inflation, $\pi$. Assuming the price of the asset rises in line with the general price level, this will result in an annual rise in the nominal value of the asset of $\pi.£C$. Fourth, allowance will also have to be made for taxes on profits of the project, less any capital grants. This can be done by either deducting from the MRP or adding to the estimate of the rental cost of capital. Amalgamating the first three factors gives us an equation for the rental cost of capital, R, as follows:

$$R = (i.£C + \delta.£C - \pi.£C) = £C(i + \delta - \pi)$$

The profit rule states that the firm should continue investing up to the point where this R equals MRP.

To summarise, an investment decision involves the acquisition of an asset which will provide a flow of future benefits, which has to be weighed against an up-front capital outlay and future annual costs. *A key variable in determining the rental cost of capital, and hence the profitability of investment and the demand for investment capital, is the rate of interest.* This negative relationship is the analogue of the relationship between the wage rate and the demand for labour.

The rental cost of capital approach is an intuitively reasonable, but unfamiliar, way of assessing investment. We now proceed to other ways of calculating returns on investment which draw on the same basic framework but which are more widely used in business.

## Techniques for investment appraisal

Any firm has a large number of projects in which it might invest. Each of these projects is an option available to the firm. Some of these options are profitable and some are not. Economic principles offer guidance as to which ought to be chosen. In this context, three main techniques are used for measuring the return on investment:

- net present value
- internal rate of return
- pay-back.

One of the most important techniques for the evaluation of investment projects is that of *net present value (NPV)*. This approach can be defined as follows:

$$\text{NPV} = x_0 + \frac{x_1}{(1+r)} + \frac{x_2}{(1+r)^2} + \ldots + \frac{x_n}{(1+r)^n} + \frac{J}{(1+r)^n}$$

where NPV = net present value, $x_i$ is the net cash flow from the project in year $i$ (i.e. after correcting for inflation), $r$ is the interest or discount rate, $n$ years is the life-span of the project and $J$ represents the scrap value of the investment at the end of the investment period. This technique involves prediction of the annual net cash flows of the project over its lifetime. The cash flows exclude interest payments, since the corporation is assumed to supply all investment funds from debt and equity sources. They are then discounted back to the present in order to give the present value of the investment. In NPV calculations, the interest or discount rate to be used for the test is selected in advance. Management decides the appropriate discount rate. It is the minimum rate of return on capital employed which the firm is prepared to accept. As such it includes the cost of capital and also a risk premium. (For some projects, e.g. oil in politically unstable parts of the world, the risk premium could be a multiple of the firm's cost of capital.) Projects may receive the green light if the NPV discounted at this rate is positive. If there are more such projects than the firm is able to finance, it will most likely choose those projects which have the highest return. The NPV technique, by translating future net cash flows of an investment into current value, represents the capitalised values of this stream of cash. In financial appraisals of investments, this technique is usually referred to as *discounted cash flow (DCF) analysis*.

Another indicator of the return on a project is the *internal rate of return (IRR)*. This is closely related to the NPV technique and is defined as the discount rate ($r^*$) that reduces the net present value of a project to zero:

$$\text{NPV} = 0 = x_0 + \frac{x_1}{(1 + r^*)} + \frac{x_2}{(1 + r^*)^2} + \dots + \frac{x_n}{(1 + r^*)^n} + \frac{J}{(1 + r^*)^n}$$

where the $x_i$ are the net cash-flows after subtracting input costs, and $r^* = $ IRR. This is similar to the formula used for NPV calculations, except that the discount rate $r^*$ is computed so as to equate NPV to zero. A decision rule might be to approve the project provided the IRR is equal to or greater than an agreed discount or interest rate.

The internal rate of return seems to be a convenient way of summarising the returns of a project, and in practice it sometimes makes no difference whether one uses IRR or NPV to rank projects. However, in the cases where it does make a difference, notably when there are negative cash flows later in the project's life (e.g. strip mining and oil industry projects), the IRR can give the wrong ranking. Also, some projects may have more than one IRR, so it is not clear which specific one to choose. Problems with IRR can arise where a project receives positive cash flows in some years, followed by negative cash flows. All in all, NPV is the more reliable indicator (Box 10.1).

In a large company with many investment opportunities, there are two stages in the process of investment appraisal: first, screening, and second, ranking. Oil companies, for example, usually set a high IRR threshold (screening) and then use NPV and some form of Profitability Index (such as NPV/Capital Expenditure or NPV/Maximum Exposure) to rank projects and decide which to accept (ranking). With high inflation it is important to distinguish between MoD (Money of the Day) and RT (Real Terms or constant purchasing power) cash flows.

IRR is widely used, but it should not be relied on as the sole decision criterion for investment projects.

The *pay-back period* is another common guide for investment appraisal. The pay-back technique simply considers the number of years that must elapse before the net income from the investment pays back the initial outlay – in other words, the number of years before the cost of the investment is recovered. An investment goes ahead if the pay-back is less than some prespecified number of years – two years, say, for a small project, longer for a really major, strategic project. Because of the increasing uncertainty of future revenue estimates beyond a certain period, this technique is often regarded as a valid way of appraising investments. The

## Box 10.1   Weakness of pay-back and IRR techniques

The annual flow of revenue for three projects is shown below. Each project involves an initial outlay of €1 million. Project A pays back quickly (four-year pay-back period if undiscounted, five years if discounted at 5 per cent) but has a short lifetime. Project B pays back more slowly (five-year pay-back period undiscounted) but continues to provide net revenue for many years. Clearly, it would be a mistake to select project A over project B because of its shorter pay-back period.

Project C illustrates some of the pitfalls that may be encountered by the user of IRR. This project is the same as project B except that there is a large negative flow in the last period, reflecting, say, environmental clean-up obligations. In fact, project C has two IRRs, at 9.68 and 12.75 per cent. If the discount rate were 5 per cent, the analyst might be inclined to recommend proceeding with project C. But this would be a serious mistake. Because of the last period's negative flow, the NPV of project C is negative for any discount rate below 9.68 per cent. A lower discount rate implies that relatively greater attention must be paid to distant events, such as the clean-up cost. Depositing the funds at 5 per cent will be a better strategy than investing in project C, given the clean-up costs that would be faced in 20 years. The IRR of such a project shows the rate at which the project will break even; it fails to reveal that, at a lower discount rate, the project may be unprofitable.

### Annual cash flows for three projects

| Year | [A] | [B] | [C] |
|------|------|------|------|
| 0 | −1.00 | −1.00 | −1.00 |
| 1 | 0.25 | 0.20 | 0.20 |
| 2 | 0.25 | 0.20 | 0.20 |
| 3 | 0.25 | 0.20 | 0.20 |
| 4 | 0.25 | 0.20 | 0.20 |
| 5 | 0.25 | 0.20 | 0.20 |
| 6 | | 0.20 | 0.20 |
| 7 | | 0.20 | 0.20 |
| 8 | | 0.20 | 0.20 |
| 9 | | 0.20 | 0.20 |
| 10 | | 0.20 | 0.20 |
| 11 | | 0.20 | 0.20 |
| 12 | | 0.20 | 0.20 |
| 13 | | 0.20 | 0.20 |
| 14 | | 0.20 | 0.20 |
| 15 | | 0.20 | 0.20 |
| 16 | | 0.20 | 0.20 |
| 17 | | 0.20 | 0.20 |
| 18 | | 0.20 | 0.20 |
| 19 | | 0.20 | 0.20 |
| 20 | | | −4.50 |
| Pay-back (years) | 4 | 5 | 5 |
| Pay-back (discounted) | 5 | 6 | 6 |
| NPV at 5 per cent | 0.08 | 1.42 | −0.28 |
| IRR (%) | 8.0 | 19.3 | 12.8; 9.7 |

*Source*: Alan W. Gray, *EU Structural Funds and Other Public Sector Investments: A guide to evaluation methods* (Dublin: Gill & Macmillan, 1995), pp. 28–31.

advantages of the technique relate to its simplicity and its use in highlighting the risks in a project.

Pay-back rules have, however, several limitations. One is their short-termist bias. By ignoring cash flows beyond the specified cut-off date, the pay-back technique biases investment decisions against projects with long-term benefits. Thus, take two projects with different estimated lifetime scales. The pay-back technique automatically tends to support the project with the shorter pay-back period. If the first project was at the end of its life after five years, while the second project provided annual benefits for another 15 years, the mistake of ignoring benefits after the pay-back period is clear. For this reason, use of the pay-back period criterion is not to be recommended. Yet it remains widely used in the UK and the US.

Both the NPV and the IRR method indicate that the relationship between the interest rate and the demand for investment funds is negative. Consider two projects, 1 and 2, with NPV and IRR as in Figure 10.4. Project 1 has an IRR of 23 per cent, Project 2 of 30 per cent. At low rates of interest, however, NPV is superior on Project 1, while at rates above 15 per cent, the NPV of Project 2 is above that of Project 1. Which project do we choose? At any discount rate below 15 per cent – say 8 per cent – it may be better business to choose Project 1, even though its IRR is lower than that of Project 2. If, however, Project 1 had more time-dependent risk (e.g. a change in government or in legislation were in the offing), some further risk analysis would be required before making a final decision. Project 2 has the advantage of earning its revenue earlier than Project 1.

## Extensions

The investment decision involves a great deal of uncertainty. Future net flows are subject to wide margins of error. Among the sources of uncertainty are:

● price trends/exchange rates
● changes in tax rates

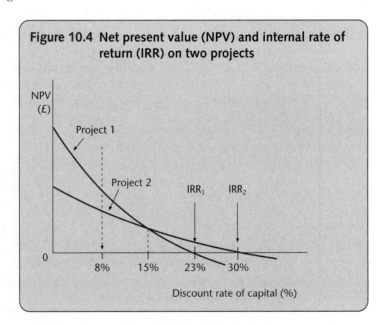

**Figure 10.4 Net present value (NPV) and internal rate of return (IRR) on two projects**

- cost trends
- depreciation
- scrap value of the investment
- interest rates
- catastrophic loss due to accidents/acts of God
- risks of nationalisation.

This endemic uncertainty, combined with the greater openness of capital markets, has made business conscious of the need to earn a healthy return on capital employed. Some firms expect new investment to earn as much as 20 per cent on shareholder capital. The profitability of the project can be critically influenced by the interest rate on borrowed funds. For example, the present value of £100 in 10 years is £56 at a 6 per cent discount rate, but only £39 at a 10 per cent discount rate and £16 if discounted at a 20 per cent rate.

Firms use many techniques for dealing with uncertainty. One possibility is to take a range of likely outcomes and assign probabilities to each. For example, suppose you judged that a project, at best, might yield an NPV of £20,000, and at worst a loss of £4000, and that you considered each outcome equally likely. Then, by weighting each outcome by its probability of realisation, an *expected return* can be computed as:

$$E(R) = 0.5(£20,000) + 0.5(-£4000) = £8000$$

Further refinement may be necessary to take account of risk aversion on the part of the firm, i.e. it may want to weigh losses more heavily than gains of the same size.

The expected return can then be compared with the riskless return on a government bond. If the return on the investment project is less than the bond rate, the firm should give the money back to its shareholders rather than invest it itself. In practice, executives are extremely reluctant to do this. They would regard it as a serious reflection on their own entrepreneurial acumen.

Another way of dealing with risk is by investing abroad in different markets with non-synchronised cycles. Then, when one market is experiencing a slump and is causing the firm to lose money, there is a good chance that the other market is performing well and adding to profits. Firms also reduce risk by investing in different products, although as we have seen in Chapter 6, conglomerate investments have tended to yield disappointing returns – risk reduction is bought at a heavy price in average returns. Risk can be diluted by joint ventures or by pooling. Dozens of banks, for example, shared the risk of the Channel Tunnel.

## Equilibrium

So far we have addressed the determinants of demand for investment funds. Given a world of full information and certainty, one could laterally summate all individual firms' demand functions to derive an industry or economy demand for capital as a function of the rate of interest.

The classical model also postulates a link between the supply of capital and the rate of interest (allowing for risk). It is generally assumed that the two are positively associated, but the relationship is not well defined. Level of income is clearly another important determinant of the supply of capital, as are expectations regarding inflation and tax.

Putting demand and supply factors together, we can sketch out a theory of the rate of interest analogous to the theory of pay determination. The equilibrium interest rate is one which brings the supply of investment capital into balance with the demand for investment capital. The interest rate, like the level of pay, plays an important role in determining the structure of an economy and is highly pertinent to the conduct of monetary policy. We shall return to this aspect in Part II of the book.

## 10.3 Conclusions

This chapter has shown that, under certain assumptions, the profit-maximising firm will pay factors of production the value of their marginal product. It is a short step from this to asserting that, under a free market system, labour and machines and other inputs are paid what they are worth to society. The marginal productivity theory invites such normative inferences. Some nineteenth-century economists concluded from it that workers who formed trade unions were in effect trying to extract a reward for their labour in excess of their 'true' contribution to society, as determined by the invisible hand. Left to itself, the market determines each person's salary. Everyone gets paid what they are 'worth' – as decided by the market. If anyone believes they are being paid too little, the theory suggests an immediate remedy: move to another job where your output would be more highly valued. If no such job can be found, the market is conveying a clear message: you are not being underpaid.

As we have seen, the marginal productivity theory is an incomplete theory of how factors are rewarded. Unlike machines, people need to be motivated and the structure of their pay packet over time plays an important role in this. Marginal productivity is not determined by technical factors only, but also by a firm's total remuneration package. Also, free competition does not prevail in labour markets. To understand how pay is determined in any real situation, careful attention must be devoted to analysing market structures. Nevertheless, the fundamental principle that, *ceteris paribus*, pay levels and the demand for labour are negatively correlated is a good starting point for discussions of employment and unemployment policy. It has practical, far-reaching implications.

Likewise, the negative association between interest rate and investment emerges from the marginal productivity theory of capital. Different types of problem arise in applying this rule to the real world. Account must be taken of the extreme uncertainty of marginal productivity estimates in the context of long-run projects. Nowhere is this uncertainty more evident than in the valuation of 'new economy' firms. Prior to its going public, accountants valued Netscape at $112 million. A few months later, after it went public, the market valued it at $2.1 billion. Such astonishing lack of concordance between accounting and market valuations is commonplace in the knowledge economy. Uncertainty about projected future earnings is only part of the problem. Evaluating the human capital assets of a firm also presents novel, and as yet unresolved, problems of valuation.

## Summary

1. Profit maximisation and competition lead the firm to hire labour up to the point where the cost of hiring equals the marginal revenue product to the firm. The cost of hiring includes all direct and indirect costs associated with an additional member of staff. Marginal revenue product equals the extra output produced by the marginal employee multiplied by the net marginal revenue derived from it.

2. This analysis carries the important inference that pay and numbers employed are negatively correlated. A rise in pay, other things being equal, leads to a fall in employment. By allowing pay to fall, employees can price themselves into a job. The labour market model has been influential in persuading some governments to view with suspicion 'social' initiatives which could threaten jobs.

3. Labour market analysis has to take into account the increasing similarities between hiring labour and the investment decision. A firm's decision to employ a person involves a commitment over time, involving costs and benefits to the firm. These need to be properly calibrated and discounted.

4. Economics takes marginal product of labour as exogenously determined by technology and by the amount of cooperant factors at its disposal. In fact, labour productivity is often highly endogenous. Management's task is to convert 'compelled performers' into 'willing contributors'. Pay levels and pay structures can contribute to this transformation.

5. The investment decision is driven by the need to equate return on capital with the cost of capital. The cost of capital can be defined as the rate of return expected by shareholders and the return on capital can be interpreted as return on shareholder capital. Firms ration investment funds by insisting on a minimum rate of return on capital employed (ROCE).

6. Three widely used techniques for investment appraisal are net present value, internal rate of return and pay-back period. Of these, the net present value – or discounted cash-flow method – is superior on analytical grounds.

7. No appraisal method can conceal that investment involves heavy risk. There are ways of coping with risk, but not of eliminating it. The riskiness of investment explains why investment spending fluctuates so markedly relative to other types of spending.

## Questions for discussion

1. Why does marginal revenue product decline as the quantity of labour employed by the firm increases? How do you reconcile this with the observed increase in the productivity of labour over time? How useful is the 'pay = marginal revenue product' rule as a guide to business?

2. Does the practice of paying an employee increments for each year of service conflict with the profit-maximising rule: wage = marginal revenue product?

3. How, in your view, would a monopoly trade union determine its objectives in pay negotiations? Would it aim to maximise pay per person employed or the number of

➔

persons employed, or something in between? How would the answer affect the level of pay demanded by the trade union for its members?

4. The Cambridge economist Alfred Marshall wrote that 'highly paid labour is generally efficient and therefore is not dear labour'. Do you agree?

5. The principal–agent problem was discussed in Chapter 4. The way of resolving it is to draw up contracts which will protect the principal from the opportunism of the agent through (a) provision of incentives to the agent, (b) monitoring of the agent's performance, and (c) penalising the agent if there is non-performance. Compare and contrast the agency theory approach with the standard demand and supply model of the labour market in this chapter.

6. Is the economist's approach to the investment decision consistent with the analysis of a corporate finance or management accounting specialist?

## Exercises

1. Suppose a firm's output–labour input relationship was as follows:

| Number of employees | Total output produced |
|---|---|
| 1 | 20 |
| 2 | 50 |
| 3 | 90 |
| 4 | 120 |
| 5 | 145 |
| 6 | 165 |
| 7 | 180 |
| 8 | 190 |
| 9 | 195 |

(a) Calculate the marginal product of labour at each employment level.
(b) If price per unit was £1000 and the pay level was £20,000 per year, how many employees would the firm hire?
(c) If pay levels increase to £31,000 per year, what would be the impact on employment?

2. Suppose the price of a computer is £10,000. Its effective life is two years. Its marginal revenue product to the firm is £5000 for each year and its scrap value at the end of the period is £2000. The interest rate is 6 per cent per year. Calculate (a) the present value of the flow of marginal revenue product, and (b) the net present value of the investment.

3. Suppose you are asked to decide whether a new machine should be purchased. Projected net returns (sales less costs) over the four-year life of the machine are: year 1, £2000; year 2, £4000; year 3, £4000; year 4, £6000. The machine costs £10,000. The firm uses a 10 per cent discount rate. Should it proceed with this project? Assess by reference to (a) NPV, (b) IRR, and (c) a two-year pay-back period.

**4.** An investment project yields a revenue stream of £100 per year for 10 years. The cost of the project is £500. Supposing the pay-back period is four years, would you accept this project? What is the NPV if the discount rate is 10 per cent? What is the IRR?

## Further reading

A good textbook on labour economics is D. Sapsford and Z. Tzamatos, *The Economics of the Labour Market* (Basingstoke: Macmillan, 1993). P. Milgrom and D. Roberts, *Economics, Organisation and Management* (Hemel Hempstead: Prentice Hall, 1992), begins where the standard analysis ends and shows how useful economic concepts can be in explaining pay structures. This new approach to explaining pay, hiring and pensions policy is developed in E.P. Lazear, *Personnel Economics for Managers* (New York: John Wiley, 1998). Useful sources on investment appraisal include S.A. Ross, R. Westerfield and B. Jordan, *Fundamentals of Corporate Finance*, 4th edn (Boston: Richard D. Irwin, 1998), and Richard Pike and Bill Neale, *Corporate Finance and Investment: Decisions and strategies* (Harlow: Prentice Hall, 1999).

# Part II

# The macroeconomic framework

(11) Aggregate supply, aggregate demand and the price level

(12) Price stability and central banks

(13) Understanding interest rates and monetary policy

(14) Unemployment and the labour market

(15) Fiscal policy, budget deficits and government debt

(16) Business fluctuations and forecasting

The overriding task of macroeconomic management is to provide a stable economic framework. This means price stability, fiscal responsibility and steady economic growth. Price stability is needed so that the price system can carry out its functions efficiently. Fiscal responsibility is necessary to ensure that a sustainable tax and government spending regime is in place that will encourage enterprise and innovation. Fiscal balance is also required in order to maintain price stability. Steady economic growth is desired in order to avoid the misery of another Great Depression similar to that of the late 1920s and early 1930s, and to escape from the cycle of boom and bust. Business fluctuations are a reality, but we need to minimise their amplitude and encourage business investors to take a long-term perspective. The implicit assumption of macroeconomics is that steady growth will mean a higher long-run trend growth.

This is a perspective which modern business would strongly endorse. Most firms have to cope with enough uncertainty at market level, without the addition of gratuitous uncertainties arising from government mismanagement of the macroeconomy. In preparing their sales and profit forecasts, however, firms cannot simply assume that the macro-environment will remain stable. They must contribute to making such stability happen by influencing economic policy. To do this effectively requires an understanding of how the macroeconomy operates, and of the dogmas and assumptions which influence economic policy.

Our starting point (Chapter 11) is a discussion of how output is determined in the short run. We study the determinants of aggregate supply and aggregate demand, and consider the relationships between the real part of the economy and monetary variables. The contribution of Keynesian analysis of demand to our understanding of the economy is explained.

With this analytical foundation, we proceed to analyse two key macroeconomic problems: price instability (Chapter 12) and unemployment (Chapter 14). Inflation has for a long time been a central preoccupation of modern macroeconomics, but it has eased considerably in most countries, to the point where the question 'Is inflation dead?' has been seriously raised. In some countries, deflation rather than inflation has become the focus of concern.

Unemployment has reached chronic proportions in many developing countries and notwithstanding aggresive labour market policies it remains an acute problem in large parts of Europe. The danger to economic and social stability from a persistently high level of long-term unemployment has obvious implications for business.

The nature and effectiveness of fiscal and monetary policies is the subject of Chapters 13 and 15. We argue that the primary focus of monetary and interest rate policies should be on maintaining price stability. This places the duties of central banks, as the relevant authority, in a higher profile than before. Fiscal policy, traditionally considered as a solution to the problem of unemployment, is now seen as having contributed to the problem. The reduced effectiveness of fiscal measures can be traced to the growth of public debt, itself the consequence of excessive budget deficits incurred over many years (Chapter 15).

This leads to an analysis of business fluctuations and economic forecasting (Chapter 16). Initially, we assume that government intervention is completely absent. Is the system very unstable in such circumstances? Or are there strong self-adjusting mechanisms at work? Then intervention by the authorities is allowed for. We conclude that intervention is desirable in cases of severe shocks to demand or supply (such as, for example, the collapse in the stock exchange on 'Black Monday', 19 October 1987, the currency crises of the 1990s, Japan's collapsing aggregate demand since 1991 and the downturn in the world economy post-2000), but that the scope for counter-cyclical action is much less than it used to be.

Business forecasting is then discussed. Managers need to understand how forecasts are formulated and to develop some 'feel' for the important qualifications attached to them. The task of converting macroeconomic forecasts to company forecasts involves analysis not only of GDP growth, inflation and interest rates, but also of overall market developments, evolution of the company's market share and specific marketing or product quality initiatives.

The objective of this section is to provide the reader with an understanding of:

- Key economic concepts: GNP, GDP, purchasing power parity, aggregate supply and demand.
- Recent economic thinking on the role of central banks and governments in dealing with inflation, unemployment and other macroeconomic problems.
- A knowledge of how monetary policy is formulated, and its implications for interest rates.
- The extent and causes of unemployment and possible solutions.
- The strengths and limitations of fiscal policy, and how it impacts on the economic environment.
- The reasons for business cycles, the scope for reducing their amplitude, the nature of economic forecasting and how to translate macroeconomic forecasts into meaningful information for the company.

## Chapter 11

# Aggregate supply, aggregate demand and the price level

## Introduction

Macroeconomics differs from microeconomics in a number of respects. First, macroeconomics is concerned with the functioning of the economy *overall*. Instead of examining how an individual market works it studies how markets interact. It focuses on aggregate variables such as national output, employment and the general price level.

Second, government and public institutions occupy a more central place in macroeconomics than in microeconomics. The high profile of government in macroeconomics stems in large part from the intellectual origins of the subject. Macroeconomics developed from the writings of the British economist John Maynard Keynes on the Great Depression of the 1920s and 1930s. Keynesians argued that state intervention on a macro-scale was necessary if capitalism was to be saved from self-destruction. They showed how the amplitude of business fluctuations could be reduced by macroeconomic policy and that higher long-term growth could be achieved as a result.

Third, macroeconomics is a more controversial subject than microeconomics. There are disagreements about the role of monetary variables, the causes and cures of unemployment, and the effectiveness of fiscal policy. The reader must not expect to find a single 'right' answer to current macroeconomic problems. There are numerous schools of macroeconomic thought.[1] Because macroeconomics is closely involved with government policy, political, social and economic objectives intermingle and can sometimes conflict. Controversy also arises because of the intrinsic complexity of the subject. There is no single 'true' model of the economy.

Readers often complain that, in macroeconomics, 'everything seems to depend on everything else'. The complex chain of interdependence between macro-variables explains why macroeconomics is so difficult and, at times, frustrating.

---

[1] No fewer than seven (respectable) schools of macroeconomic thought have been identified: Keynesian, traditional monetarist, new classical, new Keynesian, supply-side, neo-classical and structuralist. See Edmund S. Phelps, *Seven Schools of Macroeconomic Thought* (Oxford: Clarendon Press, 1990).

Yet macroeconomics, at its best, can provide solutions to practical problems. These solutions have had a tremendously positive impact on living standards during the past five decades.

### Chapter outline

1. Description of gross domestic product (GDP), gross national product (GNP) and how they are estimated.

2. Analysis of the concepts of *potential* GDP and *GDP at purchasing power parity*.

3. Outline of a simple (classical) economic framework, beginning with the aggregate supply (AS) curve. The shape of this curve has a direct bearing on the effectiveness of standard macroeconomic policies.

4. Derivation of the aggregate demand (AD) curve. The role of monetary variables enters the analysis at this stage.

5. How the equilibrium level of output and the equilibrium price level are determined. Equilibrium occurs at the point where the AS and AD curves intersect.

## 11.1 How is gross domestic product (GDP) calculated?

Gross domestic product (GDP), as we saw in Chapter 2, refers to the output of goods and services produced in an economy during a specific period of time.[2] GDP estimates are published on an annual, and sometimes a quarterly, basis. Output *less* depreciation is *net national product*. The latter is equivalent to *national income*, which in turn is defined as the total of all payments for productive services accruing to the residents of a country.

GDP statistics matter to business for at least four reasons. First, forecasts of future aggregate demand are usually expressed in terms of projected growth in GDP. These forecasts are relevant to the firm's forecast of its own future sales. Second, assessments of the current state of the economy are based on the current and recent past level of GDP. The financial markets scrutinise GDP growth trends with particular care. An acceleration in growth, for instance, could signal an increase in inflation and, in due course, a tightening of monetary policy and higher interest rates. Likewise, slower growth could mark the beginning of a recession. (A recession is technically defined as a fall in GDP in two successive quarters.) Third, movements in GDP can have political implications. Fast growth is perceived as an electoral plus, weak growth an electoral minus. Fourth, international comparisons of aggregate market size are based on GDP data.

---

[2] GDP can be defined formally as:

$$p_1 x_1 + p_2 x_2 + \ldots + p_n x_n$$

where $x_i$ = quantity of the $i$th good or service produced
$p_i$ = price of the $i$th good or service
$n$ = number of goods produced
$i = 1, 2, \ldots, n$.

## Real and nominal GDP

Nominal GDP is the current value of goods and services produced in an economy. It is the product of two variables: price and quantity. If we are analysing the change in nominal GDP between one year and another, we need to separate the effect of price changes from volume of output variations. The concept of *real* GDP is designed to provide this information. Change in real GDP is computed by valuing the quantities of goods and services produced in the two periods with the same set of prices. It acts as an indicator of changes in volume of output.

Suppose two goods, $x$ and $y$, are produced. In year 1, GDP comprises 10 units of $x$ and 12 units of $y$, at prices €5 and €8 per unit respectively. GDP equals:

$$5x_1 + 8y_1 = 5.(10) + 8.(12) = 50 + 96 = €146$$

In period 2, quantities produced of $x$ and $y$ increase to 11 and 14 units. At the same time, the price of good $x$ rises to €6 and the price of good $y$ rises to €9. Nominal GDP rises to:

$$6x_2 + 9y_2 = 6.(11) + 9.(14) = 66 + 126 = €192$$

Nominal GDP has increased by $(192 - 146)/146$ or 31.5 per cent. This increase reflects the combined effects of a rise in the average price level and a rise in volume of output. To calculate real GDP in period 2, we compute the value of period 2 quantities at period 1 prices, i.e.:

$$p_{x1}x_2 + p_{y1}y_2 = 5.(11) + 8.(14) = 55 + 112 = €167$$

The increase in real GDP is given by $(167 - 146)/146$, or 14.4 per cent.

Dividing nominal GDP by real GDP yields a figure known as *the implicit GDP deflator*. This indicates by how much the *average* level of prices of goods and services included in GDP has risen since the base year. The implicit deflator closely resembles the more familiar consumer price index which will be discussed in the next chapter.

GDP price deflator = (nominal GDP ÷ real GDP)×100

|  | Nominal GDP (1) | Real GDP (at $p_1$) (2) | Implicit GDP deflator (1)/(2) × 100 |
|---|---|---|---|
| Year 1 | €146 | €146 | 100 |
| Year 2 | €192 | €167 | 115 |
| % increase | 31.5% | 14.4% | 15% |

Since there are different ways of measuring the increase in an economy's price level, care must be taken in choosing the index itself and the base period from which the calculations are made.

## GDP and GNP

Gross national product (GNP) refers to output produced by productive factors *owned by permanent residents of a country*. Gross domestic product (GDP) is output produced by productive factors *located in the country*, regardless of their owners' nationality. The need for this distinction arises when domestically owned productive factors generate income for domestic residents from economic activity carried out abroad. For example, the repatriated profits of a Japanese automobile subsidiary located in the UK are included in Japan's GNP, but excluded from its GDP. In the UK's accounts, they are included in GDP, but excluded from GNP. For most countries, the gap between GDP and GNP is very small (for instance, it is only 0.1 per cent of GDP in the US). But for countries with large net income from migrants (Philippines, Palestine), or with an extensive presence of multinationals (Malaysia, Ireland) or with high dividend income from capital held abroad (Kuwait, Switzerland), the gap can be as high as 10 per cent of GNP and more. Both measures are useful in their own way. GDP is a better measure of the amount of productive activity in a country; GNP is a superior measure of a country's standard of living. Summing over all countries, global GNP is in principle exactly equal to global GDP.

## How to compute GDP

Statisticians compile GDP statistics using three separate data sources: (1) output, (2) income and (3) expenditure. In principle, all three sources should yield the same answer, since they measure the same thing, but because of statistical discrepancies this rarely happens in practice. The details of each method of compilation need not concern us, but the methodology throws light on the different components of these important national account aggregates.

The *output method* calculates the value of the output of goods and services produced in the economy over a specified period of time. Given that many firms' output is another firm's input, to avoid double-counting, only the value added at each stage of the production process is counted. *Value added* is defined as gross sales minus cost of raw materials and intermediate inputs. For an individual firm, value added equals, by definition, wages and salaries plus rent plus interest payments plus profits.

Since value added comprises wages, salaries and profits, GDP estimated by the output method should give exactly the same figure as the sum of wages and salaries, rents and corporate profits. The *income method* of computing GDP focuses on this latter aspect. In turn, since income is earned as a result of someone else spending, the addition of all sources of national spending should in theory provide the same GDP estimate as the previous two. (The pro forma statement of the national accounts using the income approach is presented in Box 11.1 for illustrative purposes.) The *expenditure method* adds up all spending on final goods and services, i.e. on investment goods, on consumer products, and on government-supplied goods and services. These three approaches underline the essential circularity in the flow of income and output through an economy. Firms generate value added, the counterpart of value added is wages and profits, and wages and profits, in turn, are the mirror image of national consumption and investment. These interlinkages are an important feature of an economy.

## Box 11.1    National income, gross national product (GNP) and gross domestic product (GDP)

There are three key elements in the national account totals: national income, gross national product (GNP) and gross domestic product (GDP). This table shows how they are derived, using the *income* approach.

| |
|---|
| 1.  Employees' compensation |
| 2.  Income of self-employed |
| 3.  Corporate profits |
| 4.  Rents and interest |
| *National Income* |
| 5.  Indirect taxes (+) less subsidies (−) |
| *Net National Product at Market Prices* |
| 6.  Capital depreciation |
| *Gross National Product (GNP)* |
| 7.  Net payments (+)/Receipts (−) of income from abroad |
| *Gross Domestic Product (GDP)* |

The main components of the accounts are:

1. *Employees' compensation* includes pay (before income tax) and employees' social tax contributions. In industrial countries, this amounts to over 60 per cent of national income.
2. *Income of self-employed* refers to income of farmers, retailers, professionals (lawyers, doctors, etc.), partnerships, etc.
3. *Corporate profits* are profits before tax as defined by the tax authorities.
4. *Rents and interests* represent the returns to land and capital, respectively.

*National income*, the sum of the above items, is defined as income earned by residents from current production of goods and services in the economy. National income is significantly lower than GNP at market prices. To derive GNP, two further items must be added: net indirect tax revenues and capital depreciation.

5. *Indirect taxes less subsidies*. Output valued at current market prices includes indirect taxes and excludes subsidies. Indirect tax represents a transfer to government which is collected by business on behalf of the state. It is not part of business income nor is it a receipt in respect of a service rendered. Hence, to reconcile national income and national production data, an adjustment must be made for these indirect taxes and subsidies.

Adding indirect taxes to national income yields an estimate of *net national product (NNP)*. To derive GNP, one further adjustment is required.

6. *Depreciation* is defined as the amount set aside for the maintenance of capital stock. It is computed as the amount of depreciation allowed for tax purposes in the case of business firms. In the case of government-owned assets, depreciation has to be estimated.

Net national product plus depreciation equals *gross national product*.

Finally, *gross domestic product* is obtained by adding to GNP income earned by non-residents in the national territory, such as repatriated profits of foreign subsidiaries, and subtracting income earned by nationals abroad. GDP can be higher or lower than GNP.

## Composition of GDP

There are five components of national expenditure:

**1.** Consumption            $= C$
**2.** Investment             $= I$
**3.** Government purchases $= G$
**4.** Exports                $= X$
**5.** *Less* Imports           $= M$

$$GDP = C + I + G + X - M$$

Note that exports are entered with a positive sign and imports with a negative sign. GDP does not measure total spending *by* domestic residents, but total expenditure on *goods and services produced by domestic residents*.

*Consumption* consists of purchases of non-durable goods, such as food and fuel; consumer durable goods, such as washing machines and cars; and services, such as holiday spending, insurance and travel. The main determinant of consumption expenditure is the level of national income.

*Investment* consists of additions to capital stock or, in economics jargon, increases in *real* capital formation. (This is not to be confused with financial investment, which consists of the transfer of existing assets from one person or institution to another.) Investment is divided into three categories: (a) plant and machinery investment, (b) residential and office investment, and (c) additions to inventories. Government spending on infrastructure, such as roads, railways and ports, is also included. Forecasters watch investment in inventories carefully – an unplanned build-up of inventories is a classic signal of a weakening in demand.

*Government spending* consists of current spending on goods and services, such as health, justice, security and education. Only spending which involves a direct purchase of goods and services is included in the GDP figure. Social welfare payments, industrial subsidies and interest payments on the national debt are omitted. Such transactions are called *transfer payments*, i.e. they involve the transfer of purchasing power over existing resources, from one household to another, rather than spending on additional production. Rather misleadingly, education is treated as current spending although arguably, being investment in human capital, it should be included as part of national investment.

*Exports* refer to spending by foreigners on domestically produced goods and therefore must be included in GDP, whereas for the same reason *imports* are excluded.

In summary, GDP represents total spending on domestically produced goods and services by both residents and foreigners:

$$GDP = [C + I + G - M] + X$$

| Spending by residents on home-produced goods and services | Spending by foreigners on home-produced goods and services |

These statistical conventions for measuring GDP have many conceptual and practical limitations. Practical measurement problems are particularly acute in the services sector. Outputs of the health and education sectors, for instance, are often estimated from data on inputs (number and cost of employees) rather than outputs. This is because the unit of output is such an elusive concept to measure in these sectors. Similar problems arise in measuring the output of e-commerce activities. The major conceptual issues have already been discussed in Chapters 2 and 3: (1) the omission of unpaid household and other voluntary work; (2) the incomplete coverage of shadow economy activities; (3) the classification as outputs of what arguably are inputs, such as expenses on crime prevention and depletion of the environment; and (4) the absence of specific provisions for the run-down of non-renewable resources. These qualifications are not trivial. The value of unpaid (non-market) housework in the major industrial countries has been estimated to be worth more than one-fifth of GDP.[3]

## 11.2 Potential GDP, actual GDP, and GDP at purchasing power parity (PPP)

### Potential and actual GDP

Potential GDP is a concept of crucial significance in macroeconomics. It is defined as:

> the maximum output that an economy can produce if capital, labour and other factors of production are fully utilised, consistent over the medium term with low inflation.

Potential GDP is not the same as the maximum attainable level of output in an engineering sense. The qualifying clause 'consistent with low inflation' suggests that potential GDP will be lower than the engineering maximum. As the physical maximum is approached, productive factors become more scarce, prices are bid up and an inflationary cycle could be set in motion. Deviations from potential GDP in either direction can cause problems.

> If actual exceeds potential GDP, price stability is placed in jeopardy; if it is less than potential GDP, there is unemployment and resources are being wasted. Macroeconomics studies ways in which divergences of both types can be minimised.

There are two main ways of estimating potential GDP. One is to estimate a trend growth rate from past data. This method can be sensitive to choice of base year and takes no account of new resources. Another method is the 'production function' approach, which relates potential output directly to changes in available factor resources and their utilisation rate. To estimate potential GDP by this method, output is divided into a business sector and a government component.[4] Given the difficulty of measuring government output, actual output in this sector is usually assumed to be equal to its potential. Attention then focuses on ways of measuring the business sector's potential output. This exercise involves four

---

[3] See A. Chadeau, 'What is households' non-market production worth?', *OECD Economic Studies* (Spring 1992). In the UK, unpaid household work has been estimated to have a value equivalent to one-third of consumer expenditure. See T. Jackson *et al.*, *Sustainable Economic Welfare in the UK 1950–1996* (London: New Economics Foundation, 1997).

[4] R. Torres and J.P. Martin, 'Measuring potential output in the seven major OECD countries', *OECD Economic Studies* (Spring 1990). Potential output has also been defined as the level of output which the economy could produce if capital and labour were fully utilised, with a margin of slack to accommodate short-term increases in demand.

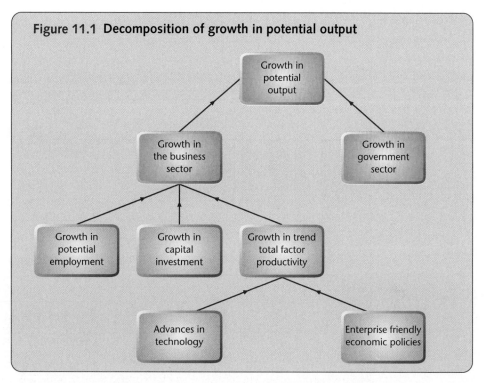

Figure 11.1 Decomposition of growth in potential output

steps: (1) the growth of productive inputs, such as labour, capital and energy, is estimated; (2) an estimate is made of the utilisation levels of these inputs consistent with low inflation; (3) the productivity of these factor inputs is assessed, i.e. an estimate of total factor productivity growth is derived; (4) these three steps are combined to obtain an estimate of the potential growth of business sector output. The process is illustrated in Figure 11.1.

Estimates of potential output based on the production function approach are regularly published and are used as a guide to macroeconomic policy. Attention is paid to the sign and size of the *output gap*, defined as the difference between actual and potential GDP. OECD estimates for 2002 show that Japan was operating at 3 per cent short of its potential, Italy at 2.3 per cent and Belgium 1.6 per cent (Figure 11.2). In other cases, actual economic growth exceeded total potential growth. But no one knows for sure what the potential growth rate in an economy is. Estimates for the US economy used to cluster in the range 2–3 per cent, but increases in productivity fed by technological advances have spawned a series of 'new economy' estimates of 3–4 per cent. To determine the level of potential GDP, one has to depend on judgement as well as on technical analysis.[5]

Macroeconomic policy focuses on the relationship between actual and potential GDP. By maintaining a stable economic framework, governments hope to achieve close concordance between the two series, thereby also ensuring that the trend growth rate will reach its optimum level.

---

[5] For instance, Professor Kazuo Sato argues that Japan's output gap was over 9 per cent instead of the OECD-estimated 3 per cent on the grounds that insufficient account had been taken of a potential output derivable from Japan's high investment rate during the 1990s (K. Sato, 'Japan's potential output and the GNP gap', *Journal of Asian Economics*, Summer 2001).

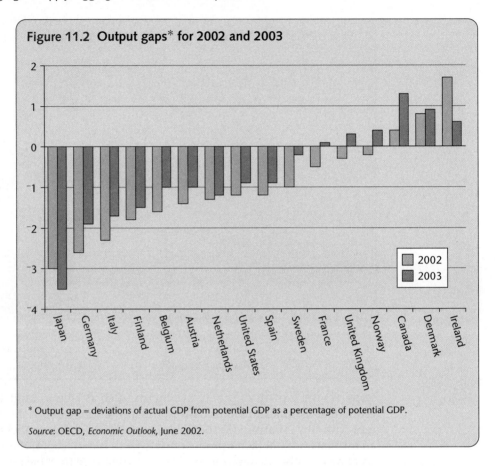

**Figure 11.2 Output gaps\* for 2002 and 2003**

\* Output gap = deviations of actual GDP from potential GDP as a percentage of potential GDP.

*Source*: OECD, *Economic Outlook*, June 2002.

## GNP at purchasing power parity (PPP)

In making international comparisons it is necessary to convert all nominal GNPs into a common currency. More often than not, the common currency will be the US dollar. In this context, it is common to distinguish between *GNP at current exchange rates* and *GNP at purchasing power parity* (PPP). The two GNPs often diverge quite markedly. For instance, India's GNP per head in 2000 was US$450 at nominal exchange rates but $US2340 at PPP (World Bank, *World Development Indicators*, 2002). Which statistic is 'right', and why do they differ? To understand the difference, imagine this simple four-step experiment.

1. Begin by compiling a *representative basket* of goods and services. Such a representative basket might, for example, contain:

> 2 kilos of rice
> 1 kilo of beef
> 5 inner city bus rides
> one month's rent of a two-bedroom apartment
> 1 personal computer
> 2 visits to doctor
> etc.

The list could run into hundreds of items; Eurostat's PPP calculations covered more than 200 product groups, and new price surveys are made at three-year intervals.

2. Ask an individual to purchase this basket in Washington, DC. Assume that the cost happens to amount to the convenient figure of US$1000.

3. Find out the cost of buying *exactly the same basket* in India. Suppose it turned out to be 8640 rupees. Then we say that the *Purchasing Power Parity (PPP)* rate of exchange is 8640 rupees divided by $1000, i.e.

$$PPP\ 8.64\ rupees = \$1$$

4. India's national accounts show that GNP per head in 2000 was 20,225 rupees. Divide by 8.64 to derive GNP per head in US dollars at PPP as *$2340*. This is the World Bank figure. To derive GNP per head in US dollars at current exchange rates, divide 20,225 by 45 to get *$450*.

The main reason for the difference is that current rates are determined by trade in goods and by mobile capital flows. Services (cost of drivers, barbers, helpers, etc.) that cannot be traded do not enter the picture. But they are invariably much cheaper in developing countries than in better-off countries. Poor countries are still poor, but much less so than comparison on the basis of current exchange rates would appear to suggest. World Bank PPP estimates indicate that countries such as China and India are three to four times better off than would appear on the basis of GDP at nominal exchange rates (see Table 11.1).

To compare living standards in different countries, purchasing power parity is the more accurate indicator. Thus, executives or diplomats from a relatively poor country posted to a relatively rich country have a strong interest in consulting the type of dedicated purchasing power parity indexes that are available from consultants, since they will require an upward adjustment in their salaries if they are to provide equivalent living standards to those available at home. For foreign investors interested in repatriating profits from a developing country, nominal exchange rates are what matter, not PPP. We discuss purchasing power parity again in Chapter 21.

---

**Table 11.1 Comparison between GNP per capita at current exchange rates and at PPP**

| Country | GNP per capita ($) (current prices and exchange rates) | GNP per capita ($) (PPP) |
|---|---|---|
| India | 450 | 2,340 |
| Morocco | 1,180 | 3,450 |
| Argentina | 7,460 | 12,050 |
| Mexico | 5,070 | 8,790 |
| China | 840 | 3,920 |
| UK | 24,430 | 23,550 |
| France | 24,090 | 24,420 |
| Canada | 21,130 | 27,170 |
| US | 34,100 | 34,100 |

*Source*: World Bank, *World Development Indicators* (Washington, DC, 2002). Figures relate to year 2000.

## 11.3 The aggregate supply (AS) curve

Our next step is to construct a model showing the determinants of aggregate supply and demand. Aggregate supply (AS) can be regarded as a rough proxy of potential GNP.

The aggregate supply (AS) curve shows combinations of real output ($y$) and the price level ($p$) which are consistent with equilibrium in the economy. A vertical AS curve shows that a given level of real output, $y_0$, is consistent with many possible price levels (Figure 11.3(b)). A positively sloped AS curve shows that a rise in the price level from, say, $p_0$ to $p_1$ is consistent with a rise in output from $y_0$ to $y_1$ (Figure 11.3(a)).

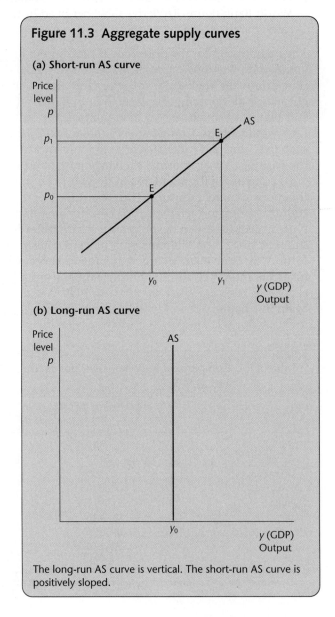

**Figure 11.3 Aggregate supply curves**

**(a) Short-run AS curve**

**(b) Long-run AS curve**

The long-run AS curve is vertical. The short-run AS curve is positively sloped.

The price on the vertical axis of the AS curve is the *general price level*. This contrasts with the industry supply curves in Chapter 3, where price of the industry's output is on the vertical axis. The industry supply effect arises because the price of the industry's output is defined relative to prices in other sectors. All other prices are assumed to remain constant. In the case of the AS curve, the general price level is defined relative to prices of productive factors such as labour. A rise in the general price level relative to nominal wages would, on this reasoning, have a positive effect on aggregate supply. The AS curve will be positively sloping. If, on the other hand, one believes that the price of labour (and other productive factors) is linked to the general price level – because, say, employees demand higher pay to compensate for inflation – it will be impossible to have any relative price effect and the AS curve will tend to be vertical. This interaction between pay demands and the inflation rate, as we shall see, has important implications for macroeconomic policy.

The AS curve provides a conceptual framework within which the viewpoints of the various schools of macroeconomic thought can be analysed. The shape of the curve is a controversial subject. The new consensus view depicts it as being near-vertical. Keynesian economists, by contrast, believe that the AS curve is near-horizontal up to the point of full capacity output. The debate hinges critically on one's view about the response of employees to changes in the cost of living and of firms to changes in costs.

## Derivation of the AS curve

To derive the classical AS curve, we start with the assumption that individuals are utility-maximising, firms are profit-maximising and that they operate in a competitive market. Markets for factors of production are also assumed to be competitive. Hence each productive factor will, in equilibrium, be paid the value of its marginal product. Figure 11.4 illustrates the case with respect to labour. Supply of labour depends upon the real wage ($w/p$). As we saw in the last chapter, the curve slopes upwards because employees supply more hours of work if the real wage rises. Demand for labour is determined by the value of its marginal product. We recall the rule that a profit-maximising firm hires labour up to the point at which the value of the output produced by the marginal employee equals the cost of hiring that employee:

*wage = marginal product of labour × price of output*

Assuming that all markets clear smoothly, equilibrium in the labour market occurs where the demand and supply curves for labour intersect. In Figure 11.4, this occurs at a real wage $(w/p)^*$, and with OL\* units of labour employed.

Having determined equilibrium real wage, the level of output can be read off from the production function. The production function indicates the level of output that can be produced by each level of labour input, assuming it is combined with a fixed capital stock ($K$), technology and other factors ($A$). Thus, it shows that an output of $y^*$ can be produced by the input of labour, L\*.

The next question is to determine how equilibrium output, $y^*$, changes in response to changes in the price level. A fundamental assumption of the model is that *in the long run, equilibrium output ($y^*$) is invariant with respect to the general price level $p^*$*. This conclusion draws heavily on the belief that most individuals and

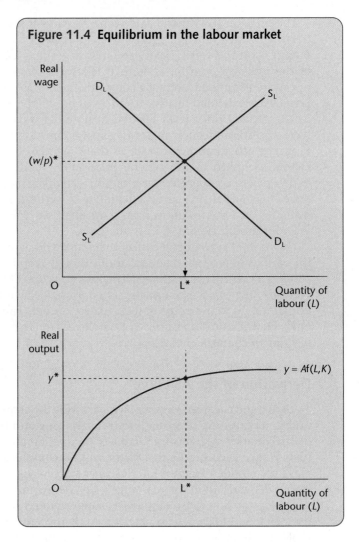

**Figure 11.4 Equilibrium in the labour market**

firms behave *rationally*. They calculate, bargain and decide whether and how much to work, on the basis of the real wage ($w/p$), not the nominal money wage ($w$). In technical jargon, market participants are assumed to be free from *money illusion*.

The role of money illusion can be clarified by drawing nominal wage, instead of real wage, on the vertical axis (Figure 11.5). Then, *for any given price level, $p_0$*, we can draw a demand and supply curve for labour as before. Consider now the effect of an increase in the price level from $p_0$ to $p_1$.

Initially, the rise in the price level shifts the demand curve for labour outwards to $D_1(p_1)$. This happens because firms will observe that price of output has increased relative to nominal pay. Profits will increase and firms will want to hire more labour. If workers were ignorant or unconcerned about the fact that prices had gone up, a new equilibrium could happen at point T. At T, more labour

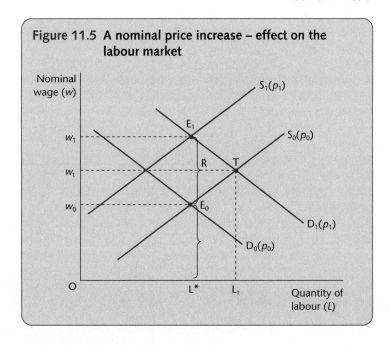

**Figure 11.5 A nominal price increase – effect on the labour market**

would be employed ($OL_t$) and the nominal wage would rise to $w_t$. Since the rise in nominal pay (measured by the vertical distance $E_0 R$) is less than the rise in the price level, $E_0 E_1$, the real wage has fallen.

However, $w_t$ is not a sustainable equilibrium point. Employees are not ignorant of the price increase and, being rational, are not indifferent to it either. As prices rise, they will demand an equivalent compensation in nominal wages. Over time, employees' supply curves will shift upwards by an amount which exactly compensates for the rise in prices. A long-run equilibrium is reached at $E_1$. The nominal wage is $w_1$, but prices have risen to $p_1$ and hence the real wage is unchanged: i.e. $w_1/p_1 = w_0/p_0$.

The rise in prices has changed *nominal* values, but has not affected any *real* variable. The only effect of the higher price level has been to prompt a compensating rise in pay. Since the amount of labour employed has not changed, the volume of output remains unaffected. Hence the long-run AS curve is vertical, indicating a complete independence between prices and real output.

Suppose that employees are 'irrational' and behave as if only the *nominal* wage level matters. This behaviour might be the result of money illusion or of rigidities in the institutional system (such as minimum pay) which prevent employees from accepting or being offered a wage below $w^*$. This situation is illustrated in Figure 11.6, where the *nominal* wage is measured on the vertical axis and the supply of labour is assumed to be perfectly elastic at the going money wage, $w^*$. In this situation, an increase in the price level from $p_0$ to $p_1$ shifts the demand curve for labour outwards. Employers respond positively to the fall in the real wage. But employees do *not* respond to the fall in their real wage. A new equilibrium occurs at $E_1$. The amount of labour employed increases to $L_1$. There is a corresponding increase in output. Using the production function, the consequent increase in output can be estimated. The new equilibrium point is reached at output $y_1$ and price $p_1$. The price level is higher and so is output. The rise in the

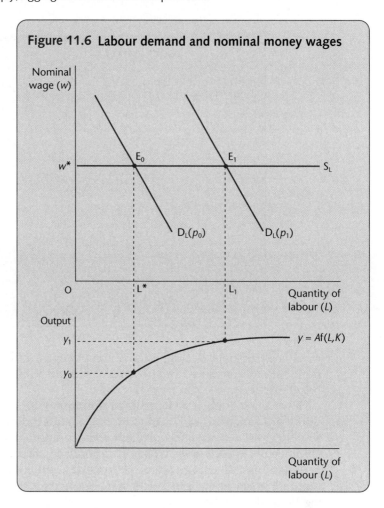

**Figure 11.6 Labour demand and nominal money wages**

price level has a significant *real* effect in that the quantity of real output produced has increased. By tracking the effects of different price levels and joining the points together, the short-run AS curve can be derived. It is positive-sloping and becomes steeper as full employment is approached.

While the labour supply curve is assumed to be horizontal with respect to the nominal wage initially, this assumption becomes more and more untenable as the economy approaches full employment. As the labour market tightens, employees' bargaining power increases and they are quicker to demand compensation for inflation. Once full employment is attained, the AS curve becomes vertical, even in the short run (Figure 11.7).

## Short-run vs long-run AS curve

The distinction is often drawn between the long-run AS curve, which is vertical, and the short-run AS curve, which is upward-sloping. A rise in prices could lead to higher output if wages were 'sticky' in nominal terms in the short run. This 'stickiness' might be present because the rise in price was unanticipated, or

Figure 11.7 Short-run aggregate supply curve

$y_f$ = full employment level of output

because of fixed-term pay deals. Employees might require time to absorb the implications of the rise in price and may react more slowly than firms to the new price level. For these reasons, price changes can have 'real' effects on output and employment in the short term.

The existence of rigidities and short-term 'wage stickiness' may be intuitively acceptable as a working assumption of how the labour market operates in the short run. But such irrational behaviour cannot be indefinitely sustained. Eventually, employees will respond in the 'classical' manner. That still leaves open the question of how long it will take them to respond. The length of the short run is not generally agreed; it is likely to vary from country to country, and even from region to region. Empirical evidence suggests that a period of 1–2 years is a reasonable definition, although some economists of the 'new classical' school argue that it is much shorter than that. They believe that economic agents react so quickly that the short-term concept has no practical relevance to economic policy.

## 11.4 Aggregate demand (AD) and money

We now turn to the demand side of the economy. As we have seen, aggregate demand comprises consumption, investment, government spending and net exports (exports *less* imports). To keep matters simple, assume a *closed* economy, i.e. one which conducts no foreign trade. Since the larger the economic entity, the lower the trade:GNP ratio, the closed economy assumption approximates the position of the larger industrial countries or blocs, such as Japan, the US and the EU.

We shall return to the determinants of the components of aggregate demand in later chapters. For the present, we focus on identifying *the relationship between aggregate demand, money and the price level*. The aggregate demand (AD) curve traces this relationship. And the intersection of AS and AD indicates the equilibrium level of output and price level in the economy.

## Money and the price level

Virtually all economic transactions in an industrial economy involve the use of money. Suppose we define money as the stock of notes and coins held by the public plus deposits in commercial banks and building societies. If people do not have 'enough' money, they cut back spending in an attempt to add to their money balances. If they feel they have 'too much' money, they go out and spend it on goods, or equities or bonds, etc., in an effort to reduce their money stock. This link between desired money balances and aggregate spending is a major focus of attention in this analysis.

Money can be defined in several different ways. One commonly used measure (known as M0) defines it as including (a) notes and coins held by the public, and (b) commercial bank balances with the central bank. The definition can be broadened to include a greater range of financial assets. For example:

M1 = currency held by public plus current accounts held by deposit-taking institutions

M2 = M1 + deposit accounts

M3 = M2 + deposits with a wider range of financial institutions and a broader definition of deposits

M4 = M3 + deposits of building societies.

Definitions differ between countries, but it is unnecessary for the reader to grapple with these fine distinctions. Suffice it to say that the boundary line between money and non-money assets is arbitrary.

## The demand for money

Consider now what determines the amount of money people want to hold. This is not just an academic question. In the euro area, the stock of money (M3) amounts to €6000 billion compared with a GDP of €7200 billion. If, tomorrow, people were for some reason to feel that they had 'too much' money and decided to spend half of their money stock on goods or equities instead, this would have a dramatic impact on the level of aggregate demand.

Individuals hold a certain amount of cash on hand and a balance on deposit in the bank. The decision to hold this amount has been influenced by three main variables:

1. *The level of GDP.* As GDP rises, the volume of commercial transactions also rises and hence the more money individuals and firms are likely to hold in absolute terms (though the proportion of total assets held as money may fall). Individuals hold currency to finance daily transactions. They use bank accounts to cover items such as monthly credit card charges, telephone and other bills which fall due for payment on a regular basis. Companies require money for much the same reasons. We call this the *transactions* motive for holding money.

2. *The price level*. If, tomorrow, all prices were to double, you would feel that you did not have 'enough' money, and to get more you would cut down on spending. If, tomorrow, all prices fell by 50 per cent, people would have a surfeit of money and would most likely embark on a shopping spree. Hence the close link between the price level and aggregate demand: for a given money stock (or money supply), the higher the price level, the lower the volume of spending and the lower the level of aggregate demand. And the lower the price level, the higher the volume of spending and the higher the level of aggregate demand. The AD curve is downward-sloping.

3. *The interest rate*. No interest is paid on currency, and demand deposits often receive only a token rate of return. Higher interest rates, therefore, increase the opportunity cost of holding money and reduce the demand for it.

Other variables, such as inflationary expectations and credit card technology, also affect the demand for money but we will ignore them for now in order to avoid unnecessary complications.

## The supply of money

The supply of money is assumed to be determined 'exogenously'. By this we mean that the central bank can decide how much to provide. If it thinks there is too much money in the system, it can reduce the stock. If it thinks there is not enough money in the system, it can add to the stock.

The central bank controls the supply of notes and coins. By law, it is the body with authority to issue them. But currency today accounts for only a small fraction of total money supply (around €300 billion in the euro area; under 5 per cent in most countries). Hence, the really important question is how deposits in commercial banks are controlled.

Assume an economy with a central bank and one commercial bank, the latter to be taken as representative of the whole commercial banking system. *Deposit creation* refers to the process whereby the commercial banking system is able to create new deposits and hence increase the money supply. The methods by which money is created can be described as follows.

Suppose an individual places €300 cash in a current account in the commercial bank. This deposit creates an asset and a liability for the bank. The deposit is a liability in that the amount is owed to the depositor, who can demand repayment at any time. The deposit is also an asset of the bank in that it has more currency in its vaults. So far, this transaction is not profitable for the bank. It has to bear the cost of managing the customer's account, while it earns nothing on the currency deposited. Hence it has an obvious incentive to use the asset. One profitable way is to give a loan to another customer.

By lending to customers, the bank creates a further asset and a liability. The asset is the customer's obligation to repay the loan to the bank at some date in the future. The corresponding liability is the credit balance placed on the customer's account with the bank. This is a profitable transaction from the bank's point of view, since it charges interest on the loan. Clearly, the bank will want to make as many loans as it prudently can. Its ability to make loans in practice will be constrained by one key obligation: the bank has to stand ready to convert deposits into cash at the request of the customer, more or less on demand. While the bank knows that only a fraction of loans will translate into a demand for cash at any one moment in time, it has to be able to satisfy that demand as required. To be safe, it must maintain a certain *reserve ratio*, i.e. ratio of reserves to deposits. The reserves in question are cash in vaults and balances with the central bank. If a bank has excess reserves, it is able to create money by making loans. If it is short of reserves, it must cut back on loans. Since the counterpart of loans is a deposit, changes in loans directly affect the money supply. The amount of new deposits the banking system as a whole can create depends on the size of its reserves and its required reserve-asset ratio.

Suppose that on average a 10 per cent reserve ratio is sufficient to meet all normal demands for cash. This means that the bank will have to keep 10 per cent of its deposits in cash on hand or as deposits with the central bank. The balance sheet of the commercial bank might then be as below:

**Commercial Bank Balance Sheet**

| Assets | € | Liabilities | € |
|---|---|---|---|
| Cash (notes and coin in vaults and balances with central bank) | 300 | Deposits | 3000 |
| | | Capital employed | 500 |
| Advances | 3000 | | |
| Fixed assets | 200 | | |
| | 3500 | | 3500 |

Suppose now that reserves were increased from €300 to €400. Assuming the reserve ratio remained constant, the bank would have an incentive to lend more to its customers since interest on loans exceeds the return on reserves. With reserves of €400, deposits could increase to €4000 without breaching the reserve requirement. These additional deposits could be created by the extension of new credit to customers. We could expect the new balance sheet to look like the following:

**Commercial Bank Balance Sheet**

| Assets | € | Liabilities | € |
|---|---|---|---|
| Cash (notes and coin in vaults and balances with central bank) | 400 | Deposits | 4000 |
| | | Capital employed | 500 |
| Advances | 3900 | | |
| Fixed assets | 200 | | |
| | 4500 | | 4500 |

Deposits have increased by €1000, advances by €900 and reserves by €100. Supply of money has increased and the bank has created money by making loans. Clearly, therefore, the amount of reserves or the *monetary base* has a pivotal role in determining money supply.

## The monetary base and the central bank

Let us now assume that the central bank can control the monetary base. This is not wholly true, but it is close to the truth.[6] The monetary authorities can affect the monetary base in several ways. We outline the main ones briefly here, leaving further discussion until Chapter 13 on monetary policy.

First, the central bank could require the commercial bank to hold a certain minimum ratio of reserves to deposits. By raising the *reserve requirements*, say from 10 per cent to 15 per cent in our example, the amount of deposits which can be sustained by a given monetary base will decline and money supply will fall. (In practice, reserve ratios are much lower than this.) If the required reserve ratio is lowered, the commercial bank will be able to lend more and money supply will rise.

Second, the central bank may resort to *open market operations*. Open market operations involve the sale or purchase of government bonds, which alters the amount of cash held by the commercial banks and thus their ability to create credit (Box 11.2). The central bank could, for instance, purchase a government bond from an individual and pay for it in currency notes. The seller of the bond will deposit the notes in the commercial bank, and the process of lending and deposit expansion, as described in the numerical example above, gets into motion. If the central bank wishes to expand the money supply, it will *purchase* bonds, so increasing the reserves available to the banking system. If its intention is to reduce the money supply, it will *sell* bonds, so reducing the liquidity base of the banks. In each case, there is a pronounced multiplier effect. Money supply expands or contracts by a multiple of the original injection, the precise amount depending on the reserve ratio.

Third, the central bank could change the *interest rate* attached to the commercial bank's balances with it. Commercial banks cannot always judge their required reserves with perfect accuracy and, when they run short, they have to borrow from the central bank. The interest rate the commercial banks pay when borrowing from the central bank is called the *discount rate* or *marginal lending facility*. By raising the discount rate, the central bank is making such emergency loans more expensive. This induces the commercial banks to hold more of their assets in liquid form, i.e. as reserves, and hence to restrict the expansion of their non-liquid assets, such as loans to customers. In that way, the supply of credit is restricted. In addition, banks will try to pass on the extra interest cost to the customer by charging higher interest on loans. This will make borrowing less attractive to businesses and households. A similar sequence of events follows, *mutatis mutandis*, in the case of lowering the discount rate.

The above analysis of money supply consists of a simple sketch of what is in fact a complex process. The multiplier approach can be extended to take account of both the bank's reserve ratio and the public's propensity to hold cash relative to deposits (Appendix 11.1), and more complicated multipliers can easily be imagined. A key issue for monetary policy is to find out how stable these multipliers are. Another complication flows from the various degrees of 'moneyness' of

---

[6] An insider view of the operational difficulties in controlling the money supply in the case of the Bank of England is provided in J. Dow and I. Saville, *A Critique of Monetary Policy and British Experience* (Oxford: Clarendon Press, 1990).

## Box 11.2    Open market operations

Suppose the central bank purchased bonds worth €105 million from the public and paid for this purchase in newly issued notes. This might lead to the following sequence of effects:

1. The public decides to hold an extra €5 million in cash and to deposit the remaining €100 million with the commercial banks.
2. The commercial banks' balance sheet initially rises by €100 million.

| Assets | | Liabilities | |
|--------|--------|-------------|--------|
| Notes on hand | (+) 100 | Deposits | (+) 100 |

3. The commercial banks now have excess reserves.
4. They will seek to expand credit by advertising the availability of loans and by reducing lending rates.
5. An equilibrium will be reached when the correct reserve ratio of, say, 10 per cent is restored. Loans of €900 million will have been generated by the initial injection of €105 million.

| Assets | | Liabilities | |
|--------|--------|-------------|--------|
| Notes on hand | +100 | Deposits | 1000 |
| Loans | +900 | | |
| | 1000 | | 1000 |

different financial assets. So far, we have distinguished between the monetary base and the larger monetary aggregate represented by deposits in commercial banks. There are, however, many intermediate types of deposits and correspondingly diverse definitions of money supply. Many types of money are aggregated in the broad money supply and, for this reason, this statistic must be interpreted with care. Sometimes shifts between different components of 'the' money supply can be as significant as shifts in the aggregate figure itself. The dividing line between financial assets which fall within the definition of money and those which fall without is quite blurred. The essential point is the importance of the monetary base. If we assume that this variable can be controlled by the monetary authorities and that the behavioural and money reserve ratios used in the money multiplier do not change too unpredictably, the authorities will be able to control the broader money supply. The significance of this power will be explained later.[7]

## Money supply, money demand and the interest rate

Interest rates come in different forms – short run, long run, nominal and real – but we assume for simplicity that there is only one (see Chapter 13 for more). The equilibrium interest rate is the rate of interest that equates the supply of money and the demand for money.

---

[7] Different monetary variables are used as indicators or objectives by central banks. The ECB uses M3; the UK, M0 and M4; the US, M2, M3 and TNDS (total domestic credit); Japan, M2 plus CDS.

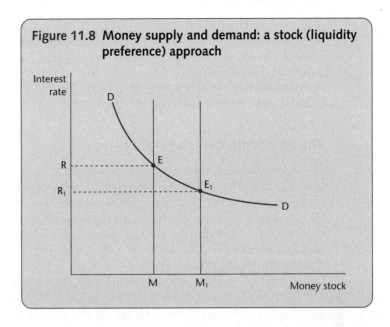

Figure 11.8 Money supply and demand: a stock (liquidity preference) approach

The relevant supply and demand curves are drawn in Figure 11.8, with stock of money (M) on the horizontal axis and interest rate (R) on the vertical axis. We assume that prices are constant and that the supply of money is determined by the central bank. Money supply can thus be depicted by the vertical curve in Figure 11.8.

The demand curve for money is determined by the interest rate and other factors such as output, technology and so on. Assuming these other factors are constant, and focusing just on the interest rate relationship, the demand curve for money (DD) will be downward sloping for reasons already discussed. Hence equilibrium will be at E, with interest rate R.

Suppose the central bank wanted to reduce the interest rate. It could use open market operations to expand the money supply, shifting it from OM to $OM_1$. The economy is now far more liquid than before; people have an incentive to put their excess cash balances into more remunerative outlets such as government bonds. Money starts flowing into the bond market, bond prices rise and the interest rate falls to $R_1$. The fall in interest rate in turn will have a positive impact on aggregate demand. The transmission mechanism running from money supply to interest rate to aggregate demand is in practice very complex; it occupies a central role in studies of monetary policy.

Two further observations are necessary at this stage. First, the analysis, although simplified, illustrates the basic thinking behind central bank policy. By increasing money supply, the bank reduces interest rates and stimulates demand. By curbing money supply, it raises interest rates and reduces demand. Central banks seeking to stimulate an economy in recession, where potential GDP exceeds its actual level, must try to work out how much of an interest rate cut is needed to achieve balance between the two. This requires in-depth knowledge of money demand curves and, further down the line, detailed understanding of the interaction between interest rates and the different components of aggregate demand. No wonder central banks have large research departments.

Second, in Figure 11.8 we use what is known as the liquidity preference framework to explain interest rates. This is a stock approach. Another approach is the loanable funds or credit flows analysis used in Chapter 13. There we focus on supply and demand for credit and the role of the interest rate in bringing them into equilibrium. This is a flow approach. To achieve equilibrium, both markets must be in balance. Hence the two approaches are complementary.[8]

## The aggregate demand (AD) curve

The aggregate demand (AD) curve shows the relationship between real expenditure, or output ($y$), and the price level ($p$) consistent with equilibrium in the money market. That is, at each point on the AD curve, money demand equals money supply. The curve is based on the assumptions that (1) the level of money supply (M) is determined by the monetary authorities, and (2) that money demand depends on the level of output and the price level. The AD curve is downward-sloping (Figure 11.9).

Suppose that the initial equilibrium at ($Y_0$, $P_0$) is disturbed by a fall in the price level to $P_1$. This brings the economy to point A in Figure 11.9. Point A, however, is not an equilibrium point. The fall in the price level has reduced the transactions demand for money. Given that money *supply* remains unchanged, the fall in money demand implies that money supply is greater than money demand. There are excess money balances in the economy which individuals will want to convert into goods or other assets. Assuming the price level stays at $P_1$, the excess demand can only be eliminated if real spending increases from $Y_0$ to $Y_1$. At this

Figure 11.9 **Aggregate demand curve**

---

[8] To see this, think of something closer to individual experience than monetary economics: house prices, for example. The equilibrium house price does two things: (a) it keeps demand for the housing stock equal to the supply for it, and (b) it ensures equality between supply of new houses (housing completions) and demand for new houses. Equilibrium in market segment (b) is not sustainable without equilibrium in (a).

higher level, people will want more cash to finance their transactions. The increase in real expenditure, by increasing the demand for money, yields a new equilibrium point $E_1$. By joining all such points together, we derive the AD curve.

The negative relationship between change in price and change in aggregate demand can also be explained by the *real balance effect*. This effect can take two forms:

1. A fall in the price level means an increase in the purchasing power of financial assets. As the price level declines, the 'real' value of these assets, including the money stock, increases, people feel better-off and want to spend more. Hence a fall in prices will be associated with a rise in real expenditure.
2. A rise in real money balances resulting from a fall in the price level causes an outward shift in the money supply. This leads to a fall in the interest rate. Investment and consumer spending will be stimulated. Again, the fall in price will be associated with a rise in aggregate demand.

## Equilibrium occurs when AD = AS

The final step is to put the AD curve and the AS curve together (Figure 11.10). We then obtain the equilibrium price and income levels in the economy at $(y_0, p_0)$. At that point $(E_0)$,

AD = national expenditure = national income = national output = AS

At any point other than $(y_0, p_0)$, aggregate supply and aggregate demand will not be equal. For example, suppose the price level was $p_1$ instead of $p_0$. At that price level, aggregate demand corresponds to $y_1$. However, aggregate supply remains at $y_0$. The excess of aggregate demand over aggregate supply means that prices must rise in order to restore equilibrium. The rise in the general price level will have the effect of reducing real money balances. People will find that they do not have enough money and will cut back spending. Aggregate demand will fall. By

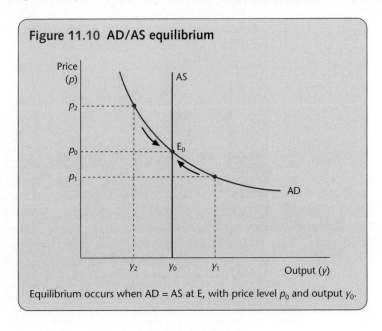

**Figure 11.10 AD/AS equilibrium**

Equilibrium occurs when AD = AS at E, with price level $p_0$ and output $y_0$.

analogous reasoning, it can be shown that a price level $p_2$, greater than $p_0$, is not sustainable. At this price level, aggregate demand will be below aggregate supply and the price level will have to fall.

The AD curve could shift outwards or inwards as conditions change. For example, an outward shift could be caused by any of the following:

- An upsurge in business expectations leads to higher investment
- Consumers decide to increase their spending
- People's preferences for holding money change
- The monetary authorities increase the supply of money.

Referring to Figure 11.11, an outward shift of AD means that, at the original price level $p_0$, demand will increase from $y_0$ to $y_1$. However, at this level of demand, aggregate supply is only $y_0$. Hence the price level must rise. Sustainable equilibrium is not reached until prices reach $p_1$. A shift in the demand curve to the left of $AD_0$ will, by similar reasoning, be consistent only with a lower price level than $p_0$. Hence the conclusion of the model: *shifts in the aggregate demand curve change the price level; they do not affect real output and real living standards.*

In the long run, changes in demand affect the price level, not 'real' variables. 'Real' output can be increased only by 'real' factors – by shifts in the production technology, by more investment, or by the better operation of the markets for productive factors, especially labour.

The model sketched above is a *classical model*. It captures some of the essential features of the modern approach to macroeconomic problems. *Its central message is that sustainable increases in aggregate supply can be achieved only by shifting the aggregate supply curve to the right.* The implication is that governments should concentrate on encouraging efficient use of existing resources, on fostering entrepreneurship and investment, and promoting technological change. Aggregate demand does not feature in this model as an independent force for growth. Because the long-run aggregate supply is assumed to be vertical, interaction between aggregate demand and supply affects only the price level. The model is

**Figure 11.11 Shift in aggregate demand**

simple, but the policy conclusions emanating from it are powerful. They dominate contemporary discussion of economic policies.

To dismiss aggregate demand as a factor relevant to the objective of securing higher output is to push the argument too far. Shifts in demand can, and do, affect output in the short run. The assumption of independence between real and monetary variables rests on the assumption that AS is vertical. If the AS were positively sloped, shifts in AD would affect the price level and *there would also be effects on real output*. Even if these effects are transitory, they could have a significant influence on an economy's trajectory. Much current macroeconomic controversy concerns arguments about the shape of the AS curve, the demarcation between the short run and the long run, and the interconnections between short-run and long-run economic growth.

## 11.5 Conclusions

> The ideas of economists and political philosophers, both when they are right and when they are wrong, are more powerful than is commonly understood. Indeed, the world is ruled by little else. Practical men, who believe themselves to be quite exempt from any intellectual influences, are usually the slaves of some defunct economist. I am sure that the power of vested interests is vastly exaggerated compared with the gradual encroachment of ideas. (J.M. Keynes, *The General Theory*, p. 383)

The above passage from the *General Theory* is by now so celebrated as to have become almost a cliché. Yet it contains an enduring truth: ideas about how an economy works matter. The study of macroeconomics provides an opportunity for engaging in dialogue with those who determine economic policy. This chapter sets the scene for later discussion by outlining the main features of the classical macroeconomic model which dominates today's economic thinking.

Macroeconomics grew out of two 'priors': (1) that deviations between actual and potential GNP occur and can persist, and (2) that something can be done to bring them closer together. That 'something', according to the Keynesian school, was management of aggregate demand. In recent times, the consensus has shifted to the view that attempts to manage aggregate demand can easily be counterproductive. Furthermore, attempts to manage it distract attention from aggregate supply, which *is* susceptible to policy initiatives. An extreme view is that aggregate demand hardly matters at all. Knowledge of the classical model enables us to understand why. If we do not agree, there are useful analytical tools with which to criticise the model and to explore alternatives.

The nub of the classical position is that the AS curve is vertical in the long run. If this is true, shifts in aggregate demand affect prices, not quantities. They affect not real output and employment, but inflation. Anyone who studies the speeches and statements of central bankers will detect a familiar echo at this juncture. An expansion of the money supply or a fall in interest rates, they say, will do nothing for long-term unemployment, or for economic growth, if it endangers price stability.

In the next chapter we study the topic of price stability. Inflation threatens when the economy 'overheats' and when growth temporarily exceeds its long-run potential. But, in certain circumstances, inflation can occur even if the economy is operating below capacity. Supply-side shocks can generate pass-through effects and, in economies with rigid structures, these shocks can generate an inflationary spiral. 'Stagflation' is how this conjunction of stagnant economic conditions and inflation has been described. A central platform of the current orthodoxy is that inflation, whatever its origin, is a 'bad thing', to be resisted if necessary at some short-term cost. In recent years, attention has shifted to deflation, a breach of the price stability objective that is every bit as damaging to an economy as inflation. Argentina (up to 2001), China and Japan have all had first-hand experience of its deleterious consequences and it constitutes a potential threat to the EU. We study these issues in the next chapter.

## Summary

1. GDP refers to the output of goods and services produced by residents of a country. Nominal GDP is the current value of these goods and services produced. Real GDP measures volume of output and is computed by valuing the quantities of goods and services produced in two periods with the same set of prices, thereby neutralising the influence of changing prices.

2. Potential GDP is defined as the maximum output that an economy can produce when factors of production are fully utilised while maintaining low inflation. This will be less than the maximum attainable level of output. It can be estimated by extrapolating growth from past trends or, alternatively, by a production function method. Macroeconomic policy focuses on minimising the gap between actual and potential GDP. Estimating potential GDP is a critically important exercise for economic authorities and central banks.

3. The distinction is made between GDP at nominal exchange rates and GDP at purchasing power parity (PPP). For less well-off countries, the difference can be appreciable. GDP per person at PPP is the better measure of real living standards across countries.

4. The aggregate supply (AS) curve can be regarded as a rough proxy of potential GDP. It shows the combinations of real output and the price level which are consistent with equilibrium in the economy. A near-vertical AS curve is based on a classical model of long-run equilibrium. Because all market participants are assumed to be free from money illusion, the model concludes that equilibrium output is invariant with respect to the general price level. A distinction is drawn between the long-run AS curve, which is vertical, and the short-run AS curve, which is upward-sloping. Keynesian economists concentrate on the short-run AS curve, which they believe is relatively flat up to the point of full employment. Nowadays, many economists argue that the AS curve is near-vertical, even in the short run. Important practical policy conclusions flow from different views on this question.

5. Aggregate demand (AD) comprises consumption, investment, government spending and net exports. The AD curve is downward-sloping and shows the relationship between real income and the price level consistent with equilibrium in the money market. Thus, at each point along the AD curve, money demand equals money supply. The assumptions underlying the AD curve are that (1) the level of

money supply is determined by the monetary authorities, and (2) money demand depends primarily on output, the price level and the interest rate.

**6.** Money supply can be regulated through a number of mechanisms: reserve requirements, open market operations and the interest rate, all of which affect the monetary base.

**7.** Equilibrium levels of price and income are determined by the intersection of the AD and AS curves. The AD curve can move outwards or inwards as economic conditions change. If the AS curve is vertical, shifts in the AD curve change the price level but not 'real' variables. Output can be increased in a sustainable way only through outward shifts in the AS curve. Aggregate supply in the economy can be increased when technology improves, more capital becomes available, labour supply increases or the labour market becomes more flexible. In the short run, shifts in the AD curve can affect output. There are disagreements about how great that effect can be. The new consensus urges circumspection in deploying aggregate demand management, while acknowledging its valuable role in circumstances where the private sector is in a state of serious recession.

## Questions for discussion

**1.** Considerable resources are spent by the statistical authorities in deriving estimates of GDP. From a business perspective, would you say that this exercise is a worthwhile and valuable one?

**2.** What is the difference between *actual* GDP and *potential* GDP? How is potential GDP calculated? Of what practical use are potential GDP estimates?

**3.** Discuss reasons why the aggregate supply curve might be vertical. Do you find them convincing?

**4.** What is the aggregate demand (AD) curve? Why does it slope downwards? What might cause it to shift outwards?

**5.** What is money supply? How might it be controlled by the authorities? What forces in the economy tend to bring money supply and money demand into equilibrium?

**6.** In the short run, the AS curve is often drawn as upward-sloping. What is the reason for this? What is the economic significance of this?

## Exercises

**1.** Which of the following transactions should be included as part of GDP?

(a) A consumer pays €10 for a meal at a restaurant.
(b) A company buys a plant from another firm for €1 million.
(c) A supplier sells computer chips to a firm that makes personal computers.
(d) A person buys a second-hand car from a dealer for €5000.
(e) A person buys a new car for €15,000.
(f) A factory exports €2 million worth of PCs and sells €5 million on the domestic market. It imports €2 million worth of component parts for the PCs.

➡

2. A person saves €10,000 of this year's income and spends it on new machinery. Explain how this would be recorded in the national accounts. Another person takes €10,000 from under the mattress and buys shares on the stock market. Would this be recorded in GDP?

3. Consider an economy with only three goods. Their market prices are $P_1 = 5$, $P_2 = 10$ and $P_3 = 15$. The production (and consumption) of each good during 2002 was $Q_1 = 20$, $Q_2 = 25$ and $Q_3 = 10$.

   (a) What is the value of nominal GDP?

   (b) Assume that in 2003 prices rise to $P_1 = 6$, $P_2 = 12$ and $P_3 = 17$, and quantities produced (and consumed) go to $Q_1 = 21$, $Q_2 = 27$ and $Q_3 = 11$. Calculate the value of nominal GDP. Compute real GDP, using 2002 prices as the base year. What is the rate of inflation? What is the real rate of growth of the economy?

   (c) Calculate the change in real GDP using 2003 prices as the base year. Explain why your answer is different from that in (b).

4. Take any country listed in Table 11.1. Explain the difference between its GDP per head at purchasing power parity and at nominal exchange rates. Using data on the actual 2000 nominal exchange rates, compute the implicit PPP exchange rate for any three countries. Comment on the results.

5. Use diagrams to explain the following statement:

   Outward shifts in the aggregate demand curve affect output only temporarily, whereas outward shifts in the aggregate supply curve affect output permanently. And, whereas a positive demand shock raises prices, a positive supply shock reduces them.

6. Suppose the national accounts for a small country showed the following figures (in millions):

   | | |
   |---|---|
   | wages and salaries | €400 |
   | investment | €200 |
   | money supply | €450 |
   | corporate profits | €100 |
   | rents and interest | €150 |
   | depreciation | €50 |
   | indirect taxes less subsidies | €70 |
   | dividends sent abroad | €50 |
   | income from agriculture | €70 |

   Compute the value of GNP and GDP.

7. Explain how you would expect a stock market boom to affect (a) aggregate supply and (b) aggregate demand. Is a stock market boom 'good' for an economy? How would a fall in the stock market affect the macro economy?

8. 'Inflation does not always rise when the economy grows; nor does it always fall when the economy decelerates. The future path of inflation depends crucially on the size of the output gap.' Give examples and discuss.

## Further reading

There is no shortage of macro textbooks, but it is difficult to find one that combines comprehensiveness with accessibility for a business-oriented reader. Perhaps this is because the subject-matter of macroeconomics is so difficult. M. Burda and C. Wyplosz, *Macroeconomics: A European text* (Oxford: Oxford University Press, 2001), has a welcome emphasis on the open economy, with useful case studies of European economic problems. C. Pass, B. Lowes and A. Robinson, *Business and Macroeconomics* (London and New York: Routledge, 1995), covers some of the same ground as Parts II and III of this book. A concise, historically minded account of the development of macroeconomics is provided by J.A. Sawyer, *Macroeconomic Theory: Keynesian and neo-Walrasian Model* (Hemel Hempstead: Harvester Wheatsheaf, 1989).

## Appendix 11.1 The money supply process

A simplified model of the money supply process can be formalised as follows:

**1.** $M = C_p + D$

where: $M$ = money supply
$C_p$ = currency held by the non-bank public
$D$ = deposits of the commercial banking system.

**2.** $C = C_p + C_b$

where: $C_b$ = currency held in bank vaults.

Next we assume that:

**3.** $C_p = cD$ and $C_b = bD$

where $c$ is the fraction of deposits the public holds in cash and $b$ is the fraction of deposits the commercial banks hold in cash.

Substituting 3 into 1 and 2 gives:

**4.** $M = cD + D = D(c + 1)$

**5.** $C = C_p + C_b = cD + bD = (c + b)D$
$M/C = (c + 1)/(c + b)$
$M = C(c + 1)/(c + b)$

This is the formula for the *money multiplier process*.

For $c = 0.05$ and $b = 0.1$, it tells us that an increase in *high-powered money* ($C$) will increase the money supply by a multiple of that initial increase, i.e. by a factor of 7, using the formula:

$$M/C = (0.05 + 1)/(0.05 + 0.1) = 1.05/0.15 = 7$$

This multiplier formula is a useful teaching device. However, in practice the ratios can prove highly unstable, thereby making the size of the multiplier difficult to predict.

## Chapter 12

# Price stability and central banks

## Introduction

Virtually all countries have endorsed price stability as an important objective of economic policy. Its two opposites are inflation (persistent increases in the general price level) and deflation (decreases in the price level). Until recently inflation was considered the most immediate and insidious threat to price stability and the attention of policy has almost exclusively been concerned with ways of controlling inflationary pressures. But for the past few years the possibility of a deflationary spiral has entered the policy frame. Declines in the general price levels have been recorded in Japan and China. Measured prices are still rising in the euro area but at such a low rate (less than 2 per cent) as to warrant serious concern. Questions have even been asked about the probability of the US economy succumbing to a deflationary downturn.

From a historical perspective, the big story of the past 50 years has been the battle to restore price stability, a battle that seems to have been decisively won in the developed world. A newspaper in the mid-1990s proclaimed Britain's success in controlling inflation with the celebratory banner headline 'INFLATION HITS A 27-YEAR LOW'. Similar headlines greet inflation figures in most other industrialised countries (Table 12.1). For them the challenge is no longer to reduce inflation, but to ensure that the success in restraining it is maintained. *Price stability in the medium term* has become the new mantra of central bankers and policymakers.

### Table 12.1 Average annual inflation rates in major industrial countries

|         | 1971–80 | 1981–90 | 1991–2000 | 2001–04 | Peak rate since 1970 |
|---------|---------|---------|-----------|---------|----------------------|
| Germany | 5.2     | 2.6     | 2.3       | 1.3     | 8.8 (1974)           |
| UK      | 13.3    | 6.1     | 3.2       | 2.5     | 23.5 (1974)          |
| France  | 10.0    | 6.3     | 1.7       | 1.8     | 14.8 (1974)          |
| US      | 7.1     | 4.7     | 2.7       | 2.0     | 10.7 (1980)          |
| Japan   | 8.7     | 2.1     | 0.9       | −0.7    | 21.0 (1974)          |

*Source*: IMF, *World Economic Outlook*, successive issues.

Developing countries have had a more turbulent experience. Brazil struggled with an inflation rate exceeding 2400 per cent as recently as 1994 (Table 12.2). Happily, it has since subsided to single figures. The former socialist countries also suffered serious depredations on the value of their currency with adverse consequences for their economies and the business environment. The situation there has much improved in recent years and price stabilisation programmes have been successfully introduced into the Baltic States and into most countries of Central and Eastern Europe (Table 12.3). But inflation still remains an acute problem. In 2002, we find high price increases in many parts of the developing world: 75 per cent annually in Angola, 450 per cent in Zimbabwe, 43 per cent in Belarus and 45 per cent in Turkey.

Price stability is important for the efficient operation of the market system. This explains the high priority afforded to it by governments. Moreover, because it is a public good the free market cannot be counted upon to provide it.[1] Hence the need for sustained involvement by the authorities.

### Table 12.2 Average annual inflation rates in Latin America

|  | 1980–85 | 1986–90 | 1991–2000 | 2001–04 | Peak rate since 1970 |
|---|---|---|---|---|---|
| Chile | 21.3 | 19.3 | 8.5 | 3.1 | 505 (1974) |
| Bolivia | 611.0 | 46.5 | 12.7 | 2.1 | 11,705 (1985) |
| Mexico | 60.8 | 69.6 | 15.2 | 4.7 | 132 (1987) |
| Argentina | 322.5 | 584.0 | 9.0 | 15.0 | 4,924 (1989) |
| Brazil | 149.0 | 657.5 | 434.2 | 8.7 | 2,407 (1994) |

Source: IMF, World Economic Outlook, successive issues; Bank of International Settlements, 64th Annual Report, Basle, 2000.

### Table 12.3 Average annual inflation rates in Central and Eastern Europe

|  | 1991–95 | 1996–2000 | 2001–04 | Peak rate since 1989 |
|---|---|---|---|---|
| Albania | 75.4 | 16.9 | 3.6 | 226 (1992) |
| Czech Republic | 21.5 | 6.9 | 2.6 | 57 (1991) |
| Estonia | 290.7 | 9.9 | 4.1 | 1,076 (1992) |
| Hungary | 104.9 | 15.0 | 6.1 | 35 (1991) |
| Latvia | 258.4 | 7.1 | 2.6 | 951 (1992) |
| Lithuania | 353.5 | 8.2 | 1.5 | 1,021 (1992) |
| Poland | 41.7 | 12.7 | 2.7 | 586 (1990) |
| Slovak Republic | 23.6 | 8.2 | 6.7 | 61 (1991) |
| Slovenia | 78.5 | 11.2 | 6.6 | 1,306 (1989) |

Source: IMF, World Economic Outlook, successive issues; European Bank for Reconstruction and Development, Transition Report 1999.

---

[1] For a definition of the term 'public good', see Chapter 8. Price stability is non-rivalrous (one person's enjoyment of its benefits does not limit any other person's) and non-excludable (people cannot be prevented from enjoying the benefits of price stability, regardless of whether or not they have contributed to its provision). Hence, a market system will not on its own produce an optimal supply of this good.

Another feature of price stability is that deviations from it tend to be self-perpetuating and difficult and costly to control. Thus the *inflationary spiral* arises as price increases feed into pay claims, which raise costs and prices, thereby generating further compensatory pay claims and so on. A similar, and perhaps even more damaging, sequence of self-sustaining events accounts for the *deflationary spiral* that is currently inhibiting the restoration of price stability and economic recovery in Japan. Price stability is an essential element in a healthy business environment and a major challenge for governments to preserve.

## Chapter outline

This chapter proceeds as follows.

1. Price stability: definition and measurement.
2. Deviations from price stability: inflation.
3. Deviations from price stability: deflation.
4. The economic benefits of price stability.
5. Policies for achieving sustainable price stability.
6. Price stability and exchange rate 'anchors'.

## 12.1 What is price stability?

Price stability is defined as the sustained absence of both inflation (prices rising too fast) and deflation (falling prices). Since inflation is more common than deflation, and since some degree of price increase may be consistent with price stability, we focus initially on inflation.

Inflation is a *persistent* rise in the *general* level of *money* prices. Consumer price inflation is defined by reference to the total money cost of a *basket* of consumer goods and services. The components of the basket and the weights attached to them are designed to reflect the type of goods and services consumed by a typical individual or household. In 1914, the UK retail price index (RPI) contained 80 items, most of them food products, but also including necessities such as candles, starch and washing soda. Nowadays, the index contains around 650 items. Many new products have been added such as video recorders, CD players, microwave ovens and mobile phones. In all, some 140,000 price quotations are obtained each month from various types of sales outlets in different regions of the country. The US consumer price index (CPI) is derived from price quotations on 71,000 goods and services collected at about 22,000 retail outlets.

The number of goods and services in the sample basket is necessarily an incomplete inventory of output in the economy. Opinions differ as to what should be included in the price index. For example, the UK is one of the few countries to include mortgage interest payments in its index. The method of introducing new goods is also problematic, though much of the improvement of living standards in modern economies derives from new products. Another issue is the weighting to be attached to the various items in the basket. As the standard of living rises, basic necessities – such as food and fuel – become proportionately less important in household consumption. Although the composition of the household 'basket' is revised periodically in order to reflect the changing pattern of household spending, the timing and extent of such revision can create biases in the resultant price index.

Inflation statistics are affected by three main sources of bias:

1. *Composition bias* arises because of the delay in incorporating new goods into the consumer basket. They tend to be included in the CPI only after some years have elapsed. Typically, their price will have fallen during this period, sometimes by 80 per cent or more. (Mobile phones were not included until 1998, thus the index missed the substantial price reductions of this product during the previous decade.) The delay in including new products in the CPI basket leads to a systematic overestimation of true inflation.

2. *Quality bias* occurs because there is insufficient adjustment of price increases for improvements in quality. Thus, a new car model might be more expensive than the old model, but if the rise in price is due to higher quality living standards the CPI should register no change. The statistical authorities try to adjust for quality improvement, but generally the adjustment has been found to be insufficient, particularly in the case of personal computers, household appliances and medicines – where quality improvement is occurring at a very rapid rate.

3. *Substitution bias*: As prices increase, people shift spending from goods which have become relatively dear towards cheaper goods and services, and from more expensive to less expensive retail outlets (this is called *outlet bias*). The share of spending on individual components of the consumer basket changes in response to changes in relative prices. Since spending tends to shift from goods with the most rapid price increase towards goods with the lower price increase, failure to take account of this will result in an upward bias in the inflation index.

The precise empirical importance of these various sources of measurement bias is not known. Studies of the consumer price index suggest a total upward bias of around one percentage point each year. Although this bias may seem small, if inflation is running in low digits the bias may amount to a large fraction of actual inflation. A study of the UK retail price index concluded that substitution bias was not a substantial source of error, but that composition and quality biases could lead to a 'significant', but at present unquantifiable, overstatement of the true price increase. In the US, the Advisory Commission to Study the Consumer Price Index (CPI) concluded that the CPI overstated the change in the cost of living by about 1.1 percentage points per year: 0.5 percentage points due to substitution bias and the remainder due to quality and composition bias.[2]

*Because of these biases, price stability is defined as a sustainable, medium-term average annual rise in prices in the range 1–3 per cent.*

---

[2] M.J. Boskin *et al.*, 'Consumer prices, the Consumer Price Index and the cost of living', *Journal of Economic Perspectives* (Winter 1998); N. Oulton, 'Do UK price indexes overstate inflation?', *National Institute Economic Review* (May 1995); the Japanese CPI has been estimated to have an upward bias of at least 0.5 per cent (K. Ariga and K. Matsui, 'Mismeasurement of the CPI', *NBER Working Paper 9436*, January 2003).

The consumer price index can be a politically sensitive statistic.[3] It has a direct bearing on the living standards of the majority of households and employees. Pay, pensions and social welfare increases are often directly tied to this index, with significant consequences for public finances. Three issues arise because of this.

First, should there be a different 'representative basket' to reflect the spending pattern of different segments in society? A senior executive has a different consumption pattern from that of a young trainee. A poor person's consumption basket will be more affected by changes in prices of basic necessities than that of the representative household. However, because, in the long run, most prices rise more or less proportionately, the biases arising from these different consumption patterns will usually be small.

A second issue is whether *asset prices* such as house and share prices should be included in the index. Many people might feel that changes in house prices, for instance, would impact significantly on living standards, yet they are excluded from the consumer price index. The statisticians would reply that what matters for living standards is the cost of *housing services*, i.e. rents on rented accommodation, the cost of housing repairs and in some countries (the UK, for instance) mortgage payments, rather than the price of a house *per se*. Likewise a stock market boom means that buying shares is more expensive, but share prices are not included in the consumer price index. Were they to be included a problem would arise in so far as a rise in share prices, unlike a rise in food prices, may not be a 'bad' thing for the consumer. Changes in asset prices are by no means irrelevant to inflation. They can impact in an important way on pay costs and total spending. But their impact is measured indirectly rather than directly in the consumer price index.

Third, how should changes in the price index that are caused by government indirect taxes on alcohol, cigarettes, petrol and suchlike be treated? There is certainly a good case for separate computation of these effects on the CPI. They represent government tax policy more than 'core' underlying price trends. For this reason, energy, food and drink prices are often excluded in analyses of future price trends. The difference between core inflation and measured CPI can sometimes be appreciable. But the possibility of interaction between the two measures needs to be borne in mind. Past changes in core inflation can increase government costs and hence oblige governments to raise indirect taxes in order to balance the budget. Thus changes in indirect taxes may reflect not just an exogenous decision by the government but an endogenous response to core inflationary pressures.

## 12.2 Deviation from price stability 1: inflation

In 2003, 95 countries out of a total of 182 recorded price increases in excess of 3 per cent. Why has this happened and what can be done about it?

---

[3] So much so as to cause the resignation of Brazil's finance minister in September 1994. In a private conversation mistakenly broadcast by satellite television to a bemused audience throughout Latin America, he remarked that when it comes to inflation indices: 'I don't have any scruples. What is good, we use – what is bad, we hide' (*Financial Times*, 5 September 1994).

To control inflation, we must understand its causes. The *monetarist* view of inflation, encapsulated in Milton Friedman's dictum, *inflation is always and everywhere a monetary phenomenon*, has been enormously influential. Inflation occurs when the growth of the money supply persistently exceeds the growth of real output. Theories of inflation focus on (a) how 'shocks' on the demand side (a rise in confidence) or the supply side (a commodity price boom) can impart an upward twist to the general price level; and (b) how that initial price level rise can generate an inflationary spiral through accommodating monetary supply increases.

## Money supply and inflation

If each of us woke today with twice as much money as yesterday, two things could happen: (1) we could spend some of the extra money on goods and services to celebrate our good fortune; or (2) we might invest part of the money in government bonds or similar financial assets. In the latter case, the resultant upsurge in asset prices would boost demand for goods and services. Hence prices would be 'driven' up – assuming a fixed aggregate supply.

This higher level of spending does not reduce the *total* holding of money, but merely transfers money from one person to another at a more rapid rate than before. Nominal money stock remains at twice its original level. As prices rise, however, a given amount of money will buy fewer goods and services. The real purchasing power of money declines. The initial equilibrium is restored when prices and income in money terms are about twice as high as they were originally. Only then will people be willing to hold the higher supply of money. This explains why inflation cannot continue without a sustained increase in the money stock and why continued excessive increases in the money stock are invariably followed by inflation.

The chain of causation may be sketched using the AS/AD framework of Chapter 11. A rise in money supply from $M_0$ to $M_1$ shifts the AD curve outwards

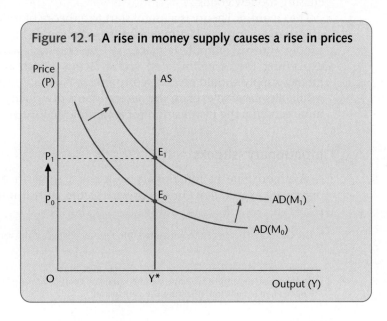

**Figure 12.1  A rise in money supply causes a rise in prices**

from $AD(M_0)$ to $AD(M_1)$. The eventual equilibrium will move from $E_0$ to $E_1$ and prices will rise from $P_0$ to $P_1$ (Figure 12.1). Further increases in money supply will lead to corresponding price increases, and so on.

In the short run, as we have seen, the AS curve may be positively sloped rather than completely vertical. In that event, a rise in the money stock will cause higher prices, but it will also lead to more output. The output effect occurs because of short-term rigidities, reflecting employees' inability to respond instantaneously to the decrease in the real wage caused by the increase in the price level. In the longer term, pay levels will 'catch up' on inflation and, over time, they will respond more quickly to it. The economy then approximates more and more closely to the vertical AS.

This approach is consistent with the *Quantity Theory of Money*. This theory is constructed on the basis of the highly simplified equation:

$$MV = PT$$

where $M$ is the money supply, $V$ is the velocity of circulation of money, $T$ is the amount of transactions, and $P$ is the price level. The amount of transactions can be approximated by the volume of real output ($Y$).

Suppose that the money stock ($M$) in an economy is £1000 and the velocity of circulation ($V$) is 2. The Quantity Theory tells us that, in equilibrium, the annual value of GNP (i.e. $PY$) must equal £2000. This is consistent with any number of combinations of price and quantities. If the price ($P$) is £4 per unit, then $Y$ must be 500 units. If price falls to £2 per unit, volume of output can rise to 1000 units, and so on.[4] Clearly, a great deal of theorising is going on behind the equation, but for the present we simply accept it at face value.

If the further assumption is made that $Y$ and $V$ are given, a direct link is established between changes in $M$ and changes in $P$. This can also be expressed in percentage terms. Other things being equal (notably, the velocity of circulation and trend growth in income), the higher the growth of money supply, the higher the rate of inflation. Hence the popular description of inflation as 'too much money chasing too few goods'.[5]

The Quantity Theory is a useful start to a theory of inflation, but it leaves many questions unanswered. It oversimplifies the causal interactions between money supply and real output. It places all the emphasis on money supply without explaining the economic and social factors which determine how and why money supply should be allowed to increase. A fully fledged theory of inflation would also have to explain the determinants of velocity of circulation and probe more carefully the justification for assuming that it remains 'constant'.

## Inflationary 'shocks'

A common type of inflationary shock is a surge in demand caused by over-optimistic expectations in the private sector. British inflation in the late 1980s,

---

[4] The Quantity Theory can be converted into rates of change of the variables as follows:

$$m = p + y - v$$

where lower-case letters refer to rate of change over time.

[5] To keep matters simple, we have assumed that the coefficients of $p$ and $y$ are unity. This assumption can be changed without affecting the conclusion.

for example, was fuelled by a housing boom, stimulated by tax cuts and a feel-good factor, and financed by excessive credit expansion. Deregulation had loosened the Bank of England's control over lending by financial institutions. It took time before the monetary authorities were able to rein in the money supply.

Demand-pull inflation can also be sparked off by excessive *government budget deficits*. For example, the government might try to stimulate demand in order to achieve a reduction in unemployment. As demand expands, labour and commodity markets tighten, and prices could be driven up. Also the deficit could affect the liquidity base of the economy, in effect increasing the money supply, lowering interest rates and giving an additional boost to the economy. In transition economies, the sudden liberalisation of the economy was associated with a huge increase in the deficits of state firms and a corresponding build-up of overdrafts in the banking system. Governments were unable to stem these deficits (the soft budget constraint). Being underpinned by state guarantees, these overdrafts were in effect 'monetised'. The resultant expansion of credit constituted a significant demand shock to the economy and directly contributed to inflation.

Another source of shocks is supply-side disruption. *Energy-price shocks, sudden shortages of key materials* and *trade unions* can 'cause' inflation by persistently raising costs ahead of the level of productivity. Traditionally, this was termed *cost-push inflation*. But the verb 'cause' has in each case to be carefully qualified.

From an inflation perspective, the key point to remember is that, in each case, inflation will be sustained only if the rise in spending is accompanied by an increase in the money supply.

## The inflationary process

In order to translate a one-off general price increase into sustained inflation, the Quantity Theory tells us that something else must happen: money supply also has to rise on a sustained basis. The monetary authorities have to acquiesce in a continuously rising money supply. A political decision might be taken that the short-run costs, in terms of civil strife, unemployment and disruption, of refusing to validate the inflation are greater than the economic costs of inflation (about which more later).[6] Nothing better illustrates this point than the contrast between the reactions of the UK and West Germany to the oil crisis of the 1970s. Up to 1973, the UK inflation rate had been only marginally higher than West Germany's. After 1973, UK inflation rose to more than double Germany's. The UK authorities decided to validate the inflation, whereas in Germany the authorities made clear their intention not to validate it, and German employers and trade unions responded by keeping tight curbs on prices and nominal incomes. In Germany, determination not to increase the money supply dampened inflationary expectations and moderated pay claims. This made it easier to curb inflation. In the UK, responses to the initial price rise appeared to weaken the authorities' will to control the money supply, which made control of inflation harder, and inflation escalated.

---

[6] Exchange rates have to be introduced in order to explain inflation in open economies. These economies are exposed as much to external as to internal inflationary pressures. The extent to which inflation is imported from the rest of the world, then, hinges crucially on the exchange rate regime adopted by the small country. We consider this issue later.

An anti-inflation strategy should be based on a proper understanding of the economic costs of inflation. This will help to provide the authorities with a democratic consensus needed to take the sometimes unpleasant actions required to make the strategy work. West Germany's successful postwar inflation record, for example, owes as much to the public's aversion to inflation as to the skill of its monetary authorities in regulating the money supply. But institutions also play a vital role. Monetary institutions and fiscal policies must both be geared to give a high priority to price stability. Monetary institutions derive their status, power and priorities from government, and are heavily influenced by societal values.

A key element, therefore, in understanding inflation is to understand why a price shock in one country translates into an inflationary spiral, whereas in another it leads to a one-off rise followed by a return to price stability. The answer seems to be that the capacity of a country to resist inflation depends on its institutions, and on their credibility and reputation in restraining inflationary impulses. These institutions include, of course, the monetary authorities, but trade unions and government also form a vital part of the relevant institutional infrastructure.

The proximate economic causes of inflation are comparatively easy to analyse in the context of a Quantity Theory approach. Its ultimate causes are more complex. Nobody believes any more that inflation is exclusively associated with excess aggregate demand – the prevalence of *stagflation*, i.e. recession combined with inflation, has seen to that. Nor is it inevitable that a supply-side shock will generate an inflationary spiral. Excessive money creation does not take place in a vacuum. Inflation is caused by the interaction between monetary policy, institutions and political calculation.

## 12.3 Deviation from price stability 2: deflation

Deflation is defined as a persistent decline in the general price level. Because of the upward bias in the measurement of the consumer price index, deflation could be present at any time when the CPI is rising by less than 2 per cent, although we cannot be precise about the actual cut-off point.

Deflation has been a comparatively rare phenomenon during the past century. The Great Depression of the 1930s is, of course, a searing exception, but the tendency has been to regard it as a problem solved, relegated to economic history, rather than as a source of lessons for contemporary policy-makers. Such might still be the case were it not for the unleashing of a stubbornly persistent deflationary spiral in Japan where prices have been falling since 1995. A diverse group of other countries, including Germany, Switzerland, China, Thailand and Saudi Arabia, are experiencing either actual declining prices or something dangerously close to it. *The Economist* (17 May 2003) pronounced the risk of deflation in the USA to be greater than at any time since the 1930s. Around the same time, the IMF found evidence of prices increasing at an annualised rate of below 1 per cent for significant periods of time in several industrial and large emerging economies.[7] And in a press release on 6 May 2003, the Federal Reserve, with the

---

[7] International Monetary Fund, *World Economic Outlook*, Washington, DC, May 2003.

Delphic circumspection one expects of central bankers, commented on the probability of 'an unwelcome substantial fall in inflation' posing a threat to US economic recovery. Suddenly, deflation has become a hot research topic (Figure 12.2).

Deflation is the mirror image of inflation and we can use the same analytical framework to study it. Like inflation, it can be caused by supply or demand shocks. Supply shocks include such factors as sustained productivity improvements and technological innovation that lower the prices of inputs and output. These supply shocks have a benign aspect; they are not inconsistent with strong economic growth, although they can have undesirable income distribution and transaction costs effects.

Demand shocks can arise for several reasons: a collapse in the stock market or in property prices, a sustained strengthening of the exchange rate, wars or rumours of wars that undermine business confidence. Governments are generally more prone to overspending than underspending, and hence in normal circumstances are unlikely to be the source of a deflationary demand shock.[8] Deflation caused by demand shocks causes not just a loss of static efficiency in the market system. It is usually accompanied by a slowdown in economic activity and this slowdown, by what the Federal Reserve calls *a process of adverse dynamics*, increases the gap between aggregate demand and supply and exacerbates the deflation.

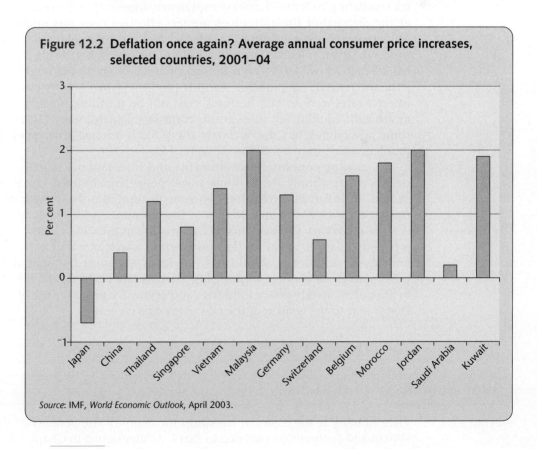

**Figure 12.2 Deflation once again? Average annual consumer price increases, selected countries, 2001–04**

*Source*: IMF, *World Economic Outlook*, April 2003.

---

[8] As we shall see in Chapter 22, an exception to this rule is the European Union's stability and growth fiscal guidelines, which have been criticised for having a deflationary bias.

In assessing the economic effects of deflation, the problem stems less from the shock itself than from the sequence of events that follow and magnify its initial impact. Price declines become self-reinforcing. If consumers expect prices to fall by 5 per cent next year, they have a strong incentive to postpone purchases this year. But this postponement weakens demand, ensures that the expected price decline actually happens and strengthens expectations of even greater declines in the future. Weakening consumer demand passes into investment. Investors begin to lose nerve. Sales forecasts are cut back. The appetite for risk weakens. Faced with declining sales, corporate debt that once looked rock-solid now begins to look less secure. As investment is curtailed, firms cut back on the number of employees, which accentuates business and consumer pessimism. It is easy to see how a period of sustained price and output decline can kick a deflationary spiral into operation. In an open world economy, there is the added fear that deflationary impulses in a large economy could be transmitted across countries through trade and investment linkages.

Deflation is a particular concern because it is intrinsically difficult to resolve, and there is no storehouse of experience in dealing with it comparable to that for inflation. There is also a worry that too many of today's monetary generals are focused on fighting the last war (against inflation) instead of devising a strategy for combating deflation. Japanese experience suggests that the policy instruments at the disposal of the authorities are less effective than was originally hoped. Monetary policy is constrained by the fact that the nominal interest rates cannot be less than zero. Hence, if prices are falling, the cost of borrowing for investment can be high in real terms, even though nominal interest rates might be very low – the *zero interest floor* problem. Another problem is the liquidity trap. Even if real interest rates were to fall, business may still be unwilling to invest. Banks are awash with liquidity but there are no borrowers. Expansionary fiscal policy offers some possibilities, but after a certain threshold is reached it becomes part of the problem rather than a solution (Chapter 15).

The growing concern of governments and international organisations about deflation has already led to some novel policy conclusions: (a) central banks should set inflation targets high enough to minimise the danger of deflation (taking account of the upward bias of the consumer price index and the heavy costs of deflation); (b) they must consider a rise in the CPI of below 1 per cent as a potential danger signal for deflation, not as a welcome respite from inflation; and (c) the authorities should not just focus on prices but should also move pre-emptively to counter output gaps. There is talk of the desirability of 'unconventional' monetary policy initiatives and aggressive proactive use of fiscal policy that is new to the lexicon of the new economic consensus.

## 12.4 Benefits of price stability

Price stability is the essential backdrop for many of the benefits of the market system and competition outlined in Part I. As mentioned in Chapter 3, without a secure medium of exchange, prices cannot perform the signalling function that is key to the efficiency gains of a market system, and hence the market cannot deliver on its potential. Exactly the same argument applies in the case of the gains from trade. A stable domestic price system helps to ensure that international exchange is conducted on the basis of a correct knowledge of prices and alternatives.

The economic benefits of price stability are analysed by considering the costs that arise when such stability is absent, i.e. when the economy is subject to periods of inflation or deflation.

(1) *Rapid changes in the general price level obstruct the efficient working of the market system.*
Faced with these changes, consumers and producers will often suffer some degree of 'money illusion'. They confuse general price level changes with relative price movements. This leads to a blurring of the signals and a distortion of the incentives on which the market economy depends. A World Bank report commented that:

> Rapid and accelerating inflation undermines allocative efficiency because it increases uncertainty and induces savers to invest in unproductive 'inflation hedges' such as real estate, consumer durables, gems and foreign currency deposits. Some countries have developed complex systems for indexing wages and prices to compensate for inflation, though this is administratively costly and tends to penalise those (mostly poor) people outside the indexation system. Where indexation does not exist, the 'inflation tax' contributes to a growing sense of social and economic injustice.[9]

In addition to making the price system function less efficiently, inflation and deflation both impose an administrative cost. The *menu cost* refers to the time and bother of having to change prices frequently in markets where price, in the normal course of events, is kept unchanged for some time. Examples of such 'customer' markets include labour markets, retail and wholesale trade, pay telephones and parking meters. Another type of efficiency loss consists of what are known as 'shoe-leather costs'. These arise because of the extra complexity and inconvenience of transacting business when price stability is absent.

(2) *Effects on the distribution of wealth.*
Unless loans are perfectly indexed, inflation will redistribute resources from lenders to borrowers by reducing the real value (in terms of goods and services) of debt which is denominated in money terms. It will also tend to redistribute income from those whose incomes are fixed in nominal money terms, or which lag behind inflation, to those whose incomes are indexed to inflation. The elderly (who have accumulated assets) may also lose from inflation to the young (who are, in general, net debtors). Most of these redistributions reflect either an inability to adjust to a higher rate of inflation or, more likely, a lag in adjustment. Inflation-indexation schemes are not only administratively costly, but also likely to be applied only to a proportion of the workforce, more often than not those in secure sectors of the economy with strong trade unions. The income-distributive effects of inflation are not just a simple question of reallocating income from poor to rich, elderly to the young, government to private sector. What is really damaging is the haphazard and uneven incidence of this redistribution within and between different classes. The

---

[9] World Bank, *World Development Report* (Washington, DC, 1983), p. 59.

Hungarian economist, Janos Kornai, described inflation as a disaster which *descends mercilessly on the population, leading to perpetual unrest as people see the savings they have scraped together melt away in their hands.*[10]

(3) *Inflation hinders economic growth.*
The causal link between inflation and growth is easier to establish in theory than to identify empirically. Multi-country studies of inflation and growth suggest two main conclusions:

1. Low inflation is positively associated with growth.
2. Hyperinflation is associated with economic decline.[11]

For countries in between, with moderate rates of inflation, statistical analysis is less conclusive. China and India, for example, have experienced fast growth, notwithstanding annual inflation rates of 6–10 per cent (Figure 12.3). Some studies reported reductions in productivity growth in the range 0.05–0.10 per cent for each additional percentage point of inflation, which implies significant losses from inflation in the long run. However, some scepticism about the reliability of these precise estimates is justified.[12]

The unstable environment produced by rapidly rising prices can easily lead to the shortening of the time horizons within the community. Rather than focusing

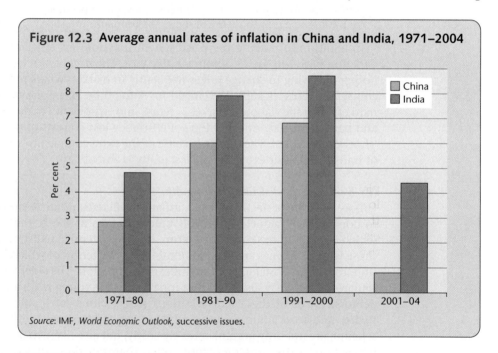

**Figure 12.3 Average annual rates of inflation in China and India, 1971–2004**

*Source*: IMF, *World Economic Outlook*, successive issues.

---

[10] Janos Kornai, *The Road to a Free Economy* (London: Norton, 1990), p. 108.
[11] International Monetary Fund, *World Economic Outlook* (Washington, DC, May 1990).
[12] T. Gylfason, *Principles of Economic Growth* (Oxford: Oxford University Press, 1999) concludes: 'Experience thus seems to indicate that high inflation hurts growth, but where the threshold between high and low inflation lies in this context – at 40 per cent per year? 20 per cent? 10 per cent? – is not yet known' (p. 93). This degree of agnosticism might appear somewhat alarming to devotees of a price stability target of 0–2 per cent! However, few economists would argue that inflation is good for growth, even if evidence that mild inflation is bad for growth is hard to establish.

on opportunities with a medium-term or long-term pay-back, attention and effort is switched to short-term, speculative 'deals'. Thus, inflation impacts negatively on the capacity of society to generate wealth, by causing the misuse of capital and by distorting the behaviour of entrepreneurs.

(4) *The economic turmoil associated with price instability can cause major social tensions and threaten democratic institutions.*

Resentment among the losers and uncertainty among other members of the population can enhance the appeal of populist and totalitarian parties which provide simplistic answers to economic problems. There are many examples of democratic regimes that collapsed in the aftermath of inflation. Italy during the 1920s when Mussolini took control, and Germany in 1933 when Hitler gained power, are instances of this. Some Latin American countries have experienced similar crises. Inflationary spirals, where prices, salaries and wages chase each other upwards in a mutually self-reinforcing circle, have had dire social and economic consequences. The disastrous consequences have been summed up in a famous quote from Keynes (himself drawing on Lenin):

> There is no subtler, no surer means of overturning the existing basis of society than to debauch the currency. [13]

Sustained deflation can likewise be damaging to enterprise and can cause unemployment, stagnation and widespread dissatisfaction with a political regime.

(5) *Inflation and deflation 'spirals' are costly to reverse.*

Because of slow adjustment in labour and goods markets to continuing uncertainty, there are substantial economic costs in restoring price stability once it is lost. For example, the restrictive policies in the UK during the period 1989–93, which were introduced in order to reduce inflation, led to an increase in the unemployment rate from 7 per cent to 12 per cent from 1990 to 1993, and to real short-term interest rates exceeding 9 per cent in 1990. If the monetary authorities proceed too rapidly in trying to cut the inflation rate, without the necessary complementary policies being in place and public opinion being properly primed, lower inflation will be secured at the cost of unemployment in the short run. [14] In the case of deflation, the problem can be that the authorities do not react rapidly enough. By the time they do respond, the deflationary spiral has gained momentum. At this stage, reversing the momentum becomes very problematic. Conventional monetary and fiscal policies lose effectiveness, thereby generating more delays – incurring heavy costs – in resolving the problem.

Writing 60 years ago, Keynes observed that:

> each process, inflation and deflation alike, has inflicted great injuries. Each has an effect in altering the distribution of wealth between different classes. Each has an effect in over-stimulating or retarding the production of wealth. *Both evils are to be shunned.* [15]

---

[13] J.M. Keynes, 'The social consequences of changes in the value of money', in *Collected Economic Writings*, Vol. IX (London: Macmillan, 1971), p. 60.

[14] The process of reducing inflation is called *disinflation*, and the relationship between inflation and unemployment is measured by the *Phillips curve* (see Chapter 14, Appendix 14.1).

[15] J.M. Keynes, 'Economic consequences of the peace', in *Collected Economic Writings*, Vol. II (London: Macmillan, 1971), p. 149.

Inflation creates problems. For similar and symmetrical reasons, so does deflation, defined as a persistent fall in prices (Box 12.1). The solution is for governments to ensure that price stability, once restored, is thereafter maintained.

Some qualifications to the case against inflation can be made without detriment to the general thrust of the argument. The harmful effects of inflation will be reduced to the extent that inflation is correctly anticipated, and contracts and loans are properly indexed. But this is not easy to do. Inflation is mostly unpredictable and uncertain. In the case of deflation, full indexation is not possible because nominal interest rates cannot be reduced below zero. While in principle deposits could be taxed to achieve negative interest rates, there would be many practical difficulties. Currency notes could not be taxed.

Another extenuating argument relates to inflation. Rising prices help business by lowering the real value of debt and thus large nominal rises in company profits resulting from inflation may flatter managers and keep shareholders happy. Also, it may be easier to save jobs in weak firms by freezing nominal wages in conditions of rising prices than by reducing real wages by the same amount through nominal pay reductions in conditions of price stability. Employees resist nominal wage cuts, for understandable reasons. For governments, tax bands are often not indexed and so, if inflation occurs, extra revenue may be generated without the political cost attached to raising tax rates. Mortgage holders on fixed-interest and inflation-indexed salaries will not be unhappy at the prospect of higher inflation. However, all these are short-run arguments. It is questionable if 'money illusion' can persist for long among consumers, producers and voters in the face of a persistently rising level.

---

### Box 12.1 The costs of deflation

Japan's prolonged and widespread price decline that started in the mid-1990s was a novel experience for a modern industrial country. The experience throws light on the difficulties created for business by falling prices.

Between 1990 and 1995, Japanese commercial property prices tumbled more than 50 per cent, while by August 1995 the Tokyo stock market had fallen 54 per cent below its recorded high in 1990. Land prices more than halved in value. The collapse of asset prices has continued into the 2000s. Consumer prices started to slide in 1994, affecting a diverse range of products: food, drink, clothing, machine tools and computers.* Since then, prices have continued to fall and deflation shows no sign of loosening its grip on the Japanese economy. The CPI fell for four consecutive years, 1999–2003.

The case for price stability is usually made by reference to the economic costs of inflation. But the case could equally be made by reference to the cost of deflation. Some of these costs are evident in Japan. Among the problems attached to a falling price level are the following.

1. Declining prices lead to major, haphazard changes in the distribution of wealth. Borrowers find that the real burden of debt has escalated beyond their expectations. High debt:income ratios, combined with falling asset prices, lead to a 'debt trap',

whereby servicing debt becomes increasingly difficult. Problems of negative equity for households can have disastrous consequences for consumer confidence and business expectations.

2. The counterpart of borrowers' real loss is lenders' gain. But lenders benefit only if the borrowers are able to pay. Japanese banks have suffered huge write-offs from non-performing loans. Older people who had paid off their mortgages have done well. They now control 80 per cent of Japan's $22 trillion in household savings. As prices fall, their wealth increases.

3. Profits have been squeezed between price declines and wage and other costs, which are relatively inflexible. Industry is experiencing a 'Darwinian shake-out'. Market shares are under threat.

4. Unemployment has risen and there is a general feeling of job insecurity and uncertainty.

5. Nominal interest rates have fallen. Deposit rates are near zero. Yields on 10-year government bonds fell below 0.6 per cent in 2003, a record low. But interest rates cannot be negative. If prices fall, real interest rates become higher than appears. Real long-term interest rates in Japan reached as high as 5 per cent. This has an adverse impact on investment.

6. Deflationary Japan is not a comfortable place to be. Deflationary expectations are becoming more pervasive and there is a significant risk of crisis in the country's financial institutions.

7. Consumers find it difficult to estimate relative price changes against a backdrop of rapid overall price declines.

It is still unclear whether and how Japan will pull out of its deflationary slump. Japan suffered from having a very high initial level of household and corporate debt, and the combination of debt and deflation is a lethal cocktail. GDP growth remains stagnant. Fears are expressed that the sustained fall in prices could initiate a further vicious circle of lower domestic consumer spending and even greater pressure on prices, profits and the battered financial system. The Bank of Japan has been urged to take unconventional action, even to initiate a small inflation and increase inflation expectations – a rather uncongenial policy prescription for a central bank.†

While deflation has been unusual, *disinflation* – defined as reducing a high rate of inflation to an acceptable 2 per cent level – has been a common experience in recent decades for both developed and developing countries. It involves a milder version of the problem of deflation.

Price stability is clearly the best recipe for deriving maximum benefit from 'new consensus' economic policies, and avoiding problems of deflation and inflation. But achieving this objective can be a major challenge.

*Source*: IMF, *World Economic Outlook* for statistics.

---

* Although the consumer price index showed inflation in the range 0–1 per cent, the Japanese consumer price index tends to overstate inflation for two reasons. First, like all such indices, it fails to take full account of quality improvements and substitution possibilities. Second, the upward bias in inflation statistics is thought to be bigger in Japan than elsewhere because of the shift in spending from traditional retailers to cheaper discount stores. Some estimates suggest that average consumer prices, when measured correctly, may have fallen by as much as 5 per cent in 1995.

† G. Eggertson, 'How to fight deflation in a liquidity trap: committing to being irresponsible', IMF Working Paper, Washington, DC, March 2003. M. Kumar *et al.*, 'Deflation determinants, risks, and policy options', IMF April 2003 provides a comprehensive overview of the problem.

## 12.5 Central banks and institutional reform

Price stability involves a broad spectrum of economic policies.

(1) *There must be political commitment.*
An informed public opinion is also important. Popular aversion to inflation, fed by the memories of the disastrous hyperinflation in the inter-war period, was the hallmark of Germany's successful anti-inflation strategy. Widespread understanding of the costs of both inflation and deflation is necessary in order to ensure sufficient public support for the sometimes unpalatable measures needed to maintain price stability.

(2) *There must be an appropriate institutional framework to buttress this political commitment and to give it credibility.*
The elements of such an institutional framework have been the subject of much debate in recent years. The proposed new institutions of the EU provide an interesting case study in this matter. In seeking to establish a single currency, the requirement that such a currency would be stable was deemed of paramount importance. The Maastricht Treaty (1993) specified procedures for restraining government borrowing and for ensuring that the European Central Bank (ECB) should be independent of governments, with price stability as its primary objective (Box 12.2). These conditions provided a strong bulwark against inflationary pressures. The institutional framework to cope with deflationary pressures is considerably less impressive. That is because inflation, not deflation, was, until recently, widely regarded as the more pressing issue.

(3) *Central banks should be largely independent of political control.*
Until recently, many central banks played a clearly subordinate role to government, as for example in the relation of the Bank of England to the Chancellor of the Exchequer up to the early 1990s. In other instances, for example in the case of Germany, the monetary authorities have enjoyed considerable autonomy.

The evidence indicates that independence rather than management by politicians is the optimal strategy for price stability (Figure 12.4). The thinking behind this is that monetary policy should be dictated by the needs of the economy, not by political considerations such as the timing of elections or the need of governments for extra finance that a compliant central bank could all too easily supply. The worldwide trend has been to try to avert this danger by enhancing the autonomy of the monetary authorities. EU governments, for example, have significantly extended the independence of their national central banks. The European Central Bank enjoys complete independence. New Zealand has been to the fore in delegating responsibility for maintaining stable prices to its central bank.

(4) *Central banks need a clear statement of their policy objective.*
Ideally, this objective should be to maintain price stability. Central banks, as the guardians of monetary policy, may be asked to carry out unpopular tasks. For instance, the objective of maintaining low inflation may require higher interest rates at a time when the government's desire to be re-elected might dictate keeping interest rates low. New Zealand gave a strong signal to its central bank by

## Box 12.2  The European Central Bank

A landmark event in Europe's monetary history was the establishment of the European Central Bank (ECB) on 1 January 1999. The ECB, with its unqualified objective of price stability and elaborate guarantee of independence, incorporated new thinking on monetary economics as well as the old-fashioned commitment to sound finance of the Bundesbank.

The primary objective of the ECB is to 'maintain price stability' (art. 105). It must also 'support the general economic policies of the Community', but this is to be done 'without prejudice to the objective of price stability'. The ECB is independent from political control. Community institutions and the governments of the Member States undertake 'not to seek to influence the members of the decision-making bodies of the ECB in the performance of their tasks' (art. 107). Reflecting the strong liberal market principles of the Community's founders, Europe's new monetary authorities are enjoined to act 'in accordance with the principle of free competition, favouring an efficient allocation of resources' (art. 105).

The Governing Council of the bank consists of:

(a) an executive board, appointed by common accord of the Member States, for an eight-year non-renewable term, consisting of a president, a vice-president and four other members;
(b) governors of the national central banks.

The ECB is required to submit an annual report to the Council and to present it to the European Parliament. Members of the executive board may be asked to appear before the European Parliament.

Given the numerical weight of the national governors in the decision-making process, it is necessary that their independence from national governments must be clearly established, hence the Commission's concern to ensure that national central banks are independent.

The ECB's tasks are:

- to define and implement the monetary policy of the Union,
- to hold and manage the official foreign reserves of the Member States,
- to promote the smooth operation of the payment systems,
- to conduct foreign exchange operations in a manner consistent with 'the general orientations for exchange rate policy' as laid down by the Council (i.e. the finance ministers of the Member States).

One of the Governing Council's first tasks was to decide on an operational definition of price stability. Price stability was defined as *a year-on-year increase in the consumer price index of below 2 per cent*, maintained over the medium term. In May 2003, the Council announced that the objective was to maintain an *inflation rate below, but close to, 2 per cent*. This clarification was made in response to criticism that the original formulation of the objective had a potential deflationary bias.

The tasks of the ECB are similar to those of national central banks. Note that the European Council not the ECB, retains control of exchange rate policy, though it is specifically stated that the Council shall do so without prejudice to the primary objective of maintaining price stability (art. 109). This is a sensitive issue and the relationship between the Council and the ECB is not one which can be defined precisely in formal treaty language. Only by practical experience will the balance of responsibilities be determined.

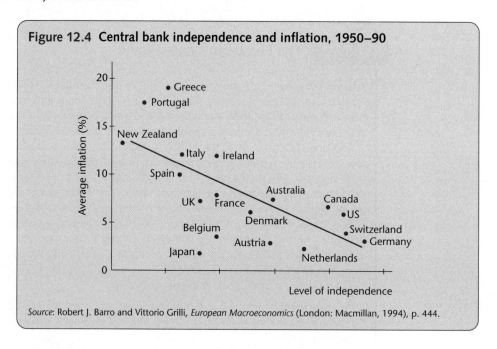

Figure 12.4 Central bank independence and inflation, 1950–90

*Source*: Robert J. Barro and Vittorio Grilli, *European Macroeconomics* (London: Macmillan, 1994), p. 444.

linking the pay and job security of the governor and staff to their success in achieving price stability.[16]

(5) *Governments must not finance their budget deficits by borrowing from the central bank.* Borrowing from the central bank is, as we have seen, equivalent to printing money. It directly increases the money supply. If excessive money creation is the cause of inflation, a primary requirement for controlling inflation is control of the money supply.

These general principles are useful guides for a price stability strategy. However, the detailed requirements will vary from country to country. (See Box 12.4 below for a discussion of the Argentinian experience.) Procedures for pay negotiations or *incomes policy*, agreed between the state and the private sector, may be important in some countries as a direct means of curbing an inflationary wage–price spiral and of defusing inflationary expectations.[17] Maintaining a strong competition policy can also be a way of restraining inflation. For example, the British economy was able to grow quickly during the past decade without igniting pay inflation because labour markets have become less influenced by trade union monopolies, and more flexible in relation to types of work and hours worked. Improved efficiency at the micro level and breaking up monopolies make it hard to pass on price increases to the consumer.

---

[16] For a review of the evidence, see J. Berger, J. de Haan and S. Eijffinger, 'Central bank independence: an update of theory and evidence', London: CEPR Discussion Paper 2353, 2000.

[17] Incomes policy can be particularly useful in countries with strong and highly organised labour unions. If a large section of the workforce pre-commits to a low level of pay increase, that ensures a broad level of support for anti-inflation policies. Austria has used a form of national pay agreements as part of its successful price stabilisation strategy. Incomes policy can also be used as a way of minimising the costs of disinflation.

## Box 12.3   Forecasting by lead indicators

The main objective of monetary policy is to maintain price stability. This is the core responsibility of a central bank. However, there is a significant time-lag between the implementation of a monetary policy change (say, a rise in the interest rate) and the subsequent effect that change has on the rate of inflation. For this reason, it is vital that central banks have early advance warning of price changes so that countervailing action can be taken in good time. To this end, monetary authorities monitor a wide range of indicators of future inflation. These are called *lead indicators*. Movements in these indicators tend to precede movement in the price level. Sometimes a composite leading indicator is derived which combines individual indicators into a single index.

The most widely used lead indicators are:

- overtime payments,
- order books,
- capacity utilisation (usually available for manufacturing only),
- growth of aggregate money supply and private sector credit,
- commodity prices (oil and non-oil),
- stock market indices,
- labour earnings in service industries,
- house prices (new and second-hand),
- long-term bond yields (nominal),
- exchange rates.

Statistical techniques are used to estimate the power of these possible indicator variables in predicting future changes in price level. The calculations will associate each indicator with a certain 'lead' value. Thus, new house prices '*with a lead of two years*' may be chosen. This tells us that house price changes this year correlate closely with changes in the consumer price index in two years' time. Sometimes it is possible to go further and estimate by how much and over what precise time-period the consumer price index will be affected by a change in a lead indicator, e.g. 'a 5 per cent devaluation in the exchange rate will lead to a 2 per cent increase in the CPI within 18 months'.

In particular, it is important to identify lead indicators that will be effective in picking up *turning points*, i.e. points when a recession is turning into a boom, or a boom turning into a recession. Straightforward extrapolation techniques will give satisfactory estimates of what prices would be, given a combination of past trends. The major contribution of lead indicators is their ability to signal changes from past trends or turning points. Needless to say, no indicator is perfect, and the length of the 'lead' time and the significance of variables will change as the economy changes. For example, the increasing flexibility of labour markets has weakened the hitherto very close relation between movements in the exchange rate and subsequent inflation. In former days, employees might have received full and automatic compensation for any rise in the CPI following devaluation. The rise was then 'passed on' to other domestic prices, promptly and entirely. Nowadays, the pass-through mechanism operates much more weakly.

Lead indicators are not plucked from the air. Rather, they derive from systematic thinking about the economic system. Sometimes formal multi-equation models of the economy are constructed, from which inflation forecasts are derived. These are a natural complement to the lead indicator approach.

Lead indicators are used for many purposes other than predicting inflation: for example, for predicting business fluctuations.

Equally important is the need for capable policy-making *within* central banks. Central banks must know *when* to intervene and *how* to intervene. Although central bankers like to affect an aura of omniscience, the decision of when to 'put on the brakes' or to relax monetary policy is a matter of judgement as well as science.[18] A prime requirement for a central bank, therefore, is to develop an early warning system of impending deviations from price stability. Macroeconomic forecasting models and *lead indicators* are used for this purpose (Box 12.3). Experience has also shown the importance of asset prices, in particular stock price indices and house prices, in influencing the general price level. We need better understanding of these processes. It is also important to have reliable information on *actual* and *potential* GDP.

The next task is to decide on the policy instruments to use in controlling the money supply – interest rates, open-market operations, reserve requirements – and to understand their likely effects on the economy. These are discussed in the next chapter. As we shall see, controlling the money supply has been made difficult by deregulation and global capital mobility, further compounded by technical advances. For example, automatic teller machines (ATMs) enable a fixed supply of cash to be used more efficiently. Other innovations, such as smart cards and credit cards, substitute for cash. The ratio of cash to consumption spending in Europe has fallen from 13 per cent in 1970 to under 8 per cent in 2002. The possibility of a cashless society has become closer as technology advances. The evolution of mutual funds has also impaired the capacity of central bankers to control money supply. In terms of the Quantity Theory of Money equation, all these changes in the financial system have led to a higher and less predictable velocity of circulation ($V$), and hence have weakened the relationship between money supply ($M$) and the price level ($P$).

Central banks are beginning to adopt a more pragmatic approach to controlling money supply than in the past. Nowadays, many central banks use inflation targeting rather than control of the money supply as the primary instrument for maintaining price stability.

## 12.6 Price stability and exchange rate anchors

Monetary policy as described above is relevant mostly to large countries with autonomous monetary policies. The euro area, Japan and the US obviously fall into this category. For smaller countries, however, a different approach may be necessary. One major difference is the importance to them of exchange rate policy as a means of attaining price stability. By attaching its currency to an anchor currency, that is, by tying its currency to a stronger and more stable currency, a small country can 'lock' its inflation rate into that of the anchor currency. Provided the anchor currency's monetary authorities remain firmly

---

[18] A Swiss authority on monetary economics, Professor Jürg Niehans, expressed the view that 'economists should be under no illusion that central banking will ever become a science. ... However far monetary theory may progress, central banking is likely to remain an art': J. Niehans, *The Theory of Money* (Baltimore, MD: Johns Hopkins University Press, 1978), p. 294.

committed to price stability, the smaller country attached to it will enjoy this benefit also.

To understand this process, we begin by noting that small open economies (SOEs), being heavily dependent on trade, are highly vulnerable to external price changes. The extent to which inflation is 'imported' from the rest of the world then hinges crucially on the exchange-rate regime adopted by the small country. If the exchange rate is *fixed* relative to a weighted average of its trading partners, domestic inflation is largely determined by inflation in these countries. If they have high inflation, it will be transmitted to the small country; if they have low inflation, the small country will have low inflation. (The theory behind this is explained in Box 12.4.)

---

**Box 12.4**  **Price stability lost and gained: lessons from Argentina**

Most countries, once they become rich, stay rich. Argentina is the exception that proves the rule. From being one of the world's richest countries a century ago, Buenos Aires rivalling Paris in ambition, scope and wealth, the country had declined to Third World status by the middle of the last century.

Chronic inflation ravaged the Argentine economy for most of the postwar period. It peaked at over 3000 per cent per annum in 1990. The rich survived by carrying out their transactions in US dollars. The poor suffered. In 1991, a major effort was made to restore financial equilibrium. A key element in the new strategy was exchange rate stabilisation, by anchoring to a strong currency. Countries with strong trade links with Europe anchored to the Deutschmark (and now the euro). Argentina, like several other South American and West Indian countries (Panama, Ecuador, etc.), linked to the US dollar. In 1991 the Convertibility Act ordained a fixed and immutable parity of one US dollar for every one peso.

According to theory, provided the exchange rate remains fixed, inflation in the smaller country will tend to converge to the inflation rate in the anchor currency. To see why this is so, suppose that inflation in Argentina were 10 per cent annually compared with 2 per cent in the US. With the passage of time, Argentina's exports become steadily more expensive relative to American goods. Argentina loses competitiveness in world markets and exports fall. For exactly the same reason Argentina's home market becomes vulnerable to US competition. Import prices compare more and more favourably with Argentine domestic products. Activity in Argentina falls, and unemployment rises. *All this puts severe downward pressure on domestic prices.* As long as the chain to the anchor holds, Argentina's 10 per cent inflation will have to decline. Business, unions and government, knowing there is no possibility of being bailed out by devaluation, will curb domestic cost increases. The process will continue until market forces bring about a convergence towards the US inflation rate.

Such is the theory. Initially, practice followed the textbook remarkably well. Within a short period of three years Argentina progressed from four-digit hyperinflation to price stability. By 1994, the inflation rate had fallen to 3 per cent, and it stayed down for the remainder of the decade.

In addition, the economy turned from negative growth to a sparkling 6 per cent average during 1991–95. The fiscal situation also improved. In the mid-1990s Argentina was running a fiscal surplus, enjoying fast growth and, for the first time in a generation, stable prices.

→

Box 12.4 continued

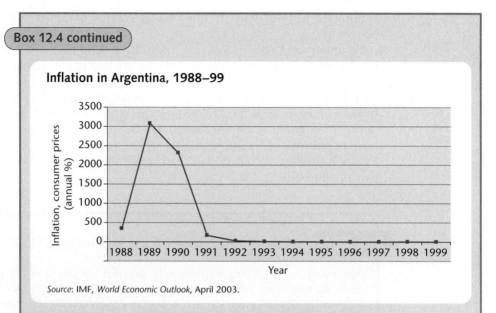

### Inflation in Argentina, 1988–99

Source: IMF, *World Economic Outlook*, April 2003.

Things began to go terribly wrong towards the end of the 1990s. First, the US dollar had proved too strong an anchor currency. It strengthened against the European currencies that happened to be important customers of Argentina. Argentina's output became steadily less competitive relative to its competitors. Second, the substantial devaluation of the Brazilian real in 1999 led to a further significant loss of competitiveness for Argentina in one of its largest markets. The peso was becoming more and more overvalued and questions started being asked about the sustainability of Argentina's peg with the dollar. This led to the third problem. As nervous peso holders started shifting into US dollars, interest rates in Argentina began to rise. Higher interest rates deterred investment and made matters only worse. Argentina, having conquered inflation, began to suffer from deflation, thus further fuelling speculation about the sustainability of parity with the dollar. Pressure built up during 2001 and the government implemented *de facto* exchange controls and a freeze on deposits, all to no avail. After more than a decade of parity, the peso was officially devalued in 2002 and in a few weeks the exchange rate surpassed 3 pesos to the dollar.

The devaluation was quickly transmitted to domestic prices. Inflation rose to 26 per cent in 2002 and is not expected to regain single-digits for several years. Following the default on debt repayments to the IMF, confidence in the economy has been severely dented. GDP has fallen and widespread misery has been caused. An IMF economist described it as a case of moving from triumph to tragedy.

One major lesson from Argentina's debacle is that fixed currency commitment without strong natural trading and investment links with the anchor currency can be highly destabilising. Argentina's trade amounted to only 10 per cent of GDP and only a small fraction of that trade was transacted with the US. It was bad luck for Argentina that the dollar sustained its upward surge for so long, contrary to expectations right up to 2002.

Some argue that the dollar link was over-ambitious. Once the fixed link had done its work of eliminating inflation and improving confidence, it should have been quietly abandoned. It was a good policy but was adhered to for too long. Another view is that the policy was not strong enough. Argentina, they argue, should have gone the whole

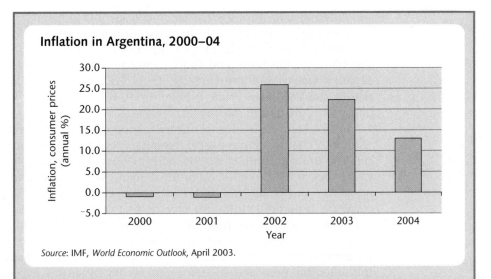

**Inflation in Argentina, 2000–04**

Source: IMF, *World Economic Outlook*, April 2003.

hog and 'dollarised' the economy. This would have entailed withdrawing the peso and replacing it with dollars.

Argentina's experience contains lessons for all countries contemplating currency union with another. It shows how quickly costs can get out of line and how difficult it is to regain lost competitiveness in a low-inflation world environment. It also demonstrates the importance of the distinction between a single currency and a fixed currency link. The break factor in Argentina was not just the unsuitability of the dollar link. The penal interest rates needed to support that link in times of currency turmoil – outside the control of the authorities – also proved costly. In a common currency area, this interest rate penalty is likely to be much lower. The Argentine government has also been criticised for fiscal laxity that is inconsistent with the strong monetary/exchange rate regime. There is some truth in this, but when an economy is growing slowly, and tax revenues are sluggish, it is difficult to impose restrictive policies. The IMF recommendation that public sector salaries should be cut was politically impractical and inequitable.

Sources: M. Mussa, *Argentina: From Triumph to Tragedy*, Institute for International Economics, Washington, DC, 2002; A. Kruger, 'Crisis prevention and resolution: lessons for Argentina', Conference on Argentina Crisis in Cambridge, 17 July 2002.

Why choose another currency as an anchor? One reason is that anchoring the value of your currency in terms of a major currency gives a great degree of credibility to your committment to price stability. It is an easily understood signal to impress the public and trade unions. It provides a clear message to the market that the state is serious about stabilising prices. If successful, product and factor prices will adjust quickly to the lower inflation regime and expectations will be moderated accordingly. Using a single-currency anchor is, for this reason, superior to using a trade-weighted multi-currency anchor. The single-currency anchor gives a much clearer signal of a government's anti-inflationary intentions and thus garners credibility in the capital and labour markets.

There are many examples of countries using exchange rate anchors to combat inflation. In the past, Austria, the Netherlands and Belgium have all used a Deutschmark link to achieve consolidated low inflation rates. They have been succeeded by countries such as Denmark, Estonia and Bulgaria which peg their currency to the euro. In West Africa, the former French colonies were linked with the French franc through the CFA currency zone and since 1999 with the euro. The US dollar has been used as an anchor to achieve stabilisation by Argentina, Ecuador, Mexico and Brazil among others. For a period, the Canadian dollar was tied to the US dollar. From 1922 to 1979, the Irish pound was maintained at parity with the pound sterling.

Not all anchor regimes work out well. Adoption of a fixed exchange rate anchor without a complementary fiscal, monetary and microeconomic reform package can lead to major problems. One danger is loss of cost competitiveness. Suppose employees in the domestic economy demand salaries over and above productivity gains – this could lead to domestic costs getting out of line with the anchor currency. If domestic inflation exceeds that of the anchor economy, cost competitiveness of domestic producers will be eroded. Another difficulty arises if the anchor currency revalues and this erodes cost competitiveness of the domestic economy relative to its third country competitors. Thus, a strong dollar pulled up the Argentine peso and created problems for Argentine exporters and import-competing firms (Box 12.4). The French franc zone in West Africa delivered price stability, but may have damaged these countries' long-term competitiveness. A second consideration follows from this. It is important that the link with the anchor currency is credible. Credibility in this context requires that the exchange rate is in line with the government's capacity and political determination to deliver complementary anti-inflation domestic policies. We shall return to this topic in the discussion of exchange rate systems and regimes.

## 12.7 Is inflation dead?

Following many years of struggle, by the mid-1990s inflation appeared to be under control in most industrial countries. So great has been the success in achieving price stability, in both developed and developing countries, that some have concluded that inflation is 'dead'. By this they mean that structural and institutional changes in the global economy have made a resurgence of inflation so unlikely that inflation can effectively be written off as a problem solved. There are several powerful factors behind this line of reasoning.

First, there is *strong public support* for price stability. In part this is explained by unhappy memories of past inflation and its association with low growth and high unemployment. Even more important, in developed countries, is the ageing of the population. The proportion of people relying on pensions that are not inflation-indexed and who have a strong interest in price stability has increased dramatically. Older people also tend to be lenders rather than borrowers, and – as we saw earlier – lenders are hurt by inflation.

Second, *changes in the financial system* have been conducive to price stability. Capital markets, not monetary authorities, exercise the dominant influence on long-term interest rates. The international market in bonds is highly inflation-averse. Policies that endanger long-term price stability in the pursuit of short-term economic goals will be swiftly 'punished' in the market through falling bond prices and higher interest rates. This will not be popular with domestic voters. Finance ministers have consequently become as fearful of market perceptions as of the censure of their own monetary authorities. The more open and competitive financial environment, in both national and international markets, has encouraged monetary authorities to take pre-emptive action against incipient inflation sooner than they might if they had full control over the domestic market.

Third, liberalisation of markets has led to *greater competition*. The power of special groups to pass on cost increases to the customer has diminished. Resistance to price hikes, whether by trade unions or oligopolies, has stiffened considerably in recent years.

Fourth, the major economies are now *less vulnerable to commodity price shocks* than they were in the 1970s and 1980s. In part this is because of the growth of the services sector, in part because advances in technology have reduced independence on material inputs. GDP becomes lighter as countries become richer.

Fifth, the potentially harmful effects of price instability on their nascent democracies have motivated many developing and transition economies to adopt cautious monetary and fiscal policies.

At a theoretical level, we have seen that economists have become increasingly convinced that inflation must be confronted rather than accommodated. Politicians, motivated by practical considerations, have reached exactly the same conclusion, and price stability has now become a political priority:

> There is now more conviction among politicians of the electoral advantages of running an economy in a way that keeps inflation under wraps, with ageing populations in many countries providing a growing constituency in favour of low and stable inflation. Politicians seem increasingly more content to leave monetary policy to independent central banks. This favourable political background is enabling central banks to engage in pre-emptive strikes against inflation – a strategy that is, in the long run, likely to be much less painful than allowing inflation to emerge (possibly into double figures), then stamping hard on the brakes and bringing the economy crashing to a sudden halt. This new approach can only be good for inflation and, since low inflation and high output growth go together in the medium to long run, good for the overall economy.[19]

Although this may appear a reassuring conclusion, experience warns against complacency for two quite different reasons. The spectacular decline in the UK inflation rate from around 16 per cent in 1980 to under 4 per cent in 1986 was succeeded by a return to double-digit inflation five years later, a relapse for which macroeconomic policy had a large share of responsibility. Perhaps it is safer to say that inflation is now dormant, rather than dead. It is always only too ready to oblige with an encore.

By the end of 2003 the risk of deflation had begun to dominate thinking. With it there is the belief that deflation is more damaging than inflation and may be harder to defeat. And, as we shall see in the next chapter, today's central bankers are in many respects ill prepared to fight on this new battleground.

---

[19] F. Browne and J. Fell, 'Inflation – dormant, dying or dead?', Technical Paper, Central Bank of Ireland (October 1994).

## 12.8 Conclusions

The painful experience of inflation has enhanced the status of price stability as a policy objective. It has also strengthened our understanding of the link between money and inflation.

Weak monetary authorities failed to deliver price stability by:

- misjudging the timing of monetary policy – being too lax when the economy is booming and too restrictive when the economy operates below capacity,
- pushing too hard on the brakes once inflation has emerged, thereby raising the costs of disinflation,
- accommodating excessive pay demands and price increases,
- failing to control public spending,
- financing deficits by monetary means.

The world economy is now seeing a focused and determined effort on the part of the authorities to provide price stability – more so than ever before. One would hope that the decline in inflation has been associated with a demonstrable improvement in economic efficiency and social stability. Many experts believe that it has, and for good reason. However, causality is never simple in economics. Price stability facilitates, but does not guarantee, good economic performance.

## Summary

1. Central banks define price stability as an inflation rate in the range 1–3 per cent, sustainable over the medium term. Price stability is *not* zero per cent inflation because inflation statistics are affected by composition, quality and substitution biases.

2. Price stability is measured by the consumer price index. This index indicates changes in the cost of a representative 'basket' of goods and services. The composition of this basket is periodically reviewed.

3. Inflation (persistent rises in the price level above 3 per cent) and deflation (declines in the price level) represent deviations from the goal of price stability.

4. The monetary view of inflation, associated with Milton Friedman, asserts that inflation occurs when the growth of the money supply persistently exceeds the growth of real output. This approach is consistent with the Quantity Theory of Money: the higher the growth of money supply, the higher the rate of inflation, other things being equal. However, the Quantity Theory leaves many questions unanswered, such as explaining the economic and social factors which determine how and why money supply should be allowed to increase.

5. A sound strategy for price stability must be based on a proper understanding of the economic benefits derived from stability. Rapid changes in the general price level obstruct the efficient working of the market system. Inflation and deflation can impact adversely on the distribution of wealth, as well as hindering economic growth. The redistribution of wealth and the economic turmoil which accompany

price instability can in turn cause major social tensions which threaten democratic institutions. Finally, once started, inflation and deflation are both costly to reverse. The solution is for governments to ensure that price stability, once restored, is thereafter maintained.

6. The price stability objective is motivated by three fundamental premises:

   (a) price stability yields economic benefits by making markets operate more effectively,

   (b) deviations from price stability, once started, tend to be self-perpetuating,

   (c) halting the inflationary or deflationary spiral can be costly and problematic.

7. Price stability involves a broad spectrum of economic policies. There must be political commitment to this objective and, to buttress this political commitment and give it credibility, there must also be an appropriate institutional framework. The evidence indicates that independence rather than management by politicians is the optimal strategy for achieving price stability. For this reason central banks are being given independence from political control. Equally important as the need for capable policy-making within central banks is the need for government restraint in fiscal policy (Chapter 15).

8. Exchange rate policy has important implications for price stability in small economies. Some countries have attached their currency to a stronger, low-inflation currency in the hope of locking their inflation rate into a lower level. The advantage of such anchoring is that it can deliver price stability with a high degree of credibility. However, adoption of a fixed exchange rate anchor without the adoption of a complementary monetary, fiscal and microeconomic reform package can lead to major problems. Also, the anchor should be with the trade patterns of the smaller economy.

9. There are many factors explaining the priority being given to price stability: changes in public support, openness of financial system, more intensive competition, less vulnerability to 'shocks'. Inflation may not yet be 'dead', but it is certainly dormant. During the first years of this century, deflation, not inflation, has taken centre-stage as the main potential threat to price stability in the developed world.

## Questions for discussion

1. What is price stability? How is price stability calculated? Why might the consumer price index overestimate the 'true' rate of price increase?

2. Discuss the reasons why one might expect, over the long run, countries with price stability to enjoy faster growth than those with high inflation or deflation.

3. It is sometimes said that business prefers an environment of rising prices to one of static or declining prices. Do you agree?

4. Why do monetarists believe that sustained inflation is impossible without the explicit or implicit acquiescence of the monetary authorities?

5. Inflation targeting by the monetary authorities involves three steps:

    (a) deciding on a target inflation rate,

    (b) forecasting inflation, and

    (c) formulating and implementing a policy response should the forecast inflation rate deviate from its target level.

    Comment on each of these steps.

    (*Note*: Further details relevant to part (c) of this question are provided in Chapter 13.)

6. Is inflation 'dead'? Evaluate the arguments in Section 12.7 of this chapter.

7. Discuss the nature of the deflation problem facing many countries and the difficulties this creates for business and for investors in these countries.

## Exercises

1. What has been the inflation rate in your country in the past decade? What have been the determinants of this inflation?

2. The price stability objective is motivated by several fundamental premises. Critically evaluate each of these premises by reference to the experience of (a) a developed economy, and (b) a developing economy, of your choice.

3. Suppose the UK inflation rate were to rise from 2 per cent to 10 per cent. Indicate three sections of the community that would lose and three that would gain from this. List three reasons why a resurgence of inflation might be bad for the UK economy.

4. Identify any developing country that has experienced high inflation and has implemented a successful stabilisation programme. Evaluate that experience in the light of the arguments of this chapter in favour of price stability.

## Further reading

Central bank reports are the best source of up-to-date statistics and analysis of price stability – see the *Bank of England Quarterly Bulletin* for instance. Roger Bootle's *The Death of Inflation* (London: Nicholas Brealey, 1996) explores the causes of inflation. J. Kornai's *The Road to a Free Economy* (London: Norton, 1990) looks at inflation from the perspective of the transition economies, while A. Blinder, who (like the author of this book) spent several years on a central bank's board, gives an intriguing account of life in the Fed in *Central Banking in Theory and Practice* (Cambridge, MA: MIT Press, 1998). A detailed assessment of the measurement of price stability is provided in the *Economic Journal* (June 2001). The linkage between asset prices, the price index and economic activity is explored in C. Borio and P. Love, 'Asset prices, financial and monetary stability: exploring the nexus', *Bank of International Settlements Working Paper*, no. 114, July 2002, and C. Goodhart, 'What weight should be given to asset prices in the measurement of inflation?', *Economic Journal*, June 2001.

## Chapter 13

# Understanding interest rates and monetary policy

## Introduction

Interest rates are important to business. Although interest payments constitute a small proportion of most firms' total costs, they are often highly significant in relation to profit. Because the corporate sector tends on average to be a net borrower, a rise in interest rates involves a direct deduction from profits. For a highly geared firm with a heavy debt, a rise in interest can lead to bankruptcy. Even a financially strong firm can find its bottom line severely dented by a change in lending rates.

Changes in the interest rate also impact on business indirectly. If a rise in interest rates causes an economic slowdown, the demand for products which are interest rate-sensitive (new houses, for example) will fall and firms supplying these products will suffer, even if they were net lenders. Some firms are vulnerable to this type of interest rate exposure; for them, the interest rate (and, by extension, monetary policy) must be factored into their value at risk. The large and growing volume of trade in interest rate futures is testimony to the importance business attaches to interest rate fluctuations.

Business and central banks frequently clash over the conduct of monetary policy. They have radically different perspectives on interest rates. Central banks are likely to regard fluctuations in economic activity with far greater detachment than the business sector. A central bank might even regard a slowdown in economic growth as a necessary, if regrettable, cost of maintaining price stability. A company put out of business by a recession is unlikely to take such a philosophical view of the matter.

This chapter explores the complex and circumscribed relationship between monetary policy, interest rates and economic activity. Although monetary policy was discussed briefly in the last chapter, the details of such policy and its relation to interest rates have yet to be fully examined. Our starting point is the Quantity Theory of Money from which are derived propositions about both the long-run 'neutrality' of money and the monetarist dictum that *inflation is always and everywhere a monetary phenomenon*.

Public opinion easily overestimates the power of the monetary authorities in relation to interest rates. They *influence*, rather than determine, the level of interest rates. Their power has been particularly circumscribed in the long end of the market, by mobile capital and financial technology. Price expectations are crucial in explaining nominal interest rates, while at the same time nominal rates and monetary policy can play a key role in forming these expectations.[1]

A related issue is the effectiveness of interest rate changes in determining the level of economic activity. Lowering the interest rate might encourage economic activity but does not make it happen. If business expectations are depressed, nothing at all might happen. The potency (or lack of it) of monetary policy is a subject that has risen to the top of the agenda of central banks in recent years.

Monetary policy and interest rates are analysed in this chapter in the context of a closed economy. The analysis is primarily applicable to policy in the US, Japan and the euro area. In such circumstances, foreign considerations exert only a subsidiary influence in determining domestic policy. By contrast, in smaller countries, the relationship between domestic interest rates and the exchange rate is far closer and would have to be viewed in the context of global capital markets. The analysis is extended to the open economy in Part III.

## Chapter outline

1. Definition of different types of interest rate: nominal vs real, short-term vs long-term, and the meaning and significance of the term structure of interest rates.

2. The determinants of interest rates.

3. The effect of changes in interest rates – the chief weapon in the central bank's armoury – on levels of consumer spending and investment activity.

4. The framework of monetary policy in terms of the instruments at the central bank's disposal, and the use of intermediate targets and instruments.

5. The design of monetary policy, paying particular attention to the need to achieve balance between the long-term objective of price stability and short-run discretionary action.

## 13.1 Which interest rate?

Interest is payment for the use of funds over a period of time. The interest rate is defined as *the amount of interest paid per unit of time as a fraction of the balance outstanding*. Although, for convenience, we refer to 'the' rate of interest, in practice there are many different rates of interest, according to their maturity, marketability and risk of the financial instrument. 'The' interest rate is in fact a continuum of interest rates, extending from the short to the long run across a wide spectrum of degrees of riskiness.

---

[1] Higher interest rates might be caused by fears of future inflation, but they could also be the consequence of a tight monetary stance designed to prevent such inflationary expectations taking root. The authorities can engineer a rise in interest rates only to find that the market drives them higher still, fuelled by a fear that the initial rise was not enough!

## Nominal vs real interest rates

Suppose interest on a £1000 government bond is 10 per cent per year. An investor in this bond will receive £1100 at the end of the year. The *nominal* return is £100 and the nominal interest rate is 10 per cent. Assume inflation is 4 per cent p.a. and is expected to stay at that rate. This means that, at year-end, £1040 will be needed in order to maintain the real purchasing power of the £1000 principal. In other words, £40 of the £100 nominal return represents compensation for rising prices. To derive the *real* return, this £40 must be subtracted from the total nominal return. The real return is defined, according to the *Fisher relation*, as £$(\frac{100-40}{100}) \times 100 =$ £60, or 6 per cent per year.[2]

Real interest rate ($r$) = nominal interest rate ($i$) *minus* inflation rate ($\pi$)

Now suppose people expect that inflation will rise from 4 per cent to 8 per cent per year. A 10 per cent bond will still yield a nominal return of £100. However, the expected 8 per cent inflation rate implies that to buy the equivalent of £1000 worth of purchases this year will cost £1080 next year. In such circumstances, the real return will fall to (£100 − £80) = £20 per year. The real interest rate becomes (10 per cent − 8 per cent) = 2 per cent.

The fall in the prospective real interest rate will not go unnoticed. Financial markets are paid to be aware of such developments. As inflation expectations are adjusted upwards, they will be less willing to lend at 10 per cent since the expected real return has fallen. The fall in demand for government bonds will drive down the price and cause nominal yields to rise. Assuming that market participants do not suffer money illusion, bond prices will continue to fall until the nominal yield (or nominal interest rate) increases to 14 per cent. At that rate, the real interest rate has returned to its initial (equilibrium) level.

The real rate of interest is not directly observable. It is defined by reference to an *expected* inflation rate. However, one can infer its value by subtracting *current inflation* from nominal interest rates. Defined this way, real interest rates can be negative. Real interest rates in Europe and the US fell to −4 per cent in 1973, but rose to a level of 4–6 per cent in the 1980s.[3] Since then, they have fallen. The range of variation across countries is quite marked. By the early 2000s, real long-term interest rates were as low as 1–2 per cent in the developed countries compared with 4–7 per cent in emerging-market countries (Russia, Brazil, Egypt and Turkey).

The Fisher equation implies that 10 per cent interest with 4 per cent inflation is equivalent to 14 per cent interest and 8 per cent inflation. Since the real rate of

---

[2] The relationship is named after Irving Fisher who was the first to provide a systematic analysis of the issue in 1896. This relationship holds exactly in theory. In practice, when tested against past experience, we find that, over long periods, changes in inflation have a less than point-for-point effect on nominal interest rates.

[3] The negative real interest rate of the 1970s poses some intriguing questions. Why would anyone lend money at a negative real rate of interest? The most likely answer is that the lenders did not intentionally do so, but simply made a mistake in their inflation forecasts. The steep rise in inflation may have taken them by surprise; and, as the value of their fixed nominal interest bonds fell in real terms, they lost money. This loss in real earnings had an important implication for future behaviour. The next time inflation threatened, lenders were determined not to be caught again. Financial markets continued to have an aversion to even the mildest threat of inflation. Any suspicion that the authorities are taking a permissive approach to inflation immediately pushes up the nominal rates.

interest is the same in both situations, borrowers might be thought to be indifferent between them. In practice, this is unlikely to be so. Cash flow is heavily influenced by the absolute level of the nominal rate. The higher the nominal rate, the greater the outflow (proportionately) in the early years of a loan. Many businesses, especially small firms, and mortgage holders are constrained by nominal limits on credit. Bankers respond to the cash-flow profile of a loan as well as to the long-run real rate of interest. The rise in the upfront burden of a rise in nominal rates, therefore, can affect business in ways which are ignored in the Fisher relation.

Another implication of the Fisher equation is that low nominal interest rates do not necessarily translate into low real rates. In June 2003, Japan's prices were falling by 0.5 per cent. This meant that the real interest rate on a 10-year government bond with nominal interest of 0.4 per cent was 0.9 per cent annually. (The equivalent nominal rate on a 10-year US bond was 3.2 per cent but US prices were increasing by 1.7 per cent.)

## The term structure of interest rates and the yield curve

Interest rates differ according to the maturity of the loan. Bonds with a maturity of less than 1 year are considered short term; those with a maturity of 1–3 years, medium term; and those over 3 years, long term. The *short-term* rate is usually defined by reference to the yield on a 3-month interbank deposit or treasury bill; the *long-term* rate by reference to a 10-year government bond. Statistics for these rates in 2000 show that nominal long-term interest rates in the industrial countries exceeded short-term interest rates in most countries (Table 13.1). Real yields are also higher in the long run. Interest rates differ markedly between countries, but more so in the case of nominal rates than long-run real rates.[4]

### Table 13.1 Interest rates and inflation in industrial countries, June 2003

| | Nominal interest rate | | | Real interest rate | |
| | Short term (1) | Long term (2) | Inflation (3) | Short term (1) – (3) | Long term (2) – (3) |
|---|---|---|---|---|---|
| US | 1.0 | 3.2 | 1.7 | −0.7 | 1.5 |
| Japan | 0.0 | 0.4 | −0.5 | 0.5 | 0.9 |
| UK | 3.6 | 3.9 | 2.0 | 1.6 | 1.9 |
| Euro area | 2.1 | 3.5 | 1.5 | 0.6 | 2.0 |

*Notes:*
Short term = 3-month interbank or certificates of deposit. Long term = 10-year government bonds. Inflation = consumer prices forecast for 2004 (author's estimate).

*Source*: OECD, author's own estimates.

---

[4] Given high capital mobility, this is what one would expect. Theoretically, if inflation expectations were correctly measured and national governments were all equally creditworthy, market forces would tend to force real interest rates in different countries to converge.

Three-month and 10-year yields are just two observations on a whole spectrum of maturities. One could add 6-month, 2-year and 5-year rates, and so on. The *term structure*, or time profile, of interest rates is defined as the relationship on a specific date between interest rates for bonds with different terms to maturity that have similar risk. The curve connecting these interest rates, or yields, is called the *yield curve*.

The 'normal' shape of the yield curve is upward-sloping. The underlying theory is that people have a positive time preference. Consumption this year is better than the promise of the same consumption next year. A promise to pay next year is considered more valuable than a promise to pay in 10 years' time, even if the same guarantee is attached to each promise. Things can go wrong in the future; people discount accordingly, and require compensation for the longer 'wait' and the accompanying uncertainty. Because short-term bonds are more liquid than long-term bonds, investors buy them even though they yield a lower return. Hence, the normal expectation is that long-term interest rates will be higher than short-term rates. But this does not mean that yield curves in reality are always positive-sloping. They can have a diversity of slopes: downward-sloping, flat and, occasionally, hump-backed (Figure 13.1).

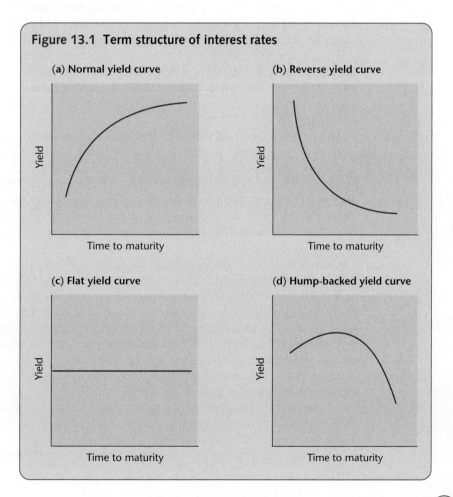

**Figure 13.1  Term structure of interest rates**

(a) Normal yield curve

Yield

Time to maturity

(b) Reverse yield curve

Yield

Time to maturity

(c) Flat yield curve

Yield

Time to maturity

(d) Hump-backed yield curve

Yield

Time to maturity

Yield curves are calculated in nominal terms. Their shape is determined jointly by 'real' variables and by expectations of future inflation. Suppose inflation is expected to rise. Following the logic of the Fisher relation, a corresponding rise in nominal interest rates will also be expected. Hence the market will *expect* the price of longer-term bonds to decline. Dealers will rush to sell long-term bonds and to hold cash, or buy short-term bonds. This drives down the price of long-term bonds and raises the price of short-term bonds. As the yield on long-term bonds rises relative to short-term bonds, the *yield curve becomes steeper* (Figure 13.1(a)).

Now take a situation when inflationary pressure has eased; inflation is predicted to fall and a consequent fall in the nominal long-term interest rate is expected. New investors want to move out of cash and to buy more long-term bonds, thereby 'locking in' to the high rate now available but not expected to last. This leads to a rise in long-term bond prices and a corresponding fall in long-term yields. The yield curve could then be downward-sloping and we obtain the 'reverse-yield' curve (Figure 13.1(b)).

The expectations theory helps to explain the shape of yield curves. But its explanatory power is limited in so far as it ignores the distinctive characteristics of bonds of different maturities. The financial market is highly *segmented*. Life assurance companies, for example, with predictable nominal future obligations, have a preference for long-term bonds with which to balance these liabilities. If these are in short supply, a succession of shorter-term bonds will make do, but will not be perfect substitutes. Other institutions have a preference for short-term bonds. Because bonds with different maturities are traded in different markets, the shape of the yield curve will to some extent reflect the particular supply–demand characteristics in each market. (Some might even have a shape like Figure 13.1(d).)

The shape of the yield curve is a matter of crucial significance for bond traders, corporate treasurers, investment banks and fund managers. Considerable resources are expended on predicting its shape. Good predictions can prove hugely profitable. If a bank believes that a positively sloped yield curve is about to flatten, it will buy long-term bonds in the expectation that long-term interest rates will fall (and the capital value of the bonds will rise), and sell short-term bonds in the expectation that short-term interest rates will rise (so avoiding the prospect of capital loss).

Central banks also keep watch on the term structure. The yield curve can serve as a lead indicator of price expectations in the market. It can also provide useful information to a central bank on market perceptions of its policy. Suppose the bank raises short-term interest rates. If the market is reassured by this signal of the central bank's determination to maintain price stability, long-term interest rates will not increase proportionally, and may even fall. In that case, a negatively sloped yield curve would reflect market confidence in the bank's anti-inflation strategy. Economic forecasters also study the yield curve for indications of the markets' perception of growth prospects.

So much for the *slope* of the yield curve. We still have to analyse what determines its *position*, i.e. what makes 'interest rates' rise or fall. To study this issue, we return to the assumption of there being a single interest rate. Like any other price, this interest rate will be determined by the forces of demand and supply.

## 13.2 What determines interest rates?

The interest rate can be regarded as the 'price' that brings demand for credit into equilibrium with supply of credit. As interest falls, investment projects become profitable, housing becomes less costly to finance and people want to borrow more. Hence the demand curve for credit is downward-sloping with respect to the interest rate. The supply of loanable funds is assumed to respond positively to the interest rate. A higher interest rate means a better return on saving. People spend less now in the expectation of earning higher interest and being able to spend more in the future.

This theory, called the 'loanable funds' theory, is illustrated in Figure 13.2. DD represents the demand for credit and SS the supply of credit. Equilibrium occurs where supply equals demand, at point E*. Suppose interest strayed from equilibrium and went to $r_2$ instead of r*. At that higher interest rate, supply of funds would increase from r*E* to $r_2v_2$; while demand would fall from r*E* to $r_2u_2$. At this interest rate, supply of credit would exceed demand. To induce people to borrow more, interest will have to fall. As it falls, supply of credit will also decline, because lending is becoming less remunerative. The interest rate continues falling until the original equilibrium r* is restored.

Changes in the interest rate in this framework are explained by shifts in the demand and supply curves of credit (Figure 13.3). An outward shift in the demand curve caused, for example, by an upsurge in profit expectations, will move the demand curve from DD to $D_1D_1$ and cause a rise in interest rates from r to $r_1$. If the savings propensity increased, the supply curve would shift to the right and interest rates would fall.

Since saving and borrowing decisions are forward-looking, the nominal interest rate ought, in principle, to be adjusted for expected inflation. Inflation expectations will affect both the demand and the supply of credit.

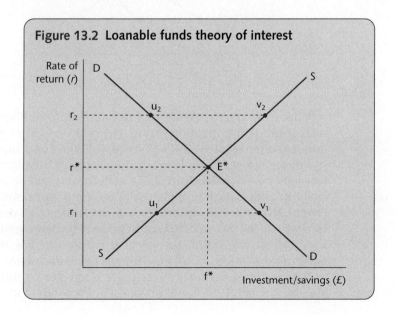

**Figure 13.2 Loanable funds theory of interest**

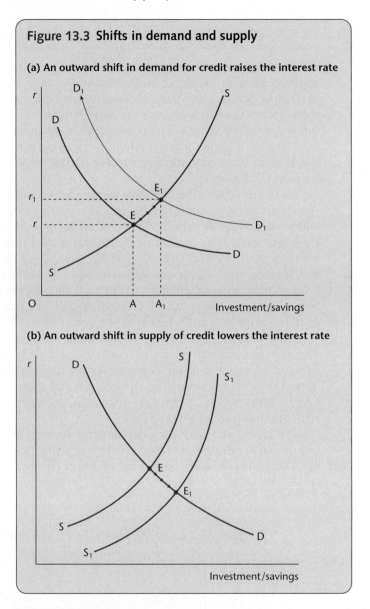

**Figure 13.3 Shifts in demand and supply**

**(a) An outward shift in demand for credit raises the interest rate**

**(b) An outward shift in supply of credit lowers the interest rate**

Suppose we start in Figure 13.4 from an initial equilibrium at $E(f^*, i^*)$. Assume that, at this point, inflation is zero. Hence the real interest rate is the same as the nominal interest rate. Now suppose that, following a supply-side shock or excessive money growth, people expect an upsurge of inflation. This shifts the demand for credit curve outwards to $D_1 D_1$, as borrowers will be prepared to pay more for credit in anticipation of higher sales revenues. But simultaneously the supply of credit curve will shift inwards to $S_1 S_1$, as lenders will demand higher interest to compensate for the expected rise in prices. The new equilibrium will be realised at $E_1(f^*, i_1^*)$. At this point, the *nominal interest rate has risen proportionally to the expected rise in prices, $\pi^e$. The real interest rate is unchanged.*

The long-term nominal interest rate is affected by inflation expectations, and also by the level of the short-term interest rate. Arbitrage between the two

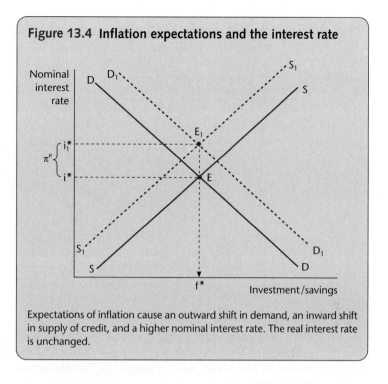

**Figure 13.4 Inflation expectations and the interest rate**

Expectations of inflation cause an outward shift in demand, an inward shift in supply of credit, and a higher nominal interest rate. The real interest rate is unchanged.

markets will create a spillover from the short-run interest rate to the long-run rate. The correlation between them is not perfect and the degree of spillover between one market and another depends on circumstances.[5]

The loanable funds model of interest rates provides an intuitively appealing and simple framework for the analysis of interest rates. But the theory needs qualification and extension in several respects.

(1) In this approach, the interest rate takes centre-stage in bringing savings and investment into equilibrium only because a *given* level of real output and income is assumed. Because of this assumption, an outward shift in savings leads to a fall in the interest rate. Behind the scenes, output is being *reallocated* from production of consumer goods to production of investment goods. Suppose, however, we remove the assumption of fixed output and that a rise in the propensity to save, represented by an outward shift from SS to $S_1S_1$, leads to a lowering of profit expectations – as in real life it easily could (Figure 13.5). The demand for loanable funds would then shift inwards from DD to $D_1D_1$. A new equilibrium occurs at $E_1$ at a lower level of investment and aggregate demand. There is a subsequent fall in real output and national income. Since savings are a function of income as well as interest rate, the fall in income leads to an inward shift in the savings function from $S_1S_1$ to $S_2S_2$. Eventually, a new equilibrium is attained at $E_2$. The interest rate may or may not fall, depending on the precise extent of the movements in the

---

[5] During the period 1970–90 the correlation between long- and short-term interest rates was 0.96 in the US, 0.51 in Germany and 0.30 in the UK. As we shall see, monetary policy operates mostly at the short end of the market. These figures suggest that the effect of monetary policy on the long end of the maturity structure will vary from country to country. IMF, *World Economic Outlook* (May 1994).

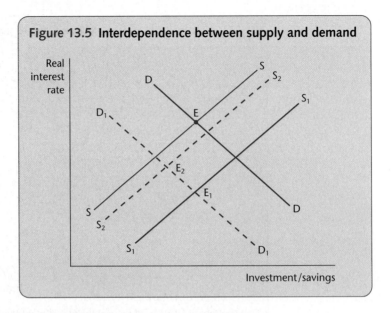

**Figure 13.5 Interdependence between supply and demand**

curves. The important point is that equilibrium has been brought about by two equilibrating factors rather than one: *changes in the interest rate* and *changes in income*. In the short run, changes in income would in fact bear the brunt of adjustment.

(2) The loanable funds theory concentrates on the mechanisms by which the interest rate brings *flows* of saving and investment into equilibrium. But the interest rate also performs an important function in relation to *stocks* of financial assets. At any one time, the term structure of interest rates determines the disposition of these stocks as between money at one end of the spectrum and long-term bonds at the other. Shifts in preferences between financial and real assets or between different types of financial assets could impact on the level of the interest rate.

(3) The loanable funds theory ignores the long-run *dynamic* relationship between interest, investment and savings. From a long-run point of view, savings are an essential prerequisite of investment. Investment generates economic growth, which will raise incomes and out of which will come future savings. This approach emphasises the importance of ensuring that savings are adequately and securely rewarded, and perceives no necessary contradiction in the long run between high real interest rates and high levels of growth and investment. A contrary view is that the propensity to invest, not the propensity to save, is in most urgent need of being protected, which implies that priority should be given to keeping long-run interest rates as low as possible. At this stage, it is unnecessary to do more than flag the issue and to note that interest rate policy has long-run as well as short-run implications for the economy.[6]

---

[6] The complexity of these relations is evident in the difficulties researchers experience in identifying any statistically robust relationship between long-run economic growth and the real long-run interest rate.

## 13.3 Interest rates and economic activity

To understand the channels through which interest rates affect economic activity, we focus on the direct links between interest rates and aggregate demand. There are also important indirect effects, via, for instance, changes in exchange rates, discussion of which is deferred to Part III.

Interest rates affect each of the components of aggregate demand in different ways. Recall that aggregate demand (GDP) can be broken down as:

$$GDP = C + I + G + X - M$$

where $C$ = consumption, $I$ = investment, $G$ = government consumption, $X$ = exports and $M$ = imports.

Of course the interest rate is only one of many factors affecting these components, but because of its relevance to monetary policy the interest rate effect is what we focus on in this section. A typical macro model, for example, would specify consumption as being dependent on disposable income ($Y - T$), wealth ($W$), interest rate ($i$) and other variables ($Z$) such as demographic change, i.e. $C = f(Y - T, W, i, Z)$.

Delving deeper, research has shown that interest rates affect *consumer spending* through three main channels:

1. *Substitution effects*: a decrease in interest rates makes saving (i.e. future consumption) less attractive for households and stimulates current consumption.
2. *Cash-flow (income) effects*: a lower interest rate increases the cash flow of borrowers and reduces the cash flow of lenders. If borrowers and lenders responded to changes in cash flow in the same manner, these effects would be symmetrical and offsetting. In practice, borrowers and lenders tend to have different spending propensities, and hence the redistribution of income following a fall in interest rates can, and does, impact on aggregate consumer spending. The magnitude of the net effect depends on household and business sector balance sheets, on the prevalence of fixed interest rate contracts and on propensities to spend (Box 13.1).
3. *Wealth effects*: a fall in interest rates raises the value of housing, equities and bonds. A rise in asset values relative to borrowing can have a powerful effect on consumer spending. In the mid-1990s, UK consumers were still feeling the aftershock of the collapse in house prices five years earlier (Box 13.2). The Federal Reserve Bank estimates that the boom in asset values during the late 1990s added 1 percentage point to US aggregate demand per year.

*Investors* tend to be more sensitive to interest rate change than consumers. This explains why business is so concerned with interest rate forecasts. Again, however, we note that interest rate is by no means the only variable to impact on the investment decision. A typical investment function would include a range of variables:

$$I = f(MPC, C)$$

where MPC = marginal product of capital,
$\qquad$ $C$ = cost of capital.

---

### Box 13.1    Interest rates and cash-flow effects

The cash-flow effects of lower interest rates depend on the net indebtedness of house-holds and firms, and on the proportion of assets and liabilities which are interest-rate adjustable. This proportion varies sharply between countries. For example, two-thirds of lending to the private sector in the US is in the form of 'predominantly fixed inter-est', as compared with less than one-third in the UK, Australia and Italy. The higher the share of variable interest loans, the greater the extent to which borrowers will be affected by a change in interest rates. The potential importance of this cash-flow effect has been significantly magnified by the rise in the debt/income ratios of households in many countries during the past decade.

The impact of a change in interest rates has been found to be quite asymmetrical between borrowers and lenders. Not surprisingly, borrowers with a high debt/equity ratio respond more sensitively to the interest rate than lenders with substantial net wealth. The age profile of borrowers and savers also has a bearing on the source of this asymmetry. Older people have a lower propensity to spend than younger people. They also have higher net savings. For example, almost 60 per cent of funds invested in British building societies are owned by investors over 55 years of age, but these account for only 15 per cent of borrowing. This may be a reason why a decrease in deposit rates may have a different effect than a decrease in lending rates of the same value.

The cash-flow effects of an interest rate change are more important in practice than the traditionally emphasised substitution effects. Cash-flow effects are especially impor-tant for business because firms in the non-financial sector are large net borrowers, while households in aggregate are net lenders.

---

Each of these variables has to be defined over a future time period and hence both marginal productivity of capital and cost of capital will be strongly affected by business 'sentiment' or expectations. In this respect, expected productivity (and hence profitability) of investment will be much influenced by prevailing ideas about the growth of the economy, so income variables also enter the picture either implicitly or explicitly. The interest rate is embedded in the cost of capital variable, along with depreciation, expected price changes in capital goods, corpo-rate taxes and investment subsidies (see Chapter 10).

Different types of investment have different interest rate sensitivities. Thus res-idential investment is very interest-sensitive because of the long lifespan of housing and the large initial outlay relative to income involved in a house pur-chase, whereas the link between interest rates and *business fixed investment* has proved surprisingly hard to quantify.

Two approaches have been used to study total business investment: the *neo-clas-sical* model and *Tobin's q-theory*. The neo-classical model draws on the marginal pro-ductivity theory outlined in Chapter 10. The firm chooses a minimum cost combination of inputs to produce a given output. The desired level of the capital stock depends on the level of output and the cost of capital, where the cost of capital depends on the nominal interest rate, the price of capital goods, expected inflation, and tax rates and allowances. A negative relationship between interest rate and investment is predicted by this model. Tobin's *q*-theory of investment comes to the same conclusion by a rather different route. It hypothesises that new investment

Box 13.2 **Effects of interest rate changes on consumer wealth**

Interest rate changes affect investment levels. They also impact on consumer spending through net wealth effects. The latter are measured by changing asset prices. Asset prices in turn change because the discounted present value of future income pertaining to that asset has changed.

Take, for example, the bond market. Because of the fixed coupon rate on bonds, bond prices and the rate of interest are inversely related. Consider a one-year bond, sold for £1000 and on which the borrower/issuer offers an 8 per cent return. After one year, the bond yields £80 to the lender, as well as the redemption of the original £1000.

The price of the bond equals the present discounted value of the bond. The present value is what would be paid today for the promise of money in one year's time and it is discounted because the value today is less than the promised payment in a year's time. Denoting the one-year interest rate by $i$, the actual yield payment by $U$ and the redemption value of the bond by $B$, we can write the present discounted value of the bond as:

$$PDV = \frac{U+B}{1+i} = \frac{80+1000}{1.08} = £1000$$

Now, supposing that the interest rate on one-year bonds increases, how much would anyone be willing to pay for the promise of receiving £1080 in one year's time? Because this promise will be discounted at the now higher rate of, say, 10 per cent, this must mean that the present discounted value, and hence the price of the bond, will fall:

$$PDV = \frac{U+B}{1+i} = \frac{80+1000}{1.10} = £981$$

Because the market yield rate has increased from 8 to 10 per cent, the value of this bond must fall until the yield rates are equalised. *An increase in interest rates will therefore lead to a fall in bond prices.* Likewise, *a fall in interest rates boosts bond prices.* Higher bond values will enhance consumer wealth. Given that wealth is an important determinant of spending, a rise in consumer wealth will be followed by an increase in consumption expenditure.

Interest rates also affect the equities market. A fall in the interest rate on financial assets leads to a decline in the returns investors require from equities. Lower returns on bonds give equity holders an incentive to move their wealth into equities. By adding to their equity shareholdings they drive up equity prices. Share prices will continue rising until equity returns are brought into equilibrium with bond returns. Conversely, a rise in interest rates will lead to a switch from equities to bonds and a fall in share prices. According to the direction of the interest rate change, asset holders are likely to feel either wealthier or poorer and, in consequence, either expand or reduce their spending.

Further effects will also be evident in the housing market. Most prospective home owners require mortgages to buy their homes and the interest rate is the cost of these loans. Hence, a reduction in the interest rate will lead to a corresponding rise in housing demand. This will be felt in the new housing sector, but it will also encourage people to 'trade up' to larger houses. Even home owners with no mortgages will respond to the interest rate, because it represents the opportunity cost of holding their wealth in housing rather than in, say, financial assets. Hence, a reduction in the interest rate raises housing demand and consequently house prices. As housing forms a large proportion of people's individual wealth, this will feed into higher spending.

depends on the gap between the market value of industry's capital assets and the replacement cost – the quotient of these two values is the $q$ ratio. If the market value exceeds the replacement cost, profitable opportunities exist for new investment to exploit this gap. A rise in the interest rate, by lowering the market value of capital, therefore weakens the incentive to invest. A fall in the interest rate, by raising the market value of capital, stimulates investment. Although intuitively appealing, neither of these theories has stood up well to empirical testing. Even the association between interest rates and *inventory investment*, which one would have expected to be very strong, has proved hard to pin down.

The impact of interest rates on *government spending* is a comparatively neglected topic, but for heavily indebted governments, a potentially important element in the overall picture. The direct impact of an interest rate change falls on debt-servicing costs. A rise in these costs tends to have a negative impact on public sector spending as well as on general market sentiment. Relations between central banks and governments can become quite tense when the latter are heavily indebted. A decision to change interest rates can have a major impact on budget arithmetic in such countries. Interest payments on debt still account for over 20 per cent of government revenue in countries as diverse as India (28 per cent), the Philippines (22 per cent), Pakistan (32 per cent) and Turkey (42 per cent). The ratio often exceeds 10 per cent in developed countries too, for example the US (10 per cent), Canada (15 per cent) and Denmark (11 per cent).

The modest effects revealed by econometric investigations into the effect of interest rate changes contrast with the weight attached to interest rate changes by the media, business organisations and politicians. Taken at face value, they suggest that we might agonise too much about the interest rate. The occasional much publicised disagreements about interest rate policy are usually about proposed adjustments in the interest rate of less than 1 percentage point. Why so much fuss if the impact on total spending is not appreciable?

There are several ways of answering this question. First, the cumulative effect of an interest rate change on aggregate demand may be greater than the sum of the effects of each component of demand. The UK Treasury's model, for instance, suggests that a 2 percentage point reduction in the interest rate causes consumption to be $1\frac{3}{4}$ per cent higher after two years than it would otherwise be. Add in the hard-to-quantify investment effects and one is talking about a significant effect on aggregate demand. Second, movements in interest rates have a strong effect on expectations. The interest rate acts as a signal. An interest rate increase comes with an implicit warning that, if the economy does not slow down, further action will be taken by the authorities. Likewise, a lowering of interest rates by the monetary authorities could be interpreted as a signal of easier money and more aggressive stimulation of aggregate demand should the monetary measures fail to provide the desired stimulus to economic activity.

## 13.4 Monetary policy and interest rates

Interest rates are an important tool in a monetary authority's armoury. Sometimes the central bank may directly change the short-term rate; at other times its actions will have an indirect effect on the interest rate structure. In assessing and guiding monetary conditions, the bank has regard not just to the level of interest, but also to money supply, lead inflation indicators and the exchange rate. To implement their policies and alter monetary conditions, monetary authorities have a variety of instruments at their disposal, both direct controls and 'market-based' instruments.

## Price stability – the ultimate objective

The ultimate objective of monetary policy is price stability.[7] Most central banks publish explicit inflation targets; virtually all regard control of inflation as a high priority (Box 13.3). This objective is based on the conviction that price stability is conducive to economic growth and full employment. An explicit price stability objective for monetary policy minimises uncertainty.

Monetary policy operates with a delayed reaction of 1–2 years. If inflationary pressures are building up, central banks need to take countervailing action before these pressures are translated into actual inflation. Prevention is better than cure. From a central bank's view, early response to a build-up of inflation signals a determination to maintain its *credibility*. If the proposed measures are seen as effective, the bank's credibility is strengthened. As a result, the bank's advice and opinions will carry greater weight with business, employees and government. By accurate diagnoses of what needs to be done, and implementation of the necessary measures, a central bank over time builds up *reputation*. This further strengthens its influence.

Experience shows that well-judged monetary policy can combat incipient deflation such as that threatened after the 2001–02 stock market collapse. The chain of causation is outlined in Figure 13.6.

Central banks have learnt much from their past mistakes. For example, the Bank of Japan reacted far too slowly to the downturn in the Japanese economy in the 1990s. This persuaded the Federal Reserve of the necessity to take aggressive stimulatory action before a deflationary psychology took hold. The 3-month deposit rate tumbled from 6.5 per cent in 2000 to 1.1 per cent in June 2003 as a consequence. The Fed could not be accused of inaction, though it remains to be seen how effective the action taken will be.

## Intermediate targets

Intermediate targets are variables that the central bank seeks to control in order to achieve its objective. The Bank of England, for example, has identified long-run price stability as its ultimate objective. Its main focus, however, is not *current* inflation, which is given and which it is powerless to do anything about, but *future* inflation, 1–2 years ahead, which can be changed by today's policy actions. Money stock and credit aggregates are used as intermediate targets. Published monetary objectives include a wide diversity of measures. In using money supply

---

[7] The Federal Reserve's objective is specified differently as that of ensuring full employment, rapid growth and price stability. Of course, US central bankers assert that price stability is the best way of achieving full employment and that there is consequently no conflict between these objectives. From time to time there have been proposals to redefine the objectives of the Fed in order to give price stability specific priority.

### Box 13.3 How central banks define their objectives

#### Euro area

Price stability is the primary objective of the European Central Bank. The Bank has defined price stability as

> a year on year increase in the harmonised index of consumer prices for the euro area of below 2 per cent.

Neither price increases persistently above 2 per cent, nor price declines, could be deemed consistent with price stability. In 2003, the ECB respecified the target as *medium-term inflation below but close to 2 per cent*.

#### UK

The Bank of England Act 1998 also defines the objectives of the Bank as being to maintain price stability. But the Chancellor of the Exchequer, not the Governor, determines the operational expression of the price stability target. Since December 2003, the target has been specified as an underlying inflation rate of 2 per cent in the consumer price index. Deviations of more than 1 per cent in either direction will require special notification to the Chancellor.

#### US

The mandate of the Federal Reserve System was most recently defined in the *Humphrey–Hawkins Act*, passed by Congress in 1978. The Act requires the Fed to

> maintain long-run growth of the monetary and credit aggregates commensurate with the economy's long-run production potential so as to promote effectively the goals of maximum employment, stable prices and moderate long-term interest rates.

The Federal Reserve does not offer a quantitative definition of price stability. The chairman of the Fed argued in 2001 that, because of the margin of measurement error in price indices, a specific numerical inflation target would represent an unhelpful and false sense of precision.

#### Japan

The new Bank of Japan Law was passed by the Diet in June 1997. The objective of monetary policy under the new law is

> to contribute to the sound development of the national economy through the pursuit of price stability.

The Bank has no explicit inflation target. It has been under pressure to introduce one in order to trigger more forceful action against current deflation.

*Source*: ECB *Monthly Bulletin*, May 2003 (press release on ECB's monetary policy strategy); M. Kieler, 'The ECB's inflation objective', *IMF Working Paper*, Washington, DC, May 2003.

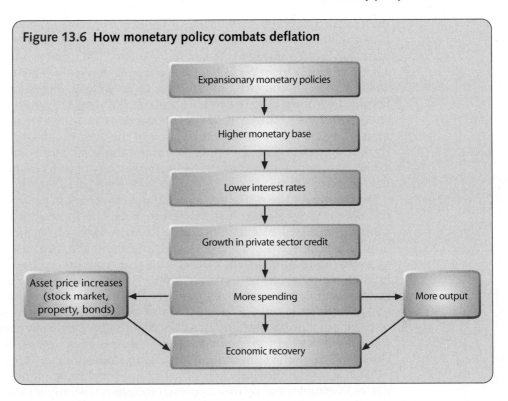

**Figure 13.6 How monetary policy combats deflation**

as an intermediate target, some central banks derive an estimate of money demand (consistent with its inflation target) and then announce a target money supply to match it. A typical demand for money function will take the form:

$$\log m = a + b \log y + c \log p - d \log i$$

where $m$ = nominal money supply, $i$ = nominal interest rate, $y$ = real income and $\log p$ = per cent annual increase in the price level.

The monetary authorities proceed by (a) estimating the parameters of the demand for money function ($a$, $b$, $c$, $d$), (b) inserting values for potential economic growth ($y$) for the coming year, and (c) specifying its target (or maximum) level of inflation. The rate of interest is a policy instrument, which can be taken as given for the initial calculations. From this exercise will emerge the level of money demand in the economy, and hence the required money supply increase to match this demand, resulting in the published money supply target.

Money supply targeting was the central tool of counter-inflationary policy during the 1970s and 1980s. To be applied successfully, two conditions are necessary. First, the money demand function has to be stable and predictable. That is, the parameters of the money demand equation must be constant. If they change in an unpredictable way from year to year, a rate of money supply growth which was just correct in one year might be quite inflationary in another year. The central bank would be unable to predict the 'right' rate of expansion of money supply. Second, money supply obviously has to be controllable by the authorities. They must be able to achieve the announced target.

The relationship between money supply and the national income has become less predictable than it once was. In the course of a review of UK monetary policy, the present Governor of the Bank of England concluded flatly that *there is no longer any time-invariant mechanical link between the change in a given monetary aggregate and the subsequent out-turn for inflation.*[8] The speed at which money circulates (the *velocity of circulation*) has changed markedly. This means that the amount of economic activity which a given money supply can sustain has become highly variable. To complicate matters further, the velocity of circulation appears to have changed in different directions for different parts of the UK money supply. The velocity of circulation of the narrow money supply (M0) has *risen*, as new ways are discovered of economising on money balances (which attract zero, or minimal, interest), while the velocity of wider money supply (M4) has tended to *decline.*

One reason for the weakening association between money supply and prices is the deregulation of the financial sector. Financial innovation has also contributed. Increased competition has led to new ways of obtaining credit, and innovations have enabled a given supply of currency to finance a larger amount of transactions. The globalisation of capital markets has further weakened the hold of central banks on domestic money supply. Given these difficulties, the usefulness of money supply as an intermediate target has been questioned. Also, the private sector often deliberately takes action to circumvent the monetary restrictions set by the authorities. As Goodhart's Law warns: *any monetary variable which the authorities seek to control instantly becomes meaningless.* Yet some central banks, including the ECB, continue to specify a money supply target.

*Inflation targeting* is widely used either as an alternative to money supply targeting, or to complement it.[9] This approach focuses on identifying lead indicators of inflation that will help to alert the authorities when inflationary or deflationary pressures are building up. These can then act as signals for pre-emptive action on monetary policy. Inflation targeting requires good inflation forecasts. Hence, care must be taken to establish the variables that impact on future prices and the time lags between change in the target and change in the price level. Obvious candidates are output gaps, price trend expectations (derived from survey data on business and consumers), the yield curve and credit trends. For small countries such as New Zealand with floating exchange rates, the exchange rate will be a leading indicator; commodity prices such as oil are another. Capacity utilisation, unemployment, yield curves, earnings increases are others that can be useful. To work well, inflation targeting requires an independent central bank that has discretionary power to take unpopular action (and raising interest rates almost never pleases the public or the markets) when it believes action is necessary. Also there must be consistency among policy objectives. A government might want to have both price stability and a fixed exchange rate *vis-à-vis* its trade partners. But if the trade partners have high inflation, these two objectives are mutually inconsistent.

---

[8] M. King, 'Monetary policy in the UK', *Fiscal Affairs* (August 1994). Work continues unabated on estimating demand functions for money. Some are able to find stable values of the parameters, but only with the help of considerable ingenuity in constructing special variables to capture innovation, deregulation and tax effects: R. Thomas, 'Understanding broad money', *Bank of England Quarterly Bulletin*, 36(2) (May 1996).

[9] See M. Artis, P. Mizon and Z. Kontolemis, 'Inflation targeting: What can the ECB learn from the recent experience of the Bank of England?', *Economic Journal* (November 1998); L. Svensson, 'Inflation-forecast targeting: implementing and monitoring inflation targets', *European Economic Review*, 41 (1997).

The European Central Bank has adopted both inflation forecasts and money supply in setting its monetary policy. The two pillars of its strategy for price stability are (a) an assessment of the outlook for future price developments and (b) a 'reference value' for growth of money supply.

## Policy instruments

The monetary policy instruments at the disposal of the central bank can be classified into two broad categories: *direct controls* and *market-based controls* (see Figure 13.7).

*Direct controls* were once used very widely but, since the 1970s, they have become increasingly unfashionable and ineffective. They include measures such as:

- overall credit ceilings or guidelines, sometimes imposed on a bank-by-bank or sectoral basis,
- administrative controls on the level of interest rates and the spread between retail and wholesale rates,
- bank-by-bank rediscount quotas,
- moral suasion (sometimes called 'window guidance').

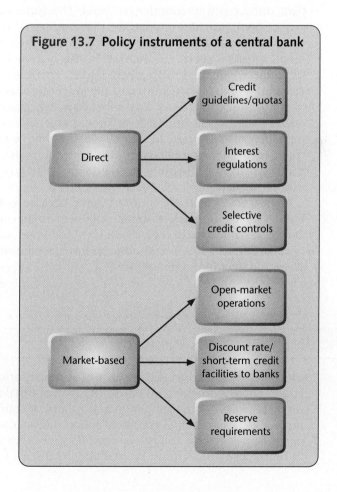

**Figure 13.7 Policy instruments of a central bank**

Direct →
- Credit guidelines/quotas
- Interest regulations
- Selective credit controls

Market-based →
- Open-market operations
- Discount rate/ short-term credit facilities to banks
- Reserve requirements

Direct controls seek to bypass the market mechanism. As such, they suffer from the predictable problems of all quantitative controls. They tend to be inefficient and their effectiveness tends to erode over time. This is because of the problem of *disintermediation*. This term originates from the definition of the function of the banks, which is to intermediate between savers and lenders. Regulation gives lenders and borrowers an incentive to bypass the banks and get together directly through other means. Hence they are engaged in *dis*intermediation. If domestic banks' lending is restricted by central bank guidelines, borrowers will seek funds directly from the public or from banks overseas, or from financial institutions not covered by a central bank's regulations. While direct controls are still used in developing and transition economies, greater reliance on market-based controls has become a universal trend.

*Market-based controls* consist of open-market operations, the discount rate and reserve requirements. *Open-market operations* are used extensively and are the most effective means of supplementing or withdrawing liquidity from the system. The most common method of effecting open-market operations is through repurchase agreements (repos). Repos involve the purchase of assets by the central bank under a contract providing for their resale at a specified price or on a given future date. Reverse repos involve the sale of assets by the central bank.

Liquidity can also be controlled by altering the terms on which the central bank offers credit to commercial banks. The *discount rate* is the rate at which the central bank provides reserves for the commercial banks. A decrease in the discount rate, in addition to lowering the cost of credit to banks, has an 'announcement' effect. It alerts the market to the central bank's view of the liquidity situation. Combined with open-market operations, we expect a fall in the discount rate to be transmitted to the longer-term end of the interest spectrum.

Third, the central bank may affect liquidity directly by altering the *minimum reserve requirements* imposed on the commercial banks. Reserve requirements have become less used in recent years. Many countries have dispensed with them entirely for monetary control purposes. Changes in these requirements can be costly and disruptive to banks and, like direct controls, they encourage disintermediation.

Fourth, *unconventional measures* have been recently included in the central banks' repertoire, such as direct increases in the monetary base, purchase of corporate debt to make it easier for firms to obtain loans (introduced by the Bank of Japan in mid-2003), and absorption of government bonds in order to drive down the long-term interest rate.

## 13.5 The design of monetary policy

Monetary policy grows out of history and institutions as much as out of rule-books. There is no universal blueprint for an optimal monetary policy. The search for better ways of managing monetary affairs, of course, continues. It has centred on four key issues: active vs passive policy; rules vs discretion; the supervisory role of the central banks; and the optimal balance between secrecy and transparency in central bank operations. We shall briefly discuss each of these in turn.

## Active vs passive

An *active* monetary policy is one which adopts a strong counter-cyclical role. It seeks to adjust monetary policy in accordance with short-term variations in economic circumstances. If the economy appears to be heading for a recession, an active monetary policy would loosen conditions; if the economy was heading for a boom, it would tighten monetary conditions. By contrast, a *passive* monetary policy focuses on the medium to long term and disclaims any responsibility for correcting short-term cyclical downturns.

The justification for a passive policy is not that cyclical downturns are a matter of no concern, but rather that monetary policy will prove to be ineffective in offsetting them. This pessimistic assessment of the role of short-term monetary policy is based on four considerations:

1. *Monetary policy operates with long and variable lags.* Monetarists argue that, because of these lags, stabilisation policy will be ineffective at best, and damaging at worst. Because of the inability to predict precisely the time profile of its effects, an activist policy could be destabilising.
2. *Information on the present state of the economy and on future trends is insufficiently precise,* given our current understanding of the economy, *to guide counter-cyclical monetary policy,* even if problem (1) did not exist.
3. There is a danger that *repeated and unsuccessful efforts at short-term stabilisation will cause monetary policy to lose touch with its primary objective of price stability.* The economy might then end up with a double negative: no price stability and no stability in output.
4. *Maintaining price stability will itself reduce the incidence of cyclical fluctuations.* Surges of inflation cause booms, and disinflation causes recessions. If inflation is controlled, the need for counter-cyclical policy will diminish.

Despite the weight of these arguments, complete passivity in the face of short-run shocks is not always a realistic policy option. At a time of crisis, activism is obviously justifiable and may be essential. One such episode was the reaction of the Federal Reserve Bank to the Wall Street crash of October 1987. On 'Black Monday', 19 October, the Dow Jones fell by 23 per cent – the largest one-day decline in stock market prices of the twentieth century. In order to keep the stock market functioning, brokers needed to extend massive amounts of credit on behalf of their customers for their margin calls. But banks were understandably reluctant to lend to the securities industry. To avert a threatened liquidity crisis, the Federal Reserve announced its readiness to serve as a source of liquidity to support the economic and financial system. This deliberate loosening of the money supply was paralleled in other countries. A major crisis of confidence, and a potentially damaging recession, was averted. Here was a case of successful monetary activism. Again, following the stock market collapse of the early 2000s, monetary policy was used aggressively in the US and elsewhere in order to stave off the dangers of recession.

The 'right' amount of activism in any particular situation is a matter for judgement. Generally, one can say that by the end of the 1990s central banks had become sceptical about the scope for successful short-term intervention. Thus, they feared that forcing interest rates down too quickly, if it were to fuel expectations of inflation, would raise long-term interest rates and deliver precisely the opposite of the intended effect. Too much scepticism, however, is also a fault and may prevent central banks from taking action when it really is needed. There is a strong case for monetary policy being focused primarily on medium-term targets, while standing ready to make short-term adjustments in case of necessity.

## Rules vs discretion

The dichotomy 'rules vs discretion' is somewhat artificial, although it raises interesting issues from a policy view. One rule advocated by monetarists in the 1960s is that money supply should be increased by the same fixed percentage amount each year, determined by reference to the expected long-run growth potential of the economy. It was assumed that potential growth changed only gradually and that the demand curve for money was stable. Given these assumptions, the monetarist rule would ensure price stability in the long run. [10]

Pre-commitment to policy rules, 'tying one's hands', has the advantage of discouraging speculation. If adhered to rigidly, a rule 'never pay blackmail to a kidnapper' will deter kidnapping much more effectively than a policy of treating each case individually on its merits. Similarly, a rule that monetary policy will *never* accommodate inflation means that economic agents know where they stand. Public commitment to rules also guards against what is known as *the time-inconsistency problem* in economic policy. This problem arises because, having promised to achieve something ('inflation will never be allowed to exceed 2 per cent') and having convinced everyone to believe in it, a government will have an incentive to renege on this promise. It can use discretion to push up inflation and thereby gain a transient increase in output (and, in the process, perhaps win an election). Time-inconsistency tells us that this use of discretion, by catching people unawares, may well result in a one-off advantage. But, understanding that policy-makers may be inconsistent over time, private decision-makers are led to distrust policy announcements. Next time, the authorities will not be believed. People will see that the government has an incentive to use discretion. Those who lost out from their misplaced trust will come to regard the authorities' discretionary power as a threat, not an advantage. To be effective, monetary policy would have to become increasingly unpredictable, making it harder for the private sector to make informed decisions. *Such discretionary policy choices will be inefficient.* They will tend to generate higher average rates of inflation, with no compensating increase in output. [11] Only by adherence to a fixed rule, publicly committed to and from which it can only deviate with the greatest difficulty, will the policy become fully credible.

The time-inconsistency literature draws attention to the adverse long-term consequence of apparently successful short-term policy expedients. Reference has been made already to the high real interest rates of the 1980s and 1990s which penalised governments for the high inflation and negative real interest rates suffered by holders of fixed interest bonds during the 1970s. Countries with a

---

[10] Another example of a monetary rule is that domestic currency must be fully backed by foreign currency. It is comparable to exchange rate 'rules' such as those whereby one currency is pegged at a fixed rate to another.

[11] The 'time-inconsistent problem' was first analysed in F. Kydland and E. Prescott, 'Rules rather than discretion: the inconsistency of optimal plans', *Journal of Political Economy* (June 1977).

historical record of broken promises may obtain a larger pay-back from fixed and binding rules than more stable countries. The latter may conclude that, used prudently, discretion is preferable to fixity, given the many uncertainties involved in interpreting monetary conditions. Recognition of these uncertainties has prompted central banks to adopt a more 'eclectic' approach to monetary policy, drawing on a number of indicators besides money supply, and to use 'evolutionary' money supply targets that take account of changes in velocity of circulation.

## Central bank as supervisor of credit institutions

The central bank is concerned with the stability and efficiency of the financial sector. This is the context in which monetary policy functions and the structure of financial markets affects the way in which central bank policies operate. The supervision of the financial markets is entrusted to a central bank in some countries, to the ministry of finance or a separate institution in others. The liberalisation of international markets and the demise of unspoken rules of good behaviour have made the supervision of credit institutions an exacting responsibility. Such supervision includes the design and implementation of regulations covering bank operations, limits on competition perceived as dangerous to the stability of banks, rules on what banks can own, who can own them, and even the type of business they can engage in. The collapse in 1995 of Barings Bank, one of the City of London's most prestigious and respected merchant banks, and the near-collapse in 1998 of the no less prestigious US hedge fund Long Term Capital Management (with two economics Nobel prizewinners on its board), demonstrated the potential vulnerability of financial institutions to speculative ventures. Central banks are drawn into the resultant crises and have to be prepared to deal with them. The supervisory duties of a central bank are absorbing increasing amounts of time and attention.

## Transparency vs secrecy

Central banks are often very secretive. Critics accuse them of using secrecy to conceal a lack of clarity in their objectives and as a means of absolving themselves from the necessity of having to explain, and justify, their policy stance. Secrecy can be a means of concealing mistakes. An argument in favour of explicit policy objectives is that they neutralise these problems. Thus, money supply targets, or a transparent obligation to give priority to price stability, are examples of measures to tie the hands of the monetary authorities, to discourage them from over-ambitious targets, and force them to take unpopular action when necessary. Most important of all, published inflation or money growth targets are a way of exposing the authorities to monitoring and criticism.

Central banks have become conscious of the need for transparency and accountability in communicating their policy stance to the public. An instance of this is the publication of the minutes of the monthly meetings between the Governor of the Bank of England and the Chancellor of the Exchequer. The chairman of the Federal Reserve is frequently called to address Congress. In the course of 1999, the Bank of Japan's Governor went to the Diet no fewer than 115 times to explain his bank's policies. Central bank governors regularly appear before parliamentary committees. Central bank reports are widely circulated and are often informative on the bank's views of the economy and on the direction of policy. The advantage of such transparency has to be weighed against the downside, from the central bank's view, of occasionally getting egg on its face because of poor forecasting – or tendering what, in hindsight, turns out to be bad advice.

Secrecy and reticence are still required, however, in some areas. First, the precise timing of its market-sensitive actions must be kept confidential. Any information leakages on such matters could call into question the bank's standing and weaken its reputation. Second, policy stances should not be made so transparent and specific as to give markets an incentive to test them and enjoy the luxury of a one-way bet. There is sometimes a need for a calculated degree of vagueness, especially in relation to exchange rate targets. Uncertainty about where exactly the central bank's break-points lie can help it to manage the market more effectively. Third, the central bank, as the government's banker, must afford government the same confidentiality as to any other customer, and many communications have to be kept secret for this reason.

## 13.6 Conclusions

Monetary policy is in practice conducted by using a mix of formal models, rules of thumb and market intuition. Monetary policy interacts with business in many different ways, most visibly through its effect on interest rates, and ultimately through its success or otherwise in delivering a stable price level. Business needs to understand the factors determining interest rates in order to understand the monetary policy debate. While monetary policy is only one of many determinants of interest rates, it is crucially important in the short end of the market and can also exert a perceptible impact on the long end.

Interest rates affect the cost of working capital and the viability of long-term investment projects. They affect mergers and acquisitions activity, and can have an important bearing on stock market trends. Interest rates have a critical influence on the fortunes of bond traders, managers of hedge funds, mutual funds and other financial companies. The growing share of leveraged funds in the bond market makes that market highly vulnerable to unexpected changes in both the level and spread of interest rates. For instance, the rise in the 30-year US Treasury rate from 6.2 per cent at the start of 1994 to 7.75 per cent in mid-September 1994 was estimated to have reduced the value of bond holdings by as much as $600 billion. This massive loss was headlined by *Fortune* as 'The Great Bond Market Massacre'.[12] The initial hike in interest rates was prompted by the Federal Reserve's tightening in the short end of the market to head off incipient inflation.

While there is agreement that monetary policy operates through interest rates, there is continuing controversy about the channels through which interest rates affect household and business spending, the speed at which monetary policy affects real variables, the appropriate instruments and targets of monetary policy, and the optimal form of monetary policy. Notwithstanding these controversies, however, there is broad agreement on the analytical framework for analysing these issues.

---

[12] *Fortune* (17 October 1994).

In response to the question, 'How much do we really know about monetary policy?', Professor David Laidler replied: 'Enough to prevent it doing harm, but not enough to use it to do good.'[13] There is a valid political demand for short-run stabilisation policy, he argued, but this demand should not be met by monetary means. Adherence to this self-denying ordinance would prevent monetary policy from 'doing harm'. Not only that, but, by forging clear anti-inflation credentials, the central bank can 'do good' and provide a stable framework for growth. Now that price stability has been widely secured, however, Laidler's reply seems rather negative and inadequate. There are calls for a more active monetary response to the danger of an economic downturn. Many fear the possibility of monetary policy being too dominated by conservative central bankers who are fighting the last generation's war against inflation whilst ignoring the danger of deflation. The critics worry not just about monetary policy being too restrictive for too long, but about the effectiveness of monetary policy even if it were to be loosened. Drawing on ideas generated by Keynes in the 1930s, concern focuses on the build-up of a *liquidity trap*. Money supply can be increased, interest rates lowered and the economy can be awash with liquidity. Additional money supply becomes 'trapped' in the liquidity pool because (a) business is unwilling to borrow at *any* interest rate, (b) banks, beset with negative perceptions of the future, are unwilling to lend to business even if it did want to borrow, and (c) *real* interest rates remain high despite *nominal* interest rates being low.

Macro-stability is a necessary, but not a sufficient, condition for prosperity. A central bank's actions are based on a repugnance towards inflation which, in many real-life situations, may seem to take insufficient account of the cost of unemployment and recession. Its actions are based on economic reasoning, accompanied by assumptions about the future. The penalty for mistaken judgements can be heavy. Together with the movement towards more independence for central banks, we can expect to see greater efforts to ensure accountability, and public explanations of the theory underlying central bank actions and of the methodology of its forecasts. Business has a part to play in this ongoing debate. If business desires a relaxation of monetary conditions, it needs to understand the motivation, and the instrumentalities, of monetary policy in order to make a convincing case for such a strategy to the monetary authorities.

Given the limitations of monetary policy on the one hand, and the political demand for counter-cyclical actions on the other, we must consider what other policies might be used to stabilise the economy. The obvious candidate, and the subject of Chapter 15, is fiscal policy.

## Summary

1. The interest rate is defined as the amount of interest paid per unit of time as a percentage of the balance outstanding. The real rate of interest is the nominal rate of interest minus the expected inflation rate. Although the real rate of interest is not directly observable, its value can be inferred by subtracting the current or forecast

---

[13] David Laidler, *Taking Money Seriously* (New York and London: Philip Allen, 1990), p. 129.

inflation rate from the nominal interest rates. Interest rates vary according to the maturity of the loan and its degree of riskiness. The term structure of interest rates is defined as the relationship on a specific date between interest rates for bonds with different terms to maturity that have similar risk. The curve connecting these interest rates is called the yield curve. Yield curves are calculated in nominal terms and are normally upward sloping.

2. The loanable funds theory postulates that interest rates are determined by supply and demand of credit in an economy. Changes in the interest rate in this framework are explained by shifts in the demand and supply curve of credit. The theory is a useful starting point, but it ignores the long-run dynamic relationship between interest, investment and savings. Thus a lower interest rate increases the demand for credit, and this in turn increases the supply of credit by raising aggregate demand in the short run and potential output in the long run. Furthermore, the effects of changes in income and the influence of interest rates in relation to stocks of financial assets must also be considered. Finally, interest levels are influenced by the action of central banks and monetary policy.

3. Interest rates affect aggregate demand through three channels: substitution effects, where cuts in interest rates make saving less attractive for households relative to consumption; cash-flow effects, where lower interest rates increase the income of borrowers and reduce the income of lower-spending lenders; and wealth effects, where changes in interest rates affect the value of housing, equities and bonds.

4. The ultimate objective of monetary policy is price stability. Its intermediate targets are primarily money supply, interest rates and exchange rate levels. The monetary policy instruments at the disposal of the central bank can be classified as either direct or market-based controls. Direct controls seek to bypass the market mechanism, and include measures such as overall credit ceilings and administrative controls on the level of interest rates. Market-based measures act primarily through their effect on the interest rate. These include open-market operations, altering the discount rate and minimum reserve requirements.

5. There is no universal blueprint for an optimal monetary policy. The search for better ways of managing monetary policy continues. This has centred on issues concerning active vs passive policy, rules vs discretion, the supervisory role of the central banks, and the optimal balance between secrecy and transparency in central bank operations.

## Questions for discussion

1. In the present macroeconomic situation, the requirements of non-inflationary growth point to the importance of monetary policy in moderating demand where margins of spare capacity have virtually disappeared. ... It [monetary policy] should support a recovery of activity only where such margins remain large and there is little risk of inflation.

This is the OECD view as reported in the *OECD Observer*, August–September 1995, p. 48.

Suggest the changes in wording that would reflect the consensus view of the appropriate monetary policy in 2003–04.

**2.** An investment report opened its 'investment outlook' section with the comment:

> We expect the global economic environment to be characterised by moderate economic growth and relatively low inflation, a combination which should lead to relatively low interest rates also.

Is this statement referring to (a) the real interest rate, (b) the nominal interest rate, or (c) both? Explain.

**3.** An investment report written in 1996 warned that:

> There is a fear that, for political reasons, the UK government will *'go for growth'* over the life of this Parliament by increasing spending and cutting taxes while being more lax about interest rates, thus fuelling inflation. That said, the feeling that interest rates have been raised at an earlier stage than in previous recoveries improves the likelihood that inflation will be kept under control.

(a) Discuss the extent to which price stability has been achieved in the UK since 1996.
(b) Analyse the extent to which monetary policy of the Bank of England can take credit for this price stability.

**4.** A recurrent theme of the European Central Bank is that 'the best contribution monetary policy can make to growth and employment is to maintain stability in the general level of prices'. Does attaining price stability implicitly mean that interest rates have to be relatively volatile?

**5.** At the end of June 2003, the Federal Reserve cut interest rates by a quarter-point to 1.0 per cent, their lowest level in 45 years. This was the 13th reduction in short-term US interest rates, from 6.5 per cent at the start of 2001. Explain the three main channels by which the fall in interest rates would be expected to translate into higher aggregate demand. Comment on their applicability to the US economy during the period 2002–04.

## Exercises

**1.** On 25 June 2003, the financial press reported:

(i) The Federal Reserve sought to revive the US economic recovery by cutting the discount rate by 0.25 percentage points to 1.0 per cent, the lowest level in 45 years.
(ii) The Fed explained that the interest rate was cut against a background of 'sluggish' expansion of the monetary and credit aggregates, and 'abating inflationary pressures'.
(iii) The Fed's action was preceded by statistics indicating poor employment growth and faltering economic activity.
(iv) It was claimed that lower interest rates would help the economy, but that there might be a lag of one or two quarters.
(v) The financial press applauded the Fed's action as a valid response to the threat of a stalled economic recovery. It followed pressure from the White House which was worried by polls indicating loss of support for President George W. Bush's handling of the economy.

➡

Comment on (a) the reasons advanced for the Fed's cut in the discount rate, (b) the likely effects of this action, and (c) the sectors likely to have been most affected by it.

2. 'Monetary policy must be defined in terms of its final goal. For us, this final goal is, without any shadow of doubt, price stability' (Dr H. Tietmeyer, President of the Bundesbank, address to the Zürich Economic Society, November 1993).

   (a) What does price stability mean?
   (b) Comment on the usefulness of money supply targets as a guide for monetary policy.
   (c) In the speech from which the above quotation is taken, Dr Tietmeyer noted that 'the German money demand function has turned out to be stable'. Explain the significance of this remark.
   (d) Suppose money supply exceeds its target in a particular period. What action could or should a central bank take in response?

3. What variables should a central bank use as indicators of risks to price stability? Suppose these indicators indicate a forthcoming departure from price stability. Should central banks respond by changing the interest rate according to a given rule (as advocates of the Taylor rule recommend) or should they adopt a broader and more discretionary set of responses?

4. Write an assessment of the successes, failures and challenges of the European Central Bank since it began operations in 1999.

5. During 2003–04, as nominal interest rates fell to near zero, there was much discussion of the need for central banks to have recourse to 'unconventional measures' in order to stimulate aggregate demand. These measures included:

   (a) Direct increases of the monetary base.
   (b) Purchase of corporate debt with the aim of helping smaller firms to obtain loans.
   (c) Purchases of government bonds to reduce long-term interest rates.
   (d) Buying private securities to boost asset prices.
   (e) Explicit commitment to a higher inflation target of 3 per cent.

   Analyse how each of the above measures might be expected to impact on aggregate demand.

## Further reading

The big story in the late 1990s was the setting up of the ECB. See European Central Bank, *Monthly Bulletin* (January 1999), 'The stability-oriented monetary policy strategy of the Eurosystem', for a concise outline of initial ECB policy. An independent, readable and forthright appraisal of issues facing the ECB since then is provided in D. Begg *et al.*, 'Surviving the slow-down', *Monitoring the European Central Bank 4*, London: CEPR, 2002. This can be supplemented by checking on speeches of the Governor of the ECB and its chief economist, Dr Otmar Issing, on www.ecb.eu.int. M. King, 'The inflation target ten years on', *Bank of England Quarterly Bulletin*, Winter 2002, outlines Bank of England thinking on monetary policy objectives and instruments. Meanwhile, the main players in the world's monetary policy continue to be the heads of the three most powerful central banks: the US, Japan and the ECB. Although carefully sanitised, readers will derive insights into the practicalities of monetary policy from the minutes of meetings between the Governor of the Bank of England and the Chancellor of the Exchequer (www.hm.treasury.gov.uk). There has been an explosion of interest in the causes of Japan's deflation and in the lessons for policy-makers in economies threatened by a similar fate. A paper released by the Federal Reserve in June 2002 attracted David Beckham-type attention to its unsuspecting authors (all 13 of them!): Alan Ahearne *et al.*, 'Preventing deflation: Lessons from Japan's experience in the 1990s', Board of Governors of the Federal Reserve System, *International Finance Discussion Papers 729*, June 2002.

## Case study 13.1

# Taylor's rule for monetary policy

Central banks adjust the short-term nominal interest rate (or what the ECB calls the short-term deposit rate and the marginal lending rate) in order to change the borrowing rates for business and hence the level of economic activity. The Taylor rule throws light both on the indicators that a central bank consults before changing the interest rate and on how much of an adjustment in the interest rate it should make in response to movements in these indicators.

A conventional linear formulation of the Taylor rule is:

$$i_t = r^* + \pi_t + \alpha(\pi_t - \pi^*) + \beta(y_t - y^*)$$

where $i_t$ is the nominal interest rate determined by monetary policy. It is set to track its long-term level (given by the sum of the long-run equilibrium real interest rate $r^*$ and a long-term inflation objective $\pi^*$), unless contemporaneous inflation $\pi_t$ is out of line with its long-term objective $\pi^*$ and/or output $y_t$ deviates from its potential level $y^*$. In this formulation the values assigned to $\alpha$ and $\beta$ measure how sensitively monetary policy responds to deviations in inflation from its target and in output from its potential level.

Supposing prices deviate from the desired inflation rate (say 2 per cent), by how much should the bank change the interest rate in order to correct this deviation? By observing past behaviour of the Federal Reserve Bank, Professor John Taylor derived the eponymous rule below:

Real interest rate = 2.0 + 1.5(inflation – 2.0) – 0.5(GDP gap)

Recall that the real interest rate is the nominal rate of interest minus inflation and the GDP gap is the percentage excess of potential GDP over actual GDP.

Taylor's rule states that, if inflation is 2 per cent and there is a zero output gap, the real interest rate will gravitate to 2 per cent and the nominal rate towards 4 per cent. For each point by which inflation rises above 2 per cent, the real interest rate will tend to be raised by 0.5 percentage points equivalent to a nominal rate increase of 1.5 percentage points. Also each percentage point rise in the output gap will prompt the central bank to change the interest rate by 0.5 percentage points. Thus monetary policy responds to both the inflation rate and the output gap.

In his original paper, Taylor inserted assumed values for $\alpha$ and $\beta$. Subsequent studies estimated them using historical time series and also added an error correction term to give expression to the likelihood that central banks adjust the interest rate gradually to its desired level as determined by the rule. Thus the short-run response to inflation above 2 per cent might be less than the long-run response. There is ongoing discussion about how to measure the GDP gap and which inflation index to use (actual vs forecasted, core vs measured and so on).

Professor Charles Goodhart found that the Bank of England's behaviour is well explained by Taylor rules. Distinguishing between intermediate and long-term effects, the Bank's response to UK output gaps and deviations from price stability was quantified as follows:

| Event | Interest rate response | |
|---|---|---|
| | Intermediate | Long-term |
| 1 per cent deviation from inflation target | 0.79 | 1.32 |
| 1 per cent increase in GDP gap | 0.13 | 0.2 |

*Source*: Goodhart (1999).

Taylor rules help us to *describe* how monetary policy has been conducted. They show how interest rate movements are related to (a) changes in actual (or expected) inflation and (b) actual (or expected) output gaps. They can also be used normatively, to suggest how a central bank *ought to set* short-term interest rates in order to stabilise prices and economic activity. They also enable us to compare the behaviour of central banks. Thus the Federal Reserve has been given credit for moving aggressively to cut interest rates during the period 2001–03. Did this represent a daring new policy stance or simply the same policy as before, reacting to different inflation and output gap expectations? A Centre for Economic Policy Research study in 2002 concluded that monetary policy remained the same. The other question was whether the ECB should have followed the Fed's example and cut interest rates at a faster pace. Here the CEPR study found, rather surprisingly in view of generally unfavourable comparisons between the two central banks' reactions, that the ECB responded appropriately to a different economic conjuncture: 'the much larger reaction of interest rates in the US reflected a response to a much larger problem. A Fed-in-Frankfurt would not have cut interest rates much more in total than the ECB' (CEPR, 2002, p. 3). A follow-up study some months later was slightly less complimentary to the ECB.

*Sources*: Professor J. Taylor's seminal paper is 'Discretion versus policy rules in practice', *Carnegie Rochester Conference Series on Public Policy 39*, 1993. For application to the UK, see C. Goodhart, 'Central banks and uncertainty', *Bank of England Quarterly Bulletin*, February 1999. The strengths and limitations of Taylor rules are elegantly dissected in the *ECB Monthly Bulletin*, October 2001. The Fed and the ECB are compared in the CEPR's study *Surviving the Slowdown: monitoring the European Central Bank 4* (London, 2002). Ahearne *et al.* in their much-acclaimed Federal Reserve study use a forward-looking Taylor rule to show that the estimated monetary policy reaction functions of the Fed and the Bank of Japan were *quite similar*, the coefficient on the output gap being close to zero and on inflation high. The Bank of Japan loosened monetary policy too slowly because its inflation forecasts were consistently too high during the crucial period 1990–95 (details at end of chapter).

## Chapter 14

# Unemployment and the labour market

## Introduction

High and prolonged unemployment is a sign of a malfunctioning economy. Being unemployed is, for most people, a highly distressing experience, and fear of becoming unemployed is a potent source of unhappiness and disutility. Moreover, unemployment causes damage in ways that cannot be measured by sheer numbers. Yet despite economic growth and rising per capita incomes, it is a more acute problem now than it was 40 years ago. The number of unemployed people in the OECD countries peaked at 38 million in 1994, up from just over 10 million in 1973. Although the OECD total has declined slightly since then, unemployment remains particularly high in Europe. France has seen the numbers unemployed increase from 530,000 in 1970 to over 3 million. Germany also has suffered a dramatic increase, from its level of below 2 per cent in the 1960s to 9 per cent at present. Meanwhile, unemployment has risen at a disturbing pace in the countries of Central Europe. This is a humbling reversal of fortune for Europeans who, for several decades after the Second World War, prided themselves on their low rates of unemployment.

An OECD study, published in 1994, described unemployment as the most widely feared phenomenon of the time:

> High unemployment creates insecurity and resistance to organisational and technical change. Long-term unemployment lowers self-esteem, is demotivating and self-reinforcing, and is associated with health problems. The rise in youth unemployment means that many young people are losing skills and employability. Groups in society that have never before faced a high risk of unemployment, such as white-collar workers, are losing jobs, with all the personal and societal costs that implies in terms of lost potential and lost investment.[1]

The ill-effects of unemployment continue to pose serious problems and represent a major challenge to economic policy.

The adverse consequences of unemployment impact on business in several

---

[1] *The OECD Jobs Study: Facts, analysis, strategies* (Paris, 1994), p. 41.

ways. They affect attitudes in the workplace, by making people less inclined to take their jobs for granted, but any advantage to business accruing on this score must be balanced by three offsetting factors. First, unemployment imposes heavy social welfare costs which have to be met by taxation; second, it places a great strain on government's economic policy; and third, it can be a cause of social and political instability.

Unemployment is a special problem of the industrialised countries because the unemployed in such countries are provided with an income by the state (unemployment benefit), but not a job. In order to qualify for unemployment benefit, the recipient must not be in paid employment. Sometimes the state benefit can amount to a significant proportion of the going pay rate, especially that available to an unskilled and poorly motivated worker.

In poorer countries, by contrast, unemployment benefit either is not provided at all or is provided at a very low level. As a result, most people are forced to find work. They are employed, but often at very low productivity levels. They may encounter extreme difficulty in finding a suitable job. Some experience long periods of involuntary inactivity (hawkers, casual labourers), but are not recorded as unemployed. This is the endemic problem of *underemployment*. Some middle-income developing countries have high rates of both unemployment *and* underemployment. South Africa has an unemployment rate of 30 per cent and Morocco of 18 per cent.

Socialist systems tended to be free of unemployment. People without work were assigned to state organisations. The state provided them with a job, regardless of whether there was any useful work for them to do. (In many cases there was not, as subsequent privatisation of socialist enterprises has revealed.) The unemployment problem, therefore, must be analysed in the context of specific institutions and societal values.

The problem of unemployment can be tackled in several ways. Much depends on the characteristics of the economy and its labour and product markets. This chapter provides the analytical framework needed to understand both the problem of unemployment itself and the rationale behind suggested ways of resolving it.

## Chapter outline

1. The nature and extent of the unemployment problem.

2. The market approach to unemployment, drawing on the supply and demand analysis outlined in Chapter 10.

3. Short-run versus long-run perspectives on the unemployment problem.

4. The Keynesian contribution to solving the unemployment problem.

5. The relationship between technological change and unemployment.

6. Policies to alleviate unemployment.

## 14.1 Facts about unemployment

### Definition

The standard international definition, developed by the International Labour Organisation, identifies the unemployed as *those of working age who, in a specified period, are without work and are both available for, and have taken specific steps to find, work.* This sounds relatively straightforward, but numerous small differences of interpretation, compilation and data sources mean that national estimates often differ from international estimates. Even at the national level, estimates of unemployment differ, depending on whether one measures it according to the 'standardised' definition above or according to the number actually collecting unemployment benefit.

Standardised rates of unemployment in the main developed economies since the 1960s are provided in Table 14.1.

The standardised definition of unemployment is not a comprehensive measure. For example, it excludes the following groups:

- Many part-time workers who would prefer to work full-time but are unable to find opportunities. Yet these 'involuntary part-time workers' are counted as fully employed.
- So-called 'discouraged workers'. These are people who report in the labour force surveys that they would like a job but are not currently searching for work, as they believe no suitable job is available.
- Older workers who are permitted to claim unemployment benefit even though not seriously searching for work.

The net impact of these various influences on the recorded unemployment rate is not known for certain. According to one study, discouraged workers and invol-

### Table 14.1 Unemployment rates in selected countries, 1960–2004

|                 | 1960s | 1970s | 1980s | 1990s | 2004 |
|-----------------|-------|-------|-------|-------|------|
| **United States** | 4.7   | 6.4   | 7.1   | 7.0   | 5.6  |
| **Japan**       | 1.2   | 1.8   | 2.5   | 3.7   | 5.3  |
| **EU-15**       | 2.0   | 3.8   | 8.5   | 9.6   | 7.5  |
| France          | 1.8   | 4.1   | 9.0   | 10.8  | 8.6  |
| Germany         | 0.7   | 2.2   | 6.0   | 8.3   | 7.9  |
| Italy           | 4.8   | 6.1   | 8.6   | 10.6  | 9.0  |
| Netherlands     | 0.9   | 4.3   | 8.1   | 5.0   | 3.6  |
| Spain           | 0.8   | 2.8   | 14.9  | 16.0  | 10.7 |
| United Kingdom  | 1.7   | 3.8   | 9.6   | 7.9   | 4.9  |
| Austria         | 2.0   | 1.3   | 2.8   | 3.9   | 4.0  |
| Finland         | 2.3   | 4.0   | 4.6   | 12.5  | 9.1  |
| Sweden          | 1.7   | 2.1   | 2.6   | 7.7   | 5.1  |
| **Australia**   | 2.0   | 3.9   | 7.5   | 8.5   | 6.6  |
| **New Zealand** | 0.9   | 1.5   | 4.1   | 7.9   | 5.6  |

*Source*: OECD, *European Economy*.

untary part-timers could amount to 3 per cent of the labour force.[2] But numbers unemployed are overestimated by virtue of the inclusion of people as unemployed who are in fact actively engaged in the 'shadow' economy.

## Geographical distribution

Unemployment is a much more acute problem in Europe (10 per cent) than in the US (4 per cent) or Japan (5 per cent). In Japan, up to the mid-1990s, unemployment (at less than 3 per cent) could hardly be described as a major problem at all, but since then the situation has worsened. Within Europe there are wide variations in unemployment rates between Spain, Finland and France at one extreme, and Austria, the Netherlands, Norway and Switzerland at the other. There are also wide regional variations within countries. In the US, California has half the unemployment rate of Mississippi. In Britain, unemployment tends to be much higher in the north than in the south. Germany also has major regional disparities not only between east and west (17 per cent versus 8 per cent in 2000), but also within western Germany, where unemployment rates in northern regions like Bremen were up to three times higher than those found in areas of the south such as Bavaria.

Transition countries have also suffered high unemployment. Starting from negligible or zero unemployment during the socialist regime, Bulgaria, Lithuania, Poland and the Slovak Republic had unemployment rates of 15–20 per cent by the early 2000s. For transition countries, the problem of unemployment is closely linked to structural change. Following the change in regime, whole sectors of industry proved to be unproductive and incapable of withstanding exposure to outside competition. Workers lost their jobs and became unemployed. In countries such as the Ukraine and Russia, there was less explicit unemployment. Workers continued in their jobs but were not paid or were forced to take administrative unpaid leave or decreased work hours. In the latter case, wages took the hit and the unemployment rate as such rose less than might be expected. There were many underemployed or unregistered workers. However accounted for in the statistics, much hardship and disillusion was caused. Transition from 'old' to 'new' competitive sectors continues to prove difficult. As Table 14.2 shows, high unemployment is endemic in these countries and, were it not for widespread labour hoarding and non-payment of wages, the position would be much worse still. Unemployment may have different origins in these countries than in the West, but it is no less painful for that.

## Time dimension

Unemployment in industrialised countries was extremely low in the postwar period until the first oil price shock in the early 1970s. Since then, it has risen in 'waves', corresponding to the two oil price supply 'shocks' of 1972–73 and 1979–80, and the demand 'shocks' of 1990–92 and 2001–03 (Figure 14.1). In

---

[2] John P. Martin, 'The extent of high unemployment in OECD countries', Federal Reserve of Kansas Symposium on 'Reducing unemployment: Current issues and policy options', Jackson Hall, Wyoming, 25–27 August 1994 (p. 11).

**Table 14.2 Unemployment rates in transition economies**

|  | 2003 |  | 2003 |
| --- | --- | --- | --- |
| Estonia | 10.0 | Slovak Republic | 18.2 |
| Latvia | 11.1 | Slovenia | 6.3 |
| Lithuania | 16.2 | Poland | 20.6 |
| Albania | 17.0 | Russia | 8.0 |
| Czech Republic | 7.0 | Bulgaria | 16.5 |
| Hungary | 6.2 | Romania | 8.7 |

Source: European Commission, 'Economic forecasts for the candidate countries, spring 2003', Brussels, April 2003.

many European countries, a strong ratchet effect was evident: unemployment rose after each shock, but did not revert to its original level once the shock had been reversed. The difficulty of a quick reversal is illustrated by the case of Finland. Following the break-up of the Soviet Union, Finland's unemployment rate rocketed from 3 per cent in 1990 to 17 per cent in 1994. It took six years to reduce it to 9 per cent. During the last decade, as Figure 14.1 shows, due in part to the implementation of better labour market and macroeconomic policies unemployment has fallen steeply.

## Composition

*Young people*, defined as those in the 15–25 age group, typically experience higher unemployment rates than other age groups, reflecting difficulties in the transition

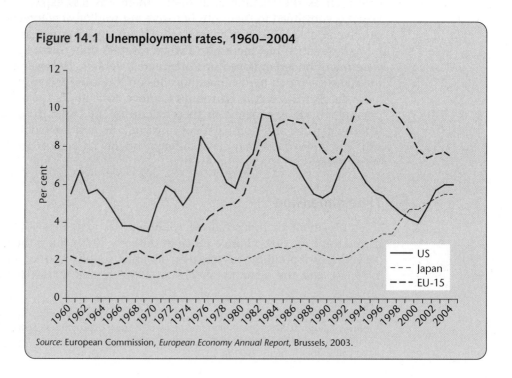

**Figure 14.1 Unemployment rates, 1960–2004**

Source: European Commission, *European Economy Annual Report*, Brussels, 2003.

from school to first work experience. *Older workers* also experience an above-average incidence of unemployment, partly because they have to bear the brunt of job loss as industries are restructured. However, this does not always convert fully into the official unemployment figures because of early retirement schemes. *Females* experience higher unemployment than males in some European countries, but lower in many others, such as the UK, Japan and North America. *Lone parents* appear to be particularly vulnerable to unemployment. It also appears that *immigrants* experience more unemployment than nationals, a fact ascribed to their concentration in sectors which are cyclically sensitive and undergoing structural change. The figures also show that, with the passage of time, immigrants integrate more easily into the national workforce and their unemployment rate tends to converge towards the national average.

Unemployment is closely correlated with level of skills. *Unskilled workers* face a higher risk of unemployment than skilled workers – whether defined by reference to occupation (blue-collar vs white-collar) or to educational attainment (years of schooling, university degree, etc.).

## Duration

There is constant movement into and out of unemployment as people lose jobs and find replacements. In the US, it is estimated that 15 per cent of all jobs are wiped out every year and replaced by new ones. The impact of these inflows and outflows on the unemployment rate depends on two separate factors: (1) the proportion of the labour force which becomes unemployed between one time-period and the next, and (2) the average length of a completed spell of unemployment. The number of unemployed could rise between one date and another because an unusually large number of new people become unemployed, or because those who were unemployed at the first count remained unemployed longer than normally.

In a steady state, where inflows into and outflows from unemployment are stable and cancel out, the unemployment rate will be constant and the following identity will hold:

Unemployment rate = rate of inflow into unemployment
× average completed duration of period unemployed

Thus, a given unemployment rate could be consistent with a high inflow rate and relatively short duration, or a low inflow rate and relatively long duration. This distinction can be important when analysing the causes of a change in the unemployment rate.

*Long-term unemployed* are defined as *those who have been unemployed continuously for one year or more*. The long-term unemployed typically suffer greater economic and personal costs than the short-term unemployed, e.g. through deterioration of their skills and loss of work motivation (loss of 'human' capital). Also, employers tend to use the duration of an unemployment spell as a screening device in their hiring decisions. As a result of these two factors, the long-term unemployed become 'outsiders' in the labour market, have little or no influence on wage determination and find it progressively harder to re-enter the workforce.

The incidence of long-term unemployment is particularly high in Europe (40 per cent of the unemployed in the EU are long-term, compared with only

12 per cent in Canada and 9 per cent in the US). Once unemployed, a worker in the EU has a relatively small probability of finding another job quickly. However, the comparatively low inflow rate into unemployment in Europe implies that the probability of *becoming* unemployed is lower for the European worker than in other industrial countries. Those with jobs – the 'insiders' – enjoy reasonable job security, while prospects for the long-term unemployed – the 'outsiders' – of getting a job remain comparatively bleak. The US labour market has quite different characteristics. There, employees experience a more fluid, less secure situation where people lose jobs and find them more rapidly. It is hardly a coincidence that unemployment in the US is at less than half the EU level. A European-style system of legal and collectively bargained restraints on hiring and firing, high levels of income support and high cost of employing labour has many attractions. But the cost can often be higher unemployment.

Unemployment is not the same thing as 'not working'. A particular concern in Europe is the growing number of workers taking early retirement. *Only 40 per cent of Europeans aged 55–64 participate in the labour force.* The present effective age of retirement is below 60. These people are not at work but, because they are not seeking employment, they cannot be classified as unemployed. The facility of being able to retire early is a huge advantage to the individuals concerned, but it comes at a heavy cost in terms of both output foregone and cost to the taxpayer (pensions in Europe are largely financed by the government). The European Council has called for the extension of the age of retirement to 65 and there is even a proposal to go further by linking the statutory age of retirement to changes in life expectancy. Traditionally economists have focused on unemployment as the major problem of the labour market. Nowadays the remit has been broadened to *labour force participation*, including in this not just the problem of unemployment but also the broader issue of the rate of engagement in the labour force by older workers and women.

The measurement and interpretation of unemployment is a complex exercise. If the concern is with income distribution, social exclusion and discontent, or under-use of human potential, the standardised measure should ideally be supplemented by the inclusion of discouraged workers and involuntary part-timers. If one is concerned with explaining why the excess labour supply reflected in the unemployment statistics does not price its way back into jobs by lower pay, the standardised unemployment rate should be adjusted to take account of the proportion of long-term unemployed. The uncertainty surrounding the correct definition is not really surprising.

## 14.2 Supply-side approach and the market mechanism

### The market mechanism

Unemployment can be analysed first in a demand–supply framework. The economy's demand for labour is derived from information on the production function, the stock of factors of production, and the level of output prices and wages. The demand curve for labour is assumed to be downward-sloping because of diminishing marginal productivity of labour. It shifts position in response to medium-term changes in technology, and in the quantities of capital stock and other factors of production. The supply curve is drawn with an upward slope, reflecting the assumption that labour supply responds positively to increases in real pay.[3] Employees in this model are assumed to be 'rational' – if prices rise by 10 per cent, they realise that their nominal pay will have to rise by 10 per cent in order to maintain their living standards. Agents bargain over real pay. They are free from 'money illusion'.

For a given demand curve DD, and supply curve SS, equilibrium pay is OW and, at that pay level, OL workers are employed (Figure 14.2). Supply equals demand and there is no unemployment. Shifts in demand and supply naturally occur over time. Supply can increase because of population growth, increased labour force participation, immigration and similar factors. Demand for labour could shift outwards as a result of increases in the capital stock, improvements in resource use or advances in capital-saving technology. The demand curve could also shift inwards because of a collapse in business confidence or the introduction of a new labour-saving technology. All these changes may have important implications for the level of pay. However, a central tenet of the market approach is that there is no *a priori* reason for believing that *any of these events should cause either labour 'shortages' or labour 'surpluses' (unemployment)*. Excess supply of labour can always be remedied by a fall in real pay, excess demand by a rise in real pay.

Thus, suppose there is an outward shift in supply from SS to $S_1S_1$. At the original equilibrium wage OW, labour supply now exceeds demand for labour by ET. If the market mechanism is allowed to do its work, this excess supply will drive down the real wage rate. A new equilibrium will be established at V. More workers will be employed at the new lower equilibrium wage $OW_2$. Thus, the increase in supply has been accommodated.

Figure 14.2 The labour market always 'clears' – in theory!

---

[3] Alternatively, it could be rationalised as a wage-setting schedule, showing how a higher level of employment causes pressure for higher real pay. But this would be in a union-bargaining model and/or an imperfect competition framework, not one in which the labour market clears in a classical sense.

Suppose there is subsequently a shift in the demand for labour outwards to $D_1 D_1$. Equilibrium will occur at the new pay level $OW_1$. More people will be employed at that pay level. Again, there is no unemployment.[4]

This way of analysing the market effectively treats employees in the same way as any other product or service. Price adjustments bring demand and supply into equilibrium. If the market for labour behaved like the market for goods, *unemployment would not be a problem*. This theory, of course, does not preclude the possibility that downward movements in pay might create another set of problems, notably that of poverty, dead-end and low-productivity jobs. Market-minded economists, however, are disposed to regard such problems as less insidious than unemployment. Producing something, even at low productivity, is better, in this view, than being unemployed and producing nothing.

## Labour market rigidities

If unemployment occurs, the classical model pinpoints the culprit as pay rigidities and, more generally, lack of labour market flexibility. Labour market flexibility is a term which can take many meanings (see Box 14.1). For convenience, we focus on the pay element. The flexibility problem then boils down to rigidity in real pay.

The 'real wage' or the real rate of pay (defined as the nominal cost of hiring labour deflated by the price of output) is the price which signals labour shortages or surpluses to the market. If the real wage is not flexible, the market cannot perform its function, and labour surpluses and shortages will persist. This process is illustrated in Figure 14.3.

---

### Box 14.1  Labour market flexibility

Labour market flexibility is a catch-all term (*un mot-valise*) which incorporates many different meanings. It could refer to one or all of the following:

1. Pay flexibility of a firm's employees.
2. Ease and cost of hiring and firing employees (quantity flexibility).
3. Flexibility of hours worked.
4. Ability to contract out services formerly provided in-house.
5. Functional flexibility – ability of the firm to redeploy labour within the firm between different tasks and different locations.

Complete flexibility in relative and aggregate real wage averts the danger of unemployment resulting from excessive real pay per employee. But the economy is still vulnerable to the danger of unemployment (caused by an insufficiency of demand) and also to the problems of low-paid jobs and bad working conditions.

*Sources:* Denis Clerc, *Dechiffrer l'Economie* (Paris: Syros, 1994); B. Brunhes, *La Flexibilité de la Main-d'Oeuvre dans les Entreprises: Etude comparé des quatre pays européens* (Paris: OECD, 1989).

---

[4] This point is overstated deliberately. We do not assert that there would be *no* unemployment. Once allowance is made for turnover in a dynamic economy, and the fact that a *search* by both workers and firms takes time, there will be some equilibrium (sometimes called 'frictional') unemployment.

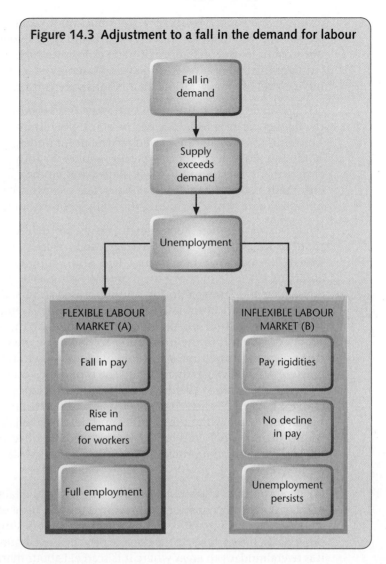

Figure 14.3 Adjustment to a fall in the demand for labour

Suppose labour demand shifts inwards because of a recession. The initial effect is to create a fall in the number of job vacancies at the going real wage. Given a constant flow of applicants, this excess supply leads to downward pressure on pay levels. As pay falls, the quantity of labour demanded increases along the lower demand curve. The process continues until eventually equilibrium is restored at a lower pay level. At that wage, everyone who wants a job will find one.

If pay does not fall, unemployment persists. A market perspective focuses on the reasons for these real pay rigidities and on methods of removing them. Among the more important rigidities are the following.

(1) *Trade union power*. Trade unions can force real wage rates above the point where supply equals demand. This pleases trade union members who retain their jobs, but limits the demand for labour and can result in lay-offs. A strong, centralised trade union movement might be able to anticipate this difficulty and pitch its demands at a level consistent with full employment. Austria is an

example of a country with powerful trade unions and a highly centralised wage-bargaining system which has enjoyed near-full employment for many decades. But sometimes the preference of trade unions for higher pay, or simple miscalculation of the trade-off between pay and unemployment, leads them to insist on a higher level of remuneration than is consistent with full employment.

(2) *Minimum wages.* If the minimum wage is set too low, it becomes redundant – the market-clearing real wage will be above the minimum. Set too high, however, a minimum wage can cause unemployment (or underground economy activity).[5] Minimum wage legislation typically applies to only a small fraction of total employment, mostly in the lower-skilled and young categories. Sometimes it has unintended effects, benefiting middle-class teenagers who get casual work at the minimum rate, while excluding the really poor whom it was intended to help.

(3) *Replacement ratios.* Replacement ratios are defined as *unemployment benefit entitlements as a percentage of average earnings after tax.* They set a floor below which the real wage rate cannot fall. Thus, suppose trade unions succeed in enforcing a pay claim above the market-clearing level. This leads to lay-offs. Laid-off workers then move into the non-unionised sectors. Pay levels in these sectors are driven down. Eventually, they reach the replacement-level 'floor' where a person is as well-off unemployed as working. At this point, additions to the supply of labour into the non-union sectors cause unemployment. Replacement ratios also affect the time spent looking for an alternative job. They put upward pressures on real wages by reducing the economic cost of being laid off.

Replacement ratios (before tax) are higher in Europe than in North America (Table 14.3). They vary considerably according to family circumstances, being higher for people with large families and the unskilled. Economic theory demonstrates the potential conflict between providing a decent safety net to a person made redundant, and providing incentives to seek work and accept a job when it is offered.

(4) *Occupational and geographical immobility.* The total labour market is highly segmented by both occupation and region. One can have excess demand for labour (shortages) in one part of the country and excess supply (unemployment) in other parts. It may take a considerable time before labour moves from areas where it is overabundant to areas where it is scarce. Labour market flexibility within the different areas may not be sufficient to enable the imbalance to be overcome by regional variations in pay. For example, if pay is negotiated through a centralised negotiating system, and if welfare benefits and employment regulations are the same through all regions of a country, labour costs will also by definition be equalised at a regional level.

---

[5] A national minimum wage was introduced in Trinidad and Tobago in 1998 – in response to a World Bank report that, contrary to stereotype, recommended a minimum wage as a means of reducing poverty. A subsequent study of its effects showed that (a) employment fell, (b) working conditions deteriorated, and (c) unemployment increased, just as economic theory would predict. The authors further found that the legislation had very little impact on the informal sector, mainly because of non-compliance. In small firms, for instance, 60 per cent of the workforce continued to be paid less than the minimum wage. Similar results were found in Ghana following the introduction of its minimum wage. See E. Strobl and F. Walsh, 'Minimum wages and compliance: the case of Trinidad and Tobago', *Economic Development and Cultural Change*, 2, 2003.

**Table 14.3  Unemployment benefit replacement rates (%), 1997**

|  | Single | Married with 2 children |  | Single | Married with 2 children |
|---|---|---|---|---|---|
| Australia | 37 | 73 | Italy | 28 | 54 |
| Austria | 54 | 70 | Japan | 32 | 65 |
| Belgium | 46 | 60 | Netherlands | 60 | 78 |
| Canada | 25 | 59 | Norway | 36 | 53 |
| Denmark | 48 | 96 | Portugal | 42 | 61 |
| Finland | 58 | 97 | Spain | 39 | 67 |
| France | 38 | 74 | Sweden | 58 | 84 |
| Germany | 57 | 68 | Switzerland | 61 | 91 |
| Greece | 8 | 11 | UK | 50 | 64 |
| Ireland | 33 | 62 | US | 7 | 48 |

*Source*: OECD web page (Social Policy: Benefit and work incentives in OECD countries).

(5) *Employment protection legislation.* Employment protection legislation is another source of labour market rigidity. In theory, its effect on unemployment is ambiguous, because it delays lay-offs (good) as well as discouraging recruitment (bad). Yet it is often cited in studies as a cause of unemployment.

(6) *Tax wedges.* Income taxes and payroll taxes drive a 'wedge' between the cost of labour to an employer and the net after-tax income of the employee. The tax wedge is defined as *tax on pay as a percentage of total pay* (Figure 14.4). When taxes increase, it often happens that businesses complain about the rising cost of labour, while simultaneously employees are aggrieved at their falling after-tax income. These two opposing perceptions are consistent. The effects of the higher

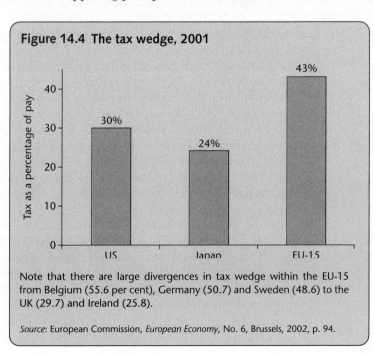

**Figure 14.4 The tax wedge, 2001**

Note that there are large divergences in tax wedge within the EU-15 from Belgium (55.6 per cent), Germany (50.7) and Sweden (48.6) to the UK (29.7) and Ireland (25.8).

*Source*: European Commission, *European Economy*, No. 6, Brussels, 2002, p. 94.

tax are to (a) raise the cost of labour relative to other factors of production and relative to product prices, and (b) lower real after-tax pay (thus raising the replacement ratio). Higher labour costs to the employer dampen the demand for labour. Again, as before, inflexibilities in the labour market may prevent nominal wages falling sufficiently to compensate for the higher hiring cost. In these circumstances, a higher tax wedge will lead to unemployment. Higher taxes are likely to aggravate the situation further by weakening entrepreneurial incentives and stimulating the underground economy.

(7) *Rigidities in the product market.* Product market rigidities exacerbate labour market rigidities. Monopoly rents extracted in final product or services markets can be shared with employees, leading to higher pay norms in these industries. This can have knock-on effects on unemployment in the same way that pay hikes in a sector dominated by trade unions can cause unemployment. Monopolies in intermediate service industries (telecoms, electricity, transport) and regulated charging scales and minimum rates in professional services (legal and accountancy professions, medicine and veterinary services) raise the cost structure of an economy, thereby reducing the competitiveness of the traded sectors. Rigidities in the distribution sector – such as limits on opening hours – can also lead to the suppression of part-time jobs which cannot be replaced in other sectors of the economy. Finally, '*menu costs*' can be another source of rigidity. Changing prices can be expensive and, as a result, prices can be 'sticky'. Firms may prefer to keep prices fixed, forgo sales and cause higher unemployment, rather than incur the costs of varying prices frequently in line with fluctuations in demand.

## 14.3 Short-run versus long-run perspectives

Labour markets are more flexible in the long run than in the short term. Thus, suppose inflation rises unexpectedly from 2 per cent to 10 per cent. In a perfectly rational and rapidly adjusting system, employees would immediately raise their pay demands pro rata. In the real world, however, the pace of adjustment will be much slower. In the short run, employees will be tied into pay agreements; they and their employers will wait and see whether the price increase is a flash in the pan or a long-run trend. Meanwhile, the sluggish response causes profits to rise, output and employment to increase, and unemployment to fall. In the long run, the story is different. Employees will insist on pay increases to compensate for the price rise. If full compensation is exacted, then real pay, employment and unemployment will revert to their original levels. A similar line of reasoning would apply in the case of an unexpected fall in prices except that now the real wages will rise, employment will decline and unemployment will increase.

The idea of the existence of a trade-off between inflation and unemployment derived from a paper written by a New Zealand economist, Bill Phillips, in 1958 (see Appendix 14.1 on the Phillips curve). Originally it was thought that there might be a long-run trade-off between inflation and unemployment. The implication was that by being a little less fussy about inflation a country could achieve a long-run lower unemployment rate. Experience showed that this belief was seriously mistaken. The trade-off, such as it is, exists only in the short run and there is considerable scepticism about how significant even those short-run gains can be.

The idea can be related to our earlier discussion of the aggregate supply (AS) curve (Chapter 11). As long as there are nominal pay and price rigidities, the Phillips argument asserts that the AS curve will be positively sloped. What Phillips failed to take account of is that, in the long run, these nominal rigidities will be washed out of the system as economic actors' pay demands catch up with price developments. 'Rationality' will prevail, and the AS curve will revert to being vertical.

Consideration of short-run versus long-run perspectives leads to several implications. The first concerns the role of aggregate demand (AD). When the AS curve is vertical, as it is in the long run, changes in AD have no impact on output or employment, only on the price level. In Figure 14.5, the shift in AD to $AD^1$ leaves output ($Y$) unchanged. Once we allow for a positively sloped AS curve, however, the same shift in the AD curve increases real output from $Y$ to $Y^1$, and in the process will reduce unemployment. AD thus becomes important in its own right as a factor in determining unemployment (a point discussed further in the next section).

A second issue concerns the location of the point at which the long-run AS curve intersects the horizontal axis, i.e. the long-run equilibrium level of output and the associated level of employment and unemployment. Nothing so far suggests that this point ($Y$ in Figure 14.5) need coincide with full employment. The actual level will depend on the amount of distortions in the labour market such as those mentioned earlier (trade union power, minimum real wages, replacement ratios, etc.) that do not have their origins in short-term money illusion but are embedded in institutions and value systems. In the jargon of economics, this long-run unemployment is called the *natural rate of unemployment*, or the non-accelerating-inflation rate of unemployment (NAIRU). The natural rate may be long run, but it is not time-invariant. It is amenable to policy action. Steps taken to reduce real rigidities in the labour market have had a significant downward impact on NAIRU in the UK, the Netherlands, Ireland and Denmark in recent years.

Third, a relatively recent discovery is that short-run unemployment can affect the long-run natural rate. The short run and the long run are not independent. Unemployment, once created, might develop its own independent dynamic. *Higher unemployment may initially be caused by short-run factors, but prolonged periods of unemployment make it progressively more difficult for the unemployed to get back into the labour market.* Here short-run and long-run considerations tend to shade into one another.

*Hysteresis* theory explains the dynamics of the natural rate in several ways. First, it refers to the fact that unemployment can be self-perpetuating both for the individual concerned (because of loss of skills and motivation) and for the economy in aggregate. The rise in the natural rate is ascribed to the erosion of human capital and the loss of the motivation of the unemployed, particularly of the long-term unemployed, the development of an underclass and a culture of dependency, and increased power of insiders (those with jobs) relative to outsiders (the unemployed). Second, physical capital too becomes run down. Once a factory closes, it is difficult to reopen. Third, as time passes, insiders are able to strengthen their position *vis-à-vis* outsiders. These explanations of hysteresis focus on social dynamics and informational deficiencies that cannot be captured in the simple analysis of demand and supply.

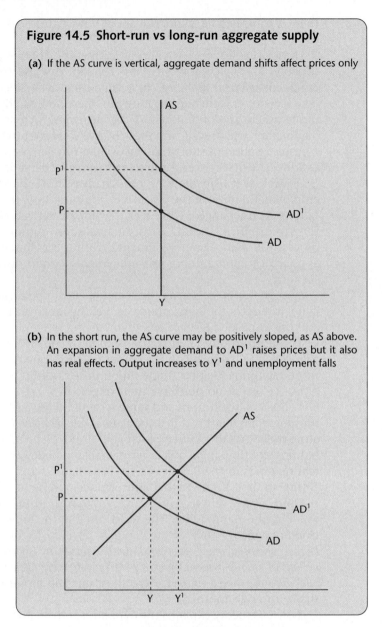

**Figure 14.5 Short-run vs long-run aggregate supply**

**(a)** If the AS curve is vertical, aggregate demand shifts affect prices only

**(b)** In the short run, the AS curve may be positively sloped, as AS above. An expansion in aggregate demand to AD$^1$ raises prices but it also has real effects. Output increases to Y$^1$ and unemployment falls

While the Phillips curve addresses the problem of short-term rigidities, many rigidities have their origins in long-term, enduring distortions in the labour market. Some are the result of market failure. The *market for lemons* case draws attention to a source of dysfunction of the market arising from asymmetrical knowledge. Suppose a person becomes unemployed, walks into another firm, enquires about the going rate of pay and offers to work for, say, 30 per cent less than this. If the market system runs smoothly, this should lead to the offer of the job. However, the market may not run smoothly. The offer to accept lower pay may arouse the suspicion of the employer. Does it signal a deficiency in the applicant's qualifications or character? The more 'flexible' the applicant, the more these suspicions may seem to be confirmed. The basic problem arises because of *asymmetric information* between the applicant's self-knowledge and the employer's perceptions of the applicant. The employer knows very little about your capabilities and reliability – only a fraction of what you know yourself – and is likely as a result to clutch at straws. Willingness to work for less than the going wage rate in this instance may signal not so much cheapness as desperation and some hidden flaw. (Hence the term 'market for lemons', lemons being an American slang word for bad quality.[6])

The *efficiency-wage theory* points to another type of rigidity deeply embedded in the market system. The theory states that employers often prefer to pay above the going rate because, in so doing:[7]

- they have a better chance of attracting and retaining better-quality employees;
- they placate trade unions – or remove the incentive for employees to join trade unions;
- they stimulate employees to work productively, with less need for monitoring (this is a variant of Henry Ford's 'economy of high wages' – Ford believed that paying higher wages gave his staff an incentive to work harder and more productively).

If one firm pays over the odds, there is no problem. But if all firms try to pay over the odds, the average level of pay rises. Eventually, equilibrium is reached at a higher-than-market-clearing wage, with residual unemployment. Efficiency-wage theory also offers an explanation of why pay levels may be rigid in the face of shifts in the demand curve – employers will be loath to be the first to cut pay.

The list of mechanisms interfering with the adjustment process of the market model can be extended, but the gist of the argument should now be clear. The different types of rigidities have different labels attached to them. Those emphasising the importance of state interference or monopoly power tend to be labelled 'classical'. Those emphasising not outside interference, but the rigidities arising from inherent failings in the market system itself (such as market for lemons, efficiency wages and menu costs) tend to be labelled (New) Keynesian. Each type of rigidity causes serious problems and is costly in a long-run dynamical sense, as well as in terms of short-run static efficiency.

New Keynesian rigidities are particularly difficult to deal with since they are less amenable to government action. They are more helpful in illustrating the complexity of the unemployment problem than in prescribing solutions for it. The policy implications of the demand and supply analysis, however, follow in a straightforward way from the diagnosis. Measures should be taken to reduce or eliminate labour market rigidities by:

- promoting awareness in trade unions of the link between pay demands and unemployment, and restraining abuses of their power,

---

[6] The concept originated with G. Akerlof, 'The market for lemons: quality, uncertainty and the market mechanism', *Quarterly Journal of Economics* (1970).

[7] J. Konings and P. Walsh identify the key feature of this model as the dual function of the wage from the employer's perspective: one function is to enable firms to attract the right type of labour, and the other is to create incentives for employees to work effectively, i.e. reduce efficiency costs: 'Evidence of efficiency wage payments in UK firm level plant data', *Economic Journal* (May 1994), p. 542.

- dispensing with statutory minimum wage legislation,
- lowering replacement ratios (by reducing income and payroll taxes, targeting social welfare to those who need it most and making unemployment assistance less open-ended),
- enhancing labour mobility through education, retraining and information,
- making product and service markets more competitive.

This list of measures resembles the standard 'supply-side' economics programme adopted by the UK, the US, New Zealand and Australia whose example has won a worldwide following. A case could also be made for introducing special measures to deal with the hysteresis problem, e.g. by programmes targeted at the long-term unemployed (community employment schemes, workfare, special training and employment subsidies).

## 14.4 The importance of demand

John Maynard Keynes (1883–1946) was the most influential economist of the last century. Because of him, macroeconomics came into existence as an independent component of economics. His masterpiece, *The General Theory of Employment, Interest and Money*, published in 1936, took five years to write. With remarkable self-confidence, he confided in a letter to George Bernard Shaw:

> I believe myself to be writing a book on Economic Theory which will largely revolutionise – not I suppose at once but in the next ten years – the way the world thinks about our problems.

The classical approach, then as now, identified the key reason for unemployment as being that real wages were too high or that 'workers were pricing themselves out of jobs'. Yet in time of recession, the main problem, from a firm's perspective, is not so much that labour is expensive, but that there is insufficient demand for the firm's output. Focusing on the demand-side of the labour market, Keynes argued that the relationship between real wages and the aggregate demand for labour was more uncertain and unstable than the market model suggested.

His basic argument can be summarised as follows. Suppose that all employees agreed to a large cut in nominal wages, with the objective of reducing unemployment. The positive effect of this action would be that, at given product prices, the real wage is lowered and demand for labour increases. Employers move downwards along the demand curve. Unfortunately, there is also a negative side. As real pay declines across the economy, workers and their families have less money to spend. Aggregate demand for goods and services in the economy also declines. Retailers, finding that sales are sluggish, cut back orders. Manufacturers have, as a result, less demand for their output and begin to cut product prices. The burden of servicing corporate debt increases and future returns on investment are discounted more heavily. Expectations about the future become depressed and business investment declines. The indirect negative effect of these factors on the demand for labour could easily offset the positive effects of lower pay. Thus Keynes's 'fundamental' objection to the classical model: there are, he stated, *no grounds for the belief that a flexible wage policy is capable of maintaining a state of full employment* (p. 267).[8]

In an economy where the workings of the price mechanism were slow and uncertain, the fundamental reason for unemployment in Keynes's view was a lack of effective demand. The *General Theory* laid the foundations for a revolution in thinking and for the evolution of the Keynesian paradigm. Key features of this new paradigm can be summarised under four headings:

1. *Investment demand tends to be highly unstable.* Investors base their decisions on expectations for the future. These expectations are volatile and are heavily influenced by what is happening now. Falling demand leads to pessimistic expectations of future demand. Pessimistic expectations tend to be self-fulfilling. What Keynes termed *'the unstable character of business expectations and investment'* lies at the root of the unemployment problem in a market economy (*General Theory*, p. 279).
2. *Investment fluctuations have repercussions well in excess of the initial change in spending because of the multiplier effect.* Investment generates income for those engaged in construction, road-building, etc. This income is spent on consumption, which in turn creates income for someone further down the line, and so on (the 'multiplier effect').
3. *Self-adjusting forces in the economy are weak and slow-moving, especially in the short run.* Keynes challenged not so much the logical coherence of the market approach as its practical relevance. Thus, he agreed that, as prices decline in a depression, the real value of money balances and government bonds increases and that, as a result, people will eventually spend more. Eventually, essential capital goods will also need to be replaced – such replacement can be postponed only for so long. Eventually, too, business expectations will improve as sentiment that 'the worst is over' takes hold. But the fact that these equilibrating mechanisms operate in the long run may be small consolation to people now unemployed. *In the long run we are all dead* is a favourite quotation of the Keynesian School.
4. *State intervention may be needed to speed up the adjustment process.* It could achieve this by ensuring consistency between the propensity of investors to invest and the propensity of consumers to save. Over time, Keynes argued, 'comprehensive socialisation of investment may prove the only means of securing an approximation to full employment'.

Keynes made a significant and lasting addition to our understanding of the unemployment problem. His work sparked off a new research programme involving intense study of the components of total demand, the interactions between them, and the linkages between aggregate demand and the monetary sector of the economy. Keynes accepted that pay rigidities could cause unemployment and that a decrease in unemployment would most likely require a fall in real pay and a high level of business confidence. He stressed the importance of maintaining a stable aggregate demand as the key to low unemployment, and he envisaged an

---

[8] Indeed, if prices fall by more than the initial nominal pay cut, real wages may end up increasing instead of falling. This is what Keynes meant by the assertion that 'there may be no method by which workers can reduce real pay through nominal wage bargains'.

**Figure 14.6 Aggregate demand and Keynesian aggregate supply curve**

active role for government in moderating fluctuations in demand via fiscal and monetary policies.

The Keynesian policy prescription can be illustrated by means of aggregate demand and supply analysis. Suppose the Keynesian aggregate supply curve (PES) is shaped like an inverted L, as in Figure 14.6. (This is, in effect, an extreme version of the positively shaped short-run AS of Figure 14.5.) Up to the point of full employment output $Q^*$, output can increase without initiating any increase in the price level. After $Q^*$, any effort to stimulate demand will lead only to higher prices. Suppose the economy were at a point like Q, with unemployed resources. This would be the appropriate time for a fiscal stimulus. If it succeeds in its aim, aggregate demand will shift outwards (from AD to AD′) and this will bring national output from OQ to OQ*, the full employment level. Thus, stimulation has been a highly effective instrument in this case. After $Q^*$ is reached, however, any further demand stimulus to AD″, say, will be inflationary.

Keynesian economics has stimulated research on the full employment level of output, on the causes of wage and price rigidities,[9] on the determinants of investment and on the different instruments which can be used to stimulate or contract the AD curve (tax reductions, direct spending by government, interest rate reductions). It provides important insights into the unemployment problem, not just in terms of short-term rigidities but also into the problem of extended demand stagnation such as that experienced in Japan during the past decade.

[9] An example of research on this topic is T.E. Bewley, *Why Wages Don't Fall during a Recession* (Cambridge, MA: Harvard University Press, 1999). Bewley confirms a long-held suspicion that opposition to nominal pay cuts emanates not just from employees but also from employers who oppose them on grounds of their adverse effect on employee morale. Using questionnaires and interviews, he found that executives were sensitive to the need to be, and appear to be, fair to their employees.

## 14.5 Technology, productivity and unemployment

At a micro-level, higher productivity and technological change often tend to destroy, rather than to create, jobs. The search for higher labour productivity and better technology, an imperative for the individual firm, leads managers to spend at least as much time analysing how to cut down the workforce as to add to it. More often than not, the decision to employ more people is taken as a last resort, after all other options have been tried. This makes the recommendations of the European Commission and the OECD urging greater investment in technology sound rather paradoxical. It is all the more puzzling since these policies are advocated as part of the solution to the unemployment problem.

Nobody denies that modern technological advance is labour-displacing in the sense that PCs replace typists, household machinery displaces domestic servants, and automation displaces operatives. This is the visible direct effect of improvements in productivity.[10] Most would also accept that, to the extent that these processes represent the replacement of boring and onerous human work by machinery, they are to be welcomed – in a sense, it is what the quest for higher living standards is all about. It would be perverse to prefer a situation in which more people were needed to complete a given task to one where fewer people were needed.

Yet technical progress can create serious distributional problems. If it proceeds too fast, those losing jobs may not be able to find alternative outlets in other industries. The problem can then be categorised as similar to that of skill or geographical mismatch and analysed in terms of the market model already described – an important transitional problem requiring flexible labour markets to resolve. Concern about the employment implications of technological advance is not something new to this generation; there have been many instances in history of opposition to new machinery on such grounds (see Box 14.2).

There is no compelling evidence to support the proposition that technical progress poses a long-term, systemic threat to the capacity of a modern economy to attain full employment. In the early 1800s, about 80 per cent of the UK working population was engaged in agriculture. The figure has now fallen to below 2 per cent. Rapid technical progress has made this massive shift possible. Fewer people are now engaged in producing food, and more are available for supplying other goods and services, such as comfortable housing and entertainment. Likewise, only 3 per cent of the US workforce is now required to supply most of America's food. Given sufficient time, major adjustment can take place without necessitating huge increases in unemployment. Such adjustment is not impoverishing: on the contrary, it is a necessary condition for attaining a higher living standard.

The main employment-creating aspects of advances in technology are indirect, and hence they are often overlooked:

1. As productivity increases, employees earn higher salaries. This leads to what are called the *income-generating effects* of higher productivity. Higher

---

[10] Although not as fast as one would think: 'we see computers everywhere but in the productivity statistics'. This statement by Robert Solow has become known as the 'Solow paradox'. Labour productivity growth fell rather than increased, despite the spread of computerisation. Only in the late 1990s did the long-awaited upsurge in productivity materialise.

> **Box 14.2** **Technological change and employment: the lessons of history**
>
> Forecasts that the next wave of technological change will cause high unemployment have frequently been made in the past. Today, these fears take a variety of forms: beliefs that computers and robots will soon take the place of unskilled labour, or that the rate of structural change in the economy is too high and will lead to overwhelming dislocations through technological unemployment. Historically, such gloomy predictions have been wrong. Increased productivity has been accompanied by rising demand for labour and rising real wages.
>
> In the 1820s, the 'Ricardian Socialists' argued that increased productivity from the introduction of machinery would reduce employment and put downward pressure on wages and on living standards. They were relying on an extended numerical example from Chapter 30 of David Ricardo's revised *Principles of Political Economy*, after which Ricardo concludes: 'the opinion entertained by the labouring class, that the employment of machinery is frequently detrimental to their interests, is not founded on prejudice and error, but is conformable to the correct principles of political economy'.
>
> Over the following half-century, capital accumulation and technical change caused average wages in the UK to more than double, while unemployment showed no appreciable rise.
>
> In the 1860s, Karl Marx wrote in *Das Kapital* that 'the greater the social wealth, the functioning capital ... the productivity of labour ... the greater the industrial reserve army [of the unemployed] ... the more extensive [are] the pauperised sections of the working class'.
>
> As capital intensity and labour productivity continued to increase, average wages in the UK once again roughly doubled, and unemployment did not appreciably rise.
>
> In the 1940s, after the Second World War, cyberneticist Norbert Weiner was forecasting that the invention of the computer would create massive technological unemployment. Over the following 40 years, average hourly wages in the US more than doubled, while unemployment increased by an average of 1 to 2 percentage points.
>
> *Source: The OECD Jobs Study* (1994).

purchasing power feeds into demand for goods and services (cars, videos, education, health). In this way, employment opportunities are created in a range of different industries. Historically, these income-generating effects on the demand for labour have tended to outweigh the direct labour displacement effects of new technologies.

2. Advances in technology are usually associated with specific machines and production processes. Demand for the products embodying the technology grows rapidly. Semiconductors, scientific instruments, aerospace and computers are the fastest growing industries in the OECD in terms of employment. Thus, technology advance, growth in labour productivity and employment growth often go together. Employment in high-tech, high-productivity industries has risen from 15 per cent of the total manufacturing workforce in 1970 to over 20 per cent at present, whereas employment in the low-tech industries has fallen from 58 per cent to 50 per cent in the industrial countries.

Higher labour productivity can be stimulated not only by technology, but also by threat of competition from cheaper imports. The liberalisation of imports into industrial countries has no doubt had such an effect, but researchers differ on the weight to be attached to each factor. What is certain is that import penetration of low-cost countries in the industrial countries' markets for labour-intensive goods is increasing. This is forcing firms to rationalise and to raise productivity. Workers, especially those with a few or outdated skills, are put under enormous pressure in these industries. The transitional effects are evident in lower wages for the unskilled, especially in the flexible labour countries like the US, and by higher unemployment in Europe.

The benefits of technological progress can be enjoyed in a number of different ways. For example, society could (a) produce the *same* output for *less* work, or (b) produce *even more* output for the *same* work, or (c) choose any number of intermediate output/work combinations. The third option seems to be the closest approximation of what has happened in most countries. Hours worked per person per year have fallen steeply, yet output per person has soared.[11]

The trend of decline in hours worked has been seized upon to argue for job-sharing (moves to a 30- or 35-hour week, 4-day work weeks, week-on/week-off, etc.). But trade unions are less keen on accepting the cut in real pay necessary to make such arrangements effective. In any event, the trend of decline in hours worked has flattened in recent years. Also, a large number of part-time workers appear to want to work longer hours. Only a modest easing of the unemployment problem, therefore, can be expected from an increased recourse to leisure. In the meantime, it makes good economic sense to ensure that labour markets are kept flexible so that workers are free to express their preferences (through flexible hours, contracting out and work-sharing), and also to ensure that the adjustment costs arising from increased labour productivity are kept to a minimum.

This analysis suggests that the best response to advances in technology and productivity change is, first, to embrace such change by *getting the right framework for the 'new economy' industries to emerge,* and second, *to shift the focus of labour market policies* away from 'passive' income support to 'active' policies (improving skills, employment subsidies and special employment schemes).

## 14.6 Labour market policies

While details of policies differ among countries, there is nonetheless a striking consensus about the broad framework of an effective strategy against unemployment. This consensus focuses on three themes:

- the importance of macroeconomic stability,
- the belief that jobs for the unemployed must be found primarily through faster growth in the private sector,
- the need to remove disincentives to work and disincentives to hiring created by the tax and social welfare system.

---

[11] Between 1938 and 1998, annual total hours worked per person fell from 2316 to 1550 in Germany, from 2267 to 1750 in the UK and from 2062 to 1960 in the US (A. Maddison, *Dynamic Forces in Capital Development*, Oxford: Oxford University Press, 1991; OECD).

Each of these themes can be found in the conclusions of most policy-oriented studies of unemployment (see Box 14.3).

## Macroeconomic policies

For a long time, roughly from the end of the Second World War to the oil crises in the early 1970s, Keynesian economics was seen as offering an effective and growth-promoting solution to the problem of unemployment. Whether it did so,

---

**Box 14.3  OECD jobs policy – 10 years later**

The OECD Jobs Study (1994) was an immensely influential project. It set the parameters for formulating, and judging, employment policy for the past decade. Its core set of policy recommendations were as follows.

1. Macro-stability – price stability and balanced budgets in the medium term.
2. Creation and diffusion of technological know-how.
3. Nurture an entrepreneurial climate.
4. Increase labour-cost flexibility.
5. Increase working-time flexibility.
6. Reform security of employment provisions (loosen mandatory restrictions on hiring and dismissals).
7. Reduce replacement ratios and other work disincentives.
8. Expand and enhance active labour policies (move from passive income support to 'active' measures such as job creation programmes for the long-term unemployed, back-to-work plans and reorientation interviews).

The first three measures could be described as output-enhancing measures. The labour market flexibility measures could be classified as labour market policies. Demand management policy gets an acknowledgement, albeit brief and cautious.

How effective has the OECD prescription been? In a 1998 survey Elmeskov *et al.* emphasise 'comprehensiveness', the need for a 'balanced mix of policies' which mutually reinforce innovative and adaptive capacity. Active labour market policies – measures initiated in order to improve the functioning of the labour market – are an important element in such a strategy. An updated version of the OECD Jobs Study would doubtless give more prominence to labour market problems arising from early retirements and pension systems, the growing polarisation of pay between skilled and unskilled, access to education and the inactivity rates of young and old workers. Note also that the Jobs Survey relates primarily to problems of the developed countries. Developing countries share some similar structural concerns. India, Morocco and South Africa, for instance, have over-regulated labour markets that hamper job creation and worsen unemployment. For countries like these, however, mass *under-employment* and pervasive low productivity represents the major economic challenge. Cyclical unemployment, which occupies much attention in the West, is a far less pressing issue in the Third World.

*Source: The OECD Jobs Study: Facts, analysis, strategies (Paris, 1994). J. Elmeskov, J.P. Martin and S. Scarpetta, 'Key lessons for labour market reforms: evidence from OECD countries' experiences' Swedish Economic Policy Review (Autumn 1998).*

in fact, is a matter of controversy. Indubitably, the heyday of Keynesianism coincided with record low unemployment. Equally, it would be hard to contest that Keynesian policies – and the widespread belief in the efficacy of these policies – kept business expectations high, helped investment and stimulated growth. Never before had the Western economies known such prolonged prosperity as that from the late 1940s to the early 1970s. Thereafter, Keynesian economics began to lose its magic touch. We discuss why in the next chapter. Emphasis has shifted to maintaining price stability so that both sides of the labour market can bargain over real prices and the forces of competition can be deployed to maximum effect. Government financial balance, it was argued, would assist by keeping taxes on labour low. As deflation replaces inflation as a perceived threat, the pendulum appears to be swinging back in favour of more proactivist macroeconomic policies. There has been a revival – with immodestly little attribution – of long-neglected Keynesian concepts such as the liquidity trap to explain why escape from recession can be so difficult.

## Supply-side measures and private sector growth

Output growth, higher demand for labour and lower unemployment are obviously interlinked. The present tendency is to emphasise 'supply-side' policies. This includes not only encouragement of private-sector growth by lower taxes, but also the elimination of rigidities in product markets such as monopoly in the services sector, or restrictive trading rules, which suppress job-creating opportunities. One conspicuous target has been state utility monopolies which stifled the development of new private industries. Their employees, sheltered from competition, have been able to set pay trends which were inappropriate for the more exposed private sector. The ultimate losers from this process were the unemployed.

## Reducing disincentives to work

This means ensuring a gap between after-tax pay and social security payments, avoidance of unemployment and poverty traps, curbing indirect costs of employing people (payroll tax, paperwork, social legislation), lowering standard income tax rates, reducing the power of trade unions, and removing biases against labour in the industrial incentive structure. There must be incentives for employees to accept jobs at competitive wages and incentives for employers to take account of the interests of the unemployed (particularly in the public sector).[12]

---

[12] These issues have been exhaustively surveyed in R. Layard, S. Nickell and R. Jackman, *Unemployment: Macroeconomic performance and the labour market* (Oxford: Oxford University Press, 1991). Dedicated to 'the millions who suffer through want of work' and citing some 500 references, the book wends its way through 580 pages of sophisticated economics to reach two broad conclusions about how to reduce unemployment. First, *reform the pay-bargaining system* in such a way as to secure lower pre-tax pay norms and achieve greater pay flexibility in response to adverse supply or demand shocks. Second, *revise the unemployment benefits scheme* by curbing open-ended duration of benefits: 'unconditional payment of benefits for an indefinite period is clearly a major cause of European unemployment' (p. 62). In place of open-ended benefit schemes, active labour market projects are recommended. These policy prescriptions have been accepted in principle, but not always vigorously implemented, in most developed countries.

## Wage formation process

Small countries have found that collective agreements can internalise labour market pressures, thus increasing the sensitivity of real wages to 'shocks'. There is ongoing debate, however, about the relevance of such agreements to larger countries. The UK and the US are resolutely opposed to them, while Germany, France and those espousing the European model are more favourably disposed. Collective agreements have certainly delivered pay restraint, and have done so effectively in the run-up to EMU; in some countries they have also been instrumental in securing broader labour market reforms.

## Active labour market policies and the long-term unemployed

Flexible markets generate jobs, but slowly. For this reason, much experimentation has been made with 'active' labour market policies, which are often designed to address the problems of the long-term unemployed by direct intervention. Active policies can be categorised into three types: (1) *job broking* – measures to improve the flow of information about vacancies such as provision of job centres; (2) *training and education* – provision of special courses designed to upgrade the motivation and skills of the unemployed, especially young 'drop-outs'; and (3) *direct job provision* through 'workfare' or public works programmes, often organised at community level, and special labour subsidies to the private sector attached to hiring long-term unemployed.[13]

The purpose of these policies is to reduce directly the number of unemployed people. One study showed that an increase in participation in active labour market programmes of 1 percentage point of the labour force reduces the unemployment rate by 1.5 percentage points.[14] But other studies show less positive results, perhaps because these programmes can have adverse as well as positive indirect effects on employment. The heavy costs to the government of implementing them (on average, active policies cost 1 per cent of GDP in developed countries) can *undermine employment elsewhere in the economy*. Also, too much emphasis on these schemes can lead to the neglect of the longer-term fundamental need to improve incentives and tackle rigidities.

## 14.7 Conclusions

A simple market approach argues that the key to reducing unemployment is (1) to enhance incentives for employers to expand their business, and (2) to achieve a reduction in the cost of hiring labour so that this extra business can be translated into more jobs. Policies are needed to address each of these requirements. In technical jargon, employers are discouraged by *product market rigidities* from expanding their business; and their extra business is not translated into enough expansion of employment because of *labour market rigidities*.

---

[13] L. Calmfors, 'Active labour market policy and unemployment – a framework for the analysis of crucial design features', *OECD Economic Studies*, no. 22 (Spring 1994).

[14] This elasticity is taken from Calmfors (1994, p. 27). See also Layard *et al.* (1991).

Labour market flexibility can be effective in generating jobs. However, higher paid and longer-lasting jobs require something more. Output-enhancing measures based on development of an entrepreneurial culture, adjustment to technological change and other 'supply-side' factors play an important role, as do effective education and training policies to upgrade skills. Incomes policy may also in certain circumstances be helpful. But if these measures are to succeed, pay bargaining must be attuned to the economy's needs. Collective pay deals can be useful in a crisis situation where one-off reforms in the labour market arrangements are being planned. They also are effective where trade unions and social partners are well informed, give genuine priority to unemployment and are able to deliver.

Market-based approaches do not imply that there is no role for government but, rather, that governments must act in concert *with* rather than *against* the market. Keynesian demand stimulation can work in certain situations. It is not coincidental that the Japanese government, the only government of a major OECD country to attempt to maintain high employment by fiscal expansion in the 1990s, started the decade with a debt:GDP ratio of only 20 per cent.

Labour market policies are not a panacea. One problem is that they tend to work slowly. Another difficulty is the limited effectiveness of labour market incentives when taken in isolation.[15] Studies of the effects of changes in payroll taxes, labour and social legislation, wage costs, income tax, employment subsidies, job training schemes and high replacement ratios often conclude that most firms are unaffected by the relevant measures, and that the number of jobs created by changes in the variable under study would be small.

It is important not to be discouraged by such findings. Even if the effects of any individual measure were negligible, the cumulative effect of a series of such measures could be extremely significant.

Some countries put more emphasis on maintaining a reasonable standard of living for the unemployed than others. But how is a 'reasonable' level to be defined and for how long should that level be maintained? The higher the level of social welfare and the more open-ended its duration, the higher the 'floor' on the wage level, since few will agree to work for less. Besides, given the high proportion of unskilled people among the unemployed, realistic alternative jobs will tend, at least initially, to be in the low-paid categories. Herein lies a serious dilemma for politicians. Another problem is that a policy of seeking to cut unemployment via labour market flexibility can often lead to an increase in job insecurity. This is not inevitable since, as we have seen, flexibility can come in many shapes besides labour turnover. Yet to many it is a worrying and unpopular outcome of the market approach. An article in *Time* magazine refers to the 'temping' of America – the increasing proportion of the workforce engaged in insecure and impermanent jobs, with little or no *esprit de corps* and diminished job satisfaction. US Secretary of Labor, Robert Reich, has referred to the 'anxious

---

[15] For example, Calmfors (1994) concludes: 'What contribution can active labour market policy make to fighting unemployment? On the basis of this exposition, my judgement would be that most countries in Western Europe could do better with more active programmes – if carefully designed – but not a lot better' (p. 38). This conclusion is consistent with those of J.P. Martin and D. Grubb, 'What works and for whom: a review of OECD countries' experience with active labour market policies', *Swedish Economic Policy Review*, Fall 2001.

class' of American workers. There is some evidence to support such a view. Part-time employment has accounted for a rising share of total employment, and the share of temporary work in total employment increased quite sharply in some countries such as the Netherlands and Spain, where legislation regulating employment contracts was relaxed.[16] As often in economics, one cannot give absolute priority to any one problem. Some compromise must be found between the brave new world of labour market flexibility, and society's need for commitment and cooperation.

Like it or not, labour market flexibility has been the dominant policy idea of recent years. Some countries find this a rather unpleasant pill to swallow and have been delinquent in following the prescription. But even in the most conservative parts of 'old Europe', the trend has been towards more flexibility. The 'tax wedge' has fallen, replacement ratios are being reduced, labour unions have become more constrained and work contracts less rigid. There has been a definite pay-off for these measures in terms of lower structural unemployment. Unfortunately this advance has been masked by the increase in cyclical unemployment in the early 2000s.

The success in restoring price stability, and the potential danger of spilling over into deflation, has changed the context of the unemployment debate. First, in a stable price environment, the labour market should run in a more efficient manner than under inflationary conditions where the price mechanism and the real wage and workers and employers' expectations are strongly distorted. Second, the asymmetric behaviour of pay and salaries (i.e. the fact that nominal pay follows prices upwards quite promptly, but is rigid downwards) has become an important reality to contend with. There has been an explosion of interest in finding explanations of this behaviour that are consistent with economic rationality. This subject used to be considered rather old-fashioned, and indeed one suspects that many old Keynesian wheels are being reinvented, and being duly published in the best journals as modern technical innovations. Third, the Phillips curve needs to be reassessed. When prices are stable or falling, it is true that an increase in the price level could be beneficial to the economy and could reduce unemployment. In this sense there is stronger medium-term trade-off between inflation and unemployment than was once believed. But the precise extent of the trade-off becomes harder to measure. This is because the Phillips curve tends to be flatter at low rates of inflation and the ratio of random factors ('white noise') to structural change becomes greater. Fourth, price stability means that the real value of pensions is no longer being eroded by inflation, and hence this element in the overall pay package and cost of labour has assumed much greater importance. The rising proportion of older people in the world's population adds further weight to this issue over time. This means that the problem of *non-active* labour is being perceived in many countries as no less important than the problem of *unemployed* labour.

---

[16] In the EU, the share of temporary contracts in total employment rose from 10 per cent in 1990 to 13 per cent in 2000, while the contribution of part-time work to jobs growth in the EU between 1995 and 2001 was over 70 per cent in Austria, Germany, Belgium and the Netherlands.

## Summary

1.  The standard international definition of unemployment identifies the unemployed as those of working age who, in a specified period, are without work and are both available for, and have taken specific steps to find, work. There are wide variations in unemployment between countries and within countries. Some sectors of the population, such as young people, migrants and lone parents, experience higher unemployment rates than others. Unemployment is also closely correlated with skill levels, with unskilled workers facing a higher risk of unemployment than skilled workers.

2.  The market model analyses unemployment in a demand–supply framework. In this model, the labour demand curve is assumed to be downward-sloping and the labour supply curve upward-sloping. Provided prices are flexible, supply equals demand and there is no unemployment. Shifts in demand and supply, of course, occur over time, but there is no *a priori* reason for believing that any of these events should cause either labour shortages or labour surpluses (unemployment). If unemployment does occur, the model pinpoints the culprit as pay rigidities and, more generally, lack of labour market flexibility, usually referring to the problem of rigidity in real pay and conditions of work. Discussion of the problem of unemployment from this perspective focuses on the causes of these real pay rigidities and on methods of removing them. Sources of such rigidities include trade union power, minimum wages, tax wedges, and replacement ratios.

3.  Nominal pay rigidities in the labour market tend to be more severe in the short run than in the long run. Because of this, inflation and deflation can impact severely on real output and unemployment in the short run. Sometimes, short-run unemployment can spill over into long-run consequences, via the *hysteresis* effect. In the long run, however, pay tends to follow prices, upwards and downwards.

4.  Focusing on the demand side of the labour market, Keynes argued that the relationship between real wages and the aggregate demand for labour was highly uncertain and unstable. In an economy where the workings of the price mechanism were too slow to ensure full employment, the fundamental reason for unemployment in Keynes's view was a lack of effective demand. While he accepted that pay rigidities could cause unemployment and that a decrease in unemployment would most likely require a fall in real pay, he stressed the importance of maintaining a high level of business confidence and aggregate demand as the key to low unemployment, and he envisaged an active role for government in moderating fluctuations in demand via fiscal and monetary policies.

5.  Technological advance can be labour-displacing and concern about its employment implications is not something new to this generation. However, there is no compelling evidence to support the proposition that technical progress poses a long-term systemic threat to the capacity of a modern economy to attain full employment. 'New economy' activities create more jobs than they destroy.

6.  Details of policies differ among countries, yet there is a striking consensus about the broad framework of an effective strategy against unemployment. This consensus focuses on the importance of macroeconomic stability, the belief that jobs for the unemployed must be found primarily through faster growth in the private sector, and the search for ways of minimising disincentives to work and to hire labour. These measures have helped to bring about a significant rise in employment opportunities.

# Questions for discussion

1. Why should high unemployment be a matter of concern for business?

2. (a) Explain how the supply and demand curves of labour are derived in the standard model. Comment on the realism of the model's assumptions relating to the labour market.
   (b) Show how technological progress might affect the labour market in this model.

3. 'Unemployment is high because wages are too high and employees are pricing themselves out of a job' (business economist).
   'Reducing pay and employing people in low-wage jobs will depress national spending and make unemployment even worse' (trade union official).
   Evaluate these two opposing views of the unemployment problem.

4. A national minimum wage has been introduced by many countries as a solution to the problem of 'underpaid' workers. How would you expect such a measure to affect the level of unemployment?

5. What is meant by hysteresis in the context of unemployment? Discuss the importance of this concept in assessing the economic costs of unemployment.

6. Who are the 'insiders' in the labour market and who are the 'outsiders'? Discuss the relevance of this distinction to current unemployment in Europe.

7. Is faster economic growth the answer to Europe's unemployment problem?

# Exercises

1. Provide statistics on unemployment trends in a country of your choice. What policies are currently being applied for reducing unemployment? What other policies would you recommend? (A useful source is the OECD's annual publication, *Employment Outlook*.)

2. Explain how business decisions might be affected by a country's unemployment rate. If you were investing in a region or a country, would you be attracted or deterred by the existence of high unemployment?

3. Suppose there was a sudden and unexpected increase in wage settlements in the economy. What policies would you propose to deal with the threatened rise in unemployment and inflation?

4. Explain why the rate of unemployment is higher for unskilled workers than for the highly skilled. List some of the implications of this different incidence for policy.

5. How would you expect the following developments to impact on unemployment?
   (a) Greater anxiety on the workers' part about job security.
   (b) A decline in the number of young entrants to the labour market.
   (c) The growing importance of Internet job listings.
   (d) A cut in income taxes.

Further reading

R. Layard, S. Nickell and R. Jackman, *Unemployment: Macroeconomic performance and the labour market* (Oxford: Oxford University Press, 1991) is a classic text, with over 500 references and a masterly review of the literature, even if it proposes less than startling policy conclusions at the end of this enterprise. Readers should also dip into J.M. Keynes's *General Theory* to savour for themselves the flavour of this masterpiece. A good, if slightly dated, source for analysis and statistical overview is *The OECD Jobs Study: Facts, analysis, strategies* (Paris: OECD, 1994). An update of the study is provided in *Implementing the Job Strategy – Assessing performance and policy* (Paris: OECD, 1999). Up-to-date statistics and commentary can be obtained from regular publications such as the OECD's *Employment Outlook* and the European Commission's *European Economy*.

# Appendix 14.1  Unemployment and inflation – the Phillips curve

## Origins

The Phillips curve (Figure A14.1) originated in a paper published in 1958 by Professor A.W. Phillips. The paper showed the existence of a strong negative relationship between inflation and unemployment in the UK for the period 1861–1957. Similar correlations were subsequently found to hold in other countries. Soon it was being suggested that governments could choose between different combinations of unemployment and inflation. Inflation-averse countries could opt for a point such as A with inflation of $OP_a$ and unemployment of $OU_a$. Unemployment-averse countries might prefer a point like B, with unemployment of $OU_b$ and inflation of $OP_b$. For some years, macroeconomic discussion focused on how to choose the most suitable point on the downward-sloping Phillips curve.

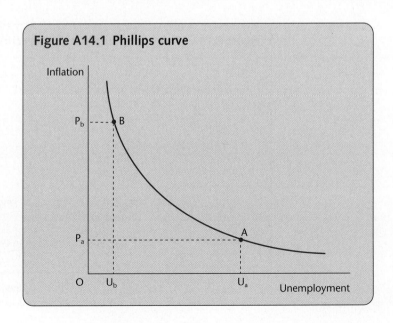

**Figure A14.1  Phillips curve**

### Two objections

From the late 1960s on, the Phillips curve came under fire on two counts. First, there were theoretical objections. In 1968, in separate articles, Edmund Phelps and Milton Friedman argued that there might be a short-run trade-off between unemployment and inflation but there was none in the long run.

Suppose the economy starts off at point A with an unemployment rate of 8 per cent and inflation of 2 per cent. The government wants to reduce unemployment from 8 per cent to 4 per cent. The Phillips curve shows that this can be achieved by allowing inflation to rise from 2 per cent to 5 per cent. In the short run the economy moves from point A to point B. At B we assume there is more inflation but wages catch up slowly and real wages fall – this is what generates the fall in unemployment. There is a 4 per cent reduction in unemployment and inflation rises by 3 per cent.

However, *this position is not sustainable*. The Phillips curve analysis above refers to the short run only. Sooner or later employees will demand compensation. They will realise that their purchasing power has been eroded as a direct result of the increase in inflation. Once compensation is achieved, real pay levels return to their original level and unemployment likewise. That is, in Figure A14.2 the economy will move back to C, identical to A, only now, employees' expectations of inflation have increased to 5 per cent and the short-run Phillips curve (SRPC) is shifted outward and to the right. Unemployment returns to its original level of 8 per cent and inflation is at 5 per cent. Thus in the long run there is no trade-off between inflation and unemployment. Expansionary policies that aim to reduce unemployment by increasing inflation will be successful only in the short run.

The Friedman–Phelps critique states that individuals learn from past experience ('mistakes'). They do not suffer from *money illusion* in the long run. It is not *nominal wages* but *real wages* (nominal wages adjusted for inflation) that matter. By incorporating price expectations into the Phillips curve, the alleged trade-off

Figure A14.2 Short- and long-run Phillips curves

between inflation and unemployment disappears: *the long-run Phillips curve (LRPC) is vertical*.

In formal terms the *expectations-augmented Phillips curve* emerges as follows. Assume expected inflation for this year is the same as last year's:

$$\pi_t^e = \pi_{t-1}$$

where $\pi$ = price inflation and superscript 'e' = expected. The Phillips curve equation then becomes:

$$\pi_t = \pi_{t-1} - \beta(\mu_t - \mu_n) + v_t$$

where  $\mu_t$ = actual unemployment rate
$\mu_n$ = 'natural' long-run rate of unemployment
$v_t$ = supply-side shocks.

Expected inflation can differ from actual inflation for two main reasons: aggregate supply-side shocks ($v$) or aggregate demand shocks, which cause $\mu_t$ to exceed $\mu_n$, the effect being determined by parameter $\beta$. Adaptive expectations implies that inflation next year will equal inflation this year provided $\mu = \mu_n$ and $v = 0$.

The second objection was that inflation could be caused by factors other than a lowering of the unemployment rate. Thus, a rise in oil prices causes an upward ratchet effect on consumer prices, which can easily feed into a wage/price spiral. Hence, inflation could increase without affecting the unemployment rate. If that level of unemployment happened to be high, we would be in a situation of *stagflation*.

## Structural unemployment and the natural rate

The long-run Phillips curve will be vertical at a point that is called the *natural rate of unemployment*. Regardless of the inflation rate, in the long run the economy will return to its underlying *natural rate of unemployment* or *non-accelerating-inflation rate of unemployment (NAIRU)*. The actual unemployment level at that point is determined by the structural factors mentioned in the text such as replacement ratios, trade union influences, minimum pay levels and so on. Thus structural unemployment and NAIRU are closely related. Note that NAIRU is not fixed. It is influenced strongly by labour market policies and structures.

## New consensus and the LRPC

The above framework laid the theoretical groundwork for new consensus macro policies. It indicated that activist demand management could not achieve any permanent reduction in unemployment. It suggested that low inflation (price stability) could be attained without any long-run impact on employment, though there would be a short-run cost.

Supposing we wish to move from high inflation point F to low inflation point G (Figure A14.3), how will this affect welfare? In the long run there appears to be no costs; we move down the LRPC to G. However, the only way to get to G might be via H. Hence, in the short run significant costs may be incurred in terms of higher unemployment. This cost will be greater the slower employers and employees are to adjust to the new policy regime. Knowledge of the Phillips curve

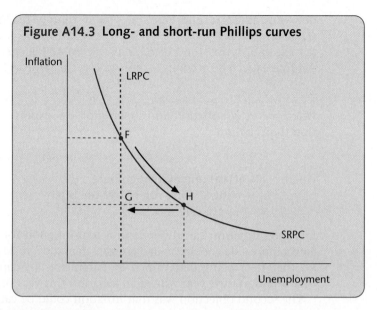

Figure A14.3 Long- and short-run Phillips curves

enables us to estimate the *sacrifice ratio*. This is defined as the percentage of real GDP that must be foregone to reduce inflation by 1 percentage point. Estimates of the sacrifice ratio range up to a value of 5, implying that to reduce inflation by one percentage point involves a cost in terms of discounted present value of about 5 percentage points of GDP. Thus, disinflation can be costly in the short run, as the experience of France and Argentina in the 1990s and of the UK and the US in the 1980s testifies.

## Revival of the Phillips curve

The Phillips curve remains an important concept. Generally, as labour markets tighten, earnings also rise and, for given productivity, this feeds into prices. During the 1990s, however, something strange happened in several Western economies (UK and US in particular). Labour markets tightened, wages increased and unemployment fell, but *without the inflation that would have accompanied such an outcome in the past*. How can this be explained? One candidate is that new consensus policies (labour market flexibility, credibility of anti-inflation commitment, and the process of globalisation) have caused a steep decline in the NAIRU. A second factor might be the rise in productivity associated with the new economy (computerisation and the Internet). This reduced unit costs, and hence held down price inflation, even though wages were rising rapidly. A third factor derives from the hysteresis argument. The boom of the 1990s led to a fall in short-term unemployment that in due course, by changing attitudes and morale of the affected workers, translated into long-run improvements in the labour market. One small indicator of this is the finding that the 2.6 percentage point fall in the US unemployment rate between 1992 and 1997 accounted for a 3.0 per cent decrease in the youth crime rate.

Another major development of recent years has been the consolidation of price stability in the global economy. Structural changes have resulted in the Phillips curve becoming much flatter than before. In the context of zero inflation and deflation, the ratio of 'white noise' to genuine price changes increases markedly. Also, there is renewed focus on the downward nominal rigidity of wages, leading to discussion of near-rational Phillips curves and a revival of interest in Keynesian analysis of this problem. In other words, at very low inflation and *a fortiori* with deflation, a reversal of trend to higher prices could well be an effective way of reducing unemployment, *even in the medium to long term*. There is thus evidence of a more enduring trade-off between inflation and unemployment than was formerly believed.

*Sources*: A.W. Phillips, 'The relation between unemployment and the rate of change in money wage rates in the United Kingdom 1861–1957', *Economica* 25 (November 1958); C.D. Romer and D. Romer (eds), *Reducing Inflation: Motivation and strategy* (Chicago: Chicago University Press, 1997); youth crime rate statistic refers to paper by Richard B. Freeman and W.M. Rodgers quoted in *Business Week*, 21–28 August, 2000. G. Akerlof, W. Dickens and G. Parry, 'The macroeconomics of low inflation', *Brookings Papers on Economic Activity*, Vol. 1, 2000, and *European Economy*, Supplement A, October/November 2001 provide excellent surveys of the literature.

## Chapter 15

# Fiscal policy, budget deficits and government debt

## Introduction

Budget deficits, excessive government debt and high taxes have become an almost universal focus of concern. Thirty years ago, governments worried much less about these matters. Management of the public finances, in the sense of balancing the books and keeping debt levels under control, was considered a rather pedestrian exercise. Fiscal policy was judged primarily in terms of its success in dampening economic fluctuations and maintaining full employment. In recent times, this counter-cyclical function of public finances has been downplayed. Keynesian economics, from which the era of fiscal activism drew its intellectual sustenance, has declined in prestige. Fiscal *balance* and fiscal *consolidation* have replaced fiscal *activism* as the conventional target of fiscal policy.

Why has *fiscal balance* become a policy priority in so many countries? It reflects a profound change in thinking about the role of fiscal policy in a modern economy. This change in perspective has had an important impact on the business environment, as is evident in the calls for smaller and more efficient government, lower taxes and more priority for the private sector.

## Chapter outline

This chapter describes and explains the origins of this new fiscal policy environment.

1. The essential features of counter-cyclical fiscal policy.

2. The limits of fiscal activism, drawing on the concept of 'crowding-out'.

3. The burgeoning size of public sector debt and the constraints this imposes on fiscal policy.

4. New perspectives on fiscal policy: case study of the European Union.

## 15.1 Counter-cyclical fiscal policy

Counter-cyclical, or Keynesian, fiscal policy ruled supreme throughout most of Western Europe, and in many other countries, from the early 1950s to the mid-1970s. This period was a 'golden age' of full employment and rapid growth, and activist fiscal policy was given much of the credit for this success. The vocabulary and mode of thinking of Keynesian economics still remains influential, although much less so than in the past.

The basic message of counter-cyclical policy is that governments should run budget deficits in times of recession, and reduce them in times of economic boom. Counter-cyclical fiscal policy proved very attractive. It proposed an antidote to business fluctuations which both had a theoretical foundation and yet which, unusually for economics, was comparatively painless to administer. It suggested that government could spend more without the private sector having to spend less. Even more radically, it raised the possibility that, *because* the public sector increased its spending, the private sector would be able to spend more also. This happy message contrasted with the image of economics as the 'dismal' science, or the science of scarcity!

The problem addressed by Keynesian theory can be illustrated with an AS/AD diagram (Figure 15.1). The Keynesian AS curve is drawn with an inverted L-shape, flat up to the point of full-employment output, then vertical once this point is reached at $y^*$. Once full employment is reached, any further increases in aggregate demand, such as that from AD to AD', will result in higher prices. Real output cannot be increased beyond the full employment level. Hence, once the output gap has been reduced to zero (i.e. actual = potential GDP), expansion of demand through budget deficits will be inflationary.

Now consider points to the left of full employment output. Keynes argued that an economy could become stuck at a point below full employment (such as $y_2$)

**Figure 15.1    The Keynesian aggregate supply curve and fiscal policy**

for considerable periods of time. At this point, output is well below its 'potential' level (recall Chapter 11 on potential GDP). The problem at $y_2$ is one of insufficient *demand*, not insufficient *supply*.

The prescription for this situation is to increase the level of aggregate demand, i.e. to shift the AD curve outwards. This could be done by raising public sector expenditure or by reducing taxation. Fiscal expansion would stimulate, through a multiplier effect, consumer and investment spending. Such action would short-cut the need to wait for the longer-term adjustment mechanisms of falling prices and wages to come into operation.

The fiscal rule suggested by this approach was *fiscal expansion* when the economy is operating below the full employment level, and *fiscal contraction* when the economy is at full employment.

One initial, and still heard, criticism of fiscal expansion is that the state could not 'afford' to raise spending. During a recession, tax revenues are low because of falling incomes and profits, while public spending is inflated because of higher unemployment payments. Expanding the deficit appears to be a recipe for making an already bad budgetary situation even worse. Also government borrowing to finance the higher deficit might pre-empt private savings, thereby leaving less funds available for private investors. Interest rates would be driven up and the private sector would be 'crowded out'. One way or another, an increase in public spending would have to be financed by a decrease in private spending. The *net* impact of a fiscal expansion, according to this view, would be to increase the size of the public sector, not the level of total output or aggregate demand.

Advocates of counter-cyclical policy argued that the 'affordability' of the fiscal expansion was the wrong issue to address. In conditions of high unemployment, fiscal expansion can be financed largely, and perhaps even entirely, *through increases in taxation revenue obtained from higher output*. This higher output could be generated through mobilisation of the unemployed. As Keynes pointed out:

> When we have unemployed men and unemployed plant, and more savings than we are using at home, it is utterly imbecile to say that we cannot afford these things. For it is with the unemployed men and the unemployed plant, and with nothing else, that these things are done.[1]

Interest rates may or may not increase as a result of higher government spending, but any adverse effects on investment and consumption through higher interest rates (the 'crowding-out' effect) would be offset by the boost to income from higher public spending, lower taxation and greater business confidence. Thus, a rise in public debt during a recession should not be regarded as a sign of government profligacy. When the economy is at the bottom of the cycle, the economy needs enterprise and spending, not saving, to restore its fortunes. When normal accounting conventions urge the government to cut back spending, that is the time to increase it.

The counter-cyclical fiscal model became an integral part of economics courses after the war. Keynesian fiscal theory transformed not only the way economists thought about fiscal policy, but also the way fiscal policy was conducted in industrial countries. Governments committed themselves to full employment and

---

[1] J.M. Keynes, article in the *Evening Standard* in 1928. Quoted in R. Skidelsky, *John Maynard Keynes: The economist as saviour 1920–1937* (London: Macmillan, 1992).

economists claimed to have the necessary technical tools to guide them to this objective, through active and vigorous use of fiscal policy.

Research on the application of fiscal policy during this period concentrated on three main issues: (1) the distinctive roles of fiscal and monetary policy had to be clarified; (2) some way had to be found of identifying accurately the shortfall, or excess, in aggregate demand that an economy was experiencing at any one time; and (3) the size of the fiscal 'injection', the net change in public spending needed to shift aggregate demand to the required degree, had to be determined.[2]

## The policy mix

Fiscal policy was generally regarded as a more effective counter-cyclical tool than monetary policy. Recall the 'long and variable lags' in the operation of monetary policy which made it unsuitable for fine-tuning. Also, monetary policy is permissive only – an economy can be flooded with liquidity, interest rates may fall, but investors cannot be forced to invest. Nor, if the economy is booming and business expectations are buoyant, will interest rates be able, on their own, to halt an excessive increase in aggregate demand. Fiscal policy, by contrast, has a direct impact on demand. The government can build a road or an airport or new schools. Equally, it can directly switch off spending. Hence, it was argued that the proper policy mix is to combine an *active* fiscal policy with an *accommodating* (i.e. supporting) monetary policy.

## How much extra aggregate demand is needed?

To be effective, counter-cyclical fiscal policy requires accurate information on the current level of GDP and on the gap between it and potential GDP. Identifying the size of the gap between potential and actual output, as we saw earlier, involves painstaking research and good judgement, and even then can be a hazardous exercise. Keynesian economics gave a tremendous boost to the development of applied macroeconomic research and national income accounting. Large econometric models of the economy were formulated, comprising hundreds of equations, and new ways of estimating their parameters were devised. The behaviour of the separate components of aggregate demand has also been extensively researched. Our knowledge of how the economy operates has been enormously enriched as a result. But, as the economy becomes more complex, the values of these parameters change in important but unpredictable ways. Hence the need for judgement. The problem for fiscal policy is that, unless the size of the required increment (or decrement) in aggregate demand can be accurately determined, active fiscal policy cannot be successfully applied.

## How much fiscal impulse?

This is another thorny issue. Suppose actual GDP was €100 billion and potential GDP was €120 billion. At first sight, it might appear that a €20 billion injection of

---

2 In terms of Figure 15.1, assuming that policy-makers knew that present output was $y_2$ and full employment (potential) output was $y^*$, how much injection of extra demand would be needed from government to ensure that the economy reached $y^*$? Recall that government intervention was needed since, by definition, the economy was locked into $y_2$ equilibrium by market forces. This was the 'under-employment equilibrium'.

government spending would close the gap. But this is incorrect. According to the *theory of the multiplier*, aggregate demand would increase by a multiple of the initial injection. To see this, suppose the government were to spend an extra €20 billion on roads and imagine the following sequence of events.

● The initial injection of €20 billion accrues to employees and suppliers of materials. Suppose they spend €16 billion and save €4 billion. The amount saved 'leaks out' of the economy, but the €16 billion stays active and now constitutes income for other sectors of the economy.
● Employees on the road project may spend their additional income on automobiles or new houses. This gives a boost to the car industry and the construction industry, and to their employees and shareholders.
● Assume that the recipients of the €16 billion of extra income decide to spend €13 billion and save €3 billion. This €13 billion now constitutes income for somebody else.
● Suppose they in turn spend €10 billion and save €3 billion, and so on.

We see that the initial outlay of €20 billion has generated spending of €39 billion (16 + 13 + 10), as well as €10 billion saving (4 + 3 + 3), and the process has by no means ended. Notice also that the additional savings will be available to buy the bonds issued by the government to finance the original €20 billion outlay on the road project.

This description of the multiplier presents an intuitive and much simplified version of what in reality is a complex process. For one thing, account should be taken of 'leakages' from income into taxes and imports as well as savings. Also, different types of spending or tax concessions have different multipliers, since the propensity to consume differs among sectors of the economy and different income groups. Moreover, the linkage between the real and financial sectors has to be incorporated in the multiplier formula.

Before deciding on the amount of fiscal stimulus to provide, information is also needed on the present fiscal stance of the government, taking account of the economy's cyclical position. As the economy fluctuates, both government spending and taxation revenues behave in a way which tends to dampen these fluctuations. Thus, at given tax rates, tax revenues automatically get larger as the economy recovers, and fall as it declines. Government spending, on the other hand, tends to fall during an upturn and rise during a recession. The budget deficit, therefore, acts as an *automatic stabiliser*, contracting when the economy is expanding, and expanding when the economy contracts. Just because a government runs a deficit does not mean that it is pursuing an active counter-cyclical policy. It may simply be passively permitting the automatic stabilisers to do their work. Active policy is reflected in changes in *non-automatic* budget balances. This can be estimated by subtracting the automatic element from the deficit. The resultant estimate is called the *structural* deficit or surplus. It indicates the extent to which government is using discretion to moderate the impact of its net spending on the economy.

Examining the pattern of deficits and surpluses during the past decade, we see a marked shift towards fiscal conservatism (Tables 15.1 and 15.2). During the 1990s budget deficits were generally more pervasive than budget surpluses, but towards the end of the decade the behaviour of the industrial countries had changed. *Thus in 1993 only three out of 29 industrial countries had budget surpluses.*

## Table 15.1 Industrial countries: budget balances (% of GDP)*

|  | 1993 | 2000 | 2003 |
|---|---|---|---|
| European Union | 6.5 | +0.8 | −3.0 |
| Japan | −1.4 | −7.4 | −7.1 |
| US | −3.4 | +1.2 | −6.0 |
| Germany | −3.3 | +0.1 | −3.9 |
| France | −6.1 | −1.3 | −4.0 |
| Italy | −9.6 | −0.6 | −2.8 |
| UK | −7.8 | +4.0 | −2.5 |
| Canada | −7.3 | +3.1 | +1.5 |
| Spain | −7.5 | −0.6 | −0.2 |
| Netherlands | −3.3 | +2.0 | −2.4 |
| Belgium | −6.6 | +0.1 | −0.5 |
| Sweden | −13.4 | +3.9 | +0.4 |
| Austria | −4.1 | −1.6 | −1.5 |
| Denmark | −4.5 | +2.6 | +1.4 |
| Finland | −8.0 | +7.0 | +2.0 |
| Greece | −12.1 | −1.9 | −1.4 |
| Portugal | −7.0 | −2.9 | −4.0 |
| Ireland | −2.7 | +4.3 | −1.1 |
| Switzerland | −4.3 | +2.6 | −2.2 |
| Norway | −1.4 | +15.1 | +8.3 |
| Iceland | −4.5 | +2.5 | −0.1 |
| Australia | −3.9 | +0.9 | +0.4 |
| New Zealand | −0.7 | +0.7 | +2.0 |

* Negative sign indicates a budget deficit; plus sign a budget surplus.

Source: IMF, World Economic Outlook (May 1996 and September 2003).

## Table 15.2 Fiscal policy stance, 1990, 2000 and 2004 (% of GDP)

|  | 1990 | 2000 | 2004 |
|---|---|---|---|
| **European Union** | | | |
| Total | −3.6 | +0.8 | −2.5 |
| Of which:  Cyclical | +1.6 | +1.4 | −1.2 |
| Structural | −5.2 | −0.6 | −1.3 |
| **United States** | | | |
| Total | −2.7 | +1.2 | −5.6 |
| Of which:  Cyclical | +1.1 | +0.6 | −0.7 |
| Structural | −3.8 | +0.6 | −4.9 |
| **Japan** | | | |
| Total | +2.9 | −7.4 | −6.5 |
| Of which:  Cyclical | +1.2 | −0.4 | −0.6 |
| Structural | +1.7 | −7.0 | −5.9 |

Source: IMF, World Economic Outlook (May 1996 and September 2003).

*By 2000, the number of surplus countries had risen to 18.* While buoyant economic conditions contributed to this turnaround (only 9 had a surplus in 2003), the adoption of new consensus policies with emphasis on macro stability played a more crucial role. In the EU in particular, the Maastricht criteria set strict limits on the size of budget deficits and Member States were urged to achieve fiscal balance over the medium term.

One must be careful about reading off a country's fiscal stance from simple examination of its fiscal balance. A budget deficit is not conclusive evidence of an expansionary budget. For example, if the economy is in recession, a budget deficit will tend to happen because of the operation of automatic stabilisers. To discover the fiscal stance, we need to delve deeper and find out what, if any, extra measures the authorities have taken in response to the situation. To do this, the budget balance is decomposed into a *cyclical* component and a *structural* component. Suppose, for example, the overall budget deficit was €1000 million and the economy was in a recession. Now replace actual GDP with potential GDP, and estimate the level of public spending, tax revenues and budget deficit corresponding to that (higher) level of output. We assume unchanged tax rates and a given set of spending rules. The deficit so estimated is termed the structural deficit. Assume it amounted to €250 million. The cyclical deficit is defined as the difference between the actual deficit (€1000 million) and the structural deficit (€250 million), i.e. €750 million.

A country's structural budget balance is a rough indicator of the extent to which discretionary fiscal measures are being applied. Thus the US and the EU both reduced significantly the size of their structural deficit during the 1990s (Table 15.2). Since then, as the recession has deepened, the downward trend in the structural deficit has gone into reverse. During 2000–04, US fiscal policy has been particularly aggressive, with the structural balance widening by 4 percentage points of GDP, from a surplus of 0.6 to a deficit of 4.9. This contrasts with the anaemic (or more cautious, depending on your view) fiscal stance of the EU. Member States of the EU were bound by the Stability and Growth pact guidelines, allowing a maximum deficit of only 3 per cent of GDP.

Since 1990, however, Japan has been a dramatic outlier. Every year it has run a budget deficit, and it is hard to believe that only a short while ago it was regarded as an icon of fiscal conservatism. Japan's commitment to fiscal activism must count as by far the most striking example of counter-cyclical policy in recent times. The use of discretionary action has not solved Japan's economic problems, nor has it restored growth, but it averted what might otherwise have been a catastrophic slump with global repercussions.

The aggressive deployment of fiscal policy in Japan contrasts with its more cautious use elsewhere in the world. Our next task is to consider why governments have generally become more conscious of the serious limitations of fiscal activism and their reluctance to resort to it except in extreme circumstances.

## 15.2 The limits of fiscal activism

The scope for using fiscal policy to stimulate economic activity in the short term, in the traditional sense of taking action that would widen budget deficits, appears to be very circumscribed at present. (OECD, *Economic Outlook*, July 1993)

Report after report on fiscal policy in the 1990s referred to the lack of *room for manoeuvre* in budgetary policy and to the likelihood that further deterioration in budget deficits *would depress overall demand through its negative effect on confidence rather than support it.*[3] The 'unsound financial position' of many industrial countries led to a conservative approach to fiscal policy. The Delors White Paper on competitiveness, for instance, concluded that, over the long term, Member States' *budgetary policy will have to contribute to increased national savings, implying budget deficits of 0–1 per cent of GDP.* Achieving fiscal consolidation forced many governments to put proposals for counter-cyclical deficits on the back-burner at least until the structural deficit problem had been resolved.

The change in perspective on fiscal activism can be explained under five main headings: knowledge gaps and time-lags, political intervention, inefficiencies of a

---

**Box 15.1** **The limits of fiscal activism**

### Knowledge gaps and time-lags
- What is potential GDP?
- Poor forecasting record
- Recognition, decision and implementation lags.

### Political intervention
- Deficits politically more attractive than surpluses
- Political (electoral) cycles – spending decisions influenced by timing of elections rather than stage of the business cycle.

### Inefficiencies of the public sector
- Growth in public spending leads to a heavy tax burden which penalises entrepreneurship and wealth creation
- High labour costs.

### Private sector response
- Lucas critique – zero trade-off between inflation and unemployment unless inflation is a one-off 'surprise'
- Ricardian equivalence considerations.

### Empirical experience
- Deficits do not cure unemployment.

### Deterrent effects of public debt overhang
- Sustainable public debt
- Generational accounting.

---

[3] These were the actual phrases used in Commission of the European Communities, *Growth, Competitiveness, Employment* (Brussels, 1993) (Delors Report), pp. 52–3. Similar views were expressed in UNICE, *Making Europe More Competitive: Towards world class performance* (the UNICE Competitiveness Report) (Brussels, June 1994).

growing public sector, private sector reactions (the Lucas critique), and historical evidence. In the next section, we address a further limitation: the deterrent effects of the public debt overhang (see Box 15.1).

## Knowledge gaps and time-lags

Fiscal activism, like any other type of policy intervention, works effectively only if the authorities have adequate information on the problem they are supposed to be addressing. In addition to accurate information on the current level of aggregate demand and reliable forecasts of aggregate demand, one also needs estimates of what are called *policy lags*. Policy lags refer to the lapse of time between recognition of the need for counter-cyclical action, actual implementation of the required measures, and the impact of these measures on the economy.

The amount of information available to the authorities often falls far short of these requirements. Fiscal policy, like monetary policy, operates with *long and variable lags*, and these lags hinder and can frustrate its effective deployment. The information problem is a valid qualification on the use of fiscal activism and is widely recognised as such. However, *on its own*, it does not amount to a compelling case against counter-cyclical policy. A dedicated Keynesian might infer that it simply signals the need to improve the quality and timeliness of the information. Also, informational deficiencies have beset the application of fiscal policy since its beginning. They have scarcely become worse over time and do not explain why counter-cyclical policies seem to have become less effective over time.

## Political interference

In theory, it should be possible to manage fiscal policy in such a way that budget deficits in recession are followed by budget surpluses in boom, with a consequent rise and fall in public debt accordingly. Yet in practice, public debt tended to rise over time as a proportion of GDP in countries that pursued active counter-cyclical policies. There has been a systematic bias towards deficits in the operation of fiscal policy. One reason for this is that deficits are more popular politically than surpluses. A government which tries to retrench during a boom will appear 'mean' and doctrinaire. By contrast, an expansionary budget will nearly always be popular.[4] Spending projects initiated during the recession tend to take on a life of their own. They become difficult to switch on and off according to the vicissitudes of the economy, as the textbooks ordain they should do.

Another limitation on fiscal activism is the intrusion of explicitly political considerations in the *timing* of fiscal action. The popularity of expansionary policies tempts governments to apply them in the run-up to election, regardless of economic circumstances. These 'political cycles' create, rather than suppress, economic instability. Also, political considerations lead to some budget measures (particularly the unpopular ones) being taken immediately *after* an election in certain circumstances. For example, a newly elected government might wish to

---

[4] Paradoxically, the time a contractionary budget becomes more acceptable electorally is during a recession, when it is inappropriate from an economic viewpoint.

administer unpleasant budgetary medicine as soon as possible after an election in the hope that the public's recollection of its actions might have receded by the time of the next election. Economic and political motivations become inter-woven. It is not surprising, therefore, that fiscal policy has often been found to operate in a pro-cyclical, rather than a counter-cyclical, manner.[5] When the gov-ernment sector is small, this is not too serious a problem. When public spending reaches over 40 per cent of GNP, politically motivated fiscal action can have serious consequences for the economy. Fiscal activism, which originated as a solution to the problem of economic stability, itself becomes the problem.

## Inefficiencies of the public sector

In Europe, government spending relative to GDP rose from 37 per cent in 1970 to over 47 per cent in 2003 (Table 15.3). In the early 1990s, the ratio in Sweden (67 per cent), Denmark (59 per cent) and Norway (58 per cent) was higher still. Most of the increase occurred during the 1970s and early 1980s. Since then, the upward trend has been halted. A similar pattern of behaviour is observable in the US, though current spending is still much higher than its 1937 level of only 8.6 per cent of GDP.

High government spending relative to GDP became a source of concern for a number of reasons. First, it was associated with excessively high taxation, which undermined incentives to hire labour and to invest. Small businesses were

### Table 15.3 Government spending (% of GDP)

| | Pre-Second World War (about 1937) | 1970 | 1984 | 1990 | 2000 | 2003 |
|---|---|---|---|---|---|---|
| EU* | 29.0 | 37.4 | 50.0 | 48.1 | 45.8 | 47.4 |
| Japan | 25.4 | 19.4 | 32.9 | 32.6 | 39.8 | 41.1 |
| US | 8.6 | 31.6 | 35.6 | 35.5 | 32.3 | 35.2 |
| France | 29.0 | 38.9 | 52.5 | 50.7 | 52.8 | 53.6 |
| Germany† | 42.4 | 38.5 | 47.6 | 45.3 | 45.9 | 48.4 |
| Netherlands | 19.0 | 42.4 | 59.6 | 54.8 | 45.3 | 47.1 |
| Ireland | ... | 39.6 | 51.3 | 43.3 | 32.0 | 35.4 |
| Italy | 24.5 | 34.2 | 49.4 | 54.3 | 46.9 | 47.8 |
| UK | 30.0 | 37.3 | 45.3 | 42.2 | 36.9 | 41.5 |

* EU figures refer to average of 12 Member States except for 1970 which include only nine Member States, and 1937 refers to five states (France, Germany, Italy, UK, Netherlands). Any resultant distortions are very small.

† The 2000 and 2003 figures for Germany include the former East Germany and are not strictly comparable with the figures for earlier years.

*Source*: *European Economy*, Annual Reports, successive years; pre-Second World War figures taken from Vito Tanzi and Ludger Schuknecht, *Public Spending in the 20th Century* (Cambridge: Cambridge University Press, 2000).

---

[5] P. Lane, 'The cyclical behaviour of fiscal policy: evidence from the OECD', *Journal of Public Economics* (forthcoming).

particularly affected, since they lacked the capacity of large multinationals to avoid taxes through 'spreading' revenues and costs in different tax jurisdictions. Second, high spending on transfer payments created problems. Excessively generous 'safety nets' for less fortunate citizens eroded incentives to work. Third, the conviction took root that government was in some vague sense 'too big' and that substantial efficiency gains could be obtained by devolving some public sector activities to the free market. Australia, New Zealand and the UK took the lead in the 1980s in rethinking and redesigning the role of the state so as to prepare their economies for the greater competition of an open trade environment. Their example was rapidly followed. Even the Scandinavian countries, long regarded as the epitome of successful market socialism, began to reshape their economies in a more market-oriented way. They are still in the process of downsizing their public sectors. The UNICE Competitiveness Report expressed a business view of the effects of public sector intervention in the European economy:

> [Growth in public spending] has resulted in a heavy tax burden which penalises entrepreneurship and wealth creation, makes labour costs too high via taxes on production, [and] is also a factor in reducing the attraction of Europe as a location for investment. (*Making Europe More Competitive: Towards world class performance*, UNICE Competitiveness Report, Brussels, June 1994, p. 51)

The report urged governments *to set a target reduction for the share of public expenditure in GDP by the end of the century*. Similar sentiments were articulated in the proposals of the Republican Party's 'Contract with America' in the US in the mid-1990s. These initiatives created a climate of public opinion that cleared the way for radical fiscal reforms. The pressure for more spending generated by the 2000s recession has put fiscal guidelines under stress but has not led to their abandonment.

## The private sector response

A fundamental premise of counter-cyclical fiscal policy is that unemployed resources can be mobilised by expanding aggregate demand, without causing inflation. Nobel prizewinner Robert Lucas challenged this theory on the grounds that an expansionary policy would cause inflation (because the aggregate supply curve was vertical). Lucas developed the *theory of rational expectations* which pointed out that rational agents' expectations of inflation are not based exclusively on past behaviour, as had been previously assumed, but take account of the future impact of present policy changes. Any attempt to use output-stimulating policy today at the cost of higher inflation tomorrow would be instantaneously recognised by alert, 'rational' agents. Their expectation of inflation would at once increase. Nominal interest rates would rise and investment would be discouraged. The hoped-for demand stimulus would be pre-empted.[6] Consequently, past behaviour is a poor guide for future policy decisions because policy decisions – and prospective changes in policy stances – affect the parameters of private sector decisions. The structure of the model is not policy-invariant. An implication is

---

[6] The Lucas critique originated in a paper by R.E. Lucas, 'Expectations and the neutrality of money', *Journal of Economic Theory* (April 1972).

that policy simulations based on models of past behaviour are, in Lucas's own word, 'worthless'. This is the so-called *Lucas critique*.

## The historical evidence

One powerful critique of fiscal activism is that it no longer seems to work. During the 1960s and early 1970s, counter-cyclical policies basked in the glow of full employment and rapid growth. After 1973, which in retrospect appears as a watershed in the debate, we saw the emergence of the decidedly un-Keynesian phenomenon of unemployment combined with inflation (*stagflation*). Evidence indicated that expansionary fiscal policy did little to raise the real level of output in the medium term, but instead stoked up inflationary pressures. These perceived failures of Keynesian remedies gave birth to a whole new set of theories which questioned, weakened and, for some, fatally undermined the theoretical case for activist fiscal policies.

Much cold water has, therefore, been thrown on earlier optimism concerning the power of counter-cyclical policies to solve macroeconomic problems. This caution has been reinforced by consideration of the long-run consequences of budget deficits – specifically the problem of escalating public debt.

## 15.3 Public debt and 'crowding out'

Public debt in the industrial countries reached a peak of 71 per cent of GDP in 1995, double the 1974 ratio. The escalation in the debt:GDP ratio began in the 1970s. Prior to that, the debt ratio had been relatively stable and, in some countries, had fallen significantly from the postwar peaks. Debt problems did not feature much in economic debate.

Opinions began to change as the 1970s progressed. Economic growth rates fell, growth in government spending continued unabated and taxation also increased, sufficiently fast to cause serious distortions in incentives, but not fast enough to keep up with spending. Finally, the debt problem hit the headlines. The cases of Mexico and Poland in the early 1980s sent shock waves through the world's financial system. Soon afterwards, a long list of developing countries had to arrange what was euphemistically called a 'rescheduling' of their debts. Lenders began to focus with greater intensity on the *sustainability* of debt. The need to reduce debt to sustainable levels 'crowded out' analyses of counter-cyclical fiscal policies. The debt crises prompted heavily indebted countries everywhere to assess their vulnerability to the market, and to review their fiscal procedures and policies. In addition to this, with the reduction and removal of international capital controls, countries have been forced to pay much greater attention to what world financial markets think of their macroeconomic policies. The ageing of the population in the developed world added a further layer of concern about the sustainability of the debt. Thus, since the mid-1990s there has been an improvement in the debt positions of most industrial countries. For example, US debt has decreased from 75 per cent of GDP in 1995 to 62 per cent in 2003 and the EU average from 75 per cent to 70 per cent (Table 15.4). There have been

## Table 15.4 General government debt (% of GDP)

|  | 1978 | 1990 | 1995 | 2003 |
|---|---|---|---|---|
| EU (15) | 23.9 | 40.8 | 75.2 | 69.8 |
| Japan* | 11.3 | 9.5 | 76.2 | 151.0 |
| US | 21.3 | 31.5 | 74.5 | 62.0 |
| Belgium | 57.2 | 124.9 | 129.8 | 101.9 |
| Italy | 62.4 | 103.7 | 123.1 | 108.1 |
| Greece | 29.4 | 89.0 | 108.7 | 103.6 |
| Netherlands | 40.2 | 75.6 | 75.5 | 50.6 |
| Denmark | 21.9 | 65.8 | 73.9 | 40.0 |
| Portugal | 37.6 | 65.3 | 65.9 | 59.7 |
| Germany | 30.1 | 42.0 | 59.1 | 63.7 |
| France | 31.0 | 39.5 | 59.3 | 68.4 |
| Spain | 14.4 | 48.5 | 68.4 | 64.6 |
| UK | 58.6 | 39.1 | 58.9 | 50.9 |
| Ireland | 65.7 | 92.6 | 80.8 | 32.9 |

* The gap between gross and net debt is extremely wide in the case of Japan; its net debt deducts social security assets from gross debt.

Source: European Monetary Institute, *First Annual Report*, April 1995; OECD, *Economic Outlook*, various issues.

some spectacular cases. Ireland, the Netherlands and Denmark have experienced reductions of above 20 percentage points over a short time frame. Nevertheless, the problem of debt overhang remains acute for several EU countries, notably Belgium, Italy and Greece, all of which have debt:GDP ratios exceeding 100 per cent. Also, Japan's debt has moved in an alarming contrarian way, rising from 76 per cent to 151 per cent in eight years up to 2003, reflecting slow growth and expansionary fiscal policy.[7]

## 'Crowding-out' problems

The scale of the debt build-up led to a radical review by economists of the theoretical interactions between debt, deficits and private sector spending. One important result of this rethink was the development of the concept of *Ricardian equivalence*. The idea behind Ricardian equivalence is that, as public debt is incurred, people realise that taxes will sooner or later have to be raised to service it. Hence, it is a matter of indifference whether the deficit is financed by taxes today or by borrowing (taxes tomorrow). In order to provide for these higher future taxes, 'rational' households will raise their savings ratio (Box 15.2). By contrast, Keynesian theory assumed that, if a tax cut was financed by bonds, these bonds would be considered by economic agents as an addition to private sector wealth. Consumption was supposed to depend on current disposable income, not on the stream of lifetime

---

[7] Japan's debt position is complex. Its gross debt:GDP ratio was 151 per cent in 2003 compared with a net debt ratio of 75 per cent. The difference arises because of the inclusion of Japan's sizeable social security assets in the latter measure. Arguably, it is misleading to include social security assets without also taking account of future claims. But, whichever measure is chosen, Japan's debt is clearly growing at an unsustainable rate.

## Box 15.2  Ricardian equivalence

Current budget deficits increase future tax liabilities. If taxpayers make full provision for them now, there is no difference between a government financing its expenditure by taxation and by borrowing. The economic impact of each option is equivalent. This insight owes its name to the nineteenth-century economist David Ricardo, but it was Robert Barro who reintroduced the idea in 1974 and explained its implications for household and business behaviour, fiscal policy and the analysis of public debt.

To see how the mechanism operates, suppose the government lowers taxes by £100 million, financed by an increase in borrowing, keeping government spending constant. Assume that the borrowing is financed by issuing a bond with a 10 per cent yield (equal to the rate of interest). Assume, further, that the government will raise taxes to pay the interest on these bonds and that repayment of the principal is indefinitely postponed. In each future year, taxes rise by 10 per cent of £100 million, or £10 million. Rational taxpayers will appreciate this and will adjust their lifetime spending plans to take account of the higher tax burden. If they could, they would like to set aside a lump sum to cover the present value of this future burden. What is this sum?

By the standard rule, the present value of the future increase in the tax burden (PV) in millions is given by:

$$PV = £10m/(1 + r) + £10m/(1 + r)^2 + £10m/(1 + r)^3 + £10m/(1 + r)^4$$
$$+ \ldots + £10m/(1 + r)^n$$
$$\Rightarrow PV = £10m/r = £100m$$

In other words, the present value of the future tax burden exactly offsets the tax giveaway in the current year. Taxpayers are neither better-off nor worse-off. The remarkable conclusion is that *whether the government chooses to finance a given level of spending by taxation or by borrowing, the effect is the same*. Hence the name for this effect: *Ricardian equivalence*.

Ricardian equivalence theory has been criticised on three main grounds. First, if public debt can be perpetually rolled over, the burden of debt servicing can be passed to future generations and will not affect this generation's spending. Second, if capital markets are imperfect, and households and firms are subject to credit limitations, they may be prevented from behaving 'rationally', even if they wished to do so. Suppose the government ran a budget surplus in order to repay public debt. Ricardian equivalence states that households, buoyed up by the anticipated decline in future taxation, will respond by spending more now. But credit controls may prevent them from borrowing enough to do so. Third, reactions to debt appear to be sensitive to its size. When the debt ratio is low, people do not worry much about it. Ricardian equivalence may apply only after debt has breached a certain threshold.

There is some limited empirical evidence in favour of Ricardian equivalence. Tests have examined the relationship between private savings and budget deficits (if Ricardian equivalence prevails, one would expect higher deficits to lead to higher savings). An indirect test of Ricardian equivalence is to check for a zero association between higher budget deficits and higher interest rates.

There is evidence of strong *threshold effects*. Only when public debt is perceived as high and threatening may budget deficits spark off a Ricardian reaction. Fear of political instability will weaken business confidence, drive up interest rates and make consumers cautious. In such circumstances, a fiscal stimulus will be ineffective and possibly

---

**Box 15.2 continued**

even counter-productive. By the same reasoning, *a determined attack on a budget deficit – what appears as fiscal contraction – can, in these circumstances, be expansionary.*

Overall, the econometric evidence appears to rule out *complete* Ricardian equivalence. Tax cuts are not entirely translated into extra savings. Budget deficits do have real effects. Hence, the real world may be one of Ricardian near-equivalence rather than literal equivalence. This still makes Ricardian equivalence an important concept for fiscal policy.

*Source*: A. Auerbach, 'Is there a role for discretionary fiscal policy?', NBER Working paper no. W9306, November 2002, provides a comprehensive assessment of US fiscal policy drawing on the core concepts outlined in this box.

---

post-tax earnings which a rational utility-maximising individual would consider the appropriate yardstick.[8] If Ricardian equivalence is right, the stimulus to aggregate demand by *government dissaving* (i.e. by a budget deficit) will be offset by a rise in *private sector saving*.

The 'crowding out' argument, like Ricardian equivalence, explores the rivalrous nature of the relation between public and private sector spending. *Crowding out* refers to the various ways by which changes in public spending impact negatively on private sector spending. A certain degree of 'crowding out' has always been recognised as a side-effect of expansionary policy. For example, a higher budget deficit might easily lead to a rise in interest rates. However, it was believed that interest rate increases could be limited by an accommodating monetary policy. The 'crowding out' problem was regarded as a qualification, rather than a fundamental criticism, of fiscal policy analysis. But Ricardian equivalence, taken literally, opened the door to a *policy-ineffectiveness* hypothesis, whereby a rise in the budget deficit could be wholly offset by contractionary private reactions which governments are powerless to counter. Thus, in a world where people take a long-run view of future liabilities, neither subtractions nor additions to public sector debt, caused by budget surpluses or deficits, will affect aggregate demand.

## Sustainable and unsustainable debt

Public debt is *sustainable* when it stops rising as a proportion of GDP. If debt is growing at a non-sustainable rate, the financial markets are likely to become alarmed. First, they fear that debtor governments will be tempted to reduce the real value of fixed-interest debt by inflation. Second, they fear the possibility of debt default, rescheduling of debt or imposition of a moratorium on interest payments.

---

[8] Robert Barro, 'Are government bonds net wealth?', *Journal of Political Economy* (November 1974), was the first to draw attention to this issue in modern times. But it was David Ricardo, a leading nineteenth-century economist, who first raised the conundrum in 1821 as a theoretical possibility. He concluded, unlike Barro, that it was of no practical importance.

Some heavily indebted countries have begun to use the attainment of a sustainable debt ratio as a target for fiscal policy. A formula for determining the stability condition is outlined in Appendix 15.1. The rule for stabilising debt is that:

$$b - (i - g)k$$

where $b$ is the *primary balance*:GDP ratio (the primary budget balance is defined as the budget surplus (+) or deficit (–) less interest payments), $i$ is the nominal rate of interest on the debt, $g$ is the nominal growth rate of the economy, and $k$ is the initial size of the debt:GDP ratio. The interest rate variable ($i$) determines how fast debt is growing. Clearly, it helps to stabilise the ratio if the interest rate is close to, or less than, growth in nominal GDP. If the nominal interest yield on government bonds ($i$) exceeds the nominal growth rate ($g$), the debt will tend to grow faster than GDP and the debt ratio will increase over time, unless there is a primary *surplus* in the budget (i.e. the value of $b$ must be positive). The bigger the initial debt ratio ($k$), the greater the required primary surplus. The advantage of the debt formula is that it helps us to identify the specific debt ratio or budget balance to target in order to achieve stability of the debt ratio.

Another issue is the *appropriate definition of a country's indebtedness*. One important item excluded from formal calculations of public debt is unfunded state pension liabilities. For many developed countries, these liabilities represent a large outstanding claim on future resources, given the projected rises in the number of elderly people over coming decades. In the US, for instance, the proportion of persons aged over 65 years is expected to rise from 12 per cent in 2000 to 21 per cent in 2050; in Japan, it is expected to rise from 17 per cent to 30 per cent (Table 15.5). In the EU, the proportion of elderly persons aged over 65 will also increase. Relative to the 'active' age group (15–64) the elderly population will more than double between now and 2040. In Germany the ratio will be 48 per cent, in Italy 55 per cent, and in Spain 49 per cent. If account is taken of the trend towards longer periods of education and earlier retirement, the dependency ratio could rise even faster. For example, the average life expectancy of a person aged 65 in America has risen from 73 years in 1940 to 84 years in 2000. Today, there are almost five working Americans for every retired person. By 2030, there will be fewer than three. This is a worrying increase in the dependency ratio, even if less pronounced than in Europe and Japan.

Several estimates have been made of the 'true' debt of the public sector, by computing the present discounted value of future pension liabilities. Unfunded pension liabilities range from less than 50 per cent of 1990 GDP for the US, to

### Table 15.5 Percentage of over-65s in the population*

|         | 1960 | 2000 | 2050 |
|---------|------|------|------|
| US      | 9.2  | 12.4 | 21.2 |
| Japan   | 6.1  | 16.5 | 30.4 |
| EU (15) | 10.6 | 16.1 | 27.6 |

* The elderly dependency ratio is the population aged 65 and over expressed as a percentage of total population.

*Source*: Eurostat.

around 200 per cent of 1990 GDP in Japan, France and Italy (Table 15.6). Clearly the link between ageing population and fiscal balance is most acute in those countries where pensions provision is primarily provided by the state on a pay-as-you-go basis.

Such calculations of the 'true' level of public debt feature just one of many unfunded liabilities of the state. If health entitlements are added to pensions, the US implicit debt:GDP ratio rises to 260 per cent.[9]

Research on *generational accounting* attempts to broaden the coverage of calculation to include all taxes and transfers, not just pension liabilities (although they omit consideration of the value of government's real investments to future generations). These accounts indicate:

● the present value of *taxes* that each generation or age cohort (say, all 30-year-olds today) will pay on average over their remaining life;
● the present value of the *transfers* each generation will receive from public sector sources, such as social security, disability, health benefits, etc.

On the basis of such calculations, it is possible to compute the net balance for each generation. These more comprehensive estimates confirm the existence of a significant intergenerational imbalance. Future generations in the US, for example, may have to pay considerably more in the form of higher taxes (111 per cent more according to one estimate) than current newborns in order to finance the same level of government benefits per person as are currently provided. The method of generational accounting was originally developed in the early 1990s. By now it has spread to over 25 countries around the globe, from New Zealand to Norway.[10]

---

**Table 15.6 Public sector debt and net public pensions liabilities, 1990 (% of GDP)*** 

|         | Public debt | Net pensions liabilities | Extended public debt |
|---------|-------------|--------------------------|----------------------|
| US      | 56          | 43                       | 99                   |
| Japan   | 70          | 200                      | 270                  |
| Germany | 44          | 160                      | 204                  |
| France  | 47          | 216                      | 263                  |
| Italy   | 101         | 233                      | 334                  |
| UK      | 35          | 100                      | 135                  |

* Estimated on the basis of earnings-related benefits indexed on prices after retirement and a discount rate in the range 3–4 per cent.

*Source*: Van den Noord and Herd (1994).

---

[9] P. Van den Noord and R. Herd, 'Estimating pensions liabilities: A methodological framework', *OECD Economic Studies* (Winter 1994). P. Heller, 'Who will pay? Coping with ageing societies', IMF working paper (September 2003).
[10] A.J. Auerbach, J. Gokhale and L. Kotlikoff, 'Generational accounting: A meaningful way to evaluate fiscal policy', *Journal of Economic Perspectives* (Winter 1994); R. Cardarelli *et al.*, 'Generational accounting in the UK', *Economic Journal*, Vol. 110 (November 2000).

On balance, the scale of unfunded liabilities and entitlements constitutes another powerful force, to be added to problems of implementing fiscal policy, the growth of conventional debt and Ricardian equivalence effects, impelling governments towards a more conservative fiscal policy (see Box 15.3). No wonder fiscal consolidation has become the guiding rule in the conduct of fiscal policy in recent years.

---

**Box 15.3** **Can fiscal contraction be expansionary?**

Policy-makers are often reluctant to cut government deficits because of the fear that withdrawing fiscal stimulus might lower aggregate demand and cause unemployment. This fear is rooted in the standard Keynesian analysis, according to which increases in government expenditures are transmitted through a fiscal multiplier into increases in aggregate demand. The standard analysis also suggests that the effects of a fiscal contraction would be broadly symmetric to those of a fiscal expansion.

This assessment of the effects of reductions in budget deficits may not apply to countries with very large budgetary imbalances combined with high debt ratios. In such economies, a fiscal contraction may *increase* economic activity in both the short and the longer run. Attempts to explain this paradoxical outcome focus on the central role played by *expectations* about future policy actions and interest rates.

Suppose that a heavily indebted government with a large budget deficit makes a firm commitment to significantly reduce its budget deficit. Provided financial market participants regard the policy measures as fully credible, long-term interest rates are likely to fall quickly. A credible policy will be seen as evidence of the government's commitment to price stability and to its own financial integrity. Hence, the risk premium in long-term interest rates will decline.

A reduction in long-term interest rates will have expansionary effects on both demand and supply. By lowering the cost of capital, it will increase investment. The debt-servicing burdens of households, firms and the public sector will be eased, stimulating consumption and investment. Diminished uncertainty about the sustainability of the budgetary situation will boost confidence of investors and consumers. These expansionary effects might well outweigh the traditional negative short-term impulse from fiscal consolidation.

Empirical identification of expansionary fiscal contraction is difficult, since account must be taken of other factors which might have been responsible for the economic growth. There is, however, evidence of a negative fiscal multiplier from the experiences of the 1983–86 Danish stabilisation programme and the 1987–89 Irish stabilisation. In both cases, the fiscal imbalances before the intensification of consolidation efforts were clearly unsustainable and risk premiums in interest rates were extremely high. Following the adoption of front-loaded fiscal consolidation programmes, which relied heavily on expenditure reductions, both countries rapidly experienced an improvement in economic performance, with stronger growth and declining unemployment. The coexistence of robust growth during periods of fiscal contraction in a number of developing and transition countries also suggests the possibility of a negative fiscal multiplier. At least for some countries, the 'macroeconomic model' used by market participants appears to be consistent with the existence of a negative multiplier.

Governments need to exploit these market sentiments in a constructive way. For countries with large fiscal imbalances and high levels of public debt, the economic

→

Box 15.3 continued

outlook can be strengthened, even in the relatively near term, by the adoption of strong deficit reduction measures. The credibility of such a fiscal adjustment programme would be enhanced by front-loaded action to achieve the necessary degree of medium-term fiscal consolidation.

The precise way in which fiscal adjustment is implemented seems to be important. Fiscal contraction by spending cuts is effective, whereas taxation increases can have a depressing effect on growth. This is because an increase in taxation raises the cost structure of the economy, worsens its competitiveness and can be read by the market as a signal of postponed adjustment.

Is contemporary Japan about to become another case of expansionary fiscal contraction? Certainly its present fiscal policy expansion has reached an impasse. Additions to government expenditure are no longer effective and fiscal injections now seem to deter rather than reassure economic actors. This weakening confidence has not driven interest rates up as in the standard form of crowding-out, nor has there been any rush out of the yen into safer havens. Rather, the confidence effect has impacted on the propensity to invest and/or to spend. Thus, the cumulative fiscal deficits are impeding economic recovery. With its debt:GDP ratio of 150 per cent (and rising) and its 7 per cent budget deficit, the Japanese economy may have reached the threshold where fiscal contraction could deliver better results than fiscal expansion.

*Sources*: For a theoretical derivation of the proposition that a fiscal deficit can have a contractionary effect, see Alan Sutherland, 'Fiscal crises and aggregate demand: can high public debt reverse the effects of fiscal policy?', *Journal of Public Economics*, 65 (1997). The issue is further explored in F. Gravazzi *et al.*, 'Searching for non-linear effects of fiscal policy: Evidence from industrial and developing countries', *European Economic Review*, June 2000. Ireland's experience is described in Dermot McAleese, 'Ireland's economic recovery', *Irish Banking Review* (Summer 1990), updated in 'The Celtic tiger: origins and prospects', *Policy Options Politiques*, July/August 2000.

## 15.4 Fiscal policy in Europe

The Treaty of the European Union 1992 (or Maastricht Treaty) laid down a number of rules governing the conduct of fiscal policy. These rules were intended to apply both in the run-up to economic and monetary union (EMU), and after EMU was established. They throw interesting light on the close links which European policy-makers believe to exist between fiscal policy and price stability. Underlying the Maastricht criteria was the conviction that the new European currency would be accepted only if price stability within the euro area was assured, and that this would be achieved only if Member States' borrowing and debt were strictly limited.

Before being admitted to the monetary union, Member States have to comply with two fiscal conditions: (a) the budget deficit:GDP ratio must not exceed 3 per cent; and (b) the ratio of government debt to GDP must not exceed 60 per cent. Under the Treaty, the Commission has to make the initial evaluation of a Member State's position, but Member States can then take a collective view on the admissibility of candidates. Considerable flexibility has been exercised in interpreting the debt:GDP rule to date: three participating states, Belgium, Greece and Italy, have debt ratios exceeding 100 per cent.

The Treaty's fiscal clauses contain other prohibitions and procedures related to fiscal policy. Thus, central banks are forbidden to provide overdrafts to governments or to purchase government securities directly in support of budget deficits. The Commission and other Member States are precluded from rescuing a Member State which defaults on its debt (the 'no bail-out' clause). Linked with this is the provision that governments cannot even have privileged access to financial institutions (such as concessionary interest rate or loan privileges).

## Stability and Growth Pact

Fiscal sanctions apply *before* membership of the euro area in so far as entry is closed to countries not satisfying the fiscal criteria.[11] Sanctions *after* membership were agreed in the Stability and Growth Pact in Dublin in 1996, and finalised in the European Council in Amsterdam in June 1997. The SGP set down procedures for enforcing the excessive deficit procedure through fines, and also incorporated detailed provision for consultation and monitoring economic policy under what is known as the Broad Economic Policy Guidelines (BEPG).

The excessive deficit procedure attracts most media attention. It is easy to understand and has political as well as economic implications. For this reason most media attention has focused on potential breaches of the 3 per cent budget deficit target. At a practical level, however, the surveillance procedures are no less important. These procedures are designed to head off difficulties at an early stage and to encourage governments to cooperate with each other in economic policy-making. They do so by obliging Member States to submit annual stability programmes to Council and Commission. These five-year programmes contain detailed economic projections over a five-year time frame, with explicit forecasts of the budget deficit and the debt:GDP ratio. In addition to the 3 per cent rule, the BEPG stipulate that:

> Each MS will commit itself to aim for a medium-term budgetary position of close to balance or surplus. This will allow the automatic stabilisers to work, where appropriate, over the whole business cycle without breaching the 3 per cent reference value for the deficit.

As Table 15.7 demonstrates, the SGP has enjoyed some success in corralling budget deficits and debt ratios. Between 1999 and 2003, despite the slowdown in economic growth, the EU average debt/GDP ratio fell from 67 to 62 per cent. Until 2003, Member States also stayed within the 3 per cent limit for the budget deficit. But increasing strains were evident. Germany and France had fallen into delinquent status with Portugal not far behind. Not surprisingly, the prospect of a country of Germany's status, long seen as the main source of fiscal stability (and at the same time generosity in terms of contributions to the EU budget), being fined by the Commission caused serious soul-searching in European circles. Why are fiscal rules necessary? And are the rules of the SGP right for Europe?

---

[11] The Maastricht criteria for membership of the euro area consist of five conditions, two of which refer to fiscal conditions, the other three referring to price stability, interest rates and exchange rate conditions.

**Table 15.7 EU fiscal targets vs actual levels***

| | Budget deficit | | Debt:GDP ratio | | Pass or fail | |
|---|---|---|---|---|---|---|
| | 1999 | 2003 | 1999 | 2003 | 1999 | 2003 |
| Austria | −2.3 | −1.0 | 63.0 | 63.0 | F | F |
| Belgium | −0.5 | +0.2 | 114.9 | 101.7 | F | F |
| Denmark | +3.1 | +0.9 | 52.7 | 42.4 | P | P |
| Finland | +1.9 | +2.4 | 52.7 | 42.4 | P | P |
| France | −1.6 | −4.2 | 58.5 | 59.3 | P | F |
| Germany | −1.5 | −4.2 | 61.2 | 61.8 | F | F |
| Greece | −1.9 | −1.7 | 105.1 | 102.0 | F | F |
| Ireland | +2.1 | −0.9 | 49.3 | 35.0 | P | P |
| Italy | −1.8 | −2.6 | 110.6 | 108.0 | F | F |
| Luxembourg | +3.6 | −0.6 | 5.6 | 3.9 | P | P |
| Netherlands | +0.7 | −2.6 | 55.8 | 50.1 | P | P |
| Portugal | −2.4 | −2.9 | 54.4 | 58.2 | P | P |
| Spain | −1.1 | 0.0 | 63.1 | 53.2 | F | P |
| Sweden | +1.5 | +0.2 | 65.0 | 51.7 | F | P |
| UK | +1.1 | −2.8 | 45.1 | 38.1 | P | P |
| EU (15) | −0.7 | −2.7 | 67.2 | 62.5 | | |

*Budget deficit target 3 per cent of GDP; debt:GDP target ratio 60 per cent. General government net lending (+) or borrowing (−) as a percentage of GDP; general government gross debt as a percentage of GDP. P and F indicate pass or fail to satisfy the two Maastricht Treaty fiscal criteria. Definitions of debt and deficits differ from those of OECD used in previous tables.

*Source*: *European Economy*, Autumn 2003.

Most discussion of fiscal policy focuses on its role as a short-term stabiliser of the economy. To understand EU fiscal policy, however, one must broaden the context to include the idea of *fiscal sustainability*. This concept draws attention to the dual transmission channel through which fiscal policy affects the economy. The first channel is directly on consumer and investor spending as outlined earlier. Here we have standard analyses of the multiplier and of the workings of automatic stabilisers, and so on. The second channel is an expectations channel whereby fiscal policy drives markets' expectations about the course of future policy (an extreme example being Ricardian equivalence). For Europe two key factors impinge on this second channel.

First, the fiscal policy framework must take account of the future demands of an ageing population on public expenditure.[12] The core statistics bear repeating: (a) the proportion of the 65+ age group to the EU active population (15–64) will double between now and 2050 from 25 to 50 per cent; (b) the number of persons aged 85+ will nearly triple, from 14 million in 2000 to 38 million; and (c) average life expectancy will increase by five years. All this will mean an added burden on

---

[12] Under realistic macroeconomic assumptions, the present value of increased spending on pensions, health and long-term care for the elderly has been recently estimated at more than 100 per cent of GDP (ECB, *Monthly Bulletin*, April 2003).

---

**Box 15.4**  **Fiscal discipline in the EMU**

Once Member States have joined the EMU, the Maastricht conditions must continue to be met and the Treaty lays down conditions to ensure this is so. The Stability and Growth Pact (1997) elaborated on these fiscal rules. Additional measures are specified in instances where governments run 'excessive' budget deficits, i.e. greater than 3 per cent of GDP. These measures are:

- The Member State at fault will have to publish additional information, to be specified by the Council, before issuing further bonds and securities.
- The Member State may be required to make a non-interest bearing deposit with the Community until the excessive deficit has, in the view of the Council, been corrected.
- Fines in the range of 0.2–0.5 per cent of GDP may be imposed.

A number of steps must be completed before the Council can decide that an excessive deficit exists:

1. Failure to meet criteria must be determined by a Commission report which takes account of 'all relevant factors'. Derogations are permitted in cases such as a 'severe economic downturn'.
2. The Commission report is sent to the Council which undertakes an assessment as to whether a failure does indeed exist.
3. The Council makes recommendations and implements sanctions.

Up to 2003 no country had been penalised for an excessive deficit. But at the end of July 2003 Mr Romano Prodi, President of the Commission, warned that Germany could face stiff fines if it continued to breach the Stability and Growth Pact. This warning was doubly ironic, first because Mr Prodi is no devotee of the Pact's 3 per cent target which he once described as 'stupid', and secondly, because Germany was the country that insisted most strenuously that the 3 per cent would have to be strictly enforced.

*Source*: Treaty of the European Union, art. 104; Stability and Growth Pact; *The Times*, 19 July 2003.

---

public finances of between 5 and 9 percentage points of GDP. Fiscal policy today must take account of this huge contingent liability in the future. The Swedish government, for example, has decided that a medium-term target of budget balance is not enough, and has adopted a 2 per cent budget surplus target instead.

Second, the forthcoming enlargement of the EU will involve integration of economies some of which have weak fiscal positions. The Czech Republic, Hungary, Poland and Slovakia all have budget deficits well in excess of 3 per cent. Strong fiscal rules are necessary in order to give these countries an incentive to continue with fiscal reform and to achieve a more sustainable balance.

The above considerations explain the EU's concern about the need to *speed up fiscal consolidation* and to *improve the quality and sustainability of fiscal policy*, and why the SGP process must be interpreted in this context.

The question still remains as to why rules are necessary. Why would the free market not take the ageing factor and all other relevant factors into account in pricing European government bonds? One argument is that the financial market will do this, but that it will assume that when one Member State gets into trouble, the EU will not be able to stand by and see it sink. In other words, the no-bail-out clause is not believed. Hence the interest penalty for bad fiscal policy will be borne by all members of the euro area, not just by the aberrant country. This is the *externality argument*. The only way to correct this negative externality is by fiscal rules. This argument has considerable weight – witness the succession of contagion crises observed in Europe, Asia and Latin America during the past 25 years.

Given that fiscal restraints are necessary, how appropriate is the specific 3 per cent target? Had the EU started off from a position of structural balance, there is evidence that this upper limit might not have proved a binding constraint and automatic stabilisers could have operated unhindered. Because of the initial structural imbalance, however, some Member States' budget deficits are at the 3 per cent limit. Thus Germany, Italy, Portugal and France are being forced to curb the budget deficit when unemployment is cyclically high and business expectations are depressed, exactly the wrong time from a Keynesian point of view. This pro-cyclical stance has attracted criticism inside Europe, and even more from outside Europe, one of its most persistent and trenchant critics being none other than the IMF!

Another issue is whether the same fiscal rule should apply to all Member States. The Irish government, with a debt:GDP ratio well below 60 per cent and a strong demand for public infrastructure, believes that a higher limit should apply in these circumstances. Account should be taken of the share of investment in government spending, since a budget deficit to finance investment has obviously different economic implications from one that is used to bolster consumer spending. Along with the UK and others, it argues that the 3 per cent limit should apply not to the *general government* budget deficit (as at present) but instead to the *current* budget deficit. Adoption of the latter would allow a country borrow for investment purposes. The usefulness of such a golden rule has been debated since the 1930s when a dual budget was proposed in order to foster the acceptance of public debt to finance investment.

Another possibility is to apply the 3 per cent limit to the *cyclically adjusted* budget deficit, allowing automatic stabilisers to work in full during a recession or a boom (when surpluses will be earned). This would be tantamount to setting an upper limit for the *structural* deficit. The argument against this is that it would defer necessary structural adjustment and, less convincingly, generate disputes about the statistical definition of the cyclical element in any given overall deficit.

Views on the appropriateness of the SGP targets differ. To Professor Paul de Grauwe,

> The Stability Pact is a vote of no confidence by the European authorities in the strength of the democratic institutions in the member countries. It is quite surprising that EU-countries have allowed this to happen, and that they have agreed to be subjected to control by European institutions that even the International Monetary Fund does not impose on banana republics. (*Financial Times*, 25 July 2002)

By contrast Professor Horst Siebert considers these fiscal restraints a necessary price to pay for the benefits of a single currency:

> Of course, the Stability Pact restricts the room for manoeuvre enjoyed by national fiscal policymakers. But this is the price that must be paid for a common currency. Historically, stability between currencies has been possible only when counries have been prepared to relinquish some national sovereignty. (*Financial Times*, 6 August 2002)

What seems clear is that those countries that failed to achieve sustainable budgetary consolidation during the 1990s boom are now finding it extremely hard to live within the confines of the SGP. Like it or not, the scope for using fiscal policy in the euro area to tackle recession is limited.

The SGP has many limitations. It reduces budget flexibility. It works asymmetrically – doing nothing to impose restraint in times of boom.[13] It makes no distinction between borrowing for investment and borrowing for consumption. The SGP makes no allowance for differences between Member States and it ignores the debt:GDP ratio. The 3 per cent rule applies as much to a well-run country with a debt:GDP ratio of 20 per cent as to a profligate with a debt:GDP ratio of 120 per cent. It has no way of dealing with one-off expenditures or tax measures needed to lay the foundations for a better framework in the future (e.g. short-term deficits might be needed to buy long-run reforms in, say, pension schemes).[14] To be sure, no set of fiscal rules is perfect. It is highly likely that, if the present economic downturn continues, changes in the details and functioning of the SGP will be enacted. Radical change is less likely, since it would be problematic from a political as well as an economic viewpoint.

## 15.5 Conclusions

The most significant factor affecting the conduct of fiscal policy in recent times has been the need to control public sector debt. Heavily indebted countries were paying what is known as the *debt penalty* – their governments were borrowing in order to stand still. As the interest burden grows, two consequences can be observed. First, any stimulatory effect of a public-sector deficit diminishes, sometimes even to the point where a deficit actually causes an economic contraction. Second, over time the deficit becomes a source of structural distortion, through rising taxes and lower investment. *The deficit, originally intended as a solution to the problem of low growth and unemployment, becomes part of the problem itself.*

As interest payments on debt increase, governments are forced to focus on the *primary budget balance*, i.e. the budget balance net of interest payments. Countries with fiscal problems and significant levels of outstanding debt – for example, Greece, Italy and Belgium – find that, in order to stabilise the debt, they must run large primary surpluses. A high, and rising, debt:GDP ratio arouses fears that a government may be tempted to 'inflate' its way out of the debt problem, thereby alleviating the real burden of its fixed interest debt. No matter how vigorously an indebted government may protest its intention not to resort to such an expedient, the financial markets will remain nervous and will demand an interest rate premium to compensate for the risk. This risk premium has adverse implications for investment which, in turn, exacerbates the deficit problem.

---

[13] Note, however, that the BEPG does address this issue – boom economies such as the Irish economy in 2001 had their knuckles rapped for adopting over-expansionist macroeconomic policies, even though none of the fiscal guidelines were in danger of being breached at the time.

[14] Source: M. Buti, S. Eijffinger and D. Franco, 'Revisiting the Stability and Growth Pact: grand design or internal adjustment?', *European Commission Economic Papers* no. 180, January 2003.

Fiscal policy is being affected by the closer integration between financial markets and the markets for real goods and services. Financial markets have become more volatile. Fiscal policy has become more constrained than previously by the sometimes fickle judgement of financial markets. The liberalisation of the financial sector has further constrained the ability of countries to run expansionary fiscal policies. Fiscal policy now has to be conducted more carefully than hitherto, particularly by countries with already high borrowing. Furthermore, EMU fiscal rules have stipulated quite specific constraints on existing and prospective Member States of the euro area.

Better control of budget deficits will, it is hoped, lead to greater efficiency in government spending and a more enterprise-friendly tax system. A lower deficit means that the government is borrowing less and more will then be available to finance private sector investment which, so it is argued, will yield greater productivity per worker than public sector spending. Professor Alan Blinder, in a presentation to President-elect Clinton in 1993, predicted that a deficit reduction programme would result in lower interest rates, more business confidence and *a 1 per cent increase in the US's standard of living after four years*.[15] Projections of this type rest on the assumption that resources released by a cutback in government will be absorbed by the private sector. In normal circumstances, deficit reduction (and structural readjustment) might lead to losses of output and jobs, just as the Keynesian model would predict. But *as the debt level increases, the potential contractionary effect of fiscal cutbacks diminishes and could even be reversed*. A key factor is the reaction of the financial markets. If they believe the deficit reduction programme will be adhered to, they will respond by buying more bonds, thus driving down long-term interest rates. The resultant relief to mortgage holders and businesses generates more investment and consumer spending.

How much more spending? A new feature of the debate on this question is the growing awareness of the importance of *private* debt as well as *public* debt in influencing expenditure by the private sector. The huge increase in household debt:disposable income ratios has had a profound effect on consumer demand in the UK, Japan, the US and the Scandinavian countries. It has enhanced the impact of real wealth effects on private-sector spending.

Fiscal policy, however, still has a role to play in stabilising the economy. Automatic stabilisers continue to perform a valuable function, and will continue to do so as long as government remains a key player in the economy. In addition, structural changes in the budget may also be required to deal with *severe* downturns or upturns. A balanced budget is not, in all circumstances, a sign of good economic management. Instead of 'fine-tuning' aggregate demand, fiscal policy may have to settle for the more modest objective of 'coarse-tuning', that is, responding only to prospective major deviations from potential output.[16] But, as the debate about fiscal policy in Europe demonstrates, there is room for disagreement about the size and likely duration of output gaps and the need and effectiveness of fiscal policy in dealing with them. By 2003, the mood has swung towards favouring a more activist stance.

---

[15] In effect, this is another instance of the expansionary fiscal contraction argument. See Bob Woodward, *The Agenda: Inside the Clinton White House* (New York: Simon & Schuster, 1994), pp. 83–6.
[16] A. Lindbeck *et al.*, *Turning Sweden Around* (Cambridge, MA: MIT Press, 1994).

The need for such intervention has been prompted by the spillover effects of the collapse in stock prices and the shift in investment demand from 'dotcom' and high-technology investors. The scope for fiscal policy being effective will, however, depend on international responses. As the economy becomes more integrated, one country on its own may find a proposed fiscal expansion through, say, a tax cut, being frustrated by leakages through imports (consumers may spend a large part of their additional disposable income on imported cars or foreign holidays) or by capital outflows (if bond holders and investors lose confidence in the government). Increasingly, fiscal policy will have to be implemented on a coordinated basis if it is to be effective. Single country fiscal initiatives are likely to be frustrated. A textbook example was the failure of President Mitterrand's efforts to spend France out of the early 1980s recession. The open-economy dimensions of fiscal policy are discussed further in Part III.

The accumulation of public debt and the growing sophistication of markets have made demand management policy more problematic and less effective. This is a fact of life, deserving neither praise nor condemnation. It is not necessarily a 'good' development for the world economy. The belief that counter-cyclical policy did work, and could be applied, kept business confidence and investment high for many decades. 'Thinking made it so' – the belief that the economy would never be allowed to slide into depression ensured that depressions were avoided. We have referred on more than one occasion to the sustained growth of the postwar economy and the much reduced amplitude of business fluctuations during this period. Fiscal policy objectives have been radically revised because of a fear of the financial collapse of heavily indebted countries, and also because of a widespread belief that the marginal productivity of public sector spending has declined. This latter belief has fuelled the movement towards 'smaller government' and to a comprehensive review of the economic role of government in the field of micro- as well as macroeconomic policy.

## Summary

1. The approach suggested by counter-cyclical, or Keynesian, fiscal policy is fiscal stimulus when the economy is operating below full employment, and fiscal contraction when the economy is at full employment. This theory transformed not only the way economists thought about fiscal policy, but also the way fiscal policy was conducted in industrial economies. Counter-cyclical policy focused on the policy mix between fiscal and monetary policy, ways of identifying how much extra aggregate demand was needed and the size of the fiscal injection needed to shift aggregate demand to the required degree.

2. Growing public-sector indebtedness has forced governments to reassess the role of fiscal policy. This change in perspective on fiscal activism can be explained under six main headings: (a) knowledge gaps and time-lags, where the amount of necessary accurate information available to authorities often fell short of their requirements; (b) political considerations, which distorted the extent and timing of fiscal action; (c) inefficiencies of the public sector, which have led to public opinion becoming more critical of budget deficits than in the past; (d) links between aggregate demand and inflation, proposed by the Lucas critique;

(e) evidence accumulated in the 1970s that expansionary fiscal policy did little to raise the real level of output in the medium term, but instead stoked up inflationary pressures; and finally (f) the adverse impact of rising public debt on interest rates and investment.

3. The escalation of public sector debt led to a radical review by economists of the theoretical interactions between debt, deficits and private sector spending. Out of this review emerged the development of the concept of Ricardian equivalence. It has also stimulated fresh investigation into the issue of the sustainability of public debt. The appropriate definition of a country's indebtedness has also received attention, since formal calculations of public debt exclude unfunded state pension liabilities. Research on generational accounting attempts to broaden the coverage of calculation to include all taxes and transfers, not just pension liabilities.

4. The Maastricht Treaty laid down a number of rules governing the conduct of fiscal policy which were intended to apply to both existing and aspiring members of the euro. Before being admitted to the monetary union, Member States had to comply with two fiscal conditions: (a) the budget deficit:GDP ratio must not exceed 3 per cent; and (b) the ratio of government debt to GDP must not exceed 60 per cent. There is general support for curbing the growth in public spending, seeking more efficient ways of managing public services and keeping public finances in good order. Serious disagreement has arisen among European governments about the practical use of the Stability and Growth Pact guidelines. Surprisingly, it is Germany, for long the bulwark of fiscal conservatism in Europe, that is leading the charge. If the world economic slowdown continues, there will be increasing calls for some modification of the fiscal rules. One possible modification is the separation of capital from current government spending in applying the 3 per cent rule.

5. Fiscal policy still has a role to play in steadying the economy and, in particular, in preventing major downturns and booms. Instead of fiscal fine-tuning, however, we shall have to be satisfied with coarse-tuning policies, applied with circumspection.

## Questions for discussion

1. Business often supports the objective of fiscal rectitude in the belief that it will lead to lower taxes. Explain how these two phenomena are linked.

2. A lobby group suggests a constitutional amendment to the effect that government budgets must be balanced, arguing that allowing politicians discretionary power leads to large deficits and escalating debt. Analyse this proposal.

3. The German government currently plans a reduction in taxes, to be financed by borrowing, with the aim of increasing demand to stimulate the economy. Forecasters claim that this could mean Germany will breach the 3 per cent excessive deficit rule in 2004 for the third year in a row. Discuss this policy proposal. In your reply, comment on the perspective of Ricardian equivalence proponents on such a proposal.

4. What are automatic stabilisers? Discuss the ways in which an economic slowdown could be moderated by these automatic stabilisers.

5. Explain why, and how, a country's public debt, if it exceeds a certain threshold level, might lead to a contractionary budget having a stimulating effect on aggregate demand (expansionary fiscal contraction).

## Exercises

1. Assume the following situation occurred in an economy:

   Unemployment rises and output falls dramatically, consumption and investment fall, and interest rates decline. The money supply declines and prices actually fall. Furthermore, the stock market crashes.

   Propose remedies for this situation.

2. The 1996 Annual Economic Report of the European Commission stated that (in reference to the French economy):

   fiscal consolidation is a necessary condition for a stable macroeconomic environment conducive to growth and employment. It should enable an easing of monetary policy, compatible with the monetary stability objective, which should offset the adverse effect on economic activity of budgetary restraint. (p. 24)

   Explain each step of this argument by answering the following questions:

   (a) What is a stable macroeconomic environment?
   (b) What is meant by fiscal consolidation?
   (c) Why is (b) necessary for (a)?
   (d) Through what mechanisms would (a) be conducive to growth and employment?
   (e) Revise your understanding of the terms 'an easing of monetary policy' and 'monetary stability' (see Chapter 13).
   (f) What evidence would you wish to consult in order to be satisfied that an easing of monetary policy would succeed in offsetting the adverse effect of budgetary restraint?

3. Would an average, well-run business agree to limit itself to a zero borrowing target over the business cycle? Why do some business lobbies urge governments to constrain government spending according to this rule? Is this a sensible rule for European governments to adopt?

4. A country has a debt ratio of 130 per cent of GDP, it pays 10 per cent interest on this debt and its nominal growth rate is 7 per cent. What primary balance (as per cent of GDP) should it be targeting if it wants to stabilise the debt ratio? You are told that its total deficit is currently running at 9 per cent of GDP. Does this country have a fiscal problem?

   Another country has a debt ratio of 40 per cent, it pays 7 per cent interest and its nominal GDP is growing at 6 per cent annually. Its present total budget deficit:GDP ratio is 1.7 per cent. Is this country's debt ratio growing or declining?

   Do these figures approximate the position in any of the countries which are listed in the tables to this chapter?

→

5. New Zealand's Fiscal Responsibility Act 1994 requires the government to identify and publish its fiscal objectives. The New Zealand government has specified prudent levels of public debt to be below 30 per cent of GDP in the short run and below 20 per cent in the longer term.

   (a) Are these targets high or low by international standards?
   (b) Would you recommend other governments to follow New Zealand's example?

## Further reading

Our understanding of fiscal policy has changed in recent years. More than before, we now recognise the importance of private-sector expectations and also of the dynamic interactions between public debt and the budget deficits in determining how effective fiscal policy will be in any given circumstance. These two themes are analysed in a thorough (albeit challenging) manner in Chapters 8 and 14 of M. Gartner, *Macroeconomics* (London: Pearson Education, 2003). For a good overview of the European fiscal policy debate, see S. Eijffinger and J. de Haan, *European Monetary and Fiscal Policy* (Oxford: Oxford University Press, 2000) and M. Buti and G. Giudice, 'Maastricht's fiscal rules at ten: an assessment', *Journal of Common Market Studies*, 2002. Fiscal reform proposals are dissected in a readable way in M. Buti, S. Eijffinger and D. Franco, 'Revisiting the Stability and Growth Pact: grand design or internal adjustment?', *European Commission Economic Papers* no. 180, January 2003. Among the many background papers on the linkage between fiscal policy and the 'greying' of Europe, 'The need for comprehensive reforms to cope with population ageing', *European Central Bank Monthly Bulletin*, April 2003, gives a good summary of the issues and a strong endorsement of the European Commission view.

## Appendix 15.1 The sustainability of debt

Let $D$ = total nominal debt, $Y$ = nominal GDP and $k$ = Debt:GDP ratio. Then:

$$k = D/Y \qquad (1)$$

Differentiating (1) we obtain:

$$\frac{dk}{dt} = \frac{\frac{dD}{dt} \cdot Y - \frac{dY}{dt} \cdot D}{Y^2} \qquad (2)$$

The growth rate of the debt, $dD/dt$, is by definition,

$$\frac{dD}{dt} = B + iD \qquad (3)$$

where $B$ = primary deficit (i.e. the budget deficit *less* interest payments on outstanding debt), and $iD$ = interest payments on debt.

By inserting (3) into (2), the growth of the debt:GDP ratio, $dk/dt$, may therefore be written as:

$$\frac{dk}{dt} = \frac{(B + iD)Y - \frac{dY}{dt} \cdot D}{Y^?}$$

$$= \frac{(B + iD)Y}{Y^2} - \frac{\frac{dY}{dt} \cdot D}{Y^2}$$

$$= \frac{B + iD}{Y} - \frac{dY}{dt} \cdot \frac{D}{Y}$$

$$= \frac{B}{Y} + i \cdot \frac{D}{Y} - g \cdot \frac{D}{Y}$$

$$= b + i.k - g.k$$

$$\frac{dk}{dt} = b + (i - g)k \qquad (4)$$

where $b = B/Y =$ ratio of primary deficit to GDP, and $g = (dY/dt)/Y =$ growth rate of nominal GDP.

The condition for $dk/dt = 0$, that is for a stabilisation in the debt:GDP ratio, is:

$$-b = (i - g)k \qquad (5)$$

If the nominal interest rate exceeds the nominal GDP growth rate, i.e. $i > g$, the stability condition indicates that there must be a primary surplus ($b$ must be positive). If the growth rate exceeds the interest rate, a primary deficit is consistent with a stable debt ratio provided it does not exceed $(i - g)k$.

Consider the case of a country with a current debt:GDP ratio ($k$) of 60 per cent, running a primary deficit/GDP ($b$) of 1.5 per cent, paying an interest rate of 6 per cent on debt and with a nominal growth rate of 4 per cent. In this situation its debt:GDP ratio will grow this year at the rate of 2.7 per cent.

$$\frac{dk}{dt} = b + (i - g)k$$

$$= 0.015 + (0.06 - 0.04)(0.60)$$

$$= 0.027$$

To stabilise the debt ratio, the primary deficit and/or the initial debt:GDP ratio must be reduced. To find by how much, we set the above equation (4) equal to zero. Suppose a debt:GDP ratio of 60 per cent is agreed, then the formula indicates that it will be necessary to convert the primary deficit of 1.5 per cent into a primary surplus of 1.2 per cent ($b = 0.012$):

$$\frac{dk}{dt} = b + (i - g)k = 0$$

$$0 = b + (0.06 - 0.04)0.60$$

$$b = -0.012$$

Interest rates on government borrowing ($i$) have often been higher than GDP nominal growth ($g$). If this is the case, and assuming positive $k$, the condition for stabilisation requires a primary budget surplus. At the time of writing (2003), nominal GDP growth in the major industrial countries is exceptionally low, but so are interest rates, which could explain the relative stability of the debt:GDP ratio in recent years.

## Government budget constraint

$$(G - T) + iD = \frac{dD}{dt} + \frac{dM}{dt}$$

$$= \text{change in debt} + \text{change in money supply}$$

where $G$ = government spending less interest on debt
$T$ = net taxation
$iD$ = interest on debt.

Since Maastricht regulations forbid monetary financing of the debt, $dM/dt = 0$, then

$$(G - T) + iD = \frac{dD}{dt} = B + iD$$

Hence the derivation of equation (3) above.

**Chapter 16**

# Business fluctuations and forecasting

The inevitability of the business cycle, as it used to be called, I take for granted. Good times bring into existence: first, incompetent business executives; second, wrongful government policies; and, third, speculators. Working together, they ensure the eventual bust.

J.K. Galbraith, 'Challenges of the new millennium', *Finance and Development* (December 1999), p. 5.

It is not enough to assert that since there have always been business cycles there always will be business cycles. Understanding what causes business cycles and how these causes have changed suggests that business cycles will not be as important in the future as they were in the past.

S. Weber, 'The end of the business cycle', *Foreign Affairs* (July 1997), p. 67.

## Introduction

Fluctuations in economic growth are an endemic feature of industrial economies. Periods of above-average growth tend to be succeeded by periods of below-average growth. Occasionally, the level of economic activity declines even in absolute terms. These economy-wide trends are mirrored across a wide range of industries. However, macroeconomic cycles must be distinguished from cycles which are particular to individual industries. The latter can sometimes be entirely independent of the former. Some industries are in long-run decline (steel, coal), while others (personal computers, mobile telephones) are enjoying sustained growth, even during economic recessions.

From a business perspective, the timing of these upturns in economic activity can have a crucial bearing on product prices and corporate profits. A takeover deal, or an investment in a new market, which might be profitable if completed at the start of an economic upturn, could prove disastrous if succeeded by an economic downturn. Property and construction are particularly prone to cyclical fluctuations, but so is the demand for many consumer goods which are dependent on discretionary spending, such as fashion clothing and household durables. Business fluctuations have a major impact on the profits of the banking sector. Non-performing loans and the number of business failures tend to move in unison with the state of health of the economy. The instability of the market system, therefore, is a matter of profound practical importance.

For this reason, companies put considerable resources into predicting the course of the cycle and estimating the implications of the cycle for their sales and costs. The most widely read, and eagerly sought, economic articles among the business community tend to be those containing economic forecasts and projections. These are prepared by international organisations, national research institutes, banks and stockbrokers. Some large corporations prepare their own projections. The demand for these forecasts fluctuates in line with the cycle itself, as many economic forecasters have had occasion to discover. When profits decline, the providers of macroeconomic forecasts and statistics tend to be among the first casualties!

In this chapter we use the terms *fluctuations* and *cycles* interchangeably. 'Cycle' implies the existence of regular fluctuations of equal size and timespan. Postwar empirical analysis suggests that economic fluctuations are, in fact, quite irregular. To be sure, there are peaks and troughs in GDP, but the time-lapse between them, and the size of the gap between peak and trough, varies markedly from case to case. The term 'fluctuations' gives a more accurate impression of the phenomenon.

The severity of economic fluctuations has moderated significantly since the inter-war period. There has been no repeat of the Great Depression (August 1929 to March 1933), which involved a 53 per cent fall in US industrial production and a 32 per cent decline in non-farm employment.[1] Yet two severe recessions occurred in the 1970s, the second of which lasted into the early 1980s, and a sharp downturn marked both the early 1990s and the early 2000s. From a systemic viewpoint, these postwar fluctuations have been relatively limited in severity. However, although mild in a macro-sense, they have had serious implications for many firms and have spelt disaster for others.

The reasons for a more stable performance of the industrialised economies have been much analysed. One explanation focuses on the growing share of sectors such as health and education in economic activity as a nation becomes more prosperous. Demand for such activities is more stable than for others. Another, not unrelated, explanation attributes a strong stabilising role to government spending, which, until the 1990s, had also been increasing its share in national output. Public-sector spending is much less dependent on the performance of the economy than private-sector spending. Demand management policies (in the 'coarse-tuning' sense described in Chapter 15 on fiscal policy) have also played an important part in stabilising the economy. Most crucial of all has been the strengthening of the financial architecture – the institution of effective lender of last resort, deposit insurance and bank supervision. This has prevented the recurrence of bank 'panics' and financial disintermediation that converted recessions into depressions in the past.

### Chapter outline

This chapter analyses the topic of business fluctuations in five steps:

**1.** The size, duration and incidence of these fluctuations. We focus on the larger economies, because many smaller economies experience upturns and downturns

---

[1] V. Zarnovitz, 'Theory and history behind business cycles: Are the 1990s the onset of a golden age?', *Journal of Economic Perspectives* (Spring 1999).

in a passive sense, buoyed up or sucked down mostly by the changing fortunes of their larger trading partners.

2. The causes of these fluctuations and the reasons for their diminished amplitude. This raises the question of whether, in today's more open and market-driven economy, we can continue to assume that the amplitude of the cycle will remain subdued.

3. The effects of business fluctuations. Obviously, they matter to individual firms. Do they still matter if all firms are taken together? In other words, is overall economic growth adversely affected by business fluctuations?

4. Predicting economic fluctuations and the accuracy of economic forecasts.

5. The link between macroeconomic forecasts and company projections.

## 16.1 Business fluctuations – the facts

Business cycles refer to fluctuations in aggregate economic activity that are widely diffused throughout the economy and have identifiable 'peaks' and 'troughs'. Recovery and expansion are followed by downturn and contraction. Identifying the precise contours of a particular business cycle, and defining its turning point and peak, can be a complex statistical exercise, but such complications are not considered here. Cyclical analysis can be performed on a large range of variables, but most macro-studies focus on industrial production, GDP and investment. In part, this choice is dictated by data availability – volume indices for services (which account for a much larger proportion of GDP than industry) are highly unreliable. Traditionally, industrial production has been regarded as the key source of instability in an industrial economy. Most modern studies focus on *growth cycles*, i.e. deviations from trend growth, whereas formerly analysis focused on the *'classical'* cycle, i.e. changes in the absolute value of the aggregate variable.

The salient features of business fluctuations can be traced with the assistance of Figure 16.1. This tracks GDP growth rates for a selection of major industrial countries during the period 1964–2004:

1. The infrequent incidence of negative growth rates is striking – over the 40-year period, only four such instances were recorded in the US, two in Japan, three in Germany and three in the UK.[2]

2. There are significant fluctuations around the average (and trend) growth rates for each of the countries. Each growth cycle tends to have a different amplitude and different periodicity than the others. The sequence of change from boom to contraction is *recurrent, but not periodic*.

3. No compelling evidence has been found to confirm the existence of systematic long-run cycles such as the Kondratieff 40–50-year cycle or the Juglar 10-year cycle. Yet the search for regularities in the data continues.

4. Sustained periods of prosperity and fast growth are followed sooner or later by a relative (or absolute) downturn. As the period of boom conditions lengthens,

---

[2] Most cyclical analysis uses quarterly data which provide a greater degree of variation than the annual data, but suggest the same qualitative conclusions.

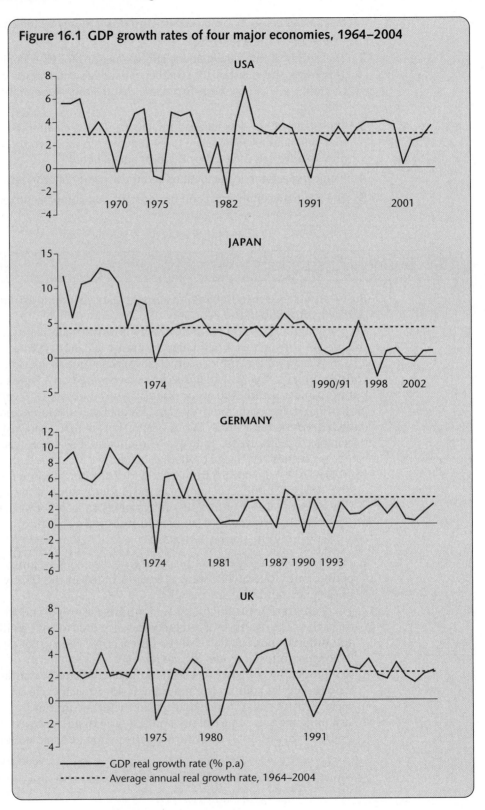

Figure 16.1  GDP growth rates of four major economies, 1964–2004

the probability of a slowdown increases. After a number of years of recession, the probability of economic recovery increases.[3]

5. Even fast-growing economies experience growth cycles. The dynamic Asian countries, which enjoyed an average annual growth rate of 8 per cent for three decades up to the mid-1990s, recorded a standard deviation in their GDP growth of 2.3 percentage points (Table 16.3 later in the chapter). This was higher in absolute terms than the industrial countries' 1.8 percentage points, but considerably lower relative to trend growth (Box 16.1).

6. Industrial economies stay on average approximately three times longer in the expansion phase of the cycle than in recession. Expansions lasted 51 months, compared with 15 months for recession (Table 16.1). Downturns tend to be shorter than upturns. Data for industrial countries show that the average cumulative loss of production due to recessions amounted to 11.7 per cent of industrial production, compared with a corresponding average gain of 25 per cent due to expansions. The typical cycle lasts about six years.

7. There appears to be a strong degree of synchronisation of cycles among individual industrial countries, but cycles in the European economies, taken as a group, are not generally synchronised with those in North America and Japan.[4]

---

**Box 16.1**　**Business cycles in the dynamic Asian economies**

Although the East Asian economies were able to sustain impressive rates of growth, they also experienced the business fluctuations characteristic of industrial countries. During the period 1967–96, there were only four years of negative growth rates. 'Growth recessions' – defined as periods in which an economy continues to grow at a rate that is substantially below its long-run trend – were more common. Nineteen cyclical downturns, in which actual GDP fell more than 1 per cent below its long-run trend, were identified. At cyclical troughs, GDP was on average about 4.5 per cent below trend. This is a larger output gap than the 3 per cent average estimated during downturns in the major developed countries over the past 25 years. But since the average growth rate of these economies was about three times higher than that of the major industrial countries, the impact was relatively mild. This successful run was shattered by the downturn of 1997–98. However, by 2000, all except Indonesia had resumed their upward track.

In the past, cyclical trends in the developing economies were linked to developments in the industrial countries. In recent years, this linkage has become weaker. The correlation coefficient between growth rates in the OECD area and in developing countries has fallen. As they have grown rapidly, domestic developments have played a larger role in determining business cycle trends. In addition, the influence of China on its neighbours has increased as a result of closer economic integration of coastal China with the other Asian economies.

---

[3] While booms are usually associated with inflation and depressions with deflation, the correlation between inflation and economic activity through moderate cyclical fluctuations is much less clear. For example, during the stagflation of the 1970s, depressed growth went hand in hand with high inflation.

[4] M.J. Artis, Z.G. Kontolemis and D.R. Osborn, 'Classical business cycles for G7 and European countries', Centre for European Policy Research Discussion Paper No. 1137 (March 1995). The 'stubbornly asynchronous' nature of UK and euro area business fluctuation is analysed in M.J. Artis and W. Zhang, 'Further evidence on the international business cycle and the ERM: is there a European business cycle?', *Oxford Economic Papers*, 1999.

## Table 16.1 Business cycle characteristics*

| | Recessions | | Expansions | |
| --- | --- | --- | --- | --- |
| | Total change in output | Duration in months | Total change in output | Duration in months |
| US | −8.672 | 15 | 22.512 | 46 |
| Canada | −9.195 | 14 | 20.330 | 35 |
| Japan | −10.095 | 13 | 28.878 | 56 |
| Germany | −11.373 | 24 | 33.708 | 77 |
| France | −7.862 | 11 | 12.350 | 42 |
| UK | −9.810 | 14 | 18.445 | 45 |
| Italy | −13.742 | 15 | 35.491 | 63 |
| Spain | −16.529 | 13 | 26.535 | 90 |
| Belgium | −11.417 | 14 | 17.323 | 39 |
| Netherlands | −9.247 | 20 | 15.408 | 30 |
| Ireland | −10.641 | 15 | 39.219 | 53 |
| Luxembourg | −21.821 | 16 | 30.362 | 39 |
| Average | −11.7003 | 15 | 25.046 | 51 |

* Total output change equals the average monthly decline (rise) in industrial production, multiplied by the average duration of contractions (expansions). Changes are expressed in terms of logarithms, while 'duration' refers to months. All figures are averages over completed recessions or contractions.

*Source*: M.J. Artis, Z.G. Kontolemis and D.R. Osborn, 'Classical business cycles for G7 and European countries', *Journal of Business* (April 1997).

Apart from the UK, business fluctuations follow a broadly similar path between European countries. With the increasing intensity of intra-European trade and capital mobility, cyclical trends are rapidly transmitted from one economy to another.

The less synchronised are fluctuations in the major economies, the more stable is the global economic system. If the US economy is heading towards its peak at a time when the EU is descending towards its trough, the EU will find it easier to reallocate resources, which have been made redundant by poor domestic market conditions, to the production of exports for the American market. This stabilises EU economic activity. Simultaneously, the booming US economy will benefit from the higher rate of growth in imports from Europe. These imports will divert US domestic spending from its overstretched domestic sector and will help to restrain price increases. The outcome is mutually advantageous: less unemployment in Europe and less inflation in America. The amplitude of the fluctuation in both areas is moderated. A distinctive feature of the 2000s recession is that it has been much more synchronised than earlier recessions between the US and Europe and for that reason it may prove longer lasting than its predecessors.

Economic variables respond in different ways to each stage of the cycle (Box 16.2). Some respond *pro-cyclically*, i.e. they increase (fall) as output increases (contracts); others respond *counter-cyclically*, i.e. they fall (increase) as aggregate output increases (declines). Some economic variables are *acyclical* – their values are relatively unaffected by fluctuations in aggregate economic variables.

> **Box 16.2**  **How changes in domestic activity affect economic variables**
>
> **Pro-cyclical variables:** (+) *in economic activity leads to* (+) *in these variables*:
>
> investment, commodity prices, business profits, labour productivity, imports, private sector credit, property prices, stock market index.
>
> **Counter-cyclical variables:** (+) *in economic activity in domestic economy leads to* (−) *in these variables*:
>
> unemployment rate, number of lay-offs, bankruptcies, foreign trade balance, short-term inventories, non-performing loans, the trade balance.
>
> **Acyclical variables:** (+/−) *in domestic economic activity have a zero or near-zero effect on these variables*:
>
> health services, staple foods, exports, primary education.

Sectoral responses to recessions and booms tend to be diverse. This is one strong motivation for firms to diversify sales and production into different sectors of the market. The lower the degree of synchronisation of fluctuations in economic activity at sectoral and international levels, the greater the potential gains from sectoral and geographical diversification.

While empirical studies confirm that business cycles are less prevalent and of lower amplitude than they were prior to the Second World War, these cycles have still caused significant losses of output. They add to the uncertainty of business and cause many to lose their jobs.

So much for the facts about economic fluctuations. We now consider the causes of these fluctuations and the reasons why their amplitude has become less extreme.

## 16.2  What causes fluctuations?

### Causes of economic instability

Business cycles are caused by a mixture of factors. Some theories of the business cycle focus on the *intrinsic instability of the free market*. Other theories focus on the role of *random external shocks* such as the Iraqi invasion of Kuwait (1990) and the Kobe earthquake (1995). *Policy-induced shocks* have been identified as another cause of cycles. Shifts in monetary and fiscal policy, for example, can sometimes turn out to be pro-cyclical, an eventuality which becomes more likely when government fiscal decisions are influenced by the approach of elections.[5] At several

---

[5] The term political cycle was introduced by the Polish economist Michael Kalecki, 'Political aspects to full employment', *Political Quarterly* (October 1943).

junctures during the past four decades, *banking and financial crises* have brought booms to an untimely end; South-east Asia, Brazil and Russia all suffered in this way. In the case of Argentina during 2001–03, problems in the financial sector aggravated and prolonged the downturn.

Keynesian economics attributes cycles to shifts in aggregate demand, caused primarily by the highly volatile behaviour of investment. Taken together with the assumption of pervasive nominal price rigidities, shifts in investment demand could impact on the *volume* of aggregate demand instead of on *prices*. Suppose that investment expands because of a more upbeat assessment of future economic prospects. This will be magnified, through the multiplier, into a much larger increase in sales throughout the economy. The resultant rise in aggregate demand will give a further reinforcing stimulus to investment. Firms will find that their inventories have fallen. New stocks will be ordered to keep up with extra sales. This very act, of course, adds another stimulus to aggregate demand, justifies the expectations of the original investors and makes them even more bullish. Optimistic expectations become self-fulfilling. The economy enters a boom. This continues until eventually the market begins to believe that capacity growth has been reached. Then investors become more cautious and demand for additions to inventories begins to subside. Resources employed in producing the annual additions to firms' inventories and capital stock might have to be 'let go'. A downward spiral is set in motion, fuelled by the same forces that drove the economy upwards during the boom. This process of cumulative and circular causation has been formalised in a simple but revealing way in the multiplier–accelerator model (see Box 16.3).

Real business cycle theory explains cyclical shocks in terms of spurts and starts in technological advance. An improvement in technology leads to a rise in productivity, a higher real wage and a correspondingly greater willingness to work. Hoteliers and restaurant workers in Mediterranean countries, for example, work long hours during the tourist season when the productivity of work is high, and take leisure time during winter when productivity is low. Cycles, in this view, are generated by rational economic agents and 'real' factors. We do not require nominal rigidities or money illusion to explain their existence. Random factors such as wars and natural disasters can have effects similar to the technology shocks analysed in real business cycle theory.

*Policy induced shocks* seem a rather unlikely cause of business fluctuations. The task of policy would seem to be to moderate fluctuations, not to cause them. Unfortunately, experience shows practice to be at variance with precept in this respect. Both monetary and fiscal policies have often been found to function in a surprisingly pro-cyclical way. Sometimes this is intentional (the political business cycle); at other times, the pro-cyclicality arises because of implementation and other lags or simple misreading of the economic situation by the authorities.

*Banking and financial crises* have been an intrinsic feature of the market system for a long time. During the Asian boom, banks lent too much to dubious building and other speculative projects in domestic currency on the basis of funds borrowed in dollars at what appeared to be relatively low dollar interest rates. All went well as long as confidence in the sustainability of the building boom lasted. Once confidence began to falter, however, the bubble burst. The financial sector's balance sheet began to look dodgy; dollar loans to the banks were recalled; and bank depositors began to take fright. Falling output, high interest rates and

---

**Box 16.3**  **The multiplier–accelerator model**

The investment accelerator idea was for a long time the leading theory behind the explanation of cycles. The British economist Sir John Hicks wrote: 'the main cause of fluctuations is to be found in the effect of changes in output (or income) on investment.' Although several important developments have occurred in the theory of business fluctuations during the last three decades, many economists believe that the accelerator principle of investment remains an important explanation of the business cycle.

Consider a simple model where output is determined as follows:

$$Y = C + I \tag{1}$$

Consumption ($C$) is a function of income alone, but with a one-period lag; thus, $C = aY_{-1}$. Investment ($I$) is a function of the change in income, also with a one-period lag, and an exogenous level $I_0$, determined by 'animal spirits':

$$I = b(Y_{-1} - Y_{-2}) + I_0 \tag{2}$$

Combining equations (1) and (2), we have

$$Y = (a + b)Y_{-1} - bY_{-2} + I_0 \tag{3}$$

Output is a function of its lagged levels in the two periods. Given plausible parameters, a cyclical behaviour following a rise in $I_0$ can be generated by this model.

*Sources*: J.D. Sachs and F. Larraín, *Macroeconomics in the Global Economy* (Hemel Hempstead: Harvester Wheatsheaf, 1993), Chapter 17; J.R. Hicks, *A Constitution to the Theory of the Trade Cycle* (Oxford: Oxford University Press, 1950).

---

depreciating exchange rates added to the disarray and sense of panic. In Japan, the weakness of the financial system continues to prolong economic stagnation, a decade after the bursting of the stock market and property bubbles. Serious damage was inflicted on economies such as Korea's where capital flows reversed from inflows of $5 billion per quarter in the first half of 1997 to an outflow of $20 billion in November, while the won's exchange rate was cut in half. Worse, through a process of contagion, economies with relatively sound banking and financial systems also suffered speculative attacks (the *contagion effect* for these countries is then similar to an external random shock). These types of crises indicate the presence of systemic flaws in the market system akin to the market failures discussed in Part I. Thus rational behaviour on the part of the individual lender to one of these countries (anxious to get money back quickly), once it is replicated by all lenders, leads to an irrational outcome (an unnecessary and unwarranted recession in the whole economy). And just as in the case of individuals standing up in a football stadium to get a better view, or a panic exit from a theatre, each individual's doing the 'rational' thing leads to a sub-optimal collective outcome.

These theories of business fluctuations have developed from experience of different historical cycles. In analysing any particular situation, we must use the theory that seems most appropriate in the circumstances.

## Why has the amplitude of the cycle diminished?[6]

Reference has already been made to the small number of negative annual growth rates in postwar experience. The downturns are steeper and longer-lasting for industrial production than for GDP, but even there the incidence has been mild, especially by comparison with the inter-war period of 1919–39. Why have downswings in the cycle become shallower and expansions become longer?

In answering this question, a distinction needs to be made between the incidence and size of shocks and the change in the factors that moderate or magnify their transmission through the economy. It is possible that part of the reduction in the amplitude of fluctuations is due to the less severe and traumatic nature of the shocks themselves. More important, however, have been the changes in the transmission mechanisms (*propagation effects*) that have on the whole tended to moderate the overall impact of any given shock.

First, the shift in composition of output from the industrial sector to the tertiary sector has made total GDP less volatile. The purchase of new durable goods, such as cars and washing machines, can be easily deferred or advanced, but services have to be produced and consumed simultaneously and are less easy to postpone. Demand for services such as education, basic health needs and counselling is highly income-elastic in the long term, but can be relatively insensitive to short-term reductions in GDP. Once a certain level of health provision and education is established, it proves extremely resistant to downward adjustment. A ratchet effect appears to operate. Of course, not all services are stable in this sense – tourism, theatre and real estate services are highly cyclical.

Second, the high share of government spending in GDP has added an element of stability to the economy. Government spending, including that of publicly owned corporations, is much less sensitive to cyclical conditions than spending in the private sector. This, in part, reflects the nature of the services provided by government (health, social welfare, education, interest on public debt), as well as the lesser degree of discipline exerted by market forces on state-owned corporations, which makes their investment decisions less sensitive to fluctuations in profits.

Third, automatic fiscal stabilisers tend to moderate the effect of private sector volatility. Economic booms are choked off by higher leakages to the public sector via growth in tax revenues and reductions in the social welfare bill, while budget deficits buttress private sector spending during the downturns.

Fourth, policy activism has played a role in averting major crises. Consider, for example, an early, optimistic assessment of policy activism by Arthur F. Burns, a distinguished business cycles scholar and former chairman of the Federal Reserve Board:

---

[6] We take this reduction in the severity of cycles as an established fact. It has been repeatedly affirmed by empirical researchers. But inevitably, every empirical generalisation in economics seems to invite challenge sooner or later. It has been claimed that the contrast between postwar and prewar cyclical behaviour is not as self-evident as it might appear if postwar indexes of economic activity were calculated on the same basis as prewar indexes. Research on this subject continues but, at the end of the day, the generalisation is likely to be qualified rather than refuted. Zarnovitz, for example, finds that the coefficient of variation (a statistical measure of dispersion) of America's real GDP for the period 1946–83 was one-half that of 1875–1918 and only one-third that of 1919–45: Victor Zarnovitz, *Business Cycles: Theory, history, indicators and forecasting* (Chicago and London: University of Chicago Press, 1992).

The general expectation of the postwar period has been that the government would move with some vigour to check any recession that developed, and that its monetary, fiscal and regulatory actions would contribute to that objective. By and large, this confidence has been justified by events. Not only has monetary policy in the main been shaped with a view to promoting stable prosperity, but fiscal policy – which previously had been handicapped by the convention of normally balanced budgets – has lately also been guided by the state of the economy.[7]

In retrospect, we have seen that the record of demand management has been more mixed than the above quotation would suggest. *Yet the ability of governments to take action in the event of a major disruption of demand, say, following a stock market crash, or of an unjustified and contagious bout of inflationary expansion, is an important stabilising influence on the economy.* Another, not necessarily contradictory, twist is often added to this argument. It is that the adoption by governments of medium-term stability objectives has imposed greater discipline on macroeconomic policy.

Confidence that the government would set a 'floor' below which the real economy will not fall and a 'ceiling' beyond which real growth will be discouraged helped to ensure that fluctuations stayed within manageable bounds. The readiness of governments to intervene in order to avert a financial crisis strengthens investors' confidence. Closer supervision of the financial system can also help to avert crises – although disaster has been only narrowly averted in Japan and even in the better regulated US during the past decade.

## 16.3 Business fluctuations and growth

Instability in a country's growth path seems to be negatively related to the trend rate of growth. For example, on the basis of the performance of the US economy over the past 100 years, Zarnovitz finds that *periods of high instability have been associated with lower average economic growth.* 'Growth was generally higher when stability was greater. Instability of aggregate demand and of the price level impedes growth', he concluded.[8] One reason for this finding may be that sustained growth creates a climate which is conducive to innovation, adjustment and structural change which, in turn, tends to create faster growth. Schumpeter's process of 'creative destruction' may be replicated more effectively in an economy which grows faster but experiences smaller oscillations than in a free market *laissez-faire* economy, characterised by textbook boom and slump. Fast-growing economies provide a friendly environment for innovation, new competition and reallocation

---

[7] Arthur F. Burns, *The Business Cycle in a Changing World* (New York and London: Columbia University Press, 1958), p. 49. Writing in 1969, the economic historian Angus Maddison concluded that 'government policy has obviously added greatly to the buoyancy of the economy and has been one of the main causes of rapid economic growth'. Economists nowadays describe the effects of government intervention in less glowing terms: Angus Maddison, 'Comment', in Martin Bronfenbrenner (ed.), *Is the Business Cycle Obsolete?* (New York: John Wiley, 1969), p. 500.

[8] V. Zarnovitz, *Business Cycles: Theory, history, indicators and forecasting* (Chicago: University of Chicago Press, 1992), p. 230. See also G. Ramey and V. Ramey, 'Cross country evidence on the link between volatility and growth', *American Economic Review*, December 1995. Research during the past decade has confirmed these conclusions. The effects of output volatility on growth in developing countries are particularly harmful.

of resources. There is evidence that by moderating cyclical fluctuations 'good' economic policy encourages the build-up of human capital and learning-by-doing.[9]

## 16.4 Forecasting the business cycle

The business cycle has altered in character. The amplitude of cycles, in particular, has diminished in recent decades. This has in no way diminished the demand for forecasts of variables such as GDP, interest rates, inflation and exchange rates. How are these eagerly sought and read forecasts formulated? How accurate are they? How do firms use macro-forecasts and why are they important?

### How are forecasts made?

In preparing a GDP forecast, a forecaster's first step is to study the past behaviour of the variables involved. This can be done in many different ways.

First, econometric and mathematical models are used. These models vary from small *ad hoc* models to models with literally hundreds of variables and equations. Consumption, investment, exports, imports, prices, wages and productivity all figure in such models. Some technical assumptions have to be made – about commodity prices, exchange rates, fiscal policy, and so on. One powerful advantage of a macroeconometric model is that it helps to ensure consistency of the overall forecast (especially important where several countries' performance is involved). It can also be used to test alternative policy assumptions and to identify major sensitive points of the overall projections. These models are voracious consumers of good quality, up-to-date data and are crucially dependent on such data.

Second, judgement has to be applied in interpreting the results of the model. The results need to be assessed by sectoral specialists and country experts. A good team of economists can be helpful at this stage. For instance, the Federal Reserve's track record in forecasting inflation and growth was consistently better than the consensus views of private sector forecasts – one possible explanation for which might be the expertise of the Bank's sizeable research staff (as C. Romer and D. Romer argued in the June 2000 issue of the *American Economic Review*).

Third, from these macroeconomic forecasts specific variables of interest to business, such as regional sales, can be derived. In such instances, macro forecasts will often be complemented by less formal techniques such as 'eyeballing' of past trends (Chartism) and application of rules of thumb and key historical ratios. Often, in practice, it is not just the variable itself that is closely scrutinised but how that variable has behaved *in conjunction with a selection of other variables*.

### Are forecasts accurate?

Do forecasters get it right, on average? We know that it is impossible for any forecaster to be correct all the time, but how often do they come close to the actual outcome?

---

[9] P.H. Martin and C.A. Rogers, 'Long-term growth and short-term economic instability', *European Economic Review*, 2000.

In an attempt to answer this question, Professor John Kay reported the results of a review of the record of 34 individual forecasters and forecasting organisations in the UK in the period since 1987.[10] He found that forecasters tend to cluster around a consensus – and that this consensus will more than likely be wrong. He found that all the forecasts for GDP growth in 1993 and 1994 were substantially below the actual outcome, while all the forecasts in 1991 and 1992 were above the actual outcome. The consensus forecast, he went on, 'failed to predict any of the important developments in the [UK] economy over the past seven years – the strength and resilience of the 1980s consumer boom, the depth and persistence of the 1990s recession, or the dramatic and continuing decline in inflation since 1991'.

This type of forecasting record is not peculiar to the UK. Reviews of the forecasting record of many international think-tanks reveal similar results. A study of the OECD's forecasting quantified its degree of success in prediction by means of the *root mean square error technique*. This involves finding the difference between the forecast value of a variable and the actual outcome. This difference, or 'error', is then squared in order to standardise positive and negative mistakes.[11] These squared errors are then averaged, and the square root is taken of this figure. The result is the root mean square error (RMSE) of a forecast. The larger the RMSE, the less accurate the forecast.

In Table 16.2, the RMSE of OECD forecasts since 1974 for seven major market economies are considered. For the sake of comparison, the performance of the

### Table 16.2 Forecasting errors for growth and inflation*

| | | Growth | | | | | Inflation | | |
| | | | Errors | | | | | Errors | |
| | | Actual | OECD | Random | | | Actual | OECD | Random |
|---|---|---|---|---|---|---|---|---|---|
| US | (1987–92) | 2.0 | 1.3 | 1.8 | US | (1987–92) | 3.6 | 0.5 | 0.7 |
| Japan | (1987–92) | 4.4 | 1.3 | 1.8 | Japan | (1987–92) | 1.2 | 0.6 | 1.0 |
| Germany | (1987–92) | 3.1 | 1.4 | 1.3 | Germany | (1987–92) | 3.1 | 0.4 | 0.9 |
| France | (1987–92) | 2.5 | 0.9 | 0.9 | France | (1987–92) | 2.9 | 0.6 | 1.0 |
| Italy | (1987–92) | 2.5 | 1.1 | 0.7 | Italy | (1987–92) | 6.2 | 1.5 | 1.5 |
| UK | (1987–92) | 1.5 | 1.9 | 1.7 | UK | (1987–92) | 6.1 | 0.7 | 1.1 |
| Canada | (1987–92) | 2.0 | 1.8 | 1.9 | Canada | (1987–92) | 3.3 | 1.5 | 1.5 |
| G7 | (1974–82) | 2.7 | 2.2 | 3.5 | G7 | (1974–82) | 10.2 | 3.0 | 4.2 |
| G7 | (1982–91) | 2.9 | 1.3 | 1.9 | G7 | (1982–91) | 4.3 | 1.0 | 1.5 |
| G7 | (1987–92) | 2.6 | 1.4 | 1.5 | G7 | (1987–92) | 3.8 | 0.9 | 1.1 |

* Actual refers to the level of output growth or inflation recorded in the economy or group of economies in question. OECD and Random refer to the Root Mean Square Error of forecasts of growth/inflation made by the OECD Model and a Random Walk Model respectively.

*Source*: Computed from OECD, *Economic Outlook* (June 1993).

[10] John Kay, 'Cracks in the crystal ball', *Financial Times* (29 September 1995).

[11] Suppose the forecast for output growth is 4 per cent and that growth of 2 per cent actually occurs. This error of −2 is then squared. The squared error of the forecast is 4. If, on the other hand, the forecast value is 6 per cent, the squared error would also be 4. Had the gap between forecasts been 3 per cent instead of 2 per cent, then the squared error would have been 9. Thus, the squared error of a forecast does not discriminate between positive and negative errors, and also penalises larger forecast errors.

sophisticated OECD techniques is contrasted with that of a simple naive 'random walk' technique, whereby the forecasted value of a variable next year is assumed to be the same as its actual value this year.

Four conclusions can be drawn from these tables. First, random walk models tend to perform as well as, if not better than, the OECD model when predicting GDP growth in Germany, France, Italy and the UK. Second, conventional forecasting techniques are more successful at predicting inflation than at predicting growth. The inflation forecasts clearly outperform random walk methods. Third, the overall record of forecasts with regard to *total* OECD countries' inflation and growth has been consistently better than the random walk method since 1974. Fourth, the RMSE of the forecasts has declined for both output and growth. However, since the accuracy of random walk measures has also improved, an open verdict must be recorded as to how much of this improvement has been due to improved technique and how much to a decline in the year-to-year variability of the macroeconomic variables themselves.

Instead of RMSE, one could use the mean error and the mean absolute error. One could also examine how an organisation's forecasts compare with others in terms of these efficiency indicators and the degree to which forecast errors are persistent. A comprehensive analysis of European Commission forecasts published in 1999 reveals a similar pattern of results to the OECD study.[12]

No matter how interpreted, the impression is that many key economic forecasts have proved disappointingly inaccurate. One basic problem has to do with the reliance of forecasts on past data. First, *while the past may seem like a good yardstick for predicting the future, it will fail to take account of random shocks* (internal or external) on the economy. These shocks are, by definition, unpredictable through systematic analysis, yet they happen all the time and can have a major impact on the forecast variables. For example, the Kobe earthquake had a major impact on the Japanese economy, initially most acutely reflected in the performance of the Nikkei, Japan's closely followed equity index. Yet forecasters, using historical data to forecast Japanese GDP growth or the future values for the Nikkei, could not

### Table 16.3 Growth in developed and developing economies since 1970

|  | Average rate of growth | Standard deviation |
|---|---|---|
| OECD Major Seven | 2.8 | 2.0 |
| China | 8.4 | 3.8 |
| India | 4.8 | 3.9 |
| Korea | 7.5 | 3.8 |
| Hong Kong | 6.9 | 4.7 |
| Singapore | 8.2 | 3.5 |
| Thailand | 6.6 | 4.5 |
| Malaysia | 7.0 | 3.9 |

Source: World Bank, *World Development Indicators*, 2002.

[12] F. Keereman, 'The track record of the Commission's forecasts', *Economic Paper No. 137*, European Commission (October 1999).

possibly have accounted for such a random event. Similarly, in the US, most fore-casters were unable to predict the timing of the stock market collapse. Even the most vaunted forecaster of them all, Alan Greenspan of the Federal Reserve, was a full five years premature in his famous 'irrational exuberance' speech of 1996 warning of the overvalued level of US share prices.

Second, *the use of historical data assumes that the factors which have driven each of the previous cycles are the same ones driving the present cycle. Factors which were present in past cycles may no longer be relevant in determining this business cycle.* 'New economy' factors not present in earlier cycles may be crucially important in interpreting the current cycle. Also, the roles of asset prices, household debt, computer-led productivity increases and globalisation were not nearly as prominent in earlier cycles. Forecasts based on earlier cycles will be generally off the mark, because they failed to take this into account. Even if cycles look the same, different factors may be driving each one.

Third, *past relationships between key economic variables may change over time.* For example, analysis of historical experience showed that if house prices have risen less than average incomes for a period, they will rise faster in the next period, and when the ratio of prices to incomes becomes too high, they rise less quickly. But this relationship was observed in a period when house prices consistently rose, so that the price people would pay for a house was often limited only by what they could borrow. The past relationship may not persist in an era of lower inflation and in the wake of a traumatic period when many householders become locked in a negative equity position. Forecasts based on historical data will not reflect such structural changes.

Fourth, *official forecasts are prone to over-optimism.* Cambridge economist Wynn Godley noted that the UK Treasury had never forecast a recession. Some would reply that the forecasting exercise prevents recessions by alerting authorities to the need for remedial action, but there is an undoubted element of 'cycle denial' at work also. Buyer beware!

The above analysis explains why forecasters so often seem to err in the same direction. Their forecasts are all based on the same faulty foundation of a given set of past data and estimated behavioural relationships.

Does it matter if forecasters get it wrong? Ultimately, the answer to this question will depend on the uses to which the forecast is put. In the case of the Kobe earthquake, forecasts of the Japanese economy were seriously affected. The accompanying fall in the Nikkei index led ultimately to the collapse of Baring Brothers merchant bank – because one of its traders was speculating heavily on the value of the Nikkei and made a spectacular mistake. So if forecasts are being used in this way, accuracy is important. The accuracy of forecasts may also matter at a political level, in so far as they may influence the timing of an election and the nature of political promises and programmes. But Mr Greenspan's spectacularly wrong forecast about the US stock market in his 'irrational exuberance' speech at the end of 1996 seems to have caused no harm either to the economy or to his reputation or – still less – to the stock market, which continued to rise from 6400 in December 1996 to nearly double that level three years later.

Economics is not very good at answering questions about what will happen; it is much better at answering the question: *if* something happens (be it faster growth, higher interest rates or an exchange rate depreciation), what will be the consequences for the economy? Caution must therefore be used when utilising economic forecasts. Fortunately for the economics profession, such sage advice will not stop forecasters forecasting or commentators commentating on them, or businesses demanding them. Nature abhors a vacuum. In this instance, however, it is useful to be aware that what replaces the vacuum can sometimes be as empty as the vacuum itself.

## 16.5 Macro-forecasts and the firm

A firm might have many reasons for using economic forecasts. If it was considering an investment, interest rate forecasts could help it decide how and when to borrow. If forecasts for interest rates show that they will be lower in six months' time, the firm may defer taking out the loan until credit becomes cheaper. Likewise, if forecasts point to higher interest rates in the future, the firm may decide to take the loan out now as credit is cheaper, or even may decide not to take the loan out at all if the repayments would be too high in the future. Similarly, firms with foreign transactions will regularly consult exchange rate forecasts for guidance. An exporting firm would surely be interested in the likely future direction of the relevant currency in projecting income and payment flows for the company. Firms are not interested exclusively in macroeconomic forecasts, such as those on economic growth, interest rates and exchange rates, but also in integrating these forecasts into their own sales and cost projections for the company. This integration can proceed on a *top-down* or a *bottom-up* basis. Top-down forecasts begin with macroeconomic projections and work out the implications of these projections for the firm (Box 16.4).

### Box 16.4 Top-down forecast of demand for personal computers

1. Forecast growth of GDP and other macroeconomic indicators, such as disposable income, that are closely related to PC sales.

2. Prepare PC industry forecast in volume and value terms, drawing on aggregate forecasts.

3. Regionalise forecasts and break down by product category.

4. Make use of external information regarding the competitive environment (domestic vs foreign costs; changes in exchange rates; new entrants to industry) and supplement this information with analysis of consumer preferences and company capacity. Develop market share projections for the company.

5. Review company sales forecast disaggregated by region and product line.

6. Develop market share projections and compare with *bottom-up* forecasts based on opinion surveys of regional sales offices and other micro-projections.

*Source*: Dale G. Bails and Larry C. Peppers, *Business Fluctuations: Forecasting techniques and applications*, 2nd edn (Englewood Cliffs, NJ: Prentice Hall, 1993).

Top-down methods are relevant only to a large firm or to projections for an entire industry. For a small firm, its future sales path will be determined primarily by micro-factors within its own control, rather than by macro-trends. In all cases, market share projections based on *top-down* techniques should be compared with *bottom-up* forecasts based on projections of sales managers, opinion surveys of regional sales offices and extrapolation of past sales, which take account of specific factors relevant to each element in the company's product range.

## 16.6 Conclusions

Comparison of growth rates over the past 40 years highlighted the size, duration and incidence of business cycles and fluctuations. The exercise revealed a low incidence of negative growth rates, but significant fluctuations around average and trend growth rates for the major industrial countries. There is no compelling evidence of the existence of systematic long-run cycles. Sustained periods of prosperity and fast growth, however, tend to be succeeded sooner or later by a relative or absolute downturn.

In industrial economies, downturns have been greatly moderated in recent decades. These economies have stayed on average approximately three times longer in the expansion phase of the cycle than in the recession phase. There is a strong degree of synchronisation of cycles among European economies, and a growing degree between the different continents. This synchronisation may tend to accentuate world fluctuations, unless global economic policy coordination is improved.

Business fluctuations occur in an erratic fashion. Their characteristics change over time. One important development has been that the amplitude of business cycles has diminished. In particular, downswings in cycles have become shallower and expansions have become longer. The increasing share of government spending in GDP and the shift from the industrial to the tertiary sector have made national output behave in a less volatile way. Policy measures have also helped to avert major crises, though their effectiveness in moderating smaller fluctuations is dubious.

Studies of the relationship between business fluctuations and growth suggest that higher instability is associated with lower average economic growth. However, opinion is divided as to what exactly causes this instability. For example, some theories attribute cycles to random external shocks, others to internal shocks, still others to policy-induced shocks. Real business cycle theorists emphasise the role of discrete shifts in technology such as the current information and biotechnology boom. Others focus on inherent tendencies towards self-fulfilling over-optimism and over-pessimism in a market system.

Economic forecasters try to extrapolate from what has happened in the past in order to make predictions about the future. Various methods are used to obtain these forecasts. Highly complex mathematical and statistical models are often used by central banks, the World Bank and the OECD. But using such sophisticated methods does not prevent forecasters from getting it wrong. In fact, no matter how much information forecasters have at hand, they will never be right all the time.

It is wrong, therefore, for business to expect great precision from forecasts. The forecast is only a means of attempting to reduce uncertainty; it cannot eliminate that uncertainty. Forecasts can be useful as sources of information and for teasing out issues of interest to the firm.

## Summary

1. Business cycles refer to fluctuations in aggregate economic activity that are widely diffused throughout the economy and have identifiable peaks and troughs. Most modern studies focus on growth cycles, that is, deviations from trend growth of the aggregate variable under investigation. Economic variables respond in different ways to each stage of the cycle. Some respond pro-cyclically, some respond counter-cyclically, while some are acyclical. Empirical studies indicate that business cycles are less prevalent and of lower amplitude than they were prior to the Second World War. However, these cycles have still caused significant losses of output and add to the uncertainty of business.

2. Business cycles are caused by a mixture of factors. Some theories of the business cycle focus on the intrinsic instability of the free market, others on the role of random external shocks. Policy-induced shocks have also been identified as another cause of business cycles. These shocks are amplified by various propagation mechanisms. In analysing any particular situation, we must use the theory most appropriate in the circumstances. Many factors have contributed to the diminished amplitude of cycles in the postwar period: for example, the shift in composition of output from the industrial sector to the tertiary sector, the rising share of government expenditure in GDP and – but more debatably – policy activism.

3. Instability in a country's growth path seems to be negatively related to the trend rate of growth. One reason for this finding may be that sustained growth creates a climate which is conducive to innovation, adjustment and structural change, which in turn tends to create faster growth.

4. Despite the diminished amplitude of cycles, forecasts for variables such as GDP, interest rates and inflation are still in great demand. There are many ways in which these forecasts can be developed. Usually, the past behaviour of the variable, and other related variables, is used to develop forecasts. However, the picture will always be incomplete, which explains why no forecaster can predict the future with perfect accuracy. In practice, historical data are not always a reliable guide to future behaviour. Relationships between key variables may change over time, factors driving cycles can change over time, and there will always be unpredictable random shocks. Thus, caution must be exercised when using economic forecasts.

5. Firms frequently make use of economic forecasts. For investors, interest rate forecasts are of crucial concern, while foreign exchange forecasts can be used by exporting firms with large foreign exchange risk exposure. Macroeconomic forecasts are often integrated into the firms' own sales and cost projections which can proceed on a top-down or a bottom-up basis.

## Questions for discussion

1. Why do economic cycles (or business fluctuations) occur? What are the implications of these fluctuations for business?

2. Would you expect government intervention to increase, or to diminish, the amplitude of business cycles?

3. It is often assumed that business cycles have little effect on the long-run growth of the economy. In other words, the business cycle represents transitory deviations around a given trend growth rate.

   Do you agree? If this statement were true, why should economists be concerned with business cycles?

4. Evaluate the usefulness of economic forecasts to business, especially in the light of their indifferent prediction record.

## Exercises

1. Most business cycle literature refers to industrial countries, yet developing countries are harmed more than industrial countries by these economic fluctuations. Examine the GDP fluctuations in any developing country, analyse the causes and suggest policies to reduce their amplitude.

2. Show how you would present a macroeconomic forecast of the economy (choose between the US, German, French or UK economies) to other business people. What use, if any, could a firm make of such a forecast?

3. A stockbroking firm provides your business with a quarterly review containing forecasts of GDP growth for one, two and three years ahead. You are asked to evaluate the forecasting record of this firm. How would you propose doing this?

### Further reading

A concise summary of recent research can be found in IMF, 'Modern business cycles in industrial countries – a tale of 93 cycles', *World Economic Outlook*, April 2002. A comprehensive overview is available in V. Zarnovitz, *Business Cycles: Theory, history, indicators and forecasting* (Chicago: University of Chicago Press, 1992). See also K. Mayhew and J. Muellbauer, 'Business cycles', *Oxford Review of Economic Policy*, 13(3), 1997. The close synchronisation of the most recent cycle is analysed in O.T. Dalsgaard *et al.*, 'Ongoing changes in the business cycle – evidence and causes', *OECD Economics Department Working Papers*, no. 315, 2002. A useful description of forecasting techniques is outlined in D.G. Bails and L.C. Peppers, *Business Fluctuations: Forecasting techniques and applications*, 2nd edn (Englewood Cliffs, NJ: Prentice Hall International, 1993). Theoretical aspects of business cycles are explained in F.E. Kydland, *Business Cycles Theory* (Aldershot: Edward Elgar, 1995), and M.P. Niemira and P.A. Klein, *Forecasting Financial and Economic Cycles* (New York: John Wiley, 1994).

# Part III

# The global economy

**17** Foreign trade: patterns and policy

**18** Capital flows and foreign investment

**19** Labour migration

**20** The balance of payments: what it is and why it matters

**21** Coping with exchange rates

**22** Exchange rate regimes and the euro

This part assesses how the world macro-environment impacts on business. It examines the benefits – and challenges – to the global economy arising from the growth in foreign trade, capital flows, foreign investment and migration. It also discusses the exchange rate regime that is most suitable to the needs of countries adjusting to the more liberal and open system. Excessive exchange rate volatility adds to problems of adjustment and generates large costs for business. Excessive rigidity can cause similar problems. The search continues for ways of avoiding balance of payments and exchange rate turmoil.

*Think global, act local.* As the world economy becomes more open, even small firms have to take this rule seriously. The domestic market is no longer the secure base it once was, and foreign markets are no longer as difficult to penetrate or as remote. The globalisation of the economy brings opportunities and threats to firms. There is hardly any country nowadays that is not concerned with its international competitiveness. National policies have become *more outward-looking*, as evidenced by the implemention of the Uruguay Round, the relaxation of controls on capital mobility, the globally more benign stance towards foreign investment and the establishment of the World Trade Organisation in 1995. The consolidation of Europe's 1992 single market programme marks another watershed in the move towards a liberal world trade system.

The first two chapters of Part III explore the economic implications of the globalisation of markets. By this we mean the reduction of tariff and nontariff barriers on merchandise goods, the extension of an open trade regime to the services sector, the opening of world capital markets and the decline in barriers to the exchange of knowledge and technology. This is regarded as a strongly positive development for world economic growth and employment. But there could be serious short-term adjustment costs which domestic policy needs to address. Fear of such adjustment costs underlies the resistance to immigration in host countries. We discuss how the world economy has become more integrated, what gains can be expected to follow the growth in trade and what conditions are necessary in order to ensure that these gains will be realised.

Next we discuss the balance of payments, exchange rates and the world monetary system. If trade is important for welfare, it is important that the world payments system functions smoothly. Misaligned exchange rates, balance of payments crises and foreign exchange turmoil impose heavy costs on business. Companies spend heavily trying to find ways of limiting their exposure to foreign currency risks. There has been active debate over the optimal exchange rate system for an individual country or group of countries. Europe has been deeply embroiled in that debate, first under the European Monetary System and then with the creation of the euro and a European Central Bank.

This part is designed to provide the reader with an understanding of the main ideas underlying the consensus for freer trade, liberalisation of factor movements and a multilaterally agreed world trade order governed by rules. We draw extensively on analysis and concepts of Parts I and II. For example, the gains from trade are analysed with the aid of concepts such as economies of scale and the economic gains from competition that were introduced in Chapters 3–7, while the analysis of balance of payments and exchange rates has close ties with the macroeconomic chapters on monetary and fiscal policy.

## Chapter 17

# Foreign trade: patterns and policy

## Introduction

A worldwide consensus in favour of free trade has taken hold of economic opinion. Notwithstanding setbacks such as the failed Seattle and Cancun trade summits and the disruptive effects of the 2003 Iraq war, the consensus has remained firm. Political considerations played a key part in the development of this consensus, motivated by the desire to avoid trade wars and to promote faster growth. Business has supported free trade through its representative organisations, though the reaction 'on the ground' depends greatly on whether the particular enterprise is export- or home market-oriented. Export industries tend to be enthusiastic proponents of the merits of trade liberalisation. To them, freer trade means easier access to foreign markets, profitable investment opportunities and a greater spread of fixed costs. Import-competing firms in 'sensitive' sectors of the economy tend to see things differently. To them freer trade means the erosion of domestic market shares and the danger of job losses. The views of the pro-trade group have clearly prevailed.

There is growing evidence that trade liberalisation brings benefits to those countries ready to grasp the opportunities of global markets. The resultant gains outweigh the losses caused by adjustment to freer trade. Efforts to close the domestic market to foreign competition have proved both unavailing and counter-productive. Free trade versus protection is no longer the main issue in international trade. The conditions under which liberalised trade is conducted – the maintenance of 'level playing fields' and fair trading rules among developed economies, but in particular between developed and developing countries – have become the major subject of debate.

Economics concludes that foreign trade brings major benefits, but the reasoning behind this conclusion sometimes appears counter-intuitive, or just wrong. What many businesses might consider a 'bad' thing – cheaper imports, pressure on domestic market shares and job losses in industries which compete with imports – appear in economic models as a 'good' thing: an expression of the gains that accrue to society from trade. According to the economist's view, a country sells exports only in order to enjoy more consumption of imports. Higher exports are not a gain in the true sense. They imply that goods produced at home are being enjoyed by someone else. *They are beneficial to a country only to the extent that they enable its citizens to consume more imports* – now, or sometime in the future. Hence the notion that a country with a trade surplus (i.e. which exports more than it imports) benefits more from international trade than a country with a trade deficit is based upon a complete misunderstanding of the gains from trade.

Different perspectives on foreign trade can translate into different approaches to trade policy. It is important to understand the institutional background, the assumptions and the evidence on which discussion of global trade issues is now based.

## Chapter outline

This chapter provides an analytical overview of trade issues under five headings:

1. An overview of global trade patterns and the WTO.
2. Analysis of how nations benefit from foreign trade.
3. Empirical estimates of the gains from trade.
4. Trade policy, protection and new trade issues.
5. Determinants of competitiveness in the global market.

## 17.1 Global trade and the WTO

The global trade environment has changed in three major ways in recent decades. International trade has grown rapidly in value and volume, the composition of trade has altered significantly, and trade flows have been extensively liberalised.

### Growth in trade

The total value of world exports of goods and services is close to US$7000 billion. Among the few statistical regularities in modern economies is the tendency for growth in trade volume consistently to exceed growth in output. For example, between 1973 and 2003, world trade increased by 4.6 per cent annually compared with an annual growth in world output of 2.8 per cent (Table 17.1). During the 1990s, trade grew by nearly 6 per cent annually, more than twice as fast as world output. Economic growth in the EU (2 per cent p.a.) has been below the world average, but its trade continues to expand at more than double this rate.

A feature of the world trade system is that *successful exporters tend also to be fast-growing importers*. Each of the top 10 leading exporters is included among the top 10 leading importers (Table 17.2). The export performance of Asian countries has been matched by an equally dramatic increase in imports into Asia. The share of developing Asian countries in EU exports has jumped from 7 per cent to nearly 20 per cent – overtaking, in the process, the 18 per cent share held by the US.

**Table 17.1(a) World merchandise trade and GDP, 1900–2003 (average annual % change in volume)**

|  | 1900–13 | 1913–50 | 1950–73 | 1973–2003 |
|---|---|---|---|---|
| Merchandise trade | 4.3 | 0.6 | 8.2 | 4.6 |
| Gross domestic product | 2.5 | 2.0 | 5.1 | 2.8 |

*Source*: World Trade Organisation, *Regionalism and the World Trading System* (Geneva, April 1995); *International Trade Statistics* (1995); own estimates.

**Table 17.1(b) Value of world exports, 2002 (US$ billion)**

| | |
|---|---|
| World merchandise exports | 6150 |
| Commercial services | 1460 |
| Total | 7610 |

*Source*: WTO, *International Trade Statistics 2002*. Available at www.wto.org

Foreign trade has become more important for virtually all countries, even for large countries such as the US, but trade ratios differ markedly between countries. A rough measure of the rising importance of trade is the ratio of exports and imports to GDP. Since 1990, the export:GDP ratio of low-income countries has doubled from 12 to 24 per cent. Middle-income countries have also registered a steep rise in the export:GDP ratio from 22 to 28 per cent. The range of variation in trade ratios is striking, from 8 per cent in Rwanda to 180 per cent in Singapore (Table 17.3). At any one time, however, small countries tend to have a higher trade ratio than large countries, assuming comparable levels of economic development.

**Table 17.2 Leading exporters and importers in merchandise trade, 2001**

| | Exporters | | | | Importers | | |
|---|---|---|---|---|---|---|---|
| Rank | Country* | US$bn | % share | Rank | Country* | US$bn | % share |
| 1 | United States | 730.8 | 11.9 | 1 | United States | 1180.2 | 18.3 |
| 2 | Germany | 570.8 | 9.3 | 2 | Germany | 492.8 | 7.7 |
| 3 | Japan | 403.5 | 6.6 | 3 | Japan | 349.1 | 5.4 |
| 4 | France | 321.8 | 5.2 | 4 | UK | 331.8 | 5.2 |
| 5 | UK | 273.1 | 4.4 | 5 | France | 325.8 | 5.1 |
| 6 | China | 266.2 | 4.3 | 6 | China | 243.6 | 3.8 |
| 7 | Canada | 259.9 | 4.2 | 7 | Italy | 232.9 | 3.6 |
| 8 | Italy | 241.1 | 3.9 | 8 | Canada | 227.2 | 3.5 |
| 9 | Netherlands | 229.5 | 3.7 | 9 | Netherlands | 207.3 | 3.2 |
| 10 | Hong Kong | 191.1 | 3.1 | 10 | Hong Kong | 202.0 | 3.1 |
| 11 | Belgium | 179.7 | 1.8 | 11 | Mexico | 176.2 | 2.7 |
| 12 | Mexico | 158.5 | 1.6 | 12 | Belgium | 168.7 | 2.6 |

* Figures for EU countries include intra-EU trade.

*Source*: WTO, *International Trade Statistics 2002*. Available at www.wto.org

Table 17.3  How important is trade?

| Country | Exports of goods and services as % of GDP (2000) |
|---|---|
| **The least trade-dependent nations** | |
| Rwanda | 8 |
| Uganda | 10 |
| Argentina | 11 |
| Brazil | 11 |
| Bangladesh | 14 |
| India | 14 |
| Tanzania | 15 |
| Peru | 16 |
| Albania | 19 |
| **Major industrial economies** | |
| US | 11 |
| Japan | 10 |
| Germany | 33 |
| France | 29 |
| UK | 27 |
| Italy | 28 |
| Canada | 44 |
| **The most trade-dependent nations** | |
| Netherlands | 61 |
| Estonia | 84 |
| Belgium | 88 |
| Ireland | 88 |
| Malaysia | 125 |
| Hong Kong | 150 |
| Singapore | 180 |

Source: World Bank, World Development Indicators, 2002.

The top five trade-oriented countries, with export:GDP ratios in the range 88 per cent to 180 per cent, are small countries. Paradoxically, while small countries trade more proportionately than large countries, small firms tend to be less trade-oriented than large firms. In most countries, a small minority of large firms account for the predominant share of total exports.

## Composition of trade

About 80 per cent of total trade consists of merchandise trade and 20 per cent consists of commercial services. Most of this trade is between developed countries – they trade much more with each other than with developing countries.

The product composition of trade is changing rapidly. Trade in food and primary commodities has declined relative to manufacturing. Manufactured goods dominate world trade, accounting for 72 per cent of merchandise flows. In recent decades, the share of *high-tech trade*, which includes pharmaceuticals, chemicals, precision engineering and electronics, has risen steeply. Office and telecom equipment, for example, has increased its share of world trade from 5 per cent in the early 1980s to 13 per cent – slightly higher than the share of agricultural products. Trade in commercial services, such as transport, tourism and financial services, accounts for about 20 per cent of total trade. Services trade can be especially important for countries that rely heavily on tourism – for example Egypt (64 per cent of total exports) and Greece (63 per cent). Advances in technology and deregulation have opened up large sections of the services industry to international competition. Income from foreign investment has increased in tandem with the globalisation of financial markets.

A large part of trade consists of *intra-industry trade*, defined as the exchange of broadly similar goods. Intra-industry trade has risen rapidly in the past three decades and now accounts for more than half of all trade in manufactures between the industrial countries.[1] An analysis of trade in over 2000 different manufactured goods shows that 64 per cent of trade between EU countries in 1992 was intra-industry in character. Computations for the period 1970–98 indicate that the intra-industry share of extra-EU trade has also been growing rapidly.[2] Many practical examples of intra-industry trade can be given. The UK exported US$130 billion worth of machinery and transport equipment in 1997, but in the same year it also imported US$135 billion worth of these products. Germany is the second largest exporter *and* importer of automotive products in the world. The causes of intra-industry trade, and its implications for structural adjustment and the gains from trade, have been the subject of much study.

A high proportion of foreign trade consists of trade between different branches of the same company. This is called *intra-firm trade* (IFT). A multinational, for example, might buy components for a machine from subsidiaries in one country, assemble it in another country and export it to a subsidiary in a third country. Intra-firm trade has been estimated to comprise over one-third of US merchandise trade. An estimated 26 per cent of trade in Japanese electrical machinery and 23 per cent of its transport equipment trade consists of intra-firm transactions. IFT tends to be prevalent in industries such as machinery, pharmaceuticals and telecommunications. Large firms are particularly active in intra-firm trade. US multinationals in the EU, for example, account for 22 per cent of total EU imports from the US, and about 90 per cent of these imports are from the parent group.[3] Multinational companies often undertake their own marketing, service/repair and wholesale/distribution operations in foreign markets as a way of maintaining competitive advantage while limiting exposure to outsiders. Intra-firm trade allows multinationals to profit from different national taxation systems. A free-trade environment allows a company to carry out R&D in one country (where research subsidies and R&D tax concessions are favourable), manufacture in

---

[1] *OECD Jobs Study* (Paris, 1994), p. 84.

[2] M. Brülhart and R. Elliot, 'A survey of intra-industry trade in the European Union', in M. Brülhart and R. Hine, *Intra-industry Trade and Adjustment: The European experience* (London: Macmillan, 1998); M. Brülhart and A. Matthews, 'External trade policy', in A. El-Agraa (ed.), *The European Union: Economics and politics*, 7th edn (Harlow: Financial Times Prentice Hall, 2004).

[3] OECD, *Intra-Firm Trade* (Paris, 1993); G. Navaretti, J. Haaland and A. Venables, 'Multinational corporations and global production networks: the implications for trade policy', CEPR Report, London, 2003.

another (where taxes on manufacturing are low), and export the finished product and R&D services to third countries. [4]

Another form of trade is countertrade, whereby payment for one set of goods is effected by means of another set. The most common type of countertrade is *bilateral barter*, but there are more complex forms such as *offset* (where a certain proportion of a purchase from one country is offset by corresponding sales to them) and *buy-back trade* (where a firm investing in one country undertakes to purchase part of the output of the investment). Countertrade used to be common in the trade of developing countries and in former socialist countries. By 1990, it accounted for up to 10 per cent of world trade and 20 per cent of developing countries' trade. [5] With the reform of the economic regime in these countries since then, countertrade has diminished in relative importance.

## The WTO

Foreign trade has become easier to transact. Tariff barriers have fallen drastically and so have transport and communication costs. Quotas and other forms of quantitative restrictions are used in some sectors but do not constitute a significant barrier in most. Despite ongoing concern about nontariff barriers, the general momentum has been in favour of freer exchange. But this has not happened by chance. Trade liberalisation has been given institutional force through a series of regional and multilateral trade agreements negotiated during the past five decades. And these agreements, in turn, have been founded on a growing conviction of the economic benefits of free trade.

The General Agreement on Tariffs and Trade (GATT) was founded in 1947. It established two core principles for the conduct of trade policy. First, a *non-discrimination* ('most favoured nation') clause stipulates that any trade concession extended to one member applies to all other members. Second, *national treatment* requires that the same treatment as regards taxes/subsidies should be given to foreign goods once they have entered the country as to domestic goods. Through a succession of trade rounds, GATT succeeded in putting these important principles into effect. Initially attention was focused on achieving deep reciprocal cuts in tariffs on manufactured goods. Later attention shifted to the control of nontariff barriers to trade such as voluntary export restraints and other forms of quantitative restraints. The Uruguay Round extended the coverage of the Agreement to trade in services and agricultural products. New procedures for handling trade disputes were worked out and the remit of the organisation was extended through the establishment of the World Trade Organisation (Box 17.1).

In addition to the multilateral agreements, numerous free trade area agreements, common markets and economic unions have been negotiated. The European Union was once the most conspicuous sponsor of these regional trade agreements. The North American Free Trade Agreement (NAFTA), ratified in 1993 by the US, Mexico and Canada, covers measures for trade liberalisation and the removal of

---

[4] H. Grubert and J. Mutti, 'Taxes, tariffs and transfer pricing in multinational corporate decision making', *Review of Economics and Statistics* (May 1991), pp. 285–93. These authors found that differing tax systems were an important determinant of industrial location. See Chapter 18 for discussion.

[5] W. Brown and J. Hogendorn, *International Economics: Theory and context* (Reading, MA: Addison-Wesley, 1994), pp. 356–9.

**Box 17.1** **The World Trade Organisation (WTO)**

On 1 January 1995, the World Trade Organisation was established with headquarters in Geneva. The WTO provides the contractual framework within which governments undertake to implement legislation and regulations for foreign trade. It is a platform for collective trade debate, negotiation and adjudication among member countries. By early 2003, 146 countries had joined. China became a member in December 2001. Negotiations are continuing with Russia. Over three-quarters of WTO members are developing or transition countries.

The WTO has been assigned the following responsibilities:

- to put into effect and oversee the provisions of the Uruguay Round (such as tariff reductions, services trade rules and trade-related investment programmes);
- to implement the plurilateral agreements, such as those on civil aircraft, government procurement, trade in dairy products and meat;
- to act as a forum for trade negotiations and settlement of disputes;
- to conduct periodic trade policy reviews of Member States.

The main anti-discriminatory provisions of the GATT (the WTO's predecessor) are contained in a revised format in the WTO Agreement, notably the 'most favoured nation' (MFN) clause and the principle of 'national treatment'.

WTO is basically a system of rules dedicated to *open, fair and undistorted competition*. The WTO agreement on agriculture is designed to provide increased fairness in farm trade. That on intellectual property will improve conditions of competition where ideas and inventions are involved, and the GATS (General Agreement on Trade in Services) will do the same thing for trade in services. The plurilateral agreement on government procurement will extend competition rules to purchases by thousands of government/public sector entities in many countries.

WTO is committed to ensuring better environmental protection and to promoting sustainable development. Linkages between trade policies, environmental policies and sustainable development are to be given priority. International competition policy is also high on the agenda.

The position of developing countries in the WTO is a subject of concern. In the past, their interests have been taken into account by means of escape clauses. However, many are now 'graduating' to developed status; and transition periods are running out. Despite their numerical majority, many developing countries complain about the imbalance in bargaining power between them and the developed countries. This imbalance is particularly apparent in the implementation of the WTO's dispute settlement procedures. Another complaint is that key decisions are taken 'behind doors' by the principal trading partners (the US, the EU and Japan). The WTO has promised to give top priority to resolving this issue.

Some new members of the WTO have had a high level of trade-distorting intervention through their economies. Their trading partners worry about how 'fair' trade will be in such circumstances. These controls will have to be substantially scaled down prior to membership. In the case of China, major problems arose in agreeing a mode of compliance with WTO rules on intellectual property and subsidies.

*Source*: World Trade Organisation (www.wto.org).

capital restrictions and many nontariff trade barriers. Free trade areas, unlike common markets and economic unions, do not commit their members to a common external trade policy. Many other regional trade organisations exist throughout all five continents, including ASEAN (Association of South East Asian Nations), COMESA (Common Market for Eastern and Southern Africa), MERCOSUR and APEC (Asia-Pacific Economic Community) to mention just a few. Those with a taste for them will find a bountiful selection of acronyms from which to choose. Currently the number of RTA exceeds the number of WTO members.

## 17.2 Explaining the gains from international trade

'Trade will very powerfully contribute to increase the mass of commodities and therefore the sum of enjoyments.' This is how David Ricardo, the originator of the theory of comparative advantage, described the gains from trade in 1817. Not only does trade bring material advantage, he argued, but it brings people together, forges common links and helps the cause of peace. 'Perfectly free commerce', he asserted, 'binds together by one common tie of interest and intercourse the universal society of nations throughout the civilised world.'[6] Although the wording sounds anachronistic, the same sentiments are expressed regularly by politicians and opinion leaders.

Gains from trade may be summarised as follows:

1. Traditional gains

- Comparative advantage
- Variety of products.

2. Modern extensions

- Competition and contestability
- Economies of scale and scope
- Innovation and R&D
- Product and quality improvement.

The gains from trade in one sense are easy to understand. Foreign trade results in cheaper prices and a wider range of goods available to the consumer. Freedom of trade means that buyers for department stores and retail chains can search the world for cheaper sources of supply. They do so for their own profit, and customers benefit as a result. The search for reliable and better quality automobiles led to the growth of Japanese exports to Europe and the US, thereby adding to what Ricardo called the 'enjoyments' of millions of car owners in Europe and America. But, as already remarked, there are losers as well as gainers from trade,

---

[6] D. Ricardo, *Principles of Political Economy and Taxation* (1817). Ricardo's views have been echoed by the Nobel prizewinner Milton Friedman, who argued that 'free trade would foster peace and harmony among nations' and, even more ambitiously, that 'the century from Waterloo to the First World War offers a striking example of the beneficial effects of free trade on relations among nations. As a result [of free trade] it was one of the most peaceful in human history among Western nations' (M. and R. Friedman, *Free to Choose: A personal statement*, Harmondsworth: Penguin Books, 1990).

and protection-seeking business lobbies exist everywhere. In order to assess the balance of advantage, we must analyse the four components of the gains from trade:

- *Comparative advantage* gains, arising from efficient allocation of a country's resources
- Gains from *enhanced competition and contestability* of markets
- Gains from *exploiting economies of scale*
- Gains from the *stimulus to innovation, access to knowledge and R&D, and thereby to economic growth.*

## Comparative advantage

> By means of glasses, hotbeds and hotwalls, very good grapes can be raised in Scotland, and very good wine too can be made of them at about thirty times the expense for which at least equally good wine can be bought from foreign countries. Would it be a reasonable law to prohibit the importation of all foreign wines, merely to encourage the making of claret and burgundy in Scotland? (Adam Smith, *Wealth of Nations*, Volume 1 (1776), p. 480)

The essence of comparative advantage is the idea that nations, like individuals, should concentrate on what they are best at producing. If one person is an accomplished musician and another a computer wizard, it is more efficient to allow each person to specialise in one field rather than have each of them produce their own music as well as their own computer programs individually. The musician would 'export' music to the computer specialist and the latter, in exchange for these music imports, would 'export' computer services. This seems a mutually advantageous way of trading. In this way the musician and the computer wizard will end up with more and better goods than if they try making both goods individually. As with individuals, so with nations.

The theory of comparative advantage goes one important step further. It shows that even if one nation is, in an absolute sense, more efficient than another in all activities, trade could be mutually beneficial. The essence of the theory can be illustrated by an arithmetical example.

Suppose there are two countries, England and Portugal, each producing two commodities, wine and clothing. Assume that perfect competition prevails in all markets and that there are constant returns to scale, zero transport costs and only one factor of production: labour. Add the further assumption that labour is always fully employed; if displaced in one industry, it can move costlessly to another. In our example, a worker in England can produce 3 units of wine in the wine industry, or 3 units of clothing in the clothing industry. A worker in Portugal can produce either 6 units of wine or 4 units of clothing. Note that the Portuguese worker is more productive in absolute terms in both industries. (This assumption was not as 'unrealistic' when made by Ricardo in the early nineteenth century as it would appear now.)

### Units of output per person at work

|          | Portugal | England |
|----------|----------|---------|
| Wine     | 6        | 3       |
| Clothing | 4        | 3       |

In a state of autarky (i.e. a situation of zero international trade), 1 unit of clothing will exchange for 1.5 units of wine within Portugal. In England a unit of clothing will exchange for 1 unit of wine. Clothing is more expensive in Portugal than in England. By the same reasoning, wine is cheaper in Portugal than in England.

Suppose England takes two workers out of the wine industry and assigns them to work in the clothing industry. This means that wine production falls by 6 units and clothing production increases by 6 units. The 6 units of clothing are exported to Portugal. Given that, in Portugal, 1 unit of clothing exchanges for 1.5 units of wine, the exporters of the 6 units of English clothing return with 9 units of wine. Result: *England has gained 3 units of wine: Portugal is left exactly as well off as before* (see Box 17.2). One can adjust this example to illustrate a case where Portugal gains and England is left as well off as before, or, the more likely case, where both countries gain.

The above example is capable of extension and modification in many ways. But its essential features convey what is now seen as the core message of international trade theory:

- A country can have an absolute disadvantage in all goods and yet gain from trade with the more efficient partner.
- The gain is realised through imports – they enable England to consume wine more cheaply and Portugal to consume clothing more cheaply. Exports are in a sense 'bad' (one is giving away to foreigners goods which one would like to

---

**Box 17.2   Comparative advantage in action**

This example uses the figures in the text for labour productivity and assumes a price of 1 unit of clothing per 1.5 units of wine.

### England

Two workers reallocated from wine to clothing implies:

$$-6W + 6C$$

Clothing is exported to Portugal in exchange for wine:

$$-6C + 9W$$

*Net result*: $-6W + 9W = +3W$.

### Portugal

Exports 9W in exchange for 6C from England:

$$-9W + 6C$$

To produce 9W it must give up 6C in domestic product:

$$+9W - 6C$$

*Net result*: 0.

consume at home) and imports are 'good' (they add to consumption). Exports are useful solely as a means of obtaining imports.

● Trade involves mutual gains. It is not a zero-sum game, whereby gains to one country mean losses to another. Not only is it possible for both countries to gain, it is the most likely outcome in practice, since only at the extremes of the possible price range will one country acquire all the gain.

● The total gain from trade may be unevenly shared. In the above numerical example, England gets all the gain, Portugal none. It all depends on the clothing:wine price ratio, which in turn will be determined by world demand and supply. Countries benefit most from trade by obtaining high prices for their exports and paying the lowest possible prices for their imports.

The gains from trade can also be illustrated by means of the production frontier curve, introduced in Chapter 2. Units of wine are drawn on the vertical axis and units of clothing on the horizontal axis (Figure 17.1). We look at England's production frontier. Under autarky, consumption possibilities for England are limited to that production frontier. With the introduction of trade, the range of consumption possibilities for England is expanded. The new range can be represented by curve FF. England could shift production from A to P, exporting PR of clothing in exchange for RB of wine to reach a new consumption point B. Point B is clearly a superior consumption point to A. More of each good can be consumed at that point. England has benefited from trade.

Behind these net gains are losses to factors of production. These do not emerge clearly from the Ricardian analysis, though in a broader context one could see that free trade was good news for England's clothing industry and bad news for

**Figure 17.1 How trade allows more consumption**

The production function is TT. With trade, consumption possibilities are extended to FF. A new consumption point B can be attained by exporting RP clothing in exchange for RB wine. B is a superior consumption point to that available under the autarky frontier TT.

producers in the English wine industry. Modern trade theorists have developed more complex diagrams and mathematical models to analyse these issues.

## Competition and contestability

The comparative advantage gains are derived on the assumption of perfect competition. However, when a country's domestic market is shielded from foreign competitors, competitive forces are likely to be weak. Domestic producers have an incentive to collude, safe in the knowledge that the home market will not be attacked from abroad. Small countries with strong protectionist regimes are particularly prone to monopoly influences, since in many industries the domestic market will be small in relation to the minimum efficient size of the firm.

In such circumstances, the liberalisation of trade can give a sharp boost to competition in the domestic market. As the market becomes more contestable, domestic producers have to fight hard to stay in business. The reductions in general inefficiencies and in 'managerial slack' under this process are referred to as the 'X-efficiency' gains. Increased competition in the manufacturing sector and exposure to world-class competition was considered as a major source of X-efficiency gains for the economies of the EU Member States. Today, the same processes are observed in services such as banking, insurance and transport, where radical improvements in efficiency have been recorded in response to external competitive pressures following trade liberalisation.

X-efficiency gains can be depicted as a general outward shift of the production frontier (from TT to $T^1T^1$). This does not imply that all industries gain equally – in some industries the intensity of competition among domestic producers may have been higher under protection, and the potential efficiency gains from the trade lower, than in others. The essence of the gain arises because, through elimination of waste and better utilisation, the same stock of productive factors can produce more output. This concept is given expression in Figure 17.2.

The competitive effects of free trade are not fully captured by the above static analysis. This is because competition leads to second- and third-round benefits – indeed, to an ongoing process of continuous improvement and innovation. In a globally competitive market, a firm cannot afford to stand still. It must engage in renewal and re-evaluation. This is hard work for the firm, but redounds to the benefit of the consumer. Competition confers 'dynamic' gains on the trading country in addition to the 'static' gains of Ricardian comparative advantage. Once considered relevant only to smaller countries, nowadays larger countries include the stimulative effects of more competition as a major source of gain.

## Economies of scale and scope

'The division of labour is limited by the size of the market.' Adam Smith's dictum provides the key to the third source of gain from foreign trade. While the 'competition' gains described above are derived from the opening of *domestic* markets to foreign competition, scale economies arise as a result of the opening of *foreign* markets to domestic producers. Widening the extent of the market makes it possible for domestic producers to specialise on narrower product ranges (horizontal specialisation) and to integrate the output process (vertical specialisation).

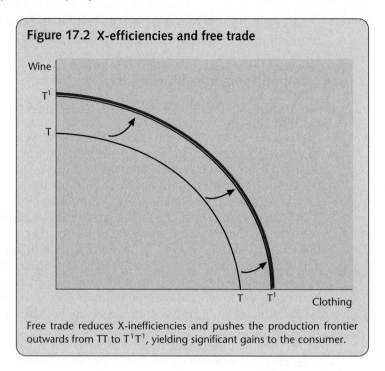

**Figure 17.2 X-efficiencies and free trade**

Free trade reduces X-inefficiencies and pushes the production frontier outwards from TT to $T^1T^1$, yielding significant gains to the consumer.

Specialisation leads to lower unit costs and, by so doing, makes it possible for domestic firms to compete in foreign markets (now assumed to be untrammelled by trade restrictions). Franchisers can export their services to foreign countries, reduce unit cost and make more profit; car manufacturers, by selling to foreign markets, can attain viable production levels.

Many small firms are able to trade globally on the basis of an extremely specialised product range. This is economies of scale in action. The exploitation of the potential economies of scale does not require huge plants. A single factory in Ireland, employing just over 200 people, provides sufficient soft drink concentrate to supply over 17 per cent of the global consumption of Coca-Cola products. A single Finnish firm, Nokia, supplies 39 per cent of the world market for mobile phones, much of it produced in Scandinavia.[7] Sweden accounts for some 40 per cent of the world paperboard market; Swiss-manufactured watches comprise one-third of world exports of watches; and 95 per cent of 'budget' bikes sold in the US are made in China.[8] By extending the size of the market, foreign trade gives producers the opportunity to exploit economies of scale. For small countries, exports provide a means of escape from the limitations of their small size.

By exposing domestic firms to competition and forcing them to improve efficiency, free trade has the effect in some countries of stimulating mergers and acquisitions. This can lead to an increase in industry concentration ratios. It

[7] *Business Week* (17 July 2000).

[8] Michael E. Porter, *The Competitive Advantage of Nations* (London: Macmillan, 1990); *The Economist* (1 June 2002). One further indicative statistic: of the 110 million bicycles built worldwide annually, over 40 per cent are made in China, India and Taiwan. Annual production in the US fell from 10 million units in 1994 to 500,000 in 2002. Much the same experience was recorded in Europe.

would obviously be wrong, however, to interpret this as evidence of a diminution of competitive pressure. 'Rationalisation' of industries is a normal part of the adjustment process, to be expected rather than resisted by the authorities. Nevertheless, it is a rather paradoxical outcome, which needs to be monitored by the competition authorities.

## Growth effects

Trade has been described as the 'handmaiden of growth'. It encourages economic growth by bringing about changes in attitudes and motivation favourable to industrialisation, by acting as a conduit for technological change, and by encouraging innovation and investment. People learn, and are influenced by, foreign commercial contacts. To survive against foreign competition, firms must invest in R&D and innovate. Imports also incorporate technical improvements; hence the positive causal link from imports to economic growth. This fourth source of gain derives, but is distinct, from the first three. It is a case of the whole effect of trade being greater than the sum of its parts. This broader canvas has been encapsulated in *The Economist* (20 April 1991):

> Liberal trade: is it a good thing or not? This is less a matter of doctrine – though the answer is exceptionally well-grounded in economic theory – as of coincidence that the expansion of global trade since 1945 went hand in hand with unprecedented economic growth. Or that the nearly closed economies of Eastern Europe and the Soviet Union failed on every measure. Or that the most protected economies in the third world (India and Argentina, for instance) squandered their potential, while neighbours (such as Thailand and Chile) embraced trade and thrived. Or that, in otherwise fairly open economies, the most protected industries are the most backward (steel in America, farming in Japan, computing in Europe).

Evidence of a positive association between export growth and economic performance continues to accumulate at a rapid rate. The World Bank has been to the forefront of research on this topic and has been a consistent and vocal advocate of outward-looking policies. Openness produces better results because it involves working *with* rather than *against* the market. In the case of developing countries, the World Bank pointed out that not only did protection deny developing countries the benefits of trade, but it led to destructive side-effects such as the substitution of capital for labour (a perverse effect given the abundant labour supply in these countries) and 'rent-seeking'.[9] Worse, as a result of their deliberate isolation from the world economy, inward looking countries tend to lose out on advances in industrial technology.

The experience of countries that have isolated themselves from international commerce alerts us to another benefit of trade, which has been emphasised in the business literature. Manufactured exports provide a powerful incentive to technological upgrading in imperfect world technology markets. The exposure of a

---

[9] *Rent-seeking* in this context refers to the diversion of entrepreneurial effort to socially unproductive activities such as lobbying for protection or for a government subsidy against foreign competition. In other circumstances this effort would be directed to innovation or tighter cost control. We have already encountered this concept in our analysis of monopoly (Chapter 6). It was originally applied to trade protection in an article by Anne Krueger in the 1970s and it has been extended into a theory of the more cumbersomely titled *directly unproductive profit-seeking* by J. Bhagwati.

firm's products to a demanding and sophisticated market forces management to improve product quality. Because firms that export have greater access to best-practice technology, there are benefits to the enterprises and spillovers to the rest of the economy which are not reflected in market prices. These information-related externalities are an important source of productivity growth. Both cross-country evidence and more detailed studies at the industry level confirm the correlation between exports and rapid productivity growth. Transition countries that exported manufactures to the Soviet Union found virtually no quality control necessary and, as a result, they had no need to engage in the continuous innovation on which long-term economic success so much depends.[10] When the Russian market collapsed, firms in those countries had great difficulty in competing against Western goods of a much higher quality.

## 17.3 Quantifying the gains from trade

Some critics argue that the expansion of trade, yields at best trivial gains which come at a heavy cost to the physical and social environment. Empirical measurement of the gains from trade contradicts this view. Trade brings gains which are far from trivial. They can be measured in several ways.

First, trade gains can be measured by reference to countries that have changed from complete isolation to free trade. Japan, for example, moved from autarky pre-1850 to trade liberalisation during 1850–74. During this period, prices of import-substitutes fell to one-third of their autarky level. According to one estimate, Japanese GDP increased by as much as 65 per cent as a result of opening its market.[11] Second, the effects of economic sanctions and blockades can be estimated. These show severe adverse effects, provided the sanctions are enforced. Significant losses were, for example, imposed on Iraq's economy as a consequence of the sanctions after the first Gulf war in 1991.[12] The standard of living of small countries can be especially vulnerable if possibilities of international trade were to disappear. Imagine a country such as Belgium having to manufacture all its own machinery, its own cars and trucks, its own

---

[10] An interesting exponent of this view is the Hungarian economist, Janos Kornai:

> The most important long-term drawback of Hungary's export ties with the Comecon countries is the low levels of quality standards in these markets. ... It is relatively easy to sell products in these markets that would be unacceptable in hard-currency markets. This is one more reason for the need to coolly but resolutely shift Hungary's sphere of interest to markets that insist on better-quality goods. (J. Kornai, *The Road to a Free Economy*, New York: W.W. Norton, 1990)

Selling to higher-quality markets is also the fourth part of Michael Porter's diamond of comparative advantage (see below).

[11] J.B. Huber, *Journal of Political Economy* (May/June 1971).

[12] G. Hufbauer, *Economic Sanctions Reconsidered – Supplemental case studies* (Washington, DC: Institute of International Economics, 1993). Ironically, in view of his many past criticisms of the unequal nature of the global trade system and its alleged tendency to harm developing countries, Fidel Castro in August 1994 blamed the disastrous condition of the Cuban economy on its lack of access to this trade system (as a result of US trade sanctions).

computers and aircraft. The cost of producing them domestically would obviously be prohibitive.

A third option – and by far the most commonly used – is to quantify the benefits of *incremental* movements towards freer trade. Consider, for example, Europe's single market programme. This programme involved the removal of nontariff barriers on trade between Member States and the opening of the hitherto protected services industries to foreign competition. Frontier controls were abolished, fiscal regimes made more compatible, and public procurement contracts opened to tender and publicised more transparently. The total gain to the Member States from the programme was estimated to be between 4.5 and 6 per cent of GDP, equivalent to about €200 billion in 1992 values. *Ex-post* studies suggest that the actual gains will be half this figure – still a substantial amount.[13]

Similar methodologies have been applied to estimating the economic effects of further multilateral trade liberalisation. Estimates of the gains of the Uruguay round, for instance, amounted to US$510 billion (see Box 17.3). A large proportion of these gains derived from the reduction of agricultural protection. This explains why the EU emerges with a gain of US$164 billion, or one-third of the total. Industrial countries see the liberalisation of agriculture as a 'concession' but, in fact, as these exercises demonstrate, protection hurts the country imposing protection much more than it does potential exporters. A complete liberalisation of trade would provide even more gains than those obtained from the partial liberalisation of the Uruguay Round. Patrick Messerlin, for instance, estimates that the total gains to the EU from removing all remaining external trade barriers is equivalent to around 7 per cent of GDP, or US$600 million.[14]

These figures must all be taken with a large grain of salt. They are based on a diverse range of methodologies, including computer simulations, assumed price elasticity values, business opinion surveys and arbitrary assumptions. This much is readily admitted by their progenitors. Whilst it is often asserted that the estimates are likely to underestimate the true gains, because certain dynamic benefits have defied quantification,[15] the bias can go both ways. If labour adjustment were to prove slow and unemployment to escalate, for example, the standard approach could just as easily exaggerate the gains. Besides, domestic industry needs to be stimulated to adjust, not be destroyed by foreign competition for enduring gains to be realised. Like macroeconomic forecasts, they are not flawless predictors, simply the best available, and have to be treated with caution. Unlike the macro-forecasts, however, estimates of the gains from trade are difficult to prove wrong. Because they involve comparison between actual *ex-post* trade flows and hypothetical trade flows (as they would have been had the Uruguay Round been unsuccessful or the EU's single market programme never occurred), the estimates

---

[13] European Commission, *2002 Review of the Internal Market Strategy*, COM (2002) 171 final.

[14] Patrick Messerlin, *Measuring the Costs of Protection in Europe* (Washington, DC: Institute for International Economics, 2000). A Bonёt shows that Messerlin's estimate may exaggerate the gains since it includes government tariff revenue loss as an economic loss instead of a redistribution. On the other hand, both estimates omit potential gains from the services sector (*Economie Internationale*, Vol. 89–90, 2002).

[15] International Monetary Fund, 'The Uruguay Round: results and implications', *IMF World Economic Outlook* (Washington, DC, August 1994).

---

**Box 17.3**  **The Uruguay Round and beyond**

*Market access should boost world income by an extra US$510 billion annually.*

By the time market access commitments are fully implemented in 2005, the reduction of trade barriers following the Uruguay Round agreement will have resulted in an increase in world income of US$510 billion annually. This WTO estimate relates to only one aspect of the Round, namely liberalisation of trade in goods. It ignores the beneficial impact of other aspects concerning, for example, strengthened trade rules, procedures and institutions, market access commitments, and rules for trade in services. Highlights from the empirical studies of the Round include the following:

- Estimated annual income gains:

|                      | *$bn* |
|----------------------|------:|
| US                   | 122   |
| EU                   | 164   |
| Japan                | 27    |
| Developing economies | 135   |
| Other                | 62    |
| Total                | 510   |

- Estimates by the World Bank and others indicate that the static welfare gains from removing *all* remaining barriers to merchandise trade would amount to a further $250–$620 billion per year.
- Developing countries could capture one-third to one-half of these gains – *largely by opening their own markets*.
- Removing barriers to trade in services would increase global welfare by even more. Research, reported in Laird (2001), indicates that a 40 per cent reduction in barriers to trade in services could produce welfare gains of as much as $332 billion in 2005.
- Against this, the cost of conforming to intellectual property rules could be quite high for some developing countries. This feature of the new liberal trade agenda has not received the attention it merits. No less an authority than Professor Jagdish Bhagwati, a leading exponent of the virtues of free trade, has commented that poor countries have been 'bamboozled' at the Uruguay Round into accepting intellectual property rules which could, in his view, cost them dearly.
- Opening markets not only could boost trade and global growth over time, but would also bring greater stability and predictability to the global economy.

*Sources: The Results of the Uruguay Round of Multilateral Trade Negotiations. Market Access for Goods and Services: Overview of the Results (Geneva GATT Secretariat, November 1994); Sam Laird, 'Dolphins, mad cows and butterflies – the multilateral trading system in the 21st century', The World Economy (April 2001); J. Bhagwati, The Wind of the Hundred Days: How Washington Mismanaged Globalisation (MIT Press, 2000).*

---

cannot be directly confronted with actual outcomes.[16] The manner in which these estimates are commonly presented often gives a misleading impression of precision and authority.

---

[16] The achievement of the Uruguay Round has been described by an analogy with riding a bicycle. If the bicycle stops, the cyclist falls. Had the Uruguay Round failed, the *status quo ante* may not have been maintained. The whole system might have been overwhelmed by protectionist pressures. The Uruguay Round agreement was, therefore, more important than estimates based on the assumption of the *status quo* being maintained would indicate.

A final way of estimating the effects of free trade is by comparative analysis. Countries which choose outward-looking trade regimes can be compared with countries opting for inward-looking or protectionist trade regimes. One study divides developing countries into two categories ranging from strongly outward-oriented to strongly inward-oriented and finds that the outward-looking groups have clearly outperformed the inward-looking groups. Growth in total GDP, in GDP per person, in total factor productivity (which measures the efficiency of both capital and labour inputs) and other indices all testify to the benefits of outward-looking strategies (Table 17.4). Work on this subject continues. In a 1998 study of 93 countries, Edwards, for example, finds that openness is very strongly correlated to total factor productivity.[17] The World Bank published a multi-country, seven-volume, 3000-page study of the effects of trade liberalisation in 1991. Its central finding is a ringing confirmation of previous studies: 'liberalisation clearly tends to accelerate economic growth'.[18] While differences in economic performance happen for many reasons other than choice of trade policy, the results are nevertheless consistent with a highly positive view of the benefits of trade. More recent research adds another twist to this story. Because growth helps to alleviate poverty, and trade helps growth, trade can play an

### Table 17.4 Developing countries: trade orientation and economic performance*

|  | 1974–85 | 1986–92 |
|---|---|---|
| **Strongly outward-oriented** | | |
| Real GDP growth | 8.0 | 7.5 |
| Real per capita GDP growth | 6.1 | 5.9 |
| Total factor productivity | 2.6 | 3.8 |
| **Strongly inward-oriented** | | |
| Real GDP growth | 2.3 | 2.5 |
| Real per capita GDP growth | −0.3 | −0.1 |
| Total factor productivity | −0.4 | 0.3 |
| **All developing countries** | | |
| Real GDP growth | 4.1 | 3.8 |
| Real per capita GDP growth | 1.7 | 1.5 |
| Total factor productivity | 0.8 | 1.4 |

* Annual percentage change unless otherwise noted. Developing countries are classified into two categories according to the orientation of their trade strategy: (1) strongly outward-oriented, where trade controls are either non-existent or very low; (2) strongly inward-oriented, where the overall incentive structure strongly favours production for the domestic market.

*Source*: IMF, *World Economic Outlook* (May 1993), p. 76.

---

[17] S. Edwards, 'Openness, productivity and growth: What do we really know?', *Economic Journal*, March 1998.

[18] D. Papageorgiou, M. Michaely and A. Choksi, *Liberalising Foreign Trade* (Washington, DC: World Bank, 1991), p. 85. However, see D. Greenaway, 'Liberalising foreign trade through rose-tinted glasses', *Economic Journal* (January 1993) for a warning about the validity of some of the evidence.

important part in alleviating poverty. A WTO secretariat study published in June 2000 found that developing countries that are most open to trade are catching up fastest with living standards of the developed countries. For example, 30 years ago South Korea was as poor as Ghana. Today, as a result of trade-led growth, it is richer than Portugal. In summary, globalisation is good for growth and growth is good for the poor.

## 17.4 Trade policy and protection

When imported goods are in direct competition with a firm's domestic sales, free trade poses the threat of falling prices, employment cutbacks and lower profits. The firm's existence may be placed in jeopardy and it lobbies for protection.[19]

Arguments in favour of protection have a long history. Although an ardent advocate of free trade, Adam Smith identified four cases where protection was justified (see Box 17.4). These exceptions are still considered valid. First, there is obvious justification for protecting *strategic defence industries*. The export of technically advanced products to hostile nations is often prohibited. Second, if a domestically produced good is subject to a tax, imported goods should be taxed by the same amount, if necessary by imposition of a tariff. (This is an early and rudimentary form of the *level playing field argument*.) Third, *countervailing duties on imports* could legitimately be used in order to discourage the arbitrary use of protection by others, and to encourage them to abide by international trade rules. Fourth, the case for *transitional protection* is widely accepted as a way of moderating the painful adjustment costs of freer trade. These and other possible justifications for protection have absorbed a great deal of research effort over the years.

Modern analysis, however, goes well beyond this. It focuses on sources of distortions in the system and on the *optimal form of intervention* to remedy them. Four sources of possible distortion are of particular importance in trade analysis:

1. Unemployment and the capacity of an economy to adjust
2. Foreign monopoly power
3. Failure of prices to signal future changes in comparative advantage
4. Neglect of environmental effects.

### Unemployment and the capacity to adjust

An implicit assumption of trade theory is that resources are fully employed. This means that labour and other factors of production 'released' from import-

---

[19] Economists have tended to take a jaundiced view of such lobbying, as evidenced in the conclusion of a 1903 manifesto signed by a number of distinguished British economists: 'protection brings in its train the loss of purity in politics, unfair advantage to those who wield the powers of jobbery and corruption, unjust distribution of wealth and the growth of sinister interests' (quoted in J.N. Bhagwati, *Protectionism*, Cambridge, MA: MIT Press, 1990, p. 31).

**Box 17.4** **Adam Smith's argument for protection**

Smith is usually viewed as an early champion of free trade. His masterpiece, *The Wealth of Nations*, contains a blistering attack on the protectionist philosophy of the mercantilist school. Yet Smith, as an intelligent and practical person, envisaged exceptional cases in which protection could be justified:

1. *Defence of the country* – Protection of defence industries such as shipping could be justified on non-economic grounds.

2. *Level playing field* – If a country imposes a tax on domestic producers it should levy a similar tax on imported substitutes.

3. *Retaliation* – A retaliatory tax might be a useful deterrent to protectionist practices by other countries. Smith instanced the case of the French who *have been particularly forward to favour their own manufactures by restraining the importation of such foreign goods as could come into competition with them.*

4. *Transitional protection* – 'When particular manufacturers have been so far extended as to employ a great multitude of hands, humanity may require that the freedom of trade should be restored only by slow gradations and with a good deal of reserve and circumspection' (Adam Smith, *Wealth of Nations*, Book IV (1776), pp. 488–91). Free trade agreements normally have transition periods designed to allow time for adjustment by the affected employees. This may not only be justifiable for reasons of 'humanity': it may also make good economic sense.

competing industries are redeployed elsewhere in the economy. In terms of our earlier example, workers in England's wine industry displaced by Portuguese imports move to the clothing industry where their output has a higher value. This reallocation is an integral element in reaping the gains from trade.

Suppose, however, that those who lost their jobs in the wine industry were not successfully redeployed. Then, instead of moving from A to P in Figure 17.3, the economy's production point moves to P*. This point lies below the production frontier, reflecting the fact that people are unemployed. Trade will take place at P*, but clearly the gains from trade will be reduced and may even be completely negated by this failure to reallocate. This problem is real and immediate to those affected. To argue that resources will be reallocated in the long run may be valid but can sound complacent. Referring to the communication gap between economists and the public on the merits of free trade (Box 17.5), Alan Blinder criticised the economics profession for *'speaking in a long-run equilibrium dialect to people who live in a short-run disequilibrium world. No wonder what we say sounds like Greek to them.'*[20]

Yet labour displaced in import-competing industries does generally succeed in finding alternative employment in the long run. For instance, over the past decades, there have been massive reallocations of the workforce throughout the EU. Numbers employed in European agriculture fell from 12 per cent of the workforce in 1970 to 4 per cent in 2002. Since 1984, employment has fallen by 36 per

---

[20] A.S. Blinder, *Macroeconomics under Debate* (Hemel Hempstead: Harvester Wheatsheaf, 1989), pp. 152–3.

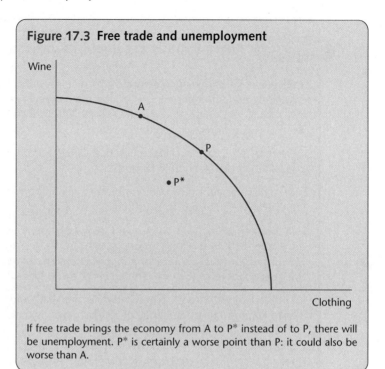

**Figure 17.3 Free trade and unemployment**

If free trade brings the economy from A to P* instead of to P, there will be unemployment. P* is certainly a worse point than P: it could also be worse than A.

## Box 17.5    Job losses and imports

Economists are often accused of having their heads in the clouds when it comes to discussing the effects of free trade. Critics say with some justification that trade theorists tend to overplay the benefits and downplay the costs. Professor Alan Blinder responds to this charge in the following passage, which demonstrates his capacity to see the trade adjustment process in a clear light rather than through rose-tinted glasses:

> Virtually all economists support free trade; but a frustrating number of non-economists do not. Members of our fraternity are constantly amazed at the depth and strength of protectionist sentiment, which we view as evidence of either rent-seeking behaviour or low intelligence. Doubtless, some protectionists qualify under both rubrics. But I want to suggest that there is more to the matter.
>
> One reason for economists' near-unanimous support of free trade is our use of the long-run, full-employment framework for policy evaluation. In our world, workers displaced by foreign competition move into industries in which our country has a comparative advantage. That can only raise productivity; so both GNP and social welfare should rise. How, except as viewed through the distorting lenses of a special pleader, could that be bad?
>
> But people unencumbered by advanced degrees in economics see trade policy differently. They live in real space and time, where unemployment truly exists and workers displaced by foreign competition often move into unemployment rather than into new jobs. So they reason that our GNP will fall if our markets are opened to free trade. How, except in the strange world of the economic theorist, could that be good?
>
> The two world-views generate different predictions. Which is right? Consider a concrete example. Korean firms learn how to make television sets efficiently and want to export them to the US. The TV industry and its workers petition Congress for a strict quota to 'save jobs'. Economists scoff at the idea. According to standard trade theory, the US can only gain by

opening its borders to Korean TVs. A quota cannot save jobs; it can only trap labour in an industry in which the United States has no comparative advantage.

Though over-simplified and missing many of the qualifications that a good trade theorist would want, this conclusion probably characterises the typical economist's view of the matter. And it is also probably the right view in the long run. It might even be right for the short run, if the unemployment rate were 4 per cent. But suppose Korea learns how to make TVs when the US unemployment rate was 10 per cent. Who can honestly assure a displaced factory worker that she will quickly find a new job at a wage close to her present one, as she would in the world envisioned by Ricardian comparative advantage? Isn't it more likely that she will suffer a spell of joblessness, perhaps a lengthy one? Aren't these short-run costs relevant to any social decision?

I anticipate your response and I agree with it: the appropriate solution is not to erect trade barriers but to pursue a vigorous full employment policy so that displaced workers will be quickly re-employed. This is precisely my point. Conditions of full employment are necessary to validate standard propositions in trade theory. High unemployment calls many of these propositions into question. Both the positive predictions of trade theory and its normative prescriptions may be wrong. For example, when unemployment results from a rigid real wage, free trade may reduce both employment and welfare. Furthermore, if unemployment were eradicated by abolishing the wage floor, patterns of trade might reverse. Those who are wary of free trade may have a valid point in the presence of unemployment, as even Adam Smith realised. At the very least, trade adjustment assistance should perhaps become a more integral part of the advocacy of free trade.

Now, I am not trying to argue for protectionism. Though we may all be dead in the long run, someone will be alive. And a nation that protects one senile industry after another winds up looking like a nursing home for state capitalism. Economists correctly seek to avoid this outcome. Besides, the mere existence of unemployment does not in itself imply that protection is better than free trade.

I am arguing, however, that trade theorists could do their job better if they paid more attention to the short run. At a minimum, it would narrow the communication gap between economists and the public. We insist on speaking in a long-run equilibrium dialect to people who live in a short-run disequilibrium world. No wonder what we say sounds like Greek to them.

*Source*: Alan S. Blinder, *Macroeconomics under Debate* (Hemel Hempstead: Harvester Wheatsheaf, 1989); first published in *American Economic Review*, May 1988.

cent in the steel industry, by 46 per cent in clothing and textiles, and by a devastating 47 per cent in coal. The compensating expansion in employment in other sectors that theory leads us to expect does indeed appear to have materialised. Employment in the services sector has grown dramatically, as has employment in different parts of the manufacturing sector: food processing, chemicals and pharmaceuticals. The millions of jobs 'lost' have to a large extent been compensated by jobs found in 'new' industries. Too much focus on the short run can lead to the neglect of the powerful productivity gains obtained by such reallocation.

Studies of the income profile of workers displaced by import competition show a wide variation in experience across sectors. The scale of adjustment depends on the countries between which trade is being liberalised. If closer integration is taking place between countries with similar income per capita and structure, intra-industry trade is likely to dominate the outcome. Firms will produce a more specialised range of output, but whole industries will not be put out of business, and comparatively little inter-industry labour adjustment may be necessary. Where trade liberalisation takes place between rich and poor countries (e.g. North–South trade), adjustment is likely to be more painful. Those with sector-specific skills lose income. The beneficiaries are those with the skills and the adaptability to fit into new employment patterns. These are usually younger and better-educated employees. Prospects for successful labour market adjustment are enhanced by factors such as:

- fast economic growth,
- flexibility of wages and openness to new entrants,
- prompt availability of retraining and re-skilling programmes for displaced employees,
- the length of time available for adjustment.[21]

Conditions of full employment are not satisfied in the labour markets of many countries around the world. This warns against any over-optimistic assessment of the adjustment capacity of a modern economy. A surge in imports may exacerbate unemployment and government intervention may well be justified to assist adjustment. *But it does not follow that import restrictions are the optimal form of intervention.* To the extent that unemployment is the fault of domestic policies rather than trade policies, the problem should be dealt with directly at source rather than indirectly through trade measures.

A more general interpretation of the unemployment argument is that *trade provides benefits only if prices reflect social opportunity costs.* When large numbers are unemployed, the wage obviously fails to reflect social cost, since the alternative to being at work in an import-competing industry is very likely being idle.

## Monopoly power

One of the oldest arguments for protection (the optimum tariff argument) states that, if a country is exposed to monopoly exploitation by importers, it can improve its welfare by (a) placing a countervailing tariff on imports, or (b) subsidising the import-competing industry. Here less trade means more welfare. (By the same reasoning, a country with unexploited *monopsony* power should impose an export tax.)

Take, for example, the subsidisation of Airbus, initially a government-backed consortium of companies from France, the UK, Germany and Spain. The market for civilian aircraft had for a long time been dominated by Boeing and McDonnell-Douglas (now merged). Airbus was set up to develop an alternative European source of supply. Subsidies played a big part in the growth of Airbus. Since its establishment in 1970, an estimated US$28 billion has been sunk into the consortium by the European taxpayer (some of that sum has been repaid from profits on the A320). In return, Airbus has become a major player in the civilian aircraft market. By 2003, its share of global production of civilian aircraft had surpassed 57 per cent. To determine the success of Airbus in economic terms is more complex. Cost–benefit studies show that (a) Airbus and its employees gained, (b) profits in the US civilian aircraft industry fell, (c) the European consumer benefited from lower airfares, and (d) the European taxpayer had to finance subsidies. The net impact of these forces on European welfare is still being debated. A good

---

[21] In the US, two-thirds of these employees who lost their jobs as a result of imports during the period 1979–99 found new work; the remaining one-third are not re-employed. More than half of the re-employed suffered a loss of pay and a quarter took pay cuts of over 30 per cent. L. Kletzer, *Job Loss from Imports: Measuring the costs* (Washington, DC: Institute for International Economics, 2001.)

case can be made that the reduction in fares and the indirect labour market and innovation spillover effects following the establishment of Airbus compensated for the cost of the subsidies from the European taxpayer. On balance, Airbus would qualify as a case of successful intervention.[22]

The justification for such intervention, of course, was not just to offset US monopoly power. In addition to this optimum tariff consideration, there were many externalities through positive spillover effects from domestic industry or from the development of indigenous technical and human capital.

## Changes in comparative advantage

In our example, comparative advantage leads Portugal to specialise in wine and England to specialise in clothing. From the viewpoint of the theory, it does not matter which country exports which good. Yet, in practice, countries do worry about this – and with reason. Britain's industrial growth drew sustenance from its comparative advantage in clothing. The factory system developed, and with it the opportunity to exploit economies of scale and technological progress; income was distributed from landowners to industrialists, who had a high propensity to reinvest; wage costs were reduced by lower food prices; and a self-sustaining cycle of industrial advance was generated. The same benign process would have been less likely had England happened to find its comparative advantage emerging in food (wine) rather than manufacturing (clothing). Hence, the industry in which a country specialises initially may have a powerful influence on its future development. In certain circumstances, government intervention may be necessary in order to ensure that a long-term view is taken of a country's comparative advantage.

Japan is often considered an outstanding example of a country where government took deliberate measures to assist and guide the evolution of comparative advantage. Opinions differ as to the effectiveness and efficiency of such intervention. But the approach taken by the Japanese authorities was described approvingly as follows:

> The Ministry of International Trade and Industry (MITI) decided to establish in Japan industries which required intensive employment of capital and technology, industries that in consideration of comparative cost of production should be the most inappropriate for Japan, industries such as steel, oil refining, petrochemicals, automobiles, electronics, computers. From a short-run, static viewpoint, encouragement of such industries would seem to conflict with economic rationalism. But from a long-range point of view, these are precisely the industries where income elasticity of demand is high, technological progress is rapid, and labour productivity rises fast. (OECD, *Industrial Policy of Japan*, Paris, 1972)

The same ideas lie behind the Cecchini Report's lapidary comment that 'comparative advantage is no longer seen as divine inheritance'.[23] 'Nor', it adds, are 'market structures and rivals' behaviour set in tablets of stone'. Concern with dynamic comparative advantage continues to motivate governments to make

---

[22] See L. Tyson, *Who's Bashing Whom? Trade conflict in high technology industries* (Washington, DC: Institute for International Economics, 1992).

[23] P. Cecchini, *The European Challenge 1992* (Aldershot: Wildwood House, 1988), p. 85.

strategic interventions, particularly in the high-tech sector. The league tables of world market share in high-tech products are monitored carefully. Indeed the perceived loss of market share in these products was one of the factors which pushed the European Commission to propose the formation of the 1992 single market programme. Protection of these industries at a national level had not succeeded, for all the reasons outlined earlier: insufficient scope for economies of scale serving national markets, suppression of competition behind import restrictions, specialisation patterns out of line with comparative advantage. To develop these sectors, a large domestic market was needed, an open market of 360 million people instead of national markets of 3 to 60 million. In addition, efforts had to be made to ensure that the educational and R&D infrastructure was in place from which comparative advantage could develop. Finally, anti-dumping and competition rules were needed in order to allow European and third-country suppliers to compete on a level playing field. The reasons for the Commission's intervention are similar to those of MITI in Japan. *Strategic trade theory*, as it is now known, draws both on externality theory and on dynamic considerations from industrial organisation to provide a framework for analysing these issues.

## Environmental protection[24]

Firms in countries with strict environmental standards worry about the impact of those standards on their competitiveness in world markets (the 'eco-dumping' problem). At the same time, governments and firms in countries with less strict standards express concern about new barriers being erected against their exports. The treatment of exports from countries which use child labour, deny freedom to trade unions, and ignore animal health and welfare rules is becoming the focus of more disputes. These are difficult issues to resolve.

The principle of non-discrimination ordains that a country cannot discriminate against imports merely because the exporting country has environmental policies different from its own. In the absence of this principle, any country could unilaterally apply trade restrictions not just for the purpose of enforcing its own laws in its jurisdiction but to impose its standards on others. In such circumstances the scope for abuse would be great. It would work against the main objective of the multilateral trade system – to provide stable and predictable market access through agreed rules. This partly explains why the US was ruled out of order in the early 1990s for placing an embargo on imports of tuna products from Mexico because Mexico's tuna fishing regulations did not satisfy the US's dolphin protection standards. On similar grounds, the WTO ruled in favour of the US in the late 1990s against the EU's ban on imports of hormone-treated beef from the US.

Another principle is that governments are free to agree multilaterally on any set of environmental restrictions they like. Trade in the products of endangered animals is outlawed by multilateral agreement. Discrimination is allowed against imports produced by prison labour. If sufficient support could be found, the rules could be extended to cover child labour and other labour market conditions. The important point is that intervention must not be unilateral.

---

[24] For a discussion of these issues in the EU context, see M. Brülhart and A. Matthews, 'External trade policy', in A. El-Agraa (ed.), *The European Union: Economics and politics*, 7th edn (Harlow: Financial Times Prentice Hall, 2004).

WTO rules also allow governments to protect their *own* environment from damage arising from domestic production or from the consumption of domestically produced *or* imported products. It is when one country's environmental problem is due to production or consumption activities in *another* that application of the rules becomes complicated. One constraint is that countries are prohibited from making market access dependent on changes in the domestic policies or practices of the exporting country. Countries are allowed to impose restrictions on imports which might endanger the health or safety of their citizens (sanitary and phytosanitary measures), but subject to the requirement that the measures do not arbitrarily discriminate between countries where the same conditions prevail and that they are not a disguised restriction on international trade.

Different national systems, whether in environmental, health, social or fiscal matters, can have a significant impact on trade flows. For individual firms this can have important implications. It is tempting to seek protection to 'compensate' for such differences and thereby create 'fair' trading conditions. The difficulty is that firms in other countries will have no difficulty in finding instances where your system hurts them and use this to justify restrictions on your exports. Hence some internationally agreed compromise is essential.

The above discussion shows that the case for liberal trade is open to challenge and must be kept regularly updated and revised. As a long-run strategy, however, the case remains strong. In any event the decline in transport costs, the information revolution and the increased ease of communication have also contributed to making international trade barriers much less enforceable than in the past. Faced with this fact, business has little choice but to adjust. In a sense, acceptance of the case for free trade between nations is the logical extension of the case for free trade within national boundaries. But this argument implies that internationally accepted 'rules of the game' must be put in place analogous to those enforced in domestic trade. The WTO is addressing this issue and has reinforced procedures to deal with government subsidies, patents and intellectual property issues, dispute settlement and dumping. An agreed international code of fair trade practices is vital if the world trading system is to gain acceptance among nations of widely different income levels and aspirations.

## 17.5 What determines comparative advantage?

Which industries and firms will prosper in a global trading system? Given the rapid pace of technological progress and the propensity of comparative advantage to change over time, this question must be addressed by firms and governments. Ultimately, it is individual firms which exploit and develop comparative advantage. They know the market better than any civil servant or economist. Yet sometimes comparative advantage can be changed as a result of government intervention.

Following Ricardo, we say that a country will export goods and services in which its comparative advantage is greatest. A country with abundant capital will export goods and services which are intensive in human and physical capital

(US); a resource-rich country will export resource-intensive goods (Argentina, Kuwait, Australia); and labour-abundant countries will export labour-intensive goods (Bangladesh, China). This approach does not imply that a country's comparative advantage remains fixed in any one category indefinitely. A country can progress from one stage to another, in accordance with what is called the Stages Theory of Comparative Advantage.[25] For example, Japan specialised in the export of low-cost, labour-intensive goods before advancing to the export of human capital-intensive goods.

The world's fastest growing industries are heavily reliant on human capital. As Professor Thurow noted:

> Consider what are commonly believed to be the seven key industries of the next few decades – microelectronics, biotechnology, the new materials industries, civilian aviation, telecommunications, robots *plus* software. All are brainpower industries. Each could be located anywhere on the face of the globe. Where they will be located depends upon who can organise the brain power to capture them. In the century ahead comparative advantage will be man-made.[26]

Ideally we need a theory of the determinants of trade which is more strongly rooted in an analysis of firms. An industry's export performance is only as good as the export performance of its firms. Usually only a minority of firms engage in exporting. Looked at this way, the issue becomes one of determining what factors explain the successful performance of this select group.

Michael Porter, author of the best-seller *The Competitive Advantage of Nations*, has identified four major determinants of national competitive advantage. The so-called Porter Diamond (Figure 17.4) consists of:

1. *Factor endowments* – countries with abundant supplies of a factor relative to another will export goods intensive in that factor.
2. *Demand conditions* – a country which has a sophisticated domestic market will export better quality goods with higher income elasticities.
3. *Firm strategy and rivalry* – vibrant domestic industries need strong competition and rivalry in the domestic market to keep them fit and lean for exporting.
4. *Related and supporting industries* – countries with industrial clusters gain economies of scale and can build on this to consolidate comparative advantage.

Each of these concepts has been discussed in general terms already. Porter skilfully puts empirical content into these abstractions and relates them to the behaviour of individual firms and industries.

In addition to these four determinants, Porter considers two further forces determining the evolution of comparative advantage: *chance* and *government policy*.

Comparative advantage of a nation can sometimes be determined by trivial and random events. Once an industry takes off, cumulative learning processes and increasing returns to scale reinforce its comparative advantage. The industry becomes 'locked in' to its original location. According to the originator of this

---

[25] B. Balassa, *Comparative Advantage, Trade Policy and Economic Development* (New York: New York University Press, 1989).

[26] L. Thurow, *Head to Head: The coming economic battle among Japan, Europe and America* (London: Nicholas Brealey Publishing, 1993), p. 45.

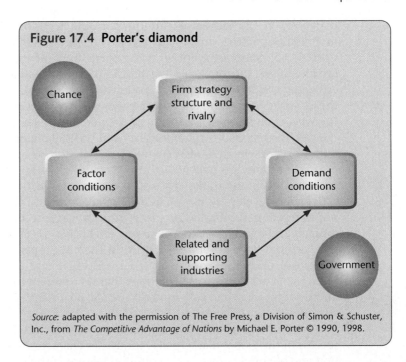

**Figure 17.4 Porter's diamond**

*Source*: adapted with the permission of The Free Press, a Division of Simon & Schuster, Inc., from *The Competitive Advantage of Nations* by Michael E. Porter © 1990, 1998.

theory, Brian Arthur, insignificant circumstances become magnified by positive feedbacks to tip the system towards the actual outcome we observe.[27] The small events of history become important. Chance, in other words, plays a vital role in determining the comparative advantage of nations, and a lucky accident can get an industry started in a particular location. Arthur instances Silicon Valley in California, and Krugman lists similar examples in his work on trade and economic geography.[28] This line of thought has given new impetus to the case for intervention and to the search for the 'right' industrial policy.

Porter assigns an important role to government intervention. He rejects protectionism as a policy option but advocates a proactive approach to building up comparative advantage. In line with current thinking, he stresses the importance of participation in global markets, but he adds an important clause *through continuous upgrading*, and sees no future for isolationist policies. He stresses the need to build on existing strengths, i.e. exploitation of scale economies through industrial clusters, the importance of encouraging competition, the need for macro-stability, and the establishment of a sound fiscal and economic infrastructure. Porter's ideas have been influential in the formation of industrial policies in many countries (including New Zealand, India and Ireland).

An interesting case where government intervention can be justified is in *export-promotion policies*. These policies comprise loan guarantees, export credit insurance,

---

[27] B. Arthur, 'Competing technologies, increasing returns and lock-in by historical events', *Economic Journal* (March 1989), p. 127.

[28] P. Krugman, *Geography and Trade* (Cambridge, MA: MIT Press, 1991). Comparative advantage is almost impossible to identify in advance. Bangladesh specialises in hat production; Ireland is a major producer of Viagra and artificial hips. How to explain? Some have linked comparative advantage to a *process of self discovery*.

marketing grants, subsidised information and technological advice, trade fairs, mobilisation of the diplomatic service to push national exports, and so on. Considerable sums are spent on such policies by some industrial countries. During the mid-1990s, the total exposure of official export credit agencies had grown to an estimated US$380 billion. Heavy losses were incurred on exports to Nigeria, Brazil, the ex-Soviet Union and Iraq. As a percentage of exports covered during the period, this was equivalent to a subsidy of 19 per cent.[29] US export subsidies granted through foreign sales corporations covered US$250 billion of US exports (and were found to be in violation of WTO rules).

Export-promotion policies are interventionist rather than protectionist and, as such, are less prone to the types of flaw associated with the latter. They are used actively by developing as well as developed countries. Governments are anxious not to repeat past mistakes on protection, yet eager to find ways of breaking into difficult and expensive export markets.[30] This issue is especially relevant to small and medium-sized enterprises (SMEs) in their attempts to take full advantage of the global market. Having won the intellectual case as regards telling governments what *not to do* in trade matters, there is room for further economic research on the topic of what governments *should* do in order to exploit comparative advantage more effectively.

*Low costs, high quality* and *continuous innovation* are the vital ingredients for success in the global marketplace. Industries characterised by product differentiation and oligopoly power are a common feature of the world trade system and for them the need to upgrade quality is particularly pressing. Instances include automobiles, aircraft, computers and telecom equipment. Competitive advantage in these cases is nurtured by a variety of forces: standard comparative costs, oligopolistic rivalry, government intervention and even corporate inertia (the firm's own history and corporate characteristics).[31] If the share of intra-industry trade were taken as an indicator of the extent of imperfectly competitive or oligopolistic influence in international trade, the proportionate share of trade influenced by the above considerations may well be as high as 40 per cent.

## 17.6 Conclusions

An increasingly high proportion of the world's output is being traded internationally. The composition of the world's merchandise trade flows continues to move from primary goods towards manufactured goods. Within manufacturing, high-tech industries are the most dynamic element. Trade in services is also growing fast. In addition to traditional service activities such as tourism and transport, new activities are entering the global market: hitherto protected activities such as

---

[29] M.G. Kuhn *et al.*, 'Officially supported credits: recent developments and prospects' (Washington, DC: IMF, March 1995); 'Export credits: giving arms a hand', *The Economist* (5 November 1994).

[30] A. MacBean (ed.), *Trade and Transition: Trade promotion in transitional economies* (London: Frank Cass, 2000).

[31] D.B. Yoffie, *Beyond Free Trade: Firms, governments and global competition* (Cambridge, MA: Harvard Business School Press, 1993).

banking and insurance and technology-led activities such as software and information processing. Three factors – income growth, improvements in transport and communications, and trade liberalisation – have been critical determinants of these developments.

The globalisation of markets has had a profound effect on the modern business environment. Firms are being driven to become more efficient and dynamic in order to survive. Global competition is bringing many benefits to the consumer in terms of cheaper and better quality goods and services. Trade has helped to bring faster growth to many countries. But there is also a downside. The relentless search for improved efficiency has imposed a heavy burden of adjustment on import-competing industries and on the people who are dependent on them for a living. To minimise this burden is a major challenge to policy.

One way to ease the adjustment burden is to liberalise by forming regional trade agreements with similarly structured economies. Another option is to arrange generous transition periods designed to give firms time to restructure. Direct and indirect protection of sensitive sectors has also been resorted to. Agriculture, steel, clothing and textiles are the most common examples. Protected pockets of economic activity exist in even the most sophisticated economies. Thus, the US summarily imposed restrictions on steel imports in 2001, contrary to WTO rules. The EU protects its farmers. The Japanese market is protected by numerous opaque nontariff barriers which make exporting to Japan problematical and expensive.[32]

A growing weight of evidence suggests that it is better to participate in international specialisation than to resist it. But because protectionism is rejected does not mean that unqualified *laissez-faire* must be embraced. First, protection is only one of many possible forms of state intervention. Even in a liberal global system, governments and industry have to consider ways of promoting comparative advantage. This exercise will entail taking a longer-term view of a nation's competitive position than free enterprise alone might adopt. Government assistance should aim to ensure that people and firms are encouraged to make full use of the opportunities of the external economy. Second, the gains from trade will be realised only if resources can be kept fully employed. Large-scale unemployment not only undermines popular support for free trade, it also undermines some of the reasoning and the theoretical assumptions upon which the case in its favour is based. Free trade, therefore, requires the existence of a price system which functions well and which has appropriate levels of government intervention to cope with externalities and income distribution. To some extent, the exposure to foreign trade will help this condition to be fulfilled. For example, trade contributes to keeping domestic markets competitive and flexible. Nevertheless, one can safely say that, far from *laissez-faire* being a condition for obtaining the gains from trade, the case for free trade is consolidated by a certain degree of state intervention. This point has been made in a different way by Peter Drucker:

> The world economy has become too important for a country not to have a world-economy policy. Managed trade is a delusion of grandeur. Outright protectionism can

---

[32] Following threats of retaliatory action by the EU against US exports, President Bush removed the steel import barriers in late 2003. Empirical studies suggest that the main cost of protection falls on the country imposing it. Japanese protection, according to one estimate, has cost consumers an amount equal to 3.8 per cent of Japanese GDP; the overall national loss is 0.6 per cent of Japanese national income. (Studies for other countries reach qualitatively similar conclusions.)

only do harm, but simply trying to thwart protectionism is not enough. What is needed is a deliberate and active – indeed, aggressive – policy that gives the demands, opportunities and dynamics of the external economy priority over domestic policy demands and problems. [33]

The specifics of this 'aggressive' policy have to be worked out on a country-by-country basis. As markets become more competitive, and production and marketing become more globalised, a new generation of trade issues is coming to the fore. Market access has been subjected to new scrutiny and the concept of the level playing field is seen to involve much more than the absence of trade barriers. [34] National competition policy, intellectual property investment incentives, labour standards and environmental regulation are areas of policy which impact strongly on trade flows. Free trade disposes of one set of trade barriers, only to move the searchlight to new, indirect, and hitherto ignored, barriers. There is a continuing need to adapt the architecture of the world trading system to ensure fairness between developed and developing countries. Fair trade is replacing free trade as the rallying cry for the twenty-first century. This in turn will involve linkage between trade issues and other policy areas, such as corporate taxation and environmental and competition policy, that were formerly considered a matter of exclusively national concern. Countries which assign priority to micro-efficiency and macro-stability, and constrain government intervention within tight parameters, will be best placed to take advantage of this evolving system.

## Summary

1. Trade continues to grow rapidly, much faster than world output. Manufactured trade is expanding fastest, much of it consisting of exchange of similar goods called intra-industry trade. Trade in services has been boosted by technological advance and by deregulation.

2. A landmark development in the world trade regime was the completion of the Uruguay Round and the establishment of the World Trade Organisation (WTO) in 1995.

3. Motivating the global trend towards freer trade was the belief that trade yields significant economic benefits. Economic theory explains these benefits as deriving from greater efficiency in the allocation of given resources (the law of comparative advantage), and also from so-called dynamic factors such as better scope for exploiting economies of scale, more intense competition, stimulus to the adoption and gestation of technological advance, and a resultant upgrading of product quality.

4. But there are downsides to an open trade environment, notably for those who lose their jobs, or the value of their share capital, in import-competing industries. Also, trade fulfils its potential and delivers gains to society only if the domestic

---

[33] P. Drucker, 'Trade lessons from the world economy', *Foreign Affairs* (January/February 1994), p. 108.
[34] OECD, *New Dimensions of Market Access in a Globalising World Economy* (Paris, February 1995); J. Bhagwati and R. Hudec, *Fair Trade and Harmonisation* (Cambridge, MA: MIT Press, 1996).

price system is functioning smoothly and reflecting domestic social costs and benefits. These caveats to the free trade case are important for many transition and developing countries.

5. Comparative advantage changes over time. Not only this, but the profile of national comparative advantage can be altered by economic policy. Comparative advantage nowadays is *made*, not *given*. Government policy can play a role in determining it, through long-term investment in human capital and physical infrastructure. Government policy can also play a role through the provision of incentives. Governments, and economists, continue to search for ways of improving the efficiency of their national industries and to build on, and consolidate, their competitive advantage.

6. The world trade system faces new challenges in developing a consistent and acceptable approach towards environment-related trade issues and towards global competition rules to ensure that trade is both free and 'fair'. The dispute settlement procedures of the WTO will be tested in coming years.

## Questions for discussion

1. According to official estimates, world income will increase by over $500 billion following implementation of the Uruguay Round. What, in your view, are the main sources of these gains? Why have so many countries, both developed and developing, participated in this major movement towards global free trade?

2. What is comparative advantage and what determines it? Can a comparative advantage be developed through judicious use of economic policies?

3. Why do smaller countries trade more as a percentage of GDP than large countries? Does this help or hinder their efforts to improve living standards?

4. The WTO's Trade Policy Review Board has on occasion expressed concern about the vulnerability of some developing economies arising from their heavy export reliance on a limited number of products and markets. Explain why such concentration might be a problem. What measures would you suggest to help a country achieve greater export diversification?

5. Adjustment to freer trade can involve heavy economic costs to the people affected, arising from financial and employment losses in import-competing industries. What measures should the government take in order to minimise these adjustment costs?

6. A group of competing firms in Italy produces 80 per cent of the world's sunglasses. Most of this production is located between Ancona and Venice, making sunglasses a remarkably concentrated one-product industry. Exports make this type of specialisation possible but, using Porter's diamond, can you think of reasons why the industry happens to be so heavily concentrated in a region of Italy rather than being geographically spread?

# Exercises

1. Suppose that in Sweden 1 unit of labour can produce 10 units of timber and 10 units of steel, whereas in the UK 1 unit of labour can produce 8 units of steel and 6 units of timber. In what product does the UK have a comparative advantage? In what product does Sweden have a comparative advantage? Would your answer be different if 1 unit of Swedish labour could produce 14 units of steel instead of 10?

2. Examine EU–Japan trade figures in recent years. In every year since 1958 (with the exception of 1961) the main European countries have experienced deficits on merchandise trade with Japan. Comment on the extent and structure of the trade imbalance. Compare this imbalance with EU trade balances with other countries and regions. In the light of your empirical findings, should Europe's merchandise trade deficit with Japan be a cause for concern? (For relevant data, see World Trade Organisation, *International Trade: Trends and statistics*, or Eurostat trade figures.)

3. There is no doubt that China's decision to join the WTO is particularly momentous. Opening its markets to foreign trade and investment will make China more prosperous, and committing China to world trade rules will foster and consolidate market-based reforms. WTO members stand to gain by better access to an economy of 1.3 billion consumers, which was growing at 8% in 2000. (WTO *Annual Report*, 2001)

   Analyse the above statement carefully. Explain how WTO membership will make China more prosperous. What does it mean to say that it will foster market-based reforms? Through what mechanisms do other countries gain? (See Case study 17.1 for further information.)

4. Japanese car imports into Europe used to be restrained by a voluntary export quota. Use a demand and supply diagram to show the effect of this quota on the price of Japanese cars in Europe. One research study found that the effect of the quota was to raise the price of the average Japanese car to the EU consumer by 12 per cent. It also found that the price of competing European cars rose by 7 per cent. How would you explain this?

5. Analyse the following assessment of the effects of protection. Can it be reconciled with the theory of the gains from trade outlined in this chapter?

   The Japanese were undoubtedly greatly helped by the building up of immense protective walls about them. Foreign car makers had dominated the Japanese market, and indeed had local plants until the 1930s when the militarists shut them out. Those doors were not opened again until the Japanese manufacturers were firmly established and becoming exporting powers themselves. Indeed, right until the 1990s there were complaints from foreign car makers – and from foreign manufacturers in other areas – that Japanese bureaucrats typically twist, bend and extend the rules, via administrative guidance or inspections or any other excuse, effectively to shut foreigners out of the market. Thus, in the case of cars, small suppliers to the Japanese market not only faced stringent safety rules different from those in their home country, but also had to pay for lengthy inspections of each individual car to make sure that it met the peculiar and usually highly particular rules and regulations of the Japanese market, all of this adding expensive cost and time to selling to Japan. (Kevin Raftery, *Inside Japan's Power Houses: The culture, mystique and future of Japan's greatest corporations*, London: Weidenfeld & Nicolson, 1995, p. 13)

6. Sometimes protection is justified on the grounds that it is good for all industries. One favourite ploy is to list all the domestic goods and services purchased by the protected industry and to compute all the extra jobs thereby 'created' as a benefit of protection. What is wrong with this approach?

7. Consider the following statement by Adam Smith. How would you explain continuing high levels of protection of the wine industry in many countries? Make the case for and against complete liberalisation of the industry.

> By means of glasses, hotbeds and hotwalls, very good grapes can be raised in Scotland, and very good wine too can be made of them at about thirty times the expense for which at least equally good wine can be bought from foreign countries. Would it be a reasonable law to prohibit the importation of all foreign wines, merely to encourage the making of claret and burgundy in Scotland? (Adam Smith, *Wealth of Nations*, Volume 1, 1776, p. 480)

8. Use a demand and supply diagram to explain the effect of an export subsidy. Is there a case for the government using subsidies to encourage the development of domestic industries by helping them win export markets? Is this fair play, or is it a form of hidden protectionism?

9. What are the three most important export industries in your country? Examine their export performance during the past decade. What factors explain your country's comparative advantage in these industries? Is Porter's diamond useful in this exercise?

10. According to Blinder (Box 17.5), 'the existence of high unemployment calls into question many of the propositions of standard trade theory'. Given current unemployment rates in Europe, is there an economic case for the EU's participation in another WTO trade round? If so, what is it?

## Further reading

There are several good textbooks on international economics for readers wishing to delve more deeply. Examples include L.A. Winters, *International Economics*, 4th edn (London: Allen & Unwin, 1991) and B. Sodersten and G. Reed, *International Economics*, 3rd edn (London: Macmillan, 1994). An influential, business-oriented interpretation of global trade which relates economic theory to strategic firm behaviour is Michael Porter's *The Competitive Advantage of Nations* (London: Macmillan, 1990). J. Bhagwati, 'Free trade: old and new challenges', *Economic Journal*, (March 1994), presents an assessment by one of the world's foremost thinkers on these matters. The impact of globalisation and trade on living standards is top of the research agenda as we enter the twenty-first century. See D. Ben-David and Alan Winters, 'Trade, income disparity and poverty', *WTO Special Study* no. 5 (June 2000), for a strong conclusion that open economies are performing better than the less open economies. For an up-to-date assessment of WTO see S. Laird, 'A round by any other name – the WTO agenda after Doha', *Development Policy Review*, 20(1), 2002. An excellent forward-looking overview of RTAs, representing the world's present spaghetti bowl of trade relationships, is given in L. Cernot and S. Laird, 'North, South, East, West: modern RTAs and their implications for trade policy', CREDIT Research Paper, University of Nottingham, August 2003. Useful websites include the WTO website (www.wto.org) and EU Trade DG (http://europa.eu.int/trade).

### Case study 17.1

# China and the WTO: the effects of trade liberalisation

## Background

Speed and trade negotiations are antithetical concepts. It took China and the WTO 12 years to agree terms of accession, which were finally concluded in November 2001. By that time China had become the fourth largest trading nation (or bloc) in the world, after the US, the EU and Japan.

**China's trade by area, 2002**

| Exports | $bn | % | Imports | $bn | % |
|---------|-----|---|---------|-----|---|
| US | 70 | 22 | Japan | 53 | 18 |
| Hong Kong | 58 | 26 | Taiwan | 38 | 13 |
| Japan | 48 | 15 | S. Korea | 29 | 10 |
| Korea | 15 | 5 | US | 27 | 9 |
| EU | 58 | 18 | EU | 48 | 16 |
| Other | 77 | 14 | Other | 85 | 33 |
| Total | 326 | 100 | Total | 295 | 100 |

*Source*: *China's Customs Statistics*

Trade agreements involve positive and negative effects, but there are differences in view about the category into which particular effects fall. For example, trade negotiators are trained to see increased imports as a concession ('negative') that is compensated by the gain ('positive') of better access for exports, whereas economists think of cheaper imports as the source of welfare gain and exports being a positive only in so far as they make it possible to purchase these imports. Similarly, as tariffs are phased out, government sees the resultant loss of tariff revenue as a negative, whereas economists deem it merely a redistribution of income. And, as we saw in Box 17.5, the effects of lay-offs in import-competing industry can validly be seen as a positive in the long run, but they are assuredly a heavy cost in the short run. These different perspectives on gains and losses should be kept in mind in evaluating the 'positive' and 'negative' effects of China's accession.

## Positive aspects

Analysis of the gains from the WTO has focused on:

- improved access to global markets for exports,
- free trade in textiles and clothing (especially important for China),
- increase in foreign direct investment inflows in response to reduced restrictions on China's export and domestic markets,
- spur to efficiency in import-competing firms in manufacturing,
- transmission of new technology and management skills

All the above are standard effects. In China's case there is one further, crucially important, non-standard gain. Trade liberalisation, it is hoped, will underpin and reinforce the entire market reform programme, improving efficiency and cultivating a market-oriented economy based on the rule of law.

## Short- and long-term costs

Short-term adjustment costs arise as reductions in protection and conformity to WTO rules lead to more imports and to inflows of foreign investment. The consequent cutback in China's domestic import-competing activities leads to:

- job losses in state-operated enterprises,
- worsening of bad asset problem in state banks (national treatment to apply in banking and much of the financial sector within five years),
- pressure on agricultural output and employment,
- unemployment and inflows of people into the cities, leading to social instability.

To these can be added two potential long-run costs:

- cost of conforming to the intellectual property agreement (copying foreign software and ignoring international patents, copyright and trademarks is a cheap way of acquiring know-how and knowledge),
- vulnerability to downturns in the world economy as China becomes more open.

## Sectoral impacts

The aggregate effect of trade liberalisation has to be built up on detailed analyses of individual sector effects. China's agriculture, for example, is likely to be significantly affected by the WTO limit on state support (trade-distorting subsidies) to not more than 8.5 per cent of the value of farm production. Duties on agricultural imports of grain, soybeans and cotton will fall from 31 per cent to 14 per cent by early 2004. There may be offsetting increases in export opportunities for fruit and vegetables.

Another strongly affected sector is telecoms. Foreign producers will be permitted to own up to 50 per cent of Chinese telecom companies and in addition tariffs will be phased out on most high-tech products.

Profound effects are expected in banking, insurance, asset management and even the stock market. The China–WTO accession terms include a long list of detailed commitments to allow foreign participation in petrol stations, retail distribution and similar activities. Is this excessively intrusive? To some it looks like bringing national treatment to the level of religious dogma rather than a rule for trade among equal partners.

## Welfare effects

On balance, taking good and bad effects, is this the right move for China? And is it the right move for WTO members? The net impact on welfare of the various and complex consequences of trade liberalisation is notoriously difficult to measure. But negotiators, political leaders and the public do need an answer.

Estimates of the effects of WTO membership on merchandise trade show gains to China of the order of $4–$30 billion per year. In terms of GDP this amounts to between 1.5 per cent and 10 per cent of China's GDP. The gains for the global economy are in the range $20–$56 billion. The range of variation of these estimates is formidably wide, but this is not at all unusual in estimates of this type.

Note that both parties, China and the rest of the world, gain. This is exactly the win–win outcome that trade theory predicts.

Barriers to trade will also decline in the services sector. A cut of one-third in these barriers has been estimated to confer a further gain to China of $2–$7 billion per year.

Potential job losses can also be estimated (by computing likely increases in imports, and multiplying the consequent displacement of domestic output by an appropriate output:employment ratio). Some estimates indicate a loss of 11 million jobs in agriculture. There will also be large lay-offs in state-owned enterprises and about 500,000 jobs are expected to be lost in the automobile industry. The hope, and expectation, is that these job losses will be compensated by the expansion in employment in the more efficient private sector firms. Not surprisingly, the view from Geneva and Beijing is upbeat. But opting for the path of trade liberalisation is anything but easy. It offers *possibilities* of gain, not certainty. That so many countries, developing and developed, have chosen this path tells us as much about the failures of protectionism as the benefits of free trade.

## China and WTO – the view from Geneva

There is no doubt that China's decision to join the WTO is particularly momentous. Opening its markets to foreign trade and investment will make China more prosperous, and committing China to world trade rules will foster and consolidate market-based reforms. WTO members stand to gain by better access to an economy of 1.3 billion consumers, which was growing at 8% in 2000. (WTO, *Annual Report*, Geneva, 2001)

*Sources*: N.R. Lardy, *Integrating China into the Global Economy* (Washington, DC: Brookings Institute Press, 2002). For a short summary of the issues and references to further literature, see R. Adhikari and Yangzheng Yang, 'What will WTO membership mean for China and its trading partners?', *Finance and Development*, September 2002.

---

( **Questions for discussion** )

1. Under the WTO agreement, the average tariff on imports of automobiles into China will fall from 70–90 per cent to 25 per cent by mid-2006. Use demand and supply analysis to illustrate the effects of this tariff reduction on automobile imports. What will be the effect on:

   (a) the price of imports in Chinese currency?
   (b) the dollar price of imports?
   (c) employment in import-competing industries?
   (d) government tariff revenues?

2. The WTO negotiations took place against the backdrop of a large and persistent Chinese trade surplus (US$31 billion in 2002) and fear in many developed *and* developing countries (e.g. Mexico, the last WTO member to sign off on China's accession) that China

had the capacity to out-compete their domestic firms on a major scale. How relevant is the existence of a trade surplus to China's actual and potential gains from trade?

3. This case study explains the effect of WTO membership from China's perspective. Set out the main issues as they would appear to:

(a)  a developed country member of WTO;
(b)  a developing country member.

4. China's trade partners complained that their access to the Chinese market would be obstructed by the pervasive state controls of firms and financial institutions. Hence the need for detailed commitments on this point. From an economic perspective, which party – China or its trade partners – had most to lose from a continuance of these controls?

## Chapter 18

# Capital flows and foreign investment

A major feature of the world economy over the past decades has been the growing integration of national economies. International trade in goods and services grew faster than gross domestic product, links between national financial markets strengthened, more people moved across borders, foreign direct investment (FDI) expanded rapidly, and so did the activity of transnational corporations (TNCs).

(United Nations, *World Investment Report 1993: Transnational Corporations and Integrated International Production*, New York: UN, 1993, p. 113)

## Introduction

In Chapter 17, we analysed the gains from foreign trade in the context of an economy where capital, labour and other factors of production are mobile *within* nations, but immobile *between* nations. Factors of production were assumed to be able to move costlessly between industries within the same country, but they could not move abroad. Trade theory shows how, in such circumstances, foreign trade can act as a partial substitute for international factor mobility. Capital-rich countries can achieve higher returns for their relatively abundant capital by exporting capital-intensive goods. Likewise, populous countries achieve higher-paid employment and more prosperity by exporting labour-intensive goods and services. The output of labour is exported rather than labour itself.

In this chapter account is taken of the growing international mobility of factors of production. Flows of international capital are increasing in volume and variety. This mobility takes many forms – mutual fund investment, lending by banks to governments, and speculative flows by hedge funds and derivatives traders. Alongside this, firms have become globalised. Few leading companies nowadays are located exclusively in their home country. Foreign investment has become an essential element in firms' investment and production strategies and is undertaken not just by huge multinationals in the conventional sense, but also by medium-sized companies in both industrial and developing countries. This globalisation involves movements of financial and physical capital across countries, as well as the mobility of cooperant factors such as know-how and technical skills. International labour mobility has grown too, although not to the same extent as capital mobility. We discuss this in Chapter 19.

Chapter 17 showed how foreign trade can contribute to growth. Can the same be said of the international exchange of capital and labour? Does factor mobility confer benefits on both the receiving country (the host country) and the sending country (the home country), or is it a zero-sum game? Does it help the process of economic development? What are the gains from such mobility and how are they measured? Should economic policy-makers remove obstacles to inward and outward movement of productive factors, or does the process of integration make such obstacles redundant?

Chapter outline

1. Recent trends in level and composition of capital flows.

2. Analysis of capital flows in a simple, general framework. This analysis shows how capital flows can potentially add to the welfare of both host and home countries. The basic analysis is extended to cover the effects of capital mobility on tax revenues.

3. Extension of the framework to analyse the extent and motivation of one important type of capital flow: foreign direct investment. The multinational firm has been the leading force behind direct investment flows. Its activities involve the transfer between countries of a 'package' of productive factors: capital, technology and skilled management talent.

4. The economic effects of foreign investment. Most research has focused on the effects on the host country, but donor countries can also gain. Witness the rush to invest in China and the complaints from some governments of being barred from investing in Japan. Policies for maximising the potential benefits from inward investment are outlined.

## 18.1 Capital flows

The past three decades have witnessed major changes in the level and composition of capital flows, both among industrial countries and between industrial and developing countries. The 1990s were described as 'the decade of equity finance', reflecting the huge increase in foreign direct investment and international equity flows during the decade. This contrasted with earlier decades where the dominant form of international capital movement was portfolio debt finance, involving both government and private sectors. Notwithstanding the steep downturn in capital market activity in the early 2000s, the world capital market has now become more integrated than at any time since the pre-1914 heyday of the gold standard. There are several striking indicators of this enhanced level of integration.

● The stock of international bank lending, which includes both cross-border lending, domestic lending and lending denominated in foreign currency, has risen to around half the value of industrial countries' GDP.

- A rising share of government bonds is held by foreigners. According to the Bank of International Settlements, the average proportion of industrial countries' government debt held by non-residents has risen to 25 per cent.[1]
- Private sector issuers of bonds and securities have frequent recourse to the international markets. Often these transactions are linked to mergers and acquisitions activity. Net issues of international bonds peaked at $1100 billion in 1999.[2]

As capital markets have become more integrated, there has been a proliferation of different types of mobile investment funds designed for the private investor. An individual with even as modest a sum as €5000 can choose from a welter of attractive and exotic investment funds, each with its own risk and geographical profile. There are funds specialising in the Far East, North America, Europe and the 'emerging' economies of Asia and Latin America.

Both supply and demand factors have contributed to the increase in capital mobility. On the supply side, there has been a huge increase in the amount of investible funds in industrial countries, representing the effects of higher incomes, an ageing population profile and a tendency to replace or enhance public sector pension schemes (often financed out of current tax revenue) with privately funded schemes. On the demand side, the growing pressure on fund managers to produce better returns has led them to search further afield for foreign investment opportunities in order to achieve both higher average returns and a more diversified portfolio. The performance of fund managers is being monitored ever more closely and regularly. Competition between them is intense. In addition, both supply and demand conditions have been affected by two further developments: (1) the gradual removal of government-imposed barriers to capital mobility, and (2) the development of information technology.

The path to capital market integration has, however, not been entirely smooth. Nowhere was this more evident than in the emerging economies during the late 1990s. Up to then, private capital had flowed in generous amounts into the rapidly growing and profitable markets of the Asian tigers and countries in transition. By the mid-1990s, East Asia was the recipient of over US$100 billion of private capital annually. Transition economies absorbed a further US$45 billion out of a total flow to emerging economies that peaked at US$229 billion in 1996 (Figure 18.1). Following the 1997 currency crisis in Thailand, capital inflows quickly converted into capital outflows as foreign lenders to these countries ran for cover. In the space of two years, the five most exposed Asian economies (Thailand, Korea, Indonesia, Malaysia and the Philippines) suffered a dramatic reversal from net private capital inflows of US$63 billion in 1996 to a net outflow of US$30 billion in 1998. The reverberations of the shock were felt throughout the developing world and, for a while, capital market disintegration rather than integration was the main theme of debate. The collapse of equity markets since 2000 exacerbated the situation further, with investors becoming more risk averse. As Figure 18.1 shows, by 2003 net private capital flows to emerging economies were at one-third of the 1996 level. During this time, capital flows between different parts of the developed world have also been adversely affected.

---

[1] Bank of International Settlements, *Annual Report*, Basel (June 2000); US Treasury Department, *Treasury Bulletin*.
[2] Data from IMF *World Economic Outlook* (October 1999).

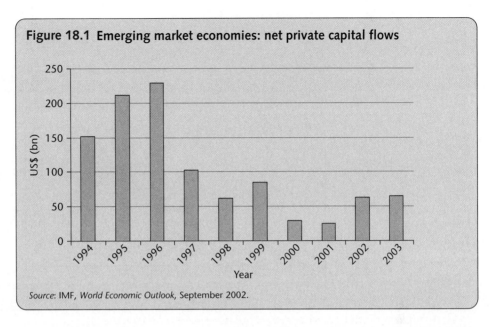

**Figure 18.1 Emerging market economies: net private capital flows**

Source: IMF, *World Economic Outlook*, September 2002.

Governments still try to persuade their citizens to keep their savings at home through various tax devices and through limits on the deployment of pension fund assets, but these measures have become less pervasive in recent years. When average returns on capital and their variances differ systematically between countries, investors will want to hold a portion of their total assets abroad, and it has become increasingly difficult to prevent them doing so.

## 18.2 Basic model

Imagine a world divided into two areas, the North and the South. Capital earns a low rate of return in the North where it is relatively abundant and a high rate of return in the South where it is relatively scarce. Initially, there is zero capital mobility between the two areas. Now assume restrictions on capital mobility are eliminated. Capital will be expected to move from the North towards the South, where returns are higher. These flows will continue until the rate of return is equalised in the two areas. Economic welfare is increased by such mobility because capital is deployed where it is most productive. In a sense, the argument is a rerun of the theory of comparative advantage.

The effects of capital mobility can be illustrated by means of Figure 18.2. Assume a fixed world supply of capital, measured by the distance $O_nO_s$. The richer North is endowed with $O_nK$, and the poorer South with $O_sK$ of capital. Curves showing the marginal product of capital at each level of capital stock in each area are drawn as the downward-sloping lines, $MP_n$ and $MP_s$. As more capital is added to the stock, its marginal productivity declines. (The information required to draw these curves is derived from the production functions for each country.) Initially there is zero capital mobility between N and S. Hence at $O_nK$, the marginal return on capital in the North is measured by the vertical distance

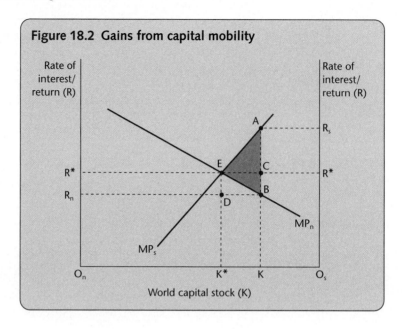

**Figure 18.2 Gains from capital mobility**

$O_n R_n$. For the South, with capital stock $O_s K$, the marginal product is the vertical distance $O_s R_s$. The marginal product of capital is lower in the capital-abundant North than in the capital-scarce South.

Suppose restrictions on capital mobility are removed. Capital now flows from North to South in response to the higher rate of return in the South. As capital flows into the South, its marginal product declines. At the same time, the marginal product in the North rises. Eventually equilibrium is reached, at the point E ($K^*$, $R^*$). Capital no longer has an incentive to migrate. Returns are equalised in both areas.

The global economic gains from this redeployment of the world's capital stock are represented by the triangular area ABE. It represents the difference between what the redeployed capital produced in the South and what it had been able to produce in the North. Thus at K, the marginal product of one unit of capital was KB in the North. By shifting to the South the same unit of capital produced an output of KA. With respect to that unit, the gain from mobility was AB. Similar gains accrue, at a declining rate, as a result of each unit movement of capital until we reach $K^*$. At this point the value of the marginal product in each region is the same. The gain from the exchange of capital, represented by the triangle ABE, is a gain of economic efficiency, analogous to the gains from trade (Chapter 17) and to the welfare gain of moving from monopoly to competition (Chapter 6).

The distribution of the gain between the two areas and between capital owners (capitalists) and the rest of the population (workers) can also be worked out from Figure 18.2.

The South attracts capital $K^*K$, for which it pays interest of $OR^*$ per unit, amounting in total to $K^*KCE$. The sum of the marginal products of $K^*K$, however, equals $K^*KAE$. Hence the net gain to the South is ACE. From the North's point of view, it has exported $K^*K$ capital for which $K^*KCE$ has been received from the South. Had this capital stayed in the North, it could have produced only $K^*KBE$. Hence the North gains BCE. Thus *both areas gain from capital mobility*. Like trade, a mutually beneficial exchange is being transacted, not a zero-sum game.

This win–win outcome at an aggregate level, however, masks the existence of losers and gainers within regions. Capitalists in the South lose – the return on their capital has fallen by $AR_sR^*C$. The effect of capital mobility has been to make their capital less scarce. By contrast, capitalists in the North clearly gain. The capital they deploy at home now earns a return of $R^*EK^*O_n$ instead of $R_nDK^*O_n$, while their exported capital earns ECBD more than it was earning at home. Hence, the total gain to northern capital owners amounts to $R_nBCR^*$. There are corresponding losses and gains for non-capital factors of production (for convenience often described simply as labour) in each region. Thus, labour in the South gains relative to capital – workers there become more productive as a result of the capital inflows – while workers in the North lose relative to northern capital – capital per worker declines as a result of the North's capital outflows.

## Capital mobility and taxes

Because each region is better-off as a consequence of capital mobility, it is possible for the government in each region to compensate the losers while still leaving some of the population better-off than before. The theory does not assert that compensation *will* happen, only that it *could* happen, given political commitment to this objective and an appropriate tax regime.

Paradoxically, redistribution through taxation, although strictly speaking required in order to make a cast-iron case for capital mobility, is made more difficult by the international mobility of capital itself. As many governments are learning, the scope for taxation of capital has become increasingly circumscribed. Capital mobility, by redistributing income, creates a case for public intervention if compensation of the losers is considered desirable. But it also makes the policies needed to effect such transfers more difficult to implement.

Suppose the equilibrium rate of return was OR and that capital was immobile internationally (Figure 18.3). Suppose further that the government decided to levy a tax, equal to RT, on capital earnings. If capital were immobile, a tax on capital equal to RT would be an effective way of transferring income from capital owners to others. The capital stock could be considered fixed at $OK_0$, hence the vertical supply curve $K_0S_k$. The interest rate charged to borrowers cannot exceed OR because at any higher rate, supply exceeds demand and the rate of return will fall. The incidence of the tax falls entirely on capital and there is a transfer of REGT from capitalists to the government. In the long run, domestic savings might be affected by the tax. But even if the supply curve were not completely vertical, the sensitivity of savings to the net of tax return is likely to be low.

By contrast, when capital is mobile, foreign and domestic investment funds compete actively for the same capital. Any gap between domestic and foreign interest rates will be immediately competed away. If domestic interest rates were higher than the foreign interest rate, capital would flow into the country, driving down the domestic rate. In other words, the supply curve of capital becomes horizontal instead of vertical. The equilibrium rate of interest, OR, is set by international supply and demand.

In these circumstances, suppose a tax of RT were imposed. Capital would leave the country until the *net return*, that is OT less tax RT, equalled the 'ruling' rate attainable elsewhere, OR. The objective of the tax has been frustrated. True, tax revenue RTDF has been collected. But capitalists have not lost income. All that

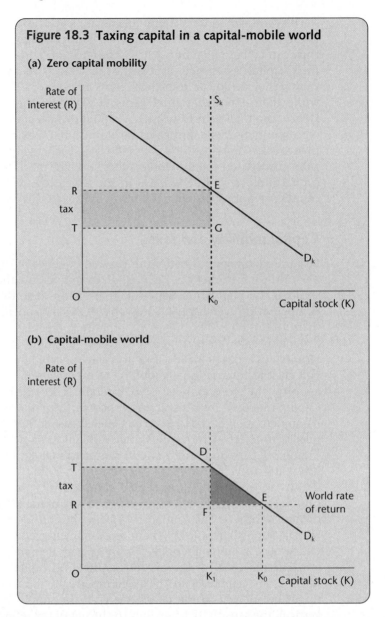

**Figure 18.3 Taxing capital in a capital-mobile world**

**(a) Zero capital mobility**

**(b) Capital-mobile world**

has happened is that the price of capital to domestic borrowers has been raised – the tax has been fully 'passed on'. The portion of capital staying in the region continues to earn the higher gross return while capital which has left the country earns the world rate of return. The outflow of capital has led to a loss of national welfare of DFE, representing the distortionary effect of the tax.

The above example reaffirms two significant lessons which are already familiar to the reader. First, the revenue collected from a tax tells us little about the incidence of the tax (i.e. who is truly paying it). Second, the incidence of a tax must be calculated before reaching a conclusion about its economic effects. In a world of increasing tax-consciousness and greater capital mobility, the possibility of avoiding tax through relocation must be kept in mind by the authorities.

## ◯ Extensions and qualifications

Capital inflows, if utilised properly, offer a welcome opportunity to build up infrastructure and to tackle bottlenecks to development in a capital-scarce economy – much as is envisaged in a more formalised and abstract way in the basic model. Such inflows offer not just a higher rate of return to the providers of capital but also the opportunity of spreading risks. America and Australasia owed their initial development to huge capital flows from Europe and, to this day, the EU provides significant capital to the peripheral regions of Europe.

One indirect spillover effect of global capital mobility is to improve the macro-management of an economy. A mobile capital stock obliges governments to manage their finances carefully. There is no longer a large captive pool of domestic savings which remains impervious to the conduct of domestic policy. Finance ministers have to frame their budgets and control government finances in a way that will not frighten capital markets. Capital markets take a dim view of spend-thrift policies. If these policies persist, domestic and foreign investors will move their assets to safer havens. Domestic interest rates will rise, the government will be blamed and there will be a negative political fallout. Capital flows, therefore, act as an external and impersonal discipline on macroeconomic policy.

In line with the theory, interest rates in practice play an important role in determining capital flows. The surge in capital to middle-income countries in the early 1990s, for instance, was largely a response to low interest rates in the US, which gave American and other investors a strong incentive to seek higher returns in new locations. Obviously, in addition to the interest rate, political and economic risk and the growth prospects of the host country must also be factored into the calculation. Thus, 'interest rate' is shorthand for a compendium of several factors affecting the expected return on capital flows.

The above qualifications help to explain several surprising and counter-intuitive features of the global capital market. First, *capital does not in general flow from rich to poor countries*. Table 18.1 compares the investment:GDP ratio with a country's savings:GDP ratio. If investment exceeds saving, the country is a net borrower, i.e. it receives capital from the rest of the world. On this basis, the US emerges as a major net borrower (3.6 per cent of its GDP in 2003) from other countries, not a lender as its wealth would lead one to expect. Capital outflows from Japan amount to 2.8 per cent of its GDP, but only a small part of this goes to poorer countries, most being allocated to US government debt. The developing countries collectively *export* capital to the rest of the world. Only Africa conforms to the model's expectations, with capital inflows amounting to 2.4 per cent of its GDP.

Second, although capital mobility has increased, *the vast bulk of the world's capital still remains more attached to its domestic market than a literal interpretation of the model of global capital markets would suggest is optimal.* (This is known as the Feldstein–Horioka puzzle.) Only 11 per cent of Europe's pension funds are invested outside the EU. US pension funds invest 92 per cent of their assets in the US, even though the US stock market accounts for only 48 per cent of global market capitalisation.[3] National savings and national investment are also closely

---

[3] A. Ahearne, W. Grieve and F. Warnock, 'Information costs and home bias: an analysis of US holding of foreign equities', *Federal Reserve System, International Finance Papers*, November 2001.

| Table 18.1 Saving, investment and net lending, 2003 (% of GDP) | | | |
| --- | --- | --- | --- |
| | Investment | Saving | Net borrowing/lending* |
| US | 18.8 | 15.2 | +3.6 |
| EU | 20.0 | 20.5 | −0.5 |
| Japan | 22.9 | 25.7 | −2.8 |
| **Developing countries** | 26.5 | 26.9 | −0.4 |
| of which: | | | |
| Africa | 21.2 | 18.8 | +2.4 |
| Asia | 30.2 | 31.3 | −0.9 |
| Middle East and Turkey | 23.4 | 24.4 | −1.0 |
| Latin America | 19.4 | 18.5 | +1.1 |

* A plus sign indicates net borrowing, a minus sign net lending.

Source: IMF, World Economic Outlook (September 2002), Table 44.

correlated in the developing countries. Their investment ratio was 26 per cent during the period 1993–2003, of which 24 percentage points came from domestic saving and only 2 extra percentage points from foreign investors. Even at the peak of the boom, less than 1 percentage point of the Asian Tigers' 33 per cent investment:GDP ratio was provided by foreign capital.[4]

Third, *a feature of capital mobility is the preponderance of two-way exchange between industrial countries* rather than the unidirectional movement analysed in the basic model. Total direct foreign investment outflows from the developed countries at their peak reached $1271 billion in 2000, whilst inflows in the same year came to $1227 billion. Western Europe exported $1018 billion of capital and imported $832 billion. This pattern parallels the intra-industry trade ratios noted in Chapter 17 and can be explained in a similar way. One obvious factor is product differentiation. Investments in different locations have different characteristics in terms of yields and risks and therefore investors view international diversification as an important vehicle for risk spreading. Investment funds managers like to have a diversified portfolio and modern telecommunications technology is making this cheaper and easier to achieve.

While it is possible to finesse the gains from capital mobility, account should also be taken of certain adverse effects associated with it:

1. *International capital flows can be volatile.* What flows in can just as easily flow out. In former times, a larger proportion of capital inflows were 'rooted' in the host country, taking the form of direct investment in enterprises, property and infrastructure. Nowadays capital flows are easily realised and carry no loyalty or longer-term commitment. This is 'the crisis-prone downside' of portfolio

---

[4] Interestingly, the originator of comparative costs might not have been surprised by this. Ricardo took the view that feelings of *fancied or real insecurity ... check the emigration of capital* and *induce most men of property to be satisfied with a low rate of profit in their own country, rather than seek a more advantageous employment for their wealth in foreign nations*: D. Ricardo, 'Principles of political economy and taxation', in P. Sraffa, *The Works and Correspondence of David Ricardo*, Vol. 1 (Cambridge: Cambridge University Press, 1953), pp. 136–7.

capital mobility that leads Bhagwati, Stiglitz and others to caution developing countries against premature liberalisation of capital flows.

2. *Capital inflows can cause unsustainable inflationary pressures.* Foreign investors can cause unsustainable property and equity booms. They also cause problems through increasing the supply of high-powered money. This creates difficulties for the monetary authorities in the host country, particularly if that country is trying to establish an anti-inflation reputation.

3. *Capital flows can lead to short-term misalignments of the exchange rate.* These lead to distorted price incentives and inefficient trade and investment decisions. Hence many countries continue to impose restraints on these flows. Because of its restrictions on short-term capital inflows, Chile was spared much of the disruption that Asian countries suffered during the currency crisis of the 1990s.

4. *Capital mobility can weaken a country's tax base by forcing governments to offer excessive enticements to investors.* Tax competition among governments can lead to a 'race to the bottom' with suboptimally low tax revenues and public investment.

## 18.3 Foreign direct investment and multinationals

Foreign direct investment (FDI) involves the acquisition of a controlling interest in a domestic enterprise by foreign capital owners. It differs from simple capital movements in that a mix of productive factors, such as technical know-how, marketing, managerial and financial expertise, is transferred alongside financial capital. Often the financial transfer is the least significant element in the package.

The main agent of FDI is the multinational enterprise (MNE).[5] Examples of FDI include the establishment of a subsidiary plant in a foreign country, the takeover of a domestic firm by a foreign corporation, creating a joint venture with a domestic firm (as part of a privatisation programme), and a licensing agreement with a domestic company to manufacture a brand owned by a foreign company. FDI by its nature tends to involve a stronger and longer-term commitment than portfolio capital movements. While fund managers respond to short-term profit opportunities, direct investment responds to longer-term assessments of prospective returns. These assessments take account of the future economic growth of host countries, taxation policy, trade and currency regimes, labour costs, environmental regulations and political stability – in short, the entire gamut of variables that influence the business climate.

FDI has the potential to play a major direct role in a country's development. Because it involves a package of productive inputs, some of which are in very short supply in the host country, governments have devised elaborate schemes for attracting such investment, comprising tax incentives, capital grants and labour training programmes. But FDI also has its critics, and the multinationals have been a subject of controversy for many years. Some argue that FDI inhibits development, or that branch plants contribute less to the national economy than appears.

---

[5] Foreign investment is undertaken not just by huge multinational enterprises, but also by many medium-sized enterprises.

## Trends in FDI

There are two ways of measuring FDI. One way is to focus on the *stock* of capital at a particular date. Each country has an inward stock representing capital owned by foreigners in the economy and an outward stock representing capital owned by the country's nationals in foreign countries. An alternative approach is to study annual *flows* of inward and outward investment. FDI flows fluctuate a good deal more than the stock indices; even the direction of the net flow can change from year to year. A large mergers and acquisitions deal, for example, can exert a disproportionate impact on the annual flow data. Nevertheless, capital flow data can highlight changes in investment patterns which capital stock indices will be much slower to reveal.

Using investment position as a criterion, the world's major outward investors are the US, EU and Japan (Table 18.2). The rapid growth in the world outward stock is also evident from this table. Within the EU, the UK, followed by Germany, France and the Netherlands, are the largest outward investors. The value of capital stock abroad has risen 15-fold in Europe since 1980. In 2000, stocks of gross outward direct investment reached 83 per cent of GDP in the Netherlands, 63 per cent in the UK and 25 per cent in Germany (Table 18.3). A

**Table 18.2  Inward and outward stock of foreign-owned capital, 2001 (US$ billion)**

|  | 1980 | 1990 | 2001 |
|---|---|---|---|
| **European Union** | | | |
| Inward | 217 | 733 | 2649 |
| Outward | 215 | 799 | 3440 |
| **United States** | | | |
| Inward | 83 | 395 | 1321 |
| Outward | 215 | 431 | 1382 |
| **Japan** | | | |
| Inward | 3 | 10 | 50 |
| Outward | 20 | 201 | 300 |
| **Latin America and the Caribbean** | | | |
| Inward | 50 | 117 | 693 |
| Outward | 9 | 19 | 128 |
| **East, South and South-East Asia** | | | |
| Inward | 161 | 284 | 1243 |
| Outward | 5 | 41 | 590 |
| *of which* | | | |
| **China** | | | |
| Inward | 6 | 25 | 395 |
| Outward | n/a | 2 | 28 |
| **India** | | | |
| Inward | 1 | 2 | 22 |
| Outward | 0.2 | 0.3 | 2 |

*Source*: UNCTAD, *World Investment Report 2002*, available at http://r0.unctad.org/wir/contents/wir02_dl.htm

### Table 18.3 Stocks of FDI (% of GDP)

| | Outward | | Inward | |
|---|---|---|---|---|
| | *1980* | *2000* | *1980* | *2000* |
| **US** | 7.8 | 13.2 | 3.0 | 12.4 |
| **UK** | 15.0 | 63.2 | 11.8 | 30.5 |
| **Japan** | 1.8 | 5.8 | 0.3 | 1.1 |
| **Germany** | 4.6 | 25.2 | 3.9 | 24.1 |
| **Netherlands** | 23.7 | 83.3 | 10.8 | 65.9 |
| **Developing countries** | 1.3 | 11.9 | 10.2 | 30.9 |

*Source*: UNCTAD, *World Investment Report 2002*, available at http://r0.unctad.org/wir/contents/wir02_dl.htm

10 per cent return on this investment could translate into a significant fraction of annual income in these countries.

Developed countries with a large outward capital stock also tend to have a large inward capital stock. Thus, the US has an outward stock of $1382 billion and an inward stock of $1321 billion, while in the EU inward capital is over three-quarters of outward capital. Japan is a clear exception to this rule (as is Germany to some extent also). Japan's outward stock is high, having grown very rapidly in the 1980s, but its inward stock is abnormally low. The rapid growth of Japan's outward investment seems to follow logically from its strong export performance and its sustained series of balance of payments surpluses since the early 1980s. Less easily explained, in economic terms at least, is the minimal growth of Japan's inward investment. Historically, the Japanese have preferred to license foreign technology in the belief that this was a better way of developing indigenous expertise. This approach was implemented by imposing government restrictions and institutional barriers on inward investment in Japan (see Box 18.1).

Developing countries are net recipients of foreign direct investment. As Table 18.2 shows, China has become a major actor in the field with a foreign capital stock of US$395 billion. Annual foreign direct investment flows into China exceeded $50 billion in the early 2000s. China has now become the third largest recipient of foreign direct investment in the world, behind only the US and UK.

Industrial countries tend to be significant net outward investors. In this respect, experience conforms with theory-based expectations. Their outward flows exceed inflows and amount to 93.5 per cent of total global outflows (Table 18.4). The flow figures, however, show only part of the picture. They exclude capital mobilised by borrowings and equity partners in the host country. The total flow of capital associated with global investment could be three times the flows recorded in Table 18.4.

Underlying these statistics, and perhaps representing the greatest change, is the transformation in policy towards FDI in host countries. Controls over the foreign ownership of domestic assets have been progressively liberalised and in many cases abolished altogether. Foreign investment is now welcomed by countries that until recently had viewed it with suspicion and worried about the loss of autonomy implied by the increased reliance on foreign decision-takers. European governments are no longer concerned about the influence of American multinationals,

## Box 18.1  Why is inward foreign direct investment to Japan so low?

Japan receives a remarkably low volume of inward investment relative to its economic size and influence. At the end of 2001, the stock of capital accumulated by Japanese residents abroad (outward stock) exceeded the capital of foreigners in Japan (inward stock) by a factor of 6. Most other industrial countries have ratios of between 1 and 2 (Table 18.2). Investment flow data reveal a similar picture. Japan absorbed only 0.8 per cent of world FDI inflows in 2001, while accounting for 6.1 per cent of outflows. Is this low share a function of market forces, or does it represent the effects of formal and informal barriers to inward investment?

Historically, the Japanese government has placed a high priority on promoting indigenous technical and managerial strengths. It pursued this objective by encouraging Japanese firms to license foreign technology. As recently as 1987–91, the value of Japan's technological imports (defined as payments of royalties and licence fees to foreign owners of patents, copyrights and other non-financial intangible assets) was nearly 10 times greater than inflows of FDI. The value of these technological imports was two or three times that of other major developed countries, such as France, Germany, the UK and the US.

Direct manufacturing investment by foreigners in Japan was discouraged. Until 1990, the Foreign Exchange and Foreign Trade Council Law enabled the government to restrict inward FDI, on the grounds that the investment might adversely affect similar domestic business activities or the smooth performance of the Japanese economy. Foreign firms faced special difficulties in merger and acquisition activities because of Japan's institutional framework. An inward investor had to contend with the large share of corporate stock owned by financial companies and *Keiretsu* firms (large conglomerates), the lifetime employment and seniority system, and the complex, multi-layered distribution networks. Preferential group trade practices decrease the transparency of business transactions and discriminate against the prospective foreign investor. Furthermore, hostile takeovers were institutionally difficult since, up to 1990, prior notification was required. Thus, targeted companies had time to prepare their defences.

Japan is not the only country to have adopted a guarded position regarding foreign investment. Switzerland and Norway also closed off, explicitly or implicitly, easy access to their domestic markets by outside investors, particularly in cases where foreigners seek to purchase equity in domestic firms, natural resources or residential property. All three countries also happen to have built up strong industrial sectors.

Japan's favourable approach to outward investment contrasts with its restrictive policy towards inward investment. A European Commission report argued that: 'the benefits for the economy of its FDI and other activities have helped Japan become one of the world's most powerful economies.'[1] Whilst Japan's inward investment policies have been liberalised in recent years, the implementation process has been slow and the economy's slow growth has deterred investors.

Japan's policy towards foreign investment raises the question of who benefits from FDI. Pressure for change is coming from outside Japan, from potential investors in the US and Europe, which suggests that gains accrue to them from establishing a presence in the Japanese market. This pressure has undoubtedly had an impact. The inward stock of foreign-owned capital has increased five-fold since 1990 in dollar terms. But if the theory of this chapter is correct, and gains from FDI are mutual, Japan should lose from a restrictive policy in investment, as it has from its trade restrictions.

[1] European Commission, 'Trade and investment', *Discussion Paper* (Brussels, December 1994), p. 16.

*Sources:* United Nations, *World Investment Report* (New York, 2002); R.Z. Lawrence, 'Why is foreign investment in Japan so low?', *Transnational Corporations* (December 1992); OECD, *The Performance of Foreign Affiliates in OECD Countries* (Paris, 1994).

**Table 18.4  Regional distribution of FDI inflows and outflows (% of world total)**

| | Inflows | | Outflows | |
|---|---|---|---|---|
| | *1995* | *2001\** | *1995* | *2001* |
| **Developed countries** | **63.4** | **68.4** | **85.3** | **93.5** |
| of which: | | | | |
| US | 17.9 | 16.9 | 25.7 | 18.4 |
| Japan | – | 0.8 | 6.3 | 6.1 |
| EU | 35.1 | 43.9 | 44.7 | 58.8 |
| Other | 10.4 | 6.8 | 8.6 | 10.2 |
| **Developing countries** | **32.3** | **27.9** | **14.5** | **5.9** |
| of which: | | | | |
| Asia | 20.7 | 13.9 | 12.3 | 5.1 |
| Latin America | 10.0 | 11.6 | 2.1 | 1.2 |
| Other | 1.5 | 2.4 | 0.1 | –0.4 |
| **Rest of world** | **4.3** | **3.7** | **0.2** | **0.6** |
| **Total** | **100** | **100** | **100** | **100** |

\* Total FDI inflows for 2001 amounted to US$735 billion.

*Source*: UNCTAD, *World Investment Report* (2002).

but now actively seek ways of encouraging investment regardless of nationality. The UK government offers generous incentives to Japanese and Korean investors, and is pleased to have captured the leading share of inward investment from the Far East into the EU.

Increased flows of direct investment have been especially prominent in the services sector. Outward FDI has been growing at 15 per cent for tertiary industries, compared with 10 per cent for secondary industries and 6 per cent for primary industries. The services sector represents 64 per cent of the FDI inward stock and nearly one-half of global inward capital stocks.[6] Examples include banking and insurance, airlines and tourism, distribution and telecommunications. New markets for services have opened up in cellular phones, satellite-based television, data communication and long-distance networks, which provide attractive opportunities for multinationals to exploit their competitive technological advantages and spread development costs. India, in particular Bangalore, has, for example, a thriving software industry to which virtually all the major US software producers have contributed by direct investment. Growth in services FDI is expected to continue, because of the fast underlying growth of such high income-elastic activities, trade liberalisation, and the tremendous scope for exploiting cheap production capabilities abroad for many high-value service functions.

[6] European Commission, Eurostat, *European Union Direct Investment Yearbook 2000*; European Commission, 'Trade and investment', *Discussion Paper* (Brussels, December 1994), p. 6.

### Box 18.2 Why do firms invest abroad?

Dunning states that three conditions are critical to the foreign investment decision.

- *Ownership advantage*: the firm must possess some special proprietary knowledge, trademark, or skilled management and human capital.
- *Location costs*: there must be an ongoing cost advantage to the firm in locating abroad, sufficient to compensate the firm for the heavy start-up costs of a foreign subsidiary.
- *Internalisation*: 'market failure' must be such as to make it profitable to operate abroad through wholly owned subsidiaries rather than by selling production rights to independent firms.

Recent approaches use the same variables as Dunning's models but integrate them into a more rigorous theoretical framework. FDI is classified into two main categories.

The first category is *horizontal FDI*. Here the motivation is to serve the local market more efficiently by establishing a new plant in the host country. The subsidiary saves expense through cutting transport costs, avoiding import restrictions ('tariff jumping'), and in some cases having lower labour costs (though this would not be a relevant consideration for FDI in rich countries). Establishing a market presence might also have a strategic motivation, especially if the host country's market is large and rapidly growing. Thus, the subsidiary might help the parent to keep in closer contact with market developments and with the behaviour of key market competitors. It might also make it easier to extract monopoly profits from its intangible assets in the host market. EU and US multinationals invest a huge amount in each other for these reasons. Note that the savings must offset the economies of scale derivable from adding to production in the home country. Much FDI between developed countries could be categorised as horizontal. Likewise a large share of investment in China is driven by the desire to gain an early foothold in what is seen as one the world's most dynamic markets.

It has been said that *increasingly competitive advantage in a global economy lies in local things that distant rivals cannot touch*. In former times, these 'local things' were cheap labour, large domestic market, and availability of raw materials. Nowadays we must add factors such as knowledge, business networks, environment and government motivation.

*Vertical FDI* is the second type of FDI. A significant amount of multinational activity nowadays takes the form of firms shifting production of one or more stages in the value chain to low-cost locations with the intention of serving the global market from there. A precondition for attracting vertical FDI is a competitive cost structure in the host country and reliable access to home and third-country markets. Different parts of the production process have different input requirements, and since input prices vary across countries it becomes profitable to split production, undertaking unskilled activities in the low-cost host countries and perhaps leaving much of the highest-skilled activities at home. Through outward processing, export platforms and strategic location of affiliate production, multinationals enhance profits and incidentally exert a strong influence on global production and trade patterns. Small countries like Ireland and Singapore attract a disproportionate amount of vertical FDI. As the country becomes more prosperous, and labour becomes more expensive, economic logic drives the multinational to move to cheaper locations (e.g. most clothing and textile subsidiaries in Ireland have moved production to developing countries). Host countries of vertical FDI need to encourage the multinational subsidiary to move steadily up the value chain.

*Source*: John Dunning, *Explaining International Production* (London: Unwin Hyman, 1988); J. Markusen and A. Venables, 'Foreign direct investments as a catalyst for industrial development', *European Economic Review*, 43 (1999); UNCTAD, *World Investment Report 2001*, Geneva; G. Navaretti, J. Haaland and A. Venables, 'Multinational corporations and global production networks: the implications for trade policy', Report prepared for the European Commission (London: CEPR, 2003).

## Why invest abroad?

Most large firms have some international involvement, and the extent of such involvement is continuously increasing. It has been estimated that 30–40 per cent of the sales of the leading industrial companies are produced outside their national boundaries. Their combined sales exceed the value of global trade.[7] The globalisation of production and markets by MNEs has been helped by three major influences: growth in world trade, capital market integration and technological advance, including innovation in managerial structures and techniques.

A business can 'go international' in many ways:

● export from the home country,
● license a foreign business to produce the good or service, or
● engage in production abroad.

Only when it chooses the last step does it enter the statistics for FDI. At this point a further decision has to be taken regarding the mode of control over its foreign production. For instance, the MNE could decide to start by building a new factory from scratch, i.e. a 'greenfield' operation. Alternatively, it could organise a takeover of an indigenous company, or it could arrange a joint venture or a merger with a local company.

An enterprise chooses the direct investment path because it expects a higher return from exploiting its advantages itself than from selling its know-how to an indigenous company. The latter has the advantage of greater familiarity with local customs, culture and business environment but there are offsetting problems with a firm selling its know-how. To make it profitable for a firm to engage in production abroad, Dunning has set out three sets of conditions which must be satisfied (see also Box 18.2).

(1) *Ownership advantages*. The firm must possess some special monopoly advantage – such as proprietary knowledge, a trade mark or brand name, a patent, access to cheaper inputs, access to customers, or economies of scale and scope – which cannot be replicated by other firms. If this condition is not satisfied, an indigenous company could start up independently and produce an equivalent good locally. FDI would not exist. Ownership advantages comprise all the competitive advantages of a firm.

(2) *Location advantages*. To explain why an investor sets up abroad or in one host country rather than another, the chosen host country has to offer some special location advantages (as compared with the cost of exporting from the home country, for instance). The list of significant locational variables includes labour costs (defined in the broadest sense to include the industrial relations climate as well as direct labour costs), the availability of skilled labour, transport and communication costs, R&D capability, the size of the domestic market, access to the domestic and other markets, government incentives and taxation policy, in short, the 'investment climate'. Assigning precise weights to these variables is a crucial concern to any industrial promotion authority. Studies of the determinants of FDI tend to find that the most influential factors in the host country are corporate tax rates, trade union activity and R&D capability. Regional labour

---

[7] J.H. Dunning, *The Globalization of Business* (London: Routledge, 1993), p. 107.

costs, unemployment and transport infrastructure are also important in determining which particular country in a geographical region is chosen as a location for the investment.

(3) *Internalisation advantages*. Lastly, there must be some source of 'market failure', which impedes the sale of these ownership advantages to a local bidder. These internalisation advantages often arise in knowledge-intensive industries. Take, for example, the case of a drug company which discovers a new formula for treating a disease. To understand and evaluate the product – in short, *to be able to make a well-informed bid* – the buyer must know how useful the drug is and how much it would cost to produce. However, by divulging such information to every prospective buyer, the firm is undermining its own commercial advantage, and soon it would find that its specialised knowledge is no longer exclusive enough to qualify as an ownership advantage. The only solution to this market 'failure' is for the firm to set up a subsidiary to manufacture the drug abroad under the direct control of the parent company.[8]

Often a firm can avail itself of economies of scale or scope or reputation *only by producing the good itself*. Automobile companies for this reason usually insist on joint ventures or full ownership of foreign production facilities rather than licensing others to produce on their behalf. By selling production rights, the firm would inevitably lose some degree of control and endanger its reputation. People buy a Mercedes because it is made by Mercedes. Their attitude might change if they were told that it was made by a local manufacturer *for* Mercedes. Another reason for internalisation might be the weakness of the legal system in host countries. If know-how is franchised or licensed, a fraudulent foreign partner could be difficult to prosecute and, hence, the MNE might feel safer retaining complete control over the foreign operation itself.

In many cases, the choice between licensing and direct provision can be finely balanced. If the particular advantage can be 'de-bundled', licensing and franchising are likely to become more attractive. The possibility of de-bundling a brand name from its production may explain why franchising is common in the international retail trade. The parent firm may have an ownership advantage (such as ownership of a brand name – McDonald's, for instance, or Coca-Cola) but, since this can be sold on to local businesses at a realistic price, there is no internalisation advantage relative to the local franchisee.[9]

The logic behind internalisation advantages draws on the transaction cost approach (discussed in Chapter 5). Whenever transactions such as establishing a relevant price through licences can be organised and carried out more cheaply within the firm than through the market, they will be internalised and undertaken by the firm itself.

---

[8] There is a strong link between technology and outward investment: countries and sectors with the greater propensity to generate know-how prove to be the most significant sources of outward FDI (J.A. Cantwell, *Technological Innovation and the Multinational Corporation*, Oxford: Basil Blackwell, 1989).

[9] However, there is no clear-cut boundary between FDI and franchising/licensing; rather, a continuum of degrees of control and ownership. Furthermore, control can be confined to a number of different organisational areas and does not necessarily relate positively to the size of the stake held by the parent. Modern practice is for MNEs to leave their subsidiaries considerable operational leeway, even if they are majority-owned by the parent. A subsidiary of AAB in Indonesia, owned 100 per cent by AAB International, might be more independent than the local McDonald's, even though the latter is tied to its parent only through a franchise agreement.

Dunning's carefully composed scheme indicates that all three elements are necessary for a direct foreign investment decision to be profitable. The company must *own* something valuable that cannot be costlessly replicated. Market failure must dictate that this advantage should be *internalised* rather than be sold for others to exploit. And the host country must present a *locational* advantage to the company to induce it to set up business abroad in preference to supplying from a home base.

## 18.4 Effects of foreign investment

Direct investment embodies a package of potential growth-enhancing attributes, including technology, managerial and technological know-how, and access to international markets.

Most countries welcome *inward* investment, even those which formerly regarded it with mistrust. Virtually all recent legislation on foreign investment has been intended to liberalise the regime applied to FDI.[10] A majority of governments also believe that *outward* investment benefits their economies. But there is some residual ambivalence about this. Host countries continue to worry about the long-term consequences of foreign investment on the domestically owned sector of the economy, and are concerned with the fiscal costs of attracting the multinationals. Within home countries too, there is concern that the internationalisation of production will mean the 'export' of jobs.

At the level of the firm, there is less ambiguity. The majority of firms regard freedom to establish abroad as an important facility which allows them to exploit their competitive advantages. Apart from the internalisation factors outlined above, there is the practical matter that, as firms get bigger, they start to outgrow the domestic market. As their domestic market share approaches saturation point, further expansion could cause trouble with competitors, or suppliers, or might be blocked by monopoly legislation. Going international is a means of diversifying the firm's operations, and of keeping in touch with new markets and new ideas in a direct way.

A business strategy of globalisation works to the firm's advantage but does it also contribute to the national economy? The answer is generally yes. The static gains from foreign investment are the same as those from capital mobility outlined in Figure 18.1. Through foreign investment, capital and its associated resources are deployed where their productivity is highest. This brings mutual benefits to both home country and host country parties. But, in addition to these static gains, there are important dynamic gains which are specific to direct investment flows and which therefore require separate analysis. A European Commission report describes FDI as *a dynamic process which raises total wealth to the advantage of all those involved*.[11] This dynamic process has motivated countries

---

[10] According to the 2002 *World Investment Report*, 208 changes in FDI laws were made in 2001 by 71 countries, over 90 per cent of which were aimed at making the investment climate more favourable to inward FDI.

[11] European Commission, *op. cit.*, p. 14.

as diverse as Singapore, Poland, Mexico and Ireland, and regions as diverse as Scotland and North Carolina, to rely heavily on inward investment for economic development.

Foreign investment is sought for many reasons, some more substantive in economic terms than others.

(1) *Multinationals generate externalities.* FDI involves the import of productive factors such as marketing know-how, training facilities and technological expertise. Multinationals, for example, account for some 80 per cent of private R&D spending in the world.[12] The host country benefits from the spillover effects of these activities. The head office of the multinational, of course, charges its subsidiaries for inputs of productive factors supplied by the parent, so the mere fact that know-how is passed on does not constitute proof of net gain to the host country. A gain to the host country occurs only when the price charged (the private cost) is less than the social benefit (the full economic benefit from the operation). Spillovers and externalities arising from the multinational's activities reflect the potential dynamic gains from foreign investment. Typical spillovers include labour training, upgrading the production skills and motivation of local component suppliers, stimulus to competition, and development of managerial skills and of knowledge about foreign markets and other types of demonstration effects.[13]

(2) *Multinationals create more jobs.* Or, in the case of a takeover of an ailing domestic firm, they 'save' jobs which would otherwise be lost. This argument seems reasonable, but in economic terms it is badly articulated. Just because an activity 'creates' jobs is not an automatic indication of its merits. If the activity did not exist, jobs might be created elsewhere in the economy. Furthermore, the new activity might be responsible for the displacement of existing jobs in other sectors of the economy. The relevant comparison is between what is produced with foreign investment versus what would have been produced in its absence. If, in the absence of foreign investment, labour would have remained unemployed, questions must be asked about the labour market. If the host country's unemployment originates in labour market inflexibility, it would be better to tackle this problem at source (through the type of labour market policies described in Chapter 13) rather than by attacking the symptoms.

(3) *Foreign investment generates tax revenues.* Foreign subsidiaries pay corporation (profits) tax to the host government and their workers pay income tax and indirect tax on their spending. The sum of all these taxes can amount to a sizeable contribution to the exchequer, which can, so the argument goes, be offset against any grants or incentives paid to the foreign firm. Exercises of this type win high marks in popular debate but they suffer the defect of neglecting the alternatives forgone. Thus, alternative domestic activities to those of the foreign firm would also have generated tax revenues. It is the net addition to tax revenues by

---

[12] Dunning, *op. cit.*, p. 287.

[13] See, for example, T. Ozawa, 'Foreign direct investment and economic development', *Transnational Corporations* (February 1992); J. Cantwell, 'Foreign multinationals and industrial development in Africa', in P. Buckley and J. Clegg (eds), *Multinational Enterprises in Less Developed Countries* (London: Macmillan, 1991); and S. Young, N. Hood and E. Peters, 'Multinational enterprises and regional economic development', *Regional Studies*, 28(7) (1994).

comparison with this hypothetical alternative, not the gross tax revenues, against which the cost of fiscal investment incentives should be offset. Another qualification to keep in mind is that tax revenues can be artificially boosted by 'transfer-pricing' activity (see Box 18.3). In this instance, one exchequer's gain is another's loss and, from a global point of view, the position could be suboptimal.

### Box 18.3 Transfer pricing

*Transfer pricing* is an accounting practice used by multinational enterprises to limit their overall tax burden. It arises because of the existence of different national tax regimes. Profits earned in a high-tax country are 'transferred' for tax purposes to a low-tax country. To reduce its overall corporation profits tax burden, a multinational can arrange for its subsidiary in a low-tax country to be undercharged (or overpaid) for goods and services purchased from (sold to) another subsidiary located in a higher tax jurisdiction. In this manner, profits in the subsidiary in the low-tax country are artificially inflated, while profits reported for the operation in the high-tax country are reduced.

For example, suppose that a US multinational company has a plant in Ireland, which produces an intermediate product for export to another subsidiary of the same multinational located in a high-tax country, say Germany. The Irish subsidiary pays corporation profits tax at 10 per cent; the German subsidiary pays 30 per cent. If the two tax rates were identical, the Irish plant would sell the components to the German plant for €10 million at an arm's length price of €20 per unit. However, with different tax rates, the multinational has an incentive to inflate this price. Suppose it charged €40 per unit instead of €20; the Irish subsidiary would be paid €20 million instead of €10 million. The amount of profit reported in Ireland would increase by €10 million; profits attributed to Germany would fall by the same amount.

Assume that, in the initial situation, the subsidiary in each country earned €5 million profits. Total tax paid would amount to €2 million (€1.5 million in Germany and €0.5 million in Ireland). Now, after the higher transfer price, €10 million profits are transferred to low-tax Ireland. Tax is paid in Ireland at 10 per cent and the tax bill on its €15m profits amounts to €1.5 million. Results: (a) the company's overall tax bill is reduced to €1.5 million, not counting the write-off in respect of losses of its German subsidiary; (b) the Irish government gains an extra €1 million in tax revenue; and (c) the German authorities are less happy – they lose €1.5 million of tax revenue.

#### Effect of transfer pricing on profits and taxes

|  | Without transfer pricing | With transfer pricing |
|---|---|---|
| Per unit price | €20 | €40 |
| Sales revenue | €10m | €20m |
| Profits – German operation | €5m | −€5m |
| Profits – Irish operation | €5m | €15m |
| Total tax payable | €2m (€1.5m + €0.5m) | €1.5m (€0m + €1.5m) |

Transfer pricing is a touchy subject. There is a limit to the amount of tax-motivated transfer pricing that can be done. Tax authorities are alert to the possibility of profit-switching from one jurisdiction to another, and will if necessary 'see through' such transactions if they are made too blatant. However, this leaves plenty of scope for

→

**Box 18.3 continued**

discretion and for honest disagreement as to the 'true' costs of goods and services supplied from one part of a multinational to another.

Proposals for a system of unitary taxation have been recommended, whereby a multinational would pay a single tax on all its sales, such revenue to be assessed by some proportional formula. Hence, if 60 per cent of a firm's sales revenue was earned in the US, the authorities would assume that 60 per cent of its global profits originated there also, and levy tax accordingly. The idea does not seem to have taken off. Yet the problem will not go away, and there is continuing pressure within the EU, for example, to proceed to greater coordination of corporate tax regimes as the only really effective mechanism for dealing with the problem.

(4) *Foreign investment generates foreign exchange*. The initial investment may take the form of loans from the parent company or from a foreign bank. Once the subsidiary is in operation it may generate exports or displace imports. Against this, one would have to deduct outgoings of dividends and loan repayments. If the net result is a positive contribution to the balance of payments, this seems like a reason for supporting the project. However, this argument too is deficient. First, it ignores the foreign exchange earnings and outgoings if the resources had been used in an alternative way. Second, even if the foreign investor makes a positive net contribution to foreign exchange earnings relative to, say, alternative investments, this is not the only economic criterion on which to judge the desirability of foreign investment. As in the 'create jobs' argument, there may be more efficient ways of achieving foreign exchange balance. If shortage of foreign exchange is a problem, adjusting the exchange rate may be a better policy than offering incentives to foreign investors.

*To assess the net gains from foreign investment, therefore, a fully fledged cost–benefit analysis is needed.* The benefits from FDI should be compared with costs such as capital and training grants, tax incentives, rent allowances, interest rate subsidies and other forms of implicit or explicit assistance. Theory helps us to ask the right questions in carrying out such an exercise and to avoid major conceptual errors in the definition of benefits and costs, but in the end there is no substitute for detailed assessment of each project under alternative scenarios. Such assessments can prove controversial – different assumptions about the hypothetical or counterfactual situation lead to different conclusions.

Empirical studies are plagued by the problem of trying to assess the counterfactual, i.e. the difference between the actual impact of MNEs and the situation that would have prevailed in their absence. Recent research emphasises that FDI is an important vehicle for the transfer of technology and that it can generate significant productivity growth in host countries, provided that they have the necessary skills to utilise that technology.[14]

---

[14] E. Borzenstein, J. De Gregorio and J. Lee, 'How does foreign direct investment affect economic growth?', *Journal of International Economics*, 4, 1998.

Increasingly, attention is being focused on the contribution of MNEs to developing the innovatory capabilities of host countries and on ways in which governments can maximise this contribution. To maximise the potential spillovers, the host country needs to develop the following.

1. *An integrated policy approach*: efforts to attract FDI must be complemented by stable macroeconomic policies and by supportive microeconomic policies on linkages, industrial clusters, education and R&D, rather than being pursued in isolation. Higher levels of educational attainment in the host country enhance the positive spillovers of high-tech inward FDI by raising the host countries' absorptive capacity.

2. *Export-oriented FDI* should be given priority over foreign investment directed at the home market. Employees and local managers learn how to access export markets and how to manage in a globalised environment.

3. *Competition policy* needs special attention if multinationals are being given incentives to produce for the domestic market. Multinationals can cause losses to the host country if they are allowed to operate in a monopoly environment. Repatriated monopoly profits, earned through sales on the home market, involve a direct loss to the nationals of the country, and not just a redistribution of income. The most efficient way to handle the difficulty is to bid away monopoly profits by opening the market to foreign competition. Guidelines for multinationals were adopted by governments of the 29 members of the OECD in June 2000 that address these issues.

4. *Targeted incentives*: FDI promotion agencies should target the sectors most concordant with the country's evolving comparative advantage, and calibrate the incentive package to achieve the desired mix of foreign investors. Competition for investment projects means that countries and regions offering below the 'market' level of incentives will lose projects. On the other hand, incentives above the market rate are costly. Cost–benefit analysis can provide valuable guidance. Also governments should think of providing attractions other than financial incentives – a pleasant environment, and a one-stop shop to liaise with host authorities and reduce hassle (see Box 18.4).

5. *After-care policies*: the authorities should keep in touch with the foreign firms, discuss their plans and prepare the groundwork for expansion, extension of linkages with the local economy and structural change. Included here is the need to upgrade the economic and physical infrastructure in order to maintain the attractiveness of the host country for international business. The foreign subsidiaries themselves should also be encouraged to invest and upgrade. The 'branch-plant' or 'screwdriver industry' syndrome can lead to an over-dependent and poor-quality productive base.

6. *Support for indigenous industry*: the search for foreign investment projects must not lead to a neglect of indigenous firms. An innovative and competitive economy needs plenty of small and medium-sized enterprises (SMEs); the externalities of the multinationals are mostly delivered through the agency of these firms.

Foreign investment continues to engender feelings of disquiet and suspicion. Looked at objectively, there are indeed circumstances in which multinationals can impose costs on an economy. These costs are, however, avoidable, and the consensus among economists is that the potential benefits significantly outweigh the potential losses.

### Box 18.4 Incentives and foreign direct investment

Foreign investors are strongly influenced by investment incentives. Although they often express reservations about projects whose potential profitability relies solely on host country incentives, once a company has narrowed its choice of sites, incentives *do* count. Studies on foreign investment incentive criteria have found that, although incentives are a secondary consideration in corporate strategic planning, an attractive incentive package can influence the final decision on where to invest.

Many developing countries and regions offer extremely generous incentive 'packages'. However, incentive competition between governments is costly and can generate inefficient investments, with disappointing results for the 'victor'. If it goes too far, the 'winning' country obtains no net benefit – all of the 'rent' goes to the foreign investor. European countries bidding for foreign investment are similar to the prisoners in the prisoners' dilemma case outlined in Chapter 7. If all refused to offer incentives, foreign investors would invest in Europe anyway, attracted by the need for market access. But in the absence of cooperation, each country will compete against the other.

In the automobile industry, for example, regions of the US have found that the scale of incentives required to induce FDI lies between $120 million and $325 million per plant, well in excess of the financial capacities of many developing countries. The UK government has provided grants amounting to more than £20,000 per job to attract 'greenfield' subsidiaries of multinationals to designated regions.

Reducing incentives requires cooperation among governments. Efforts to date have focused on the regional level. In particular, the OECD has long sought closer harmonisation of investment policies among its members. The EU has placed a ceiling on total incentive packages, while allowing for some regional variation. Under WTO rules, financial subsidies that distort trade have to be curbed.

International harmonisation of incentives is difficult to achieve. The main problem is that of ensuring transparency. Incentives come in all sorts of guises and national and regional authorities are adept at concealing exactly how much has been provided. Also, there is disagreement about how the incentives to the investor, such as tax breaks or training grants, should be measured. The value of an incentives package may depend on a firm's tax situation, for example, and some types of training may be more firm-specific than others. But the diminishing effectiveness of the incentives as their use widens, their tendency to distort trade flows and the danger of an incentives war are factors encouraging the authorities to put a concerted effort into controlling their level.

*Source*: UNCTAD, *Incentives and Foreign Direct Investment* (New York: United Nations, 1996); United Nations, *World Investment Report* (New York: United Nations, various years).

## 18.5 Conclusions

This chapter has discussed the role of mobile capital, focusing on the extent to which this mobility might contribute to higher living standards in host and home countries. We started with a simple analysis and gradually introduced more realistic conditions. We concluded that openness to exchange of productive factors has the potential to provide important net static and dynamic gains to the world economy. But theory also warns that not everyone gains, and we should not be surprised if national and sectoral interests are differently affected.

Capital and labour mobility are to some extent interrelated. The point is often made, in the context of discussion of underdeveloped regions, that one can choose between *bringing capital to people, or bringing people to capital.*

One way to bring capital to people is through foreign investment. Foreign direct investment brings the technical and marketing know-how (human capital) which host countries need if they are to convert the opportunities of the free market into real achievements. Another form of capital inflow is portfolio capital that enables the host country to invest more rapidly and to upgrade its labour force. Convergence is then achieved not by a process of levelling up the poorer countries and levelling down the richer ones to a single average, but primarily by raising the performance of the poorer countries to the high standards of the richer countries. Finally, the ability to invest abroad provides one other gain that is becoming increasingly important: spreading risk through portfolio diversification.[15]

Liberalisation of trade and foreign investment go hand in hand. Some FDI, such as outward processing, is directly trade motivated. Here access to the home country market and also to third markets from the host country is essential. Equally, the host country must be able to assure the foreign company that it will be able to repatriate its profits and even to liquidate its investment if necessary.

## Summary

1. International trade in factors of production generates economic gains in much the same way as international trade in goods and services. Both parties to the transaction can benefit. It is a positive-sum game.

2. Capital has become increasingly mobile internationally. This applies to both portfolio flows and direct investment. Transaction costs of moving capital have been reduced as a result of information technology and the removal of official restrictions. The supply of funds has increased as a result of greater prosperity and the growth of the pensions industry. Demand for international investment has been stimulated by intense competition among fund managers for high returns and diversified portfolios.

3. The gains from capital mobility derive from the allocation of capital to sectors and locations where its productivity is highest. Two indirect effects of capital mobility are that domestic capital has become harder to tax. High taxes lead to capital flight. Also capital mobility places constraints on governments' fiscal policy. There are potential downsides: speculative inflows and outflows of capital can be destabilising, can lead to exchange rate misalignments and can erode a country's tax base.

4. Foreign direct investment is a special form of capital mobility in that it involves a 'package' of factors – know-how and skilled management alongside capital. Firms

[15] P. Lane, 'International trade and economic convergence: the Credit Channel', *Oxford Economic Papers*, 53(2), 2001.

produce abroad in response to ownership advantages, locational incentives and internalisation economies. In addition to standard economic gains, multinationals bring to the host country what the United Nations describes as 'a package of potential growth-enhancing attributes'.

## Questions for discussion

1. 'The international mobility of capital, both in the form of portfolio capital and direct foreign investment, can make a significant positive contribution to economic welfare.' Evaluate this statement. Examine some of the problems associated with enhanced capital mobility.

2. 'The international mobility of factors of production can contribute significantly to the reduction in international differences in income and wealth.' Discuss in the context of portfolio capital mobility.

3. Explain the contribution made by multinational enterprises to (a) a host country, and (b) a home country of your choice. Is it possible for you to conclude that both host and home country benefited from investment by multinationals?

## Exercises

1. Theory gives *a priori* reasons why capital would be expected to flow from rich to poor countries. Does this in fact happen? Why not?

2. A foreign firm is proposing to set up a new 'greenfield' manufacturing plant in your country. List the economic benefits which you would expect to be generated by the plant, then draw up a list of likely costs.

3. What is the difference between 'direct' investment and 'portfolio' investment? Explain why the economic effects of the two types of investment are likely to differ.

4. Outline the main 'locational' advantages of your country for a foreign investor. How can/should these be improved?

5. Box 18.3 analyses transfer pricing in response to differences in corporate profit tax. Show how firms could also use transfer pricing to exploit country differences in tariffs and subsidies.

6. European Firm A proposes to establish a subsidiary in China to serve as a production base for components that will be exported to Firm A's final production plants in the EU. European Firm B plans to establish a production plant in China, the output of which will be sold exclusively on the domestic Chinese market. Explain why and how the expected benefits and costs might be expected to differ between these two activities.

## Further reading

Most international economics textbooks contain a chapter or two on the economics of factor mobility between countries. P. Lindert, *International Economics*, 9th edn (Homewood, IL: Irwin, 1991) is particularly useful. A leading authority on direct investment and multinationals, Professor John Dunning, *Governments, Globalization and International Business* (Oxford: Oxford University Press, 1997) provides a flavour of where the debate is on this topic. Another good source is P.J. Buckley, *Foreign Direct Investment and Multinational Enterprise* (Basingstoke: Macmillan, 1995). John Stopford, 'Multinational corporations', *Foreign Policy* (Winter 1998–99) provides a readable, pointed overview of multinationals from the perspective of strategic management. Today's multinationals, he argues, bear little resemblance to their forebears as they reinvent themselves to adapt to new competitors and new organisational structures, including strategic alliances. An influential and widely read critique of the case for portfolio capital liberalisation in developing countries is provided in J. Bhagwati, 'The capital myth: the difference between trade in widgets and dollars', *Foreign Affairs*, no. 3, 1998. 'Only an untutored economist', he remarks, 'will argue that free trade in widgets is the same as free capital mobility' (p. 8). UNCTAD's annual *World Investment Report* is a goldmine of FDI statistics and analysis.

## Chapter 19

# Labour migration

## Introduction

Because of its humanitarian and cultural dimension, labour migration is a sensitive and controversial topic. Yet, in economic terms, it can be visualised as another example of international exchange of a factor of production leading to mutual gains. Professor John Kenneth Galbraith, no starry-eyed admirer of the free-market system, describes migration as *a process that helps those who go, the place they go to and those they leave behind.*[1]

This chapter considers only voluntary migration induced by economic circumstances. We exclude forced migration from totalitarian regimes or war zones. Economic analysis, drawing on the same framework used to analyse capital movements, provides important insights into the consequences of migration for each of the parties concerned. However, many aspects of the migration process are ignored in the simple model. When they are taken into account, the net balance of advantage and disadvantage becomes more complex to assess, and it becomes easier to appreciate the ambivalence both of host countries to immigration and of sending countries to emigration. Business is often caught in the middle: it has to cope with a welter of immigration laws and regulations on the one hand, and on the other with the necessity of competing with firms that employ illegal immigrants.

Most countries tend to encourage migration *within* their national boundaries – domestic labour mobility is generally regarded as a good thing – but they display less enthusiasm for mobility between nations.[2] Thus, the EU encourages labour mobility between Member States through reciprocal recognition of educational and professional qualifications, anti-discrimination rules and equality of social welfare treatment. But strict limits are applied to applications by non-EU citizens for admission to the EU labour market. Many other host countries, such as Australia, Switzerland and the US, place restrictions on the number of immigrants.[3]

---

[1] J.K. Galbraith, *The Nature of Mass Poverty* (Cambridge, MA: Harvard University Press, 1979).

[2] This is not to deny that regional policy is active in these countries, and that after a point internal migratory flows can also be seen as a problem.

[3] Since the mid-1990s there has been a limit of 150,000 visas in Australia and 700,000 in the US. Add to this a flow of illegal immigrants, believed to be around 300,000 per year in the US.

( **Chapter outline** )

This chapter examines the economics of migration in the following steps:

**1.** Recent trends in migration.

**2.** Standard model showing how migration can yield gains to home country, to host country and to the migrants themselves.

**3.** Extension of model to include wider considerations of an economic, social and political nature.

## 19.1 Recent trends

Three trends are evident in the pattern of migration in recent years.

- The number of people migrating has increased. Over 100 million people reside outside the country of their citizenship today compared with 80 million in the late 1980s.[4] Two-thirds of these are economic migrants, one-third refugees.
- Migration has become more globalised. African emigrants move to Europe, Asians migrate to the Middle East and Australia, and Europeans migrate to North America.
- Emigration patterns have been influenced by the regionalisation of the world economy, as evidenced by migratory flows from East to West Europe, from Thailand and the Philippines to Japan, and from South and Central America to North America.
- Migration is not just a developed country phenomenon; developing countries (South Africa, Pakistan, Argentina) attract 60 per cent of all migrants.
- Although the number of immigrants has increased in absolute terms, their *share* of total population is still relatively modest. The share of immigrants in the UK workforce averaged 3.9 per cent during 1995–98 (Table 19.2). The share of immigrants is below 5 per cent in most countries and exceeds 10 per cent in only four. However, these figures, being derived from official sources, omit unrecorded or illegal migration. In some countries this may imply a significant underestimation of the scale of migration. The number of illegal immigrants smuggled into Europe has been estimated at 400,000 per year, and into the US at 300,000 per year.

During the past two decades the share of foreigners in total population rose rapidly in several European countries (see Table 19.1). Foreign residents have increased by almost 3 million in Germany since 1980, by 1 million in Italy and by over 700,000 in the UK. Absolute numbers of foreign residents are greatest in Germany, France and the UK. Austria has experienced the greatest increase in foreign residents in percentage terms, up from 4 per cent to 9 per cent of the population, most of this increase occurring during the 1990s. Not surprisingly, given the scale and speed of change, the issue of immigration has aroused much controversy in that country. The most cosmopolitan country in Europe is Luxembourg (not shown in Table 19.1); over one-third of its population and

---

[4] S. Stanton Russell and M.S. Teitelbaum, 'International migration and international trade', *World Bank Discussion Paper*, No. 160 (1994); D. Papademetriou, 'Migration', *Foreign Policy* (Winter 1997–98).

**Table 19.1 Foreign population resident in main host European countries**

| | Thousands (% of total population) | |
|---|---|---|
| | *1980* | *2000* |
| Switzerland | 893 | 1397 |
| | (14.1) | (19.1) |
| Belgium | 879 | 862 |
| | (8.9) | (8.4) |
| Germany | 4453 | 7297 |
| | (7.2) | (8.8) |
| France | 3582 | 3263 |
| | (6.3) | (5.5) |
| Austria | 282 | 758 |
| | (3.7) | (9.3) |
| Netherlands | 521 | 668 |
| | (3.7) | (4.2) |
| UK | 1601 | 2342 |
| | (2.8) | (3.9) |
| Italy | 299 | 1388 |
| | (0.5) | (2.4) |

*Source*: J.-P. Garson, 'International migration: facts, figures, policies', *OECD Observer* (June/July 1992); OECD, *Trends in International Migration* (Paris, 2002).

over a half of its workforce is foreign-born. Most (89 per cent) of Luxembourg's migrants are well-paid EU civil servants and bankers from adjacent countries who are easily assimilated and cause minimal friction. Countries such as Australia, Canada and the US have traditionally given succour and opportunity to immigrants (see Table 19.2).

In the early postwar years immigrants into Europe were welcomed as a source of much-needed labour, willing to undertake work that nationals shunned. Latterly, too, the contribution of skilled foreigners to the development of key economic sectors has become recognised. More than one-third of those employed in Silicon Valley are foreign born, many providing essential services in lower-paid sectors but many others at the cutting edge of the new industries. Nevertheless, there are also strong undercurrents of unease and resistance to large-scale inflows of immigrants. In Europe the high unemployment rate has no doubt contributed to this change in attitude, while in the US concern about ethnic and linguistic mix and assimilative capacity have been central to the debate.

Migration patterns must be evaluated in the context of world population trends. Between 2000 and 2025, the world's population is expected to increase from 6 billion to 8 billion. During this period, and notwithstanding the immigration levels observed to date, the number of people in Europe is projected to decline marginally from 582 to 580 million. This forms a stark contrast with the increase in population of North Africa from 170 to 249 million and in Asia from 3.6 to 4.9 billion. The populations of the US, Canada and Australia are expected to increase by over 20 per cent over the next 25 years – an increase that is largely related to their higher rates of immigration.

**Table 19.2 Foreign-born labour force in selected countries, 1995 and 2000 (thousands and %)**

| | Thousands | | % of total labour force | |
|---|---|---|---|---|
| | 1995 | 2000 | 1995 | 2000 |
| Australia | 2,139 | 2,365 | 23.9 | 24.5 |
| Canada | 2,839 | n.a. | 19.2 | n.a. |
| US | 14,083 | 17,384 | 10.8 | 12.4 |
| Germany | 3,505 | 3,429 | 9.1 | 8.8 |
| Sweden | 186 | 205 | 4.2 | 4.8 |
| UK | 1,011 | 1,220 | 3.4 | 4.4 |
| Italy | 100 | 246 | 0.5 | 1.1 |

*Source*: OECD, *Trends in International Migration* (Paris, 2002).

## 19.2 Effects of migration – the basic model

We begin with the model used earlier to analyse capital flows. World labour supply, assumed to be fixed, is depicted on the horizontal axis and wage per hour on the vertical axis (Figure 19.1). The world is divided into two regions, the North and the South. Each region has a fixed stock of capital (shorthand for all productive factors other than labour). Within each region there are two sets of individuals: workers and employers. Employers own the nation's stock of capital and land. Initially, there is no mobility between North and South. The North has a labour stock of $O_N L$. Because of the North's superior infrastructure, level of human capital investment and technology, labour productivity is relatively high in the North and wage is $O_N W_N$. By contrast, labour productivity is relatively low in the South. Labour supply of $O_S L$ earns a wage equal to $O_S W_S$.

The existence of this wage differential provides a powerful incentive to migrate from the South to the North. As migration proceeds, the wage gap

**Figure 19.1 Labour migration in the basic model**

narrows. Eventually, a new equilibrium is reached at L*. At that point, wages are equalised and nobody has any incentive to migrate. Complete convergence has been achieved. The wage level falls in the North, and it rises in the South. The equilibrium wage lies between the initial North and South level.

The effects of migration can be worked out as follows:

- Southern workers who remain at home obtain a rise in pay to $O_S W^*$ and gain $W^* E R W_S$ in increased wages.
- Workers in the North experience a pay decline of $W_N W^*$ and lose $W^* C A W_N$ as a result.
- Migrating Southern workers, who were initially earning $O_S W_S$, now earn $O W^*$, a gain of ECBR.
- Employers in the South do badly. They have to pay an extra $W^* E R W_S$ to their employees and they also lose profits of EBR because of the reduction in output.
- Employers in the North make additional profits of $W^* C A W_N$ as a result of the fall in the wage level. In addition, they earn a profit of ACE on the output produced by the immigrants.
- Global welfare increases by the triangle ABE, of which CEA accrues to the North, and CEB to the South (including therein the higher income received by the South's emigrants).

The profile of the effects of migration parallels that of the effect of capital mobility. There are gainers and losers in each country, but by appropriate income redistribution the gainers could compensate the losers. Because of this, freedom to migrate, according to this model, is welfare-enhancing. The world as a whole gains because people go to the country where their marginal productivity is highest.

Although the model is based on many simplifying assumptions, it yields some remarkably realistic predictions. First, it predicts that workers and employers in the North are likely to adopt different positions regarding immigration. Trade union representatives are likely to advocate restrictions, while employers would be expected to adopt a more permissive approach. Immigration for them means lower labour costs. Second, the model predicts some ambivalence in the home region. Workers remaining in the South benefit in so far as their real wage increases, but owners of other productive factors tend to lose as higher labour costs eat into profits. The South's GNP will fall. The emigrants themselves are of course better-off, but they will no longer be around to vote in the home country elections.[5]

## Making the model more realistic

### Wages are not everything

There are psychic and economic costs associated with migration. Also potential migrants will have to weight the northern wage $O W_N$ by the probability of their getting a job at that wage. When the North's unemployment rate is high, this probability will be less than unity. Potential emigrants will also care about the quality of life, which is often thought to be superior in one's native country, due to proximity to friends and relatives and a familiar lifestyle. Hence, migration will

---

[5] For all that, there are few instances of countries trying to restrict emigration, whereas controls on immigration are the norm. This may be due to governments assigning higher weights to the incomes of (native) workers relative to other income groups.

continue to a point where the *expected value* of the pay in the North (i.e. the wage rate multiplied by the probability of getting a job at that wage) equals the expected value of pay in the South, after taking account of the psychic advantages of being employed at home:

$$W_n(1 - \phi U_n) = W_s(1 - \phi U_s)f$$

where:  W = wages

U  = the unemployment rate

$\phi$  = a parameter by which the unemployment rate is weighted

f  = the non-pecuniary advantage of staying in the South for the marginal migrant.

Subscripts n and s refer to North and South.

This equation shows how the unadjusted North–South wage gap can give a misleading impression of the intensity of the incentive to migrate. For example, suppose the non-pecuniary advantage of staying at home (f) was valued at 1.5, i.e. 50 per cent of $W_s$, and that the rate of unemployment was the same in the two areas. The incentive to migrate would disappear when wages in the South had risen to two-thirds of the level in the North.

### Time dimension

Migrants respond not just to *current* pay differences but to the expected profile of earnings over time. The migration decision can be conceptualised as depending on the balance between, on one side, a stream of benefits over time (higher real income, job security, better promotion prospects) and, on the other, a stream of costs (absence from home, psychic disutility of migrant status) and a significant upfront cost (removal expense, travel expenses, uncertainty). This 'human capital' approach emphasises that migration is an investment decision, involving a fixed irrecoverable cost (of movement) and an uncertain future stream of returns.[6] Four important implications follow from this approach.

- Since young people have a longer period in which to write off initial costs than older people (the duration of the investment is longer), young people are more likely to migrate than older people.
- More clever and dynamic persons have a greater prospect of future promotion and advancement in the host country, and hence have a greater incentive to migrate than those less talented.
- Two-way flows can be expected, younger workers emigrating, older workers returning and also among highly skilled and highly specialised individuals.
- As incomes equalise, less migration will take place. This explains the fall-off in migration for the Iberian countries to northern Europe. By the same token, greater income divergence encourages migration. This crude economic imperative underlies the continuing flows from North Africa and eastern Turkey to the EU.

---

[6] In formal terms, the present value of staying at home (PV) can be represented as:

$$PV = \sum_{t=0}^{n} \frac{w_t - f_t}{(1 + r)^t}$$

where:  $w_t$ = the real income difference at time $t$, adjusted for unemployment

$f_t$  = the financial/psychic cost of migration at time $t$

$t$  = the time in years

$n$  = the duration of the investment horizon in years

$r$  = the rate of discount.

## 19.3 Migration, public finances and jobs

Migration has many spillover effects on the economy. Sometimes migrants prove to be more educated, innovative and enterprising than the norm. If so, they may bring positive externalities to the host country, and their departure involves negative externalities for the sending countries. India and Morocco, for example, complain that their electronics graduates are being lost to Europe and North America. Sending countries such as Mexico argue that they lose twice in so far as they have to provide education to their migrants, and then this is followed by post-retirement social services for many who return to Mexico late in life.

Market-size effects can be another source of externalities. Immigration to the US, Canada and Russia in the nineteenth century was essential to the development of the immense natural resources of these areas. Productivity increased with numbers up to a critical minimum point, such that the social benefit of an individual immigrant exceeded the individual earnings. If, on the other hand, immigration leads to the development of congested suburbs and shanty-towns, the externalities become negative. The argument that migration promotes cultural diversity is also double-edged. Such diversity can, of course, be an advantage, but it can also become a source of serious social friction, especially if the migrants are of markedly different race, language and religion to the majority and are slow to integrate.

Two other important externalities relate, first, to public finances and, second, to the job displacement and wage effects of migration.

### ◯ Public finance effects

There are good reasons for believing that immigration would have a positive impact on public finances in the host country. People tend to migrate at an age when they are unlikely to draw heavily on the education and health facilities of the host country. Also, the cost of certain indivisible public expenditure, defence being a classic example, can be spread over a larger working population, to the advantage of all. If migration policy is applied selectively, giving preference to the better-educated, this will further improve the probability of fiscal gains by reducing the likelihood of unemployment, and maximising the probability that the immigrant will be a net contributor to the public finances.

On the other hand (and on complex issues there nearly always is another hand), where migrants are mainly unskilled, as is predominantly the case with South–North migration, the net impact on the public finances is less clear. Unskilled migrants are likely to have more difficulty finding work in the host country. For instance, the unemployment rates of foreign workers in Belgium, France, Germany and Sweden have been between 50 and 100 per cent higher than for nationals (see Chapter 14), although by no means all migrants to these countries are unskilled. A serious fiscal burden falls on the host country if people move solely in order to avail themselves of its better standard of social services (Box 19.1).

The net impact on the host country's public finances thus depends upon the motivation, skills and circumstances of the migrant – all of which are likely to change over time. For example, European experience shows that although many migrants arrive on their own, intending to return home, the majority of migrants who stay eventually send for their families.

## Box 19.1 Migrants and government finances

The economic theory of migration, like the theory of trade outlined in Chapter 17, stresses the potential for mutual gains from migration. This emphasis tends to favour a liberal approach to immigration policy. But clearly, in view of the widespread restrictions on immigration, the arguments in favour of free movement of labour have proven less persuasive than arguments for free trade in goods.

One reason for this is that the model treats 'labour' as if migrants and natives consisted of homogeneous units of labour. But in reality labour is highly differentiated. When account is taken of different segments of the labour market, one sees that migration can have significant income distribution effects. This on its own would not make immigration a distinctive problem – trade also has potentially strong effects on income distribution. The real contrast arises from the dynamic and spillover effects. In the case of trade, they are generally accepted as positive, but the dynamic and spillover effects of migration are much less clear. They are certainly more ambiguous and controversial than the dynamic effects of trade.

The impact of migration on government finances is an example of one such spillover effect. A theme of this chapter is the contrasting fiscal impact of skilled and unskilled migrants. Educated migrants bring with them a stock of human capital, much of it paid for by the government of the sending country. They are likely to find work quickly and to pay taxes in excess of their drawings on government sources. An immigrant with less than a high school education, by contrast, is likely to cause a net drain on public finances. They are likely to have a larger family, have weak language skills and poorer job prospects. Largely because of the preponderance of low-skilled immigrants, foreign-born residents of the US have a 35 per cent higher probability of receiving public assistance than native-born Americans. By 1998, almost a quarter of immigrant households were receiving some type of assistance, as compared to 15 per cent of native households.

From time to time, efforts are made to quantify the fiscal effects of migration. One way of doing so is to compare the stream of taxes paid by an average immigrant over his or her lifetime in the host country and subtract from it the stream of government assistance absorbed. The OECD presents the following estimates of the net present value:

| Education level of immigrant | Net present value of contribution to US government finances (US$) |
| --- | --- |
| Below high school | –89,000 |
| At high school | –31,000 |
| Above high school | 105,000 |
| *Average all groups* | *–3,000* |

These estimates confirm that (a) better-educated immigrants are hugely advantageous to the host country, and (b) less-educated immigrants tend to be net recipients of state assistance. The estimates further implied that the US public purse was $15 billion to $20 billion worse off in 1996 as a result of immigration.

The general gist of these findings mirrors the experience of most host countries. When immigrants are skilled and motivated, they can make a significantly positive contribution to the economy. Well-educated immigrants have helped spearhead the 'new economy' sector, in many US and European regions. Host countries have learnt from

→

Box 19.1 continued

experience and immigration restrictions have been framed accordingly. Many host countries use a points system weighted towards the better-educated immigrants who will provide the most economic benefit to the host country.

Two points, however, should be noted in qualification of the above. First, if the estimates were extended to later generations of immigrants (the majority of whom will advance up the fiscal ladder to become net contributors) the net fiscal effect changes radically. Then even unskilled immigrants can be shown to have a positive fiscal impact. Second, while economic cost–benefit is important, humanitarian and political considerations are also important in determining policy towards immigrants.

*Sources*: *OECD Economic Surveys United States* (Paris: OECD, 1997); *The Economist* (29 November 1997); George Borjas, *Heaven's Door: Immigration policy and the American economy* (Princeton, NJ: Princeton University Press, 1999). The Ethical Globalization Initiative, headed by former UN Human Rights Commissioner Mary Robinson, is addressing human rights aspects of global migration.

For the sending country, emigration can reduce the burden of public goods provision. However, this gain must be balanced against the loss of potential future tax revenue from the emigrants. The lifecycle patterns of migration and of the consumption of public goods mean the sending country is more likely to suffer a net fiscal loss. People tend to migrate in early adulthood. This means that emigrants tend to be concentrated in the age-group that has just received public schooling at taxpayers' expense, yet the migrants will not be around to pay taxes from their adult earnings. Also, the more skilled the migrants and the more income they could earn, the greater the future income forgone in the sending country.

> Once migration has become an established option for educated people, more people will want to become educated. Higher education will attract as many people as can get an adequate yield on their education by staying at home plus the extra number flowing abroad. This can be major public expenditure with no offset in future tax yields. (Richard Layard, *East–West Migration*, Cambridge, MA: MIT Press, 1992, p. 39)

A 'brain-drain' tax has been proposed to deal with this problem. Emigrants would pay an extra education-related tax in the 'North' that would be passed back to the governments in the 'South'. The control and supervision needed in order to implement such a proposal would, however, be extremely costly. Other variations of the 'brain-drain' tax have been proposed, but none has yet been implemented.[7]

## Migration, wages and job displacement

Many efforts have been made to quantify the areas of loss and gain indicated in Figure 19.1. The estimates, however, tend to be subject to large margins of error.

---

[7] Numerous efforts have been made to quantify the economic value of the brain-drain transfer from South to North. Estimates suggest that it may exceed by many times the total value of all official development assistance in the opposite direction. According to a 1994 OECD report, 'the most skilled, talented and motivated people represent a wholly disproportionate share of those who migrate from the less-developed countries ... this haemorrhaging does much to widen the gaps between regions' (OECD, *Migration and Development: New partnerships for co-operation*, Paris, 1994, pp. 142, 150).

Furthermore, generalisation is difficult, given the distinctive characteristics of migration in different parts of the world. In a comparatively inflexible labour market, such as Europe's, immigration may increase the unemployment rate of unskilled native workers. In the flexible US labour market, immigration is unlikely to cause unemployment but can have a depressing effect on unskilled wage levels. Underlying these hypotheses is the fear that, in a completely open labour market, industrial wages would tend towards some global average level. While this would appeal to the poorer countries, better-off countries worry about the possibility of a decline from their present levels to a world average wage of about $2500 per annum.

Take, for example, the case of the US. Immigration into the US during the 1980s consisted preponderantly of low-skilled and poorly educated people. As a result, the supply of unskilled workers increased. The fraction of the US labour force that had completed less than high school education rose significantly. Towards the end of the decade, the proportion of less educated workers was 7 per cent higher than it would have been if, in each skill group, the ratio of immigrants to natives had been the same as it had been in 1980. Having estimated that the relative wages of the less educated fall by over 3 per cent with each 1 per cent rise in their relative numbers, one study concluded that immigration between 1980 and 1988 cut the relative wages of less educated Americans by 21 per cent. Although there is continuing controversy about the reliability of such estimates, more recent studies confirm that the fears of some threatened groups about the effects of immigration are not unfounded.[8] Of course, the native lower-paid workers could be compensated out of the extra output generated by the immigrants. A practical way of implementing such compensation would be through an improved education system for the children of the lower paid, thus leaving them less vulnerable to competition. But will compensation actually be provided? The real incomes of the lower paid in industrial countries have continued to stagnate. It is scarcely accidental that this happened to coincide with significant levels of immigration, though changing technology and freer trade must also be factored in to provide a complete explanation.

Austria is an interesting case study, of a small country which has accommodated a large population of new migrants, many from Eastern Europe in particular, since the late 1980s.[9] The share of migrants in the labour force rose from 5 per cent in 1987 to 11 per cent in 2000. Yet, the unemployment rate of Austrians remained relatively low by European standards (4 per cent). This has been explained by reference to two factors: first, migrants proved to be efficient job-seekers; and second, they competed for a different segment of the labour market from the national workforce. Natives and immigrants were not in direct competition. It does not follow that no displacement occurred. Immigration may have made it more difficult for the unemployed and other groups to enter the workforce. Nevertheless, the absence of visible detrimental effects on the group that would have been expected to be most adversely affected is significant.

---

[8] Recent studies suggest only small effects on resident workers: David Card, 'Immigrant inflows, native outflows and the local labour market impacts of higher immigration', *Journal of Labour Economics*, January 2001; W. Cline, *Trade and Income Distribution* (Washington, DC: Institute for International Economics, 1997); and *OECD Economic Surveys – United States* (November 1997) which analyses the immigration issue in relation to the US experience.

[9] R. Winter-Ebmer and J. Zweimüller, 'Do immigrants displace native workers? The Austrian experience', *CEPR Discussion Paper*, No. 991 (July 1994).

## 19.4 Conclusions

Migration involves people moving from areas where labour productivity is low to where it is high. The economic motivation for such migration is obviously very strong. Unskilled workers receive nearly 10 times more in the North than in the South, and skilled workers six times as much.[10] While those with specialised skills are welcome in most countries, there is a potential conflict of interest between host and sending countries arising from the former's preference for the skilled, well-educated migrant – precisely the type of person the sending country wants to keep at home and whose externalities could make a major difference to its development. Efforts to adjust the free market to take account of such externalities have had little success. The more skilled remain heavily represented in migration flows from developing to developed countries. Lower transportation costs, more information and a rising stock of migrants abroad are making migration more attractive to an increasing number of people in low-income countries, despite restrictions in the host countries.

As explained in Chapter 18, an alternative to migration is to bring capital to people through foreign investment. Foreign investment, combined with a liberal trade policy, acts as a substitute for migration. This line of thinking is neatly encapsulated in Layard's comment that:

> A free trade pact that ensures Eastern European countries access to Western European markets is the best single migration policy that could be put in place. (Layard, *op. cit.*, p. 51)

The potential of trade to act as a substitute for factor mobility has long been recognised in international trade theory. The theory shows that income differences between countries can be reduced through trade, even when factors of production are completely immobile between countries. The theory has been influential in persuading Western Europe of the importance of trade liberalisation with Central and Eastern Europe as an alternative to the prospect of 'catastrophic' immigration. Such considerations also carried weight among decision-makers in the US, and led them to embrace the idea of NAFTA as a vehicle for ensuring more rapid growth in Mexico and, consequently, reducing the volume of migration. This connection underlies a comment in *Business Week* following the 1995 Mexican peso crisis:

> Reviving Mexican prosperity is more politically important than ever at home because of smouldering US resentment about the influx of new immigrants into key states such as California and Texas.[11]

Whether NAFTA has succeeded in reducing the flow of illegal immigrants to the US, however, remains an open question – official US data indicate that the number of illegal Mexican immigrants in the US was 4.8 million in 2000, double the figure for 1990.

---

[10] A. Wood, *North–South Trade, Employment and Inequality: Changing futures in a skill-driven world* (Oxford: Oxford University Press, 1994).

[11] *Business Week* (16 January 1995). See also N. Lustig, 'Life is not easy: Mexico's quest for stability', *Journal of Economic Perspectives*, Winter 2001.

## Summary

1. Labour has become increasingly mobile internationally and the labour market has become significantly more 'globalised'. Demand and supply factors have both contributed to this. Advancing technology, strong economic performance and low population growth mean that current and prospective remuneration levels in the North have remained high both in absolute terms and relative to the South. On the supply side, rapid population growth combined with poor economic performance in many parts of the developing world provide a growing stream of young people eager to seek their fortune in more promising labour markets. Cheaper transport costs and easier communication through television and the web mean that people are better informed of job opportunities and comparative economic conditions than ever before. The transactions costs of moving from one labour market to another have been dramatically reduced.

2. Some countries have been significantly affected by labour migration. In Europe, Austria, Germany, Italy and the UK have experienced large inflows of migrants. The ongoing prosperity and openness of the US and Australian economies have also acted as powerful magnets for immigrants. Supplier ('home') countries such as Mexico, Morocco, Turkey, India and Eastern Europe have also experienced problems. Partly because of the nature of immigration restrictions, they find they are losing skilled people, rich in human capital that a developing country badly needs.

3. The gains from labour mobility derive from the reallocation of workers from locations where their productivity is relatively low to countries where their productivity is higher. The predominant direction of flow is from poorer to richer countries, as economic theory would predict. The gains from this movement are realised through higher global productivity.

4. In assessing the costs and benefits of migration, account must be taken of fiscal effects and externalities as well as the standard productivity effects. Also the implications of immigration for particular segments of the host country's labour market must be faced up to. Migration has potentially important consequences for the real wages of unskilled workers in host countries, but so far it has proved difficult to disentangle this effect from other more powerful influences such as technology and education.

## Questions for discussion

1. 'The value of migration as a means for enhancing economic efficiency is well known. However, at some point, it can become socially disruptive and inefficient, notably where local regimes perform so poorly that mass emigration occurs.' ('One market, one money', *European Economy*, October 1990, p. 27)

   Do you find the efficiency arguments for migration convincing? What criteria would you use in deciding the point at which migration becomes disruptive?

2. Of the EU-15's 370 million citizens, only about 5 million live outside their country of birth, and only 3.1 million work outside it in another EU state. Give economic reasons for this low degree of labour mobility.

➡

3. Free trade between the EU and its European and North African neighbours is often considered as a superior alternative (economically speaking) to mass migration. Explain the reasoning behind this belief.

4. 'If a truly global market for labour ever appears, it will be for highly skilled workers only.' What economic grounds could be used to justify this prediction?

## Exercises

1. Suppose a country's unskilled workforce increases by 10 per cent as a result of immigration. Trace out the effects on (a) resident unskilled employees, (b) capital owners, and (c) government finances, in the host country and the home country. (Use a supply and demand diagram with the number of unskilled workers on the y-axis to illustrate your answer.)

2. Is it correct to state that every additional immigrant displaces the job of his or her resident counterpart? Explain using a supply and demand diagram.

3. Suppose the marginal product of labour curve in the sending country shifts upwards and outwards from the origin. What effect will this have on the incentive to emigrate? What factors could cause the curve to shift in this way?

   Explain why free trade has been proposed, in the context of both NAFTA and EU trade relations with eastern Europe, as contributing to a reduction in international inequalities and an easing of the migration problem.

4. Outline the main fiscal effects of migration from the perspective of the home country and the host country respectively.

5. Reference is frequently made to the growth in the services sector in developed economies and the increasing share of employment in services in total employment. What impact does this structural change in northern economies have on immigration?

6. In the context of the standard model in this chapter, why are countries more likely to impose stronger restrictions on immigration than on emigration?

## Further reading

R. King, *Mass Migration in Europe: The legacy and the future* (London: Belhaven Press, 1993) offers a geographer's perspective on these matters. Julian L. Simon, *The Economic Consequences of Immigration* (Oxford: Basil Blackwell, 1989) and Richard Layard, *East–West Migration* (Cambridge, MA: MIT Press, 1992) consider the economics of movements between countries. George Borjas's *Heaven's Door: Immigration policy and the American economy* (Princeton, NJ: Princeton University Press, 1999) is a provocative, controversial and astringent book that assesses the overall effects of immigration on America. For a concise, readable overview of immigration (including the linkage between the ageing of Europe's population and future demand for young immigrants), see J. Coppel, J.-C. Dumont and I. Visco, 'Trends in immigration and economic consequences', *OECD Economic Department Working Paper*, No. 284, Paris, 2001. A good textbook account of the issues is available in R. Ehrenberg and R. Smith, *Modern Labour Economics: Theory and public policy*, Chapter 10 (Boston, MA: Addison-Wesley, 2003).

## Chapter 20

# The balance of payments: what it is and why it matters

## Introduction

This chapter provides a bridge between the analysis of 'real' international transactions and the exchange rate.[1] International trade in goods, services and factors of production can, as we have seen, bring major economic benefits. But, for these benefits to be realised, there must be an efficient payments mechanism. The balance of payments, the exchange rate and the exchange rate regime are three different but interrelated aspects of the financing of international transactions. The analysis of these issues has been motivated by the belief that the international system will work properly only if (a) business has easy and reliable access to foreign exchange, and (b) there is a relatively stable relationship between domestic and international prices.

The balance of payments is an important statement of account. It shows, on one side, all sources of supply (inflows) of foreign exchange, such as receipts from exports of goods, and services and capital inflows and, on the other side, all the sources of demand (outflows) for foreign exchange, such as payments for imports of goods, and services and capital outflows.

A company contemplating an investment or a new marketing drive in a foreign country usually seeks information on that country's balance of payments position as part of its overall economic assessment of the market. This chapter explains why. It shows how the balance of payments statement should be interpreted, and outlines the uses and pitfalls of balance of payments analysis for business.

We begin by analysing the *current* account of the balance of payments. References in common speech to 'the US deficit' or 'the Japanese surplus' or a country's 'balance of payments constraint' are shorthand for the balance of payments on current account. A country with a deficit, say, in this sense buys more from foreigners than it sells. That is, for current transactions demand for foreign exchange exceeds supply. To make ends meet, the country must obtain more foreign exchange, either by borrowing abroad or by selling its foreign assets. As

---

[1] The exchange rate is defined as the price of foreign currency in terms of domestic currency. It is the price that brings into equilibrium the demand and supply of various 'real' flows, such as the trade in goods, services and foreign investment. (See Chapter 21.)

long as there are sufficient foreign currency reserves, or willing lenders, the deterioration in the country's *capital* position creates no problems. Over time, however, as reserves decline and net foreign debt rises, two things are likely to happen. First, the country may have to offer higher interest rates in order to persuade foreigners (and its own capitalists) to hold more of its debt. Second, its exchange rate may come under pressure. Each of these outcomes could have adverse implications for anyone doing business in those countries. The choice of policies for dealing with this situation can affect economic growth and the general business climate. Moreover, since a deficit in one country implies a corresponding surplus in others, surplus countries cannot remain aloof from the deficit countries' problems.

Sometimes too much can be read into the balance of payments statement. A common misperception is that the existence of a deficit or surplus reflects the balance of advantage from trade between countries. Deficit countries in particular often accuse surplus countries of hogging the benefits of trade at the deficit countries' expense. This is another manifestation of the mercantilist fallacy that one country is doing another a favour by consuming its goods and services. Another common fallacy is the belief that a balance of payments surplus is a sign of economic strength, while a deficit is a sign of weakness. There is no logical reason for this supposed association. In any given year, some industrial countries will have surpluses and others deficits. And not all poor countries have balance of payments deficits.

### ( Chapter outline )

This chapter analyses the balance of payments in three steps:

1. Analysis of the balance of payments and its sub-components.
2. The concept of *balance of payments equilibrium* and the criteria for deciding at what stage a country has a balance of payments disequilibrium (or 'problem').
3. Policies for restoring balance of payments equilibrium.

## 20.1 What is the balance of payments?

The balance of payments is a statement of all transactions between residents of the home country and the outside world during a specified period of time. These transactions are grouped under two key headings: current items and capital items. The balance of payments statement is compiled using the double-entry book-keeping method familiar to students of accountancy (Table 20.1).

### The current account

The current account is a record of cross-border transactions in goods, services, factor income and transfers within a certain period of time. Annual, quarterly and even monthly balance of payments figures are published. Transactions involving an inflow of foreign currency are entered with a positive sign; outflows are entered with a negative sign.

> ## Table 20.1 Balance of payments statement
>
> **Current Account**
>   Goods trade
>   Services
>   Trading and investment income
>   Current unilateral transfers
>   *Balance on current account*
>
> **Capital Account**
>   Foreign direct investment
>   Portfolio capital
>   *Basic balance*
>   Short-term capital
>   Change in official reserves
>   Net errors and omissions

The current account has four major components. The first is the merchandise trade balance, often called the balance of visible trade or just *the balance of trade*. The trade balance measures the difference between the value of current exports of merchandise goods and the value of imports over the same period. This is a widely publicised part of the balance of payments. Traditionally, merchandise trade has dominated other components of the current account in value. Also trade data tend to be more reliable and up-to-date than other balance of payments statistics.

*Services trade* consists of tourism, transport, cross-border banking and insurance, and new activities such as telemarketing and software. Because services are intangible and difficult to trace, data on this trade are unreliable. Services are often delivered at their point of production and not shipped across country borders. Thus, a Japanese tourist paying to be shown around the Acropolis is said to *import* a service from Greece to Japan (without having to take the Greek tourist guide home to Kyoto). At other times, the service is delivered to the consumer. A Tokyo business consultant who travels to Sydney to advise on sales prospects in Japan is exporting a service from Japan to Australia.

The third component of the current account is the *balance of trading and investment income* (also known as factor income). It includes interest payments on foreign debt, dividends and royalties on foreign direct investment, and income flows between residents and non-residents in relationship to stocks, bonds or patents. Salaries earned abroad by domestic residents or by foreigners working in the domestic country are also included. The earnings of a British student from a summer job in a New York restaurant enters as an import of foreign factor services in the US's current account.[2] The repatriated profits of a Nissan plant in the UK

---

[2] Note, however, that the earnings of a British student who took up permanent residence in the US would no longer appear in the balance of payments. Salaries only enter the balance of payments when paid to seasonal, border and other short-term (less than a year) workers, whose main residence is outside the host country. An interesting case is embassies. Due to their status as part of the territory of their home country, the salary paid to a Japanese gardener employed by the US embassy in Tokyo enters the Japanese balance of payments as a factor export and appears with a positive sign in the balance of factor income. If, however, this same gardener were running a landscaping business and serving the US embassy as one of several clients, the activity would count as a Japanese *services* export. This example indicates that in many cases allocating individual transactions to balance of payments categories can be somewhat arbitrary.

are recorded with a positive sign in Japan's balance of services, since they involve a receipt of foreign exchange in return for the services of Japanese capital and entrepreneurship, and as a negative item in the UK's balance of payments. Developed countries tend to have positive net earnings from 'trading and investment income', because richer countries invest, or have invested in the past, more in poorer countries than the latter can afford to invest in the rich.

The fourth component is *unilateral transfers*, often referred to as the balance of international transfers. These transactions consist of unrequited payments such as foreign aid, or remittances to family members abroad. Government aid to a developing country enters the balance of payments with a negative sign for the donor and a positive sign for the recipient.

The *current account balance* is the sum of the four components: trade, services, factor incomes and unilateral transfers.[3] Among developed countries, the current account balance in 2003 ranged from a surplus of 11 per cent of GDP in Switzerland to a deficit of over 10 per cent in Portugal. Most developing countries and countries in transition tend to run current account deficits while the industrial countries as a group tend to have current account surpluses. The US stands out as a conspicuous exception to this rule, with a deficit of 5 per cent of GDP ($515 billion) (Table 20.2).

Since, by definition, one country's surplus is another's deficit, the global sum of countries' current accounts should in principle be zero. In fact, the sum of the world's current accounts added up to −$243 billion in 2003. This vast sum is a veritable 'black hole', a measure of our statistical ignorance. It reflects factors such as goods in transit (which appear as an export for the sending country but have not yet been recorded as imports by the recipient), smuggling, drug transactions, undeclared investment income and straightforward errors in statistical compilation.

## Capital account

Current account transactions account for only a small proportion of the total value of international transactions. As capital has become more mobile and investment more globalised, the capital side of the balance of payments has

### Table 20.2 Current balance of payments (% of GDP)

|          | 1980  | 1990  | 2003  | $ billion |
|----------|-------|-------|-------|-----------|
| US       | 0.1   | −1.6  | −4.7  | −514.9    |
| Japan    | −1.0  | 1.2   | 2.9   | 122.1     |
| Germany  | −1.7  | 3.3   | 2.1   | 45.5      |
| UK       | 1.2   | −3.5  | −2.3  | −37.1     |
| Norway   | 1.7   | 3.3   | 9.5   | 17.8      |
| Portugal | −3.7  | −0.3  | −7.5  | −9.8      |

*Source*: IMF; OECD.

---

[3] The current account balance corresponds to the value of $(X - M)$ in the national income equation in Chapter 11.

grown in importance. Hence considerably more attention is now being devoted to this section of the balance of payments than formerly.

We divide the capital account into four components: foreign direct investment, portfolio investment, short-term capital flows and change in official reserves.

(1) *Direct investment* refers to transactions where the investor acquires 'a significant degree of influence on the management of a foreign enterprise' (*IMF Balance of Payments Manual*, 1993, p. 86). Transactions such as the establishment of a new plant in the US by a Japanese car manufacturer or the takeover of an American corporation by a British company are classified as direct investment. Note, however, that only the amount of funds actually transferred from one country to another in respect of the transaction appears in the balance of payments. In many cases this will be a small fraction of the total cost of the plant or the takeover. Suppose, for example, that the total cost of the Japanese plant in the US was $200 million. Assume that the plant is incorporated as a separate company in the US, and will therefore qualify as a resident for balance of payments purposes. Funds borrowed from American banks by the subsidiary to finance the investment do not appear in the balance of payments. Only the amount lent to the subsidiary from outside the US is recorded.

(2) *Portfolio investment* refers to transactions in instruments of more than one year to maturity. It includes the acquisition of foreign bonds and financial securities, and investment in a minority (less than 10 per cent) stake in foreign firms. Portfolio transactions include transactions both by governments and by the private sector. Consider, for example, the acquisition of US government bonds by a Japanese bank. This would be recorded as a capital outflow in the Japanese balance of payments and a capital inflow in the US balance of payments.

(3) *Short-term capital* refers to investment in instruments maturing in less than one year. It includes huge volumes of inter-bank transactions as well as transactions undertaken to hedge against foreign exchange risk. Speculative capital movements mostly take the form of short-term capital. The rationale behind the distinction is that short-term capital is expected to be generally more mobile, less 'rooted', easier and less costly to liquidate, than long-term capital. It also tends to be the most sensitive element in the capital account to changes in interest rates. Analysis of movements of short-term capital provides valuable insights into how current account imbalances are being financed or into how vulnerable a country may be to foreign exchange speculators.

(4) *Official reserves* are held by monetary authorities, usually the central bank. They take the form of foreign exchange, balances with the International Monetary Fund and gold. About 12 per cent of world reserves are held in gold (Table 20.3). Gold has some attractions as an international reserve, but it suffers one major disadvantage – it yields no income. Hence the only return from holding it is the prospect of capital appreciation. Foreign exchange, by contrast, being held in the form of short-term government bills, does yield an income. Some 84 per cent of the world's reserves is held as 'foreign exchange'. The bulk of these reserves is invested in high-quality, liquid, short-term government securities; only a small fraction is held as actual foreign currency notes. Dollar reserves amounted to over $1515 billion out of total foreign exchange reserves of $2330 billion. The dominance of the dollar contrasts with the pound sterling, once the

### Table 20.3 Official holdings of reserve assets, all countries, end 2001

|  | US$bn | % |
|---|---|---|
| **Foreign exchange** | 2330 | 84 |
| US dollars | 1515 | |
| Euro | 466 | |
| Pounds sterling | 93 | |
| Japanese yen | 116 | |
| Others | 140 | |
| **Gold** | 320 | 12 |
| **Fund-related assets** | 110 | 4 |
| **Total reserves** | 2760 | 100 |

Source: Bank of International Settlements Annual Report, 2002; IMF and author's own estimates.

world's most sought-after reserve currency after gold, which now accounts for only 3 per cent of world official reserves. The Japanese yen also remains little used as a reserve currency, but the euro, which is expected to reach 20 per cent of foreign exchange reserves by the end of 2003, appears to be gaining worldwide acceptance.

Sometimes a distinction is made between *autonomous* and *accommodating* transactions in the balance of payments. Autonomous items refer to all current transactions plus long-term capital transactions. These respond to 'real' long-term competitiveness factors. Accommodating items consist of movements in reserves and short-term capital, and are seen as reacting passively to prior movements in autonomous items.

To illustrate the distinction, consider the example of a country which increases its demand for imports. This leads to an increase in the demand for foreign exchange. If the exchange rate is fixed, this increased demand could be financed by a drawdown of the central bank's foreign reserves. The change in official reserves is a passive transaction: it accommodates the increase in demand for imports, not vice versa. If the central bank was concerned about the depletion of its reserves, it could engineer a rise in the short-term interest rate. This would attract short-term capital inflows. Again, such inflows would be defined as accommodating transactions. However, short-term capital and a large part of portfolio capital investment move in an accommodating sense – as the direct consequence of the balance in autonomous transactions. As capital markets have become more liquid, the dividing line between accommodating and autonomous transactions has become less distinct.

Two further points may be noted. First, *different transactions in the balance of payments statement are often closely related*. For example, the establishment in the UK of a new plant by a Japanese automobile company might entail the following sequence of transactions:

● *Direct investment* inflows related to total capital costs.

- An *increase in imports* of machinery and intermediate goods as the factory is constructed.
- When the plant starts operation, an *increase in UK exports* as the subsidiary starts selling to the continental European market.
- *Trading and investment* outflow as profits are repatriated to Japan.

All these transactions are interrelated. Balance of payments analysis requires careful attention to these intertemporal connections between one section of the statement and another.

Second, since the balance of payments is drawn up on double-entry principles, the sum of the two sides of the statement must, in principle, add up to zero. In this sense, *the balance of payments always balances*, i.e. it can never be in deficit or surplus. However, because transactions in the balance sheet are measured and reported through different channels, they hardly ever match in reality. This explains the need for a balancing item (errors and omissions), appended to avoid an 'imbalance of payments' – which is a conceptual impossibility.

## The balance of payments and the indebtedness of nations

The current account can be compared to a household's current budget. If outgoings (imports) exceed earnings (exports), the resultant deficit has to be financed either by borrowing or by selling assets. Similarly, a country's current external deficit can be covered either by obtaining loans from non-residents, be it through public or private lenders, or by sale of assets to foreign investors.[4] The reverse applies in the case of a current account surplus: it can be used to give loans to non-residents, to pay back previous loans, or to buy assets abroad.

Whether a household is a net creditor or a net debtor depends on its past financial record. If it has been living beyond its means for a prolonged period, a household's debt can grow bigger than the value of its assets, thus turning the household into a net debtor. A thrifty family, on the other hand, which consistently spends less than it earns, can build up wealth in assets and credit. The same applies to countries' economic relations with the rest of the world. The sum of a country's foreign assets less the sum of its liabilities towards non-residents at any point in time is called the *international investment position*. The international investment position is a *stock* concept. It provides a snapshot picture of the situation at one particular moment in time, while the balance of payments provides a record of transaction *flows of funds* over a period of time.

The change in the international investment position between the beginning and the end of a period is equal by definition to the current account balance over that period. As a result, the international investment position is approximately equal to the cumulated sum of all past balances of the current account. (Valuation changes reflecting changes in exchange rates and asset prices can enter the equation in any one period, hence 'approximately'.)

The international investment positions of the US, UK and Japan are charted in Figure 20.1. Japan is a major world creditor; the UK has switched from being a creditor to a debtor within the past decade; and the US is a world debtor. This diversity

---

[4] Each of these forms of financing a current account deficit appears on the credit side of the capital account, which again illustrates why these two sides of the balance of payments should balance out.

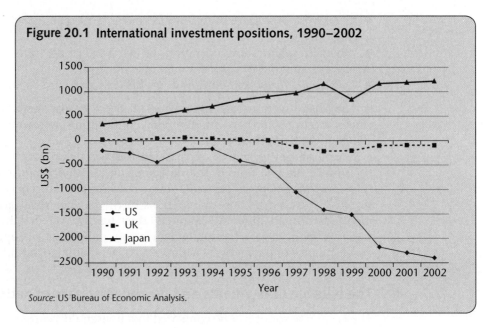

**Figure 20.1 International investment positions, 1990–2002**

*Source*: US Bureau of Economic Analysis.

of pattern is common among developed countries. Some such as Australia, Canada and New Zealand (not shown in Figure 20.1) have been sustained net debtors, utilising their access to the global capital market to build up their economies.

The big story of recent years has been the way a succession of deficits from the 1980s onwards reduced the US's net foreign wealth so that it changed from being a net creditor to the world's largest debtor. By the end of 2001, the net external debt of the US reached $2310 billion. That is a large sum in absolute terms and it is rapidly approaching 20 per cent of US GDP. Also the net debt is the balance between the $9 trillion that foreigners have invested in the US and $7 trillion that Americans have invested abroad. Until 2003, the income earned on Americans' foreign assets have exceeded the return foreigners have obtained from their US investments: foreigners have tended to invest in low-yielding US Treasury portfolios. In contrast with the US, Japan is a major world creditor. Its net investment position has continued to grow and by the end of 1998 it had become a net lender to the tune of 30 per cent of its GDP. But because much of this investment is in low-yielding foreign bonds, Japan has obtained a modest return on its foreign investments. Thus, a country like the US appears to have done well by borrowing cheap portfolio capital from foreigners and then investing this money in direct investment projects abroad.

Some oil-producing developing countries such as Kuwait, Venezuela and Saudi Arabia have adopted a deliberate policy of allocating part of their revenues to foreign direct investment projects. This policy has enabled them to build up strong creditor positions. But these are exceptional cases. Most developing countries are net creditors, some such as India mildly so (less than 20 per cent of GDP), others with deeper indebtedness ranging from Mexico and Morocco (over 40 per cent of GDP) to Sri Lanka, Jamaica and Côte d'Ivoire (over 60 per cent of GDP).[5]

---

[5] P. Lane and G.M. Milesi-Ferretti, 'The external wealth of nations: estimates of foreign assets and liabilities for industrialised and developing countries', *Journal of International Economics*, no. 55 (2001).

Not surprisingly, countries that are more open and trade-oriented tend to have larger gross flows of direct investment and portfolio equity investment.

## 20.2 Balance of payments problems

### Definition of a problem

'The balance of payments always balances.' True, but why then do countries have a balance of payments problem? When speaking of such a problem attention has tended to focus on imbalances in the *current account*, with some allowance being made for any long-term capital flows which have implications for the current account. (The concept of *basic balance*, incorporating current account and autonomous capital transactions, addresses this qualification.) Bearing this in mind,

> A country can be said to have a balance of payments problem when the current account deficit and the accumulated international investment position have reached a level where continuance of the deficit is no longer judged sustainable.

Some features of this definition have to be clarified. First, the *time dimension* needs to be specified, since a transitory deficit (as a result of a strike, earthquake or bad harvest, for example) presents fewer problems than one that is expected to persist. Second, the *size* of the deficit must be considered in relation both to the country's GDP and to its outstanding debt position. Third, the *method of financing* of the deficit has to be examined. A deficit financed by an inflow of foreign equity is less a cause of concern than one financed by foreign purchases of government bonds. In the case of equity finance, if the investment turns out to be unprofitable the liability automatically disappears. In the case of government borrowing, the liability remains, regardless of how wisely or unwisely the borrowed money was spent. The maturity of the borrowed funds would also have to be analysed. Long-term inter-governmental borrowing is obviously a more stable source of finance than short-term private capital invested for speculative reasons. Fourth, *free trade conditions* must be stipulated. A current account balance can always be sustained by tariffs or quotas or other administrative measures. Since the purpose of the international payments system is to facilitate trade, not to inhibit it, this situation could not be deemed one of equilibrium. Finally, a deficit can always be reduced by lower economic growth. A slowdown in economic activity has an immediate negative impact on import demand and as a result improves the current account. Mexico's deficit fell from 7 per cent to 0.5 per cent of GDP following the economic collapse of 1994–95 and a similar outcome accompanied Korea's downturn in 1997–98. In the latter case, a deficit of 1.5 per cent in 1997 was followed by a surplus of 12.8 per cent in 1998 (Table 20.4). Hence, *a surplus in a country's current account can indicate economic weakness rather than economic strength.*

Even with these elaborations, there remains the thorny question of how to judge whether a current account position is *sustainable*. The host country for the investment might have one view of the matter, while the foreign investors, concerned about the security and liquidity of their investment, can have another.

Table 20.4 How growth cutbacks 'improve' the current balance of payments

| Mexico 1993–96 | 1993 | 1994 | 1995 | 1996 |
|---|---|---|---|---|
| Real GDP | 2.0 | 4.5 | −6.2 | 5.1 |
| Current a/c balance (as a % of GDP) | −5.8 | −7.1 | −0.5 | −0.7 |
| Korea 1996–99 | 1996 | 1997 | 1998 | 1999 |
| Real GDP | 6.7 | 5.0 | −6.7 | 10.7 |
| Current a/c balance (as % of GDP) | −4.4 | −1.5 | 12.8 | 6.1 |

Source: OECD, Economic Outlook (June 2000).

There are also questions of political sustainability. Is one country gaining too much economic influence over another through the capital position built up as a result of sustained current account imbalances? Neither theory nor experience suggests a definitive threshold level for a current account deficit that will make it unsustainable and trigger a strong investor reaction. We know that the trigger point will depend on the characteristics of the economy in question, including its exchange rate policy and degree of openness, its saving and investment record, the health of its financial system and the structure of capital flows financing the deficit. Judgement, as well as careful statistical review, is necessary in adjudicating the issue of sustainability.

## Why does the current account balance matter?

An unsustainable current account imbalance matters for a number of different reasons. Each type of imbalance, deficit and surplus, creates its own set of problems. However, a deficit tends to result in more immediate and pressing problems than a surplus. Let us begin by considering the type of problem likely to confront a chronic deficit country.

A country with a current account deficit is absorbing more goods and services from foreigners than it is earning from export of goods and services to them. In this limited sense, a deficit signifies that a country is 'living beyond its means'. Suppose, however, that the deficit is being used to purchase capital equipment which will enhance the country's future earning capacity. In that case, running a deficit might make good economic sense. The deficit should then be financed by long-term capital inflows through the public or private sector. When the time comes for the accumulated debt to be serviced and repaid, spending will have to fall below the value of domestic production. If productive capacity has been added to, this can be achieved without any deterioration in living standards.

Ascertaining the use to which a deficit is put is obviously difficult. One must rely on a counterfactual model which would indicate the composition of GDP, in terms of investment, private consumption and government spending, as it would have been had the deficit been lower. Different macro-models often come up with radically different answers to this question. The reactions to the 1988 UK deficit and the present US deficit illustrate the distinct ways in which a deficit can be interpreted. To one school of thought they indicate economic strength, to another a sign of a chronic lack of competitiveness.

Critics of US policy have been concerned about the potentially adverse effects of the deficits on the US economy. Writing at the end of the 1980s, Paul Krugman

---

**Box 20.1** **How to interpret a current account deficit**

Nigel Lawson, former UK Chancellor of the Exchequer, attributed the UK's current account balance of payments deficit in the late 1980s to the strength of the economy. The prospect of attractive rates of return led to capital inflow, higher investment and, in turn, more imports and a current account deficit.

> Some see a current account deficit as a sign of economic weakness: 'Britain in the red' as the newspapers are wont to put it. But, of course, a current account deficit is manifestly not at all like a company running at a loss. A better analogy is with a profitable company raising money overseas – either borrowing, or reducing its holdings of overseas assets, or attracting new equity. A company with greater investment opportunities than it could finance from retained profits would look for additional funds from outside. A country in a similar position will draw on the savings of the world, particularly in today's global market. (Special lecture to the Institute of Economic Affairs, London, 21 July 1988)

In hindsight this turned out to be an unduly complacent view of what was to become a series of UK current account deficits amounting to a cumulative total of £100 billion between 1988 and 1991. Eventually restrictive monetary and fiscal policies had to be introduced which led to lower growth and higher unemployment.

This case illustrates the point that identifying a balance of payments problem is a matter of judgement. It is possible to make an incorrect judgement, and unfortunately the penalty for doing so can be severe.

---

described the deficit as involving 'a gradual mortgaging of future US income to foreigners'. The deficit in his view gives rise to

> one definite cost and some vaguer risks: the definite cost is, by definition, that you owe people money. From now on, the United States will be obliged to deliver a stream of interest payments to foreign bondholders, rents to foreign landowners, and dividends to foreign stockholders. Our payments to foreigners are a direct drain on our resources, and the longer the trade deficits continue, the larger this drain will become.[6]

A decade later, the US deficit has grown even larger, the investment position has worsened even more and economists continue to express misgivings. Their concerns are based on the type of issues outlined in Chapter 14 in the discussion of the sustainability of government debt. Many would have agreed with Dr Catherine Mann's view that the US current account trajectory as at 1999 would be sustainable for only another three years.[7] But three years later, the deficit continues to grow.

The economic costs of running an unsustainable current account deficit are threefold.

First, the greater the reliance on foreign creditors, the greater is the country's exposure to the volatility of international capital markets. This can have a

---

[6] Paul Krugman, *The Age of Diminished Expectations* (Cambridge, MA: MIT Press, 1994), p. 48.

[7] C.L. Mann, *Is the US Trade Deficit Sustainable?* (Washington, DC: Institute for International Economics, 1999). In *The World Economic Outlook*, September 2002, the IMF commented that the net asset positions of the US and Japan were *difficult to explain* and *are unlikely to maintain their current trajectories over the medium term* (pp. 73–74).

number of adverse effects. Highly indebted countries generally have to pay higher rates of interest for further credits. Worse still, if there is a loss of confidence on the part of creditors, the supply of capital can dry up regardless of the interest rate on offer. Such a collapse of creditor confidence led to successive economic crises in heavily indebted developing countries (Mexico, Indonesia, Brazil, Argentina, among many others).

Second, the loss of confidence scenario can lead to excessively large devaluations of the exchange rate, which involves both loss of real income and inflationary repercussions that only add to the problems of the deficit country. A textbook, if tragic, case is that of the Argentinian peso, which collapsed from parity with the US dollar to 4 pesos to the dollar following the 2001–02 currency crisis. Fear of such an overreaction in investment sentiment motivates current concern about the US deficit. An excessive depreciation of the dollar (25 per cent has been mentioned) would disrupt financial markets and have adverse knock-on effects on investment and consumption in the US and throughout the world.

Third, the more a country's international investment position moves into the red, the more ownership over its economic assets moves into the hands of foreigners. From a strictly economic point of view, this should not matter. The country is simply trading off future consumption in favour of present consumption, just as one would do by mortgaging one's house in order to splurge on a long vacation. But foreign ownership of domestic assets, with its overtones of a loss of national economic sovereignty, can be a politically sensitive issue.

Deficits can create special problems for developing countries with weak access to global capital markets. For this reason, countries such as India and Brazil have to pay far more attention to the current account of the balance of payments than the UK or Portugal. With globalisation of capital markets, the balance of payments has virtually disappeared from the policy agenda in many industrial countries. But, even for these countries, access to the global capital market can be fickle, capable of being turned on and off quickly. In other words, the international debt *position* of the country continues to be crucial, even if the current account *in any one year* has diminished in significance (Box 20.2).

The example of Korea is instructive in this respect. Korea borrowed heavily abroad. The big push to build up steel, chemicals and automobile industries in the 1970s, and light industry in the 1960s, was accompanied by large government-induced inflows of foreign capital. At one stage Korea's external debt:GNP ratio reached 50 per cent, giving it fourth place in the world debt league. However, its balance of payments deficits, and the resultant foreign debt, reflected high domestic investment ratios. In this way, Korea managed to maintain its growth, develop a strong export sector and enhance its creditworthiness, right up to the mid-1990s. Around that time, it fell into the trap of other Asian tigers: borrowing short abroad in order to finance domestic long-term projects of dubious economic viability. The resultant currency crisis proved costly in economic terms.

By definition, one country's surplus is simply another country's (or group of countries') deficit. Any country, whether in overall deficit or surplus, will have bilateral surpluses with some countries and bilateral deficits with others. The US has a large trade surplus with Australia (export:import ratio 1.60) and a large deficit with Japan (export:import ratio 0.44). Its overall export:import ratio is

**Box 20.2** **A tale of three deficits: the US deficit, Third World debt forgiveness and deficits in Euroland**

Three contrasting balance of payments issues face the global economy at the start of this century. One concerns the sustainability of the US current account deficit. The second concerns the sustainability of developing countries' external debt. The third issue is whether balance of payments deficits continue to have economic significance for Member States of the euro area.

### US deficit

Is the US current account deficit sustainable? The current account deficit amounted to 5 per cent of GDP in 2003. US net international indebtedness reached $2000 billion in 2001, nearly 20 per cent of GDP. Although there is currently no lack of eager lenders (foreigners investing in the US earned adequate returns during the 1990s), those taking a longer view fear that the balance of payments position will not remain sustainable for much longer.

Sustainability is ensured if the path of the current account is consistent with intertemporal solvency – in simpler words, if the economy will be able to meet the future cost of servicing its external debt. To do this, it must have the capability of changing from being a deficit country to having a current account surplus.

In assessing sustainability, the composition of foreign assets and liabilities is as important as the level of debt. Thus 90 per cent of US liabilities are denominated in dollars, not foreign currency. And equity liabilities leave a borrower less exposed in case of an economic downturn than fixed interest liabilities. These factors tend to diminish the vulnerability of the US economy.

But a current account deficit rising above 5 per cent of GDP is not sustainable over the long term. Sooner or later, global investors will switch off US assets. Perhaps they will move to the euro area instead. If this happens too quickly there could be a collapse in US asset values. To avoid a crisis, one or all of the following will be needed:

- a rise in the US household saving rate (it fell from 8 per cent in 1990 to 1 per cent a decade later),
- faster growth in the rest of the world to boost US exports,
- devaluation of the US dollar.

The difficulty with the first proposal is that 80 per cent of the income of US residents is spent on goods and services produced at home. As a result, the main impact of the rise in US saving will be a fall in demand for US goods and services. Similarly, only a fraction of an increase in expenditure in the rest of the world will be spent on US products. Dollar devaluation (expenditure switching) may therefore have to figure prominently in any programme to reduce the deficit.

### Developing countries' debt

At the other end of the spectrum to the US are the world's 53 heavily indebted poor countries (HIPC). These countries include some of the world's poorest nations. Their per capita income has declined from $400 in 1980 to $300 in 1998. Their problems have less to do with present current account deficits than with the accumulation of past deficits. They have an acute external debt problem. Their average external debt is

➡

**Box 20.2 continued**

150 per cent of GDP and debt service takes up 8 per cent of GDP. HIPCs on average allocate slightly more budgetary resources to debt service than to education and healthcare taken together. Because their debt is so high, foreign lenders have switched off and thus HIPCs are unable to run larger current account deficits. Here we speak of the *sustainability of debt* rather than the *sustainability of deficits*.

Debts are defined as non-sustainable if the ratio of debt to exports exceeds 150 per cent and debt/government revenue exceeds 250 per cent. The basis of the definition is pragmatic – any country with debt of this magnitude is unlikely to be able to ever repay the loan.

An HIPC initiative was launched in 1996 with the objective of bringing these countries' debt burden to sustainable levels, through write-offs and special terms. Under revised terms agreed in 1999, forgiveness of $110 billion of HIPC external debt was promised ($36 billion had actually been delivered by May 2003). A key issue is how to forgive debt without giving better-managed countries a signal to behave less responsibly and qualify for write-offs too. The creditors have tackled this by making forgiveness contingent upon satisfactory policy performance. This is a reasonable approach, but not without its drawbacks. Countries such as Nicaragua, with an external debt/GDP ratio of 295 per cent and receiving net aid of $117 per person, receives HIPC debt relief while a similarly poor country such as India, with a debt/GDP ratio of 20 per cent, gets only $2 net per capita aid, and no debt relief.

### Deficits in Euroland

Current account imbalances have for a long time been a policy concern of European countries. But they have not been a pressing concern for regions *within* these countries, for most of which the balance of payments position is not even recorded. Will the current accounts of the Member States of the euro area become likewise irrelevant, now that the euro has become the single currency for all?

In one sense the answer is yes. Already there is a marked reduction in interest in the balance of payments of individual Member States. Balance of payments policy, as such, is no longer a feature of national economic policy. Only the overall deficit or surplus of the euro area affects the value of the euro. The balance of payments position of the UK may have some implications for sterling, but the current account of France does not feature in the world currency markets' assessment of the euro.

However, this is not the same as saying that the balance of payments doesn't matter. In economic terms, movements in a euro country's current account will continue to have an important impact on the level of domestic aggregate demand. Also, the profile of its foreign assets and liabilities affects the stability of its national income in face of business fluctuations. Thus the GDP of a country suffering a negative domestic shock will be stabilised by foreign earnings if it has a positive net foreign asset position, and destabilised if it has net external debt.

*Source*: For the US, C. Mann, 'Is the US current account deficit sustainable?', *Finance and Development* (March 2000) and P. Krugman, *The Age of Diminished Expectations* (Cambridge, MA: MIT Press, 1990); for HIPCs, IMF, *World Economic Outlook* (May 2000, pp. 137–48) and World Bank Economic Indicators 2002.

0.62, indicating a net deficit. Similarly Japan, with an overall export:import ratio of 1.15, has ratios of 1.91 with the US but 0.23 with the Middle East.[8]

Countries with large deficits tend to blame surplus countries for their problems, particularly if the latter are large and conspicuous. In the US, protectionist lobbies used the deficit as a justification for deflecting the government's trade policy. Trading partners are put under pressure to import more from the deficit countries. They are also likely to be subjected to 'voluntary' restraints on their exports. They will be encouraged to invest more in the deficit country to relieve its balance of payments situation (while at the same time, and inconsistently, this very increase in investment may arouse nationalistic unease). Often such investment abroad may turn out to be unprofitable. This could happen because of exchange rate losses, as the surplus itself leads to a strengthening of the currency *vis-à-vis* the borrower.[9] More prosaically, there is also the possibility that investment decisions taken under pressure to placate the deficit countries may end up being poorly advised.

While surplus countries may have problems, the most pressing difficulties are likely to be felt by the deficit country. In every year between 1982 and 2003, the Japanese have recorded a large current account surplus and the Americans an even larger deficit. The US deficits have surely been more problematic than Japan's surpluses.[10]

## Can countries go bankrupt?

What happens if a country keeps running current account deficits over a prolonged period of time? If deficits are run for too long, liabilities may become a multiple of assets. Creditors might lose confidence in the ability of the country to honour its debts. When this occurs to a private firm, it is declared bankrupt and its remaining assets are liquidated and distributed among the creditors. But what happens to a country which loses the confidence of its creditors and thus becomes insolvent?

First, countries cannot be dissolved and their assets carved up among their lenders as in the case of private firms. There is no international authority through which debt enforcement can be imposed in a legally binding way. International law on this matter consists mostly of informal agreements, the adoption of which is ultimately left to the discretion of the sovereign signatories. Indeed, it is precisely the notion of national sovereignty that is protected most of all by international law. Hence, were the government of a creditor country to send out its army in order to liquidate its insolvent debtor abroad, the international community would be likely to weigh the infringement of national sovereignty as a more serious offence than the debtor's non-compliance with its contractual duties.

Second, the real problem is that even a temporary default destroys the reputation of the borrowing governments. They find it increasingly difficult and expensive to

---

[8] IMF, *Direction of Trade Statistics Quarterly* (June 2002).

[9] Of course, this will be a paper loss in terms of the surplus country's currency. Whether it also involves an economic loss is less certain since the revaluation effectively means improved terms of trade.

[10] It was precisely for this reason that Keynes proposed that the international community should impose an annual tax on balance of payments surpluses. The aim was to ensure greater symmetry in pressure to adjust as between deficit and surplus countries. The suggestion was never implemented.

obtain credit. Exactly the same happens if they are perceived to be accumulating excessive foreign debt. In order to assess debtor profiles and to determine interest premiums, international banks carry out regular analyses of 'country risk'. These profiles are constructed around various economic, social and political indicators in which the current balance of payments, the level of debt, in absolute terms and relative to GDP, and export performance carry a prominent weight (see Box 20.3). It is in the interest of every debtor country not to be rated as a risky borrower.

---

**Box 20.3** **Balance of payments, country indebtedness and country risk ratings**

A country's foreign indebtedness (private and public sector) is by definition related to the sum of its past balances on the current account. A highly indebted country has acquired its debt through running large deficits at some time in the past. As the current account worsens, foreign indebtedness increases and country risk ratings might be expected to increase.

Country credit ratings are compiled regularly by international banks and by financial service companies. Banker judgements, as represented by country credit ratings, are published regularly in *Institutional Investor*, a monthly financial journal read primarily by market professionals. The published risk rating for a country is derived by averaging approximately 100 individual bank ratings of that country.

A study by Somerville and Taffler represents bankers' country credit assessment by a linear model. It tries to identify the variables which are believed to exercise the most influence on bankers' assessment of country risk. The authors find that the *Institutional Investor* country rating is determined by the following variables:

| Variable | Impact on country credit status |
| --- | --- |
| Public sector external debt/exports (%) | Negative |
| Investment/GDP (%) | Positive |
| Import cover (number of months' imports covered by reserves) | Positive |
| Real total debt (US$m constant prices) | Positive |

The first three variables influence country ratings just as one would expect. Thus, countries that have accumulated large amounts of public external debt (i.e. government foreign debt) relative to exports tend to have higher country risk profiles. By contrast, those with high investment ratios and high reserves tend to have lower risk profiles. This means that bankers look not so much at the current account deficit in any one year (a variable not found to be significant), but at the accumulation of deficits over time by the government sector. They take solace from the fact that investment ratios are high and that reserves are sufficient to cover a reasonable proportion of imports. This model is consistent with the view that a current account imbalance must be interpreted in a broad context. According to the Somerville–Taffler view, long-term balance of payments variables do have an impact on country risk.

The reason for the positive sign on the level of real debt is difficult to explain. Perhaps, as the authors suggest, it indicates that larger economies have larger debt in absolute terms. For this reason there are more bankers who are familiar with its problems. And bankers tend to feel more comfortable about lending to those countries whose economies they feel they know well. This may well be yet another example of the triumph of hope over rational assessment.

Comparing *Institutional Investor* ratings with actual outcomes, bankers appear to be poor forecasters of debt-servicing difficulties among less-developed countries. But so is the equation used to represent their forecasts. Hence the shortcomings of banker judgement are of a fundamental and systematic nature (Somerville and Taffler, 1994).

Alternative country ratings, prepared by the Economist Intelligence Unit (EIU), are published regularly by *The Economist*. These are drawn from EIU's own estimations, based on economic and political factors. Country ratings of *Institutional Investor* and the EIU, issued before the Mexican crisis of late 1994, suggested no imminent vulnerability of the Mexican economy or currency. Yet in retrospect we know that the worsening balance of payments current account, the shortened maturity of government external debt and the pessimistic assessments of the Mexican government's ability and willingness to deal with its economic and political problems all played a role in the stampede out of the Mexican peso in late December 1994. Recent crises have included South East Asia, beginning in Thailand in mid-1997; the Russian default of August 1998; and Brazil 1998–99. In none of these cases did the *Institutional Investor* ratings show a significant dip ahead of the onset of the crisis.

*Sources:* R.A. Somerville and R.J. Taffler, 'The reliability of banker judgement in LDC credit risk assessment', *City University Business School, Working Paper Series 94/4*, 1994; R.A. Somerville and R.J. Taffler, 'LDC credit risk forecasting and banker judgement', *Journal of Business Finance and Accounting* (April/May 2001); J. Calverley, *Country Risk Analysis*, 2nd edn, (London: Butterworth, 1990).

Third, the stage could eventually be reached when credit lines were closed and a country could find it impossible to borrow. In that event, foreign suppliers demand foreign exchange guarantees and payment in advance. The supply of imports declines, factories are left idle for want of spare parts and key raw materials, transport becomes difficult because of oil and petrol shortages. Eventually the 'problem' is solved, but in a manner that accentuates difficulties elsewhere – by cutting back growth, restricting trade and devaluing the exchange rate.

Finally, political factors also play a role. A debt crisis involves rather humiliating overtures to international organisations and creditor governments, which reflect badly on the domestic government's competence. Sometimes the 'sting' can be taken out of this action by blaming the situation on the incompetence of previous governments and/or the recklessness of multinational bank lenders. This was the basis of the 1996 'debt-forgiveness' package, involving a 50 per cent write off of debt of the least developed countries.

From a growth perspective, the objective should be to maintain a sound credit rating. This will ensure that the costs of borrowing are kept to the minimum. Also it ensures that, in the event of unforeseen emergencies, a country can borrow abroad without the disruption of its investment plans which might otherwise be necessary. This can only be achieved if a sustainable current balance is maintained over time. Long-run current account deficits must therefore be matched by levels of profitable investment which will repay directly or indirectly the costs of financing them.

## 20.3 How to correct a balance of payments imbalance

Current account deficits and surpluses can each cause serious friction. Suppose some countries are running a series of chronic deficits and others apparently endless surpluses. What can be done to restore the situation to a more sustainable state? We begin by considering the effects of automatic adjustment mechanisms and then proceed to discuss policy options. Analysis of policy options, in turn, presupposes certain assumptions about the *cause* of the balance of payments problem which policy is attempting to address.

### Automatic adjustment mechanisms

Automatic adjustment mechanisms refer to the processes whereby *ex-ante* imbalances between the supply and demand for foreign exchange are brought into *ex-post* equilibrium. Starting from a position of initial current account balance, consider the effects of, say, a fall in the value of manufactured exports caused by an exogenous decline in foreign demand. Two factors are immediately set into operation which tend to reduce the deficit thereby created.

- The fall in demand for exports automatically creates a decrease in the demand for imports required as inputs for their production.
- The fall in aggregate demand generated by the decline in exports further reduces the demand for imports.

Note, however, that the adjustment mechanism is still only a partial one. The initial deficit is reduced but not eliminated. Consequently, other mechanisms must come into play in order to restore equilibrium.

One such mechanism is incorporated in the monetary approach to the balance of payments. According to this approach, the current account deficit results in a decline in deposits held in domestic banks. The balance of payments deficit, in other words, reduces the domestic money supply and, at constant prices, the value of real balances. If it is accepted that households maintain a given relation between their cash balances and levels of expenditure, a further fall in income and imports must occur in order to preserve monetary equilibrium.

There are a number of ways by which this adjustment can occur. Reduced cash balances mean less spending (the real balance effect). Also, the decline in money lends to a rise in interest rates. This causes investment to fall, leading again to a fall in imports. Financial intermediaries can also be introduced into the analysis. The adjustment process might be viewed as leading from reduced reserves in the banking system, to increases in the interest rate on overdrafts, to reduced borrowing and spending. The decrease in aggregate demand, by whatever process it comes about, must continue until full equilibrium is restored.

The automatic adjustment mechanism described above stresses the link between the current account deficit, the deterioration in the liquidity position of individuals and/or domestic banks, and the translation of the latter into a reduced level of advances and, eventually, lower aggregate demand. While relatively simple in theory, in practice the process may take a long time to work through the system. When private capital is internationally mobile, it may be that a very small increase in domestic interest rates will attract private capital inflows which offset the current account deficit and thus ease the liquidity constraint.[11] Official policy could also encroach upon the automatic adjustment mechanism by 'sterilising' the monetary effects of balance of payments disequilibrium. For example, the central bank might offset the liquidity-reducing effects of the deficit by short-term measures designed to increase domestic liquidity. Alternatively, the government might borrow abroad in order to restore the liquidity loss.

The automatic adjustment process can also operate on the supply side. Suppose we are in a world of classical full employment. To eliminate the deficit then requires more than just switching demand from imports to exports. Resources must be released from production of 'nontraded' goods and reallocated to the production of both exports and import-competing ('traded') goods. In an economy where prices are flexible, this adjustment is achieved by a change in the price of traded relative to the price of nontraded goods and services.

Thus, returning to our example of a downward shift in the demand for a country's exports, factors released in the export industry seek employment elsewhere in the economy. This will lead to a fall in the domestic price of nontraded services (taxis, restaurants, accounting and professional services, etc.). Prices in the traded sector will be much slower to fall because, at a fixed exchange rate, they will be largely determined by international market conditions. Hence the *profitability* of the traded sector will increase and resources will be drawn into it. *Domestic production of importable and exportable goods will increase relative to the production of nontraded goods and services.* The nearer an economy is operating to 'classical' conditions, the more relevant this type of adjustment will be to the process of equilibrium.

A strong automatic adjustment mechanism is particularly evident in a small open economy. Changes in the demand for exports translate into changes in the demand for imports. A shift in the demand for imports will have implications for the money supply and the level of aggregate demand, and so on. The process of adjustment may be delayed by institutional rigidities and *ad hoc* government interventions. A key issue is whether adjustment is effected through changes in real variables such as the level of employment and the growth rate or by means of changes in relative prices. Economic policy aims to ensure that the process of adjustment is carried through with minimum loss in terms of output and efficiency, and with maximum use of the price mechanism. In practice this means not waiting until reserves and foreign borrowing capacity are exhausted before taking action. Our next task is to analyse the type of action to be taken, which would give firms and individuals an opportunity to make structural changes in good time, before a crisis point is reached.

## Balance of payments policies

Balance of payments policies are concerned with maintaining balance of payments equilibrium. Effectively this means keeping the deficit or surplus at a sustainable level. As an extreme example, suppose a country with a current account

---

[11] However, private capital will continue to flow only if it is convinced that the underlying balance of payments position is secure.

deficit reaches a stage where reserves and borrowing capacity are depleted. As we have seen, in such circumstances, the country does not go bankrupt. However, it will find it progressively more difficult to secure essential imports. What policy instruments are available to the government to remedy the situation? For illustrative purposes, we consider the case of a country with an unsustainable deficit.

If the deficit country is operating at full employment and production is by definition at full capacity, *expenditure reduction* policies would be one way of resolving the deficit problem. Reductions in the real level of economic activity brought about by, say, restrictive fiscal policies will decrease the level of import demand. If the propensity to import is high, this policy can be highly effective in restoring balance of payments equilibrium.

Recall that the total income of a country is defined as:

$$Y = C + I + G + X - M$$

where $C$ is private domestic consumption, $I$ is domestic investment, $G$ is government consumption, and $X - M$ represents exports less imports.[12]

Income can also be defined as:

$$Y = C + S + T$$

where $S$ is savings and $T$ is taxes. In equilibrium the two definitions are identical:

$$C + I + G + (X - M) = C + S + T$$

Hence,

$$(I - S) + (G - T) = (M - X)$$

that is, excess investment over savings + government budget deficit = balance of payments deficit.

The balance of payments deficit has a counterpart in (a) the budget deficit and (b) the excess of investment over savings. Assuming full employment, it follows that one solution to the deficit is to cut spending. This can be done by some combination of measures such as:

● increasing domestic savings,
● reducing investment,
● restrictive fiscal policies.

*Expenditure switching policies*, by contrast, focus on the redeployment of resources. There are three standard methods of expenditure switching:

● commercial policy,
● improved competitiveness, and
● exchange rate changes.

(1) *Commercial policy* comprises price and non-price measures designed to restrict imports and stimulate exports, e.g. tariffs, quotas, export subsidies. Besides being a source of friction with a country's trading partners, commercial restrictions are rarely an efficient way of rectifying a balance of payments problem. But in a crisis

---

[12] For simplicity, we assume zero unilateral transfers and net factor income.

they may be the only practicable way of dealing with it. Hence the existence of a specific WTO provision for imposing temporary trade restrictions in cases of exceptional balance of payments difficulties. India used this clause to justify quantitative import restrictions during the 1990s. Note that these trade restraints will be effective only if there are unutilised resources available to satisfy the demand which is diverted from imports to domestic goods. If this assumption is not valid, diverted demand will meet a fixed domestic supply, domestic prices will rise, and the initial competitive advantage accruing to domestic suppliers through import barriers (or export subsidies) will be eroded.

What is needed to resolve the deficit problem is a way of altering the composition of output. In effect, we have to incentivise resources to move to the traded sector from the nontraded sector. The next two policies address this objective.

(2) *Cost competitiveness* can be defined in a broad sense to include price and non-price factors such as product quality, reliability of supply and back-up market services. Improving a nation's competitiveness involves a wide range of measures such as restraints on domestic costs and incomes, improvements in infrastructure, correcting bottlenecks in the supply of skilled labour, establishing an orderly industrial relations system and so on. A country's long-run competitive position can also be influenced by its policy towards research and development and its success in product innovation and technology. Countries with balance of payments deficits often consider themselves to be suffering from lack of *competitiveness*. Their exports and import-competing industries are unable to 'hack it' in a globalised economy. The lack of dynamism in the traded sector is perceived as holding back economic growth. Expansion of the economy is frustrated by balance of payments crises, as imports demand outstrips export revenues. The solution is to improve competitiveness.

(3) *Exchange rate changes* involve a *combination of expenditure switching and expenditure reduction*. The objective is to reduce domestic spending, to maintain output at a high level, and to reallocate output towards the traded sector, all at the same time.

*Depreciation of the exchange rate* makes imports more expensive and improves the price competitiveness of exports. For a large country, a depreciation can be far more effective than an expenditure-reducing policy as a means of cutting a current account (see Box 20.4).[13] The reason is that expenditure-reduction policies, achieved through, say, a cut in government spending or a rise in taxation, cut spending on imports (as intended) but also cut spending on domestic goods (an unwanted and potentially unemployment-creating side-effect in the short run). Expenditure switching, therefore, is needed to pick up the incipient slack in

---

[13] According to the basic macroeconomic equations, the current account balance (in this context mostly referred to as net exports) results from a mismatch between domestic savings and investment. If residents save more than they invest, or, in other words, they have a surplus of output to be sent abroad, net exports are positive. Conversely, a country turns into a net importer if its residents do not save as much as they invest, which means also that they consume and invest more than they produce. Total spending by domestic residents, i.e. the sum of consumption and investment, is called absorption. Thus, if absorption exceeds production, the current account is in deficit. These fundamental relationships underline the importance of the balance between savings and investment for the determination of the external balance.

### Box 20.4  Expenditure switching and the US deficit

'The United States has a current account deficit because it spends more than it earns.' This view of the cause of the deficit has interesting policy implications. One is that total spending might have to be curtailed. The second is that the cut in spending must as far as possible be concentrated on imports. To achieve such a reorientation requires therefore a mixture of expenditure reduction and expenditure switching. A policy which aims merely to cut US demand will not lead to the right *kind* of demand cut. Krugman explains the analysis with the aid of a simple arithmetical example.

He starts with the observation that, despite the increasing openness of the US economy over the past 40 years, most of the income of US residents is spent on goods and services produced at home. As a result, the main impact of a reduction in US expenditure will be a fall in demand for US goods and services. Similarly, only a fraction of an increase in expenditure in the rest of the world (ROW) will be spent on US products.

To see the problem this causes, consider the example illustrated in the table below. Suppose the US reduces its spending by $100 billion, while the ROW simultaneously increases its demand by the same amount. Unfortunately, this does not translate smoothly into a $100 billion reduction in the trade deficit. At least $80 billion of the reduction in US spending is likely to represent a fall in demand for domestically produced goods and services, with only $20 billion representing a fall in demand for imports. Meanwhile, no more than $10 billion of the rise in spending in the ROW is likely to be spent on US goods, with $90 billion being spent on ROW products. The outcome is a net reduction in demand for US products of $70 billion, and an equal increase in demand for ROW products. Instead of a smooth reduction in the US trade deficit, we get a combination of recession in the US and inflation abroad. To make the adjustment work, some way has to be found to switch $70 billion in spending from ROW to US products. The easiest way to do this is to lower the foreign exchange value of the dollar, which makes US goods cheaper to ROW residents and ROW goods dearer to US residents.

The lesson of this example is that devaluing the dollar can be an effective element in a deficit-reduction policy package.

|  | Total demand | Demand for US products | Demand for ROW products |
|---|---|---|---|
| US | −100 | −80 | −20 |
| ROW | +100 | +10 | +90 |
| Total | 0 | −70 | +70 |

*Source*: P. Krugman, *The Age of Diminished Expectations* (Cambridge, MA: MIT Press, 1994).

demand for domestically produced goods by stimulating exports and import-competing activities. Devaluation offers the necessary incentives for this and, in addition, provides an inducement to suppliers to shift to traded from nontraded production.

The effectiveness of a devaluation, however, is subject to certain practical and institutional constraints, which are particularly relevant to smaller countries.

First, a devaluation raises exporters' costs by raising the price of imported imports, an effect which is more pronounced in a small trade-dependent country. Second, the favourable competitive effects often come into play only in the medium to longer term. Third, depreciation of the exchange rate can lead to domestic inflation, compensatory income claims and the beginning of a wage–price spiral.

For all that, there are many instances of successful devaluations. Sometimes such devaluations are forced upon the deficit country by capital speculation. Devaluations can also help to insulate a country against competitive disadvantages arising as a result of devaluations in the currencies of its trading partners. Sometimes they are made in order to bring about what is hoped will be a once-for-all correction in a country's cost structure. Given the right circumstances, a devaluation can play a constructive part in rectifying a balance of payments deficit crisis. A detailed analysis of exchange rates will be provided in Chapter 21.

While this analysis has focused on policy measures to correct a deficit, the same framework can be applied to analyse measures for correcting a surplus. Thus, surplus countries are urged to liberalise commercial policy by dismantling non-tariff barriers on imports. For them, expenditure-expanding programmes are appropriate, provided they can be effected without giving rise to inflation. Measures can also be taken to reduce the propensity to save. The Japanese government has gone so far as to encourage employees to take longer holidays and spend more on enjoying themselves.

In the last analysis, surplus countries too are under pressure to realign their currency. Surpluses, like deficits, can often be difficult to correct. A government with a surplus can hardly be expected to instruct its producers to become less competitive. Self-interest, in fact, will lead its firms to redouble their efforts to increase competitiveness in the face of revaluation or stiffening competition from foreigners. This makes good sense for the individual corporation. But it frustrates the global system's capacity to deal effectively with a troublesome imbalance.

## 20.4 Conclusions

The structure of the balance of payments in developed countries has been undergoing profound change. Deregulation and liberalisation have led to rapid growth in services trade. The proliferation of multinationals has fuelled the growth of royalty and dividend payments and international marketing and consultancy services. Most significant, however, has been the quantum leap in capital account transactions, as technology makes it easier to transfer capital and relaxation of exchange controls legalises such transfers.

Defining a sustainable balance of payments position has, as a consequence, become more problematic. Capital flows have made it possible to contemplate a much longer period of deficits or surpluses on the current account. Eventually, however, sustained imbalances cause friction even in a capital-mobile world. In that event, the same ease of capital mobility that for long made it unnecessary to implement corrective action, can precipitate the need for it in moments of difficulty. There is, unfortunately, no ready formula for determining whether a particular country has, or is likely to have, a balance of payments problem. Balance of payments analysis involves good judgement, as well as good economics.

Balance of payments problems remain a serious constraint on development in many countries. This is particularly the case for developing countries with restricted access to world capital markets and with relatively fixed exchange rate regimes. Developed countries, however, can also be affected. Balance of payments policy continues to be preoccupied by the twin problems of the Japanese surplus and the US deficit. For decades, the UK government wrestled with the problem of 'stop–go' policies whereby economic growth was brought to a premature end by a balance of payments deficit, caused by import demand outstripping export capacity.

In the present environment, the main themes of debate focus on automatic balance of payments adjustment mechanisms, optimal levels of foreign borrowing, the changing composition of external assets and liabilities, and interdependence between one country's balance of payments deficit and other countries' surpluses. In a world still heavily dominated by the triad of the EU, Japan and the US, the development of a cooperative rather than a confrontational approach is important not only for the triad itself, but also for developing countries. The latter rely more than the richer countries on access to world markets in order to earn the foreign currency needed to achieve faster growth and to service their external debt.

Remedies for a balance of payments problem may be found in a number of possible measures: trade policy, aggregate demand (absorption) policy, improved competitiveness and changes in the exchange rate. Much balance of payments analysis has, in fact, been conducted in the context of an implicitly assumed fixed or quasi-fixed exchange rate regime. Once flexible exchange rates are introduced, the balance of payments problem evaporates – at *some* price, demand and supply of foreign exchange will be equilibrated. But in solving the balance of payments problem this way, the danger of creating another is accentuated. One danger is inflation. Devaluations can become excessive and self-sustaining (the multiple equilibrium problem). Difficulties can be caused to neighbouring countries (contagion). To understand these issues requires an analysis of the exchange rate – the theme of the final two chapters.

## Summary

1. The balance of payments consists of current transactions and capital transactions. Current transactions include trade in goods, services trade, trading and investment income and unilateral transfers. Capital transactions refer to net stock changes in portfolio capital, foreign direct investment, short-term capital and official reserves.

2. The balance of payments on current account is an important economic variable. It represents the difference between current outflows and inflows of foreign exchange. The current account balance impacts on the level of aggregate demand and on the level of a country's international indebtedness. For example, a succession of current account deficits since the 1980s has reduced the US's net foreign wealth to the point where the US has been transformed from being a major creditor country to being the world's largest debtor country.

3. A current balance of payments deficit means that a country is spending more foreign exchange than it is currently earning. In some cases, running a deficit is a perfectly defensible, even a desirable, strategy. For example, a rapidly growing economy may run a deficit, and in so doing draw on external capital, to support its investment programme. But a deficit incurred to finance extra consumption will sooner or later be judged unsustainable by the world markets. Corrective action will then have to be taken. A country running a persistent surplus could also be considered in a disequilibrium position, not least because of the objections of its trading partners. There is, however, no simple rule-book to guide us in deciding when a country has a balance of payments problem or when its balance of payments is in disequilibrium. Balance of payments analysis requires judgement.

4. There are automatic adjustment mechanisms which tend to restore balance of payments equilibrium. Surplus countries can find that the resultant rise in liquidity attracts growing import demand. By contrast, a decline in demand for a country's exports dampens that country's demand for imports. A change in the current account has other automatic repercussions on the domestic price level and the country's international competitiveness. But automatic income and price adjustment mechanisms are rarely sufficient to ensure equilibrium. Policy action may also be required.

5. Expenditure changing and expenditure switching policies are mechanisms for speeding up the adjustment process. Deficit countries can ease their balance of payments by curbing net government spending or encouraging saving; and surplus countries can stimulate import demand and reduce the surplus through expansionary budget policies (subject to the caveats about the effectiveness of such policies mentioned in our discussion of fiscal policy in Chapter 15). Expenditure switching policies refer to price incentives designed to induce a switch in spending between traded and nontraded goods and services. Three such policies are commercial policy, domestic competitiveness measures and exchange rate changes.

6. In a world of freely floating exchange rates, balance of payments problems as such are unlikely to surface. Impending deficits or surpluses, if not matched by offsetting capital flows, will bring about exchange rate fluctuations which will neutralise the threatened imbalance. Exchange rate fluctuations may, however, raise difficulties for the authorities no less acute than the balance of payments difficulties experienced by countries with a fixed exchange rate regime.

## Questions for discussion

1. Discuss the US and Japanese external imbalances and their impact on the two economies themselves and their global main trading partners.

2. How would you explain the rapid growth in capital account transactions relative to merchandise trade transactions in recent years? Does the increase in capital mobility tend to accentuate balance of payments problems?

3. What, if anything, does the fact that a country has a current account surplus tell us about the strength of that economy?

➡

4. How would you define a balance of payments disequilibrium? Discuss some of the economic forces which tend automatically to restore the balance of payments to equilibrium.

5. What problems, if any, is a country which runs a persistent current account balance of payments deficit likely to encounter? Contrast them with the problems of a country with a persistent surplus.

6. Should a tax be imposed on countries running a persistent balance of payments surplus, on the grounds that such surpluses are deflationary and a danger to the world trading system?

## Exercises

1. Under what circumstances could a country simultaneously have a balance of trade surplus and a current account deficit? Give examples of countries with this combination.

2. Classify the following transactions in the UK balance of payments:

   (a) British Airways purchases a jet from Airbus for £60 million, and receives a three-year credit from a French bank to finance the transaction.
   (b) A US tourist travels to Britain and spends £1000 financed by dollar travellers' cheques.
   (c) Mercedes Benz sells €4 million of its cars to a UK distributor, allowing 90 days' trade credit until payment is due.
   (d) Herr Schmidt in Bonn sends his grandson in London €4000 for his university fees.
   (e) A resident in Phoenix, Arizona, receives a £10,000 dividend from British Telecom plc which is deposited in a local bank.

   Specify a balancing capital account transaction in each instance.

3. Consider any country with a balance of payments deficit on current account. Reviewing the economic record of the country, should the authorities take steps to reduce this deficit? If so, how should this be done?

4. Review recent trends in the current account balance of payments of any major industrial country. What would be the likely effect on the current account balance of:

   (a) faster economic growth in the economy of its trading partners?
   (b) faster growth in its own economy?
   (c) rapid inflation relative to its trading partners?

5. Does it make sense for a developing country to run a current balance of payments surplus? In your answer, give examples of developing countries that have surpluses.

6. At the end of 2001, official foreign exchange reserves amounted to $212 billion in China, $45 billion in India, $44 billion in Mexico, but only $29 billion in the US. Explain why the US holds such low reserves by comparison with these developing countries.

**7.** Many argue that the US current account deficit, running at $2 billion per day in April 2003, poses a major risk for the world economy. The then Secretary of US Treasury, Paul O'Neill, rejected this argument. He asserted that the balance of payments on current account was 'a meaningless concept', reflecting the fact that foreigners wanted to invest in America because returns were higher. Which side of the argument is correct in your view and why?

## Further reading

Two major world balance of payments problems – the US deficit and the Japanese surplus – are dissected in a readable and enlightening way in Paul Krugman, *The Age of Diminished Expectations* (Cambridge, MA: MIT Press, 1994). Catherine Mann's 'Perspectives on the US current account deficit and sustainability', *Journal of Economic Perspectives*, 16(3), 2002, brings the discussion up to date. The IMF's *World Economic Outlook*, published twice yearly, contains information on the balance of payments and foreign position of the main countries and regions and commentary on these problems. The IMF's *Balance of Payments Statistics Yearbook* provides a wealth of detail on national balance of payments statistics. Any reader interested in the minutiae of balance of payments methodology should consult the IMF's *Balance of Payments Manual* (1993). A major contribution to the estimation and analysis of international capital flows and asset positions has been made by P. Lane and G. Milesi-Ferretti in a series of joint papers. See their paper 'External wealth, the trade balance and the real exchange rate', *European Economic Review*, No. 46, 2002. See also the European Central Bank's *Review of the International Role of the Euro*, December 2002.

## Chapter 21

# Coping with exchange rates

## Introduction

Exchange rate variations can cause major headaches for firms, especially those with a diversified sales pattern. Bilateral rates between the major currencies are subject to violent and unpredictable swings. Even in the course of a relatively quiet year currency swings in the range of 10–20 per cent would not be uncommon. Given that profit margins in most industries lie in the range of 3–10 per cent of sales, a firm's profits can quickly be eroded by unexpected shifts in exchange rates. There are ways of avoiding or minimising exchange rate risk, but they are not costless. Attempts to forecast exchange rate changes are also unlikely to be effective in protecting profits (for reasons to be explained). This chapter outlines the causes of exchange rate volatility and analyses how business can cope with it. In Chapter 22, the various ways by which government can alleviate exchange rate problems are analysed.

Business and government have conflicting perspectives on the exchange rate. At one extreme, exchange rate changes can mean the difference between prosperity and closedown for the low margin exporter, or the domestic manufacturer competing with low cost imports. At the other, to the government a 'strong' exchange rate regime connotes lower inflation, lower interest rates and high political prestige. To the consumer, a strong currency means lower prices for imported goods.

Although a weak currency helps the traded sector in the short run, it could have adverse repercussions on the long-run competitive position. Michael Porter articulated the danger in this way:

> The expectation of a lower exchange rate leads firms towards a dependence on price competition in price-sensitive segments and industries. Automation and other forms of innovation that improve productivity, and the shift to higher order competitive advantages are retarded. Thus a balance needs to be struck. *Currency pressures need to be strong enough to promote upgrading but not so great as to run ahead of factor quality and other preconditions for upgrading to succeed.* (M. Porter, *The Competitive Advantage of Nations*, London: Macmillan, 1990, p. 642)

Finding the golden mean between exerting pressure to improve quality and destroying the cost base of a nation's industry can be a difficult task. Strong, prosperous economies do indeed tend to have strong exchange rates, but it does not follow that strong exchange rates have made them prosperous. Arguably, a slightly undervalued currency provides a greater inducement to growth than an overvalued one. Certainly a highly overvalued currency has proved damaging to growth in many developing countries.

## Chapter outline

The chapter proceeds as follows:

1. The foreign exchange market and the effects of changes in the exchange rate on business behaviour.
2. Exchange rate theory. This involves analysis of purchasing power parity and other economic 'fundamentals' in influencing exchange rates.
3. Reasons for exchange rate volatility and the implications of this volatility for business.
4. Methods by which business can cope with exchange rate fluctuations. These include use of the forward market, options and other hedging devices.

## 21.1 How exchange rates work

### Foreign exchange markets

The foreign exchange (forex) market is the world's largest financial market. Currencies are traded in financial centres around the world, connected by communications systems that allow nearly instantaneous transmission of price information and trade instructions. Total net turnover averaged $1200 billion per day during 2001. The most active market was London ($504 billion per day), followed by New York ($254 billion), the euro area ($239 billion) and Tokyo ($147 billion).[1]

The *spot* foreign exchange market refers to the market for foreign exchange deliverable two days after the contract is made. The market operates by means of communications on computer screens and telephones by four categories of participants: dealers/traders (predominantly large international banks), brokers, institutions (mutual funds, pension funds, insurance companies) and central banks. In addition to the spot market, there is the *forward* market and the *futures* market, and a market for *swaps* and *options* (derivatives). Spot transactions dominate trading, accounting for half of total turnover. Information on spot rates is available in daily newspapers, usually in the form of data on *closing rates* and on the day's *spread* or *trading range*, the latter indicating the range between the highest and lowest bid during the day. A major development in the market in recent years has been the surge in swaps and derivatives transactions, as banks and their customers have become increasingly anxious to hedge their foreign exchange positions. These sophisticated instruments will be analysed later in the chapter. Further details of the forex market are provided in Appendix 21.1.

---

[1] European Central Bank, *Review of the Foreign Exchange Market Structure*, March 2003.

The exchange rate is defined as *the price of foreign currency in terms of domestic currency*. It is the amount of domestic currency needed to buy one unit of foreign currency – just as the price of apples is the amount of domestic currency needed to buy an apple. Thus, it cost a US citizen $1.99 to buy a pound sterling in 1991; 12 years later, it cost only $1.58. Looked at from the UK perspective, a dollar cost 50p in 1991 as compared with 63p in 2003. During this period, the dollar had become more expensive and sterling cheaper. On this bilateral basis, we say that the dollar has *appreciated* and sterling has *depreciated*. The percentage depreciation/appreciation lies between 22 and 28 per cent, depending on the base from which the calculation is worked out.

The pound sterling alters in value relative to other currencies as well as the dollar. To obtain an impression of the trend in sterling's overall value, one must take an average of these diverse bilateral depreciations and appreciations. For this purpose, a weighted average is used, the weights being related to the proportion of total UK trade with each country concerned. Often trade weights are modified by other *ad hoc* adjustments to take account of the degree of price-sensitivity of trade with certain countries, the currency in which trade is denominated and other factors. The resultant trade-weighted index is called the *nominal effective exchange rate* (EER) (see Box 21.1). Estimates of the EER of four leading currencies

---

### Box 21.1   The exchange rate – basic definitions

#### Nominal exchange rate

*The exchange rate* is usually defined as the price of a unit of foreign currency in terms of domestic currency. It is the amount of domestic currency needed to buy one unit of foreign currency. For example, on 26 April 2003, the price of one US dollar was 0.91 euro. A British firm had to pay 69p sterling and a Japanese firm 132 yen. These rates are *bilateral* rates.

Exchange rates change over time. The euro was worth US $1.18 at its launch in 1999 but fell to US $0.82 in October 2000. By end-2003, this lost ground had been more than recovered, notwithstanding that the US and the euro area had broadly similar inflation rates.

#### Nominal effective exchange rate (EER)

Bilateral exchange rates do not all rise or fall in unison *vis-à-vis* any particular currency. In any period the dollar might become weaker against the Japanese yen but appreciate against the euro. If we want to comment on the overall weakness or strength of a currency, some way must be found of summarising the diverse pattern of depreciation and appreciation. The nominal effective exchange rate (EER) is designed to do precisely this.

*The nominal EER* is defined as *the exchange rate of the domestic currency vis-à-vis other currencies weighted by their share in the country's trade*. It is a weighted average of the value of one currency's bilateral exchange rates with a group of other currencies. Two issues have to be decided: (a) how many currencies to include in the index, and (b) the weight to be given to each currency.

Ideally all currencies should be included but, for reasons of practicality, the number of currencies in the EER 'basket' is usually limited to those that are of major importance to the country concerned.

To determine the weights to attach to each bilateral exchange rate, the simplest approach is to consider weightings based on the amount of trade between countries. Hence in the construction of an EER index for the US more weight would be given to Canada than to the UK or Germany, since Canada is the major trading partner of the US. An alternative weighting system would take account of total payments rather than just merchandise trade. In some instances more complex formulas can be employed, which incorporate information on third-country effects and the price sensitivity of different types of trade.

## Real effective exchange rates (REERs)

Real effective exchange rates (REERs) are used to assess the competitive position of a country relative to its competitors or sometimes to make inferences about how close actual exchange rates are to their long-run equilibrium level.

Suppose a country's nominal EER had devalued by 10 per cent but, during the same period, its domestic inflation was 10 per cent while its trading partners had zero inflation. Clearly there has been no devaluation in real terms. Any competitive advantage secured by the 10 per cent nominal devaluation has been counteracted by the 10 per cent increase in domestic prices relative to foreign prices. The real effective exchange rate (REER) takes account of price level changes between trading partners by adjusting the nominal EER by the ratio of foreign to domestic inflation.

The IMF's *International Financial Statistics* contains REERs based on a nominal EER index for 18 industrial countries and weights computed from its *Multilateral Exchange Rate Model* (MERM). The Bank of England, the European Central Bank, the Federal Reserve and J.P. Morgan also publish trade-weighted nominal and real effective exchange indices.

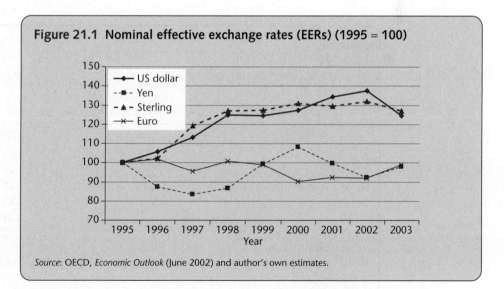

**Figure 21.1 Nominal effective exchange rates (EERs) (1995 = 100)**

*Source*: OECD, *Economic Outlook* (June 2002) and author's own estimates.

are shown in Figure 21.1 for the period 1995–2003. The EER of the yen fell by 24 per cent between 1998 and 2001. Sterling and the dollar exhibited strength up to 2002. The year 2003 saw a reversal of these trends. Thus EERs tend to fluctuate less than bilateral rates, but are still fairly volatile.

## Impact of exchange rate on firms

Imagine the case of a UK exporter selling to the US. From the point of view of the UK firm, what matters is the sterling value of the firm's export sales, but for the US consumer all that matters is the dollar price of the UK goods. The sterling/dollar exchange rate is of no relevance to the consumer's decision to buy the good. In setting price, therefore, the seller must take account of the degree of competition from competing dollar-priced goods. Suppose 100 units were sold at a price of $1.50 per unit, yielding total revenue of $150. The UK exporter converts this into sterling at the current exchange rate, assumed here to be 50p per dollar. Sales revenues in sterling of £75 can now be compared to the sterling costs of producing the exports (see Box 21.2). In the illustrative examples, profits earned amount to £5, yielding a profit/sales ratio of 7 per cent.

Consider now the effect of a sterling depreciation, from 50p to 70p per dollar. At the same dollar price of the good (i.e. $1.50 per unit), dollar sales revenue remains constant. But the sterling value of these sales rises from £75 to £105. The UK firm's export profits increase to £35, a seven-fold increase. The 40 per cent depreciation has generated a much larger percentage increase in profits. This *magnification effect* of depreciation on profit margins is a key factor in understanding why depreciation gives a strong incentive to higher exports.

A similar incentive effect applies to a domestic UK firm competing against goods imported from the US. The sterling depreciation makes the UK market *less* attractive to US exporters for exactly the same reason that it made the US market

### Box 21.2 How changes in the exchange rate affect profits

| | (A) Exchange rate $1 = £0.50 | (B) Exchange rate $1 = £0.70 |
|---|---|---|
| Sales in US market | 100 units @ $1.50 per unit = $150 | 100 units @ $1.50 per unit = $150 |
| US sales converted to sterling | £75 | £105 |
| Costs | £70 | £70 |
| Profit | £5 | £35 |

*Result*: Depreciation of sterling makes exports to the US market more profitable. It creates a strong incentive to increase export volume. This could be done by reducing the dollar price or by additional spending on marketing/distribution. Either way, sales of UK exports expand. This will lead to more jobs in the firm itself and to greater demand for intermediate goods from other British firms.

*more* attractive to UK exporters. This eases the pressure on UK import-competing firms from foreign competition. Some scope for raising sterling price may be exploitable. UK firms will have the opportunity of charging higher prices *and* expanding sales on the UK market.

Three major qualifications are needed in order to bring the example closer to reality:

- The sterling depreciation is unlikely to leave the UK firms' cost structure un-affected. The sterling price of their imported raw materials and intermediate inputs will rise as a result of the depreciation. Hence, some of their competitive advantage will be eroded.
- Employees may demand compensation for the price increases caused by the devaluation. This is especially likely to happen if prices of necessities such as food are affected.
- The appreciation of the dollar may force US producers to upgrade as a means of preserving market share. Vigorous productivity and quality improvements could compensate for the currency appreciation. This is precisely the spur which Porter sees as the advantageous side of strengthening the currency.

The combined effect of these negative factors could, in certain circumstances, offset the positive effects of depreciation on a country's cost-competitiveness.

## Taking all firms together

The arithmetical illustration above can easily be translated into the familiar demand and supply framework. Instead of confining the analysis to one firm, the various demand and supply responses of all firms can be added together by lateral summation. The UK export supply curve will be the sum of individual firms' responses to the sterling equivalent of the dollar price ($P_\$ \times$ exchange rate) while the US consumer's demand for UK exports is determined by the dollar price ($P_\$$). This situation is depicted in Figure 21.2.

A depreciation of sterling shifts the supply curve of UK goods outwards. This reflects the fact that, for each given dollar price, sterling profits rise as a result of the devaluation, and therefore more will be supplied. The depreciation has no impact on the US demand curve. The new equilibrium is at $E_1$. At $E_1$, the dollar price has fallen and the quantity exported has risen, as one would expect. An opposite effect applies to US exporters to the UK (Figure 21.3). Their supply curve moves inwards to the left. This happens because the dollar equivalent of the ster-ling price at $E_0$ has fallen as a result of the devaluation. The new equilibrium occurs at $E_1$. At this point, the sterling price is higher than its $E_0$ level but the dollar price is lower – bad news for the US exporter, but good news for the UK firms competing against imports. Exploiting the fact that import quantities have fallen from $OM_0$ to $OM_1$, import-competing firms are able to sell more at a higher sterling price.

Hence, a depreciation of sterling will, other things being equal, lead to:

- an increase in volume of UK exports,
- a reduction in the volume of UK imports,
- a fall in the dollar price and a rise in the sterling price of UK exports, and
- a rise in the sterling price and a fall in the dollar price of UK imports.

**Figure 21.2 Effect of sterling depreciation on UK exports to the US**

The depreciation shifts the UK supply curve downwards since UK exports are now cheaper in terms of dollars. The new equilibrium is at $E_1$. Total dollar value of exports may rise or fall depending on the price elasticity of demand for UK exports.

**Figure 21.3 Effect of sterling depreciation on US exports to the UK**

The depreciation raises the supply price of US goods in terms of sterling. The supply curve shifts upwards from SS to $S_1 S_1$ to give a new equilibrium at $E_1$. Quantity of imports falls from $OM_0$ to $OM_1$. Value of imports falls in dollar terms, but could fall or rise in terms of sterling depending on the price elasticity of the demand for imports.

All the above effects are favourable to the traded sector of the UK economy. This explains why domestic industry usually prefers a devaluation to an appreciation of the national currency.

## Effects on trade balance and the J-curve

So far, we have analysed the effects of devaluation on the volume of trade. The next step is to study the combined (net) effect on the value of exports and imports. Suppose the depreciation was caused by concern over the UK's current balance of payments deficit. Will a depreciation cause the gap between the value of imports and exports to narrow? The normal expectation is that it will. However, the ultimate impact depends on the price elasticities of demand in the two markets. If the export and import demand elasticities are low, then the possibility of a depreciation worsening the trade balance cannot be ruled out. In the immediate aftermath of a devaluation, the trade balance often does tend to worsen, taking a period of a year or more to improve. This rather counter-intuitive phenomenon of a negative short-term effect followed by a positive longer-term effect on the current account balance of payments is called the *J-curve effect* (Figure 21.4).

The J-curve effect can be illustrated by an extreme case. Suppose that the demand for imports into the UK had zero price elasticity of demand in the short run. In Figure 21.3, the curve DD would be vertical. A 10 per cent depreciation shifts the supply curve of US products up by 10 per cent. Despite the rise in price, the quantity sold remains unchanged. Hence, the sterling value of imports increases by the same percentage as the depreciation. Suppose now that, in the US, the demand curve for imports from the UK was also price inelastic. Then DD

**Figure 21.4 The J-curve**

Devaluation at A leads to a worsening of the current account in the initial period. After point B, the expected improvement begins to materialise. At point C, the devaluation has achieved its objective of eliminating the deficit and turning it into a surplus.

in Figure 21.2 would be vertical. The depreciation shifts the supply curve of UK exports to the right. Since the demand curve is vertical, the dollar price falls by the amount of the depreciation and export revenue in dollars falls by the devaluation percentage. In sterling terms, export receipts remain unchanged. Hence, if the elasticities of demand for exports and imports are each zero, the effect of depreciation of 10 per cent in sterling terms would be:

- a rise in value of imports of 10 per cent in sterling terms,
- no change in export receipts in sterling terms, and hence
- a worsening of the current account.

The J-curve does not relate just to devaluations: exactly the same line of reasoning might be applied to explain why an appreciation could, in the short run, lead to an improvement in the trade balance.[2] The J-curve effect will be observed whenever exporters set price in domestic currency (rather than pricing to market) and volumes react slowly to exchange rate changes.

The J-curve effect is an intriguing possibility, but it must not blind us to the fact that, in general, one can expect a depreciation to have a positive impact, and an appreciation to have a negative impact, on the trade balance. A strengthening currency will, over time, tend to erode export sales and profits. Profits may be further reduced by accounting rules which require a firm in an appreciating currency to write down holdings of foreign assets denominated in the depreciated currencies.[3]

## 21.2  Exchange rate theory

Exchange rate movements affect both the individual firm and the economy. Realignments of the exchange rate can be of positive benefit to an economy and can assist the process of adjustment to changes in a country's competitive position, to sectoral imbalances, or to a variety of demand and supply 'shocks'. However, excessive exchange rate volatility can have detrimental effects. It can lead to:

- disruption of price stability programmes,
- systemic instability, whereby changes in one country's currency cause problems for other countries ('contagion' effects),
- misalignments over periods of time leading to sub-optimal investment and marketing decisions, and
- transaction and hedging costs.

We need to understand, therefore, both how to define an equilibrium exchange rate and how to explain why large fluctuations from this level are frequently observed.

---

[2] A Rose and J. Yellen, 'Is there a J-curve?', *Journal of Monetary Economics* (July 1989).

[3] The literature on the J-curve continues to grow, and there is continuing disagreement about its practical relevance. See G. Leonard and A. Stockman, 'Current accounts and exchange rates: a new look at the evidence', *NBER Working Paper 8361*, July 2001.

## Purchasing power parity (PPP)

*Purchasing power parity* (PPP) links movements in exchange rates to differences between the price level in the domestic country and that of its major trading partners. PPP theory draws its inspiration from the *Law of One Price*. According to this law, if two goods are identical, they will sell at the same price. Otherwise it will pay someone to buy where it is cheaper and sell where it is dearer. *Arbitrage* is the process which ensures that the existence of any price differential between one country and another is exploited in order to make a riskless profit. Extended to all goods this becomes the theory of *absolute* PPP. Its central postulate is that the general level of prices, when converted to a common currency, will be the same in every country. If this were not so, arbitrageurs would have profitable incentives to trade, until the differential disappeared. From this, absolute PPP deduces that *the exchange rate will be such that the general level of prices will be the same in every country*:

$$P_d = ER \times P_f$$

where:  ER = exchange rate (units of domestic currency per unit of foreign currency)
$P_d$ = domestic price level
$P_f$ = foreign price level.

The Law of One Price, however, applies only in a rather unreal world of zero transport costs, absence of trade barriers, perfect competition and no possibility of market segmentation. If these conditions are not satisfied, price differentials will not be arbitraged out of existence.

A weaker version of PPP, *relative* PPP, states that *changes in the exchange rate are determined by the difference between relative domestic inflation rates in different countries*:

$$\%\Delta ER = \%\Delta P_d - \%\Delta P_f$$

where %Δ = change as per cent of starting level.

Proponents of this theory argue that, if the domestic inflation rate exceeds the foreign rate, exports and import-competing activities in the domestic currency will become price-uncompetitive. As a result, exports will fall, imports will increase and the current account balance will worsen. Furthermore, inward foreign direct investment will be discouraged by the high price of domestic assets and, for the same reason, outward direct investment will be encouraged. Foreign assets will become a more attractive buy; domestic assets will appear overpriced. Balance of payments pressures will eventually lead to pressures on the exchange rate. Hence, the negative relationship between relative inflation and a country's exchange rate. An alternative formulation of this principle is that *prices in different countries tend to change at the same rate over time, after correction for changes in the exchange rate.*[4]

Relative PPP is easy to understand in the context of goods which are easily traded between two countries. But the links between prices, the balance of

---

[4] This illustrates an important point: relative PPP can serve both as a theory of inflation and as a theory of exchange rate determination. The former aspect has a decisive bearing on a country's choice of an exchange rate regime, as will be seen in Chapter 22.

payments and exchange rates operate more slowly and problematically in the case of *nontraded goods and services*, such as housing, medical services, education and government administration.[5] Suppose house prices were rising faster in the UK than in the US. Since houses cannot be physically exchanged between the two countries, the rise in UK house prices will not affect the UK's balance of payments: UK imports and exports will not be *directly* affected. There could, of course, be *indirect* effects; the higher cost of housing could generate demands for compensatory pay rises, which would impact on manufacturers' costs – but these indirect effects will take time to work through. Hence, the exchange rates are likely to respond more to prices of traded goods than to the overall price index.[6]

In an open trading environment, PPP would be expected to hold at a bilateral level, and it is usually tested on this basis. Where PPP is calculated with more than one trading partner, each with a different inflation rate, a formula needs to be found for applying it at a multilateral level. Foreign inflation is then defined as the *trade-weighted average* of trading partners' inflation, and the corresponding exchange rate is the *effective exchange rate* (EER).

## Balance of payments and monetary approaches

An alternative to PPP as an explanation of the equilibrium exchange rate is the *balance of payments approach*. This theory focuses more directly on the link between the trade/current account balance, modified to take account of long-term capital flows, and movement in exchange rates. According to this view, a country with a persistent deficit is likely to devalue and a country with a persistent surplus is likely to revalue. This approach differs from, but is consistent with, PPP theory. PPP states that if country A has higher inflation than country B, A's currency will have to depreciate because it will run into a deficit if it fails to devalue. The balance of payments approach incorporates this PPP view, but allows for the possibility that exchange rates are affected by 'real' factors, as well as relative inflation rates. Examples of these factors (or economic *fundamentals*) are:

● changes in the growth rate,
● changes in the composition of aggregate demand,
● equity and bond market performance,
● size of budget deficits and public debt, and
● governance and political stability.

Each of these factors can have major implications for the balance of payments, and hence for a country's exchange rate.[7]

Probing deeper, one might ask why countries have current account deficits and/or different inflation rates. The *monetary approach to the balance of payments* emphasises the role of money supply growth rates in the home country relative to foreign countries. Recall that more money supply implies lower interest rates

---

[5] The 'price' of non-marketed public sector output is defined as the cost of producing it which in practice is often tied to the remuneration of its providers.
[6] Even this can involve minor statistical complications if the basket of goods consumed differs between countries and relative goods' prices are changing.
[7] This is not to say that PPP theory ignores such economic fundamentals, since all of these factors affect inflation, and hence PPP.

and cheaper credit. If money supply rises faster than real income, pressure builds up on domestic prices, which makes exports less competitive and imports more competitive. The real balance effect, generated by the rise in money supply relative to prices, further increases import demand. A depreciation of the exchange rate is necessary in order to restore the balance of payments to equilibrium (see Chapter 20). Hence, the chain of causation proceeds from increases in money supply to a current account deficit, to exchange rate depreciation.[8] By the same reasoning, a restrictive monetary policy reduces money supply, raises interest rates, diminishes import demand and improves the current account. Although the theory is plausible, empirical tests of the monetary theory have not been successful in explaining exchange rate variations (Box 21.3). Nevertheless, more comprehensive asset-based theories have developed from it which have been helpful in explaining short-run oscillations in exchange rate.

## Empirical analysis of PPP

Empirical studies have shown that absolute PPP does not work. Given the strict assumptions needed for the theory to be valid, this is not surprising. Readers familiar with *The Economist*'s Big Mac index will appreciate the shortcomings of the Law of One Price as applied to the price of hamburgers.[9] Comprehensive price comparisons, covering 2500 consumer goods and services, 250 types of machinery and equipment and 30 occupations in the public sector, tell a similar story. Actual exchange rates diverge considerably from what one would 'expect' on the basis of PPP.

Empirical PPP estimates nevertheless have many practical uses. They are widely used for comparing living standards between countries (as we have seen in Chapter 2). For example, the European Commission uses income comparisons based on PPP rather than current exchange rates in analysing regional convergence trends. *Eurostat* publishes data on the cost of living in the 15 capitals of the EU. PPP figures are also used to calculate cost of living allowances for staff working overseas. Imagine the case of an executive about to be posted to Tokyo. The executive's current US salary is $50,000 p.a. How much yen would be required to provide a standard of living in Tokyo equivalent to that provided by a salary of $50,000 in the US? At the 2002 market rate of exchange (125 yen to the dollar), the answer would be 6 million. Consulting PPP data, however, we find a very different answer. As Table 21.1 shows, the PPP rate was 147 yen per dollar. Hence on this basis the executive would need over 7 million yen in order to have maintained the US standard of living. Clearly there is room for negotiation![10]

---

[8] In theory, balance of payments adjustment can also occur via interest rates.

[9] In 1986 *The Economist* launched a Big Mac index. The idea was that McDonald's went to great pains to ensure consistent quality no matter where the Big Mac was sold. Hence, the Law of One Price would suggest that the domestic price in each country multiplied by the dollar exchange rate should equal the US price ($2.71 in 2003). Needless to say, no such correspondence is found. The local price of a hamburger depends on nontraded inputs such as rents and labour, and both taxes and other degrees of competition differ between countries. For these and many other reasons, the Law of One Price and, by extension, PPP do not hold.

[10] In 1985, when the dollar was strong, the PPP rate was 222 yen to the dollar, but at that time the actual exchange rate, at 237 yen to the dollar, was *higher* than the PPP rate. (In terms of our example, the firm should have paid the executive fewer yen than the market rate translation.)

---

**Box 21.3** **The monetary approach to the balance of payments**

The monetary approach to the balance of payments can formally be summarised as follows.

Begin with the standard relative PPP equation:

$$e = p - p^* \tag{1}$$

where: $e$ = the exchange rate (per cent change)
$p$ = the domestic inflation rate (per cent change)
$p^*$ = foreign inflation rate (per cent change)

(all variables are expressed in log form indicating annual percentage change; * denotes foreign).

According to the classical monetary theory, inflation is determined by the excess of money supply growth ($m$) over growth in money demand. The latter is determined by growth in income ($y$) and the level of interest ($i$), multiplied by their respective elasticities of demand, $k$ and $h$:

$$p = m - k.y - h.i \tag{2}$$

$$p^* = m^* - k.y^* - h.i^* \tag{3}$$

Putting these three equations together we obtain:

$$e = p - p^* = (m - m^*) - k(y - y^*) - h(i - i^*) \tag{4}$$

Coefficients $k$ and $h$ are assumed to be the same in each country.

Equations such as (4) have been estimated, using $e$ as the dependent variable, with mixed and generally weak results. One obvious explanation for this is that deviations of actual exchange rates from their PPP-ordained level are common. Another is that potentially crucial variables, such as exchange rate expectations based on an assessment of the economic fundamentals, have been excluded. Third, there are long and variable lags between changes in money supply and changes in prices. For these reasons, it is not surprising that econometric studies have given only weak support to the monetary approach to the balance of payments. Nonetheless, the monetary approach marks the beginning of a new theoretical perspective, an asset approach to determining the exchange rate, which has proved fruitful in explaining the volatile behaviour of current markets.

*Source*: R. Dornbusch, Foreword in J. Bhandari and B. Putnam, *Economic Interdependence and Flexible Exchange Rates* (Cambridge, MA: MIT Press, 1983).

Discrepancies between the PPP and the actual exchange rate are common. The key question is whether such discrepancies tell anything about the likely future direction of the actual exchange rate.

Relative PPP indices have yielded mixed results in analysing and forecasting exchange rates. A study of exchange rate change in major currencies published in the early 1980s referred to the 'collapse' of PPP.[11] Later studies indicate equally unfavourable results when applied to the experience of the dollar, yen and

---

[11] J. Frenkel, 'The collapse of PPPs during the 1970s', *European Economic Review* (May 1981). The opposite conclusion – that PPPs hold in the long term – is advocated in A. Taylor, 'A century of purchasing-power parity', *Review of Economics and Statistics*, February 2002.

**Table 21.1 Purchasing power parities and actual exchange rates per US dollar**

|  | Actual exchange rate | | | | PPP | | | |
|---|---|---|---|---|---|---|---|---|
|  | 1985 | 1990 | 1995 | 2002 | 1985 | 1990 | 1995 | 2002 |
| US | 1.00 | 1.00 | 1.00 | 1.00 | 1.00 | 1.00 | 1.00 | 1.00 |
| Japan | 237 | 144 | 94 | 125 | 222 | 195 | 170 | 147 |
| UK | 0.77 | 0.56 | 0.63 | 0.66 | 0.57 | 0.60 | 0.65 | 0.65 |
| Euro | n.a. | n.a. | n.a. | 1.06 | n.a. | n.a. | 0.93 | 0.88 |

Source: OECD, *Main Economic Indicators* (Paris, various editions); OECD, *OECD Economic Outlook* (Paris, various editions).

Deutschmark. Relative PPP fared better when tested against the experience of smaller European countries. This probably reflects the fact that closer trade ties, lower transport costs and policy convergence provided a more favourable environment for arbitrage, which is the key mechanism driving the PPP model. Also, PPP performs better when tested against the weighted average EER rather than against bilateral rates.

One long-held objection to the PPP hypothesis is that productivity growth in the traded sectors of a rapidly growing economy exceeds that in nontraded sectors. Wage increases in the former feed into the nontraded sector, leading to higher inflation and, by extension, a higher real EER, in the country concerned. Thus, Japan's superior growth rates prior to 1990 resulted in a systematic trend appreciation of the yen. This is the *Balassa–Samuelson effect*. It is often cited as a reason for expecting the new Eastern European entrants into the EU to experience both higher inflation than the EU average and a higher REER over time.

PPP tends to perform poorly when large structural shocks occur, such as the oil price increases in the 1970s, a rapid increase in unemployment or a deterioration in a country's fiscal position. In these circumstances the market's perception of the economy – its capacity to adhere to a low inflation regime, its commitment to finance its debts, etc. – undergoes significant change. Actual or anticipated political instability also impacts severely on the exchange rate. (These events may not necessarily affect the *present* current account balance, but they could have important implications for the *future* balance.) It is the anticipation of future difficulties which motivates capital flows and moves the exchange rate. Furthermore, PPP is not useful in the very short term, which is the trader's perspective. Most dealers regard it as at best a proximate indicator of the future exchange rate with a wide ±25 per cent of plausible variation for the exchange rate over the medium term.

Yet, for all its limitations, PPP analysis provides essential input to understanding exchange rate trends:

- It works well in the long run, especially in conditions of very large differences in inflation.
- It provides a guide to the general trend in exchange rates, in particular where the main changes underlying the trend are of monetary origin.
- In a quasi-fixed exchange rate system, inflation differences give a useful indicator of pressure for currency realignment.
- For the conduct of macroeconomic policy, it is an important reminder that the exchange rate and the price level cannot be divorced from each other. Policies

which affect the trend of domestic (relative to foreign) prices are likely to affect the exchange rate.

PPP is an important benchmark for the analysis of movements in the exchange rate, particularly in the medium to long run and as a gauge of international price competitiveness. But there is still the problem of explaining divergence from PPP. In a floating exchange rate system, short-term currency volatility tends to overpower everything else, including PPP. Why is this so?

## 21.3 Capital flows and exchange rate volatility

Knowledge of a country's economic 'fundamentals' – its inflation rate, balance of payments, growth rate, and so on – is a necessary input for understanding exchange rate movements. But it is not sufficient. To understand the reasons for exchange rate volatility, we must study the determinants of international capital flows. These flows, not sudden changes in economic fundamentals, are responsible for most of the turbulence observed in the foreign exchange markets.

The growing volume of capital movements has forced a rethink of traditional exchange rate theory. The PPP and balance of payments approaches concentrate on the equilibrating role of the exchange rate in balancing *flows* of foreign exchange. The modern approach emphasises the role of the exchange rate in bringing supply and demand of domestic and foreign *assets* into equilibrium. The assets in question consist of cash, bills and bonds of varying maturity and equities held in different currencies. Investment in these assets is highly mobile, and moves to wherever the expected return is greatest. The expected return is determined by: (a) the difference between the present interest rate at home and abroad, and (b) expected future changes in exchange rates, interest rates, probability of repayment, etc. Thus, expectations about the future play a key role in determining the present deployment of assets. Any change in these expectations will call forth portfolio adjustment by domestic and foreign investors. During periods dominated by unexpected events ('news'), asset prices will be subject to frequent and substantial change. Hence, the exchange rate will exhibit a high degree of volatility. Since, by definition, 'news' cannot be predicted on the basis of past information, *by and large fluctuations of exchange rates associated with 'news' will be equally unpredictable*. Also, if 'news' of a significant nature occurs often, exchange rate fluctuations will be not only unpredictable, but also very large.

Of course, current account transactions are also, to some extent, influenced by expectations. The decision to enter an export market or to expand capacity is based not just on present prices and costs, but also on the expected evolution of the price–cost matrix into the future. These predictions are formed under the same conditions of uncertainty as apply to capital transactions. The crucial distinction, however, concerns the *different speed of response between asset and goods prices*. As expectations change in response to unexpected events ('news' and 'shocks'), owners of capital can take lightning decisions on how to allocate their assets. Flows of goods and services are much slower to change. Companies are loath to abandon hard-won market share. They expect that exchange rate changes will be reversed, or else compensated by offsetting changes in domestic costs. Price stability for certain products can be an important attribute in itself, and price changes are costly to implement. It takes time to enter and to exit a market. For these reasons, the prices of most goods and services are less responsive than asset prices to changes in expectations. Short-run asset movements, therefore, will tend to dominate current account transactions, and the exchange rate may frequently change in response to expectations, even if relative product prices do not change. This explains why breaches of the PPP rule are common in the short run.

## Interest rate parity

There are two main determinants of international portfolio capital movements: (a) the difference between interest rates at home and abroad, and (b) expectations about future exchange rates. Suppose, for example, that the rate of interest is 5 per cent in the UK and 1 per cent in Japan. Assuming capital between these countries is free to move, the question arises as to why fund managers do not immediately reallocate capital from Japan, where it is earning only 1 per cent per annum, to the UK, where it could earn 5 per cent per annum. Rational investors must have some reason for permitting this apparent anomaly to continue. According to the theory of interest rate parity, the reason is that the yen is expected to appreciate relative to sterling. This expected appreciation compensates exactly for the interest forgone by keeping money in Japan. The equilibrium condition is:

domestic interest rate *less* foreign interest rate = expected change in exchange rate.

This relationship is known as the *Uncovered Interest Rate Parity* (UIP).[12]

What determines exchange rate expectations? Obviously, they are much influenced by systematic changes in economic fundamentals such as persistently high balance of payments deficits, inflation, money supply growth or government budget deficits. One way to quantify the effects of these different influences would be to regress the interest rate differential on a selection of 'fundamentals'. Empirical analysis, however, repeatedly yields disappointing results in such cases. Economic fundamentals do play a role, but that role is difficult to quantify, and accounts for only part of total exchange rate variation.

One problem might be that we are using the wrong dependent variable. If the interest parity condition does not hold, interest rate differences may not be a good proxy for the market's (unobservable) exchange rate expectations. An alternative approach is to use the *forward exchange rate* as a proxy for exchange rate expectations. The forward exchange rate represents the rate at which, say, dollars can be traded for pounds today, deliverable at a specific date in the *future*. If that rate were, in any one transaction, considered too high, entrepreneurs would enter the market in the expectation of making a profit. In so doing, the market price will shift in a direction closer to their expectations. Hence, the forward rate for each time-period in the future represents the market's best guess of what the future spot rate will be. It closely resembles the currency forecasts regularly compiled by financial journals.

---

[12] It is also called the International Fisher Equation, after Irving Fisher, the originator of the idea that the nominal interest rate is divisible into a real rate and a premium due to expected inflation or, in this case, currency depreciation.

The *Covered Interest Rate Parity* (IRP) theory states that there will be a close tie between the forward exchange rate and differences in the interest rates; otherwise opportunities for riskless profit arise by arbitraging between the spot and forward market.

A practical example may illustrate this point. On 31 July 2000, one-year international interest rates were as reported in Table 21.2.[13] Sterling interest rates were 0.5 percentage points lower than the dollar and 6 percentage points higher than the yen. Focusing on the sterling–yen relationship, recall that the explanation why fund managers do not move capital to the UK is that they expect sterling to fall relative to the yen. We now check if this is true, on the assumption that the forward rate is a measure of exchange rate expectations. The theory predicts that as the market expects sterling to depreciate relative to the yen – and that the amount of the expected depreciation should be just about the same as the difference in interest rates (6 per cent) – the yen should be selling at 6 per cent premium relative to sterling.

The data indicate that this presumption is approximately correct. The spot rate was 164 yen per pound. The yen was trading in the forward market at 154, a 6 per cent premium. This signalled the market's belief that the yen would appreciate relative to sterling over the year.

The next step is to ask a much researched question: how well does the forward exchange rate track future movements in the spot exchange rate? The answer can be found by comparing the forward market rate at time $t$ for delivery at time $(t + 1)$, $f_t^{t+1}$, with the future spot rate, $S_{t+1}$. *The results indicate that the forward rate tracks the future spot rate very poorly.* This means that, even if it were possible to explain the forward rate by exchange rate fundamentals, we would still be unable to explain actual movements in the spot rate. Interestingly, however, the results also show that the forward rate is an *unbiased* predictor of the future rate (see Box 21.4). This suggests that there is no systematic source of bias in the forward rate's predictions of the future.[14] But, regardless of the bias of the forecasts, the

---

**Table 21.2  An example of the forward market**

|  | Interest rate |  | Interest difference |
| --- | --- | --- | --- |
| Pound sterling | 6.5% |  | – |
| Yen | 0.4% |  | –6.1% |
| US dollar | 7.0% |  | +0.5% |

|  | Spot | 1-year forward | % change |
| --- | --- | --- | --- |
| Yen | 164.1 | 154.5 | +6.0 |
| US dollar | 1.498 | 1.507 | –0.6 |

---

[13] International money rates are the interest rates which deposits in each currency would attract on the international market (i.e. free of any distortions from domestic authorities). By 2003, interest rates had declined in both the US and UK. This has made it even more difficult to ascribe exchange rate variations to differences in interest rates. In general, the convergence of fundamentals in the major currencies has made 'white noise' and speculation more important, and fundamentals such as PPP and IRP less important, as a determinant of exchange rate changes.

[14] If bias did exist, that would be a challenge to find the missing systematic factors. Note, incidentally, that interest rate parity is not expected to hold exactly. Central bank intervention and transactions costs alone will prevent complete parity being realised.

## Box 21.4 — Are foreign exchange markets efficient?

The foreign exchange market is efficient if it fully and correctly utilises all available information in forecasting exchange rates. If the market uses the best possible forecast of future exchange rates, then no superior forecast exists, and there can be no sustained advantage to speculation. In formal terms this can be expressed as follows.

*Market efficiency* implies that:

$$f^t_{t+1} = E_t[S_{t+1}] + P_t + u_{t+1}$$

where: $f^t_{t+1}$ = forward $(t+1)$ market price at time $t$

$E_t[S_{t+1}]$ = a mathematical expectation conditional on the information set available at time $t$

$S$ = the spot rate

$P$ = the market risk premium

$u$ = a random variable.

The *efficient market hypothesis* states that $u_t$ is a random variable with mean zero (white noise). In other words:

> the gap between the forward rate and the spot rate actually ruling when the forward contract matures is the sum of two components: a completely random expectational error and a risk premium.

The forward rate is an unbiased predictor of the spot rate provided the investors are risk-neutral, implying $P$ is constant, i.e. actual change in spot rate = expected future rate plus or minus a random error.

The forward rate, however, often fails to detect key turning points. The rule-of-thumb hypothesis that $S$ follows a random walk, i.e.

$$S_t = S_{t-1} + u_t$$

has been found to slightly outperform a number of different models (Meese and Rogoff, 1983).

Is $u_t$ random? Most studies suggest that it is, but there is also some evidence that currency markets have become less efficient in the last decade, contrary to what one would expect. One way to test for this is to examine expectations, as found, say, in the *Eurocurrency Investors Review* and other summaries of exchange rate forecasts, to see if they are 'rational'. If they are, the difference between $E[S_{t+1}]$ and $S_{t+1}$ should be the random variable $u_t$.

The problem with this test is that there is a wide divergence of forecasts, they can change rapidly and they are difficult to summarise. The median forecast rate was chosen by Frankel and Froot (1987). Their survey revealed a persistent bias in respondents' expectations. But, unless we can identify an alternative which will consistently outperform the models used for such forecasts, knowing that the forecasts are biased may be of little practical use. The authors ruefully concluded that: 'there is nothing in our results to suggest that it is *easy* to make money speculating in the foreign exchange markets' (p. 295).

*Sources:* R. Meese and K. Rogoff, 'Empirical exchange rate models of the seventies: Do they fit out of sample?', *Journal of International Economics* (1983); J.A. Frankel and K.A. Froot, 'Using survey data to test standard propositions regarding exchange rate expectations', *American Economic Review* (1987).

variance of the forecasts and of the subsequent spot exchange rates is extremely high. This is because exchange rates are affected by shocks which are intrinsically unpredictable.

Attempts to relate exchange rate 'overshooting', defined as excessive volatility in relation to its long-run equilibrium value, to changes in economic fundamentals indicate that exchange rates are far more volatile than the underlying fundamentals. The fundamentals do sometimes change rapidly and unexpectedly, and 'shocks' and 'news' undoubtedly contribute to volatility. But the 'news' component in any situation is difficult to estimate, and no combination of 'news' or 'shock' variables has yet been able to explain comprehensively the volatility of exchange rates.[15] Since informational surprises about fundamentals do not explain exchange rate changes, the search for an explanation has extended in two directions.

*'Bubbles'* and *'bandwagons'* refer to the possibility that investors behave irrationally. Prices are chased upwards for no well-based reason, the upward spiral is fuelled by the bandwagon effect or herd instinct – both features of many speculative markets. Famous examples of bubbles in earlier centuries include the Dutch Tulip Bubble in 1636, the Mississippi Land Scheme in Paris in 1719–20, the related South Sea Bubble in London during the same period, and the Railway Mania in England in 1846–7. In each case frenetic and apparently irrational price surges were followed by a massive price collapse (hence the bubble analogy). Bubbles are not exclusively a phenomenon of the remote past. The property booms of the 1980s in the UK and the US had similar characteristics. Bubbles and bandwagons also affect currency markets. Much forex dealing defies rational explanation. Investors move in because everyone else is doing so. One irreverent insider described the market as 'a disparate group of highly-paid people with a common economic purpose but with the collective intelligence of a baby trout'.[16] But all investors in bubbles are not necessarily irrational. It may make good sense to invest in a bubble, provided the investor knows when to sell out! Although it was common knowledge that the dollar was overvalued in the mid-1980s, it was not rational for any one trader to sell dollars, nor for any fund committee to order its manager to sell its dollar holdings. The reason was that participants did not know the precise time at which the trend reversal would take place. The time-horizon of the investor is a critical variable – many traders and investors take a very short-run view.[17]

*Technical analysis*, or chartism, is widely used by foreign exchange traders.[18] Basically, it involves the use of graphical representations of past price fluctuations

---

[15] Often what matters is not the change in the economic fundamental, but whether it is higher or lower than 'expected' by market.

[16] M. Baker, *A Fool and his Money* (London: Orion, 1995). Inevitably, there are different views as to whether exchange markets fluctuate more than underlying fundamentals; empirical tests have been inconclusive (see R. Meese, 'Testing for bubbles in the foreign exchange markets: a case of sparkling rates', *Journal of Political Economy*, April 1986). There are, however, such things as 'rational stochastic speculative bubbles'!

[17] Another example of apparently irrational behaviour is the *peso problem*. From April 1954 to August 1976, the spot peso exchange rate was fixed at 0.08 dollars per peso. Despite the spot rate being constant during this period of over 20 years, futures and forward contracts sold at a discount. This reflected the small probability of a large, discrete shift in the value of one or more of the 'fundamentals' which would force a devaluation of the exchange rate. Up to 1976 it appeared that the forward rate was an inefficient (biased) estimator; after, the market was seen to be right.

[18] Chartism was originated around the late 1800s by Charles Dow. He formulated a basic theory of trading which is a forerunner of modern technical analysis and produced a number of rules for forecasting, all connected with the identification of trends in prices.

for forecasting purposes. Foreign exchange traders use technical analysis for general guidance. The key to successful technical analysis is the accurate and consistent determination of current trends. The aim is not to explain but to identify trends from careful examination of past data, including analysis of moving averages, past peaks and troughs. Exchange rates are often strongly influenced by support and resistance points, that is, specific rates which are hard to breach, because at that rate the market tends to consider the exchange rate too low or too high. Resistance and support points tend to congregate around whole numbers or those with a special resonance. The reasons for this resistance have to do with market sentiment rather than with meticulous examination of fundamentals. Likewise, a falling currency will often receive support from the market after a certain level of decline has been reported. Experience shows that support and resistance points are subject to change once the market is given sufficient time to adjust to a new set of parities.

Chartism has an exotic jargon of its own: *head and shoulders, reverse head and shoulders, double bottom, flags* and *pennants*. For all this, chartists have had mixed results in forecasting exchange rates. Some individual chartists have scored very highly, but the variance is high and there is a low degree of consensus among the various forecasters. Like the theories based on economic fundamentals, chartism cannot be ignored – but neither can it be relied upon. [19]

The coexistence in the foreign exchange market of chartists and 'fundamentalists', the former relying on technical analysis and the latter relying on analysis of economic fundamentals, can give rise to considerable instability of its own. Some experiments have been made to apply chaos theory to explain exchange rate gyrations. [20] Work in this area is still in its infancy.

A point of practical importance is whether exchange rate volatility 'washes out' over time. The evidence suggests that it does not. Sustained differences persist in the average annual return between different currencies. The variance is highest in the case of the dollar, yen and sterling. Over a long period, a difference of even one percentage point matters a great deal. Hence, although often a frustrating exercise, the reward for getting exchange rate forecasts right is sufficiently high to justify continuing investment into finding a better predictive model. The persistence of different long-run rates of return, after correcting for variance, reinforces the view that exchange rate volatility can lead to *exchange rate misalignments*, sustained over fairly long periods. Exchange rate misalignments cannot be predicted in advance, they cannot be cheaply covered against, and they can add significantly to the difficulties of a company trading on international markets.

---

[19] M. Taylor and H. Allen, 'Chart analysis and the foreign exchange market', *Bank of England Quarterly Bulletin* (November 1989).

[20] Systems that exhibit sensitivity to the initial conditions and that show a seeming randomness or irregularity in their trajectory are called *chaotic systems*. The outcome of a chaotic system can be predicted (it is by definition a deterministic process), but for a relatively short time only. The overall long-term evolution of the system in a general sense can also be predicted. For an application of this approach to exchange rates, see P. De Grauwe, H. Dewachter and M. Embrechts, *Exchange Rate Theory: Chaotic models of foreign exchange markets* (Oxford: Blackwell, 1993).

## 21.4 Strategies for coping with exchange rate risk

Faced with continuing uncertainty in exchange rates, the first priority of most companies is to protect themselves against the risks of unexpected exchange rate changes. Managers frequently assert that they are in business to trade and manufacture, not to speculate in foreign currency.[21] A wide range of instruments can be used to close off exchange risks. However, the more volatile the exchange rates (hence risk), the more resources have to be spent in order to hedge this risk.[22]

### Using the forward market

The forward and futures markets offer a number of instruments to companies wishing to reduce their exposure to exchange rate risk.

A foreign exchange *forward contract* is an over-the-counter (OTC) transaction between a bank and its customer (a company wishing to minimise exchange rate risk), whereby the bank agrees to buy or sell a specified amount of currency at an agreed rate for delivery at a specified future date. This is a highly flexible instrument which can be tailored to individual companies' requirements – forward contracts are flexible on the principal amount, on start and expiration dates, and they can be written in all major currencies. The foreign exchange will be transacted at the agreed forward contract rate irrespective of any exchange rate movements over the lifetime of the contract. In this way, the forward contract eliminates exchange rate risk for the company.

Returning to the Table 21.2 example of the forward market on 31 July 2000, note that the yen was trading at a premium *vis-à-vis* the pound sterling, i.e. the forward rate for delivery in one year's time was 154 yen per pound sterling, compared with the spot rate of 164 per pound. By contrast, the US dollar was trading at a *discount*, i.e. the forward rate for delivery of dollars in 12 months was 1.507 dollars per pound, compared with a spot rate of 1.498 per pound.

The forward market enables companies to close off any risk of loss from movements in the exchange rate. The downside of the transaction is that it also closes off the possibility of gain. Thus, suppose the yen were to appreciate more than the forward rate indicates; an exporter to Japan would have done better by converting yen at the time of sale (one year later) into the domestic currency. An exporter to the US who had believed that the dollar would depreciate by less than the forward rate would also have made money. Often firms worry about the danger of losing advantage to competitors that are less risk-averse and more ready to gamble on their instincts about future exchange rate developments.

Forward transactions cover the firm's exchange risk by transferring the risk to the bank supplying the forward contract. Consider a UK bank which agrees to sell euro three months forward to a domestic company at a rate of 60p per euro. The forward contract eliminates exchange rate risk for the company, but it places the bank in an exposed position. If the euro appreciates, the bank will lose money.

---

[21] J. Roberts, *$1000 Billion a Day: Inside the foreign exchange markets* (London: HarperCollins, 1995); also M. Goldstein *et al.*, *International Capital Markets: Part 1. Exchange rate movements and international capital flows* (Washington, DC: IMF, 1993).

[22] Stable exchange rates would thus benefit all firms in the long run (except banks).

Prudence dictates that the bank should take action to limit its exposure. To do this, it will engage in offsetting transactions in the wholesale market. A German bank which had offered forward contracts to its domestic customer in the opposite direction of the UK bank, for example, would be an ideal partner in such a deal. A *swap* could be arranged on the wholesale market which matched each currency exchange with a reverse exchange on a forward basis. Many forward contracts are written as part of a swap. Since the forward rate is agreed for both contracts, there is no exchange risk for the participants. Swaps are flexible and are used to hedge against specific foreign exchange (forex) risk and maturity exposures; they can also move exposure forward or back in time.[23] Thus, behind every retail transaction, there is usually a large set of associated wholesale transactions. The value of the latter greatly exceeds the value of retail foreign exchange transactions.

A foreign exchange *futures contract* is similar to a forward contract in that it secures a fixed exchange rate for receipt or payment at a future date. Unlike forward contracts, futures contracts are traded on the open market. To enhance marketability, they are standardised with regard to expiration dates and currencies. They cannot be tailored to a company's individual needs in the way a forward contract can. For this reason, futures contracts are used primarily by forex traders rather than by individual firms seeking to cover risk. Most futures contracts are 'closed out' before they mature (i.e. sold back to the bank or to another company).

## Options and hedges

Forward and futures contracts offer protection against forex risk to a company which has a definite commitment to make or receive a future payment in foreign currency. Options are resorted to in cases where future payments or receipts are uncertain.

Consider a company that is tendering for a foreign contract for consultancy work to be carried out at some future date. The company has to base its quotation on some estimated future rate for foreign currency. The company could sell its anticipated foreign currency income forward in order to cover its revenue side, but failure to secure the contract would leave it in a highly exposed position.

To avoid this risk, the company can enter into an *options contract* with the bank, securing a fixed rate for a fixed fee. A foreign currency options contract gives the company the right to buy (*call* option) or sell (*put* option) a specified amount of foreign currency *on* or *before* a specified expiration date at a fixed *strike* price. Unlike the forward or futures contract, the company is not obliged to exercise the option unless it chooses to do so. Options are written on either US or European exercise terms. Under US terms the option can be exercised at any time prior to maturity; under European terms it can be exercised only upon maturity. Corporate treasurers rely almost exclusively on options structured specifically for their needs (over-the-counter options or OTCs), while large institutional investors rely more on traded options. Option contracts have been on the market since the

---

[23] Banks in this situation reduce one set of risks but add another. This risk, called *counterparty risk*, concerns the possibility that the contracts entered into by the bank will not be honoured.

early 1980s. Because of the introduction of more stringent accounting rules, options have lost some of their appeal to corporate treasurers in recent years.

The company in our example would buy a *put* option from the bank. This confers a right, but not an obligation, to sell the foreign currency at the predetermined rate. The company could then be in a position to tender for the foreign contract without fear of exchange rate risk. If the contract is not awarded, the company merely lets the currency option expire – or, if it pays to do so, it will sell the option on at a profit. If the tender is successful, the company will hold on to its option until the payment date under the contract. Currency options are an ideal instrument for managing the downside risk arising from exchange rate movements, while leaving open the upside potential for profits. The most an options purchaser can lose is the premium paid for the contract, while potential gains depend on the spread between the contract exchange rate (the 'strike') and the spot rate.[24] An illustrative example of the possible outcomes is given in Box 21.5.

The above instruments may be used by companies to *hedge* risks associated with exchange rate changes.

> Hedging refers to the process whereby a company offsets an existing exposure in a given currency by taking an opposite position in that currency with the same or similar risk.

Given the wide array of foreign exchange instruments available and the explosion in derivatives trading, there are many possible hedging strategies: forward contracts, futures, swaps, options, cross-currency swaps and even swaptions. Trade in currency options alone is doubling every three years and new instruments are being regularly devised. An example is the foreign exchange swaps involving the exchange of the principal and interest payments backed by a loan in one currency for the principal and interest payments on a loan in a second currency. Swaps allow firms to lower their cost of foreign exchange management in situations where the firm is better known and has easier credit terms in one market than another. They are often used to provide long-term financing in foreign markets where the forward market might not be developed (Box 21.6).

## Internal methods of managing exposure

In addition to the use of market instruments, a firm might also choose to control currency risk through internal mechanisms of exposure management. These include netting, matching, leading and lagging, pricing policy and asset/liability management. These methods may not always be available to the firm – their use is restricted in some countries. For instance, in a country with no proper forex market and strict foreign exchange controls, it will be essential to develop internal methods of hedging.

Two or more companies which trade with each other might engage in a *netting* agreement, whereby they cancel out amounts payable and receivable, leaving only the difference to be settled. Similarly, it makes sense for an individual company to *match* its outflows and inflows in a given currency, using US dollar receipts to make US dollar payments, for example. Both these methods substantially reduce reliance on the foreign exchange markets.

---

[24] Hence options contracts offer significant opportunity for speculative gain.

**Box 21.5** **A foreign currency options contract**

A British company is tendering for a German contract and it enters into a *put* option, giving it the right to sell €160,000 on or before a date one year from now at a strike euro/sterling price of €1.60 per pound sterling. The cost of the option is a 3 per cent premium or fee on the capital value, i.e. €4800 or £3000.

**1. Where the tender is successful and the euro depreciates to 1.80**

(a) Company receives €160,000 as a result of the contract.
(b) Exercises its put option and receives £ at €1.60 per pound   =   £100,000
(c) Market value of €160,000 at spot rate of 1.80   =   £88,888
(d) Profit from exercising option   =   £11,112
(e) Cost of option   =   £3,000
(f) Net profit   =   £8,112

Note that this is a *notional* profit. Had the company not taken out the options contract, it would have received only £88,888 instead of £100,000, a difference of £11,112. From this saving, we must deduct the cost of the option, £3000. Thus the net gain from having the option is £8112.

**2. Where the tender is successful and the euro appreciates to 1.40**

(a) Company receives €160,000 as a result of the contract.
(b) Does not exercise option, but pays cost of option, i.e. £3000.

In the case of an appreciation of the euro, the company is better-off to let the option lapse. Under the options contract, the company would have received £100,000 for the €160,000, but by selling the euro on the spot market it could obtain £114,286. Although the £3000 premium must automatically be paid, the gain from selling at the new spot rate of 1.40 compensates for this. Thus the company makes a net gain of £11,286.

**3. Where the tender is unsuccessful and the euro depreciates to 1.80**

(a) Company does not receive contract.
(b) Cost of purchasing €160,000 at spot rate of 1.80   =   £88,888
(c) Exercises profit option and sells euro at 1.60 per pound   =   £100,000 +
(d) Profit from exercising option   =   £11,112 +
(e) Cost of option   =   £3,000 –
(f) Net profit   =   £8,112

The contract is not awarded but the company can sell the €160,000 at the more favourable rate of 1.60 as agreed in the options contract. This allows the company to make an actual profit of £8112.

**4. Where the tender is unsuccessful and the euro appreciates to 1.40**

This case is similar to case (2), except for the fact that the company fails to secure the contract. It lets the option expire.

---

**Box 21.6** **Example of a swap**

Interest rates payable on five-year loan (per cent p.a.)

|  | US$ | UK£ |
|---|---|---|
| Firm A | 8 | 10 |
| Firm B | 10 | 11 |

Assume five-year borrowing rates for Firm A and B in two currencies as above. Firm A can obtain loans at a cheaper rate in both currencies (in terms of Chapter 17, it has *absolute* advantage in both markets), but it can borrow *comparatively* cheaper in dollars relative to Firm B. We suppose further that Firm A wants to borrow sterling and Firm B wants to borrow in dollars for their respective trade and investment transactions.

An arrangement is now made by an intermediary bank as follows:

1. A borrows dollars @ 8 per cent.
2. A lends dollars to B @ 8.5 per cent which is currency that B wants to borrow.
3. B borrows sterling @ 11 per cent.
4. B lends sterling to A @ 9.5 per cent.
5. Firm A is satisfied because it now receives sterling at a cheaper rate than it would have paid had it borrowed on its own account.
6. Firm B obtains a dollar loan at 8.5 per cent, a saving of 1.5 per cent. If it lends sterling at 9.5 per cent, it breaks even. At any rate between 9.5 and 10 per cent, B makes a profit, as does A.

As a result of the swap, both firms are better off than they would be borrowing directly in the foreign currency on their own account. This is another example of mutual gains from trade based on comparative advantage. It gives an opening to banks arranging swaps for profitable arbitrage.

---

*Leading and lagging* are techniques whereby a company advances or delays foreign currency payments when a devaluation or revaluation of the domestic currency is expected, in the hope of reducing the amount of domestic currency needed to settle its debts.

In situations where a devaluation of the domestic currency is expected, a company can cover its exposure by *invoicing in foreign currency* instead of in the domestic currency.

*Geographical diversification of sales and purchases* is another technique, by which firms can diminish risk by spreading it. This is the basic argument for diversifying exports and imports.

*Asset and liability management strategy* may be deployed to ensure that assets and liabilities are as far as possible matched in the same currency. Suppose a Japanese car manufacturer decides to establish a new plant in the US. The total cost of constructing the plant is $200 million. If the Japanese investors choose to finance the new plant by borrowing yen from a Japanese bank, they take on a large exposure to the dollar, all the more so if account is taken of the value of future flow of dollar sales. If the dollar depreciates *vis-à-vis* the yen, the yen value of the company's US asset will fall, while the loan outstanding remains unchanged. The company can hedge this risk by borrowing the $200 million in dollars from a US bank. The company's dollar loan would be exactly matched by its asset of $200 million and its exchange rate exposure would be closed off in respect of that transaction.

## Company exchange rate exposures

The unpredictable and volatile nature of international currency markets explains why exposure management is such an important area of policy for any company engaged in international trade. However, many companies still do not hedge exchange rate risk. Some, especially small firms, are deterred by the costs. Others might consider the risk of exposure worth accepting. The forward rate is as likely to be above, as it is to fall below, the future spot rate (by definition since it is an 'unbiased estimator'); thus a company which chooses not to hedge exchange rate risk leaves open the possibility of making large short-run gains. This, however, is a dangerous strategy. Spectacular losses, as well as gains, have been made on forex dealings; one short-run loss on a very large receipt or payment could be enough to drive the company out of business.

Alternatively, a company may actively seek such short-run gains by using the available instruments for speculative purposes. Large multinationals nowadays tend to have their own treasury departments which undertake the trading and cover functions that banks used to carry out for them. The turmoil on international currency markets in recent years has increased the potential for short-run profit. As global competition intensifies, companies may be encouraged to use the foreign exchange markets for profit as well as for protection. This is especially likely where a company's competitors are engaged in speculative activity. However, this kind of activity among corporate treasuries has reduced lately due to increasing focus on corporate governance and the introduction of stricter accounting controls (e.g. FAF 133 in the USA, IAS 39 in Europe).

Five much-publicised examples of this activity are as follows.

- Quantum Fund, a hedge fund associated with George Soros, allegedly made profits of $1 billion out of sterling's fall from the exchange rate mechanism of the EMS in September 1992. The fund lost equally spectacular sums in the late 1990s.
- In early 1994, Metallgesellschaft, the German metals, mining and engineering group, incurred losses of more than DM 2 billion through futures contracts on oil (sometimes used as a currency hedge). A similar fate befell Ashanti Goldfields, an African gold mining firm, in 1999.
- Procter & Gamble lost heavily in 1994 from a series of complex interest rate swaps.
- The most spectacular case of all was the collapse in 1995 of one of Britain's oldest and most prestigious merchant banks, Barings Bank, as a result of unauthorised activities of an employee in Japanese stock market futures and options markets.
- A currency trader in Allfirst Bank managed to lose $691 million of the bank's money on the world currency markets over a period of six years from 1997 to 2002.

## 21.5 Conclusions

When the fixed exchange rate system was abandoned in 1973, a US dollar was worth ¥270. By mid 2003, it was worth ¥120. The pound sterling, which was worth US$4.80 in the mid-1950s, had fallen in value to US$1.50. These long-term trends have been accompanied by large variations in exchange rates over shorter (1–3-year) timespans. Exchange rate uncertainty is an important source of potential gain and loss to any business engaging in trade outside its national borders. As markets become more international, fewer firms can afford to ignore these issues.

Economic theory has no fully satisfactory explanation of exchange rate variations, but it can provide useful guidance. Relative inflation rates have certainly played a part in accounting for the strength of some currencies in the past. Other fundamentals, such as productivity growth, budget deficits and domestic investment rates, also go some way to explaining movements in the exchange rate. But as macroeconomic policy objectives and outcomes are converging, 'fundamentals' have become less valuable as a guide to exchange rate movements. We are still far short of having a theory which could provide a reliable basis for forecasting exchange rates. A survey of the literature by two long-standing experts concluded that:

> Exchange rates are moved largely by factors other than the basic, observable, macroeconomic fundamentals. Econometrically, most of the action is in the error term.[25]

The relative weights to be attached to the 'fundamentals' keep changing. Interest rates are seen as the crucial factor in some circumstances; in others it can be political stability, or inflation, or the budget deficit, and so on. The relationships are both unstable and dynamic. This conclusion amounts to a clear warning as to the inadequacy of the simple demand and supply diagram with which we began our discussion. This depicts a unique well-defined equilibrium exchange rate. If no such equilibrium exists (if we are in fact talking of a situation of a multiplicity of unstable equilibrium points), it might be better to think of equilibrium as a wide range of possible outcomes rather than a single equilibrium point. Taking a broader view might also bring us closer to the market where calculations based on purchasing power parity and suchlike are seen as providing *bounds* (of, say, ±25 per cent) within which 'the equilibrium' can be found. This approach is unsatisfactory and far short of the ideal, but may contain more intellectual honesty than chasing the will-o'-the-wisp of a unique correct value for the exchange rate – a value which time is bound to prove incorrect.

The foreign exchange market has become more similar to the stock market, the oscillations of which also continue to defy rational explanation. So much so that many market participants have become sceptical about the usefulness of economic models in exchange rate prediction and have turned instead to technical (chartist) analysis as a tool for forecasting. Some researchers are experimenting with the idea that the interaction of fundamentals and chartists in the foreign

---

[25] J. Frankel and R. Dornbusch, 'The flexible exchange rate system: experience and alternatives', in S. Borner (ed.), *International Finance and Trade* (London: Macmillan, 1988). A less restrained view of the fundamentals approach is contained in the laconic comment of a forex trader and friend of the author's: 'That's the theory. It sounds great. It doesn't work.'

exchange market introduces a significant number of non-linearities to make chaotic motion in exchange rates possible (chaos theory).[26]

The reason why exchange rate changes are notoriously difficult both to explain and to predict can be boiled down to one major factor. Capital flows, not trade, make exchange rates change. Over $1200 billion passes through the foreign exchange markets per day, compared with which world exports of $7000 billion per year fade into insignificance. Capital responds to exchange rate expectations and these are subject to seemingly irrational impulses and bandwagons. In the case of exchange rates, prediction is even more difficult than explanation. Economic and political fundamentals change in a way that even the most savvy prophets cannot foresee.[27] Even if it were possible to obtain good forecasts of the fundamentals, exchange rate forecasts generated by the 'fundamentalist' model would, as we have seen, still be subject to large error. The precise impact of changes in each of the fundamentals on the exchange rate can be difficult to determine. Hence, the cynical advice: *in exchange rate forecasts, specify the level or the date, but never both*.

Exchange rates are highly volatile – much more so than domestic prices. This underlines the need for sound corporate strategy for dealing with foreign exchange risk. Various methods of coping with foreign exchange risk have been explained. Foreign exchange cover is needed not only for current transactions, but also to cover translation exposure in firms with assets and liabilities located in different countries and currency zones.[28] The provision of this cover can be costly, but the penalty for not having it may prove even more expensive. Large corporate treasurers have departed from the past practice of leaving forex management to their banks and are now managing it themselves to a much greater extent than before. For smaller companies, some elementary knowledge of hedging options and exchange rate risk is needed to ensure that they have an adequate level of protection for their business. But 'adequate' is not the same as 'complete'. Even the best practice techniques usually give only partial cover.

The present world exchange rate system has been characterised by misalignments and periodic currency crises. This is a source of worry for the smooth functioning of the international monetary system. Currency instability in the 1980s and early 1990s gave renewed impetus to the drive for a common currency in Europe. The wild oscillations in the exchange rates of emerging economies – and the associated lasting damage done to many of them in consequence – have fuelled concern about the global financial system ('architecture'). The role of the IMF, in particular, is being re-examined. Governments have progressed from concern about the *level* of the national exchange rate to concern about choosing the right exchange rate *regime* within which that level is determined. Exchange rate regimes are the subject of the next chapter.

---

[26] Many would dismiss forecasts based on chartist analysis or chaos theory as mere guesswork. Perhaps the emergence of these forecasts is more a result of human dislike of the unknown than evidence of their superior performance.

[27] One small set of people who might out-perform a random-walk model are market movers, such as central banks or fund managers, who have access to such enormous resources that their predictions can be self-fulfilling.

[28] Also known as 'accounting exposure', translation exposure arises when a multinational company's foreign currency-denominated balances and transactions are consolidated into the group financial statements, denominated in the currency of the parent company. Exchange rate fluctuations may result in substantial translation losses or gains.

## Summary

1. Exchange rate movements can have a significant impact on a firm's bottom line. The net long-term impact depends on the extent of the 'pass-through' from exchange rate changes to the domestic price level and domestic costs and to the underlying price elasticities of demand.

2. There is no single, comprehensive theory of the exchange rate capable of explaining the violent swings in market exchange rates. Relative purchasing power parity (PPP) states that if prices in two countries change at a different rate, the exchange rate will appreciate or depreciate so as to preserve price, or purchasing power, parity between the two countries. PPP theories focus on relative inflation rates as the determinant of exchange rate behaviour. Other theories emphasise the balance of payments, different rates of money supply growth, budget deficits and portfolio asset effects.

3. Exchange rates remain difficult to predict, partly because economic 'fundamentals' change unpredictably and sometimes violently, partly because of irrational elements in foreign exchange markets such as bubbles and bandwagons and market 'sentiment'. The value of forex transactions on the market vastly exceeds the value of global trade in goods and services.

4. To cope with this volatility, business must understand its degree of exchange rate exposure and apply risk-reducing measures as appropriate. Use can be made of the forward market, swaps and options and other types of hedging instruments available on the market. Also there are *internal* mechanisms for reducing exposure such as netting, leads and lags, matching assets and liabilities. But there is no costless way of offsetting exchange rate risk, and each firm must carefully balance the benefits of risk reduction against the cost of the instruments to achieve it.

5. Because exchange rate volatility imposes costs on the trading sector, and through it on the economy, governments have begun to explore alternatives to a floating exchange rate regime such as currency area agreements or, in the limit, abolishing different national currencies and replacing them with a common currency as in Europe's euro.

## Questions for discussion

1. Purchasing power parity states that countries with high inflation rates tend to have depreciating currencies. Can you explain why?

2. Why should the discovery of a natural resource, say oil, be expected to lead to a strengthening of a country's currency?
   What effect would you expect such an appreciation to have on the oil-producing country's:
   (a) manufacturing sector?
   (b) exporters?
   (c) consumers?

3. Why do significant differences in interest rates continue to prevail between countries notwithstanding the increasing international mobility of capital which must tend to reduce them? (Consider, in your discussion, the contrast between, say, 10-year government bond yields in Japan, the US and Canada of 0.6, 4.0 and 5.1 per cent respectively in mid-2003.)

4. Why are exchange rates volatile? What can government do to try to reduce such volatility? Does government action sometimes cause volatility?

5. Foreign exchange risk is a major concern for multinationals. Is exchange rate exposure a problem just for multinationals or could a firm with a wholly domestic market orientation also be affected?

6. Explain why firms with highly price-elastic demand for their product (price-takers) are more likely to be affected by currency fluctuations than those with low price-elasticity of demand (price-makers).

7. It has been said that 'good currency risk management and good business management are synonymous'. Do you agree? Discuss the main market instruments which a firm can purchase in order to reduce its foreign exchange exposure.

8. A company can also deal with the exposure problem through internal exposure management. What does this entail?

## Exercises

1. Suppose the one-year interest rate on sterling deposits is 4 per cent, the dollar interest rate is 2 per cent, and the current $/£ spot rate is $1.50.

    (a) What do you expect the spot rate to be in one year?
    (b) Suppose both the US and UK implement new policies that lead to an expected future spot rate of $2. Suppose further that the dollar interest rate rises to 3 per cent. What spot rate would be consistent with these two changes?

2. 'Overly strong currencies cut first into profits and then into market share, fewer jobs, financial instability and social unrest.' Comments of this nature are often made when a country's currency soars and their economy declines.

    What indicators would you use to determine whether a currency is 'overly strong'? Explain the effects mentioned above (loss of profits, market share, etc.). Use data on the economy of any currency which you think might be overvalued to illustrate your answer.

3. A British company has to make a US$1 million payment in three months' time. It has a sterling balance of £550,000 available now and requires advice on whether to invest this amount in sterling or in dollars.

    Given that:

    the US three-month deposit rate is 1 per cent p.a.,
    the sterling deposit rate is 4 per cent p.a.,
    the spot dollar exchange rate is £0.63,
    the three-month forward rate is £0.66,

(a) Where should the company invest for better return over the next three months?

(b) Assuming that interest rates and the spot exchange rate remain as above, what forward rate would make the firm indifferent between the two currencies?

(c) Assuming that the US interest rate and the spot and forward rates remain as above, where would you invest if the sterling deposit rate were to rise to 14 per cent p.a.?

(d) With the originally stated spot and forward rates and the same dollar deposit rate, what is the equilibrium sterling deposit rate?

4. A director of a multinational asks why the company is spending $30m annually on currency options. How would you explain the value added to the company by such expenditure?

## Further reading

For a review of trends and theories see Richard Meese, 'Currency fluctuations in the post-Bretton Woods era', *Journal of Economic Perspectives* (Winter 1990). Robert Hutchinson, *Corporate Finance: Principles of investment, financing and valuations* (London: Stanley Thornes, 1995) provides a clear and incisive account of options and futures. Adrian Buckley, *Multinational Finance* (London: Philip Allan, 1986) is helpful on the subject of foreign currency exposure and techniques of exposure management. John Roberts, *$1000 Billion a Day: Inside the foreign exchange markets* (London: HarperCollins, 1995) is a breezy and highly informative insider's account of the dealing room. An accessible and comprehensive assessment of the ongoing literature on the topic is provided in Ken Rogoff, 'The purchasing power parity puzzle', *Journal of Economic Literature* (June 1996). An up-to-date source on the structure of the foreign exchange market is European Central Bank, *Review of the Foreign Exchange Market Structure*, March 2003.

## Appendix 21.1 The global foreign exchange market

The global foreign exchange market is the world's largest financial market. It is not a physical location; rather it comprises numerous financial centres around the world, connected via the telephone and other telecom devices which allow almost instantaneous transmission of information. The progressive liberalisation of cross-border capital flows, together with improvements in trading and settlement practices and the rapid advance of technology, have resulted in an unprecedented expansion of foreign exchange trading. Three broad categories of foreign exchange instruments are traded: contracts for spot delivery, forwards and swaps, and other derivatives. A significant development in the market has been the expansion in trade in derivatives, notably interest rate options and futures (Table A21.1). A *derivative* is an off-balance sheet agreement. It defines certain

### Table A21.1 The expansion of financial derivatives markets

| Instruments | (US$ billion) | | | |
| --- | --- | --- | --- | --- |
| | 1986 | 1990 | 1995 | 2002 |
| Exchange-traded instruments | 583 | 2,292 | 9,185 | 23,880 |
| Over-the-counter instruments | 500 | 3,451 | 17,990 | 127,564 |

*Source: Bank for International Settlements Annual Report, 1995 and 1996; Bank for International Settlements Quarterly Review (March 2003). Figures refer to amount outstanding at end of year, and at end of March 2003.*

financial rights and obligations which are contractually linked to interest rates, exchange rates or other market prices.

The foreign exchange market has expanded rapidly – net daily turnover has more than doubled since 1990. But a marked decline (19 per cent between 1998 and 2001) occurred as a result of the replacement of European currencies by the euro, the growth of electronic trading and the consolidation of exchange rate transactions in corporate treasuries.

Foreign exchange transactions are organised at wholesale (or interbank) or retail market level. There are four groups of participants: dealers (traders), brokers, customers (mainly institutional investors) and central banks. The wholesale market consists of dealers' trade both with other dealers and with non-dealing banks. Retail market transactions involve the banks and their customers. However, the rapid market developments of recent years have made the distinction between the two increasingly blurred; many larger retail customers have gained access to the wholesale market through improved communications with the dealing banks. Wholesale market activity dominates the foreign exchange market.

## Dealers

The dominance of the wholesale market reflects dealers' position-taking activity. A position is simply a market commitment. For example, a dealer who buys a futures contract takes a long position; a dealer who sells a futures contract takes a short position. Dealers buy and sell foreign exchange on their own account and may take open positions in a currency. They are employed by banks and other financial institutions that need to have a continuing presence in the foreign exchange market. These are dominated by the 40–50 large dealing banks which actually make markets. Market makers are dealers who stand ready to buy and sell assets at any time, thus satisfying the public's demand to trade immediately. Dealers can make enormous profits for the banks which employ them, but they can also make enormous losses. For this reason, most banks have internal controls, limiting the size of dealers' open positions. The limits on open positions, especially overnight positions, mean that banks try to offset the exposures that result from retail trades, either by finding another customer with exactly the reverse requirement or by trading on the wholesale market. If another bank is willing to undertake the reverse transaction, a 1:1 ratio between wholesale and retail orders is generated. If not, up to four or five wholesale market transactions may be needed to cover the risk associated with a forward, swaps or derivative contract. However, these internal controls are not as effective in some banks as in others, and some dealers may retain highly exposed positions. This can result in financial disaster, as the collapse of Barings Bank in February 1995 demonstrated. A dealer operating from the Singapore branch of the bank built up a large exposure which involved Barings in losses well in excess of the bank's equity capital. Barings was sold to a Dutch bank, ING, for a nominal sum of £1.

## Brokers

Brokers match orders to buy and sell currencies for a fee. However, unlike dealers, they cannot take positions themselves. Brokers keep a 'limit book' containing information on the public bid and ask prices of the dealers they (the brokers) have contacted, and match incoming demands for, or supplies of, foreign currency with the dealer currently offering the best price. To offer their clients the best prices, brokers must obtain the best possible information by remaining in frequent contact with the dealers. As the volume of transactions increases, this becomes increasingly difficult. Therefore, many of the larger banks have dispensed altogether with brokers; instead they maintain close relationships with the dealers themselves in order to have access to timely quotes.

## Customers

Customers include non-financial companies and financial institutions that do not maintain a constant presence in the market as dealers. Customers may enter the foreign exchange market to buy foreign exchange for imports and to sell foreign exchange received for exports. They may also use the forward, swaps and derivatives markets to hedge foreign currency exposure arising from foreign trade and investment. In addition, they may enter the market for speculative purposes.

The main players in the foreign exchange market have been the large dealing banks. These traditional players have been joined by a new set of players: institutional investors, such as pension funds, insurance companies, investment funds and bank trust departments.

Of these, pension funds are the largest players, followed by insurance companies. They are investing increasing proportions of their assets abroad in order to improve yield and reduce risk. Investment and hedge funds have also grown rapidly. Total funds managed by the world's 500 largest asset managers amounted to $35.7 trillion at the end of 2002 (Source: Watson Wyatt).

## Central bank

Central banks enter the market to satisfy the needs of their governments and to influence the exchange rate. The role of central banks becomes especially significant in times of extreme currency turmoil. A central bank might then intervene in the foreign exchange market directly, or else indirectly through interest rate policy, to relieve pressure on the exchange rate. The power of a modern central bank, however, has been much eroded in recent years by the twelvefold increase in the derivatives market since 1990 and by the associated growth of hedge funds and institutional investors in the forex market.

## Chapter 22

# Exchange rate regimes and the euro

## Introduction

In a free market, price is determined by the forces of supply and demand. As demand and supply conditions change, price fluctuates upwards and downwards. Normally such fluctuations would be seen as an expected feature of the market system, certainly not as evidence of a malfunction in the system which requires correction. We saw in Chapter 3 the danger of government attempts to suppress such flexibility. Black markets, queues and bureaucratic distortions are the unwanted and costly side-effects of such intervention.

The foreign exchange market is an unusual market. In one sense it has all the attributes of a perfectly competitive market (large numbers of buyers and sellers, full information, flexibility) from which the benefits of the free-market system might be expected to flow. The market price is flexible and volatile. To some this is by no means an unwelcome feature. Currency traders thrive when the market is unstable, since it is from hedging and speculative transactions that they derive their income. Others, notably those with a heavy involvement in real international transactions, are affected less benignly. To them, currency volatility can be costly and often threatening. They support official efforts to intervene in the market. Why should market forces be welcomed in one context but treated with suspicion in another?

Part of the answer lies in the volatile nature of the market. As we have seen, the foreign exchange market is unusually prone to destabilisation through 'overshooting' and 'undershooting' the equilibrium exchange rate. The 'herd instinct', described as 'a self-organising process of infection among traders', can lead to prices which deviate from fundamental values.[1] This volatility, in turn, can have strongly adverse repercussions on the economy, particularly in situations where there is rigidity in domestic prices and costs. Examples of such adverse effects include the following.

- Large speculation-fed devaluation can disrupt domestic stabilisation and anti-inflation policy.

---

[1]  See T. Lux, 'Herd behaviour, bubbles and crashes', *Economic Journal* (July 1995).

- Competitive devaluations by a country's trading partners can damage trade relations.
- Currency turmoil in one part of the world can spread to other countries without apparent reason, involving a headlong rush into 'safe' currencies and out of non-core currencies, with consequent unwarranted revaluations and devaluations.
- Long-term planning and investment decisions can be distorted by sustained currency misalignments.

This chapter analyses the case for government intervention in the foreign exchange market. The starting-point is that both the exchange rate *level* and the exchange rate *regime* are important for an economy. An exchange rate level which is too high creates problems for exporters; an exchange rate which is too low can lead to high costs of imported inputs and inflation.[2] An exchange rate regime which is too rigid can lock business into an unsustainable cost disadvantage: a regime which is too flexible generates uncertainty. Most businesses take the view that they have enough uncertainty to deal with as a result of global competition and open markets without having to cope with the extra expense and hassle of volatile exchange rates. Ideally the global exchange rate system should provide (a) a *level* of the exchange rate which leaves industry in a reasonably competitive state *vis-à-vis* foreign competitors, and (b) an exchange rate *regime* to ensure that this level is sustained. As we have seen, the free market has not been able to deliver either of these requirements.

*The question posed in this chapter is whether governments, through intervention in the forex market and/or through selection of a different exchange rate regime, can create a more efficient outcome in transacting international business than a wholly free forex market.*

Free market imperfections are not automatically corrected by state intervention. History suggests that this is particularly true of state manipulation of exchange rates. Many countries have suffered from ill-advised and politically motivated initiatives affecting their exchange rate. For example, the UK economy suffered serious damage as a result of Churchill's insistence on a return to the gold standard in 1925 at an overvalued rate. The delayed devaluation of 1967 by the Wilson government also caused problems. The overvalued exchange rate in the early 1980s inflicted lasting injury on large sectors of UK industry and contributed to the 17 per cent decline in manufacturing jobs in the five years 1979–84. The adherence of the UK and Italy to what many believed was an overvalued rate *vis-à-vis* the Deutschmark led to the European currency crisis of 1992–93.[3]

Exchange rate reform concerns choosing the best system for maintaining a competitive exchange rate, while at the same time maintaining price stability. The choice of regime is an active item on the agenda of many countries, not only in Europe where the debate on participation in the euro gathers pace, but also in Latin America and among transition economies.

---

[2] 'Yen's rise catastrophic, says Japanese business leaders' – under this headline the *Financial Times* (20 April 1995) goes on to report the warning of the Japan Automobile Manufacturers' Association that the strong yen (80 yen per dollar) would affect employment levels. The Japanese government was urged to take action 'to calm currency markets'. The rise in the euro in 2003 elicited much the same response from European business leaders.

[3] E. Roll, *Where Did We Go Wrong? From the gold standard to Europe* (London: Faber, 1995).

The exchange rate regime which is 'best' for an individual country is rarely self-evident, nor will adherence to it always be politically expedient. Much depends on the economy's stage of economic development, its trade patterns and the degree of economic integration with neighbouring countries. The well-being of an economy can be affected for good or ill by decisions on the exchange rate. While free-floating exchange rates lead to costly volatility, attempts to control the exchange rate, if based on mistaken analysis, can also inflict heavy costs on business.

## Chapter outline

This chapter analyses what governments can and should do to set parameters on exchange rate movements in the following steps:

**1.** Description of the global exchange rate system. Today's world is characterised primarily by a floating system, but there are different types of floating regimes, and some countries have chosen to peg their exchange rate to another currency or group of currencies.

**2.** Assessment of the experience of the *floating currencies*.

**3.** The tools of intervention and the effectiveness of proposed measures to achieve greater exchange rate stability.

**4.** Implications of the euro. For the countries of the euro area, this has involved the abandonment of something close to a free float in favour of the extreme rigidity of a single currency.

## 22.1 The global exchange rate system

Under the Bretton Woods system, which lasted from 1946 to 1973, industrial countries' exchange rates were tied to the US dollar, and through it to gold, at 'fixed' parities. The exchange rate could be adjusted, but adjustments were infrequent and reluctant.[4] Since 1973, the major currencies have operated under a floating regime, while smaller countries have adopted a range of fixed and flexible options. The present global exchange rate system has the following features (Figure 22.1).

1. The world's three major currencies, the US dollar, the yen and the euro, are 'independently floating'. By this we mean that the authorities have not committed themselves to maintaining a particular value of their currency either *vis-à-vis* each other or *vis-à-vis* any other exchange rate index. At the same time, they do intervene in the forex market, and the exchange rate is considered an important factor in the economy.

2. A growing number of countries have adopted a flexible exchange rate regime. Within this group, which includes approximately half of all currencies, a

---

[4] A brief history of the origins of the present system is provided in Appendix 22.1.

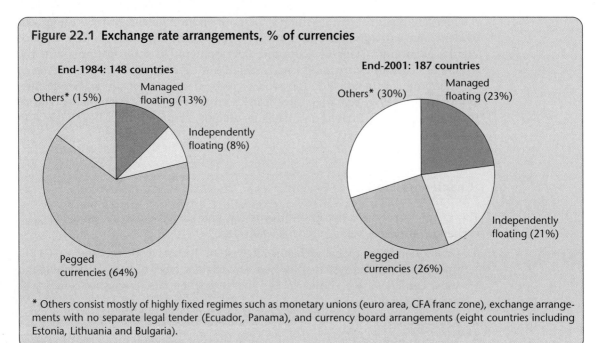

**Figure 22.1 Exchange rate arrangements, % of currencies**

End-1984: 148 countries

Others* (15%)    Managed floating (13%)

Independently floating (8%)

Pegged currencies (64%)

End-2001: 187 countries

Others* (30%)    Managed floating (23%)

Independently floating (21%)

Pegged currencies (26%)

* Others consist mostly of highly fixed regimes such as monetary unions (euro area, CFA franc zone), exchange arrangements with no separate legal tender (Ecuador, Panama), and currency board arrangements (eight countries including Estonia, Lithuania and Bulgaria).

distinction is made between currencies which are 'independently floating' and those which are 'managed floating'. Exchange rates in the latter group are allowed to float, but only within certain limits. By the early 2000s, one-fifth of all national currencies were independently floating and a further 23 per cent were managed floaters. Large developing countries such as Brazil and Turkey, small developed countries such as Norway and New Zealand, and many other small and medium-sized developing countries have converted to an independently floating system. However, the dividing line between independent and managed floaters is often blurred.

3. Some currencies are linked at a fixed rate ('pegged') to another currency or basket of currencies. Within the fixed-rate category, there are different types of arrangements. Some countries have pegged to a single currency: Barbados, China, Ecuador and Panama to the US dollar, Estonia and Bulgaria to the euro, Lesotho to the South African rand. Others have adopted a composite peg or are tied to the SDR.[5] For example, Morocco's dirham is linked to a trade-weighted basket comprising mostly the euro and the dollar.

4. The degree of fixity of a currency link can itself be quite variable. Some countries choose a relatively fixed band of variation within which their currency can fluctuate, but others adjust the band regularly ('crawling bands'). Israel, Romania and Venezuela have adopted crawling band currencies.

5. Although countries with pegged currencies are numerous, their combined economic weight in world trade is modest. They are mostly small open economies, for which a pegged system has important advantages that would not apply to a larger country.

---

[5] SDR, or *standard drawing right*, is a notional unit of currency based on the world's major currencies.

6. Countries have been moving towards more extreme exchange rate regimes. Increased capital mobility makes a floating regime more viable; but it also makes a strong commitment to exchange rate fixity more attractive, under the umbrella of sustainable monetary and fiscal policies.

The diversity of options available within the world exchange rate system is reflected in the regimes chosen by countries of the former Soviet Union (Table 22.1). At one extreme are Russia, the Ukraine and Poland with flexible exchange rates. At the other are countries like Bulgaria and the Baltic states, which have adopted a peg to other currencies.

Many countries are dissatisfied with their exchange rate regime, but each is dissatisfied for different reasons. The major industrial countries worry about the destabilising effects of large exchange rate fluctuations on national prestige, competitiveness and price stability. Developing countries have still different concerns. Many feel vulnerable to speculative attack and seek security by attaching their national currencies to *exchange rate anchors*.

### Table 22.1 Exchange rate regimes and country characteristics

| Country | Population (millions) | Openness (exports/GDP) | Currency | Exchange rate arrangement |
|---|---|---|---|---|
| Armenia | 3.8 | 23 | Dram | Independently floating |
| Azerbaijan | 8.0 | 41 | Azerbaijan Manat | Managed float |
| Belarus | 10.0 | 68 | Belarusian Ruble | Crawling bands |
| Bulgaria | 8.2 | 58 | Lev | Currency board (fixed to euro) |
| Czech Rep. | 10.3 | 71 | Koruna | Independently floating |
| Estonia | 1.4 | 84 | Kroon | Currency board (fixed to euro) |
| Georgia | 5.0 | 37 | Lari | Independently floating |
| Hungary | 10.0 | 63 | Forint | Pegged to euro |
| Kazakhstan | 14.9 | 59 | Tenge | Managed float |
| Kyrgyz Rep. | 4.9 | 43 | Som | Managed float |
| Latvia | 2.4 | 46 | Lat | Pegged to SDR |
| Lithuania | 3.7 | 45 | Litas | Currency board (fixed to euro) |
| Moldova | 4.3 | 50 | Leu | Independently floating |
| Poland | 38.7 | 27 | Zloty | Independently floating |
| Russia | 145.6 | 46 | Russian Ruble | Managed float |
| Slovakia | 5.4 | 74 | Slovak Koruna | Managed float |
| Slovenia | 2.0 | 59 | Tolar | Managed float |
| Tajikistan | 6.2 | 81 | Somoni | Independently floating |
| Turkmenistan | 5.2 | 63 | Turkmen Manat | Pegged to US$ |
| Ukraine | 49.5 | 61 | Hryvnia | Managed float |
| Uzbekistan | 24.7 | 44 | Sum | Managed float |

*Source*: IMF, *International Financial Statistics*, January 2003.

## 22.2 Floating exchange rates

> There are no major difficulties to prevent the prompt establishment by countries of a system of exchange rates freely determined in open markets, primarily by private transactions, and the simultaneous abandonment of direct controls over exchange transactions. A move in this direction is the fundamental prerequisite for the economic integration of the free world through multilateral trade.[6]

Milton Friedman's advocacy of flexible exchange rates in 1956 rested on the proposition that a system of freely floating exchange rates was 'the fundamental prerequisite' for achieving free trade. Ironically, many economists now regard floating rates as a danger to free trade. To understand why, we need to understand both the theory itself and how the system has worked out in practice.

### Floating exchange rates – in theory

Any economy is vulnerable to shocks – to 'real' shocks, such as changes in composition of demand and supply, and to 'monetary' shocks, such as the creation of excessive money supply, or foreign capital outflows. Suppose a shock leads to an outward shift in the country's demand for foreign exchange (from $D_0D_0$ to $D_1D_1$ in Figure 22.2). If the exchange rate is fixed at $E_0$, an excess demand equal to $Q_0Q_1$ will develop. This excess demand can be dealt with by:

1. central bank intervention, supplying $Q_0Q_1$ of foreign currency in each period;
2. import controls or similar trade interventions designed to bring the demand for foreign exchange back to $D_0D_0$;
3. improvement in cost competitiveness, resulting in a fall in the demand for imports. The demand curve will shift backwards from $D_1D_1$ towards $D_0D_0$;
4. cutbacks in domestic spending, leading to a lower domestic demand for imports and traded goods.

If the exchange rate were flexible instead of fixed, a fifth possibility would be:

5. a depreciation in the exchange rate, leading to a new equilibrium at $OE^*$, with value of foreign exchange transactions $OQ^*$.

The case for flexible exchange rates is that option 5 is more efficient than any of options 1–4. With respect to option 1, it is clear that central bank intervention can last only for a limited period. The case against option 2 is that the exchange rate system exists to facilitate trade, not to hinder or restrict it. To save the system by restricting the benefits of trade is to subvert its *raison d'être*. The objections to adjustment options 3 and 4 need more careful analysis. Reductions in spending will, of course, bring about equilibrium. As national spending falls, so does demand for imports. Simultaneously, there is a decline in demand for domestically produced goods, thereby releasing resources to produce more exports. Hence lower spending is associated with a lower demand for foreign exchange and a greater supply. This process is further strengthened by a fall in the domestic price

---

[6] M. Friedman, 'The case for flexible exchange rates', in *Essays in Positive Economics* (Chicago: University of Chicago Press, 1953), p. 173.

**Figure 22.2  Changes in the exchange rate and payments imbalances**

An outward shift in the demand curve for foreign currency to $D_1D_1$ results in a new equilibrium exchange rate $E^*$. The move from $E_0$ to $E^*$ represents a depreciation of the domestic currency.

level. The income and spending effects are then reinforced by a competitive effect. Domestic prices fall relative to foreign prices. Exports and import-competing industries become more competitive, at each given exchange rate. $S_0S_0$ will shift outwards, and $D_1D_1$ will shift inwards. A new equilibrium will be established at the unchanged exchange rate $E_0$, somewhere between $Q_0$ and $Q_1$. In an economy with perfectly flexible prices, a fall in domestic prices has exactly the same effect on the forex market as a devaluation of the same percentage.

If domestic prices are flexible downwards, the adjustment can take place with minimal real effects on economic activity. However, if domestic prices are inflexible, the entire burden of adjustment falls on real income. The fall in aggregate spending (demand) will lead to increased unemployment and lower output rather than lower domestic prices. In such circumstances a devaluation of the exchange rate is a more efficient way of restoring equilibrium. In a memorable analogy, Friedman likened the argument for flexible exchange rates to the argument for daylight saving time. Why, he asked, do we change the clock in summer when exactly the same result could be achieved by having each individual change routine? The reason is that:

> it is much simpler to change the clock that guides all than to oblige each individual separately to change his patterns of reaction to the clock, even though all want to do so. By the same token it is far simpler to allow one price to change, namely, the price of foreign exchange, than to rely upon changes in the multitude of prices that together constitute the internal price structure.[7]

---

[7]  *Ibid.*

Contrary to what many think, speculators are not seen as a problem in this theoretical framework. Suppose traders correctly anticipate the outward shift in the demand curve for foreign exchange. They will have an incentive to buy foreign currency now, wait for the expected devaluation, and then sell the foreign currency at a higher price in terms of domestic currency. The effect of their action will be to raise the spot price of foreign exchange in anticipation of the forthcoming imbalance between supply and demand. This gives producers advance warning of the depreciation, and spreads out the period of adjustment. The adjustment, by being anticipated, becomes less disruptive. The exchange rate depreciates gradually, instead of in a sudden discrete fall. Speculation performs a useful *stabilising* function in such instances.

## Floating exchange rates – in practice

Flexible exchange rates, therefore, have many cogent arguments in their favour, not only in theory but also in practice. Under the floating system, countries have been able to adjust their economies to new competitive realities, global trade has risen faster than world production, protection has been replaced by trade liberalisation, and the system has been able to cope with the huge increase in capital transactions.

One practical advantage of a floating system is the *increased autonomy* it gives to governments in the conduct of their monetary policies. This is seen as a major advantage by the industrial powers. Their monetary authorities are committed to price stability. Once this is achieved, the precise value of the currency can be decided by the market. Some small countries also have found this an appealing argument. New Zealand and Switzerland are among the many countries that have operated successfully under a free floating system (Box 22.1), while several transition countries such as Poland and Slovenia have also opted for flexible rates.

---

### Box 22.1  How small countries choose an exchange rate regime

The choice of exchange rate regime is never straightforward, particularly for a small country. A number of factors determine the suitability of a regime: the degree of trade openness, the geographical composition of trade, the sensitivity of industry to price fluctuations, the inflation record of the country in question and of its trading partners, and the degree of autonomy of its monetary authorities. This analysis focuses on the experience of four financially small countries in their choice of exchange rate regime.

#### Austria

A small open economy in the centre of Europe, Austria has close trading links with one dominant trading partner, Germany, which accounts for about 40 per cent of Austrian exports. Given this, the 'overriding objective' of Austria's exchange rate policy between 1979 and 1998 was to peg the schilling to the Deutschmark. (Prior to 1979, the schilling was pegged to a trade-weighted basket of currencies.) By pegging the schilling to a low-inflation anchor, it was hoped that Austrian inflation would converge to the low German level. In addition, the harmful effects of schilling/Deutschmark exchange rate fluctuations on Austrian trade and tourism would be eliminated. This was felt to outweigh the drawback that the 60 per cent of Austria's trade with countries other than Germany was left exposed to exchange rate fluctuations. The schilling remained stable *vis-à-vis* the Deutschmark and as a result, inflation also remained low. The Deutschmark peg was widely viewed as a success and was considered to have made an important contribution to Austria's strong economic performance. The decision to participate in the euro was seen as a continuation of this successful formula.

## Australia and New Zealand

On the other side of the world are two small open economies which have chosen a radically different exchange rate policy. Both the Australian dollar and the New Zealand dollar have been allowed to float since the mid-1980s. Unlike Austria, Australia and New Zealand have a wide diversity of trading partners. Europe and Japan are the main markets for primary commodities, the US for manufactures. In addition, the two countries trade significantly with each other. Their main trading partners have a mixed record on inflation. Thus, no single obvious choice of anchor currency presents itself. This may explain why the Australian and New Zealand authorities have tried almost every conceivable exchange rate regime in the recent past. Both currencies were pegged to the pound sterling until 1971; then to the US dollar, until 1973 in the case of the Australian dollar, and until 1974 in the case of the New Zealand dollar. Next they tried pegging their currencies to a trade-weighted basket of several trading partners. After experiments, the Australian authorities finally decided to float the dollar in 1984. The New Zealand authorities followed suit in 1986.

Both Australia and New Zealand have discovered that a floating regime has many advantages. It has eliminated the costly delays in realignments associated with the previous fixed or quasi-fixed regimes, and both countries had achieved a low rate of inflation and a stable effective exchange rate by the early 1990s. Tight monetary policy in the form of higher interest rates was necessary to ensure this stability. The resurgence of inflation associated with a 15 per cent depreciation of the dollar necessitated a return to higher interest rates to ensure the sustainability of the float. Concern about higher inflation arising from the weakness of the New Zealand dollar prompted an increase in New Zealand interest rates. Indeed, permanently higher interest rates might be viewed as the *premium* which has to be paid for adopting a floating regime. However, while the New Zealand authorities have adopted a *clean* float, meaning no intervention by the monetary authorities in the foreign exchange market, the Australian authorities maintain a limited role for foreign exchange market intervention, alongside a tight monetary policy.

## Switzerland

Switzerland adopted a floating regime in 1973. The obvious similarities between the Swiss and Austrian economies – both are small open economies with strong German trade links – have caused many to question their fundamentally different exchange rate policies. Why did the Swiss authorities allow the Swiss franc to float rather than pegging it to the Deutschmark and now the euro?

The answer seems to be that the Swiss found that the floating regime works well for their economy. Given that, they see no reason to change. Swiss inflation has never been significantly higher than the German level, and the Swiss authorities are confident in their ability to maintain a stable currency through appropriate monetary policy, i.e.

Box 22.1 continued

high interest rates when needed. (On two occasions, however, in 1978 and again in 1987, the Swiss National Bank departed from its strict monetary policy temporarily and intervened to reverse the appreciation of the franc.) The autonomy of the Swiss National Bank – the Swiss government is prevented by law from intervening in the realm of monetary policy – and the credibility of its monetary policy have been critical to the success of the float.

## Conclusion

Since the demise of the Bretton Woods system in 1973, small countries have had a wide variety of exchange rate regimes from which to choose. The choice is not clear cut, and many countries have experimented with a variety of regimes. Pegging requires the subordination of monetary policy to the maintenance of the exchange rate parity. A country with a good price stability record, such as Switzerland, might be better off not having its hands tied, while for a country with a poorer track record than its dominant trading partner, pegging might help by reducing the interest rate premium (because of enhanced credibility) and by ensuring that the monetary authorities will follow a stable course (important in young and fragile democracies).

*Sources*: OECD, *Economic Surveys: Australia, Austria, New Zealand, Switzerland* (various editions); Österreichische *Nationalbank Annual Report*; *Reserve Bank of New Zealand Bulletin*; *Reserve Bank of Australia Bulletin*; *Schweizerische Nationalbank Annual Report* (various editions).

A second advantage of floating is that it constitutes *a fast and effective alternative to domestic price and wage adjustment*. Changes in economic conditions are a fact of life that must be adjusted to. If prices and wages are sticky downwards, as is often the case, the adjustment process can be slow and waiting can be costly. It is much better in such circumstances to move the exchange rate than the entire spectrum of domestic prices.

Third, a floating exchange rate *reduces the need for foreign reserves*. For some poorer countries this may be a decisive consideration. They may lack the resources to finance a peg even if they wanted to.

This is the positive side of the story. The negative side comes to the fore whenever the forex markets are in turmoil. At such times, countries find their currencies shifting by large discrete amounts – with severe impacts on the real economy – for seemingly inexplicable reasons. Criticism of volatility in the real exchange rate focuses on three points:

● Volatility inhibits trade and investment.
● Destabilising speculation exacerbates the problem.
● Domestic stabilisation measures can be undermined.

### Cost of volatility

That volatile exchange rates deter international business by raising transaction costs and causing uncertainty seems a highly plausible assertion. Yet it has proven surprisingly difficult to make an accurate assessment of the effects of currency fluctuations on trade.[8] This may imply that the adverse effects of currency volatility on trade are smaller than is commonly believed. World trade has expanded faster than world GDP during the period of both fixed and floating exchange rates, which suggests that any trade-suppression effects of exchange rate variation have been overwhelmed by pro-trade influences. As we saw in Chapter 17, the ratio of the growth of trade to the growth of GDP has remained high right into the 2000s. EU countries have also experienced a continuing rise in the ratio of trade to GDP notwithstanding their different exchange rate regimes. Doubtless the currency turmoil of the 1990s involved a significant economic cost in terms of lost output and investment. One side might argue that this exemplifies the damage caused by exchange rate volatility. But the opposite case could also be made: that the damage was caused by insufficient flexibility, i.e. by government efforts to resist an exchange rate adjustment which was warranted by economic fundamentals.

Another argument is that volatility leads to currency misalignments and that this also impacts adversely on trade performance. There is little doubt that such misalignments occur and that they have an adverse impact on business confidence and trade performance in individual countries. The global impact of the misalignments tends to be harder to identify for two reasons. First, the adverse effect on one country of being overvalued has a counterpart advantageous effect on others because by definition they are undervalued. Second, misalignments can happen under fixed exchange rate systems as well as floating systems.

### Destabilising speculation

The second objection relates to the causes of currency volatility. Again there is a common belief that exchange rate fluctuations are 'excessive' and that much of this can be attributed to speculators. Supporting evidence focuses on the fact that forex traders pay limited attention to fundamentals, and chartists none at all. Irrational and speculative forces, fuelled by the fear of being out of step with others in the market, are features of a floating exchange rate system.[9]

Speculation, far from acting as Friedman's textbook stabiliser, may well be exacerbating the volatility of the market. The chairman of Sony expressed a widely held business view on this point:

> In 1973 the experts claimed that exchange rate fluctuations serve to adjust automatically the differences in industrial competitive power among countries. Now I am tempted to ask whether the experts were right in claiming this. What was not anticipated in 1973

---

[8] M.C. Thursby and J.G. Thursby, 'The uncertainty effects of floating exchange rates: empirical evidence on international trade flows', in S.W. Arndt, R.J. Sweeney and T.D. Willett (eds), *Exchange Rates, Trade and the US Economy* (Cambridge, MA: Ballinger, 1985). The effects of exchange rate volatility on trade are notoriously difficult to detect. The empirical evidence is limited and 'inconclusive'. The effects of volatility are perhaps less insidious than was once thought. Certainly the 'pass through' from exchange rates to domestic prices appears to have diminished to only 25 per cent in the case of the US. But opinions differ on this subject. See J. Frankel and A. Rose, 'An estimate of the effect on common currencies on trade and income', *Quarterly Journal of Economics*, Vol. 117, March 2002, for an upper bound estimate of the benefits of eliminating this volatility.

[9] Note that forex market participants have an interest in encouraging currency fluctuations. The more volatility, the greater are trading volumes and sales of hedging instruments and, hence, the greater are banks' incomes from trading commissions and margins (regardless of speculation on their own account).

was that the freely fluctuating rates would spawn speculation and money trading. The resulting rates did not necessarily reflect competitive power of the fundamentals of national economies. (Akio Morita, Chairman: Sony Corporation, 'How to renew the global economic framework', *International Economic Insights*, Washington, DC, March/April 1993, p. 25)

### Domestic stability

Governments do not like to appear ineffective, yet that is how they are often perceived in times of currency turmoil. Even the might of the combined intervention of the US and Japanese authorities, for example, proved unavailing against the bearish sentiment towards the dollar in March–April 1995. The headline of the *Financial Times* (30 March 1995) – 'Dollar hits record low as Japan and US fail to halt slide' – sums it up (see Figure 22.3). Official intervention in the forex market can involve the authorities in huge financial losses. Small countries feel even more vulnerable. Their efforts to stabilise the economy can be undermined by a change in market sentiment. Those most affected are countries with a poor record of consistency in the past, with a really acute inflation problem, or with exposure to large international capital flows inwards and outwards. The problem of *contagion*, arising from these global capital movements, is a dominant theme of the current exchange rate literature.

---

**Figure 22.3 Financial Times, 4 April 1995**

# Dollar hits record low as Japan and US fail to halt slide

By Philip Gawith in London and
George Graham in Washington

Intensive efforts by US and Japanese officials to halt the dollar's recent decline yesterday failed to prevent the currency falling to a record low against the yen.

Repeated bouts of dollar-buying by the Federal Reserve and the Bank of Japan failed to boost the currency. Efforts to talk up the dollar by Mr Robert Rubin, the US Treasury secretary, and Mr Masayoshi Takemura, the Japa-

neses finance minister, also had negligible impact.

At lunchtime in New York, the dollar was trading at DM1.3737 and Y86.28, having earlier touched a new low of Y86.00. Traders estimated that the Fed and the Bank of Japan together bought $2bn to $3bn. There was no evidence of any support for the dollar from European central banks.

*Source*: *Financial Times* 4 April 1995.

Stories such as the above were typical of the period from end-March to early April 1995 (and many periods before and since) when official intervention was overwhelmed by private capital flows, in this instance reflecting adverse market sentiment towards the dollar.

## 22.3 Search for stability

The problem of currency instability can be approached in a number of ways. We shall consider two approaches here. First, a country could choose an anchor currency or group of currencies, and pre-commit to some range of variation around that anchor. Second, the country could continue to float its currency, while deploying special measures to reduce exchange rate variability.

### Tying to an anchor currency

For this approach to be effective, the anchor currency has to have certain features. First, it should be the currency of a stable, low-inflation country. In this way, the anchor will serve the dual role of providing exchange rate stability as well as controlling domestic inflation. Second, the proposed relationship with the anchor must be specified clearly: single currency, fixed parity, fixed but infrequently adjusted parity, fixed but frequently adjusted parity (crawling peg), or floating within narrowly defined fluctuation margins. Third, domestic monetary and fiscal policies must be consistent with the exchange rate policy. Fourth, the authorities must be able to defend the arrangement, through appropriate intervention mechanisms. There must also be the political will to implement the measures needed to maintain the arrangement.

In practice the last requirement often proves difficult to satisfy. Political will falters when the adjustment costs imposed on an economy by its choice of anchor prove too much to bear. Realisation of this difficulty has led to renewed investigation into the conditions needed to ensure that adjustment costs are kept to the minimum. The *theory of optimum currency areas* emphasises the importance of the following additional factors.

### Trade and investment links

A substantial share of the country's trade and foreign investment flows should be conducted with or in terms of the anchor currency. Thus a currency link between Estonia and the euro makes sense; one between Estonia and the yen would not.

### Proneness to asymmetric shocks

Difficulties arise when a shock affects one part of a fixed-exchange area but not another. Suppose that aggregate demand shifts from one part of a fixed-peg area (declining area) to another part (the booming area). If exchange rates are fixed, the declining area is likely to experience a recession and unemployment, while the booming area will be threatened with inflation. These problems are not going to be easy to solve. Hence, to avoid them, economies forming a fixed exchange rate area should be reasonably similar in regard to economic structure and policy.

### Labour mobility

If asymmetric shocks arise but labour moves freely within the area, then the declining area will experience emigration, not unemployment, while immigration will relieve the over-heating problem in the booming area. Thus, extensive labour mobility within the US makes adjustment to asymmetric shocks much easier there than in, say, an area like Europe where labour mobility is comparatively limited.[10]

### Wage and price flexibility

If wages and prices are flexible, a declining economy might not have to suffer emigration. Instead it would experience a decline in prices and costs, relative to the booming area. This would boost demand for the declining area's exports and help to restore its output to the full employment level.[11]

### Counter-cyclical fiscal transfers

Adjustment is easier if mechanisms exist whereby the booming region automatically transfers resources to the declining region. In a single currency area, this is done by federal or central authority transfers. Some rudimentary transfers of this nature were provided as part of the European integration programme to strengthen the sustainability of the euro.

### Credibility of link

The degree of wage and price flexibility is not to be regarded as something given and unalterable. It can be influenced by institutions such as the exchange rate regime. When everybody knows that the exchange rate is fixed (or abolished, through a single currency), then the adverse effects of holding out for higher than equilibrium pay will be anticipated. This anticipation will lead to more flexibility than would otherwise be the case. If there is a pegged arrangement, the government must try to convince its citizens that the peg will not be altered lightly. The more persuasive it is, the less painful the adjustment to shocks. One advantage in a country 'tying its hands', through a binding and irreversible commitment with regard to the exchange rate, is that its credibility will be enhanced.[12]

The choice of an anchor requires careful economic analysis. The precise type of link between the anchor currency and the national currency also needs serious attention. Some countries use the anchor in a rather casual way (such as frequently adjusted pegs or crawling pegs); others tie themselves to the anchor more tightly.

## Measures to influence the exchange rate

A pegged system is one where limits are set on the range of variation of the exchange rate. At any time, the authorities may be called upon to intervene in order to ensure that the market exchange rate stays within the permitted range of variation. For example, a currency might come under pressure because of

---

[10] Every year 2–3 per cent of Americans move to a different state. An action plan published by the European Commission points out that only 225,000 people (or 0.1 per cent of the population of the EU15) moved between two countries in 2000 (*Commission's Action Plan for Skills and Mobility*, Brussels, February 2002).

[11] This is, of course, the standard adjustment mechanism described in Chapters 11 and 14.

[12] P. Kenen, 'What we can learn from the theory of optimum currency areas?', HM UK Treasury, 2003, Chapter 14.

speculative capital outflows. In order to forestall a depreciation of the currency, a variety of measures could be used. We consider the five main instruments: open market intervention, interest rates, impediments to short-term capital movements ('sand in the wheels'), policy coordination, and ministerial government statements.

The first line of defence is *direct intervention* in the forex market. The central bank could sell foreign exchange reserves.[13] In some instances, such intervention may 'see off' the doubters and reassure the market as to the authorities' determination to defend the currency. It may be no coincidence that China, Singapore and Taiwan, areas with large forex reserves, were least affected by the East Asian crisis. But there are limits to this policy:

- Official reserves are finite, and the capacity of government to borrow from the private sector and international agencies may be small in relation to total potential capital flows.
- Even coordinated intervention by several central banks can be ineffective (as the EMS crisis of 1992–93 and the fall in the dollar in spring 1995 illustrated). The Bundesbank reportedly spent DM 92 billion in support-purchases of EMS currencies during August and September 1992 – to no avail (*Monthly Report of the Deutsche Bundesbank*, January 1993).
- Intervention may have undesirable side-effects on money supply and interest rates.

A second line of defence is the *interest rate*. By changing the rate at which banks can borrow from the central bank, interest rates throughout the economy can be raised. This rewards those who keep their money in domestic currency and, in theory, makes it more expensive for the speculator to sell domestic currency. Yet, interest rate policy, like direct intervention, has limitations:

- A rise in interest rates affects all borrowers, not just the speculators. The corporate sector may as a result be exposed to a double blow – higher interest on borrowings and weaker consumer demand – which may not be consistent with the requirements of domestic economic balance. (At this stage the business sector becomes torn between support for currency stability and opposition to the measures necessary to achieve it.)
- Higher interest rates are particularly unwelcome in countries with high debt:GDP ratios and high budget deficits.
- Higher interest rates give markets 'a taste of blood' and can add to market nervousness. Overnight and interbank interest rates sometimes reach astronomical heights as expectations of devaluation gather strength. In September 1992, the Swedish Riksbank's marginal lending rate rose to 500 per cent and the 1-month interbank rate was 70 per cent. Yet speculators were not deterred. To understand why, consider the following case. Suppose a non-resident speculator borrowed kronor from a Swedish bank at 70 per cent, converted the kronor into US dollars and deposited the dollars at 6 per cent interest. This seems very unprofitable since devaluation at an annualised rate of approximately 64 per cent would be required to break even. But if a devaluation of 5 per cent were to take place within a week after borrowing, the annualised equivalent would be

---

[13] The author is indebted to Dominic Burke whose M.Litt thesis for Trinity College addressed this issue.

over 250 per cent, leaving a tidy profit to the speculator.[14] Hence, if the market is convinced that depreciation is imminent, even the highest interest rates may not be effective.

In most circumstances, high interest rates motivated solely by the need to defend the currency are difficult to sustain.

A third line of defence is termed *throwing sand in the wheels* of the forex market.[15] Included here are measures such as the direct controls on capital movements, taxation of gains on currency speculation, limits on open positions held by the banking system, enforcement of high capital reserve requirements against such open positions and restrictions on foreign participation in the domestic capital market.[16] While these measures are popular with the electorate (the currency speculator has few admirers), two factors restrict their long-term usefulness:

● The increased mobility of capital and the wide range of instruments for speculation have made the identification of speculative transactions increasingly difficult.

● Capital controls are a two-edged sword. They penalise *bona fide* long-term investors as well as speculators. Genuine investors, once bitten, will be twice shy. The country imposing the controls will pay a penalty in terms of higher long-term interest rates. In many countries, this is a decisive argument against arbitrary imposition of capital controls.

A fourth possibility is *enhanced international coordination of economic policy*. Governments could agree *target exchange rate zones* within which their currencies would be allowed to fluctuate, and could further undertake to coordinate their domestic economic policies so that these zones proved viable. If one currency was thought to be *depreciating* too much, the *appreciating* currency's government could respond by (a) reducing interest rates, and (b) taking other measures to expand aggregate demand. Countries can and do cooperate – via meetings of the major economic powers, the IMF and the Bank of International Settlements. Within the European Union, there are regular meetings of finance and monetary officials. But national interests take precedence over international priorities. If an economy was at full capacity, the authorities would be unlikely to stimulate demand merely to assist its neighbour with the depreciating currency.

Finally, *ministerial and government statements* on exchange rate policy can, on occasion, have a calming effect on the market. Unfortunately, they can also exacerbate the situation. Ministers do not always adhere to the carefully prepared script of their central bank and finance officials. Sometimes politicians in supposedly cooperating countries make contradictory statements. Repeated

---

[14] Developments in the derivatives markets may also have weakened the power of the interest rate defence. For some hedging strategies, a rise in the spread between domestic and foreign interest rates mandates a forward or spot sale of the domestic currency. Thus, raising the interest rate could have a perverse effect: inducing sales instead of purchases.

[15] B. Eichengreen, J. Tobin and C. Wyplosz, 'Two cases for sand in the wheels of international finance', *Economic Journal* (January 1995).

[16] Often called the Tobin tax proposal after Nobel prize-winner James Tobin, who recommended the imposition of a tax on forex transactions in order 'to throw sand in the wheels of our excessively efficient international money market'. See J. Tobin, 'A proposal for international monetary reform', *Eastern Economic Journal* (Winter 1978) (reprinted in J. Tobin, *Essays in Economics*, Cambridge, MA: MIT Press, 1982).

assurances by a government that it will not devalue can inflame suspicions that this is precisely what is being considered. Rhetoric without supporting action can be equally unproductive, since then it only serves to highlight a country's lack of resolve and possible disagreements within the government. A succession of US Presidents and Treasury Secretaries have in the past affirmed that 'a strong dollar is vital to US economic interests', just at the time when the dollar has weakened.[17] As Germany's former finance minister, Theo Waigel, remarked: 'it is an illusion to believe that government and central banks can go against the markets for any length of time'.[18] Exchange rate expectations are not subject to the whim of governments or monetary authorities. Neither intervention nor interest rate policy nor public statements will ultimately be successful unless there is real economic convergence with the countries to which one's currency is being linked. However, there are three useful lessons for governments facing speculative attacks on their currency:

- First, defence of an exchange rate position will work only if that position has a high degree of credibility. The target must not be over-ambitious, and it must be consistent with economic fundamentals and macroeconomic policies.[19]
- Second, the authorities must carefully decide which instrument or combination of instruments to use and how much reliance to place in each one.
- Third, if a strategic retreat has to be made, the authorities should retreat to a defensible position. If a devaluation proves necessary, the amount of devaluation should be substantial enough to convince the market that the traded sector can 'live' comfortably with the new rate, and yet not so substantial as to create fears of an inflationary spiral. To be sure, this is not an easy task. (See Box 22.2 on the 1994–95 Mexican peso crisis.)

Business is affected by currency instability, by the level of the exchange rate, the nature of the exchange rate regime and the methods of defending it. Business

---

**Box 22.2**  **The 'tequila effect', contagion and the Mexican peso crisis, 1994–95**

In the five years to the end of 1994, the Mexican government had built up a reputation for cautious economic management. Monetary and fiscal discipline was allied to control of wages and prices with the objective of reducing inflation to OECD levels, balancing the budget and creating sustained growth. By 1994, the strategy appeared to have been successful. Inflation had fallen from 27 per cent in 1990 to 7 per cent in 1994, and was forecast to fall to 4 per cent in 1995. Massive deficits had been eliminated and replaced by balanced budgets. Economic growth averaged 3.5 per cent per annum from 1989 to 1992, although there was a sharp reduction in 1993 to 0.7 per cent.

---

[17] March 1995 and June 2003, for example.

[18] Reported in *The Financial Times* (6 April 1995).

[19] This point was forcefully made in the conclusion of the *Deutsche Bundesbank Annual Report 1992*: 'Exchange rate expectations cannot be controlled in the long run contrary to the fundamentals by intervening in the market.' Neither intervention nor interest rate policy nor public statements, it goes on to say, will ultimately be successful unless there is real economic convergence with the countries to which one's currency is being linked.

**Box 22.2 continued**

### Mexico – economic statistics

|                         | 1990   | 1991   | 1992   | 1993   | 1994   | 1995   | 1996   |
|-------------------------|--------|--------|--------|--------|--------|--------|--------|
| *Exchange rate, peso:$* | *2.81* | *3.02* | *3.09* | *3.15* | *3.44* | *6.50* | *7.50* |
| GDP growth              | 4.5%   | 3.6%   | 2.8%   | 0.7%   | 4.5%   | −6.2%  | 5.1%   |
| Consumer prices         | 26.7%  | 22.7%  | 15.5%  | 9.8%   | 7.0%   | 35.0%  | 34.4%  |
| Trade (deficit), $bn    | (0.9)  | (7.3)  | (15.9) | (13.6) | (18.5) | +7.0   | +6.5   |
| BoP current a/c, $bn    | (7.5)  | (14.6) | (24.4) | (23.4) | (24.7) | (1.6)  | (2.3)  |
| External debt, $bn      | 104.3  | 116.6  | 117.6  | 130.2  | 139.0  | 174.0  | 175.0  |

*Note*: Parentheses means deficit.

*Sources*: IMF, *The Economist*, OECD.

In January 1994, Mexico acceded to NAFTA as a full member, joining the US and Canada. Together with membership of the OECD, this appeared to set the seal of international approval on the success of its development strategy.

### The exchange rate anchor

The anchor of monetary and fiscal policy for six years had been the establishment of a stable relationship between the Mexican peso and the US dollar by the Salinas government. Since November 1991 the peso had been permitted to depreciate by a maximum of Ps0.0004 per day against the US dollar. By setting a definite limit on the amount of depreciation, this regime encouraged business to abandon its traditional preoccupations with devaluations and inflation hedges, and to concentrate instead on 'real' business. In return for a stable peso, labour and business agreed to low wage and price increases. The stable exchange rate with the dollar enhanced the attractiveness of Mexico to foreign (mainly US) investors. Large inflows of direct investment and portfolio investment occurred.

Against these successes there were some negative developments. First, the current account deficit had increased from $4bn in 1989 to $23.4bn in 1993. As 1994 progressed, the projected deficit rose to $29bn or 8 per cent of GDP. Its causes could be traced to a consumer boom, and ominously it was financed primarily by short-term external debt.

Second, the political background in Mexico during 1994 became volatile. There were two assassinations of major political figures, one of whom was the ruling party's presidential candidate, and the Chiapas peasant revolt continued to simmer. Foreign investors were becoming uneasy and, as a result, the foreign reserves had fallen from $30 billion to $6 billion over the year.

To correct the current account deficit, some devaluation was judged necessary. It was hoped that, if the devaluation could be limited to a modest amount, the trade balance would improve and confidence could be restored, without fatal damage to the low-inflation objective. Accordingly, on 20 December 1994, Finance Minister Jaime Serra announced an immediate 12.7 per cent devaluation of the peso and the continuation of the crawling devaluation of Ps0.0004 per day.

### Aftermath of devaluation

The devaluation worked out disastrously wrong. Instead of reassuring markets that the realignment was a one-off adjustment, it aroused fears of further and deeper devaluations. The peso proved impossible to support at the new level. By March 1995, it traded at over 7 pesos to the dollar, as compared with 3.5 at the outbreak of the crisis in December. Domestic short-term interest rates rose to 42 per cent by January 1995. US investors, seeing a massive decline in the dollar value of their investment in Mexico began to take a jaundiced view of investment in Latin America generally. This led to higher interest rates in Argentina, Brazil and other dollar-dependent neighbouring countries. The consequent adverse economic impact on these economies was termed the 'tequila effect'.

## Causes of the crisis

One view is that the economic 'fundamentals' made a devaluation necessary and desirable. The relevant fundamentals would include:

● the 28 per cent rise in the real effective exchange rate between 1990 and 1993, continued into 1994;
● the weakening of fiscal and monetary policy associated with the 1994 election campaign, leading to a surge in imports; and
● the build-up of short-term Mexican debt held by foreigners, mainly US mutual funds.* There was a significant bunching of maturities around the end of 1994.

The Mexican case illustrates the problem of *excessive reliance on the exchange rate anchor strategy* to fight inflation. It resulted in an overvalued exchange rate and an unsustainable current account deficit financed by short-term capital inflows. What happened was therefore in accord with theoretical expectations. The proposed devaluation went wrong because it was too small and delayed too long. It got out of control because of the absence of appropriate 'flanking policies', i.e. carefully worked-out fiscal and monetary policy measures to ensure its effectiveness. Pegged exchange rate regimes, some argued, are inherently crisis-prone in countries like Mexico. This lesson applied with even greater force in the case of Argentina's currency debacle of 2002.

An alternative interpretation acknowledges the overvaluation of the peso but argues that the market overreacted. It sees the Mexican case as illustrating the power of speculative capital movements to disrupt stabilisation programmes. Mexican competitiveness could have been restored by any number of possible combinations of domestic inflation and devaluation (the *multiple equilibria problem*). Thus a 60 per cent devaluation followed by a 50 per cent inflation yields the same improvement in competitiveness as a 20 per cent devaluation followed by a 10 per cent inflation. On this view, market panic resulted in an excessive devaluation (overshooting). This forced a much weaker peso – and by extension a much higher inflation rate – than was objectively warranted by fundamentals.

Strong 'contagion effects', engendered by these same irrational market movements, have been a feature of foreign exchange markets to this day. A recent example is the fall of the Uruguayan peso from 7 US cents to 4 US cents between January and August 2002. Initially the decline was caused by the withdrawal of deposits by Argentinians. This forced the authorities to float the peso which promptly fell by 45 per cent. Panicky investors pushed the country's banks to the brink of collapse – this in an economy that has been called the Switzerland of Latin America and a stronghold of financial stability.

## Conclusion

As in the case of Argentina in 2001–02, the currency crisis constituted a serious setback for Mexico. Mexican inflation rose from 7 per cent in 1994 to 35 per cent in

➜

Box 22.2 continued

1995. Investor confidence was dealt a severe blow, and GDP suffered. Another effect of the devaluation was the severe impact of increased interest and financing costs on the many companies in Latin America. The depreciation of the peso could have created difficulties for NAFTA – such wild exchange rate fluctuations are not conducive to a healthy growth of trade and factor exchange. Fears were voiced that the painfully built-up consensus in favour of competition, macro-stability and openness would also be undermined. Certainly it was affected. However, Mexican governments continued their commitment to a reformist, outward-looking strategy. The Brazilian crisis of 1999 and the collapse of the Argentinian peso in 2002 caused similar misgivings and deep disquiet, the full consequences of which have yet to be revealed.

* There was a major difference between importing capital from US banks during the 1970s and importing capital from mutual and other investment funds in the 1990s. Banks lend mostly against specific projects with a long-term view, whereas fund managers regard the whole world as an investment opportunity, and their horizon is dictated by the need to publish daily asset prices. An adverse movement in fund prices can lead to large-scale redemptions – and early retirement for the fund manager!

Sources: R. Dornbusch and A. Weber, 'Mexico: stabilisation, reform and no growth', *Brookings Papers on Economic Activity* (1994), pp. 253–316; IMF, 'Factors behind the financial crisis in Mexico', *World Economic Outlook* (May 1995); B. Eichengreen, 'The morning after: the Mexican peso in the aftermath of the 1994 currency crisis', NBER Working Paper 6516 (Cambridge, MA: National Bureau of Economic Research, 1998); S. Edwards, 'The great exchange rate debate after Argentina', Austrian National Bank, Vienna, September 2002.

organisations need to understand all three aspects of exchange rate policy, and also to appreciate the sometimes unwelcome implications of such policy for interest rates.

## 22.4 Establishing a single currency – the euro

The difficulty of defending a pegged system and of preventing exchange rate volatility prompted some Member States of the EU to implement a radical alternative. Rather than floating their currencies, in January 1999 these countries adopted the most irrevocably fixed regime of all – a single currency.

The road to the single currency began in 1970 with the Werner Report (see Box 22.3). This report proposed the establishment of an economic and monetary union (EMU) in three stages over a 10-year period. The European Council accepted the proposal in 1972. However, soon afterwards came the oil crisis and the deep recession of the 1970s. Policy divergences within the European Community widened and the entire EMU project had to be placed in abeyance.

Nevertheless, concern about the adverse effects of exchange rate volatility on the process of European integration remained. Following a Franco-German initiative, the European Monetary System came into operation in March 1979. Key operational features of the EMS were:

● fixed bands around central exchange rates,
● provision for realignment,

---

<table>
<tr><td colspan="2">Box 22.3    The path to the euro</td></tr>
<tr><td>1970</td><td>Werner Report recommends implementation of economic and monetary union with single currency.</td></tr>
<tr><td>1972</td><td>All Member States (including three new members, UK, Denmark and Ireland) agree to EMU by 1980. Oil crisis later that year effectively derails programme.</td></tr>
<tr><td>1979</td><td>European Monetary System (EMS) introduced.</td></tr>
<tr><td>1989</td><td>Delors Report proposes a three-stage move to EMU.</td></tr>
<tr><td>1991</td><td>Treaty of European Union (Maastricht Treaty) sets down detailed framework for EMU (enters into force 1993).</td></tr>
<tr><td>1992</td><td>Exchange rate crisis: UK and Italy withdraw from EMS.</td></tr>
<tr><td>1993</td><td>EMS exchange rate bands widened to 15 per cent.</td></tr>
<tr><td>1997</td><td>Stability and Growth Pact introduces regulations to strengthen budgetary discipline and clarifies excessive deficit procedure.</td></tr>
<tr><td>1998</td><td>Member States eligible for participation in EMU decided by reference to four criteria of sustainable convergence (the Maastricht criteria) and central bank independence.</td></tr>
<tr><td>1999</td><td>EMU begins: European Central Bank starts operations, euro introduced. Three Member States (UK, Sweden and Denmark) do not participate.</td></tr>
<tr><td>2002</td><td>Euro notes and coins enter circulation and become legal tender in euro area.</td></tr>
</table>

---

- intervention backed by cooperative financial arrangements,
- creation of a monetary unit, the ECU.

The EMS operated fairly successfully for 12 years. Exchange rate variability was reduced and inflation rates converged to those of low-inflation members, notably Germany. Yet the system encountered a number of difficulties. First, there were problems within the system itself. Infrequent realignments during the latter years of the system gave rise to misaligned parities, which the market considered unsustainable. Second, with the liberalisation of capital controls, the volume of speculative capital flows was greatly increased. Too often, narrow exchange rate bands meant the speculators enjoyed one-way options. Third, there was a large asymmetric shock to the system – the reunification of Germany in 1990. This necessitated a huge increase in German public borrowing. To keep inflation in check the Bundesbank raised interest rates. In order to prevent their currencies depreciating against the Deutschmark, the other EMS participants had to follow suit. Thus an unwelcome hike in interest rates was forced on Germany's neighbours at a time of deep recession and high unemployment.

Considerations such as the above confirmed that the EMS was an interim measure rather than a long-term solution to problems of excessive exchange rate volatility. At a political level there was a growing conviction that, in order to complete the single market, a single European currency was essential. Jacques Delors,

President of the European Commission, reverted to the idea that EMU was the way forward. The Delors Report,[20] published in 1989, proposed a three-stage move towards EMU. The European Council endorsed the programme, out of which emerged the treaty of the European Union (the Maastricht Treaty) in 1992. To qualify for participation in the euro, a Member State had to satisfy the following *convergence criteria*:

- *price stability*: the rate of inflation could not exceed the average rates of inflation of the three Member States with the lowest inflation rate by more than 1.5 per cent,
- *interest rates*: long-term interest rates could not exceed by more than 2 per cent the average interest rates of the three Member States with the lowest interest rates,
- *government debt*: public debt could exceed 60 per cent of GDP only if the trend was declining towards this level,
- *budget deficit*: national budget deficits had to be close to or below 3 per cent of GNP,
- *exchange rate stability*: a national currency could not have devalued within the two previous years and must have remained within the margin of fluctuation.

Soon after the Maastricht Treaty was signed the EMS began to come under strain. This developed into a fully-fledged currency crisis and in September 1992 the UK and Italy withdrew from the exchange rate arrangement. There were further exchange rate adjustments and eventually it was agreed to widen the band to ±15 per cent in 1993. The new version of the EMS is very close to a floating rate system.

Pro-EMU governments inferred from these events that only complete fixity in a single currency would permanently solve the exchange problem. With this in mind and in order to complete the provisions of the Maastricht Treaty, the Stability and Growth Pact was adopted. Multilateral supervision, fines on excessive deficits and annual submission of stability reports were approved in order to ensure fiscal discipline.

In May 1998, the European Council defined the list of countries eligible for participation in the single currency, based on their satisfying the five convergence criteria and also having independent central banks. The same year also saw the establishment of the European Central Bank and the appointment of its executive committee. The final stage of monetary union began in 1999 when the euro became a currency in its own right and exchange rates between participating countries were irrevocably fixed. Four EU countries (Denmark, Greece, Sweden and the United Kingdom) did not proceed to this stage, leaving a total of 11 countries in the EMU. However, subsequently Greece applied successfully for membership and the euro area expanded to 12 countries on 1 January 2001.

The concluding phase of EMU took place in 2002 when the euro entered circulation and national notes and coins ceased to be legal tender.

---

[20] J. Delors, *Report on Economic and Monetary Union*, Report to European Council by Committee Chaired by J. Delors (Brussels: European Commission, 1989).

## The benefits of the euro

Already, it is clear that the euro is providing several types of efficiency gains.[21] First, it has eliminated the *transaction costs* of exchanging one EU currency into another. The European Commission estimated transaction costs at about one-half per cent of GDP (€13–19 billion per year) for the EU as a whole.[22] Transaction costs were estimated to be particularly high (about 1 per cent of GDP) for small, open Member States.

Second, the euro has eliminated *exchange rate uncertainty* within the euro area. Exchange rate movements add to a company's uncertainty about its future revenue and discourage trade. By eliminating the need for hedging mechanisms on intra-EU transactions, monetary union entails savings on hedging costs as well as on transaction costs. Because exchange rates are fixed, interest rates must also converge and the resultant decline in money market and bond rates was an important consideration for the more inflation-prone and weaker Member States. (However, divergences in bank lending rates still continue because of different regulatory and tax systems.) More generally, the reduction in uncertainty – not only exchange rate uncertainty but also uncertainty about monetary and fiscal policy – has encouraged investment, and thereby GDP growth.

A third efficiency gain arises from the increased *transparency in prices*. A single currency makes it easier to compare prices in different European markets. The increased comparability of prices has strengthened competition and hence increased efficiency. The transparency has also helped to enhance awareness of costs in other EU countries and over time bring about greater consistency in labour cost developments in the euro area.

Fourth, the euro has *enhanced the role of the EU in the international monetary system*. The new currency has already begun to compete with the dollar and the yen as a major international currency and reserve asset. Member States are able to economise on their holdings of external reserves, and as non-members add to their euro holdings, seigniorage gains will accrue to the euro area as a whole. In addition, the existence of the euro gives greater weight to Europe in international monetary discussions. (Member States are no longer represented by their national central bank, but by the ECB.)

These various effects of the euro are already deepening the process of trade and investment integration. More important, many argued that the absence of a single currency, and the continuance of exchange rate turbulence, could frustrate and even endanger the integration process. A strong and controversial version of the above arguments asserted that a single market without the euro would not have been sustainable – for economic and political reasons.

---

[21] For a comprehensive assessment of the benefits and costs of EMU, see P. de Grauwe, *The Economics of Monetary Union*, 5th edn (Oxford: Oxford University Press, 2003). See also European Commission, 'The euro area in the world economy – developments in the first three years', *Euro Paper*, no. 46, July 2002; and M. Buti and G. Giudice, 'Maastricht's fiscal rules at ten: an assessment', *Journal of Common Market Studies*, December 2002.

[22] See European Commission, *European Economy No. 44: One Market, One Money – An evaluation of the potential benefits and costs of forming an economic and monetary union* (Brussels, October 1990).

### Box 22.4   Economics of the euro: the story so far

The euro project continues to provide fertile ground for controversy. At one end of the spectrum, supporters of the euro stress the following advantages:

1. *Transaction costs*: A single currency eliminates all the costs arising to firms and individuals through conversions from one member currency into another.
2. *Exchange rate uncertainty*: Exchange rate uncertainty and costs of hedging are avoided. As a result, interest rates in weaker economies have converged towards the (lower) level of the stronger economies.
3. *Transparency of prices*: As goods and services are priced in the same currency, the pro-competitive effects of the single market are strengthened. Employers and employees have become more conscious of the necessary wage and price discipline.
4. *External benefits*: The euro has led to a more balanced distribution of international reserve assets, a small amount of seigniorage has been generated, and the ECB has become a powerful actor on the world stage.

Eurosceptics focus on the downsides:

1. *Loss of exchange rate autonomy*: Weakness of the euro helped some countries with high non-EU trade ratios. But a stronger euro is proving bad news for euro area competitiveness.
2. *Inappropriate monetary policy*: a single currency means a single monetary policy and a single interest rate for all participating states. This 'one size fits all' policy has created tension. Germany and France would prefer a more relaxed monetary policy but the majority rules.
3. *Enlargement of membership*: inclusion of weaker transition economies may result in a dilution of the ECB's commitment to price stability and/or the collapse of the system.
4. *Stability and Growth Pact fiscal targets too restrictive*: Member States have widely divergent needs and their fiscal constraints need to be determined accordingly.

After several years of operation, the general consensus is that the euro and the ECB have made a solid start. Initially, the euro proved to be weaker than expected. The US$/euro exchange rate fell from 1.12 in early 1999 to 0.85 in May 2000. It recovered to 1.20 in December 2003. Price stability has been maintained, unemployment has remained high and growth has been sluggish. A reasonable result, but clearly not overwhelming. To improve matters, the authorities must focus on structural reforms designed to enhance flexibility. Meanwhile, of the non-participating countries, Denmark remains sceptical (a report of the Economic Council in mid-2000 concluded that the purely economic costs and benefits for Denmark of EMU membership were *small and uncertain*), the UK economy is doing fine and the electorate is unlikely in the short run to see merit in changing to the euro, and Sweden continues to be wary.

A recent study shows that the euro has had a large trade-promoting effect, raising trade flows among euro area countries by about 15 per cent. Findings of this nature support the view that formation of a monetary union, by intensifying trade and financial integration between members of the union, improves the suitability of the union for these members. Thus, the conditions for an optimum currency area are not a 'given', forming a union makes them happen. The conditions themselves become endogenous. This is the 'endogeneity of optimality' argument.

*Sources: Report of Economic Council on Danish Economy*, Spring 2000 (www.dors.dk). For an excellent overview of the implications of EMU for the UK economy, see 'submissions on EMU from leading academics', EMU study, HM UK Treasury, June 2003, available at www.hm-treasury.gov.uk. See also A. Micco, E. Stein and G. Ordonez, 'The currency union effect on trade: early evidence from EMU', *Economic Policy*, 2003 (forthcoming).

## Drawbacks of the euro

Critics of the euro animadvert on the *loss of autonomy in economic policy* for Member States. Use of the exchange rate as an instrument of economic adjustment at national level is precluded. This loss of the exchange rate option involves a definite cost. In addition, passive control over monetary policy is surrendered to the ECB. Some governments disliked the idea of losing autonomy over monetary policy, regardless of how well the new ECB might work. This concern was accentuated by a separate but related concern that the Stability and Growth Pact could prove to be contractionary and divisive.

Three questions hang over the long-run impact of the euro. The first concerns the nature of the economic shocks affecting different Member States. Since these are often asymmetric, i.e. affect different states to a markedly different degree, some adjustment mechanism must be found to restore balance. In the absence of exchange rate change and monetary autonomy, the burden of adjustment falls on wage and domestic cost flexibility. The second question concerns the extent to which markets in Europe will be capable of evolving more flexible structures. A third issue relates to the capacity of tax and transfer mechanisms within the EU to bridge politically unacceptable gaps in living standards between Member States. While the scale of transfers required has been debated in Europe for many years, the present degree of fiscal integration is extremely modest. These queries raise doubts as to whether the proposed monetary union satisfies the criteria for a successful *optimum currency area*, given that:

- labour mobility is limited, by cultural and linguistic barriers;
- wages and prices are comparatively inflexible;
- fiscal transfers are as yet very small – less than 2 per cent of total GDP (by contrast, the tax-transfer system in the US offsets roughly 40 per cent of region-specific income shocks);
- the share of euro-area trade in some Member States is quite low (just over 50 per cent in the UK and lower still in Finland and Ireland).

Structural funds go some way towards redressing the regional imbalances arising from asymmetric shocks, but the burden of adjustment will mostly fall on domestic prices and wages or, failing that, on output and employment levels. Thus, enhanced policy initiatives continue to be needed to increase flexibility and competitiveness, supplemented with a larger pool of structural funds, if the euro is to work smoothly.

Thus the euro brings significant potential benefits and significant potential costs. These effects are being carefully monitored by the countries included in the 2004 enlargement. Initially these countries will participate in the EMS. Two years later they will decide whether to apply for full participation in the euro. To be accepted, they will have to satisfy the Maastricht criteria. Some of the new members are eager to join and have good prospects of meeting the criteria. But the choice will not be an easy one. In evaluating their options, new members will be aware that the EU at present falls short of an optimum currency area. Hence, the balance between benefits and costs will differ from country to country. We must not exaggerate the potential growth-boosting effects of a monetary union – as de Grauwe rightly warns, 'we should not expect too much additional economic growth from a monetary union'. But it must be remembered that there is a strong political backing for the euro and in the final analysis political considerations carry more weight than the economic calculus.

## 22.5 Conclusions

This chapter began with a description of the world's exchange rate arrangements. Most major currencies operate a policy of independent floating *vis-à-vis* each other. While some smaller countries adhere to managed or pegged systems, a significant number have floating currencies. But few countries are genuine 'free floaters' in the sense of being insouciant about the value of their currencies. Many try to exercise some influence over the degree of exchange rate flexibility.

Governments are concerned by the disruptive effects of excessive volatility on trade and investment, the damage caused to their economies by resulting exchange rate misalignments, and the possibility of their domestic stabilisation policies being weakened by freak, sporadic and irrational changes in market sentiment. These adverse effects are particularly likely to affect weak economies.

Business shares this concern. Of course, as we saw in Chapter 21, companies can protect themselves against short-term volatility by currency hedging transactions and by internal exposure management. But these measures are neither costless nor comprehensive. Even the best forward cover cannot insulate a firm from the effects of sustained misalignment of its currency. Such misalignments create serious problems for business. Profit calculations are thrown into disarray and investment decisions undermined. An overvalued exchange rate could enable foreign competition to establish a bridgehead in the domestic market from which it will not easily be dislodged, even when eventually the misalignment is corrected. For all these reasons, most firms consider exchange rate variations as an unpleasant fact of life, which they would rather not have to cope with.

What can be done to improve the situation? One way is to ensure that governments choose an appropriate exchange rate regime. If an anchor-currency regime is chosen, there are many criteria in addition to trade patterns to bear in mind. Labour mobility, price and wage flexibility and the nature of economic shocks are also important. In particular, the credibility of a country's choice of the anchor currency must be established by supporting fiscal policies and political support. Failure of anchor currency arrangements can usually be traced to absense of these countries.

Another response to the volatility problem was the development of quasi-fixed systems such as the EMS. After the turmoil of 1992, however, it became clear that the system would have to be either made more flexible by widening the band of variation or else replaced by some more radical form of fixity. Out of this has emerged the euro. The gains from the euro include the reduction in foreign exchange transaction costs and in exchange rate uncertainty and greater price transparency. Supporters claim that these will contribute to positive business expectations and to increased trade, investment and growth. A single currency will also allow the EU to play an enhanced role in the global economy. Only time will tell if the euro will deliver on its promise: what can be said now is that it has acquitted itself admirably well up to end 2003.

One method of assessing the implications of a single currency is to study the experience of a group of states which already have a single currency in place, such as the US. The question could be asked whether individual states like California or New England would be better off if they had their own currencies than with the dollar. The absence of active canvassing on their part for a separate currency suggests that they would not. But this observation is not a conclusive case for a single currency. Perhaps there are economic losses but the political benefits of belonging to a Union outweigh them. Besides, the preconditions for making a single currency work are nearer to being satisfied within the US than in Europe: English is the common language, labour is highly mobile between states, and the fiscal system is fully integrated. Besides the long-run growth experience of Europe, properly measured to take account of quality of life, has been in no way inferior to that of the US.

Many countries continue to opt for floating regimes, and, if anything, opinion outside Europe has nowadays come to take a more optimistic view of their operational viability. To make a floating regime work, however, consistent macro policies must be maintained. These can be supplemented by policies directed towards stabilising the exchange rate. The usefulness of forex intervention, interest rate changes, capital and regulatory controls, macroeconomic coordination and official exhortations were considered in turn. Each has a potential part to play, but we emphasised the need to ensure that the exchange rate target (be it a specific rate or a currency band) was credible. Defensive measures will not be effective if the target is perceived to be unsustainable by the market. A determined assault on a currency can be difficult to resist. In some instances, trying to resist may well be harmful to national development.

We conclude that exchange rate instability will remain a feature of the global system. It is likely that the system will evolve towards a tripolar structure around the dollar, the euro and the yen, with strong commitments within regional currency areas but loose commitment between them. Some countries will try to limit their exposure to speculative attack by pegging their currencies to an appropriate anchor and, above all, by paying attention to the conduct of macro-economic policies. As a result of enhanced capital mobility and freer trade, fund managers, corporations and individuals will seek maximum returns and will have to take on foreign currency exposures. Speculators will continue to operate, despite the best efforts of governments to 'throw sand in the wheels'. Whatever the merits of a single currency within Europe, it is unrealistic to expect any similar development on a global scale. Lack of political solidarity and economic convergence will be the dominant barrier to any such development.

## Summary

1. There is continuing debate about the type of global exchange rate system best suited to the needs of an increasingly integrated world economy. Some argue that there should be greater fixity in exchange rates between countries. Others believe that the present system of independent floating among the major currencies is, though far from ideal, the best available.

2. The three major currencies float more or less freely against each other. So do over 20 per cent of the world's currencies. But side-by-side with this flexibility, some countries are seeking more stable arrangements. One method is by pegging their

currencies to an anchor currency such as the euro and the US dollar. Another option is to adopt a composite peg whereby the exchange rate is tied to a weighted average of the currencies of major trading partners. Another possibility is to create a new currency along with one's main trading partners (e.g. the euro). Occasionally the national currency is suppressed entirely in favour of the anchor currency (e.g. Ecuador and Panama to the dollar).

3. A floating exchange rate system has many advantages: prompt adjustment, greater domestic policy autonomy and less need for international reserves. But it has one major downside – exchange rate volatility. This volatility is exacerbated by speculation and may be costly to business (though the expected negative correlation between volatility and trade volumes has proven hard to ascertain statistically) and makes governments uncomfortable.

4. The search for stability has rekindled interest in the theory of optimum currency areas, that is, in the economic characteristics of an ideal fixed exchange rate or common currency area. Among the criteria to be considered are share of trade with the area, vulnerability to shocks, price flexibility and factor mobility.

5. Attention has also focused on the policies available to the authorities to restrain excessive fluctuations in the exchange rate. These policies comprise direct intervention by the monetary authorities in the exchange market, altering domestic interest rates, imposing taxes on financial transactions ('throwing sand in the wheels'), public statements, and policy coordination in defence of target exchange zones. None of these expedients offers a definitive 'solution' to the volatility problem. Exchange rate expectations cannot be controlled by intervening in the market contrary to the long-run fundamentals.

6. The establishment of the euro represents a major initiative by the European governments to impose stability on their monetary systems. Opinions are still divided as to which constitutes the greater danger to European trade: too much currency flexibility leading to disruption of normal trade relations, or too much rigidity which will weaken the capacity of Member States to adjust to external and internal 'shocks'. There are many potential gains from the euro. But nobody can be sure of the imponderable costs which this dramatic and historic initiative might yet impose.

## Questions for discussion

1. Discuss the advantages of the system of independently floating exchange rates. Does the choice of a floating regime indicate that the authorities do not care about the level of the exchange rate?

2. Why were European politicians willing to surrender control of monetary policy and face stringent budgetary rules in return for monetary unification?

3. What criteria would need to be satisfied for the countries of the EU to constitute an optimal currency area? Does the EU at present satisfy these criteria, in your view?

4. Discuss the economic advantages and disadvantages to the UK of participation in EMU.

5. What is an 'anchor' currency? Why should a country wish to 'anchor' its currency to another?

6. Evaluate the measures available to the authorities to moderate currency variation in a floating exchange rate regime.

7. 'There is no single best currency regime for any one country for all times.' Give three examples of countries that have replaced one currency regime for another within the past two decades.

8. 'As literally hundreds of studies of exchange rate volatility have confirmed, the lion's share of short-term exchange rate movements between the euro, the yen and the dollar defy systematic explanation, much less prediction.' (K. Rogoff, Economic Counsellor IMF, *Finance and Development*, June 2002) Why is this the case? Does the same conclusion apply to long-term exchange rate movements?

## Exercises

1. The forex market is not the only market to exhibit volatility. Think of the stock market or the housing market. Why should governments intervene to stabilise prices in one but not in the other? What is so special about the exchange rate?

2. Examine the current exchange rate regime of one developed and one developing country. In each case, list (a) the advantages and (b) the disadvantages of the present regime.

3. In January 1994, the currencies of the French franc zone in Africa devalued by 50 per cent relative to the French franc. This was followed by a rise in their inflation rate from 0.5 per cent per year in 1990–93 to 33 per cent in 1994. GNP, which had been falling in real terms by 1 per cent annually in 1990–93, rose by 1.5 per cent in 1994. What happened to the real exchange rate of the devaluing countries? In your view, are these observations consistent with the predictions of PPP theory?

4. Can a country have a strong currency and a competitive currency at the same time?

## Further reading

A challenging overview of exchange rate developments and theory is provided in M. Obstfeld, 'International currency experience: new lessons and lessons relearned', *Brookings Papers on Economic Activity*, No. 1 (1995), p. 135. A more recent review is M. Mussa *et al.*, 'Exchange rate regimes in an increasingly integrated world economy', *IMF Occasional Paper*, No. 193 (Washington, DC, August 2000).

The literature on EMU ranges from the upbeat *One Market, One Money*, published by the European Commission in *European Economy* (October 1990) to the sharply critical analysis of Bernard Connolly, *The Rotten Heart of Europe* (London: Faber & Faber, 1995). P. de Grauwe, *The Economics of Monetary Union*, 5th edn (Oxford: Oxford University Press, 2003), provides a well-balanced, analytical assessment of costs, benefits and transition problems. For a detailed analysis of anchor currencies and the potential of the euro to fulfil this role, see P. Honohan and P. Lane, 'Pegging to the dollar and the euro', *International Finance* (Autumn 1999). The UK Treasury assessment (2003) of the pros and cons of Britain joining the euro is a gold mine of information and analysis by British and other economists. For a percipient insiders's view, see 'The euro after four years', Professor Otmar Issing, Member of the Executive Board of the ECB, European Finance Convention, 2 December 2002.

## Appendix 22.1  Exchange rate regimes – a brief history

International trade requires an efficient system of international payment. At one time, trade was settled via direct barter. When some commodities, particularly metals, became generally acceptable as a means of payment throughout the world, barter was replaced by the monetary system. This appendix looks at the evolution of the monetary system from the first gold standard to the present global exchange rate system.[23]

### The gold standard

Gold has been used as a means of payment for domestic and international trade since ancient times. However, until the 1870s, gold and silver coexisted as the main monetary metals. These circulated alongside bank notes, which were backed by gold or silver. Gradually, the bimetallic standard began to disappear, as gold coins drove silver coins from circulation. The UK was the first country to adopt a gold standard when, in 1819, the Bank of England was legally required to exchange currency for gold on demand. During the 1870s, most European countries, Japan and the US moved towards the gold standard, and by 1879 the gold standard had evolved from a domestic standard to an international monetary system. The UK, with its highly developed financial institutions and its dominant role in international trade, became the centre of the international financial system built on the gold standard.

The system was based on four main principles:

1. The gold standard was a *fixed* exchange rate regime. Each country set a fixed price for gold in terms of its currency, at which it stood ready to buy or sell. The relative gold values of any two currencies gave their mint parity exchange rate.
2. At that price, gold was *convertible* into currency and currency into gold.
3. Exports and imports of gold were allowed to flow freely from one country to another. This facilitated the development of highly integrated goods and capital markets.
4. Central banks were obliged to back the issue of money notes with gold reserves. This rule imposed monetary restraint by limiting the authorities' ability to print money. Thus the gold standard promoted price stability.

---

[23] For a history of exchange rate regimes, see H.G. Grubel, *The International Monetary System*, 4th edn (Harmondsworth: Penguin Books, 1984) and W. Molle, *The Economics of European Integration*, 4th edn (London: Ashgate, 2001).

The system also provided an automatic adjustment mechanism, through which balance of payments disequilibria would be eliminated. This process is known as Hume's *price-specie-flow* mechanism. Gold flowed out of a country running a trade deficit (excess imports had to be paid for) and flowed into a country with a trade surplus. Thus, a trade deficit implied a shrinking money supply, and a trade surplus an expanding money supply. The declining money supply in the deficit country placed downward pressure on prices, increasing competitiveness in international markets and eliminating the trade deficit. Likewise, the gold inflow as a result of the trade surplus increased the domestic money supply and led to inflation. The rising price of domestic goods reduced competitiveness, eliminating the surplus. Thus, trade balance was restored. Capital movements could also play a role in the adjustment process. The decline in money supply in the deficit country would place upward pressure on interest rates, leading to a capital inflow which offset the initial gold outflow. Similarly, capital outflows associated with lower interest rates in the surplus country offset the initial gold inflow. Provided capital was sufficiently interest-sensitive, the two countries could continue to run a current account imbalance.

## The inter-war period

With the outbreak of the First World War, many countries suspended the convertibility of their currency into gold. The system of fixed exchange rates was replaced by a floating rate system. As governments financed their military build-up through monetary expansion, inflation accelerated. Inflation was higher in Europe than in the US. US trade expanded rapidly, and the dollar was increasingly used to finance international transactions. After the war, the European countries continued to float their currencies, and most depreciated rapidly relative to the dollar. The pound sterling fell to a low of $3.40 per pound in 1920. The depreciation of sterling and fear of consequent inflation caused the UK Chancellor of the Exchequer, Winston Churchill, to seek a return to the gold standard in 1925 at the pre-war parity of $4.86.[24] Most other currencies had followed by 1927.

However, the system proved impossible to sustain for a variety of reasons. First, many countries continued to restrict inter-country gold flows in order to alleviate their balance of payments problems. New controls on inflows and outflows of gold seriously limited the effectiveness of the automatic adjustment mechanism. Adjustment problems were further exacerbated by the downward inflexibility of domestic prices. In addition, many central banks no longer retained the bulk of their reserves in gold but kept them in currencies convertible to gold. Thus the gold standard was effectively transformed into a *gold exchange standard*. Second, the Great Depression of 1929 led to a collapse of banking systems around the world, and confidence in the convertibility of currencies collapsed.

The UK abandoned convertibility in 1931, and other countries followed suit. The world monetary system disintegrated into currency blocs, of which the sterling area (the UK and most of the British Empire) and the US dollar bloc were the most important. Some currencies floated freely. The depression worsened, reserve levels

---

[24] See J.M. Keynes, 'The economic consequences of Mr. Churchill', *Essays in Persuasion* (New York: W.W. Norton, 1931).

were eroded and there was a rise in protectionism. International trade and finance effectively collapsed. The resultant economic lessons were so severe that the prevention of such a situation became the primary aim of postwar policy-makers.

## The Bretton Woods system

In July 1944, representatives of 44 countries met in Bretton Woods, New Hampshire, with the objective of re-establishing a workable monetary system. The negotiations culminated in the establishment of the International Monetary Fund (IMF), which was intended to police a system of exchange rates known as the Bretton Woods system. The Bretton Woods system worked on a gold exchange standard, whereby countries had fixed exchange rates against the US dollar, and the price of the dollar was fixed in terms of gold (at $35 per ounce).

Like the gold standard, the Bretton Woods system was based on the principles of *fixed exchange rates* and *convertibility*. Convertibility is a term which may be used in two different contexts: convertibility into gold and convertibility into other currencies. Only the US maintained gold convertibility during the Bretton Woods era, but the agreement specified that member countries' currencies would be convertible into other members' currencies at fixed rates. The US and Canadian dollars became convertible in 1945, but it took another decade before convertibility was restored to most of the war-torn European countries. The Bretton Woods system only became fully operational in the late 1950s. The early convertibility of the US dollar, combined with its anchor position in the Bretton Woods system and its rising economic and political power during the inter-war period, made it the key global currency of the postwar period. Most European countries were willing to accept US dollars in payment for goods and services.

As far as fixity of exchange rates was concerned, the par values of any two currencies expressed in terms of US dollars (or gold) gave their official exchange rate or parity. For example, in 1946, the pound sterling was valued at 3.6 g of fine gold or $4.03. The French franc was valued at 0.75 g of fine gold or $0.84. Thus the official pound sterling/French franc exchange rate was £1:FF 4.8. Exchange rate fluctuations were limited to a narrow band (±1 per cent) around this official exchange rate. Monetary authorities were obligated to intervene in the foreign exchange market to ensure that the exchange rate stayed within this band.

Provision was made for realignment in cases of 'fundamental disequilibrium', defined by reference to chronic and persistent balance of payments difficulties. Realignments of less than 10 per cent were left to the country's own initiative; those of 10 per cent or more were subject to the approval of the IMF. Thus the Bretton Woods system did not irrevocably fix exchange rates; rather it was an *adjustable peg* system. An inherent weakness in the system was that much-needed adjustments were often delayed, with resultant bouts of heavy currency speculation and depletion of a country's reserves in the run-up to a devaluation. In addition, while deficit countries were forced to devalue, surplus countries played little or no role in the adjustment process. (This was known as the asymmetry problem.)

## The breakdown of the Bretton Woods system

The Bretton Woods system depended critically on confidence in its anchor currency – the US dollar. In the late 1960s, US public expenditure arising from the war in Vietnam and new domestic social programmes led to growing balance of payments and budget deficits. The US current account, for long in surplus, recorded a deficit in 1969. Two years later, a trade deficit of $2.7 billion appeared for the first time this century. US inflation rose, leaving the dollar more and more overvalued relative to other currencies (particularly the strong Deutschmark and yen) and pushing up the prices of all goods except gold (its price being fixed at $35 per ounce). By the mid-1960s, the growth in dollar reserves held abroad and the steady depletion of US gold reserves began to undermine international confidence that the US could sustain sales of gold for dollars.[25] At the same time, the dominance of the dollar was being challenged by the resurgence of the European economies and Japan. The parities established under the Bretton Woods system (including the price of gold) had become seriously out of line with reality.

International tension increased. As early as 1965, the French President de Gaulle protested about the ability of the US to finance its expenditure through seigniorage (i.e. the power to finance its budget deficit by printing dollars – a *'privilège exorbitant'* available only to the US by virtue of the dollar–gold link), and France began an elaborate programme of building up its gold reserves by swapping dollars for gold. In 1968, a two-tier gold market was created, with official transactions between central banks still at $35 per ounce, and private market transactions at a substantially higher price as determined by supply and demand. However, the speculative run on the dollar soon became unsustainable. The system finally broke down when President Nixon was forced to sever the gold–dollar link in 1971. Later that year, there was an attempt to return to fixed exchange rates, known as the Smithsonian Agreement, which increased the dollar price of gold and set new parities for other currencies in terms of the dollar. This arrangement was effectively abandoned in 1973.

## Developments 1973 to the present

After the demise of the Bretton Woods system, most countries adopted floating exchange rates. Although this was viewed as a temporary measure at the time, the international monetary system has been characterised by floating to a more or less managed degree by most of the major currencies ever since. This 'non-system' of managed floating is neither universal nor stable. While most industrial countries allow their currency to float, other currencies are pegged to an anchor currency or a basket of currencies. The introduction of the euro marked a dramatic change in the balance of global currency power. The short-run effects have been discussed above, in the long run the euro could prove a powerful alternative to the US dollar – particularly in light of America's ongoing balance of payments weakness and growing domestic and external debt. Also, the prospect of setting up a single Asian currency has already been mooted by several Far East governements.

Although most central banks still hold some gold reserves, gold transactions have been largely discontinued. SDRs play a minor role, and the IMF retains a surveillance role, whereby it monitors the performance of individual countries and provides them with advice. However, there is no international body with effective control over exchange rates.

---

[25] See R. Triffin, *Gold and the Dollar Crisis: The future of convertibility* (New Haven, CT: Yale University Press, 1957).

The past 50 years has seen an explosion in foreign exchange market activity, brought about by the removal of capital controls, technological advance and the increased internationalisation of business activity. It has also been characterised by considerable volatility in foreign exchange markets. This has caused discomfort and inefficiency, and prompted calls for reform of the system, particularly in the aftermath of the periodic currency crises of the past decade. But there is no consensus about what sort of reforms are needed. Some argue for restrictions on capital flows; others want fewer restrictions but better surveillance of governments' domestic policies and more focused assistance from international bodies such as the IMF and the World Bank. The prestige of these institutions has been somewhat dented in recent years. They have been accused of being overly US dominated and of being dogmatic about the application of new consensus principles in inappropriate circumstances. These criticims have some validity, but not surprisingly they are vigorously contested by the present US government. If and when the balance of global economic power shifts to the developing countries we can surely expect more institutional change and more equal balance in how the world monetary system is managed.

# Index

absolute PPP 537, 538, 540–1
abuse of dominant position 158, 163
access (natural monopolies) 174
accidents 218, 223
accommodating monetary policy 373
accommodating transaction 506
accountability 327
accountancy services 141
accounting definition of profits 105
Accounting Oversight Board 99
acid rain 207, 210
acquisitions see mergers and acquisitions
activism, policy 410
  fiscal 370, 373–6, 376–81
  monetary 325–6
actual exchange rate, PPP and 539–40
acyclical response to cycles 406
AD see aggregate demand
Adelphi Communications 99
adjustable peg system 592
adjustment
  balance of payments 518–19, 524
  costs 573
  exchange rate 584, 591–2
  fiscal 386–8
  foreign trade policy 442–6, 453
  labour/employment 62–3
  market system 55, 57
  mechanism 518–19, 524, 591
  process 55, 57
  process (unemployment) 353
administrative costs 215
advertising
  costs 110
  demand and 91
  market power 141, 143, 144, 153
Advisory Commission (USA) 279
AEG 141
Africa
  capital flows 470
  exchange rate 564
  FDI 470
  foreign trade 452
  growth/decline 5, 15, 16, 24, 30
  inflation 300
  labour migration 489, 490

market power (diamonds) 142, 143, 151–4
new economic policy 4, 5
  see also South Africa; Sub-Saharan Africa; West Africa
after-care policies 483
age
  ageing population 26, 300, 301, 390, 464, 584
  profile (borrowers/savers) 316
  unemployment by 340–1
agents 61–3, 69
agglomeration economies 118
aggregate demand
  balance of payments 518–19, 524
  business fluctuations 407–9
  curve (derivation) 247
  fiscal policy 372, 373
  inflation 284
  interest rate and 315, 318
  labour 260, 352
  money 262–71
  unemployment 348–9, 354
  see also demand
aggregate supply
  curve 256–61
  fiscal policy 371–2
  money 269–71, 275
  unemployment 348–52, 354
  see also supply
Aghveli, B. 35
Agricultural Bank of China 126
agriculture 62, 171, 211, 219, 355
  CAP 59
  foreign trade 430
  see also drinks industry; food industry
Ahearne, Alan 333, 469
air quality
  clean (as public good) 191, 195
  pollution 28, 195, 206, 207, 208–10, 215, 219, 221
Airbus 446
aircraft industry
  foreign trade 446, 450
airlines 112, 114, 169, 174
Albania 277, 340, 427
alcohol industry

taxation 60, 79
  see also wine industry
Allen, H. 547
allocative efficiency 17, 18–19, 63, 287
anchors, exchange rate
  inflation 296–300
  regimes 565, 573, 578, 586, 593
Andréosso-Callaghan, B. 179
Angola 151, 277
anti-dumping rules 448
anti-trust regulation 81, 91, 129, 131, 147, 168, 171
Antwerp 152
'anxious class' 361–2
APEC (Asia-Pacific Economic Community) 431
Apple-Macintosh 129
applications barrier 129
appreciation (exchange rate) 530, 536, 543, 551, 576
Aral Sea 207
arbitrage 61–3, 137, 312–13, 537, 543, 552
architecture
  global financial system 555
  network of contracts 141
area, cost by 112
Argentina 489
  foreign trade 427, 437, 450
  GNP 255
  growth 45
  inflation 277, 294, 297–9
  new economic policy 1, 3, 9
  unemployment 368
arithmetic of growth 32, 33
armed forces 19, 191
  see also defence industries; military hardware
Armenia 565
Arndt, S.W. 571
art galleries 191
Arthur, Brian 129, 130, 451
Artis, M.J. 322, 405, 406
AS see aggregate supply
ASEAN (Association of South East Asian Nations) 431
Ashanti Goldfields 553
Ashenfelter, O. 98

Asia
  business fluctuation 403, 407, 408–9
  capital flows 464, 470
  currency crisis 5, 6, 29, 37
  environment 207, 211, 213, 223
  exchange rate 575, 579
  FDI 471–5
  foreign trade 425, 431
  growth 15, 25, 35, 37
  labour migration 489, 490
  new economic policy 1, 4, 5, 6
  see also dynamic Asian economies (DAEs); East Asian; South-east Asia; South Asia
Asia-Pacific Economic Community (APEC) 431
assets
  and liability management 552–3
  prices 296, 317, 321, 542
Association of South East Asian Nations (ASEAN) 431
asymmetry
  information 62, 116, 181, 192–3, 197, 351
  problems 592–3
  shocks 573, 584
Atkinson, A.A. 185
ATMs 296
auction theory 146
audit, environmental 220, 221
Auerbach, A.J. 384, 386
Australia
  balance of payments 503, 508
  diamond market 151, 152
  exchange rate 569
  fiscal policy 375, 380
  foreign trade 450
  labour migration 488, 489, 490–1
  new economic policy 1
  unemployment 338, 347, 352
Austria
  black economy 51
  exchange rate 568–9
  fiscal policy 375, 390
  government intervention 186
  inflation 299
  interest rate 316
  labour migration 489, 497
  unemployment 338, 339, 345–6, 347
Austrian School 188
autarky 433, 434, 438
authoritarian regimes 73, 182
automatic adjustment mechanisms 518–19, 524, 591
automatic stabiliser 374, 410
automatic teller machines (ATMs) 296

automobiles 191, 192
  balance of payments 503–4, 505, 507, 512
  catalytic converters 29, 216, 220
  dumping (prevention) 216
  environment and 29, 208, 210, 216, 220
  exclusive dealing 162–3
  FDI 478, 484
  foreign trade 428, 445
  market power 126, 128, 147
  see also petrol
autonomy
  exchange rate 568, 570, 584
  loss of (EMU) 585
  transactions 506, 508
average cost 108
average return on capital 174
Azerbaijan 565

Bails, Dale G. 416
Bain, J.S. 179
Baker, M. 546
balance
  on current account 503, 504, 541
  fiscal 4, 370
  international transfers 503, 504
  primary budget 385, 393
  trade 503, 535–6
  trading and investment income 503–4
balance of payments
  capital account 502, 503, 504–7
  correcting imbalance 518–23
  current account 501, 502–4, 509–517, 523, 541
  deficit 502, 507, 508, 513, 518, 520, 523, 543
  definition/analysis 502–9
  equilibrium problems 502, 508–17
  exchange rate 502, 506, 511, 515, 521–3, 524, 533, 538–9, 542, 593
  monetary approach 538–9
  policies for restoring equilibrium 520–3
  statement 503
  surplus 501–2, 504, 507, 509–10, 512, 515, 516, 524
  see also debt; disequilibrium
Balassa, B. 450
Balassa–Samuelson effect 541
Balcerowitz Plan (1990) 5
Balasubramanyam, V.N. 5
bandwagon effect 546, 555
Bangalore 475
Bangladesh 211, 427, 450
Bank of England

Act (objectives) 319, 320
  exchange rate 531, 590
  inflation 283, 292
  interest rates 319, 320, 322, 408
Bank of International Settlements 506
  capital flows 464
  exchange rate 559, 576
Bank of Japan 320, 327
Bank of Montreal 101
bankruptcy 100, 305, 515–17
banks/banking 112, 408–9
  cross-border 503
  information (role) 62
  lending 464
  regulation 195
  trust departments 560
  see also central banks; commercial banks; financial services
Barbados 564
Barde, Jean-Philippe 216
Barings Bank 327, 415, 553, 560
Barrett, M. 101
barriers to entry 129
Barro, Robert J. 32, 294, 383, 384
barter 65, 429
BASF 166
basic balance 503, 509
basket of goods/services 278–9
batch production 114
Bateman, Ian 210, 214
Baumol, W. 71, 150
Bavaria 339
BCSD (British Council for Sustainable Development) 219
Begg, D. 332
Beijing 207
Belarus 277, 565
Belgium
  business fluctuations 406
  fiscal policy 375, 382, 390
  foreign trade 426, 427, 438–9
  government intervention 196
  growth 11, 253
  inflation 299
  labour migration 490, 494
  shadow economy 51
  unemployment 347
below-cost selling 107, 140, 142
Bentham, Jeremy 183
Bergson, Abram 183
Best, M.H. 118
Bewley, T.E. 354
Bhagwati, J. 437, 440, 442, 471
Bhandari, J. 540
Bhopal accident 223
bias (inflation statistics) 279
bid and ask prices 560

bid systems 146
Big Mac index 539
bilateral barter 429
bilateral exchange rates 530
bilateral surplus/deficit 512
binding commitments 146
biodiversity 210
biotechnology 35, 40, 114, 417, 450
Birch Report (1979) 131–2
black economy 50–3, 197, 252
Black Monday 245, 325
Blinder, Alan 394, 443, 445
Blow, Laura 216
Blue Circle 166, 167
BMG 128
Board of Directors 97
Boeing 446
Boeri, T. 132
Bolivia 1, 277
Bombay 152
bonds 105, 464, 505, 509
    interest rate 307, 318, 328
    investment decision 237
    open market operations 265, 267
    see also stock market
bonuses 98
books see publishing industry
Borjas, George 496
Borner, S. 554
Borzenstein, E. 482
Boskin, M.J. 279
Botswana 151, 152
bottom-up forecasting 416
bounded rationality 73
brain-drain tax 496
branch plants 483
Brazil 1, 10, 41, 408
    balance of payments 512
    exchange rate 564
    foreign trade 427, 452
    growth 31
    inflation 277, 300
    Rio Summit 222
break-even 173
breakeven chart 107–8
Brent Spar oil rig 219
Bretton Woods system 563, 570,
    592, 593
bribery 194, 202
bridges (as public goods) 192
Britain see United Kingdom
British Aerospace 171
British Airways 169
British Coal 171
British Gas 171, 221–2
British Leyland 141
British Rail 169–70
British Salt 143–4

British Telecom 169, 171
Broad Economic Policy Guidelines
    (BEPG) 389
brokers 529, 559–60
Brown, C.V. 205
Brown, W. 429
Browne, F. 301
Brülhart, M. 428, 448
Brunhes, B. 344
bubbles 546
Buckley, P. 480
budget
    constraints 100, 283
    deficit 3–4, 283, 294, 311,
        370–400, 520, 555, 582, 593
    see also fiscal policy
building societies 262
Bulgaria 300, 339, 340, 564, 565
Bundesbank 42
    exchange rate 575, 581, 585, 584
bundling 129, 137
Bureau of Census (USA) 130
bureaucracy 199, 218
    see also regulation
Burke, Dominic 575
Burns, Arthur F. 410
business
    environment and 206–26
    globalisation of 4–5
    organisation, price elasticity 79
business-to-business (e-commerce)
    41
Business Council for Sustainable
    Development (BCSD) 219
business fixed investment 316
business fluctuations/cycles 90, 125,
    401–2
    amplitude (diminishing) 410–11
    causes 407–11
    definitions/facts 403–7
    in dynamic Asian economies 405
    forecasting 412–17
    growth and 411–12
    macro-forecasts and 416–17
    see also firm
Buti, M. 393
buy-back trade 429

Cadbury Committee 99
Cairncross, Frances 219
California 339, 451, 586
call option 549
Calmfors, L. 360, 361
Calverley, J. 517
Canada
    balance of payments 508
    black economy 51
    business fluctuations 406

competition 164
environment 215
exchange rate 531, 592
fiscal policy 375
forecasting 413
foreign trade 426, 427, 430
government intervention 185
growth 31, 255
inflation 300
interest rate 318
labour migration 490–1, 494
market system 63
NAFTA 429, 498, 578, 580
new economic policy 4
services sector 63
unemployment 342, 347
Cancun trade summit 424
Cantwell, J.A. 478, 480
CAP (Common Agricultural Policy)
    59
capacity to adjust (unemployment)
    442–6
capacity utilisation 295, 322
capital
    accumulation 36–37
    depreciation 250
    impediments to short-term
        movements 575, 576, 587
    market 2, 48, 49, 322, 469
    rental cost of 232, 234
    see also capital flows; investment
capital account (balance of
    payments) 502, 503, 504–7
capital flows 255, 558
    basic model 465–71
    exchange rate 542–7
    extensions and qualifications
        469–71
    FDI 463–5, 479–84
    inward FDI 472–5, 479, 483
    net (emerging economies) 464
    outward FDI 476–9, 473–5, 480,
        485
    taxation 467–8
capital goods 353
capital mobility 49, 296, 305, 406,
    462
    gain from 465–7
    taxation and 464, 467–8
    volatility of 470–1
    see also capital flows
capitalism 130–3
carbon dioxide 28, 210, 211, 217–18
carbon emissions 28, 210–11,
    215–18, 222
carbon monoxide 210
carbon tax 217–18, 222
Card, D. 98, 497

Carrefour 126
cars *see* automobiles
cartels 138, 142–4, 175, 187
    diamond 143, 151–4
cash 265, 267, 269, 296
    *see also* currency; money
cash flow 106
    annual 235
    discounted 234
    effects 315, 316
Casson, M.130
Castro, Fidel 438
catalytic converters 29, 216, 220
catastrophic events 218, 223
catching-up controversy 32–3
Cecchini Report 188, 447
cellophane (case study) 81
Celsis 114
CEMBUREAU 167
cement industry 100, 142, 166, 167
Cement Roadstone Holdings (CRH)
    100
Central America 489
    *see also* Latin America; Mexico
central banks 3, 389
    balance of payments and 505
    exchange rate 529, 559–60, 575,
        591
    forecasting 295
    interest rate 266–8, 305, 310, 317,
        318–24
    intermediate targets 319–23
    monetary base and 265–6
    money supply and 263–4, 267
    objectives 292, 294, 319
    official reserves 505–6, 575
    policy instruments 323–4
    price elasticity and 79
    supervision of credit institutions
        327
    transparency-secrecy balance 327–8
    unemployment and 347
    *see also* Individual central banks
Central and Eastern Europe
    foreign trade 437
    inflation 277
    labour migration 489, 497
    market system 58, 67
    new economic policy 1,4
    unemployment 336
Central Selling Organisation (CSO)
    153
CFA currency zone 300
CFCs 212–13, 221
Chadeau, A. 252
Chamberlin, E.H. 176
chance, comparative advantage and
    450

Channel Tunnel 107, 108, 237
chaos theory 547, 555
Chartered Association of Certified
    Accountants 222
Chartism (technical analysis) 412,
    546, 547, 555, 571
cheating 143, 153
chemicals industry
    balance of payments 512
    foreign trade 428, 445
    oligopoly 142
    pollution 28, 188–90, 194–5, 197,
        199, 221–2
Chiapas peasant revolt 578
Chile
    capital flows 471
    environment 215
    foreign trade 437
    growth/decline 6, 24
    inflation 277
    new economic policy 1
China 44
    business fluctuations 405
    deflation 284
    environment 207
    exchange rate 564
    FDI 472, 473
    foreign trade 426, 430, 450,
        458–61
    growth 17, 26, 34
    HDI ranking 31
    inflation 288
    new economic policy 1, 4, 6
    WTO and 458–61
China National Petroleum 126
China Telecommunications 126
Chiroscience 114
chlorofluorocarbons (CFCs) 212–13,
    221
Choksi, A. 441
Chrysler 98
Churchill, Winston 562, 591
Ciba-Geigy 220
cigarettes taxation 60
cities 30, 207
civil servants/service 199, 203
Clark, Kim B. 109, 147
Clarke, Roger 124, 130
classical theory
    business fluctuations 403
    hiring decision 227–9
    unemployment 351, 355
Clegg, J. 480
Clerc, Denis 344
Cline, W. 497
Clinton administration 35, 394
closed economy 261, 437
closing rate 529

clothing industry
    comparative advantage
        example 432–5, 443, 447
    demand function 84
    foreign trade 432–5, 443, 445, 447
CMR (corrected marginal revenue)
    140
coal 28, 213
Coase, Ronald 115, 194–5
Coase Theorem 194–5
Coca-Cola 91, 99, 436, 478
cocoa 17, 24
coffee 17
coincidence of wants 65
Colbert, Jean Baptiste 182
collusion 164, 165–6
Colombia 1
Comecon countries 438
COMESA 431
command-and-control regulation
    197, 215
commercial banks 266, 324, 560
    balance sheet 263–4
commercial policy 520
commodity prices 301, 322
    lead indicators 295, 319
Common Agricultural Policy 59
Common Market for Eastern and
    Southern Africa (COMESA)
    431
common markets 429, 431
communications 114
    costs 477
    demand function 84, 85
    industries 126, 127
company exchange rate exposures
    553–4
comparability (rational consumers)
    72, 73
comparative advantage 435, 552
    arithmetical example 432–5
    changes 447–8
    development/determination
        449–52
    stages theory 450
comparative analysis 439
Compass Group 126
compensation
    for labour *see* pay
    principle 186
    schemes 231
competition 301
    benefits 156–9
    contestability 435
    definition 160
    efficiency of 63–5
    EU law 157, 160–8
    FDI and 483

firm 95–124
foreign trade 435
hiring decision 227–9, 230
intensification 131
loss-leader strategy 138–41
loss of benefits of 116
market power 125, 127–30, 134–6,
  138–41, 142, 144–7
market system 2–3, 63–5
monopoly versus 134–6, 142
new economic policy 2–3, 6
open, fair and undistorted 430
policy/law 1, 2, 35, 81, 147,
  160–8, 175–6
pricing and 144–6
Competition Act (1988) 168
competitive advantage 118, 131,
  156, 437, 450–1
competitiveness 95, 120
  cost structure 107–15
  impact of environmental policy
    222
  industrial organisation approach
    116–17
  profit-maximisation 96–107
complements 80, 139–40
compliance costs 181, 196–7, 215
composition
  bias (inflation statistics) 279
  economic activity 208
  of trade 427–9
computer industry 503
  competition 129–30, 159, 168
  cross-price elasticities 81
  demand 81, 416
  economies of scale 114
  FDI 475
  foreign trade 445, 450
  market power 129–30
  new economy 35, 40–2
  unemployment 355, 356
concentration ratios 128, 142, 159,
  436
confectionery 81
Congo 151, 152
consensus 1–10
  criticisms of 7–9
  forecasting 412
consistency (rational consumer) 73
consolidation, fiscal 370
construction industry 127, 222
  see also cement industry
consumer see
    consumption/consumers
consumer durables 84, 401
consumer goods 313, 401
consumer price index (CPI) 278,
  279, 280, 284, 290, 295, 320

Consumers' Association 62
consumption/consumers
  aggregate demand 261
  component of national
    expenditure 251
  exchange rate 532, 559
  externalities 181, 188–90
  foreign exchange market 559–60
  growth and 17, 33
  income and 262, 382, 408
  loyalty 144
  possibilities extended 20
  rational consumer 72–4
  trade and 434, 435
  wealth effects 315, 316–18
  see also preferences; tastes
contagion effects 409, 572, 579
contamination see pollution
contestability 142, 172
  competition and 159, 168, 435
contingency valuation method 213
Contract with America proposals
  380
contraction, fiscal 372, 384, 386–8,
  394
contracts 98, 116, 141
convergence criteria 582
convergence hypothesis 30–3
convertibility, currency 5, 590, 591,
  592
convexity (rational consumer) 73
cooperation
  collusion 164, 165–6
  distributional coalitions 25
  financial cooperatives 118
  restrictive agreements 163
  see also OECD
cooperatives 114, 116
  financial 118
coordination of economic policy
  576
copyright 474
core competencies 110, 116–17
corporate giantism 126
corporate governance 99
corruption 200–1
cost-increasing rigidities 230
cost-plus pricing 107
cost-push inflation 283
cost curves
  of firm 103
  shape 115, 118
costs
  administrative 215
  average 108
  competitiveness 521
  compliance 181, 196–7, 215
  external 188–90

fixed 107, 108, 120
hiring decision 227–32
labour 380, 477
menu 287, 348, 351
monopoly 133–6
motivation 116
opportunity 18, 106, 446
pollution control 206, 210,
  212–13, 216–17, 219
prices and 56
structure (firm) 107–15, 117–19,
  120
sunk 107, 108, 114, 120, 129
transaction 100, 116–17, 137, 191,
  195, 478, 537, 583, 586
transport 114, 167, 432, 449, 477
variable 105, 107
see also expenditure; marginal
  costs
Cote d'Ivoire 508
counter-cyclical fiscal policy 4, 370,
  371–6, 381, 395
counter-cyclical fiscal transfers 574
counter-cyclical monetary policy
  325
counter-cyclical response (business
  cycles) 406
countertrade 429
countervailing duties 442, 446
Courtaulds 141
Covered Interest Rate Parity (IRP) 544
Cowling, K. 188
Crafts, N. 24
Cramer, U. 132
crawling band currencies 564
crawling peg 573, 574
creative destruction 411
credibility
  of central bank 319
  of currencies 569, 574, 577
credit 324, 516–17
  balance 263
  demand/supply 268, 311–12
  expansion 283
  guarantees 452
credit cards 296
credit institutions, supervision 327
Creedy, J. 130
CRH (Cement Roadstone Holdings)
  100
crime 30, 252
cross-border banking 503
cross-price elasticity of demand
  80–2, 91, 140
crowding out 372
  public debt and 381–8
CSO (Central Selling Organisation)
  153

Cuba 438
currency
  anchors 296–300, 565, 573–4,
    578, 586, 593
  convertibility 5, 590, 591, 592
  crises 471, 517, 594
  deposit ratios 52
  floating 566–72
  misalignments 548, 555, 562,
    570–1
  options 549–50
  single see single currency
  stability/instability 571–2, 573–80
  tied to low-inflation currencies 3
  zones 300
  see also cash; exchange rate;
    money
current account 501, 502–4
  balance 503, 504, 541
  deficit 504, 517, 518–23, 538
  surplus 504
current value of goods/services see
  Gross National Product (GNP)
customer groove-in 129
customers see consumption/
  consumers
customised goods 131
cyclical trends 410–412
  see also business
    fluctuations/cycles; counter-
    cyclical fiscal policy; counter-
    cyclical monetary policy;
    instability
Czech Republic
  exchange rate 565
  fiscal policy 391
  inflation 277
  unemployment 340
Czechoslovakia see Czech Republic;
  Slovenia

DAEs (dynamic Asian economies)
  405
Daimler 98
DaimlerChrysler 126
Darwinism 291
D'Aveni, Richard 159
Davis, Steven J. 132
dawn raids 165, 168
DCF (discounted cash flow) 234
de-bundling 478
deadweight loss 190
  of efficiency 192
  of monopoly 134–5, 187
dealers 529, 559–60
Deaton, A. 84
De Beers 142, 143, 151–4
debt 463

balance of payments 512–15,
    515–17
  developing countries 381, 513–14
  forgiveness 513–14, 517
  GDP ratio 361, 379, 381, 385, 391,
    392, 393, 398–400
  government see public
  household 316, 394
  income ratios 290, 316
  indebtedness of nations 507–9,
    524
  penalty 393
  rescheduling 381, 384
  service costs 318
  sustainability of 377, 381, 387,
    398–400, 511
  see also fiscal policy; loans
defence industries 442, 443
  armed forces 19, 191
  military hardware 19
deficit
  balance of payments 501–2, 506,
    508, 513, 518, 520, 523, 543
  budget 370–400, 520, 555, 593
  current account 504, 505, 523,
    538
  financing 509
  structural 374
  trade 593
  see also debt
deflation 278
  costs of 290–1
  as deviation from price stability
    284–6
  risk of 301
deflator, implicit GDP 248
de Gaulle, Charles 593
De Grauwe, P. 392, 547
De Gregorio, J. 482
Delors, Jacques 582
Delors Report 377, 582
demand
  business fluctuations 402, 411
  for computers 81
  conditions 450–1
  elasticities of 75–82, 91
  exchange rate 533–5, 537, 540,
    555, 560–2, 573, 575
  fiscal policy 394
  forecasting 82–8
  interest rate and 315, 318
  labour market 228–9, 352–4
  management 153, 395, 402, 411
  for money 262–71
  movements in 56–61
  -pull inflation 283
  unemployment and 352–4
  see also aggregate demand

demand curve
  for credit 311–12
  derived market 75
  downward sloping 53, 95
  estimating demand function 82–8
  for labour 228–9, 230
  marginal revenue curve 89–90
  market system 53, 54, 56–7, 63
  outward shift 56–7
  pricing decision and 74
  upward sloping 74
democracy 24, 289, 301
Denmark 300
  competition 118
  euro and 581
  exchange rate, 584
  fiscal policy 375, 379, 382, 387,
    390
  government intervention 196
  growth 14
  market power 128
  shadow economy 51
  unemployment 347, 349
Dennis, William J. 130
Dennison, Edward F. 22
Department of Justice (USA) 129,
    143, 170
dependency, culture of 349
dependency ratios 385
deposit creation 263
deposit-refund systems 215–16
deposits, bank 263–4, 265
depreciation
  capital 250
  exchange rate 521–3, 530, 532–6,
    538, 544, 551, 560–2, 575–6,
    578–9
deregulation 523
  competition and 172, 175
  financial sector 322, 428
  inflation and 283, 296
  market power and 131, 147
  new policy consensus 2, 3
  see also privatisation
derivatives 462, 529, 559, 560
derived demand 75
destabilising speculation 571–2
detergents 221
Deutsche Post 126
devaluation 295, 522–3
  exchange rate 528, 533–5, 553,
    560, 561–2, 567, 577, 578–9
  Mexican peso 577–80
  see also depreciation
developing countries 301, 524
  capital flows 463, 484
  debt 381, 513–14
  environment 208

FDI 462, 484
foreign trade 430, 441–2
growth 15, 24, 37
migration trends 489
new economic policy 4, 5, 6
*see also* Africa; Asia; Latin America
Dewachter, H. 547
diamond cartel 142, 143, 151–4
*Diamond Grace* accident 223
dictatorships 24
Diederen, P. 159
Dietz, F. 218
differentiation, product 141, 452
diffusion (technology) 23
diminishing marginal productivity
    228, 342
diminishing marginal utility 73, 96
direct controls
    capital movement 575, 576
    interest rate 323, 324
direct intervention (foreign
    exchange market) 61
direct investment *see* foreign direct
    investment (FDI)
directly unproductive profit-seeking
    (DUP) activities 136
discount rate 234, 236, 237, 265,
    324
discounted cash flow 234
discouraged workers 338, 342
discretion versus rules (monetary
    policy) 326
discretionary action (budget deficit)
    376
discrimination
    in GATT 429, 430, 448
    price 136–8
diseconomies of scale 128
    avoidance (downsizing) 117
    cost structure 108, 114, 117, 118,
        119
disequilibrium 48, 61
    balance of payments 508–17
    labour market 229–31
disincentive effect (government
    failure) 181
disincentives to work 359
disinflation 291, 325, 368–9
disintermediation 324
distribution 25
    networks 112
    *see also* agents; middlemen
distributional coalitions 25
dividends 503, 523
division of labour 109, 111, 435
Doha Development Agenda 8
Dolan, R.J. 84, 138
domestic activity (business cycle) 406

domestic stability 572
dominant position 128
    abuse of 158, 163
    *see also* cartels; monopoly;
        oligopoly
Dornbusch, R. 540, 554, 580
double-marginalisation problem 116
double bottom (in chartism) 547
double coincidence of wants 65
Douglas, P.H. 202
Dow Jones 325
Downs, Anthony 199
downsizing 117, 131, 380
drinks industry
    environmental policy 220
    foreign trade 445
    *see also* alcohol industry; cocoa;
        coffee; food industry; soft
        drinks industry; wine industry
Drucker, Peter 453
drug firms *see* pharmaceutical
    industry
drug trafficking 50
dumping 137, 142, 448, 449
Dunning, J.H. 476, 477, 479
DUP (directly unproductive profit-
    seeking) 136
Du Pont 81, 221
durables, consumer 84, 401
Dutch Tulip Bubble 546
dynamic Asian economies (DAEs)
    405
dynamic efficiency 64, 171

e-commerce 41, 42
Earth Summit (Rio) 222
East Asia 10, 575
    capital flows 472
    FDI 472
    growth 25, 32, 34–5
    inflation 288
    new economic policy 4, 5
    *see also* China; Japan; newly
        industrialised countries (Asia);
        Tiger economies
East Germany 68
Easterly, William 24
Eastern Europe *see* Central and
    Eastern Europe
EC *see* European Union
ECB *see* European Central Bank
eco-dumping problem 448
eco-labelling 221
ecology *see* environment
econometric analysis 88, 317, 373,
    384, 412
economic activity, interest rates and
    315–18

economic definition of profit 105–6
economic growth *see* growth
economic instability (causes) 407–9
economic and monetary union
    (EMU)
    fiscal policy 388
    proposal (single currency) 580–6
    *see also* European Monetary
        System
economic performance (developing
    countries) 441–2
economic policy consensus 1–10
economic unions 429, 431
economies of increased dimension
    111
economies of scale 6, 44–5, 95, 172
    competition and 95
    cost structure 108–15, 117–19
    external 118–19
    foreign trade 435–7, 447, 451
    gains from trade 435–6
    market power 129, 135, 141
    sustaining monopoly power 141
    *see also* mergers; monopoly;
        oligopoly
economies of scope 44–5, 108–13,
    435–7
economies in transition *see*
    transition economies
Economist Intelligence Unit 517
ECU (European Currency Unit) 580
Ecuador 564
education 251, 448
    demand function 84
    government intervention 198, 202
    growth and 15, 25, 31, 37
    HDI and 31
    innovation and 23
    migrant labour 496, 497
    training 118, 129, 360
    of women 25
    of workforce 25
effective exchange rate 538
    nominal 255, 530–1
    real 531
efficiency
    allocative 17, 21–2, 63, 287
    competition and 64–5, 159
    dynamic 65, 171
    economic 466
    equity trade-off 182–7, 197, 203
    loss 188, 189, 192
    market power 136
    privatisation and 170, 171
    productive 17, 63
    resource allocation 159
efficiency-wage theory 351
efficient component pricing rule 174

efficient market hypothesis 545
effluents 208–10
egalitarianism 183
Egypt 211, 428
Eichengreen, B. 576
Eijffinger, S. 393
El-Agraa, A. 160, 448
elasticities of demand 75
  cross-price 80–2, 91, 140
  income 80, 84–8, 91, 447
  price 76–9, 84–90, 136
elderly dependency ratios 385
electricity industry 137, 173, 174
electronics industry 35
  *see also* computer industry
Elliot, R. 428
Elmeskov, J. 358
Embrechts, M. 547
emerging market economies 555
  net capital flows 464, 465, 469,
    470
EMI (European Monetary Institute)
  128
Emilia-Romagna region 118
emissions 195
  carbon 215–17
  carbon dioxide 28, 211, 217–18
  CFCs 211–13, 221
  fossil fuels 208
  greenhouse gases 207, 211–13
  lead 208, 216, 219
  nitrous oxide 211
  smoke 208, 219
  sulphur dioxide 208
employees *see* labour/employment
EMS *see* European Monetary System
  (EMS)
EMU *see* economic and monetary
  union
endowment effect (of tax) 61
energy
  consumption patterns 67
  costs/tax 222
  demand 84, 85
  prices 5, 17, 68, 283
  privatisation/deregulation 147,
    172
  *see also* electricity industry; fossil
    fuels; gas industry; oil
    industry
England (foreign trade example)
  432–5, 443, 444, 447
Enron 99
Enste, D. 52, 53
enterprise-friendly environment 3
entertainment industry 169
entitlement programmes 4, 385–6
entrants *see* new entrants

entrepreneurship 35, 380
environment
  business and 206–26
  economic growth and 208–11
  GNP and 31
  human welfare and sustainable
    development 31
  impact studies 213, 219–22
  objective setting 211–13
  policy instruments 207, 208,
    211–18
  protection 448–9
  *see also* air quality; emissions;
    natural resources; pollution;
    waste/waste disposal; water
environmental audit 220, 221
equilibrium 104
  balance of payments 520
  investment decision 237
  labour market 257–8
  market 48, 55, 61
equities market 317
  *see also* bonds; stock market
equity
  competition and 157
  efficiency trade-off 182–7, 197,
    203
  egalitarianism 183
  externalities 194
  fairness and 157
  government intervention 197, 203
  income distribution 182–7
  market power 147
equivalence, Ricardian 377, 382–4,
  387
Estonia 277, 300, 340, 427, 564, 565
Estrin, S. 150
ethical mutual funds 221
ethics 66
EU *see* European Union (EU)
euro 3, 300, 320, 506, 563, 581, 586
  benefits of 583
  drawbacks of 585–6
  economics of 584
Europe, Eastern *see* Central and
  Eastern Europe
Europe, Western 68, 464, 489
  new economic policy 1, 3, 6
  *see also* European Union (EU)
European Cement Association
  (CEMBUREAU) 167
European Central Bank (ECB) 292,
  293, 320, 322–3, 423, 581,
  582, 583
European Commission
  business fluctuations 402, 413
  competition policy 157–8, 160–8,
    176

  environment 216–17
  FDI 474, 479
  foreign trade 448
  government intervention 196–7
  unemployment 355
European Council 580, 582
European Court of Justice 164, 167
European Currency Unit (ECU) 581
European Monetary Institute (EMI)
  128
European Monetary System (EMS)
  423, 581–2, 586
European Observatory for SME
  Research 132
European Parliament 293
European Union (EU)
  balance of payments 503, 504, 524
  business fluctuations 406
  CAP 59
  capital flows 469, 470
  competition policy 160–8, 175
  environment 208, 213, 215–17,
    222
  exchange rate 539, 577, 580–6
  FDI 472–3, 484
  firm size 127–8, 132
  fiscal policy 376, 379, 381–2,
    385–6, 388–93
  foreign trade 425, 428, 439–40,
    448
  government intervention 196–7
  growth 15, 21, 45–6
  hiring decision 230
  industrial subsidies 196–7
  inflation 292
  interest rate 307, 320
  labour migration 488, 489–90, 498
  market power 126–8, 132
  market system 62–3
  new economic policy 4
  services sector 62
  shadow economy 51
  single market programme 439,
    448, 584
  Social Charter 230
  Treaty of European Union *see*
    Maastricht Treaty
  Treaty of Rome 160
  unemployment 341–2, 346, 355,
    357, 361, 362
  *see also individual member states*
*Eurostat* 539
Evans, Chris 114
exchange rate
  anchors 296–300, 565, 578
  balance of payments 502, 503,
    506, 508, 511, 515, 521–3,
    523–4, 542, 593

business fluctuations 409, 412, 415
capital flows 542–7
changes affecting profits 532–3
definitions 530–1
demand 533–5, 537, 540, 555, 560–2, 573, 575
description 529–36
exposures 550–3
FDI 471, 482
fiscal policy 578, 579, 583
flexible/floating 322, 524, 541, 560–2, 563–4, 566–72, 587, 591, 593–4
forecasting 529, 544, 545, 554–5
global market 558–60
GNP 255
impact on firms 532–3
inflation 537–8, 541, 543, 554, 562, 568–70, 573, 577, 584
interest rate and 307, 538, 543–7, 552, 554, 559, 560, 569, 575–80, 582, 591
misalignment 547, 555, 562, 571
monetary approach 538–9
monetary policy 538–9, 566, 568–70, 575, 578, 579, 583, 584
nominal 255, 530–1, 584
options/hedges 529, 549–50, 559–60
perspectives on 528–9
risk 548–54, 555
stability 573–80, 582
supply 533–5, 537, 555
theory 536–42
uncertainty 562, 583, 584
volatility (cost) 570–1
see also appreciation; depreciation; devaluation; effective nominal; effective real
exclusive dealerships 162
expectations augmented Phillips curve 367
expected inflation rate 307
expected return on investment 237
expected value of pay 493
expenditure
consumer 317
entitlement 4, 386
government see government expenditure
method (computing GDP) 249, 250
reduction 520, 521
switching policies 520–3
see also costs; inflation; price/pricing

exports 424
balance of payments 507, 512, 516, 518
capital see foreign direct investment (FDI)
component of national expenditure 252
exchange rate 532–6, 567
growth and 4, 17, 24
leading exporters 425, 426
promotion policies 452
value of 426
see also foreign trade
exposures, exchange rate 550–3
external benefits (positive externalities) 188, 494, 584
external costs (negative externalities) 188–90, 494
external economies of scale 118–19
externalities 139, 194, 446
environmental 206–7
FDI 469, 480
fiscal policy and 392
market failure 181, 188–90
migration of labour 494, 495
see also global economy
extractive industries 127
diamond cartel 142, 143, 151–4
sunk costs 107
Exxon Valdez accident 223

factor endowments 450–1
factor income 503–4
factors of production
endowments 450–1
global trade in 4–5
mobility see capital flows; foreign direct investment (FDI); migration of labour
productivity 23–5, 38, 41, 170, 441
quantity of inputs 20–2
factory system 110, 447
failure
government 5–6, 155, 181, 198–202, 218–19
market 181, 187–93
fair trade 430
fairness 157
Falvey, R.E. 85
family size 26
fast food outlets 130, 478
FDI see foreign direct investment (FDI)
Federal Reserve Bank 284, 285, 315, 319, 320, 325, 327, 410, 412, 531
Feldstein-Horioka puzzle 469

Fell, J. 301
financial derivatives 462, 529, 559, 560
financial services
adjustment 55, 57
bancassurance 112
bank collapse 327, 415, 553, 560
business fluctuations 407, 408–9
cooperatives 118
deregulation 322, 428
liberalisation 394
market power 130
money supply 262–8
regulation 195
see also banks/banking; insurance sector; stock market
financial system, changes in (price stability) 300–1
financing deficit 509
Fingleton, J. 179
Finland 14
fiscal policy 375, 390
unemployment 338, 339, 340, 347
firm
in competitive market 95–124
cost functions 117–18
cost structure 107–15, 117–19
impact of exchange rate 532–3
industrial organisation approach 116–17
macro-forecasts and 416–17
market system and 48, 49
profit maximisation objective 96–101
strategy/rivalry (competitive advantage) 450–1
supply curve 117–19
see also business
firm size 115, 118–19, 126–33, 407
advantages see economies of scale
disadvantages see diseconomies of scale
market price and 127–30
micro-firms 127
statistics 126–7, 130
trends 131–3
see also large firms; multinational enterprises (MNEs); small and medium-sized enterprises (SMEs)
fiscal activism 370, 371, 393–4, 376–81
fiscal balance 4, 370
fiscal consolidation 370
fiscal contraction 372, 384, 386–8, 394
fiscal expansion 372, 387, 394
fiscal impulse 373–6

fiscal policy 3, 246, 284, 289
  business fluctuations 407, 410
  counter-cyclical 4, 370, 371–6, 381, 395
  crowding out 372, 381–8
  in Europe 388–93
  exchange rate and 565, 578, 583
  fiscal activism (limits) 376–81
  Ricardian equivalence 377, 382–4, 387
  sustainability of debt 377, 381, 384–8, 390, 398–400, 511, 513–14
  see also debt; taxation; automatic stabiliser
Fisher, Irving 307, 543
Fisher relation 307–8, 310, 543
fisheries 28, 206, 448
fixed costs 107, 108, 120
  see also economies of scale
fixed exchange rate 322, 524, 541, 571
  anchors 296–300, 565, 573, 578, 586
  Bretton Woods system 563, 570, 592, 593
  gold standard 463, 562, 590–1
  pegged 564, 568, 569, 573, 574, 587
  quasi- 569
fixed interest rate 315, 316
flanking policies (definition) 579
flexibility
  batch production 114
  exchange rate see flexible exchange rate; floating exchange rate
  labour market 6, 344, 355, 357, 361
  loss of (in firms) 114
floating exchange rate 322, 541, 563, 587, 591, 593–4
flow of funds 507
  see also capital flows
fluctuations see business fluctuations; counter-cyclical fiscal policy; instability
focused factory 110
food industry
  demand function 84, 85
  environmental policy 220, 222
  fast food outlets 130, 478
  foreign trade 445
  subsidies 193
  see also agriculture; alcohol industry; drinks industry; soft drinks industry; wine industry
football stadium example 88–90, 137

Ford, Henry 351
forecasting
  accuracy 412–16
  aggregate demand 247
  business cycle 412–16
  demand 82–8
  exchange rate 529, 544, 545, 555
  inflation 295, 296, 319
  macro-forecasts 416–17, 440
  techniques 412
foreign-owned capital 472–3
foreign aid 504
foreign currency see currency; exchange rate
foreign direct investment (FDI) 131, 462, 464, 498
  balance of payments 503, 505, 507
  basic model 465–71
  definition/role 471
  effects of 463, 479–84
  incentives and 483, 484
  inward 472–5, 479, 482, 483, 538
  to Japan 473, 474
  MNEs 471–9
  outward 475–9, 485, 538
  reasons for 477–9
  regional distribution 472
  taxation and 463, 480–1
  trends 472–6
  see also capital flows
foreign exchange 480–3
  efficiency 545
  markets 529–32, 555, 562
  official reserves 503, 505–6
  see also balance of payments; foreign direct investment (FDI)
Foreign Exchange and Foreign Trade Council Law (Japan) 474
foreign population (resident patterns) 489–90
foreign receipts (income from abroad) 250
foreign reserves see foreign exchange official reserves
foreign sector 49
foreign trade 4–5
  capital markets 2, 48–9, 322, 469
  comparative advantage 432–5, 435, 447–8, 449–52
  competition and contestability 435
  composition of 427–9
  -dependent nations 24, 426–7
  economies of scale/scope 435–7
  environmental protection 448–9
  foreign exchange markets 529–32
  gains from 431–42

in gold 590, 591
  growth effects 15, 425–7, 437–8, 441–2
  liberalisation 2, 167–8, 301, 424, 429, 435, 439–42, 445–6, 453
  market power 131
  monopoly power 446–7
  new economic policy 1, 4, 6
  orientation (developing countries) 441–2
  policy and protection 442–9
  regimes 439–42
  unemployment and capacity to adjust 442–6
  -weighted exchange rate 299
  windfalls 25
  WTO and 425–31
  zero (autarky) 433, 434, 438
  see also balance of payments; capital flows; exchange rate; foreign direct investment (FDI); migration of labour; protectionism
forests 28, 206
formal economy 49, 51
forward market/contract 529, 543–4, 545, 548–9, 552, 558, 560
fossil fuels 206, 211, 218, 219
  see also coal; oil industry
France 51, 63, 255, 514
  business fluctuations 406
  competition policy 166, 167
  exchange rate 592, 593
  FDI 472
  fiscal policy 375, 379, 382, 386, 389, 390, 392, 395
  forecasting 413
  foreign trade 426, 427, 443
  government intervention 185, 196
  growth 14, 15, 22, 30, 31
  HDI ranking 31
  inflation 276
  labour migration 490, 494
  unemployment 336, 338, 339, 347, 368
franchises/franchising 114, 116, 162, 436, 478
Franco, D. 393
Frankel, J.A. 545, 554
Franks, T. 100
free-rider problem 99, 100, 192, 197
free lunch maxim 18–19
free trade see foreign trade
free trade area agreements 429, 431
Friedman, Milton 281, 302, 366, 431, 566, 567, 571
Friedman, R. 431
Froot, K.A. 545

fuel *see* energy
Fujimoto, Takahiro 109, 147
full-line forcing 137, 162
full employment 260, 319, 345–6,
    349, 352–4, 371–3, 381,
    444–5, 446
fund managers 464, 544
fundamental disequilibrium 592
fundamentals, economic 539, 543,
    546, 547, 554, 571
futures market/contracts 529, 549,
    553, 559–60

gains from trade
    comparative advantage 432–5
    competition and contestability
        435
    economies of scale/scope 435–7
    explaining 431–42
    growth effects 437–8
    quantifying 438–42
    *see also* comparative advantage
Galbraith, John Kenneth 205, 401,
    488
game theory 144–6
gaps
    income 6, 36
    knowledge 377, 378
    output 253, 254, 375
Garson, J.-P. 490
gas industry 137, 171, 173, 174
gases *see* emissions
Gates, Bill 129
GATS (General Agreement on Trade
    in Services) 430
GATT (General Agreement on Tariffs
    and Trade) 429, 430
    *see also* Uruguay Round
GDP *see* Gross Domestic Product
    (GDP)
Gemmell, N. 85
General Agreement on Tariffs and
    Trade (GATT) 429, 430
General Agreement on Trade in
    Services (GATS) 430
General Electric 128, 152
General Motors 128
general price level 246, 257, 258–9,
    262, 287
*General Theory* (Keynes) 261, 352
generational accounting 386
geographical immobility 346
Georgia 51, 565
Germany
    balance of payments 504
    business fluctuations 403, 404
    competition 118, 168, 176
    deflation 284

environment 216, 220–1
exchange rate 531, 541, 562,
    568–9, 577, 581
FDI 472–3, 481–2
fiscal policy 375, 379, 382, 389,
    390, 392
forecasting 413
foreign trade 426, 427, 428
GDP growth rate 404
government intervention 185,
    186, 196
growth 14, 21, 22, 25, 31, 41, 46
HDI ranking 31
inflation 276, 283–4, 289, 292
labour migration 490, 494
market system 51, 63, 67, 68
reunification 581
unemployment 336, 338, 339, 347
*see also* Bundesbank
Ghana 24, 442
Ghoshal, S. 124
Giffen good 80
Gilbert, R.J. 179
Gini coefficients 185–6
GKN 141
global convergence 33–5
Global Crossing 99
global economy 1, 422–3
    balance of payments 501–27
    capital flows and FDI 462–87
    exchange rate regimes 561–94
    exchange rates 528–60
    foreign trade 424–61
    labour migration 488–500
global exchange rate system 563–5
global foreign exchange market
    558–60
global trade *see* foreign trade
global warming 207, 211–12
globalisation 3, 4, 10, 368
    of capital markets 322
    competition policy and 131,
        168–9
    of trade *see* foreign trade
GNP *see* Gross National Product
    (GNP)
Godley, Wynn 415
Goizueta, Roberto 99
Gokhale, J. 386
gold 590–1, 593
    reserves 505–6
gold exchange standard 591
gold standard 463, 562, 590–1, 592
Goldstein, M. 548
Goodhart, Charles 334
Goodhart's Law 322
goods
    capital 353

consumer 313, 401
consumer durables 85, 401
    trade in 4–5, 503
    value *see* gross domestic product
        (GDP); gross national product
        (GNP)
    *see also* manufacturing industry
governance 25
government
    aid programme 504
    borrowing 3, 509
    dissaving 384
    environmental policy *see*
        environment
    exchange rates *see* exchange rate;
        exchange rate regimes
    failure 5–6, 155, 181, 198–202,
        218–19
    FDI and 479–81
    finances, migrants and 494–6
    foreign trade policy/protection
        442–9, 451–2
    growth and 25, 33, 35
    intervention (methods) 181,
        193–8
    market system and 5–6, 49,
        180–205
    monopoly power and 141
    price elasticity and 79, 85
    procurements policy 430, 439
    smaller 2, 6
    state aid 165, 196–7
    *see also* deregulation; fiscal policy;
        income distribution; politics;
        privatisation; regulation;
        taxation
government debt *see* public debt
government expenditure
    aggregate demand 261
    GDP and 251
    growth 25
    inefficiencies 379–80
    interest rates and 318
    market system and 49, 180, 181
    new economic policy 2, 3–4
    on public goods 197
    stabilising role 402
Gravazzi, F. 388
Gray, Alan W. 235
Great Depression 244, 246, 284, 402,
    591
Greece 51, 196
    balance of payments 503
    exchange rate 584
    fiscal policy 375, 382, 390, 393
    foreign trade 428
    unemployment 347
green products 220

Greenaway, D. 441
Greenbury Report (1995) 99
greenfield operations 477
greenhouse gases 207, 210, 211–13
greenmail 100
Greenspan, Alan 415
Grieve, W. 469
Grilli, Vittorio 294
gross domestic product (GDP) 181
  balance of payments 504, 509,
      513–14
  business fluctuations 403–6, 414,
      416
  calculation of 247–52
  composition of 251–2
  computing 249
  debt ratio 361, 379, 382, 385, 392,
      393, 398–400
  definition 247, 248
  environment and 222
  FDI and 472–3
  fiscal policy 373, 379–80, 382,
      384–6, 388
  foreign trade 426–7, 441
  growth rates 17, 403–6
  HDI 29–31
  inflation and 296, 298, 301
  interest rate and 315
  investment ratio 21, 22
  per capita 441
  purchasing power parity 254–5
  real 248
  services excluded 62
  shadow economy 50–3
  terms of trade 24
  unemployment and 361
  world merchandise trade and 426
gross national product (GNP) 2
  balance of payments 512
  business fluctuations 402
  criticisms 26–30
  definition 14, 248
  environment and 28–9
  exchange rate 255
  fiscal policy 372, 378
  global convergence 30–3
  GNP versus GDP 248
  growth 14–17, 20, 24, 25
  HDI 31
  human welfare 29–33
  per capita 14, 15, 20, 27–8, 34
  at purchasing power parity 254–5
  quality of life 32–3
  shadow economy excluded 28, 51,
      52–3
  world output (trends) 15
gross profit 105
Grossman, G. 210

groundnuts 17
growth 13, 319
  business fluctuations 401, 403–6,
      409, 410–15, 416–17
  catching-up process 32
  cutbacks 510
  economics of new economy 40–2
  environment and 208–11
  forecasting 413, 414
  foreign trade 425–7, 437–8, 441–2
  inflation and 288–9
  investment and 21
  policy prescriptions 33–5
  production functions and 20–1
  sustainable 26–33
  theories 17–26
  trends 14–17
growth accounting approach 22
Grubel, H.G. 590
Grubert, H. 429
Gulf War 438
Gylfason, Thorvaldur 40, 288

Ha-Joon Chang 7
Haaland, J. 428
Haldi–Whitcomb rule 112
Haltiwanger, John 132
Hamel, G. 112, 117
Harberger, Arnold 188
Harsanyi, John 146
Hay, D. 150
Hayek, F.A. von 67
Hayes, H. Michael 143
HDI (Human Development Index)
      29–30, 31
head and shoulders (in chartism)
      547
health 30, 386
  demand function 84, 85
  see also pollution
heavily indebted poor countries
      513–14
hedge funds 328, 555, 560
hedges/hedging 530, 537, 549–50,
      553, 561, 583, 584
hedonic pricing techniques 213
Heitger, B. 67
Herd, R. 386
HHI (Hirschman-Herfindahl index)
      128
Hicks, John R. 188, 409
high-tech industries 129, 427–8,
      448, 452
  Silicon Valley 118, 451, 490
  see also computer industry;
      electronics industry;
      technology
Hine, R. 428

hiring decision
  classical theory 227–9
  disequilibrium in labour market
      229–31
  extending model 231–2
  from firm to industry 229
  investment decision and 232–8
Hirschman-Herfindahl index 128
historical rates of return 547
Hogendorn, I. 429
Hollywood 118
Hong Kong 17, 34
  business fluctuations 414
  foreign trade 426, 427
Hood, N. 480
horizontal restraints 162, 163
horizontal specialisation 435
hotel industry 141
  elasticities of demand 86–7, 137
hours worked 357
household economy
  debt in 394
  excluded from GNP 27
  leisure and 27–8
  in market system 48, 49
housing
  demand function 84, 85
  inflation 280, 295, 296
  prices 280, 296, 315, 317, 415, 538
  services 280
Huber, J.B. 438
Hufbauer, G. 438
Hughes, Helen 35
human capital 17, 447, 450
  growth 26, 28
  investment 232
  see also education;
      labour/employment;
      population; skills
Human Development Index 29–30
human welfare and sustainable
      growth 26–33
Humphrey-Hawkins Act (1978) 320
Hungary
  exchange rate 565
  fiscal policy 391
  growth 30
  inflation 277
  market system 67, 68
  unemployment 340
hyperinflation 288
  Argentina 65
  Poland 5
hysteresis theory 349–50, 352, 368

IBM 128, 141
Iceland 37, 375
ICI 143, 221

IFT (intra-firm trade) 428
illegal immigrants 489
illegal income/goods 51, 52
IMF *see* International Monetary
    Fund
immigration
    laws 488
    trends/patterns 489–91
    *see also* migration of labour
imperfect commitment 116
imperfect information 140, 199
implicit GDP deflator 248
imports 17, 507, 512, 567
    capital *see* foreign direct
        investment (FDI)
    countervailing duties 442, 446
    job losses and 424, 444–5
    leading importers 425, 426
    -substitution policies 4, 438
    *see also* foreign trade; tariffs
impulse purchases 81
incentives
    to cheat (cartel) 153
    effect (taxation) 60
    environmental policy 212–13
    FDI and 483, 484
    to innovate 23
    prices as 56
    regulation 173
    unemployment and 361
    to work 25, 183
incidence of taxation 59, 468
income/income distribution 211,
    222
    consumption and 261, 382, 408
    distribution 25, 32, 67
    effects (interest rate) 316
    elasticity of demand 80, 84–8, 91,
        447
    excluded from GNP 28
    expenditure method (shadow
        economy measurement) 52
    gap 6, 33
    -generating effects 355–6
    global convergence 30–3
    government intervention 181,
        182–7, 193
    growth 15, 27, 30–2
    human welfare and sustainable
        growth 26
    inflation 287–8
    labour migration and 495
    level of (demand for money)
        262–3
    method (computing GDP) 249,
        250
    monopoly 136
    per capita 4, 15, 33

privatisation and 170–1
redistribution 181
taxation 199, 347–8
*see also* gross domestic product
    (GDP); gross national product
    (GNP); pay
incomes policy 294–6
incremental movements (free trade)
    439
independence (rational consumer)
    73–4
independent utilities 73–4
independently-floating exchange
    rate 564
India 318, 494
    balance of payments 508, 521
    environment 207
    FDI 471, 475
    foreign trade 427, 437, 452
    GNP 255
    growth 21, 31
    inflation 288
    new economic policy 1, 4, 5, 6, 9
indigenous industry (support) 483
indirect taxation 199
    alcohol, tobacco and petrol 60, 79
    less subsidies 250
    price elasticity 79–80
individualism 182, 183
    *see also* utility
indivisibilities 108
Indonesia 31, 34–5, 464
Industrial and Commercial Bank of
    China 126
industrial countries *see* OECD
industrial organisation approach
    115–19
industrial relations 25, 114, 202
    *see also* trade unions
industrial reserve army 356
Industrial Revolution 13
industrial subsidies (in EU) 196–7
industrialisation 437
industry associations 79
inferior goods 80
inflation 4, 252, 381
    anchors 296–300
    asset prices and 280
    balance of payments 524
    central banks 3, 292
    core 280
    cost-push 283
    definition/measurement 278–80
    deviation from price stability 280–4
    exchange rate *see* exchange rate
    expectations 307–8, 310, 312–13
    FDI and 471
    forecasting 295, 296, 412, 413

hedges 287
indexation schemes 287, 290, 300
interest rate *see* interest rate
lead indicators 295, 296, 319
monetary policy and 319
money supply and 281–2
rates (comparison) 276–8
statistics (bias) 279
targeting 322–3
tax 287
unemployment and 365–9
*see also* hyperinflation; stagflation
influence costs 136
information
    asymmetry 62, 116, 181, 193, 197,
        351
    costs 139
    failure 181, 193
    imperfect 140, 199
    industry 62
    price as source of 56
    requirements 114
    revolution 35, 449
    technology 44–6, 112, 114, 169,
        416, 464
infrastructure 35, 166, 202, 469
    *see also* transport
ING 560
Ingham, A. 218
innovation 437
    costs 114
    definition 23
    demand and 91
    environmental policy 220
    financial 322
    foreign trade and 446, 452
    government intervention 197
    growth 23, 24
    market power 132, 135, 141
    offsets 220
    spillover 447
    *see also* patents; research and
        development
inputs (quantity) 20–2
instability 411
    *see also* business fluctuations
institutions
    context of economic growth 24, 35
    in market system 66–7
    reform 292–6
    stability 24
insurance sector 112, 130, 503, 529,
    560
    regulation 195
integration
    FDI policy 483
    vertical 116
    world capital 462, 463–4

intellectual property rights 449, 454
inter-war period (exchange rate
        regimes) 591–2
interest rate
    aggregate demand 263, 267
    balance of payments 518–19
    business fluctuations 413, 415
    cash-flow effects 315, 316
    central bank see central banks
    definitions 306–10
    determinants 311–14
    economic activity and 315–18
    equilibrium 265
    exchange rate and 307, 539,
        543–7, 552, 554, 558–60,
        569–70, 575–80, 582, 591
    fiscal policy 372, 382, 385, 386–8
    forecasting 413, 415
    GNP calculation 250
    inflation 307–8, 310, 312–13
    investment 233–4, 237, 238
    loanable funds theory 311
    monetary policy 305–6, 319–24
    money supply/demand 266–8
    nominal 265, 291, 307–8, 310,
        312–13, 381, 412
    real 265, 291, 307–8, 310, 312,
        326–7
    term structure 308–10
    wealth effects 315, 316–18
Interest Rate Parity 543–4
intermediaries 63, 137
intermediate targets 319–23
internal exposure management
        550–3
internal rate of return 234–6
internalisation advantages 478
international investment positions
        507–9
International Monetary Fund (IMF)
        8, 9, 10, 21, 29, 284, 375, 402,
        441, 505, 517
    exchange rate 531, 548, 556, 576,
        592, 594
Internet 40, 42, 129, 368
interventionism see government
intra-firm trade 428
intra-industry trade 428, 445, 452
invention 22
    see also research and development;
        technology
inventory 111, 114, 251
    investment 318
investment
    aggregate demand 261
    component of national
        expenditure 251
    definition 232

foreign see foreign direct
        investment (FDI)
    funds 560
    GDP ratio 24, 25, 469
    goods 313
    growth and 22–4, 32–3
    interest rate and 316–18
    international positions 507–8
    managed 100
    private 4
    savings and 21–2, 24, 36, 314,
        469, 470
    unemployment and 353, 358–9
    see also capital
investment decision 232–8
    appraisal techniques 233–6
    equilibrium 237–8
    extensions 236–7
    rental cost of capital 232
invisible hand 61, 65, 214, 238
invoicing (in foreign currency) 552
inward capital flows 472–5, 479,
        483, 538
Iraq 407, 438, 452
Ireland 51, 196
    business fluctuations 406
    FDI 480, 481
    fiscal policy 375, 379, 382, 390
    foreign trade 427, 451
    growth 249
    unemployment 347, 349
IRP (interest rate parity) 543–4
IRR (internal rate of return) 234–6
irrational behaviour 259–60, 546
isolationism see protectionism
Issing, Otmar 332
Israel 564
Italcementi 166, 167
Italy 118, 186, 196
    balance of payments 504
    business fluctuations 406
    competition policy 166, 167
    exchange rate 530, 562
    fiscal policy 375, 379, 382, 386,
        390, 392, 393
    forecasting 413
    foreign trade 426, 427
    growth 14, 21, 31, 253
    HDI ranking 31
    inflation 289
    interest rate 316, 318
    labour migration 490
    market system 51, 63, 68
    output/GDP 253
    unemployment 338, 347

J-curve 535–6
Jackman, R. 359

Jackson, P.M. 205
Jackson, Judge Thomas 168
Jacobson, D. 179
Jamaica 508
Japan 249, 508
    aggregate demand 261
    balance of payments 501, 503–4,
        506–7, 512, 515, 524
    business fluctuations 403, 404,
        405
    capital flows 470
    competition 101, 176
    deflation 290–1
    exchange rate 531, 539, 541, 544,
        572, 583, 590, 593
    FDI 472–5, 484
    fiscal policy 375, 376, 379, 382,
        385, 386, 394
    forecasting 413, 414
    foreign trade 426, 427, 430, 431,
        437, 447–8, 450
    GDP growth rate 404
    government intervention 203
    growth 14, 15, 25, 28, 31, 36, 253
    inflation 276, 296
    interest rate 307, 308
    labour migration 490
    market power 128
    market system 63
    monetary policy 320
    unemployment 338, 341, 347, 354
Japan Automobile Manufacturers'
        Association 562
job(s)
    broking 360
    creation 132, 196–7, 210, 358
    displacement 496–7
    labour migration and 494–7
    losses, imports and 444–5
    security 6
    see also labour/employment
Johnson Matthey 220
joint ventures 237, 471
Jordan, B. 241
Juglar long-run cycle 403
Jutland region 118

Kalecki, Michael 407
Karoleff, V. 51
KAS (Keynesian aggregate supply)
        curve 257, 371–2, 373
Katz, M.L. 179
Kay, John A. 68, 71, 142, 150, 160,
        413
Kazakhstan 565
Keereman, F. 414
Keiretsu firms 474
Keynes, J.M. (and Keynesianism)

aggregate demand 244, 271
aggregate supply 244, 257, 371–3
balance of payments 515
economic cycles 408
exchange rate 591
fiscal policy 371, 372–3, 381, 387, 394
*General Theory* 271, 352–3
government intervention 181, 246
inflation 289
New 351
unemployment 351, 352–3, 359, 361, 362
Kieler, M. 320
King, Mervyn 322, 332
kinked oligopoly curve 144
know-how mobility of 462, 477
ownership of 140
*see also* skills; technology
knowledge gaps 377, 378
known-value items (KVIs) 138–41
known options 73
Kobe earthquake 407, 414
Kol, Jacob 118
Komiya, R. 176
Kondratieff long-run cycle 403
Koni 118
Konings, J. 351
Kontolemis, Z. 322, 405
Korea
balance of payments 509, 512
business fluctuations 409
capital flows 464
FDI 484
forecasting 414
foreign trade 442
growth 15, 37–8
Kornai, Janos 288, 438
Kotlikoff, L. 386
Krueger, Anne 210, 437
Kruger, A. 299
Krugman, Paul 451, 511, 514, 522
Kuhn, M.G. 452
Kuwait 249, 407, 450, 508
KVIs (known-value items) 138–41
Kydland, F. 326
Kyoto conference (1997) 212
Kyrgyz Republic 565

labour/employment
adjustment 62, 344–5
costs 380, 477
demand 228–9, 259–60, 344–5
direct job provision 360
employment protection 347
FDI and 477, 480
flexibility 6, 344, 355, 357–8, 361
hiring decision 227–32

job broking 360
job creation 132, 196–7, 210, 358
job security 6
mobility *see* migration of labour
morale 219
motivation 20, 25, 28, 231
part-time work 339, 342, 357, 361
quality of 24–5
supply 228–9
technological change and 355, 356
*see also* education/training; full employment; industrial relations; pay; skills; trade unions
labour market 2, 6, 33, 48, 49
active policies 360
clearing 343
disequilibrium 229–31
equilibrium 230, 257–8
flexibility 344–5, 361, 368
nominal price increase (effect) 258
reforms 361–2
rigidities 344–8, 360, 368
Lafarge 166, 167
lags (monetary policy) 325, 373, 377, 378, 540
Laidler, David 329
Laird, Sam 440
*laissez-faire* policies 36, 411, 453
Lal, Deepak, 205
landfill tax 217
Lane, P.R. 25, 379, 508
Langrangean function 74
Lanquedoc-Roussillon region 118
La Poste 126
large firms
downsizing 116, 131, 380
FDI 474
foreign trade 428
market power 127, 130
*see also* diseconomies of scale; economies of scale; mergers and acquisitions; monopoly; oligopoly
large numbers, law of 111
Larrain, F. 409
lateral summation 75, 117, 229, 237
Latin America
balance of payments 515, 517
capital flows 464, 470
Earth Summit 222
exchange rate 579
FDI 471
foreign trade 429, 431, 448
growth 17, 37
income distribution 29
inflation 277, 289

labour migration 498
new economic policy 1, 4, 5, 6
Latvia 277, 340, 565
law/legislation
competition policy 1, 2, 33, 81, 82, 147, 157, 160–8, 175
environmental policy 208, 211–19
framework/institutions 66, 68
litigation 220
*see also* regulation
Lawrence R.Z. 474
Lawson, Nigel 511
Layard, Richard 360, 498
leads and lags 552
lead emissions 208, 216, 219
lead indicators (inflation) 295, 296, 319
Leadbeater, C. 42
lean production 114
learning-by-doing 110–11, 113
leasing 107
Lee, J. 482
legal framework/institutions 66, 68
legislation *see* law/legislation; regulation
Le Grand, Julian 186
leisure 199, 357
demand 85, 86–7
football stadium example 88–90, 137
growth and 20, 27–8
*see also* hotel industry; tourism
lemons, market for 350, 351
lending *see* loans
Lenin, V.I. 289
Lesotho 564
level playing field 168, 187, 442, 443, 454
leveraged funds 328
liabilities 263–6, 316, 552–3
liberalisation 394, 523, 558
foreign trade 2, 33, 167–8, 301, 424, 429, 435, 439–42, 445–6, 453
liberalism 182
licences/licensing 116, 163, 471, 474, 478
*see also* franchises/franchising
life assurance 310
life expectancy 15, 30, 31
Lima 30
limit book 560
limit pricing 142
limited liability 66, 96
Lindbeck, A. 394
linked currencies *see* anchors, exchange rate
liquidity 324, 325, 373, 518–19

liquidity preference 268
Lithuania 277, 339, 340, 565
litigation 220
living standards 247, 249, 255, 270,
        343, 355, 394, 438, 442
    exchange rate and 539, 585
    growth and 14, 20, 31, 32
    inflation and 278, 279, 280
    new economic policy 1, 6
    population growth and 26
loan guarantees 451
loanable funds theory 268, 311,
        313–14
loans
    by banks 263, 264, 265
    capital mobility 469, 470
lobbying 187, 197, 218
location advantages 477
London 118, 153, 208, 529
lone parents 341
long-run cost 113, 115, 120
long-run price elasticities 79, 85
long-run supply 260–1, 348–52
long-term bond yields 295
long-term unemployment 336,
        341–2, 348–52, 360
Long Term Capital Management 327
long and variable lags (monetary
        policy) 325, 373, 378, 540
Lorenz curve 184–5
loss
    competition 138, 139–40
    efficiency 188, 189, 192
    monopoly 134–5, 188
    in profit and loss account 104, 105
loss-leader pricing 138, 139–40
Louis XIV 182
loyalty, customer 144
LSEs see large firms
Lucas, Robert E. 23, 380
Lucas critique 378, 380
Lux, T. 561
Luxembourg 118, 196, 406, 490
    fiscal policy 390
luxury goods 80

Maastricht Treaty 3, 195, 292, 400
    exchange rate 582
    fiscal policy 376, 388, 389
McAleese, Dermot 388
McDonalds 130, 478
McDonnell-Douglas 446
McDowell, Moore 81
macro-forecasts 416–17
macroeconomic framework 244–5
    see also aggregate demand;
        aggregate supply; business
        fluctuations; fiscal policy;

global economy; gross
        domestic product (GDP); gross
        national product (GNP);
        inflation; interest rate;
        unemployment
macroeconomic management 191,
        246, 257, 271
macroeconomic policies
        (unemployment) 358–9
macroeconomic stability 1, 3–4
Maddison, Angus 14, 22, 357
magnification effect 532
Malaysia 249, 464
    forecasting 414
    foreign trade 427
    growth 17, 34–5
Malthus, Thomas/Malthusianism 26,
        36–7
managed floating exchange rate 564,
        565, 593–4
management
    buy-outs 171
    control 114
    incentives 97–9, 100
    pay 97–9
    principal-agent problem 96–7
    profit-maximisation 97–9, 99–101
managerial culture 172
managerial slack 135, 136, 435
Manila 30
Mann, Catherine L. 511, 514
Mannesman 141
manufacturing industry 62, 114
    firm size 127, 130
    foreign trade 427–8, 437, 452
    state aid 196–7
    see also goods
Marche region (Italy) 121
marginal benefit 192
marginal cost 63, 64–5, 136, 140,
        173
    MR = MC rule 102–7, 117, 133–4,
        137
    social 190, 192, 214
marginal lending facility 265
marginal product of capital 315–16
marginal product of labour 104
marginal productivity 228, 231, 238,
        395, 465
    of capital 315–16
marginal revenue 136, 139–40
    curve 89–90
    MR = MC rule 102–7, 117, 133–4,
        137
    product of labour 227–8, 231, 233
    sales 78
marginal utility 63, 64–5, 182–3
marginalisation problem 116

Marin, A. 150
mark-up pricing 107, 139–40
market
    -based controls (interest rate)
        323–4
    control (diamond trade) 153
    demand see demand
    economy 49–53, 66
    equilibrium 48, 55, 62
    failures 181, 187–93
    niche 88, 109, 125, 220
    price see price/pricing
    segmentation 86–7, 89–90, 136,
        137, 310
    share 96, 99, 448, 542
    -sharing (cartel) 142–4
market mechanisms 1, 2
    unemployment and 342–4
market power 95, 116, 118, 125
    competition and 163–5
    diamond market (case study) 151–4
    fewer firms 142–6
    firm size 126–33
    underestimation of 130–2
    see also cartels; monopoly;
        oligopoly
market supply curve 95, 117–19
market system (in action) 2–3, 21,
        287
    agents and middlemen 61–3, 69
    demand and supply 56–61
    description 48–53
    efficiency of 63–5
    prices (functioning/role) 53–6
    social context 65–7
    threats to 153–4
    traders and arbitrage 61–3
marketing 452
    see also advertising
Marks & Spencer 141
Mars 81
Marshall, Alfred 56, 62
Marshallian adjustment process 55
Martin, John P. 252, 339, 358, 361
Martin, P.H. 412
Marx, Karl/Marxism 131, 356
Matthews, A. 448
maximisation
    of profit see profit-maximisation
    of utility see utility
    of value 67–8
Mayer, B. 100
Mayes, D. 163
MC see marginal cost
McDonald's 126
medium-sized enterprises see small
        and medium-sized enterprises
        (SMEs)

Meese, R. 545, 546
Megginson, W. 179
menu costs 287, 348, 351
mercantilism 443
Mercedes/Mercedes-Benz 478
merchandise trade 426, 427, 428,
    452, 503
MERCOSUR 431
mergers and acquisitions 131, 328,
    436
  capital flows 464, 472, 474, 477
  competition policy 165–8
  control of 165, 168
  profit-maximisation 100
merit bads/goods 192
MES see minimum efficient scale
    (MES)
Messerlin, Patrick 439
Metallgesellschaft 553
Metcalfe, Robert 42
Mexico 10, 215, 381, 480, 494
  balance of payments 508, 509,
    512, 517
  exchange rate 255, 498, 577–80
  foreign trade 426, 429, 448
  growth/decline 14
  inflation 277, 300
  labour migration 498
  new economic policy 1, 4
  peso crisis 498, 577–80
MFN see most-favoured nation
    (MFN) status
Michaely, M. 441
micro-firms 127
microeconomic framework see
    competition; government;
    growth; market; new
    economic policy
microelectronics 450
Microsoft 42, 129–30, 142, 158, 168
Middle East
  balance of payments 508, 515
  capital flows 470
  labour migration 489
middlemen (role) 61–3, 69
migration of labour 462, 488–500,
    573–4, 585
  effects (basic model) 491–3
  job displacement and wages 496–7
  public finances 494–6
  rural–urban 26
  taxation 496
  trends 489–91
  unemployment and 341, 490, 496,
    496–7
Milesi-Ferretti, G.M. 508
Milgrom, Paul 116, 124, 241
military hardware 19

minerals see extractive industries
minimum efficient scale (MES) 114,
    118
minimum reserve requirements 324
minimum wages 230, 259, 346
mining see extractive industries
ministerial statements 575, 577
Ministry for International Trade and
    Industry (MITI) 176, 447, 448
Mirus, R. 51
Mississippi 339
  Land Scheme 546
MITI (Japan) 176, 447, 448
Mitterrand, François 395
Mizon, P. 322
MNEs see multinational enterprises
mobile phones 42, 84, 114–15, 146,
    279, 436
mobility
  capital see capital flows; capital
    mobility; foreign direct
    investment (FDI)
  labour see migration of labour
Mogadishu 30
Moldova 565
monetary aggregates method
    (shadow economy measured)
    52
monetary approach (balance of
    payments) 538–9
monetary base 265–6
monetary policy 237, 265, 373, 407,
    410
  active/passive 325–6
  balance of payments 538–9
  design of 324–8
  exchange rate 538–9, 565, 570,
    575, 578, 583, 684
  inflation and 292, 294–6, 319
  interest rates and 305–6, 319–24,
    328
  intermediate targets 319–23
  price stability and 292–6, 319,
    327
  rules/discretion 326
money
  aggregate demand and 261–71
  definition 262
  demand for 262–3, 266–8
  illusion 258, 259, 287, 290, 307,
    343, 349, 366
  multiplier process 275
  price level and 262, 281–2
  quantity theory 282, 283, 284,
    296, 305
  see also cash; currency
money supply 265, 275, 538, 543,
    566, 591

central banks and 263–4, 265,
    267–8
  inflation and 280–4, 294–6
  targeting 321
Monopolies and Mergers
    Commission 143–4
monopolists
  market power and 133–4
  multi-product/multi-plant
    138–41
monopoly
  competition and 160, 166–7, 168
  consequences 134–6
  dead-weight loss 134–5, 187
  market power 129–30, 133–41
  market structure and 162
  natural 171–3
  price discrimination 136–8
  profits 125, 136, 173, 187–8, 483
  rents 136, 348
  theory 133–41, 146
monopoly power 10, 81, 129–30,
    137–8
  competition and 166–7, 168
  foreign trade 446–7
  market failure 181, 187–8
  regulation of 171–3, 174
  sustaining 141–2
  trade unions 351
monopsony power 446
Montreal Protocol (1987) 212, 221
moral suasion 323
Moran, Peter 124
Morita, Akio 572
Morocco 9, 31, 255, 337, 494, 508,
    564
Morris, D. 150
mortality rate (of small firms) 132
Moscow 58
most-favoured nation (MFN) status
    429, 430, 448
motivation costs 116
  labour 20, 25, 28, 231
  pollution reduction 215
  for privatisation 169–71
motor vehicles see automobiles
motorways 191
MR see marginal revenue
Muelbauer, J. 84
Mueller, D.C. 165, 188
Mühleisen, Martin 21
multi-currency approach 299
multi-plant monopolists 138–41
multi-product monopolists 138–41
Multilateral Exchange Rate Model
    (MERM) 531
multilateral trade agreements 429,
    448

multinational enterprises (MNEs) 168, 428, 523, 553
  FDI and 462, 471–9, 480, 482, 483
  see also large firms
multinationals see multinational enterprises
multiple equilibria problem 579
multiplier
  -accelerator model 409
  effect 265, 275, 353, 374, 387, 407
Murphy, Kevin M. 98
Murray, J.A. 100
museums 191
Mussa, M. 299
Mussolini, Benito 289
Mutti, J. 429
mutual funds 221, 296, 328, 462, 529, 579

NAFTA (North American Free Trade Area) 429, 498, 579, 580
NAIRU (non-accelerating inflation rate of unemployment) 349, 367, 368
Namibia 151
Nash, John 146
Nash equilibrium 145–6
National Freight Corporation 171
national income 25, 247, 250, 321–2
National Institute of Economic and Social Research 98
national product (net national product) 247, 250
national sovereignty 512, 515
national treatment (under GATT) 429, 430
nationalised industries 141, 169–71, 181
  see also deregulation; privatisation
natural monopolies 171–3
  see also utilities
natural rate of unemployment 349, 367
natural resources 17, 23
  depletion 28, 206–7
  excluded from GNP 27, 28–9
  ownership of 141
  see also air; environment; fossil fuels; water
Navaretti, G. 428
Neale, Bill 241
necessities, income elasticity and 80
negative-sum game 148
negative externalities 188–90, 494
negative production externality 188–90
neo-classical model (interest rate) 316

Nepal 213
net capital flows 464
net errors and omissions 503, 507
net investment 232
net national product 247, 250
net present value (NPV) 233–4, 235, 236
Netherlands 51, 118, 299, 406, 490
  environment 211, 215
  FDI 472
  fiscal policy 375, 382, 390
  foreign trade 426, 427
  government intervention 185, 196
  growth 14, 31
  HDI ranking 31
  unemployment 338, 339, 347, 349, 362
Netscape 130, 168, 238
Netter, J. 179
netting agreement 550
network economies 42
network effects 41, 130
networks 112, 141
new economic policy 1–10
New England 587
new entrants 125, 141
  attraction of 118
  threat of 141
New York 30, 529
New Zealand 1, 508
  exchange rate 322, 564, 568, 569
  fiscal policy 375, 379
  foreign trade 451
  government intervention 183, 186
  inflation 292
  new economic policy 1, 9
  privatisation 155, 169
  unemployment 338, 347, 348, 352
newly industrialised countries (Asia)
  growth 15–16, 25, 32, 34–5
  market power 128
  new economic policy 1, 4, 5
  see also Indonesia; Malaysia; Thailand
Nicaragua 514
niche markets 88, 109, 125, 220
Nickell, S. 359
NICs see newly industrialised countries (Asia)
Niehans, Jürg 296
NIESR (National Institute of Economic and Social Research) 98
Nigeria 26, 452
Nikkei 414
Niskanen, William 198, 205
Nissan 503–4
nitrogen dioxide 208

nitrous oxide 211
Nixon administration 593
NNP (net national product) 247, 250
'no bail-out' clause 389, 391–2
'no regret' principle 212, 216
noise pollution 213
Nokia 436
nominal effective exchange rate 530–1, 577
nominal exchange rate 255, 530, 584
nominal GDP 248
nominal interest rate 307–8
nominal money wages 259–60
non-accelerating inflation rate of unemployment (NAIRU) 349, 367, 368
non-automatic budget balances 374
non-discrimination clause 429, 430, 448
non-excludable (public goods) 191–2
non-KVIs 138, 139–40
non-marketed sector 49, 51–3
non-price competition 144
non-renewable resources 31, 206
  see also fossil fuels; oil industry
non-satiation (rational consumer) 73
nontariff barriers 188, 429, 431, 439
non-rivalrous (public goods) 191–2
nontraded goods and services 538
non-use value of resource 213
Noord, P. Van den 386
normal profits 104
Norsk Hydro 221
North Africa 490
North America 1, 9, 338, 341, 489
  capital flows 464
  see also Canada; United States
North American Free Trade Area (NAFTA) 429, 498, 579, 580
North Carolina 480
Norway 51, 185, 474
  environment 221
  exchange rate 564
  fiscal policy 375, 379, 386
  unemployment 339, 347
Nozick, Robert 183
NPV (net present value) 233–4, 235, 236
nuclear power/industry 107, 218, 222

occupational immobility 346
O'Driscoll, A. 100
OECD 484
  business fluctuations 402, 413–14
  employment 63

environment 215, 216
exchange rate 539, 578
fiscal policy 376
forecasting 413–14, 417
foreign trade 447
GDP 252
growth 414
labour migration 490, 491,496
unemployment 336, 339, 347, 355, 356, 360, 361
Office of Fair Trading (UK) 142, 168
official reserves 503, 505–6, 575
Ofgas 173
Ofgen 173
Ofwat 173
O'Hagan, John 73
oil industry
OPEC 142
prices 5, 17, 24, 218, 283, 322, 339, 541, 580
resources 28
Okun, Arthur M. 184, 186
older workers (unemployment) 341
oligopoly 452
government intervention 188
kinked curve 144
market power 125, 130, 142–6
Olson, Mancur 25
One Price, Law of 537, 539
OPEC 142
open-market operations 265–6, 296, 324
open economies 4, 128, 297
operating profit 105–6
Oppenheimer, Sir Ernest 151
opportunistic behaviour 96, 116
opportunity cost 21–2, 106
social 446
opt-out clause (Social Charter) 231
optimum currency areas 573, 585
optimum tariffs 447
options/options contract 529, 549–50, 559
order books 295
Organisation for Economic Cooperation and Development see OECD
Osborn, D.R. 405
Oswald, A. 27
OTC transactions 548, 549
see also forward market/contracts
Oulton, N. 279
outcomes, process and 187–8
outlet bias 279
output 59, 102, 282
average cost 112–13
decline 17, 24
fixed cost 108

gap 253, 254
method (computing GDP) 249
productive efficiency 17, 21–2
productivity 20, 21
specialisation 110
trends 14–17
see also gross domestic product (GDP); gross national product (GNP); growth
outward capital flows 476–9, 482, 483, 538
over-the-counter (OTC) transactions 548, 549
see also forward market/contracts
overshooting (exchange rate) 561, 579
overtime payments 295
Overy, R. 19
Owens, Jeffrey 216
owner-manager 96, 118
owners
monopoly 136
principal-agent problem 96–7
ownership
advantages 477
of natural resources 206
Ozawa, T. 480
ozone layer 207, 210

Page, J. 35
Pakistan 318, 489
Palestine 249
Panama 564
Papademetriou, D. 489
Papageorgiou, D. 441
paper industry
competition 165–6
environmental policy 220–1
foreign trade 436
parallel price behaviour 164
Pareto, Vilfredo 186
Pareto efficiency 19, 186
Parkinson's Law (government intervention) 198–9
part-time work 338, 342, 357, 360
passive monetary policy 325–6
patents 23, 66, 449, 474
sustaining market power 141, 141
see also innovation
path-dependent growth 23
pay
cost of living allowance 539
exchange rate and 573, 574, 578, 584
free trade and 446
hiring decision 227–8, 228–31
incomes policy 294–6
inflation 290

labour migration and 491–3, 496–7
management 97–8
minimum wages 230
nominal wage 257, 259–60, 290, 343, 348, 352, 366
real wage 257–60, 290, 343–4, 346, 352, 366
rigidity 230
in services 295
unemployment 342–8, 355–6, 359–60, 361
wage-price spiral 523
wage formation process 360
wage stickiness 260–1
see also income
pay-back period 234–6
Paye, Jean-Claude 206, 210
payroll tax 347–8
PCs see computer industry
Pearce, David 210, 214
pegged currencies 564, 568–9, 573, 574, 587
see also anchors, exchange rate; Exchange Rate Mechanism (ERM)
Pemberton, John 91
pennants (in chartism) 547
pension funds 100, 465, 529, 560
pensions 300, 464
liabilities 385–6
Peppers, Larry C. 416
perfect competition 47, 88, 95, 135, 146, 186, 432
personal computers see computer industry
Persson, Torsten 186
Peru 427
peso crisis 498, 576, 577–80
Peters, E. 480
petrol 208, 216, 218
see also automobiles
pharmaceutical industry
competition 169
diseconomies of scale 114
FDI 478
Phelps, Edmund S. 246, 366
Philippines 249, 318, 464, 489
Phillips, A.W. 348, 365, 369
Phillips, Bruce D. 130
Phillips curve 289, 348, 350, 362, 365–9
physical capital 23, 349–50, 450, 462
physical investment 232
Physiocrats 61–2
Pike, Richard 241
pin factory (Adam Smith) 111

poison pills 100
Poland 68, 480
  exchange rate 565, 568
  fiscal policy 381, 391
  growth/decline 17, 31
  inflation 277
  stabilisation plan 4–5
  unemployment 339, 340
police 30, 51
policy
  consensus 1–10
  -induced adjustment mechanism
    524
  -induced shocks 407, 408, 417
  -ineffectiveness hypothesis 384
  instruments (environment)
    214–19
  instruments (monetary policy)
    323–4
  lags 325, 373, 377, 378
  mix (fiscal/monetary) 373
  see also government
politicians 199, 301, 576
politics 1, 24, 378–9
  inflation and 292
  parties 199, 300, 301, 380–1
  see also government
polluter pays principle 216
pollution 188–90, 194–5
  air 195, 207, 209–10, 216–17, 219,
    221
  chemical 28, 188–90, 194–5, 197,
    199, 221–2
  control (cost) 206, 208–11,
    214–16, 219
  economic growth and 208–11
  environmental policies 211–13
  higher levels 28
  reducing (policy instruments)
    214–19, 222
  taxation and 2–3, 194, 215–18
  waste disposal 28, 206, 210, 220,
    222
  water 28, 194–5, 199, 206, 207,
    210
  see also emissions; environment
Polygram 128
population
  ageing 26, 300, 301, 390, 464, 584
  growth 26, 35, 37
  see also human capital;
    labour/employment;
    migration of labour
Porter, Michael E. 118, 135, 220,
  436, 438, 450–2, 528
Porter diamond 438, 450–1
portfolio capital/investment 485,
  503, 505–6, 508, 543, 578

Portugal 196, 347
  balance of payments 504, 512
  fiscal policy 375, 382, 389, 390,
    392
  foreign trade 432–5, 442, 447
position goods 74
positive externalities (external
  benefits) 188, 494, 584
Posner, R.A. 156
post-Fordism 114
postal services 147, 167
potential GDP 252–5, 296, 372
poverty 22, 32, 183, 186, 222, 344,
  442
  trends 15, 17
Powell, Enoch 202
Powell, J.E. 202
power, market see market power
power industry see energy
PPP see purchasing power parity
Prahalad, C.K. 112, 117
Pratten, C.F. 111
precautionary principle (no regret)
  212, 216
predatory pricing 142
prediction see forecasting; future
preferences 74, 182
Prendergast, Mark 91, 99
Prescott, E. 326
present discounted value 234
price/pricing
  aggregate demand/supply 262–71
  capping 173, 174
  ceiling 58, 153
  competition 138–41, 144–6
  decision 72–94, 137
  discrimination 136–8
  elasticities 76–9, 84–90, 136
  energy 5, 17, 67, 79, 208, 283
  firm size and 127–30
  flexibility 574
  general price level 246, 257,
    258–9, 262, 287
  hedonic techniques 213
  leader 143–4, 146
  loss-leader 138, 139–40
  marginal cost/utility 63–5, 173
  market system 47, 49, 53–6, 65, 66
  mechanism 2, 216–17, 519
  natural monopolies 172
  roles/functioning 53–6
  as signals 47, 56, 65–7
  specie-flow mechanism 591
  system 116
  transparency 583, 584
price stability 3, 276, 305, 388, 582
  benefits of 286–91
  definition/measurement 278–80

  objective of monetary policy
    292–4, 319, 328
  public support for 300
primary budget balance 385, 393
primary commodities 17
principal-agent problem 96–7
printing see publishing industry
prisoners' dilemma 145, 484
Pritchett, Lance 24
private debt 394
private goods 191, 198
private property 67, 68
private savings see savings
private sector
  growth, unemployment and 359
  response (fiscal activism) 380–1
privatisation 1, 2, 147, 155, 171,
  181, 471
  effects of 169–71
  government intervention 195–7,
    203
  reasons for 170
  regulation after 171–4
pro-cyclical variables 406, 407–8
  innovation 215–16
  money supply 275
  outcomes and 186–7
Procter and Gamble 220, 553
procurement policies 430, 439
producer quotas (diamond trade)
  153
product
  cycle 90
  design 109, 215–16
  differentiation 141, 452
  market system and 56
  quality 101
  range 142, 417
  see also goods
product market 48, 49
  rigidities 348, 360
production cost 56
  externalities 188
  frontier 17, 32, 434, 435
  function 23–4, 214, 253, 257, 435
  see also factors of production
productive efficiency 17, 21–2, 63
productive factors (quantity) 20,
  23–5
productivity 20
  labour 25, 40, 41, 111, 170, 231,
    355–7, 491
  technology and 355–7
  total factor 23, 25–7
professional associations 24
profit maximisation 56, 68, 95, 118,
  138, 139, 142, 214–15
  aggregate supply 257

cartels 142–4
management 97–9, 101
market structure and 155
objective of firm 96–101
rules for 101–7, 117, 134, 137–8
takeover threat 99–101
profit and loss account 105
Profitability Index 234
profits 250
definitions 105–6
exchange rate changes 532
monopoly 125, 136–7, 170, 173,
187–8, 483
repatriation 249, 250, 483, 503–4
-seeking 65, 136
transfer pricing 481–2
promotion (of employees) 116
propagation effects 410
property rights 24, 68, 194–5
protectionism 9, 592
effects 424, 435, 437, 439, 443,
446, 452–4
psychic costs (of migration) 493
public choice theory 198, 199
public debt 4, 582
budget deficit 3–4, 283, 294,
311–12, 370–400, 520–1, 555,
582, 593
crowding out 372, 381–8
sustainability of 377, 381, 384–8,
398–400, 511, 513–14
public finances, migration and
494–6
public goods 181, 190–3, 197–8
public opinion, inflation and 299
public sector
inefficiencies of 379–80
see also government
public works programme 360
publishing industry
books (private goods) 191
demand function 85
economies of scale 118
printing press industry (Germany)
118
purchasing power parity 14, 254–5
empirical analysis 539–42
explanation of 537–8
pure private good 191, 278
pure public good 191, 192, 198
put option 549, 551
Putnam, B. 540

quality
assurance 114
bias (inflation statistics) 279
control 114, 438
of labour force 24–5

of life 29–30
of services 174
quantity
changes (adjustment process) 55
of inputs (productive factors) 20–2
theory of money 282, 283, 284,
296, 305
Quantum Fund 553
quasi-fixed exchange rates 569
quotas 429

R & D see research and development
radiation exposure 29
Rail Directive 166
Railway Mania (1846–7) 546
railways 166–7, 170, 173
rainforests 28, 206–7
random external shocks 407, 409,
414, 417
random walk model 414
rate of return on capital 173, 234
rational consumer 72–4
rational expectations theory 380
Rawls, John 183
RCA 128
Reagan, Ronald 1
real balance effect 269, 518
real effective exchange rates (REERs)
531, 584
real GDP 248
real interest rate 265, 291, 307–8,
310, 312, 326–7
real wage 257–60, 290, 343–4, 346,
352, 366
recession 284, 295, 325, 401, 405,
406, 417
budget deficits 371, 372, 378
definition 247
Great Depression 244, 246, 284,
402, 591
recreation see leisure
recycling 220
redundancy payments 98
reference value (money supply) 322
regional distribution (of FDI) 472
regional trade agreements 429, 431
regressive taxes 222
regulation 141, 171–4, 195–7
competition 1, 2, 33, 81, 82, 147,
160–8, 174
environmental policy 214–15,
216–17, 219, 221–2
market system and 49
see also government;
law/legislation
regulatory capture 174, 175, 218
Reich, Robert B. 35, 361
relative PPP 537–8, 540, 541

remuneration see pay
remuneration committees 98, 99
rents 280
GNP calculation 250
monopoly 136–7, 348
rental cost of capital 232, 233
seeking 35, 202, 218, 437
see also profits
replacement ratios 350, 358, 361, 362
unemployment benefit 346, 347
repurchase agreements (repos) 324
reputation 141, 146, 197, 219, 319,
477
research and development 23, 33, 118
costs 110,114
FDI 477, 479
foreign trade 428, 437, 448
government intervention 197, 202
reserve requirements 264, 265, 296,
570
minimum 324
reserves
official 503, 505–6, 575
ratio 264, 265
residual factor 21
Responsible Care programme 219
restrictive agreements 163
retail industry 62, 130
firm size 127
foreign exchange market 559
pricing 138–41, 173, 278–9, 320
retail price index (RPI) 173, 278
see also consumer price index
retaliation tax 443
retirement, early 341
return on capital employed (ROCE)
106, 237, 239
return on investment 105, 237, 239
revenue
cost structure 107–8
government see taxation
-maximisation 88–9
see also marginal revenue
reverse head and shoulders (in
chartism) 547
Ricardian equivalence 377, 382–4, 387
Ricardo, David 356, 383, 431
capital flows 470
foreign trade 435, 445, 449
Riksbank 575
Rio Summit (1992) 222
risk
country ratings 515, 516–17
exchange rate (coping strategies)
548–54, 555
investment 234, 237, 470
premium 105–6, 234, 393, 545
rivalry 141, 146, 191, 450–1

RMSE (root mean square error) 413
Roberts, D. 241
Roberts, John 124, 548
Roberts, R. 116
robotics 35, 356, 450
ROCE *see* return on capital employed
Roche 166, 168
Rodgers, W.M. 369
Rodrik, Dani 7
Rogers, C.A. 412
Rogoff, K. 545
Roll, E. 562
Romania 24, 51, 340
Romer, C.D. 369, 412
Romer, D. 369, 412
Romer, P.M. 23
root mean square error technique
    (RMSE) 413
Rose, A. 536
Ross, David 179
Ross, S.A. 241
Rothschild, K. 176
Roy, Noel 81
royalties 474, 503, 523
RPI (retail price index) 173, 278
rules (monetary policy) 326
    discretion versus 326
    profit-maximisation 101–7, 117,
        134, 137–8
    *see also* regulation
Russia 10, 17, 58, 408, 430, 517, 565
    diamond market 151, 152
    labour migration 494
    new economic policy 5
    privatisation 170, 171
    unemployment 340
    *see also* Soviet Union, former
Rwanda 426, 427

Sachs, Jeffrey D. 4–5, 409
sacrifice ratio 368
Sala y Martin, X. 32
sales revenue 76–8, 89
Salvadori, D. 163
sand in the wheels strategy 575, 576,
    587
Santer, W. 160
Sapsford, D. 241
Sarbanes–Oxley Act 99
satellite communications 114
Saudi Arabia 284, 508
savings 25, 469–70
    confiscation 24
    fiscal policy 374, 382–4, 385, 394
    investment and 21, 24, 35, 268,
        311, 314, 469–70
    loanable funds theory 268, 311,
        313–14

Sawers, D. 73
scale effect 208
    *see also* diseconomies of scale;
        economies of scale; firm size
Scandinavia 164, 436
    environment 215, 218, 221
    fiscal policy 379, 394
    new economic policy 4, 5
Scarpetta, S. 358
Scherer, F.M. 179
Schmalensee, R. 130
Schneider, Friedrich 51, 52, 53, 71
Schuh, Scott 132
Schuknecht, Ludger 379
Schumpeter, J. 159, 411
scope economies *see* economies of
    scope
Scotland 480
screwdriver industry 483
SDR (standard drawing right) 564,
    594
search unemployment 232
Seattle Conference (WTO) 6, 424
secrecy (central banks) 327
SEDs (selective and exclusive
    dealerships) 163
segmentation, market 86–7, 89–90,
    136, 137, 310
seigniorage 583, 593
selective and exclusive dealerships
    162, 163
self-employment 250
self-interest 67, 68, 146, 192, 198,
    523
Selten, Reinhard 146
Serra, Jaime 578
services sector 301
    balance of payments 503
    employment 62, 63
    firm size 127, 130, 146
    foreign trade 427–8, 430, 445, 452
    market power 127, 130, 131
    new economic policy 2, 4–5
    price and income elasticity 84–5
    value of *see* gross domestic
        product (GDP); gross national
        product (GNP)
    *see also* financial services;
        transport
shadow economy 28, 50–3, 199, 252
Shank, William F. 81
share flotations 170, 171
share options 98
share prices 280, 317
shareholding *see* stock market
Shaw, George Bernard 352
Shell 219
Shepherd, William 127, 150

shirking 116
shoe-leather costs 287
short-run aggregate supply curve
    260–1
short-run cost curves 108, 114, 120
short-run price elasticity 79, 85
short-run supply curves 260–1,
    348–52
Siebert, Horst 392
Siemens 126
Silicon Valley 118, 451, 490
silver 590
Simon, Herbert 84, 96, 138
Singapore 508, 575
    FDI 480
    forecasting 414
    foreign trade 426, 427
    growth 34, 249
single-firm monopoly *see* monopoly
single currency 292
    anchor 299, 573
    EMU proposal 580–6
    *see also* euro
single market (EU) 439, 447–8, 584
single parents 341
Sinopec 126
size of firm *see* firm size
Skidelsky, Robert 372
skills 42, 118
    growth and 20, 22, 23, 25, 35
    migration 495–6, 497, 498
    unskilled labour 341, 494, 495,
        496
Skinner, Wickham 110
Slovak Republic 17, 277, 339, 340
    fiscal policy 391
Slovenia 17, 277, 340, 565, 568
small industrial countries (exchange
    rate regime) 568–70
small and medium-sized enterprises
    (SMEs) 175
    cost structure 117–19
    FDI 462, 483
    foreign trade 452
    government intervention 199
    market power 126–7, 131, 132
    technology 131, 146
small open economies (SOEs) 128,
    297
SMC (social marginal cost) 190, 191,
    192, 214
SMEs *see* small and medium-sized
    enterprises (SMEs)
Smith, Adam 19, 24, 61, 65, 145,
    163–5, 180, 187, 214
    division of labour 110, 111, 435
    foreign trade 432, 442, 445
    invisible hand 61, 65, 214, 238

self-interest 67
*Wealth of Nations* 19, 111, 124,
    180, 443
Smith, R.S. 51
Smithsonian Agreement 593
smoke emissions 210
Social Charter (of EU) 230–1
social context (market system) 65–7
social cost
    marginal 190, 191, 192, 193
    opportunity 446
social security 232, 359
socialist economies
    demand/supply 58
    growth 15, 17, 32
    market system 58, 62, 66, 67
    Poland's stabilisation plan 4–5
    unemployment 337
    *see also* Central and Eastern
        Europe; Soviet Union, former
Sodexho Alliance 126
SOEs (small open economies) 128,
    297
soft drinks industry
    competition 99
    demand and pricing 91
    FDI 478
    foreign trade 436
software *see* computer industry
Solow, Robert 355
Solow paradox 355
Somerville, R.A. 516–17
Sony Corporation 128, 572
Sony Walkman 88
Soros, George 553
South-East Asia 408, 471, 517
South Africa 30, 489
    diamond market 142, 143, 151–4
    exchange rate 564
    HDI ranking 31
    unemployment 337
South America *see* Latin America
South Asia 17, 32, 37, 471
South Korea *see* Korea
South Sea Bubble 546
sovereignty 512, 515
Soviet Union, former 67, 151
    exchange rate 565
    foreign trade 437, 452
    new economic policy 1
    unemployment 1
Spain
    business fluctuations 405
    environment 207
    fiscal policy 375, 383, 385, 390
    government intervention 196
    market system 51
    unemployment 338, 339, 347, 362

spatial monopoly 138
specialisation 110, 111, 435–6, 448,
    453
    flexible 114
speculation (function) 568, 571–2,
    575
spending *see* expenditure
spillover effect *see* externalities
spot foreign exchange market 529,
    543–4, 545, 558, 568
spread (trading range) 529
Sraffa, P. 470
Sri Lanka 508
stability/stabilisation domestic 572
    exchange rate 573–80, 582
    institutional 24
    macroeconomic 1, 3–4
    Poland's plan (1980s) 4–5
    programmes 4
    search for 573–80
    *see also* anchors, exchange rate
Stability and Growth Pact 389–93,
    582, 584
Stages Theory of Comparative
    Advantage 450
stagflation 272, 284, 381
Stalin, Joseph 67
standard drawing rights 564, 594
standard of living *see* living
    standards
Stanton Russell, S. 489
Starr, Edward 130
state
    aid 165, 196–7
    provision 197–8
    *see also* government
static efficiency 65
steel industry
    balance of payments 512
    foreign trade 445
    sunk costs 107
sterling 506, 532
Stiglitz, Joseph 7, 8, 35, 471
Stiroh, K. 41, 42
stock approach (liquidity preference)
    268
stock inventory rule 111
stock market 40, 290, 415
    exchange rate 558–9, 578
    interest rate 317, 325, 328
    prices 280, 295, 296, 317, 325
    share flotations 170, 171
    share options 98
    shareholders 96–101, 105–6, 237
    *see also* bonds
stop-go policies 524
Stoneman, P. 159
Storey, D. 132

Storey, J. 114
strategic alliances 168–9
strategic entry deterrence techniques
    136
strategic quality management 114
strategic trade theory 448
structural adjustment programme 4,
    428
structural deficit/surplus 374–6
Structural Funds 235, 584
structural unemployment 367
structure, firm 141
Sub-Saharan Africa 15, 24
subcontracting 116, 118
subsidiaries 142
    foreign 471, 480–3, 505
subsidies 61, 193–5, 202
    China and 459
    environmental 216–17, 219
    on exports 440
    foreign trade 440, 446, 449, 452
    indirect taxation less 250
    industrial (in EU) 196–7
substitutes 79
    elasticities 80–2
substitution
    bias (inflation statistics) 279
    effects (interest rate) 315
sugar 17
sulphur dioxide 208, 210
sunk costs 107, 108, 114, 120, 130
supermarkets 138, 139–40
supernormal profits 104, 106
supply
    excess 55
    exchange rate 533–5, 537, 555
    of labour 228–9
    of money 263–4, 266–8, 275
    movements in 56–61
    *see also* aggregate supply
supply-side approach
    (unemployment) 342–8,
    359
supply curve 53, 54
    for credit 311–12
    for labour 228, 229
    market 117–19
    market system 54, 57, 63–5
    money supply 266–8
    outward shift 57
    upward-sloping 95
supporting industries (competitive
    advantage) 450–1
surplus balance of payments 501–2,
    504, 507, 509, 512, 515, 518,
    523
    structural 374
survivor technique 118

sustainability
  of current account position
      509–10
  of debt 377, 381, 384–8, 387,
      398–400, 511, 513–14
  fiscal 390
sustainable growth 26–33
Sutherland, Alan 388
Sutton, J. 144, 202
Svensson, L. 322
swaps 529, 548–9, 552, 558, 560
Sweden 185, 494
  exchange rate 575, 584
  fiscal policy 375, 379, 390, 391
  foreign trade 436
  growth 14, 31
  HDI ranking 31
  market system 49, 51
  unemployment 338, 347
Sweeney, R.J. 571
swing producer 153, 154
Swiss National Bank 570
Switzerland 153, 176, 249, 375
  deflation 284
  exchange rate 568, 569–70
  FDI 474
  foreign trade 436
  growth 31
  HDI ranking 31
  income distribution 183, 185
  labour migration 488
  market system 51
  unemployment 339, 347
synchronisation of cycles 406, 417

Tabellini, Guido 186
Taffler, R.J. 517
Taiwan 575
  forecasting 414
Tajikstan 565
takeovers 95, 116
  threat of 99–101
  see also mergers and acquisitions
Tanzania 427
Tanzi, Vito 379
target/targeting
  exchange rate zones 576
  incentives 483
  pricing 107
tariffs 440
  basket method 173
  countervailing duties 442, 446
  GATS 430
  GATT 429, 430, 448
  see also protectionism
tastes 74, 219
taxation 1, 67
  on alcohol/petrol/tobacco 60, 79

avoidance 202
  capital mobility 464, 467–8, 471
  carbon 217–18, 222
  environmental policy 215–18, 222
  evasion 201
  FDI and 463, 480–1
  fiscal policy 372, 374, 380, 382–4
  foreign trade 442, 443, 446
  incentive effect 60
  incidence of 59, 80
  income 197, 347–8
  indirect 196–7
  labour supply and 230
  pollution and 2, 194–5, 215–18
  price elasticity 79–80
  profits and 105, 106
  regressive 222
  shadow economy and 28, 51, 52,
      197
  unemployment and 347–8, 359
  wedges 347–8
Taylor, John 334
Taylor, M. 547
Taylor rule 334–5
technical analysis (chartism) 412,
      546, 547, 555, 571
techno-parks 196
technology
  deregulation and 172
  diffusion 23
  division of labour 111
  economies of scale 109, 112, 114,
      120
  foreign trade 436, 437, 447
  growth and 20, 23, 25, 26
  information (IT) 40–2, 112, 114,
      169, 417, 464
  pollution reduction 208, 216
  SMEs 131, 146
  transfer 23, 35, 42, 481–2
  see also high-tech industries
Teitelbaum, M.S. 489
telecommunications industry 137
  competition 160, 165–6
  economies of scale 112, 114
  foreign trade 436, 450
  privatisation/deregulation 147,
      170, 172, 173, 174
telemarketing 503
television industry 444–5
temporary work 362
tequila effect 579
terms of trade 17, 22, 24, 25
textiles see clothing industry
Thailand 517
  capital flows 464
  deflation 284
  forecasting 414

foreign trade 437
  growth 17, 34
  labour migration 489
Thatcher, Margaret 1
Thomas, R. 322
threat of litigation 219
3Com 42
3M 219
threshold effects 383
thrift see savings
throwing sand in the wheels strategy
      575, 576, 587
Thurow, L. 450
Thursby, J.G. 571
Thursby, M.C. 571
Tiger economies 464
  growth 34
  see also Hong Kong; Korea;
      Singapore; Taiwan
time
  balance of payments 509
  -inconsistency problem 325
  lags (fiscal activism) 377, 378
  long and variable lags 325, 372,
      378, 540
  migration and 493
  pay-back period 234–6
  unemployment duration 336,
      339–40, 348–52, 360
  see also forecasting
Time–Warner 42
TNCs (transnational corporations)
      462
tobacco industry
  health effect 193
  taxation 60, 78–9, 194
Tobias, J.J. 30
Tobin, James 576
Tobin's q-theory 316, 318
Tokyo 30, 290, 529, 539
Tonioli, G. 21
top-down forecast 416
Tornell, A. 25
Torres, R. 252
total costs 107–8
total economic activity 50
total factor productivity 20, 22–4,
      41, 42, 170, 441
total quality management (TQM)
      114
total sales revenue 76–8, 101–2
tourism 428, 452, 503
  see also hotel industry
Toxic Release Inventory 221
TQM (total quality management)
      114
trade
  balance 503, 535–6

global *see* foreign trade
links 573
policy and protection 442–9
-weighted exchange rate 538, 568
trade associations 25, 80, 118
trade fairs 452
trade unions
  growth 25
  hiring and 230, 238
  inflation and 283, 284
  new economic policy 2
  power 345–6, 359
  public sector 199
  unemployment and 345–6, 347,
    351, 359, 362
tradeable permits 215
traders 61–3, 529, 559–50, 561
trading and investment income
  503–4, 507
trading range (spread) 529
training *see* education
transaction costs 100, 137, 191, 195,
  478
  cost structure 115–17
  exchange rate 537, 586
transactions motive (for holding
  money) 262
transfer
  counter-cyclical fiscal 574
  payments 194, 251, 380
  pricing 481–2
  unilateral 503, 504
transition countries 65, 301, 464
  foreign trade 452
  output decline 17
  protection 442, 443
  unemployment 339
  *see also* Central and Eastern
    Europe; Soviet Union, former
transnational corporations (TNCs)
  462
  *see also* multinational enterprises
    FDI
transparency
  central banks 327–8
  FDI incentives 484
  prices 583, 584
transport 222
  companies 126, 127
  competition 166
  costs 114, 167, 432, 449, 477
  demand function 84, 85
  motorways 191
  privatisation/deregulation 147, 172
  railways 166, 170, 173, 546
  subsidies 61
  *see also* automobiles
Treasury (UK) 415

Treasury (USA) 464, 576
Treaty of Amsterdam 160
Treaty of European Union *see*
  Maastricht Treaty
Treaty of Rome 160
Triffin, R. 593
Trinidad and Tobago 346
Tulip Bubble, Dutch 546
Turkey 4, 277, 318, 493, 512
  exchange rate 564
Turkmenistan 565
Turner, R. 210, 214
turning points (recession) 295
TV industry 444–5
two-firm oligopoly 142–3
two-part tariffs 137
Tyco international 99
Tyson, L. 447

U-shaped cost curves 108
Uganda 427
UIP (Uncovered Interest Rate Parity)
  543
Ukraine 17, 51, 339, 565
Ulph, A. 218
'unbiased estimator' 553
uncertainty 65, 220, 237, 418, 542
  exchange rate 562, 583, 584
Uncovered Interest Rate Parity 543
UNCTAD 473, 484
underclass 349
underground economy *see* shadow
  economy 50–3, 197, 252
undershooting (exchange rate) 561
unemployment 2, 4, 6, 231, 372,
  381, 387
  capacity to adjust 442–6
  composition 340–1
  definition 338–9
  demand 352–4
  duration 336, 339–40, 348–52,
    360
  FDI and 494
  foreign trade 453
  free trade and 443
  geographical distribution 339
  imports and 444–5
  inflation and 283, 289, 348–9,
    365–9
  long-term 341–2, 348–52, 360
  natural rate of 349, 367
  policies 357–60
  search 232
  supply 342–8
  technology and 355–7
  time dimension 336, 339–40,
    348–52, 360
unemployment benefit 337

replacement ratios 346, 347
UNICE 175
  Competitiveness Report 377, 380
unilateral transfers 503, 504
Unilever 81, 126, 128
United Kingdom 51
  balance of payments 503, 505,
    507–8, 511, 514, 524
  business fluctuations 403, 404,
    405
  central bank *see* Bank of England
  competition 98, 100, 166, 168
  environment 216–18, 222
  FDI 472–3, 475
  firm size 130
  fiscal policy 375, 380, 383, 390,
    394
  forecasting 412–13
  foreign trade 426, 427, 432–5,
    446, 452
  GDP growth rate 404
  GNP 255
  government intervention 196
  growth 14, 15, 21–2, 25, 26, 31,
    42
  HDI ranking 31
  income distribution 183, 185, 186
  inflation 276, 282–3, 289, 292,
    295
  interest rate 308, 316, 321–2
  output/GDP 253
  price stability 278
  privatisation/regulation 155,
    169–71, 173
  services sector 62, 63, 84, 85
  stock market 100
  unemployment 338, 341, 347,
    352, 355, 360, 365, 368
United Nations
  FDI 462, 484
  Human Development Index 30
  population growth 26
  UNCTAD 473, 484
United States
  balance of payments 501, 503,
    504, 505, 507–8, 510–11, 515,
    522, 524
  business fluctuations 404, 405
  capital flow 470
  cellophane case 81
  competition 98, 100, 164
  environment 207, 215, 221–2
  exchange rate 530, 531, 538,
    539–41, 544, 549, 563, 572,
    573, 576, 583, 587, 590–1,
    593
  FDI 472–3
  firm size 126, 127, 128

United States (*continued*)
  fiscal policy 375, 376, 379–80, 383, 385, 394
  forecasting 413, 414, 415
  foreign trade 425–31, 440, 448, 450
  GDP growth rate 404
  GNP 255
  government intervention 183, 185–6
  income distribution 183, 185, 186
  inflation 276, 296
  interest rate 307–8, 316, 318, 325, 328
  IT development 40–2
  labour migration 488, 489–90, 494, 495, 496, 498
  market power 126–7, 128
  market system 49, 51, 62, 63, 67
  new economic policy 2, 4, 6
  output/GDP 253
  Postal Services 126
  privatisation 169, 170
  services sector 62, 63, 84, 85
  stock market 100
  unemployment 338–9, 341–2, 347, 352, 355, 360, 361–2, 368
unlimited wants 73
unskilled workers 341, 494, 495, 496
up-front costs 130
Uruguay Round 422
  foreign trade 429, 439–40
utilitarianism 182–3
utilities
  monopoly power 167
  price discrimination 137
utility
  diminished marginal 73
  externalities 188–90
  income and 182–3
  marginal 63, 65, 73, 74
  maximisation 56, 58–9, 63, 72–4, 86–7, 182, 191–2, 199, 230, 232
  rational consumer 72–4
Uzbekistan 565

value
  of goods/services *see* gross domestic product (GDP); gross national product (GNP)
  maximisation 67–8
  net present 233–4, 235, 236
  present discounted 234
  of world exports 426
value added 249
value added tax 79, 222
Van den Noord, P. 386
van der Linde, Claas 220

van der Ploeg, F. 218
Van der Straaten, J. 218
variable costs 105, 107
VAT 79, 222
velocity of circulation (money) 282, 296, 322, 327
Venables, A. 428
Venezuela 508
vertical integration 116
vertical restraints 162, 163
vertical specialisation 435
Vickers, John 150
Vietnam War 593
Vivendi 126
Volkswagen 126
voluntary activities 50
voluntary export restraints 429, 512
voluntary unemployment 232
voracity effect 25

Wade, Robert 7
wages *see* income; pay
Waigel, Theo 576
Wal-Mart Stores 126
Wall Street crash (1987) 245, 325
Walrasian adjustment process 55
Walsh, P.P. 140, 351
Warner 128
Warnock, F. 469
wars 25, 591
waste/waste disposal 28, 206, 210, 220, 222
watch industry 436
water
  industry 173
  pollution 28, 194–5, 198, 206, 207, 210
wealth 6, 10, 35, 62, 182–3
  distribution 67, 287–8, 289–90
  effects (interest rate) 315, 316–18
  trends 15
*Wealth of Nations* (Smith) 19, 111, 124, 180, 443
Weber, A. 580
Weber, S. 401
Weiner, Norbert 356
welfare
  China and 450–60
  loss of monopoly 135, 136, 188
  maximisation 182
  state 181
  transfer payments 194, 251, 380
  unemployment benefit 337, 346, 347
Werner Report (1970) 580, 581
West Africa 300
Westerfield, R. 241
Western Europe *see* Europe, Western; European Union (EU)

Wheatcroft, A. 19
Whelan, Ciara 140
white knights 100
wholesale 62, 127, 130
  foreign exchange market 559
Willett, T.D. 571
Williamson, O.E. 124
Wilson government 562
windfalls 25
window guidance (moral suasion) 323
Windows (Microsoft) 129–30
wine industry 432–5, 443, 447
Winter-Ebmer, R. 497
Wood, A. 498
*Woodpulp* case 163, 164
Woodward, Bob 394
workfare programme 360
workforce *see* labour/employment
working conditions 230–1
World Bank 9, 10, 183, 209, 254–5, 594
  balance of payments 517
  business fluctuations 402, 417
  corruption and 200
  East Asia 30–2, 34
  foreign trade 427, 437, 441
  growth 15, 17, 26, 30–2, 34, 41–3, 202
  inflation 287
World Economic Forum 200
world output (trends) 15
world trade *see* foreign trade
World Trade Organisation 1, 4, 8, 176, 422, 440, 442, 448–9, 484, 521
  China and 458–61
  global trade and 425–31
WorldCom 99
Wyplosz, C. 576

X-efficiency 435
X-inefficiency 136, 173, 188

Yamaha 112
Yellen, J. 536
yield curve 308–10, 322
Yoffie, D.B. 452
Young, S. 480
young people
  crime 368
  unemployment 336, 340–1, 368

Zaire (Congo) 24
Zambia 31
Zarnovitz, Victor 402, 410, 411
zero interest floor 286
Zimbabwe 277
Zweimüller, J. 497